# International Human Resource Management

## Second Edition

This is an ideal foundation text for anyone studying or working in the International Human Resource Management (IHRM) arena. This text incorporates most of what is currently known in the field. It features data and examples from academic research, international business, consulting firms, and interviews with HRM managers in multinational and global firms. The book offers both a theoretical and practical treatment of this important and constantly evolving area.

Thoroughly updated and revised, this second edition now includes key terms, learning objectives, discussion questions and an end-of-book integrative case study. It has been designed to lead readers through all of the key topics in a highly engaging and approachable way. The book focuses on IHRM within multinational enterprises (MNEs) and covers topics including:

- MNE and country culture
- Organizational structure, strategy, and design
- International joint ventures and cross-border mergers and acquisitions
- Employment law and labor relations
- Labor standards, ethics, and codes of conduct
- Selection and management of international assignees
- Training and management development
- Compensation and benefits
- Health and safety and crisis management
- IHRM departments and professionals.

Uncovering precisely why IHRM is important for success in international business and how IHRM policies and practices function within the multinational enterprise, this outstanding textbook provides an essential foundation for an understanding of the theory and practice of IHRM. This book is essential reading for all students, professors and IHRM professionals.

**Dennis R. Briscoe** is Professor of International Human Resource Management at the University of San Diego, where he has taught for over twenty years.

**Randall S. Schuler** is Professor of Strategic International Human Resource at the School of Management and Labor Relations at Rutgers University and Research Professor at GSBA Zurich.

## Routledge Global Human Resource Management Series

*Edited by Randall S. Schuler, Susan E. Jackson, Paul Sparrow, and Michael Poole*

**Routledge Global Human Resource Management** is an important new series that examines human resources in its global context. The series is organized into three strands: content and issues in global Human Resource Management (HRM); specific HR function in a global context; and comparative HRM. Authored by some of the world's leading authorities on HRM, each book in the series aims to give readers comprehensive, in-depth and accessible texts that combine essential theory and best practice. Topics covered include cross-border alliances, global leadership, global legal systems, HRM in Asia, Africa, and the Americas, industrial relations and global staffing.

**International Human Resource Management – Second Edition**
Policy and practice for the global enterprise
*Dennis R. Briscoe and Randall S. Schuler*

**Globalizing Human Resource Management**
*Paul Sparrow, Chris Brewster, and Hilary Harris*

**Managing Human Resources in Cross-Border Alliances**
*Randall S. Schuler, Susan E. Jackson, and Yadong Luo*

**Managing Human Resources in Africa**
*Edited by Ken N. Kamoche, Yaw A. Debrah, Frank M. Horwitz, and Gerry Nkombo Muuka*

**Managing Human Resources in Asia Pacific**
*Edited by Pawan S. Budhwar*

# International Human Resource Management

## Second Edition

Policy and practice for the global enterprise

Dennis R. Briscoe and
Randall S. Schuler

Routledge
Taylor & Francis Group

LONDON AND NEW YORK

First published 1995
by Prentice Hall

Second edition 2004
by Routledge
29 West 35th Street, New York, NY 10001

Simultaneously published in the UK
by Routledge
11 New Fetter Lane, London EC4P 4EE

*Routledge is an imprint of the Taylor & Francis Group*

Typeset in Times New Roman by
Florence Production Ltd, Stoodleigh, Devon
Printed and bound in Great Britain by
The Alden Group, Oxford

*British Library Cataloguing in Publication Data*
A catalogue record for this book is available from the British Library

*Library of Congress Cataloging in Publication Data*
Briscoe, Dennis R., 1945–
    International human resource management: policy and practice
    for the global enterprise/by Dennis R. Briscoe and Randall S. Schuler. – 2nd ed.
        p. cm. – (Routledge global human resource management series ; 5)
      Includes bibliographical references and index.
    1. International business enterprises – Personnel management.
    2. International business enterprises – United States – Personnel management.
    I. Schuler, Randall S.   II. Title.   III. Series.
    HF5549.5.E45B74 2004
    658.3 – dc22                                                    2003026520

ISBN 0–415–33835–2 (hbk)
ISBN 0–415–33834–4 (pbk)

"Briscoe and Schuler have created the benchmark by which other IHRM texts will be measured. The book is remarkable in its breadth of coverage of the IHRM field and the authors' in-depth knowledge of the topics they write about reflects their academic and applied expertise. Students, lecturers, and others interested in IHRM will be enriched by the contents of this volume."

Wayne Cascio, *Professor of Management, University of Colorado at Denver*

"The second edition of Briscoe and Schuler's *International Human Resource Management* is an outstanding addition to the literature. It will not only serve as an excellent university text but also provide a comprehensive overview of the field for IHRM practitioners and other interested professionals."

Cal Reynolds, *Consultant*

"To have the right staff at the right time is a safe recipe for business success. Although this is easier said than done the second edition of *International Human Resource Management* provides the appropriate tools to achieve just that. The book brings together highly relevant perspectives on the effective management of human resources on a global scale by two internationally renowned scholars on the leading edge of research and practice. This fully updated new edition should be mandatory reading for any student and practitioner of international business."

Professor Jan Selmer, *Hong Kong Baptist University*

This book serves as a basis for many other books in the **Global HRM Series** edited by Randall S. Schuler, Susan E. Jackson, Paul Sparrow and Michael Poole. This series contains books that discuss in more detail the many IHRM policies and practices introduced in this book such as compensation, staffing, legal systems, training and development, and structure, strategy, and design. The **Series** also includes books that are dedicated to specific topics such as managing human resources in cross-border alliances, and the HR profession in global organizations. In addition, the **Global HRM Series** contains many books that describe country characteristics and IHRM policies and practices within regions of the world such as Latin America, Asia, Africa, and Europe and countries therein. The books in the **Global HRM Series** form a series that is comprehensive, useable, and accessible. For further information about this book and the other books in the **Series**, please visit our website at www.routledge.com or email info.business@routledge.co.uk.

# Contents

# Illustrations

## Figures

## Tables

## Boxes

## IHRM in Action

# Foreword

Global HRM is a series of books edited and authored by some of the best and most well known researchers in the field of human resource management. The series is aimed at offering students and practitioners accessible, coordinated, and comprehensive books in global HRM. To be used individually or together, these books cover the main bases of comparative and international HRM. Taking an expert look at an increasingly important and complex area of global business, this is a groundbreaking new series that answers a real need for serious textbooks on global HRM.

Several books in this series, Global HRM, are devoted to human resource management policies and practices in multinational enterprises. Some books focus on specific areas of global HRM policies and practices, such as global leadership, global compensation, global staffing, and global labor relations. Other books address special topics that arise in multinational enterprises such as managing HR in cross-border alliances, developing strategies and structures, and managing legal systems for multinational enterprises. This book, *International Human Resource Management – Second Edition: policy and practice for the global enterprise*, serves as the foundation book for all the other books that focus on specific areas of global HRM policies and practices, and for the books that address special topics such as cross-border alliances, global strategies and structures and global legal systems. As such its fifteen chapters provide the broadest possible base for an overview of all the major areas in the field of international human resource management. As with all the books in the series, the chapters are based upon the most recent and traditional research as well as numerous examples of what multinational enterprises are doing today.

In addition to books on various HRM topics in multinational enterprises, several other books in the series adopt a comparative approach to understanding human resource management. These books on comparative human resource management describe the HRM policies and practices found at the local level in selected countries in several regions of the world. The comparative books utilize a common framework that makes it easier for the reader to systematically understand the rationale for the existence of various human resource management activities in different countries and easier to compare these activities across countries.

This Routledge series, Global HRM, is intended to serve the growing market of global scholars and professionals who are seeking a deeper and broader understanding of the role and importance of human resource management in companies as they operate throughout the world. With this in mind, all books in the series provide a thorough review of existing research and numerous examples of companies around the world. Mini-company stories and examples are found throughout the chapters. In addition, many of the books in the series include at least one detailed case description that serves as a convenient practical illustration of topics discussed in the book.

Because a significant number of scholars and professionals throughout the world are involved in researching and practicing the topics examined in this series of books, the authorship of the books and the experiences of companies cited in the books reflect a vast global representation. The authors in the series bring with them exceptional knowledge of the human resource management topics they address, and in many cases the authors have been the pioneers for their topics. So we feel fortunate to have the involvement of such a distinguished group of academics in this series.

The publisher and editor also have played a major role in making this series possible. Routledge has provided its global production, marketing, and reputation to make this series feasible and affordable to academics and practitioners throughout the world. In addition, Routledge has provided its own highly qualified professionals to make this series a reality. In particular we want to indicate our deep appreciation for the work of our series editor, Francesca Poynter. She, and her predecessor Catriona King, have been behind the series from the very beginning and have been invaluable in providing the needed support and encouragement to us and to the many authors in the series. She, along with her staff, has helped make the process of completing this series an enjoyable one. For everything they have done, we thank them all.

Randall S. Schuler, Rutgers University and GSBA Zurich
Paul Sparrow, Manchester University
Susan E. Jackson, Rutgers University and GSBA Zurich
Michael Poole, Cardiff University

# Acknowledgments

There are many individuals who have provided valuable information, insights, and assistance in completing this book. They include: Susan E. Jackson, Rutgers University; Paul Sparrow, Manchester Business School; Michael Poole, Cardiff University; Chris Brewster, Henley Management College; Paul Evans, INSEAD; Vlado Pucik, IMD; Yadong Luo, University of Miami; Andrew Inkpen, Thunderbird; Hilary Harris, Cranfield School of Management; Gary Florkowski, University of Pittsburgh; Cal Reynolds, Calvin Reynolds & Associates (particularly for his original article written for the website); Hugh Scullion, Strathclyde University; Stu Youngblood and Rob Rhodes, Texas Christian University; Bruno Staffelbach, University of Zurich; Martin Hilb, University of St Gallen; Christian Scholz, University of Saarlandes; Gerold Frich, Fachhochschule, Aachen; Michael Morley, Limerick; Charlie Tharp, Ibraiz Tarique, Paula Caligiuri, and Rucha Hardikar, Rutgers University; Shimon Dolon, ESADE; Georges Bachtold, Blumer; Darryl Weiss, Director of IHR and Corporate Attorney, Orincon; Jerry Edge, Director of International Compensation, Callaway Golf; Joann Stang, VP of HR, Solar Turbines; Bernie Kulchin, VP of HR, Cubic Corporation; Ben Shaw, Bond University; Lisbeth Claus, Willamette University; Ed Watson, KPMG; Gardiner Hempel, Deloitte & Touche; Wayne Cascio and Manuel Scrapio, University of Colorado–Denver; and Bob Grove, San Diego Employers' Association. For use of the Lincoln Electric in China integrative case in Chapter 15, we thank Ingmar Björkman of INSEAD and the Swedish School of Economics and Charles Galunic and Isabel Assureira of INSEAD. Dr Schuler thanks many students at Rutgers University in the Department of Human Resource Management for their input into the creation of the Global HRM website for use in his class, "Managing the Global Workforce" (http://www.ghrm.rutgers.edu). In the creation of this website the students were greatly assisted by the department's webmaster, Joanne Mangels, and we all thank her for this contribution. And Dr Briscoe thanks his graduate students at the University of San Diego School of Business for help in research into IHRM and country HR practices and in development of Dr Briscoe's website, www.internationalhrm.com, particularly Mario D'Angelo, former graduate assistant and now web designer at Globe[3]. Finally we thank many fine individuals at Routledge for their wonderful assistance and support throughout the project. These individuals include: Francesca Poynter, the editor for the Global HRM Series, Natasha Mary, Nicola Cooper, and Kristen Sensenig.

Dr Briscoe would also like to provide special acknowledgments to his wife, Georgina, who provided the inspiration, support, and example for "going for the summit" and completing this second edition, and without whom the climb would have been much harder, and to Randall Schuler, who was great to work with, who provided the support necessary to complete the project within tough deadlines, and who improved beyond measure the final product.

# Introduction

This book is about International Human Resource Management (IHRM). That is, it is about human resource management in the international environment. IHRM is an important enough topic to warrant its own text because the conduct of business is increasingly international in scope and managing human resources is critical to the successful conduct of global business. The majority of this book discusses the IHRM issues faced by multinational enterprises (MNEs), primarily from the perspective of the parent company or headquarters. A concerted effort has been made to internationalize this presentation to make it apply to most MNEs. That is, the information is presented from the perspectives of as many different MNEs, from as many different countries, as possible, although much of the reported research and writing has come from an American perspective. The focus is placed on IHRM problems created in an MNE performing business in more than one country, rather than those posed by working for a foreign firm at home or by employing foreign employees in the local firm. These latter two foci, however, will be addressed as they become important for particular IHRM policies and practices.

## Parts and chapters

This book is divided into three parts, with each section addressing a major component of the topic of the book. Part I describes a number of key components of the environment in which IHRM takes place. The first part of the book sets the scene for *International Human Resource Management – Second Edition: Policy and Practice for the Global Enterprise* and explains why international human resource management is important for the success of international business, describing the environment of global commerce as it relates to IHRM. A number of critical components in the environment of international business help create the context for the policies and practices of IHRM. The first seven chapters of this book describe these critical components. These chapters include (1) introduction to international business (IB) and to IHRM; (2) Strategic IHRM and its role in the pursuit of IB; (3) design of international organizational structure and the crucial role of IHRM in the design of global organizations; (4) the role of IHRM in the success of cross-border alliances, international joint ventures, and international mergers and

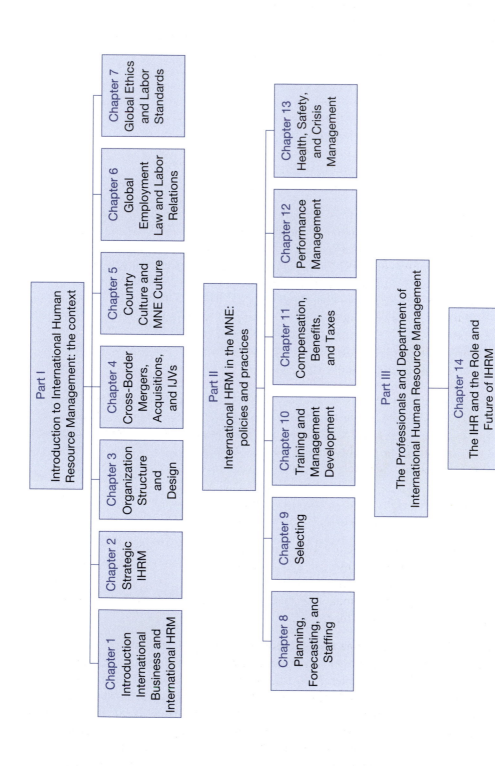

*Figure 1* Chapter map

acquisitions, and in learning across borders in the global enterprise; (5) national and corporate cultures and their overriding importance in the conduct of IB and IHRM, including their specific impact on research in IHRM; (6) global employment law and labor relations; and (7) international labor standards and ethical codes of conduct in the conduct of IHRM.

Chapter 1 introduces the reality of the ever-increasing internationalization of business and links it to the rising importance of human resource management within global business. That is, the first chapter of this book describes why international business is growing in importance and ties IHRM to that importance. Chapter 1 describes the basic nature and development of IHRM, differentiates IHRM from domestic HRM, and discusses some of the difficulties experienced in that development.

Chapter 2 describes the various responsibilities of International Human Resource management and links them to the pursuit of international business strategies. The strategic decision to "go international" is one of the most important components of the IHRM environment. IHRM must understand these strategic choices and should contribute input to them in order to contribute to their successful achievement. Chapter 2 explains how this interaction between HRM and IB leads to the many areas of responsibility that are now labeled "International Human Resource Management" and describes many of the linkages between corporate international business strategies, IHR functional responsibilities, and the various outcomes that IHRM must seek for business success in the global arena.

Chapter 3, on the environmental context of IHRM, discusses the growing complexities in designing the structure of multinational firms and the important role that IHRM plays in those design decisions. The conduct of international business is increasingly complex, involving the need to – at the same time – focus on central control and influence and local adaptation to customers and culture. Too often these efforts fail, at least partially because of inadequate attention to issues within the responsibility of IHRM. This chapter describes the contributions that IHRM can and should make to the success of these organizational choices.

Chapter 4 describes the role of IHR in cross-border alliances, international joint ventures, and international mergers and acquisitions. Cross-border acquisitions, joint ventures, teams, and alliances of various sorts are increasingly the means by which firms choose to go international and thus they constitute one of the most important components of the context for IHRM.

Chapter 5 expands the theme that is revisited frequently throughout the text: the critical importance of country and corporate culture. Cultural differences impact everything that is done in international business and are, if possible, even more important to everything that IHR managers do. Success in international business requires a thorough understanding of cultural factors and IHRM is involved both with helping provide that expertise to the firm as well as having to incorporate such understanding in its own global activities. Thus this introduction to IB and IHRM, by necessity, includes an introduction to the concepts of country and corporate culture.

The chapter also discusses the importance of culture in the both the conduct and the interpretation of IHRM research, explaining how culture impacts both our understanding of IHRM and its impact. Like everything else, culture influences what we know and what we think we know about IHR.

Chapter 6 describes international aspects of the legal, regulatory, and labor relations environment, another of the key components in the context of IHRM. Just as is true for HRM in a domestic context, there are many aspects of law that impact the practice of human resource management when working in the global arena. This chapter discusses six of these aspects: (1) international employment law and the institutions that develop and apply it; (2) application of US laws outside the US; (3) application of US laws to foreign-owned firms in the US; (4) US immigration law; (5) a short discussion of non-US perspectives on employment law and non-US immigration and work visas; and (6) elements of the international labor relations environment that are especially important to MNEs. All of these areas of the legal, regulatory, and labor relations environment related to the conduct of IHRM are increasingly important to the successful contribution of IHR managers and all have a growing impact on IHR and firms operating in the global business environment.

The last chapter in Part I (Chapter 7) focuses specifically on the problem of ethical behavior and decision making and labor standards in the international arena, particularly as they impact human resource management. This chapter discusses the nature of the problem from an IHRM perspective and describes a number of solutions that have been or are being developed by companies, governments, and non-governmental organizations and special-interest groups.

All of these components of the environment constitute the context within which IHRM performs its policies and practices and, therefore, also sets the stage for the rest of the text, which provides a comprehensive overview of the policies and practices of International Human Resource Management. These IHRM policies and practices are provided both in the context of the operation of an MNE from its home country, headquarters, perspective as well as from the perspective of IHRM at the local level, which is important to the operation of foreign-owned firms and subsidiaries and other forms of cross-border ventures and alliances.

Part II begins the detailed description and analysis of the major international human resource policies and practices of IHRM professionals (managers and staff). Part II is concerned with the management of all employees of the MNE. The chapters in this section include (as applied to MNEs):

- Planning, forecasting, and staffing (discussed in Chapters 8 and 9).
- Training and development (Chapter 10).
- Compensation, benefits, and taxes (Chapter 11).
- Performance management (Chapter 12).
- Health, safety, and crisis management (Chapter 13).

Each of these chapters describes these policies and practices as they are performed in the MNE.

The first chapter in Part II, Chapter 8, provides an introduction to the overall concern with planning, forecasting, and staffing the global enterprise. Chapter 8 begins by providing a description of the constantly changing labor markets around the world and discusses how MNEs plan for creating their workforces from those labor markets. The nature of those markets in various countries, in terms of their demographic characteristics, the skills and abilities of their individuals, and their accessibility and cost varies dramatically from country to country and region to region and can be a major determinant in the success of IB decisions such as where to locate operations. Chapter 8 also provides an overview of the many options that MNEs have available to them for that staffing.

Chapter 9 discusses the staffing issues in the MNE with primary focus on the selection of international assignees (IAs) or expatriates. It also describes many of the issues confronted in the IA selection process and best practice in dealing with those issues. Chapter 10 describes the function of training and development in the MNE, focusing on training and preparation issues for expatriates as well as local employees in foreign operations and on management development in MNEs. Chapter 11 discusses compensation and benefits issues in MNEs, again primarily focusing on these issues for expatriates, but also on describing MNE attempts to design and apply common compensation and benefits programs for their operations around the world. Chapter 12 focuses on the many issues related to the management of employee performance in the international arena. And Chapter 13 describes the many issues surrounding health, safety, and security for global business travelers and international assignees and their families and the design of crisis management programs to deal with these issues.

Part III of the book is a single chapter. It takes a look at the IHRM department and its professionals. Chapter 14 examines the role of the IHR department, including international support services that IHR departments are expected to develop and provide, the continuing internationalization (globalization) of HRM as it parallels the continuing internationalization (globalization) of business, the increasing professionalization of IHRM (including issues such as the codification of the "body of knowledge" of IHR, the development of IHR competencies and certification, the increase in training and experience in IHR, and the inclusion of IHR in career development plans of HR managers), and possible scenarios for the development of what some firms are calling "global HRM."

## Chapter features

Each chapter begins with "Learning objectives." These are the main objectives that we would like to see you focus on as you consider the material in the chapter. Similarly, the "Key terms" are those we would like you to know very well by the end of the chapter. Of course you will learn more than these particular objectives and terms. Each chapter contains a number of "IHRM in Action" illustrations of current experiences of multinational enterprises, as well as many shorter examples integrated within the text, itself. All of these examples are drawn from the enterprises of many countries, providing additional global focus for the text. At the end of each chapter there are "Points for further discussion" that might be done individually or in small teams. These are provided to allow the reader to apply many of the ideas in the chapter to other situations, especially those of the Lincoln Electric Company in China, the integrative end-of-book case that forms the last chapter.

The integrative case, "Lincoln Electric in China," describes many experiences of a company over the past fifteen years as it expanded from primarily a domestic company to a multinational enterprise. It illustrates the challenges in trying to become a successful MNE, the importance of international human resource policies and practices, and the impact of the local country environment on the effectiveness of those policies and practices. The reader may also wish to visit the company website (http://www.lincolnelectric.com) to learn more about the history and products of Lincoln Electric and also its current activities. The website also contains an original article by Cal Reynolds, one of the pioneers of IHRM, that describes the origins and early history of IHRM.

The end-of-book materials include the notes that are used in each of the chapters. These materials reflect the relevant classic and contemporary academic research worldwide and the experiences and stories of multinational enterprises. To add even more relevant information as it unfolds, the reader is encouraged to visit numerous websites that are available and suggested here. Additional websites and other materials are found on the website designed for this book (www.routledge.com/textbooks/0415338344).

Finally there is a subject and author index. This is to provide the reader with further information about the various topics covered in this book as well as the many authors whose work has been used to compile this book.

## Terminology

In this text, a number of terms are used to refer to businesses with international commerce. In general, the more traditional term MNE (multinational enterprise) is used to refer to organizations that conduct business outside their countries of origin.[1] The term MNE is used in this text, rather than MNC (multinational corporation), because in many countries there is no form of ownership equivalent to the American corporation, from whence derives the term MNC. For example, an internationally active firm may be family-owned or a member of a trading group and be owned by members of the group, or even be a government-owned enterprise. Thus, in this text, the generic term "enterprise" is used to refer to any type of organization involved with international business. For small and medium-sized MNEs, the term SME is sometimes used. Generally the term MNE will be used throughout this book. When appropriate, the term SME will be used to highlight special characteristics of small and medium-sized MNEs.

MNEs can be described as operating multinationally, internationally, or globally (or transnationally). While these terms seem to be used interchangeably, some distinctions can be made. For example the term "global" or "transnational" normally refers to MNEs with a high percentage of international sales (over 50 percent outside their home countries) and a high percentage of employees outside their home countries as well, with operations in a large number of countries, and a global perspective and attitude reflected in their mission statements. These firms tend to have highly centralized (or, at least, regionalized) policy, at least as it applies to financial issues and sharing of resources and innovations and world-class standards for products and services, but highly decentralized and localized marketing and operations. That is, they take advantage of their global presence to gain access to resources (ideas, technology, capital, people, products, and services) and develop economies of scale, while at the same time maintaining a local presence that is seen as comparable to that of domestic competitors. The other terms, such as "multinational" or "international," generally refer to MNEs that have not yet developed their level of international operations to this extent. Because more and more enterprises are moving in the direction of being more global, in thought at least, if not in action, we have chosen to use the word "global" in both the title of this book as well as in the title of the entire series. Thus many of the topics, policies, and practices discussed throughout this book are currently applicable to many enterprises and may soon be applicable to many others. In this text, if the terms global, multinational, or international enterprise make a difference to the particular topic, policy, or practice being discussed, then an attempt is made to make it clear through explanation or the use of terminology as to what type of enterprise is being described.

# Introduction to International Human Resource Management: the context

# International business and International Human Resource Management

**1**

## Learning objectives

After considering this chapter, the reader will be able to describe:

- The internationalization of business
- The internationalization of HRM
    - The three major forms of IHRM
    - The state of development of IHRM
    - Differences between international and domestic HRM
- HRM problems experienced by MNEs
- The global role of the HRM professional

## Key terms

- International business (IB)
- International Human Resource Management (IHRM)
- Multinational enterprises (MNEs)
- Small and medium-sized enterprises (SMEs)

The first edition of this book began: "The conduct of business is increasingly global." This is still the case. Today, the pace of "globalization" is increasing faster than ever. Not only – as stated in the first edition – are markets for most goods and services global, but investment across borders continues to increase, the number and value of cross-border mergers and acquisitions and international joint ventures and alliances continue to increase, and the amount of money and number of people that crosses borders is on the rise. Thousands of firms and millions of people work outside their countries of citizenship and millions of people work at home for companies with foreign ownership. Competition almost everywhere is global in scope, meaning businesses of all types in most countries face real or potential competition from foreign products or services or from foreign-owned subsidiaries and domestic firms that are now foreign-owned. In addition, inputs to business activity (including capital, materiel, ideas, technology, parts, insurance, legal services, office equipment, employees, etc.) are pretty much available everywhere from sources that can – and do – come from almost anywhere at world-class quality, cost, and speed.

What this means is that there is "no place to hide" for any business, local or multinational. Even the old assumptions that only the biggest of firms from the most developed countries can be and are involved with international business no longer hold. No business can any longer "pretend" that it doesn't have to understand and react to the global marketplace. The conduct of "business" has become a truly global activity for many general reasons, including these new realities for MNEs:

- *Increased travel*. International travelers observe and use products and services that are available in other countries and often bring many of them back home, helping to develop global demand for these products and services.
- Rapid and extensive *global communications*. Because of satellite television, global distribution of movies, music, videos, CDs, and DVDs, the Internet and World Wide Web, and global print media, people everywhere have access to information from around the world, again learning what is available and developing global demand and expectations.
- Rapid *transfer of new technology* of all forms, making it possible to produce world-class products and provide world-class service almost everywhere in the world.
- *Growing trade* and, thus, exposure to *foreign competition*. With increasingly limited exceptions, companies from all countries can buy and sell in all other countries, exposing all firms to increased competition and making it necessary to seek lower costs and new markets outside one's traditional national boundaries.
- *Improving education* around the world, enabling firms everywhere to produce world-class products and services and raising expectations for those products and services.
- The *emigration* of large numbers of people – again, exposing millions of people to standards of living in other countries, raising expectations worldwide.

Two seemingly conflicting things happen because of all these reasons, although both reinforce the point that business today is global in scope. The first of these is that every organization – regardless of its size, location, or scope of activity – is impacted by the varying attitudes, values, and behaviors that come from the many countries and cultures that provide its inputs, markets, and employees. And, second, customers (individuals or businesses) and employees worldwide also now expect the same world-class products and services and treatment available in the best firms and in the most developed countries, making firms everywhere have to compete on the basis of world-class speed, quality, service, and management.

One measure of how important international business has become is to look at just the issue of exports. Even though they represent only a relatively small portion of the

US economy, the US is the largest exporter and importer. (Germany is No. 2, Japan No. 3, and the UK is No. 4, with imports and exports representing much larger shares of these economies[1].) In addition, the US is the largest recipient of immigrants. But, having said all this, the reality is that the degree of actual internationalization of the US economy has probably only reached about 10 percent of total economic activity (as measured by gross domestic product (GDP)). Indeed, the level and pace of change in the global economy worldwide is at the early stages, yet the pace of change in this economy is accelerating rapidly. It is estimated today that, globally, there are approximately 60,000 MNEs with 800,000 subsidiaries and US$16 trillion in sales and that by 2010 there will be 90,000 MNEs, 15 million subsidiaries and US$25 trillion in sales.[2] The challenge to everyone, including, and maybe particularly, IHRM, will become only stronger and more complex. The goal of this book is to aid IHRM students and IHR professionals to more successfully meet that challenge.

## The internationalization of business

Just as many large companies such as Lincoln Electric (described in detail in our integrative case) have been required to go global over the past decade, small and medium-sized firms (SMEs) have done the same, such as Harry Ramsden's, reported in IHRM in Action 1.1.[3] It is the smaller and medium-sized firms, such as Harry Ramsden's Fish and Chips (from the UK), that illustrate what is happening to extend the impact of international business throughout the world. Other examples to illustrate this point could include (clearly there are thousands of such examples, from most countries around the globe) firms such as Overland Data (a small manufacturer – 250 employees – of high-capacity data storage disks, in San Diego) with a small assembly operation in England, sales forces in Germany and France, and a joint venture with a small high-tech manufacturer in Norway, or Badger Manufacturing, that controls about half of the market for production of plastic wrap for supermarkets in the US and Latin America, that is owned by a family business from El Salvador in Central America, or G.W. Barth, a manufacturer of cocoa-bean roasting machinery based in Ludwigsburg, Germany, that employs only sixty-five people but controls 70 percent of the global market for such equipment.

Hermann Simon's 1996 book, *Hidden Champions: Lessons from 500 of the World's Best Unknown Companies,* focused on relatively little known SMEs with worldwide market shares of 50 percent, 60 percent, even 90 percent.[4] And, interestingly, these SMEs, which include only a few US firms, often follow management and organizational practices that are not always consistent with the practices of most large, well known US MNEs.[5] For example, most have authoritarian leaders/founders who delegate day-to-day management, avoid alliances and outsourcing in favor of using their own internal strengths, and engage in limited professional marketing. These practices are contrary to those typically described as common among the major MNEs (US and non-US-based) suggesting the importance of paying attention to a firm's size and country of origin, as well as its prominence in international business,

# Harry Ramsden's goes international

Deep-fried fish and chips have been a perennially popular food in England. But they have historically been very local in their operation. One of England's premium fish-and-chip shops, Harry Ramsden's, though, founded in Guiseley, Yorkshire, in 1928, is one of the few that have opened shops at multiple locations. By 1994 the company had eight branches in Britain, with four more scheduled for opening, and one in Dublin, Ireland. Its busiest UK location is in the resort town of Blackpool, generating annual sales of £1.5 million (US$2.3 million). Harry Ramsden's managers, however, were not satisfied with this success, they wanted to turn Harry Ramsden's into a global enterprise.

To this end, in 1992 the company opened its first international operation in Hong Kong. According to finance director Richard Taylor, "We marketed the product as Britain's fast food, and it proved extremely successful." Within two years the Hong Kong venture was already generating annual sales equivalent to its Blackpool operations. Half of the initial clientele in Hong Kong were British expatriates, but within a couple of years, more than 80 percent of customers were ethnic Chinese.

Emboldened by this success, Harry Ramsden's has (as of 1999) opened additional branches in Singapore, Dublin, Ireland, Dubai, United Arab Emirates, and Melbourne, Australia; but its biggest potential target market is seen as Japan. In an experimental shop in Tokyo, the Japanese took to this product, despite their traditional aversion to greasy food. So Harry Ramsden's began to look for a Japanese partner to establish a joint venture in Japan.

As for the future, Richard Taylor states their international strategy: "We want Harry Ramsden's to become a global brand. In the short term the greatest returns will be in the UK. But it would be a mistake to saturate the UK and then turn to the rest of the world. We'd probably come a cropper when we internationalized. We need experience now."

and making it obvious that lessons to be learned about the nature of international business are not only to be learned from the large MNEs. It is in these types of examples from the SMEs that one finds real proof of the extent of the internationalization of business.

The next few paragraphs illustrate some additional reasons for growing globalization, demonstrating why it changes many of the traditions in conducting business, why it makes international business so complex and "chaotic," and why it makes the role of IHRM so important.

In addition to the general reasons mentioned earlier, there are a number of more specific business drivers of globalization.[6] These include:

- Increased pressure on costs (so firms move to where labor and other resources are cheapest and most readily available).
- The search for new markets (for growth and to be able to compete more effectively with global competitors, but also because firms and consumers around the world also seek foreign products and services).
- Greater customer demands on product and service qualities.
- Government policy (that can come in many forms, such as encouraging foreign investment through tax benefits, or the opening up of markets through regional trade treaties, or through privatizing industries such as telecommunications, health care, and the mass media, or encouraging local firms to export to develop better trade balances and to earn hard currency).
- Technological development (which impacts globalization in a number of ways, e.g., multinational firms searching the globe for the best technology, the best technology being made or copied everywhere, and new technology allowing smaller, more flexible manufacturing plants to be placed close to markets, no matter where those markets are).
- Worldwide communication and information flow (which at least partially creates global knowledge of and demand for world-class products and services).
- The interdependence of nations in trading blocs, such as the European Union, the Association of South East Asian Nations (ASEAN), Mercosur (Brazil, Argentina, Uruguay, and Paraguay), and the North American Free Trade Agreement (NAFTA – Canada, the US, and Mexico).
- The integration of cultures and values through the impact of global communication and the spread of products and services such as music, food, and clothing, which have led to common consumer demands around the world.
- A larger, more highly educated workforce worldwide.
- Decreasing trade barriers and opening markets (which expose more firms to foreign competition – often presenting higher-quality products and services at a lower cost – and which present – if not make necessary the search for – "overseas" opportunities for markets and investment).
- E-commerce (that makes firms "global" from the moment they have a web site up and running, as customers from around the world log on to that web site and order whatever product or service is being offered).

Together, these drivers have created a new set of global realities for MNEs. In turn these realities and their drivers impact every aspect of the MNE, including its human resource management activities. When businesses internationalize, human resource concerns, such as staffing (finding the best and lowest-cost employees anywhere in the world), executive development (ensuring the management group has the knowledge and ability to operate effectively in the international arena), compensation (being globally competitive), and labor relations (which can vary dramatically from country to country) require globally savvy IHRM professionals to facilitate international business (IB) success. This chapter introduces and explores this connection between IB and IHRM and the rest of the book explains in detail the nature of the IHRM connection with IB success.

## The increasing importance of international business

The evidence for the increased importance of international business comes from many fronts. The following paragraphs describe only some of this evidence. The numbers, sizes, types, and countries of origin of enterprises involved in various forms of international business have all continued to expand.

### *Numbers*

Today, the approximately 60,000 MNEs employ more than 45 million people worldwide. This is about twice as large as in 1990. And this number is predicted to increase up to 75 million people by 2010.[7] The overall level of foreign direct investment has expanded rapidly to where it is now estimated to total at least US$3.2 trillion, with approximately 80 percent coming from (and going to) developed countries. But the amount going to (and coming from) developing countries, particularly Brazil, Mexico, India, China, Singapore, Hong Kong, and the countries of Eastern Europe (primarily countries with ties to developed countries), is also increasing quite rapidly. Even though the total value (in dollars and in percent of the economy) of exports from a large country like the US also continues to increase (now about 10 percent of the US gross domestic product), there are many countries, such as Belgium, the Netherlands, Austria, Switzerland, Denmark, Germany, Sweden, Canada, and Great Britain, whose exports represent 30 percent or more of their GDP.

To further illustrate the expansion of global commerce, fifty years ago the US accounted for 53 percent of global GDP; but today it accounts for only 18 percent, albeit both of a very much larger US GDP and of a very much larger global economy. Not only is the world economy much larger in absolute terms, but an ever-increasing number of countries are developing a significant presence in that economy. It is no longer just the few large countries, such as the United States, Great Britain, Germany, France, and Japan, that play important roles in the global economy. Information in the following paragraphs illustrates the ever-growing number of countries whose enterprises are among the world's largest MNEs and the thousands of SMEs which are also playing significant roles in the conduct of international commerce.

The *Fortune* Global 500 (the largest public firms in the world, based on revenues) includes firms from an ever-increasing number of countries.[8] The 2003 list (for the year 2002) includes firms from twenty-five countries, employing some 40 million employees with a total of US$13.73 trillion in annual (2002) revenues, US$133 billion in profits (it was a bad year for profits, particularly in the US), and approximately US$45 trillion in assets (last reported in 2000). The enterprises included are not all from what has been traditionally viewed as the most developed countries, either. They include South Korea, Mexico, Russia, China, Brazil, India, and Malaysia, as well as firms from a number of small, but developed, economies, such as Canada, Belgium, the Netherlands, Norway, Australia, Singapore, Sweden, and Finland.

The *Business Week* Global 1000 (the largest public firms in the world based on capitalization, i.e., their market value based on their stock prices times the number of shares outstanding) ranked firms from twenty-one countries in their 2001 rankings (there were twenty-two in their 2000 rankings).[9] In the top 200 firms (2002 data) 105 were from the US and the other ninety-five were from fifteen other, non-US, countries.[10] In 2000, *Business Week* also included a ranking of the top 200 "emerging market" firms (this list grew from 100 firms the year before), at least half of which had market capitalization large enough to qualify them for the rankings of the top 1,000 firms from the twenty-one developed countries that *Business Week* studies. This emerging market list included enterprises from twenty-five additional countries, for a total of forty-six countries represented.

It is important to keep in mind, however, that these lists include only publicly traded firms. Many of the larger enterprises in developing countries are either state-owned or family-owned. Thus many more firms and countries would be represented if these types of enterprises were included. This means that various statistics about globalization may vary because of the types of MNEs included and the year the estimates were made.

Beginning in 1998, *Business Week* started compiling a ranking of the top 100 information technology firms in the world.[11] Even though most of the companies on this list are from the US (forty-three in 2003), the 2003 list also included firms from twenty-five other countries (up from nineteen in 2001), such as Indonesia, Greece, Taiwan, Hong Kong, Denmark, Russia, Spain, India, and Mexico.[12]

In 2001, *Business Week* compiled a list of the global top 100 brands.[13] Of these top 100 brands, sixty-two were American, but the remaining thirty-eight came from twelve other countries, including large countries such as Germany, France, and the UK, but also including smaller countries such as South Korea, Denmark, Finland, and Bermuda.

*Forbes* magazine also develops a ranking of international firms, ranking the top 500 based on a composite of sales, net income, assets, and market value.[14] In the world "Super 50", i.e., the fifty largest firms on their composite rankings for 2002, twenty-seven were from the US while the remainder were from eight other countries. On the *Forbes* list of the top 500 firms (outside the US), presented on their web site, there were thirty-two countries represented and fourteen nations with at least five companies on the list.[15] Again, these countries include not just those that are normally referred to as developed, but many "developing" or emerging economies, as well, including Austria, Bermuda, Brazil, China, Greece, India, Ireland, Mexico, Russia, Singapore, South Africa, Thailand, and Turkey. (This is a shorter list than the year before when firms from Argentina and Israel were also on the list.)

## *Sizes*

As indicated above, these lists include only publicly traded (listed on stock exchanges) firms and, by definition, include only the largest of international enterprises. In many countries (including the most developed ones), many of the largest firms are family-owned, such as those owned by the overseas Chinese in Taiwan, Thailand, Hong Kong, Indonesia, Malaysia, and Singapore and family groups in Latin America, enterprises which do not appear on these lists.[16] In addition, in many countries, the largest enterprises are government-owned; yet they, too, engage in international commerce. And in some countries, such as Germany, many of the firms that conduct international business are quite small. For example, it is estimated that in Germany there are about 350 small to medium-sized firms (SMEs with fewer than 300 or so employees) that still dominate their global niche markets. This reinforces the point that the number of firms and the number of countries involved with international commerce is continuing to expand at a rapid rate, making the world of business increasingly competitive and complex – and increasingly international in nature and scope.

## *Types*

Adding to the complexity is the growing number of firms that derive over half of their revenues outside their home countries and the increasing number of local firms whose ownership is held by firms from another country (with that parent firm possibly coming from a country like El Salvador, such as Badger Manufacturing, mentioned above, as well as from Japan or England or France or the Netherlands or Australia, all of which are countries which house firms with extensive overseas investment). Some of the larger (and more familiar) firms with greater than 50 percent of their revenues from outside their home countries include Hewlett-Packard, Intel, Xerox, Dow Chemical, McDonald's, Manpower, Eastman Kodak, Nestlé, Exxon, Royal Dutch Shell, Unilever, IBM, Siemens, Volkswagen, Asea Brown Boveri (ABB), Coca-Cola, and Gillette. In addition, many well known firms are now owned by firms from another country, including Firestone Tire (owned by Bridgestone, Japan), Chrysler (owned by Daimler Benz, Germany), Guinness (owned by Diageo, UK), Holiday Inn (purchased by Bass but now a part of Intercontinental Hotels, Great Britain), RCA (owned by Thompson, France), Ben & Jerry's Ice Cream and Best Foods (owned by Unilever, Netherlands/UK), Braun (owned by Gillette, US), Tropicana orange juice (acquired by Seagram, Canada, but recently acquired by Pepsi, US), Godiva chocolate (owned by Campbell Soup, US), Jolly Green Giant (owned by Grand Met, Great Britain), and Volvo and Jaguar (owned by Ford Motor Company).

The point is that the nationality of products and services is becoming ever more difficult to identify and, for practical purposes, even irrelevant. The concept of the "national" identity of firms is becoming obsolete. As indicated in the first edition of this book, firms on the original version of the above list of companies had been purchased by firms from other countries between the time the list was compiled and when it was published, such as Häagen-Dazs ice cream, a product line of Pillsbury, a long-time American firm, which is on that list but had been purchased by Grand Metropolitan of the UK (which is now Diageo, a result of the merger between Grand Met and Guinness, an Irish firm). (Indeed, as this list was retyped for this edition it became obvious that there are still firms on this list that are no longer "American." And some have been reacquired by a company in their original country of origin, like Tropicana.) This continuing acquisition of firms in one country by firms from another country is an ongoing reality and will continue to be a risk with the development of lists like this. As multinational firms acquire (or are acquired), merge with, and carry out joint ventures and alliances with firms in other countries (or their shares or stock are purchased by individuals and funds from all over the world), it becomes increasingly problematic to identify any large firm (or, maybe, even any small firm) as purely American or Japanese or British or French. The economy of the world is becoming thoroughly interconnected and global.

As a result, all of these factors combine to create an ever-increasing sense of chaos and unpredictability. No longer is any organization or employee (at any level) able to ignore this reality. To use the analogy expressed by a number of authors, businesses now confront a situation that feels a lot like "permanent white water."[17] That is, conducting business feels a lot like being caught in permanent rapids, in permanent turmoil, where the environment is constantly changing and past practices often do not provide a guide to how best to respond to problems and changes.

The economic linkages between countries and across borders take many forms, and all appear to be increasing in importance. These include exporting and importing (which is now growing even more rapidly through e-commerce), licensing, subcontracting, foreign-owned subsidiaries (either developed through acquisition or through start-up), joint ventures, alliances (such as research collaborations), foreign ownership of stocks, and foreign investment and participation in local firms at a less than controlling-ownership level, etc. It is hard to tell who owns what, what the country of ownership is for any given firm or product, and from where the various inputs come for products and services. The examples of this are many and increasing, from Cathay Pacific Airlines out of Hong Kong that outsources many inputs, such as aircraft maintenance to China and computer services to Australia and accounting and reservation services to India, to Boeing that outsources parts manufacturing all over the world, including Japan, South Korea, Singapore, and France, to General Motors that outsources assembly and parts manufacturing for various US cars to places like South Korea, Germany, Great Britain, and Ireland (as do also all other car manufacturers, like Hyundai, Toyota, and Volkswagen), or the many car companies that just directly manufacture their cars in their foreign markets – and sometimes, even, export them back "home", to Swan Optical, a US$30 million manufacturer and distributor of eyewear that subcontracts design and manufacturing to a number of countries outside the US.[18]

However, the most interesting – and important – story, here, may be told by the thousands of small to medium-sized firms (SMEs) that sell all types of products and services in other countries, supply materials and parts or services or do subcontracted or licensed manufacturing for firms from other countries, or distribute products from manufacturers in – or own franchises from – countries other than their own. And with the advent of sales via credit cards and the internet, and the improving ability to ship parcels from source country to country of the customer via services like UPS and Federal Express, anyone can sell any product to anyone else, anywhere in the world. And they are. And it involves business activity of every sort.

Because most early international business was conducted by firms involved in extraction (oil, mining) or manufacturing for export (often manufactured from imported raw materials), much of the writing about international business has been from the perspective of industrial enterprises. (The evolution of international business is covered in more detail in the next chapter, as it relates to the development of international business and HR strategy.) But today the reality is that every type of firm is conducting or can conduct business internationally. And in doing so every type of firm becomes more involved in the internationalization of human resource management.

## The internationalization of Human Resource Management

The above paragraphs make the point that business is global. All aspects of the enterprise are affected. This book is about one specific function of business, the international nature and implications of the management function termed human resource management (HRM). Thus the focus of this text is International HRM (IHRM). The more broadly defined field of IHRM *is about understanding, researching, applying and revising all human resource activities in their internal and external contexts as they impact the process of managing human resources in enterprises throughout the global environment to enhance the experience of multiple stakeholders, including investors, customers, employees, partners, suppliers, environment and society.*

As the global economy expands, as more products and services compete on a global basis and as more and more firms operate outside their countries of origin, the impact on various business functions becomes more pronounced. Practitioners in all business functions must develop the knowledge, skills, and experience in the international arena which will enable them and their firms to succeed in this new environment. This new reality is just as true (if not more so, as this book will demonstrate) for the HRM function as it is for other business disciplines, such as finance or marketing, which often get more attention. The purpose of this book is to describe the knowledge, skills, and experiences necessary for the successful management of the IHR function, a function that is increasingly performed by all employees in companies, including HR professionals (in the HR department), managers and non-managers (see Sparrow *et al.*, *Globalizing Human Resource Management*, in this series).

# Forms of International HRM

In the case of HRM, internationalization can take many forms. For practical purposes, HR managers in most types of firms can or will confront at least some aspects of internationalization. This is to say, the globalization and technology factors that have led to there being "no place to hide" for business, in general, have also led to there being no place to hide for the HR professional. Human resource professionals can find themselves involved in – and therefore must understand – IHRM issues in *any* of the following possible situations (which include HRM positions in all types of firms, not just international HR positions within the types of firms usually focused on, i.e., working at the headquarters of an MNE or in the parent-country operations).

In all cases, the international aspects of the situation increase the exposure and liabilities for HR managers and place on them ever-increasing demands for new, internationally focused competencies. This text is dedicated to helping develop the understanding and competencies necessary for HR managers to succeed (personally and professionally as business contributors) in the international arena.

## *The operation of parent-country firms overseas*

This situation involves working as a parent-country HR professional in the main or regional headquarters of the traditional multinational enterprise (MNE), such as depicted by firm X in Figure 1.1. Increasingly, this could also mean working as an expatriate HR manager in a foreign subsidiary of an MNE. This is the best-known of the international business situations and includes, for example, a parent-country HR manager working in the headquarters or parent-country operations of firms like Coca-Cola, Ford, Motorola, Bechtel, and Citibank from the US, or Nestlé, Shell, Ericsson, and Unilever from Europe, or Sony, Samsung, and Acer from Asia, all firms that have extensive foreign business activity. Typical headquarters IHRM responsibilities include selecting and preparing employees for and transferring them between the various country locations of the firm, determining and administering compensation and benefit packages for these international assignees, and establishing HRM policies and practices for the firm's foreign operations. Usually the parent firm either applies its parent-country HRM practices directly to its foreign subsidiaries, or it tries to merge its personnel practices with those that are common in the host countries.

In terms of HR management in the foreign subsidiaries of MNEs, as a matter of practice and probably necessity, local HR managers are almost always host-country nationals (HCNs). That is, these positions do not tend to be filled with HR managers from the parent firm (although these subsidiaries are usually established through the efforts of parent-country managers and HR managers). The use of local HR managers as part of the subsidiary management team makes sense because the host-country workforce is normally hired locally and work rules and practices must fit local laws and customs. Host-country nationals are more likely to be effective in the subsidiary

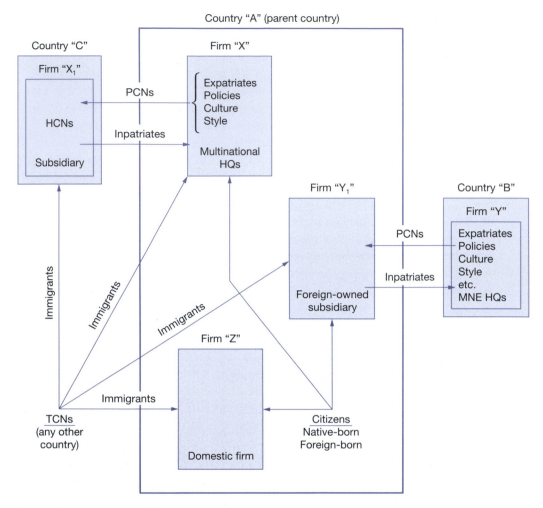

*Figure 1.1* International Human Resource Management

HR position than are expatriate HR managers from the parent firm, even though HR policy is often "dictated" from the parent-company headquarters. (However, HR policy is typically – though not always – adapted to fit local law and custom.) This centralization of HR policy can create problems with interface for host-country (subsidiary) managers – including local HR managers – who will differ in their orientations from the parent-country (HQ) HR managers.

An additional complexity, however, for IHRM, involves the increasingly common headquarters strategy in global firms that wants as many managers as possible to acquire international experience. This often also includes HR managers. So MNEs are beginning to send HR managers on foreign assignments as well as other types of managers. The result of this is that increasingly it may be possible to find HR managers serving in HR positions outside their countries of origin which could involve an HR manager either from headquarters or from a foreign subsidiary being posted to another country (that is, being an expatriate HR manager on assignment to a foreign subsidiary or regional office, in the case of a parent-country national or to another subsidiary or to headquarters, in the case of a host-country national). This situation, working as a parent-country HR manager for an MNE, at headquarters or on foreign assignment, is the first – and most commonly studied and written about – role in IHRM (see Sparrow *et al.*, *Globalizing Human Resource Management*, in this series).

## The operation of foreign firms in the home country

The second possibility for IHR involves the HR manager who works at home in the foreign subsidiary of a foreign MNE, such as firm Y in Figure 1.1 (or the HCN HR manager mentioned in the previous paragraphs). Increasingly, this could also involve working for a home-country firm that has been purchased by a foreign firm and thus is now a foreign-owned firm. In either case, the HR manager is now on the receiving end of corporate policy as it relates to HR practices. This will include working with a foreign headquarters (and, often, expatriate managers sent from the foreign – now parent – company) and typically will involve having to integrate into the local operations – the HR manager's home country – a philosophy and organizational culture and practices that are different and/or unfamiliar. This situation involves HR management as practiced by, for example, an American working in the US subsidiary of a foreign firm such as Sumitomo Bank, Sony, or Volkswagen, or in the now foreign-owned (previously US-owned) firm, such as Combustion Engineering (now a subsidiary of Asea Brown Boveri, ABB) or Häagen-Dazs ice cream (now owned by Grand Met of Great Britain), or Chrysler Group (now owned by Daimler Benz). Or it applies to the German HR manager working for Ford Motor Company in Germany or for Braun, in Germany (now owned by Gillette), or the Japanese HR manager working for the Japanese subsidiary of IBM in Japan or for Nissan, now with majority ownership by Renault from France.

The different communication and business practice styles, motivation philosophies, and organizational structures and frequent lack of understanding of the host-country cultures, markets, employment laws and practices, and language, by the parent company, can cause difficulty for the local HR manager, and thus force that host-country HR manager to confront aspects of internationalization that are just as difficult as those confronted by the home-country HR manager working at headquarters and dealing with the "export" of policy and practice.

## The employment of foreign citizens (or recent immigrants and/or their families)

The situation of firm Z in Figure 1.1 depicts what is "on the surface" a purely domestic firm, such as a hospital, farm, dry cleaner, ski resort, or restaurant (or the purely domestic operations of an MNE, such as the local fast-food franchise for

McDonald's or a local petrol station for Shell or BP). In many countries (particularly true in most locales in the US) even these types of firms confront many of the complexities of international business. These complexities include: (1) the hiring of employees who come from another country, culture, and language (recent immigrants) or their families (who may have been born in the new country, and are, therefore, now citizens, but who may still be more familiar with the language and culture with which they grow up at home than with that of their family's new country); as well as (2) having to deal with competition from foreign firms for customers and supplies, or for capital which may well come from foreign-owned firms, or competition from these firms for resources, including employees.

Sometimes this "domestic" firm hires, or even relies on, foreign-born or first-generation immigrant employees because the employer can't find an adequate number of "traditional" citizens to fill positions. Or it is done simply because these individuals make up a large percentage of the local labor force. In any case, the local firm needs knowledge of local laws that govern such employees (such as visa requirements) as well as the ability to integrate these employees with a different language and cultural background into the domestic firm and its workforce.

Examples of this situation include the Boulder, Colorado, McDonald's that had recent immigrants from El Salvador, Mexico, Russia, and Vietnam on its payroll, none of whom spoke much English, the community hospital in Seattle that hires nurses from the Philippines and doctors from Europe and Asia, the local government computer services agency in Lansing, Michigan, that recruits programmers from India and Pakistan, and the local college in North Carolina that employs professors from other countries. Of course, there are local organizations with equivalent workforces in many countries other than the US. The hiring – or recruiting – of immigrants (or, even, the first generation since immigration) in local, domestic firms can lead to many of the same internationalization concerns as those faced by an MNE, such as how to merge the cultures, languages, and general work expectations of employees from different countries, and such as how to respond to employees who bring to their new work situations sometimes very different attitudes toward supervision and have very different expectations related to the practice of management. The point is that there is no place to hide, even for HR managers of such "domestic" firms. They, too, must develop all the knowledge and experiences necessary to succeed in an internationalized environment.

IHRM in Action 1.2 illustrates how the firm Barden of Danbury, Connecticut, dealt with the challenge of hiring recent immigrants and the payoffs for the firm in terms of improved employee commitment and performance and easier recruiting.[19] Barden's experience with recent immigrants from many different countries shows that through creative efforts to integrate these types of new employees a firm can reap unforeseen yet significant benefits. But it also illustrates that in some (maybe many) communities, even in quite small firms, employers (and their HR managers) must rely on the hiring of recent foreign immigrants to fill job openings and thus have to cope with many of the same international issues as do larger international firms.

# Internationalization of a local manufacturer

The experiences of Barden, a precision ball-bearing manufacturer located in Danbury, Connecticut, illustrate how global issues can impact even a local firm. In the late 1980s, Barden had an opportunity to significantly increase its business. In order to achieve this, it had to increase its hourly labor force by about 125 employees in one year. However, the local Danbury labor market was experiencing an unprecedented low unemployment rate of about 2.5 percent. The Human Resource department thought they could do this, but indicated they would have to be very creative (using bonuses to employees for successful referrals, open houses to recruit applicants, etc.) and, importantly, by recruiting workers whose English was very poor.

In the past, Barden had found that, for example, Portuguese immigrants became very reliable, long-term employees. Barden had used a "buddy" system to help them learn their jobs and to acquire an adequate "Barden" vocabulary. But it was clear that this would be inadequate to prepare – in a short period of time – the large new group of potential employees that had been identified. It turned out that there were a significant number of bright recent immigrants from a large but diverse number of countries (e.g., Laos, Cambodia, Brazil, Colombia, the Dominican Republic, Guatemala, Chile, Lebanon, Pakistan, Thailand, and Yemen), but who spoke little or no English.

To become functioning, qualified Barden employees, newcomers would have to master the basic "Barden" vocabulary and be able to look up standard operating procedures as well as material safety data sheets, and master basic shop mathematics, measurement processes, and blueprint reading. This was a tall order for the immigrants (many of whom, it was discovered, had received a surprisingly good education in their home countries). In order to teach these new employees enough English to pay their way, a language training firm, Berlitz, was retained to develop a special, intensive course in cooperation with Barden's training unit. In a fairly short period of time six groups of eight new employees were taught through this special program. All the students were put on the payroll while they met with a Berlitz instructor for four hours a day for fifteen consecutive workdays during work hours.

The program had a number of effects, beyond enabling Barden to fill its employment needs to meet its new corporate growth strategy and to integrate this veritable United Nations group into its workforce. The confidence level of the students soared as they used their new language ability. Barden's supervisors were impressed. And the word spread to the community with the positive result of attracting new high quality recruits.

In the US and the European Union, shortages of certain types of employees, particularly ones with technical backgrounds, has made it necessary to even recruit such employees from other countries. This contributes to the global complexities that HR managers in all types of firms must now confront and learn to deal with.

### Government agencies and non-governmental organizations

Even though this text primarily discusses IHRM in the business context, many other types of organizations are also international or have to deal with many of these international issues. For example, government agencies such as the State Departments from all countries and their embassies in other countries and NGOs such as the Roman Catholic Church (and any other religion that sends representatives to other countries), World Vision or Habitat for Humanity, which has low-income housing projects in some sixty countries, all send hundreds of people from their parent countries and from their "headquarters" operations to their overseas operations (and usually also employ many local and third-country people to staff their activities around the world). Many international HR activities for these organizations are similar to those faced by their commercial counterparts. The point is, problems associated with locating, compensating, and managing employees in multiple countries are not much different for IBM than they are for the International Red Cross or the World Health Organization. Human Resource managers, even in these types of organizations, must also become globally savvy.

## The development of IHRM

The intention of the above discussion was to illustrate that HR managers in essentially all forms of organization can and do confront aspects of international HR. The extent of this involvement will vary according to a number of factors (discussed in more detail in the next chapter) and will invariably increase with time. But as internationalization of business increases in extent and intensity, HR managers will be called upon to contribute increasing expertise to that internationalization.

All of these situations create new and special concerns for HRM. One of the fundamental problems in all of these situations is to find (recruit and/or train) HR managers who, although they are raised and experienced in one culture, can effectively interact with and manage people raised in one or more different cultures, and who can develop effective HRM practices and policies in all of the various business environments in which the employer operates (as well as helping the firm's executives plan for and manage effectively in these environments, as well).

Decisions have to be made concerning issues such as: (1) from a labor force perspective, which countries make the most sense for locating international operations; (2) the numbers and proportions of international assignees versus host-country employees needed to staff plants and offices around the world; (3) where and how to recruit these individuals and how to compensate them for their performance; and (4) whether HRM practices and policies will be uniform across all locations or will be tailored to each location (or some combination of centralized and localized).[20] Whether the local HR manager is from the country of the parent company, from the country of the local subsidiary, or from a third country, he or she is sandwiched between his or her own culture and the "foreign" cultures of the firm. Human resource managers at the local, regional, and headquarters levels must integrate and coordinate activities taking place in diverse environments with people of diverse backgrounds. And they are usually looked to for expertise in helping other managers be successful in their international endeavors, as well.

The point is, today most firms experience one or more aspects of international HR management, and the successes or failures of these firms are often a function of how well they handle their international HRM concerns. Because of these pressures, a whole new set of responsibilities within the human resource function have developed. This book discusses these international human resource responsibilities.

Even though some firms – such as Nestlé, Unilever, and Royal Dutch Shell in Europe or Ford Motor Company, IBM, and Eastman Kodak in the US – have quite long traditions of being international (going back about 100 years), and thus their human resource functions – at least at the headquarters level – have also had to develop at least some international expertise, for practical purposes the identifiable business function of "International Human Resource Management" is relatively new. A professional society devoted to IHRM (the Global Forum, a division of the US's Society for Human Resource Management) held its twenty-seventh annual conference in 2004. However, it is only since about 1991 that this annual meeting has involved much more than a fairly small group of senior IHR managers from the large US MNEs, primarily involved with the management of expatriates and the establishment of local subsidiaries, who got together once a year to network and share stories and to learn from each other. (There has not been until quite recently any other way to gain expertise.) Similar professional HR associations are found in many countries of the world. The World Federation of Personnel Management Associations has fifty-one member associations, including SHRM. For details of the Chartered Institute of Personnel and Development (CIPD) in the UK see Sparrow et al., Globalizing Human Resource Management, in this series.

As a business discipline and an academic field of study, IHRM is in its infancy; yet it is very real and firmly established.[21] There are many reasons for its youth, some of which have to do with the generally limited role of HRM within many large firms, including the large MNEs, and some of which have to do with HR managers themselves. Suddenly, in the last twenty years or so, as business in general has rapidly internationalized, HR professionals have been called upon to manage a number of new activities, such as the management of international assignees, to work alongside HR professionals from other countries, and to adapt their HR practices to multicultural and cross-cultural environments.[22] In general, HR professionals have failed to embrace globalization as part of their development, and, indeed, have only recently begun to see the necessity (and business schools and professional HR societies have also been slow to add offerings in international HR to their curricula).

Often, HR managers are the last ones in their firms to focus on the increasing globalization, the last ones to take on international assignments, and thus often the last ones on the management team to contribute as fully fledged strategic partners in the internationalization of their companies.

There have been a number of reasons put forth to explain this late awakening to the importance of international business in US firms and its impact on human resources.[23] They include the lack of professionalization of IHR; the deep fragmentation into functional areas within HR practice, so that what limited international responsibilities there might be were not "seen" or evaluated as important by other HR practitioners; the lack of awareness and understanding among domestic HR practitioners of cross-cultural and international HR issues; the preoccupation with domestic legal and other practice issues; and the tremendous gap between the academic international HR body of knowledge and the international HR practitioner's expertise and concerns.

Clearly there is an identifiable body of knowledge and practice that provides an important starting point for studying IHRM. A few journals focus specifically on this subject, such as the *International Journal of Human Resource Management*, others that are more generically devoted to HR have added either specific sections devoted to IHR or have added newsletters or more frequent articles devoted to IHR. (See our web site for a list of such journals as well as professional associations.) And gradually, the number of texts and readings books has increased while the number of courses and seminars at universities and provided by consulting firms and training organizations has also gradually increased.[24]

In general, there are two quite different perspectives to the subject of IHRM.[25] These include (1) discussions of HR policies and practices and the HR function and department within the multinational enterprise, focused on the management of its employees, and also focused on the strategy and structure of its operations; and (2) discussions of HR policies and practices in various countries as well as characteristics of those countries, focused primarily on what is often referred to as "comparative" human resource management.

This text focuses mostly on perspective 1, with some discussion of the external characteristics of countries such as culture, laws, and demographics, that impact and shape the IHR policies and practices of MNEs (including SMEs). While many examples in this book reflect experiences of US-based MNEs, the experiences of non-US-based MNEs are also used. Other books in this series contain many more examples of non-US-based MNEs, so in total there is a great global coverage of MNEs (including SMEs).

## Differences between International and domestic HRM

In the early years of writing about IHRM, a number of surveys and authors suggested that IHRM differed from its domestic counterpart in terms of a number of factors.[26] The following updates this perspective.

As will become more than evident throughout this text, the practice of HRM in the international context is different from its domestic counterpart in a number of ways.[27] This includes the IHR department in a multinational firm (1) being responsible for a greater number of activities, such as the management of international assignees that includes such things as foreign taxes and work visas and detailed assistance with family relocations to foreign locales; (2) having to expand its areas of expertise to include a much broader perspective, including knowledge of foreign countries and their employment laws; (3) having to get much more closely involved – than is ever necessary in a purely domestic situation – with employees' (and their families') lives as the firm moves employees from country to country; (4) being involved with a greatly expanded and constantly changing mix of employees, adding considerable complexity to the IHR management task (Chapter 8 discusses in some detail the twenty-one types of employees encountered in the international arena, each requiring different staffing and compensation and benefits practices); (5) having to cope with more external influences, such as having to deal with issues stemming from multiple cultures and countries; and, as a result, (6) having to face much greater exposure to problems and difficulties, and, thus, exposure to much greater potential liabilities for making mistakes in HR decisions (for example, the cost of a failed international assignment can be as high as US$1 million).

In addition to these complexities, the geographic dispersion and multiculturalism that the international firm faces adds a need for competency and sensitivity that is not found in the domestic firm.[28] The personal and professional attitudes and perspectives of the IHR manager must be greatly expanded to handle the multiple countries and cultures confronted in the international arena – both to manage their IHR responsibilities and to contribute to successful international business strategies by their firms – beyond those which the domestic HR manager must develop. The typical domestic US HR manager does not have the contacts or networks that become necessary to learn about and to handle the new international responsibilities. He or she doesn't typically have any experience with the business and social protocols needed to interact successfully with foreign colleagues or with the forms of organizational structure used to pursue international strategies (such as joint ventures or cross-border acquisitions). And the still relatively limited body of literature and publicly available seminars and training programs make it much more difficult to develop the competencies needed to manage successfully the IHRM function.

The next chapter focuses on HR issues that firms confront when their international operations mature from basic export activity to becoming truly global firms with multiple activities and alliances around the world. The amount of international activity (as a percent of a firm's revenues) and experience as well as the nature of the industry in which a firm is engaged all can influence the nature of the organizational problems that MNEs confront. Chapter 3 discusses many of the issues created by the variety of national, social, cultural, educational, managerial, and governmental systems with which MNEs must interact.

In terms of the HRM function, the impact of international activity will vary according to these many considerations. At times, there may be considerable demand for international services from the HRM function (for example, when the need for increased numbers of expatriates arises), but these activities may not be housed within the essential core of the HR function – partially because many of these services can be provided by consultants or through other forms of temporary assistance. The main role for HRM at the typical MNE is to support the activities of the firm (and the local HR function) in each domestic market in which the parent company is engaged. That is, the HRM function is likely to be fairly well decentralized. However, when the firm is involved with a global industry and is pursuing a worldwide business strategy, the need for coordination and centralization for worldwide consistency of HR policy and practice will become more important. This tension between decentralization (localization) and centralization (consistency) often becomes the major conflict within the multinational enterprise's strategic management planning and, specifically, within IHRM's support of those plans.[29]

> In order to build, maintain, and develop their corporate identity, multinational organizations need to strive for consistency in their ways of managing people on a worldwide basis. Yet, in order to be effective locally, they also need to adapt those ways to the specific cultural requirements of different societies. While the global nature of the business may call for increased consistency, the variety of cultural environments may be calling for differentiation.[30]

The end result of trying to cope with this dilemma is that IHRM is left with a number of problems to resolve. These problems and their resolutions provide much of the foci for the rest of this book. Some of these key issues include:[31]

- How does HRM fit into and contribute to an international strategy?
- Which HRM practices should be *designed* at headquarters? Which locally? By whom? When are international HR teams to be used?
- How does the firm reach agreement on company objectives while allowing variable (national, local) paths to achieving them?
- How much *consistency* in HRM policies should be insisted on? Which policies should be global and which local? If global, whose laws and cultural practices take precedence? Which are best (for organizational results)? What are the benefits to consistency versus decentralization?
- Which *nationalities* should be represented by key managers at headquarters and in the main subsidiaries?
- How much and which *expatriation* should be used? Parent country to foreign subsidiary? Foreign subsidiary to parent company? Third-country nationals? Foreign subsidiary to foreign subsidiary?
- How should the whole expatriation process be managed? How are management potential and performance judged when criteria differ from country to country?
- How should the management of careers be orchestrated internationally?

These issues have to be addressed in the midst of managing the day-to-day IHRM policies and practices of staffing, training, compensation, and performance management. In the end, the IHR manager, in order to develop a truly global view, must:[32]

- Explicitly recognize how home-country ways of managing human resources are a function of cultural values and assumptions.
- Recognize that these ways are neither better nor worse than others around the world.
- Take action to make cultural differences discussable, and, therefore, usable.
- Develop a genuine belief that more creative and effective ways of managing human resources can be learned from other cultures.

The value of this sort of comparative awareness lies in the comparison of the various systems, the analysis of the causes that have produced these differences, and then the study of the different solutions found to similar problems. The diversity of solutions can then be applied to the more effective management of the global enterprise.

The extent to which corporate and parent-country cultures can or should override national cultures is at the forefront of the discussion throughout this text. MNEs and global firms have a need for (and benefit from) worldwide integration and coordination while retaining responsiveness to local customers and employees. At the local level this means determining what needs to be done differently in the context of requirements for integration. The push from headquarters to conform to a global culture often is met with an equal push at the local or subsidiary level to preserve uniqueness. (This issue is discussed in more detail in the next chapter in the context of fitting IHRM practices to the strategic plans of the firm.)

As discussed earlier and developed more fully in Chapters 3 and 5, research and experience demonstrates that even within large MNEs, famous for their strong cultures and socializing efforts, national cultures continue to play a major role in differentiating work values. These issues are at the forefront of discussions within the IHRM function, as it helps employers to develop the balance between localization and globalization, and as it tries to figure out how to do that within its own areas of responsibility. This text describes IHRM practices and policies in managing international assignees, local workforces, and global managers in the context of trying to find a balance between these pressures for localization and centralization.

Sensitivity to local conditions can be quite complementary to strong corporate loyalty, rather than these being mutually exclusive orientations. Each corresponds to important but fundamentally different strategic requirements in the running of various businesses. As a result, most businesses require that their managers (and their IHR managers) provide a blending of sensitivity to local interests *and* loyalty to overall corporate (i.e., global) interests.

> The ideal, then, is to differentiate in such a way as to make integration more effective, or to decentralize activities in such a way that an ever broader diversity gets coordinated by the "central nervous system" of [the] corporation. In matters of cultural diversity, there is always a challenge, but, where this challenge is met, valuable connections result.[33]

## The global role of the IHR professional

In order to enhance the competitive advantage of global firms, their human resource professionals (managers and staff) need to focus on developing their own international competencies.[34] At the same time, the IHRM function needs to shift from an administrative orientation to one that places primary attention on the processes of internationalization (described more fully in Chapter 2) so that it can help reconcile the types of organizational paradoxes described above that are inherent in the activities of global firms. This not only creates new demands on how specific HR activities are performed but also sets a new agenda for HR professionals and their global roles. (For more detail on the professionalization and internationalization of the HR manager see Chapter 14 and Sparrow *et al.*, *Globalizing Human Resource Management*, in this series.)

First, HR professionals need to learn about the fundamentals of global business. They cannot assume a global strategic role without understanding global strategy. Second, a solid knowledge of strategy must be complemented by the globalization of their individual professional expertises. This rests primarily on the acceptance and understanding of the cultural relativity of many HR practices. And that in turn is complemented by an understanding of how their firms' principal global competitors plan and execute their global HR strategies, what tools and methods they use to build their organizational competencies, and what implications for competitiveness arise from their actions.

This understanding of global strategy, cultural differences, and HR capabilities requires a thorough globalization of the HR function by developing a cadre of HR professionals with international perspective, knowledge, and experience. Presently, however, the number of HR executives with multicountry experience or who are on an international promotion and development track is quite limited, even in the largest of MNEs.

The lack of international experience among US HR professionals is not surprising, but this must change if IHRM is to be recognized as a strategic partner in the management of global firms. Global firms will need not only to set up regional HR positions and assign global responsibilities to corporate HR managers but also to select, develop, and motivate IHR professionals with very much the same intensity and approach that is currently used for global executives in other areas of management. Chapter 14 in this book will address specifically this issue: the future professionalization of IHR managers and departments.

Firms that have successfully globalized their human resource activities share several important characteristics:[35]

- The global HR role has the strong support of top management in terms of high expectations about the contributions the IHRM function can make to the formulation and implementation of effective global strategies and the readiness of the IHRM function to step up to its responsibilities.

- The expectations and support of top management for the IHRM role are usually derived from a longstanding commitment to dedicate management energy and resources to human resource issues as a reflection of a people-oriented corporate culture.
- Cultural diversity (including national diversity) is encouraged as a natural way of life.
- Ambiguity as a way of dealing with the many paradoxes imbedded in global HR issues is also accepted as normal. Not much is seen or accepted as "black or white."
- The final condition for a successful implementation of IHRM strategies is the competence and credibility of the IHRM staff. To earn that credibility, IHR managers must accept the risk and responsibility for putting forward policies and practices that make a difference in the achievement of corporate global strategies.

These characteristics are described, explained, and discussed throughout this text, particularly in the next chapter. They essentially provide the framework and orientation within which this text presents the current state of international human resource management.

## Conclusion

This chapter has introduced International Human Resource Management and the context of international business. It provided an overview of the globalization of the economy and discussed how that has impacted the function of international human resource management. The chapter showed how economic activity around the world has become increasingly integrated and, thus, increasingly global in nature. One of the most difficult challenges to international operations is the management of human resources. An effective and informed HRM function is vital to the success of all firms with international operations. Conducting business successfully in more than one country – at any level of activity above import–export – requires the development of culturally sensitive HRM programs. The purpose of this book is to describe and explain the scope and practice of the emerging field of international human resource management.

This chapter explains why all HR professionals must confront at least some aspects of internationalization in their jobs and describes how International HRM differs from traditional "domestic" HRM. The chapter makes the point that IHRM encompasses and reflects many international business and management characteristics such as the determination of strategy and structure. These characteristics of international business and management impact the day-to-day operations of core IHR policies and practices of selection, training and development, compensation, employee relations, and health and safety. Other policies and practices such as HR planning, HR information systems, job analysis, performance measurement and appraisal, and HR research that support core IHRM policies and practices, are also impacted by characteristics of international business and management. The characteristics of international business and management that impact IHRM policies and practices are described throughout this book.

## Points for further discussion

1 Describe why Lincoln Electric had to become more global. What were the major factors?
2 Will these factors continue to require even more globalization?
3 What is the impact of globalization on the management of its employees?

# 2 | Strategic International Human Resource Management

## Learning objectives

After considering this chapter, the reader will be able to describe:

- The development of international business strategy from three different perspectives
- The development of Strategic IHRM
- The links and relationships between strategic international business and Strategic IHRM
- The critical international strategic decision involving the centralization or localization of strategic IB and Strategic IHRM policy and practice
- The extent and nature of research into the practice of Strategic IHRM

## Key terms

- Strategic International Human Resource Management
- Strategic management
- Strategies, forms, and stages
- International orientation

This chapter is about Strategic International Human Resource Management (SIHRM). While the first chapter described the new global business realities and introduced international HRM,[1] this chapter describes international business strategy and how international HR management supports and enhances the international business strategies of the firm.

MNEs, in order to be successful in the global marketplace, must develop strategies to conduct business that take advantage of global resources and markets. In order for international HR managers to make an effective contribution to that success, they must contribute to and be a part of the global strategic management of the business. Since firms differ in their levels of international development and in the extent of their international operations, IHR managers must develop the capabilities to assist in that development and in those various levels of global operation. This chapter provides an introduction to how these variances in the strategic development of the international activities of firms influence IHRM and how strategic IHRM supports those varying strategies and activities.

As outlined in Chapter 1, the new realities for MNEs, including reduced transportation and information costs around the world and the removal of social and political barriers to trade, are making the globalization of business proceed at unexpected and unprecedented rates.[2] The opening of markets and the appearance of competitive foreign firms place pressures on virtually every major (and most minor) industry in virtually every country. These developments impact human resource management on a number of fronts.[3] The increased intensity of competition places great pressure on firms to develop the capacity to operate at lower costs and with greater speed, quality, customer service, and innovation, both at home and abroad. HR is called upon to hire, develop, and retain the workforce that can achieve this global competitiveness, often in dozens of countries. Therefore, this chapter introduces the contribution of IHR to the strategic management of the MNE and introduces the ways in which the global strategy impacts the management of IHR.

The chapter starts with a general description of the process of strategic management and then follows with an explanation of the evolution of international business strategy and describes how IHRM fits into the overall strategic management of an MNE. This includes describing the links of global business strategy with the performance of HR responsibilities in international business and discussing the outcomes that a strategically managed international business might expect from effectively tying together an international business strategy and strategic IHRM. The chapter then summarizes the findings of research studies on the nature and role of strategic IHRM and closes with a short introduction to one of the most critical (and difficult to resolve) strategic international decisions: whether and to what extent to centralize or to localize international policy and practice of the MNE.

## Strategic IHRM

In an *ideal* world, a firm conducting international business will be actively engaged in strategic planning and strategic management. The firm will regularly perform an environmental analysis or scan (of its external threats and opportunities and its organizational strengths and weaknesses) and from that analysis develop its global strategies (Figure 2.1) which are then implemented for global success. Still in this *ideal* world, all components of the firm will be closely integrated into that planning and will be involved with similar strategic planning within their own areas of responsibility (See Pucik and Evans, *People Strategies for MNEs*, in this series, for more detailed discussion).

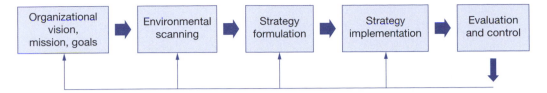

*Figure 2.1* Basic elements of the strategic management process

Strategic management, in general, is the array of competitive moves and business approaches that managers employ in running a company and that are derived from the firm's vision and objectives. In crafting a strategic course, management is saying that "among all the paths and actions we could choose, we have decided to go in this direction and rely on these particular ways of doing business."[4] A strategy signals an organization's commitment to specific markets, competitive approaches, and ways of operating. A company's strategy is thus the "game plan" its management has for positioning the firm in its chosen market arena, for investing money and people in the development of particular business capabilities, for developing sustainable competitive advantage, for pleasing its customers, and, thus, for achieving superior business performance. These strategies are developed in either or both of two ways: proactively, as a forward-looking plan to deal with anticipated market forces, or reactively, as a response to what the firm is experiencing in the marketplace. In most firms, strategies that are developed stem from a combination of these forces.

Senior executives devise specific strategies for their organizations because of two very compelling needs. One is the need to *actively shape* how their firm's business will be conducted. The second need is that of molding the independent decisions and actions initiated by departments, managers, and employees across the company into a *coordinated, company-wide* game plan. Both motives have become increasingly complex in today's global business environment. Yet

> Among all the things managers do, nothing affects a company's ultimate success or failure more fundamentally than how well its management team charts the company's long-term direction, develops competitively effective strategic moves and business approaches, and implements what needs to be done internally to produce good day-in/day-out strategy execution. Indeed, *good strategy and good strategy execution are the most trustworthy signs of good management.*[5]

In terms of HR, many of the same issues arise – albeit in a much more complex way – when a firm's strategic planning "goes international" as when its strategic planning is concerned only with domestic issues. When managements begin to develop and implement global strategic plans, they also begin to concern themselves with global human resource issues.[6] Indeed, the HR issues are among the most critical issues for successfully competing in the international marketplace. And because of that, HR should be providing input to the international strategic decision making at every step, helping with mission and goal setting, the environmental scan, design of specific strategies, and, of course, helping to implement the chosen strategies.

The new, global, complex, and often chaotic world of the MNE requires a new strategic focus and new structures from Human Resources just as it does from other management functions. The next section of this chapter introduces the evolution of international business strategy. The rest of the chapter is about strategic international human resource management (SIHRM), which, to a large degree concerns creating and implementing human resource (HR) practices that help achieve an MNE's international vision and objectives, that is, its international strategy. It also involves the strategic management of the IHR function and department itself.

Only limited studies have been made of the extent to which multinational firms involve their HRM functions with their global strategic planning, and what studies have been made suggest that HR does not tend to be nearly as involved as the need suggests is necessary. Often the Human Resource department is one of the last areas of management to be impacted by internationalization and HR managers are among the last to personally internationalize. However, HR can and should provide input to strategic decision making and choices at the highest levels, including decisions about going international.[7] (See Sparrow *et al.*, *Globalizing Human Resource Management*, in this series for more detailed discussion.)

Once the decision is made to go international (whether it is a proactive or reactive choice), the task of all managers – including HR managers – is to implement that decision, to convert the strategic plan into action and get on with whatever needs to be done to achieve the international vision and targeted objectives.

## Evolution of the multinational enterprise

In order to place IHRM in the context of the MNE and to link with the MNE, it is necessary to have an appreciation for the development of the international firm. There have been a number of approaches to this issue. The following provides a short synthesis of these various approaches.

This discussion of the development of the MNE and its international business strategy begins with a discussion of its evolution and then is organized around three issues at the center of IB strategy: (1) the degree of internationalization and geographic scope; (2) the basic choices (by a firm) for entry into international business; and (3) the extent of global mind-set or global orientation of the firm and its executives. All three issues create important perspectives for viewing the development of IHRM, itself, and its strategic ties to the MNE.

## Degree of internationalization (geographic scope)

Increasingly for most businesses and in most locations, strategic business decisions involve choices to go in an international direction. Often a firm has no choice but to "go international," either because it is facing competition from outside its national borders or it seeks cheaper resources or expanded markets in other countries. When strategic decisions are made to go international, it obviously affects every function of the organization, including human resources.

One approach to IB strategy categorizes the degree of internationalization of the firm, that is, the degree to which the firm is: (1) international; (2) multinational or multi-domestic; (3) regional; (4) global; or (5) transnational.[8] The following provides a brief overview of these types of basic strategies that a firm can choose in order to internationalize. These choices range from relatively "hands off" strategies to full integration into the global economy. This section describes the most common of these choices, which are described in more detail in Chapter 4.

As the reader will observe while reading these three sections, these various strategies or stages to understanding international business strategy are interrelated.[9] Just as firms differ in their stages of international development, so too do they differ in terms of the structures they adopt in their international operations. The specific international strategy chosen or developed influences the choice and design of organizational structure. Coping with the complexities of the design of global enterprises turns out to be one of the most difficult areas in which IHRM can make a strategic contribution to a firm's international business strategy.[10] Thus, this section includes some of the issues related to international organizational structure. (Most of these issues of structure are discussed in more depth in Chapter 4, devoted specifically to issues of international organizational design and structure.)

## *Internationalization*

At this stage, a firm makes the initial decision to "go international." In the beginning, this choice will probably involve only export to foreign customers in one country, or import of one or a few products, again probably from only one supplier or one country. The international business activity at this level will have very little impact on the overall business and will not receive much management attention. In recent years, this level of strategic involvement has extended beyond concerns for finding new markets or cheap raw materials to licensing and subcontracting of manufacturing and sourcing of manufacturing inputs, in order to meet rising cost pressures caused by increased global competition. The HR impact will be fairly limited, with the firm relying on a few key managers and technical experts to negotiate overseas linkages and to transfer technology, if necessary, to a licensee or subcontractor.

## *International division or global product division*

When foreign sales reach over 10–20 percent of total revenues, or global sourcing reaches an equivalent level of impact, firms often choose to form international divisions that will be responsible for all international operations.[11] Many service-oriented businesses begin at this stage, with a significant number of stores or offices or service centers established in one or more foreign countries. If the firm has a large number of products being sold overseas, it may choose to create product lines with worldwide responsibility. Under this strategy, the MNE will begin to consider local (foreign) assembly and, eventually, complete manufacturing of its products and/or services, either for sale in the foreign country or for export back to the home market or other foreign markets. This division may initially be located within the marketing function; but as sales and involvement increase, it may become an independent division, equivalent to domestic product or regional divisions and with little integration with the domestic operations.

At this level of development, the international responsibilities of the HR department expand dramatically and become much more complex. Not only will the number of parent-company employees on international assignment increase dramatically (creating the demand for new skills in the HR department) but now the HR department will need to become involved with development of HRM policies, practices, and decisions for the foreign operations.

## Multi-country/multi-domestic

At this level of international strategy, a firm decides to establish subsidiaries in multiple countries, with these subsidiaries typically operating independently within each country, independently of operations in other countries, and often fairly independent, even, of the parent-company headquarters. This is referred to as a "multi-domestic" or "multi-country" strategy. Lincoln Electric (described in the end-of-book case study) pursued this strategy through much of the 1990s.

As independent as subsidiaries often become, in this strategy the organization's operations in a number of countries may reach such size and importance that there is increased need for integration with corporate headquarters. The firm may develop global product divisions that provide global coordination of finance, HRM, marketing, and research and development. Or the MNE may organize into major country subsidiaries with regional headquarters to coordinate operations on a regional basis. Nevertheless, at this level of international strategy, the MNE will have significant operations (assembly, manufacturing, service centers, R&D, branch offices) in many countries and may well reach the condition where half or more of its sales and employment is in foreign countries.

Key personnel in the subsidiaries and regional offices are usually from the company's home office with many decisions made at corporate headquarters. Thus, although the subsidiaries are largely staffed by people from the countries in which they are located, managers from the home office may retain authority in key areas (such as profitability and compensation bonuses). The MNE at this level of development generally views each national market as a specialized market for its particular subsidiaries' products. Each subsidiary concentrates its efforts on the nation in which it is located. This was certainly true in the case of Lincoln Electric in the 1990s.

The HR department's role at this stage becomes even more complex and difficult. Now HRM must not only provide services – such as relocation, compensation, and benefits for often hundreds of employees (international assignees) working in foreign (to them) locations – but it must also coordinate the HRM activities and practices of the many subsidiaries, seeking both consistency with the culture and policies of the parent company and accommodation of local values and practices. In addition, training for international assignees (from the parent company or from foreign locales), local nationals, and parent-company employees to handle foreign assignments and interaction with foreign counterparts will increase dramatically.

## Regionalization

In an alternative to the multi-domestic strategy, a firm may decide initially (or, possibly after first pursuing the multi-domestic strategy) to conduct its international business on a regional basis, as Ford Motor Company has done, described in IHRM in Action 2.1.[12] This will probably involve first organizing to conduct business in only one or two regions, such as Europe or Latin America (for an American firm) or maybe North America (for a European or Asian firm) or Asia (for an Asian or European firm). This is essentially what Lincoln Electric did after learning that a multi-domestic strategy was too inefficient. The HRM impacts here are similar to those in the previous strategy, although they will be managed from a regional headquarters. An assumption made is that countries within a region share some common characteristics such as country culture, geographical proximity or stage of economic development.

## The global firm

In recent years, many MNEs have reached the state of internationalization where their operations are becoming blind to national borders. Even though most businesses still organize on a regional basis and adaptation to local customer preferences may still be necessary, products and services are increasingly designed for and marketed to customers all over the world. This is particularly true for industrial products, that is, for products sold from business to business, such as computer chips. The best technology and innovative ideas are sought everywhere and applied to markets throughout the world. Products and services are created where costs are the lowest, quality is the highest, and time to delivery is the shortest, and delivered wherever demand is sufficient. And resources (money, material and parts, insurance, even people) are sought from wherever the best quality for cost can be found.

These firms are increasingly referred to as "global."[13] Reaching this stage of development is not merely a matter of company size or experience in internationalization. Sometimes it is a reflection of the nature of the pressures of the particular industry, but often, it reflects a purposeful, strategic, decision to

# Ford Motor Company goes international

Ford Motor Company has been in business for over 100 years and when it comes to a global mind-set, Ford is ahead of most of its competitors.

For a number of historical reasons, over the years Ford evolved into a collection of country and regional fiefdoms. Early in its history, Ford was like many large US companies, which often sent someone off to the UK, Canada, or Argentina to run a company just like the one back home. The first Henry Ford was in many ways an internationalist, because within a very few years of establishing the company in the US, he was quickly opening assembly plants all over the world that were essentially smaller versions of the original company in Detroit.

But by the mid-1920s, and all around the world, a sense of national pride developed. Countries began to develop their own automotive companies. Suddenly, there were automotive companies in the UK, in France, Germany, Australia, and they were all making their own vehicles. Nations wanted to assert their independence and saw the automotive industry as a means of investing in their own economies. The Europeans exported, the Americans exported, and that's how the competitive game was being played. (This was the beginnings of the "multi-domestic" structure for large multinational corporations, which is explained earlier in this chapter.)

In the 1960s, though, regionalism began to develop, with the emergence of the European Common Market, NAFTA, ASEAN, and other regional trading groups. Countries kept their own political systems and social values but formed economic trading blocks. So big companies established regional headquarters within the various major trading blocs. Ford Europe was established in this period. This was when most of the regional and functional fiefdoms (with each region becoming very independent) became firmly entrenched at Ford. (This is what is referred to in this book as the "regional" corporate structure, an extension of the "multi-domestic" structure.) The fiefdoms were excellent at what they did: they squeezed every last ounce of efficiency out of the regional model. For example, back in the period of nationalism, Ford had multiple accounting activities around the world – there were fifteen in Europe alone. The regional model got it down to four: one in Europe, one in the United States, one in Asia-Pacific, and one in South America. But even with that efficiency, Ford felt that the model didn't work any more.

Today Ford is moving to a fourth stage of economic evolution with the globalization of all aspects of its international operations: capital, communications, economic policy, trade policy, human resources, marketing, advertising, brands, etc. The auto industry around the world has become globalized. Germany and Japan produce cars in the US, Korea produces cars in Eastern Europe, and Malaysia and Mexico export cars and parts. In addition, the automotive industry has become an electronics-driven industry. It is increasingly a business that requires huge investments in technology and intellectual capital.

So the leadership of Ford feels there is no longer a choice about globalization. For a company of Ford's background and size, remaining a national or regional company is no longer a viable alternative. Auto companies around the world have global ambitions, and many of them are world-class players, such as Toyota, Honda, Volkswagen, and Daimler–Chrysler. In this environment, Ford sees an incredible challenge: more markets open for business, more competitors fighting for dominance, more need for very smart people and fresh ideas.

Ford feels that it can't build such a company if it holds on to a mind-set that doesn't respond swiftly to (the global) consumers' needs or pay attention to the (global) capital markets. So, under the leadership originally of Jacques Nasser and now of William Ford III, Ford has begun to reinvent itself as a global organization with a single strategic focus on consumers and shareholder value. Ford realizes that, in this process, it must not try to eliminate the role of national cultures or eliminate the idea that it makes sense to have people with expertise in one function or another, but it wants to develop a sort of Ford-wide corporate DNA that drives how it does things everywhere. That DNA has a couple of key components, including a global mind-set, an intuitive knowledge of Ford's customers around the world, and a relentless focus on growth. Many large, experienced, multinational firms are now trying to develop a global structure and frame of mind similar to what Ford is doing, as they all see it as necessary for successful operation in today's globalized economy. And it is IHR which must take the responsibility to develop this corporate DNA.

"go global." IHRM in Action 2.2 describes a moderate-sized firm, the Ferro Corporation of Cleveland, which made a powerful shift to being a global MNE.[14]

> The experiences of global MNEs suggest that running a global company is an order of magnitude more complicated than managing a multinational or international firm. The global corporation . . . looks at the whole world as *one market*. It manufactures, conducts research, raises capital, and buys supplies wherever it can do the job best. It keeps in touch with technology and market trends all around the world. National boundaries and regulations tend to be irrelevant, or a mere hindrance. Corporate headquarters might be anywhere.[15]

At this level of development, the role of the HR department must again shift. Employees are hired everywhere in the world, wherever the necessary skills, training, and experience can be found. Worldwide policies are developed and implemented for many aspects of HR responsibility, possibly based on practices followed in numerous places around the world. Management promotions will require international experience and managers and executives will be developed from all major countries or regions of operation. At the same time, increased sophistication in locating certain HRM practices will become even more important, as the firm tries to be a global enterprise.

## The shift to being a global company

The Cleveland-based Ferro Corporation, a $1 billion manufacturer of coatings, plastics, specialty chemicals and ceramics, has been a successful international enterprise for almost three-quarters of a century and is now becoming a model for being a global company. Several of its foreign operations, particularly those in Europe and Latin America, have existed for as much as seventy years. About two-thirds of its employees are non-US nationals, and over 60 percent of its revenues and profits are derived from foreign operations.

Despite its impressive international record, only recently has Ferro begun to see itself as a global company. According to David B. Woodbury, vice-president of human resources, "There was quite a bit of sharing of information and technology among our operations in various countries, but each foreign division or subsidiary operated highly independently, formulating much of its own strategy for manufacturing, marketing, finance and human resources."

Since then Ferro has reorganized its corporate structure to focus on products and business lines across international borders. "Each business thinks of the world as its marketplace now," says Woodbury. "We're developing broad-based global strategies, with increased communications and a greater sharing of assets throughout the world."

High on that list of "shared assets" is human resources. "We realize there is a strong need for global managers," says Woodbury. "We have to identify, train and develop people with an international outlook, skills and experience. Like all other facets of the corporation, Human Resources has to evolve into a global operation."

This usually means fewer expatriates in local subsidiaries, an increased use of third-country nationals, and broader-based multinational composition of corporate boards and top management and technical teams. And in most firms this means trying to develop or maintain an international corporate culture that transcends national boundaries and national cultures. Key employees need to be multilingual, experienced in a number of countries, and culturally sensitive, and their countries of origin make little difference.

The Bechtel Corporation of San Francisco provides a good example of this globalizing of a firm's workforce. In the aftermath of the 1991 Gulf War against Iraq, the Bechtel Corporation was given a major part of the contract to squelch the fires in the oilfields of Kuwait.[16] Bechtel's HR staff in San Francisco had to sift through 30,000 employee files and 105,000 phone inquiries to mobilize 16,000 Americans, Britons, Filipinos, Australians – people from thirty-seven countries in all – in order to get the skills they needed to deal with the Kuwaiti disaster. "We're almost nationality-blind," says Patrick Morgan, human resource manager for special projects at Bechtel. "A person's passport is about as meaningful to us as the name of the bank on their savings account passbooks."[17] When human resource managers develop the ability to operate effectively at this level of globalization, they and their departments will have become global.

## The transnational firm

A decade ago, Bartlett and Ghoshal suggested that many firms were evolving into a new form of international business, that they termed "transnational."[18] In the sense that the transnational firm has a global focus, it is similar to the global firm, described in the previous section. But it differs from the global firm in that, rather than developing global products and services, the transnational works hard to localize, to be seen, not as a global firm, but as a local firm, albeit one that draws upon global expertise, technology, and resources.[19] IHRM in Action 2.3 describes a major transnational firm – Cap Gemini-Sogeti – and the IHR implications of "going transnational."[20]

Most of the discussion in this book will be focused on IHRM policies and practices as they apply to multinational/multi-domestic (traditional) MNEs and the newly emerging global and transnational MNEs. However, this difference between multinational/multi-domestic and global/transnational firms is significant. In the traditional multinational company, free-standing subsidiaries or stand-alone foreign operations may be so loosely affiliated that valuable opportunities for economies of scale, joint marketing efforts, or shared technology and innovations may be lost. As illustrated in the Ford Motor Company description (see IHRM in Action 2.1), country or regional operations and functional experts can develop attitudes of strong independence that can result in the loss of the benefits that arise from sharing product ideas and technologies across national boundaries.

The MNE philosophy of primarily staffing with locals (which is one of the consequences of pursuit of a multi-domestic or regional structure) sounds reasonable. But if only Frenchmen work in France, only Chinese in China, and only Americans in the US, a firm may well lose the input of talented individuals with different backgrounds and perspectives on products, services, organizational and management practices, markets, and international needs and limit its ability to learn, innovate, and adapt skills which are absolutely critical to success in a global economy. This may limit the firm's awareness of new technologies and product ideas enough so as to create a definite competitive disadvantage relative to more global competitors. Such diverse perspectives are also important to IHRM, bringing multiple viewpoints and experiences to bear on human resource problems in the parent company as well as in the foreign subsidiaries and partnerships.

At this stage of international development (particularly the transnational firm), which is often put forth as the direction in which all international firms are headed, the salient management and HRM question may be how to manage the complex, national

## Cap Gemini-Sogeti: a transnational organization

Cap Gemini-Sogeti (CGS) is Europe's biggest computer software and services group. CGS has taken all available means (organic growth, acquisitions, and alliances) to become Europe's No. 1 in computer services and consulting. The original merger of Cap, a computer services group, and Sogeti, a business management and information processing company, brought together operations in the UK, the Netherlands, Switzerland, and Germany, with a head office in France. Further acquisitions brought in a large number of small groups throughout Europe and the US. This expanded its coverage to IT consulting, customized software, and education and training. CGS is already highly decentralized, but when any of its branches reaches 150 personnel, it splits it in two. This gives the firm greater flexibility in responding to variations in local demand.

CGS has developed information pooling systems to ensure that innovative solutions developed in one country or business will be rapidly disseminated to other countries and businesses. These include electronic bulletin boards and extensive electronic and voice mail facilities, plus the organizational culture of informal networks of professionals who work frequently together in project teams.

The challenges for this fast-growing transnational have major HR components, e.g., integrating its wide variety of organizations into a group with a common culture capable of working within a complex web of ownership relationships, while benefiting from the strengths of the relationships that exist between its "family" of committed, semi-autonomous professionals. Internally, CGS and its IHR team worked to clarify and coordinate roles, objectives, systems, and resources, particularly its skilled professional staff, across countries and markets. Its Genesis project took two years to achieve this, but now CGS sees itself as coming much closer to achieving its aim to be a modern transnational company.

(cultural) diversity that this level of global business activity experiences.[21] When integration is needed (as in joint ventures and in the development of global workforces), cultural diversity needs to be valued and utilized while minimizing its impacts; but when cultural diversity is needed to differentiate products and services, for instance to meet the needs of local markets, other corporate practices and organizational designs are required.

The first chapter introduced this concern with the conflicting pressures for centralization versus localization. It will arise throughout this text as various aspects of IHRM are discussed, such as here. It is addressed specifically, again, and in more detail, at the end of this chapter and is a key component of Chapter 5, which discusses the nature and importance of national and organizational culture, which lies at the base of these conflicting pressures.

## Choice of business form for entry into international business

Once a firm has made the decision to "go international" (either through a formal strategic choice or through informal reaction to market pressures) it is faced with a number of choices for implementing this strategy. The level of involvement, as described in the previous section, interacts with these choices, as the simpler levels of global activity involve much less complex organizational structures.

For the purposes of identifying general IHR strategies for staffing and helping to achieve organizational IB strategies, this specific set of business choices for going international provides fruitful categories for understanding the way businesses pursue international strategies. These would include exporting, licensing or subcontracting, forming joint ventures or alliances and partnerships, or using foreign direct investment (FDI) through wholly-owned subsidiaries, in any of their many forms (e.g., assembly, manufacturing, offices, retail establishments, etc.) and established in any of a number of ways (e.g., through acquisition, a greenfield exercise, or a turnkey project, etc.).

The intent here is not to provide detailed information or description of these various forms of activity and structure for conducting international business, but rather to provide a very short introduction to the possibilities. Often, IHR is expected to provide expertise in helping the executive team make these choices and to evaluate which choices work best and under which circumstances, including assessing the particular strengths and weaknesses of the firm and its managers and evaluating labor force issues in various international options.

### Portfolio investment

At the simplest level of involvement, a firm may just decide to make financial investments in foreign firms, buying shares of stock, much as it could do within its own domestic equities markets. Except for a general need to assess foreign firms (including their workforces and HR practices) and markets (including the quality of country labor forces), HR is not likely to be very involved in this form of international business activity.

### Partial ownership

A common form of international participation that evolved at the end of the Cold War, particularly in Central/Eastern Europe, was partial ownership of enterprises, particularly those which had been state-owned in formerly Communist countries. The newly privatized firms needed capital, technology, and management and marketing skills and often sought partial ownership from Western firms. Indeed, it was not uncommon for these enterprises to seek capital and technology but not want necessarily to release ownership or seek management advice, figuring that they could run their own firms. As it turned out, HR practices were one area that needed significant change and thus needed the import of expatriate management and HR skill. The degree of control and influence held by the Western contributors was often very controversial, not unlike the situation in the more common cross-border joint ventures and alliances, discussed in a later section. Generally, the Western firms making this sort of capital and technology contribution were large multinationals with extensive international experience and had managers available to be assigned to these firms. Thus this was an extension of HR's already pretty extensive international experience in these firms, albeit in the very different context of previously controlled and planned economies and enterprises.

## Export

Historically, this has been the initial step of internationalization for most firms and usually occurs while the firm is relatively small. Owing to a foreign inquiry (often unsolicited) as to the possibility of buying or selling the firm's product(s), or the desire by the firm to expand beyond its domestic markets, many firms begin to export their products or services to foreign markets through the use of direct sales to foreign customers (via direct mail or internet sales, for example), or they sell through import/export firms or through foreign distributors. Franchise-based businesses, such as McDonald's, Midas Muffler, or Century 21, will establish franchises or company-owned operations to export their services. Retail establishments, such as insurance companies or department stores, often merge with, acquire, or set up joint ventures with local enterprises to begin their foreign sales.

At this stage, the firm has very few people (if any) involved extensively with foreign sales (although more than a few dot.coms found in recent years that as soon as their web sites were up, they unexpectedly received high volumes of foreign orders and inquiries and had to commit more people and resources to foreign sales than they ever anticipated). Initially, foreign sales are typically a small fraction of total sales and thus are handled by domestic sales people. Because of this, the HRM department – if there is one (since the firm is typically pretty small) – will have very little if any international responsibility. As foreign sales increase in importance, the firm will assign a sales manager responsibility for international sales. This individual may travel to foreign countries in which the firm has sales but is likely to be chosen purely for reasons of sales experience or product knowledge. Indeed, often employees with little experience or competence are chosen to handle the foreign sales because at this stage the foreign sales are not considered important nor does anyone in the firm yet perceive that they might become important.

## Wholly-owned sales subsidiary/local sales office

If direct export sales are successful enough, the firm is likely to next establish its own sales offices in those countries where sales are large enough to warrant such efforts.

These offices are most likely to be managed by a sales manager from the home office, chosen, as before, for sales and/or product knowledge, not for any foreign experience or capability.

## International division or global product division

Eventually, as indicated in the previous section, an internationalizing firm will choose to establish an international division or global product division. This organizational structure carves out the international business as a separate and distinct part of the business, with the corresponding staffing issues related to hiring and developing employees with a purely international focus to their jobs. This structure is still primarily a marketing activity.

## License

Licensing the rights to manufacture and/or market one's product(s) is an option for "going international" that does not involve the setting up of directly owned subsidiaries. In this strategy, the firm usually locates foreign firms that have the experience to manufacture (and sometimes market) its products – with minimal technology transfer, in order to bypass import duties and to provide the simplest avenue to local sales. Normally, the only person from the parent firm involved with this option is the person who negotiates the license agreements and/or handles whatever technology transfer is required. The parent firm may still choose to handle the marketing of the product or it may choose to license that, too. IHR will play a very minimal role in the licensing of manufacturing.

## Contract/subcontract

A similar strategy for entrance into IB is to subcontract the manufacture or assembly of a firm's products. Increasingly, as firms manage their supply chains on a global basis, they subcontract all or most of their manufacturing to firms abroad, in order to take advantage of lower labor and operating costs. Typically the firm will have only a few individuals who will travel to the foreign locales in order to transfer whatever technology is necessary and to monitor the quality of the manufacturing and final products. Usually this will involve manufacture for export back to the home country or to other global markets. Marketing will still be handled by the firm.

## Manufacture/assembly

The next step in the evolution of at least manufacturing firms is the assembly and then manufacture of products directly in wholly-owned subsidiaries or in joint ventures owned fully or in part by the firm. The subsidiaries can be established either through "greenfield" exercises (i.e., building them "from the ground up") as the Japanese auto companies have done, or through acquisition of existing facilities or operations as Lincoln Electric has done. This is often the stage of development for "traditional" manufacturing firms at which major new, international responsibilities are thrust on the HR function. Now HR has to get involved with selecting and preparing employees for overseas assignments, designing and administering compensation and benefit programs for international assignees and foreign (host-country) employees, coping with very different labor relations as practiced in other countries, etc. The learning process for HR was and is rarely smooth or easy, as will be discussed throughout the rest of this text.

## Service

Traditional service businesses, such as insurance, banking, department stores, hotels, and restaurants, and firms that provide supplies and maintenance, typically "go international" by acquiring local businesses or they build new stores and offices to provide their services, first to their home-country customers that are active in the foreign locale, and then, eventually, to local customers. This step for service businesses is in many ways equivalent to the previous step for manufacturing firms and involves the same new complexities for HR.

## International joint venture

In recent years, the structure of choice for many businesses, including Starbucks and Lincoln Electric, as they go international is the international joint venture (IJV), in which two or more firms (at least one from each of at least two countries) create a new business entity with shared ownership and managerial responsibilities. This entity is often created with limited objectives and a limited life. Employees will normally be assigned to the new entity from each of the partners, with specific managerial and employee responsibilities (hopefully) negotiated prior to the establishment of the joint venture. Many new problems arise here for HR, from the adoption or development of HR practices for a multinational workforce to issues concerning the merger and interaction of two or more national and corporate cultures (or, as sometimes happens, the design of a new culture). This international business form has become so common and important that it is covered in more detail in Chapter 4. The issues of national and corporate cultures are discussed in Chapter 5.

## Alliances, partnerships (e.g., research), and consortia

Firms utilizing this structure do not necessarily replace their traditional multi-domestic or global/transnational structure. But increasingly multinational firms are developing and using alliances, partnerships, joint ventures, and other kinds of linkages to "go international." Sometimes these structures are used to gain access to technology, research, and laboratories that the firm might not otherwise have access to (and that can give it competitive advantages in the global economy) or as a strategy that can provide additional flexibility in a fast-moving global economy.

For example, MCI Corporation, a provider of global telecommunications services, gets its technology from more than fifty major subcontractors located all over the world, including its major competitor, AT&T. MCI owns a $65 million R&D complex but doesn't develop new technology there. Instead, this is where MCI takes leading-edge technologies developed by the independent contractors and tests, perfects, and integrates them into the MCI telecommunications network. In an industry where new products routinely become obsolete in about thirteen months, MCI finds it more efficient to spend time looking for innovative subcontractors than developing its own technology. MCI's executive vice-president explains, "I have access to the intellectual assets of [other firms'] 9,000 engineers. If I did my own development, what would I have? Five hundred engineers?"[22]

Cross-border linkages of various types are becoming increasingly the organizational choice for many multinational enterprises.[23] In these international business structures, the human resource problems associated with coordinating workforces and managements from firms in different countries remain the primary stumbling blocks to gaining the desired benefits (see Chapter 3).

## Franchise

For firms that use the franchise form of business structure in their domestic operations, such as restaurants and specialty food shops, real estate offices, and other forms of service businesses, such as petrol stations and repair shops, it is typical to use this form of structure in foreign operations, as well. Because franchises, such as McDonald's, are usually owned locally, the impact on HR, other than a role in training local franchisees in staffing and other HR practices and skill training of new employees, is pretty minimal.

The point of this section has been to demonstrate that businesses typically pass through a number of stages as they increase their degree of internationalization, although this pattern is changing with the increase of service businesses and the development of internet-based and dot.com businesses that can follow different patterns and because of the increased use of cross-border partnerships and alliances. Not all businesses pass through all of these stages as they progress from being purely domestic firms to global ones. In general, though, most companies experience most of these stages. These stages are important to the discussion of IHRM because each stage makes unique demands on the HR department. The HRM function in a firm just beginning to internationalize faces very different responsibilities and challenges than does the IHRM department in a multinational, global, or transnational firm.

As firms increase their levels of international activity, their organizational structures and HRM responsibilities become increasingly complex. Many older, large multinational (particularly manufacturing) firms that now have numerous subsidiaries all over the world began their foreign activities by exporting (see Figure 2.2). As this stage became successful for them, they typically proceeded to establish sales offices overseas to market their exports. Where and when the sales offices were able to develop sufficiently large markets, plants to assemble imported parts were established, and, finally, the complete product was manufactured locally, sometimes for local sales and sometimes for export. These overseas operations typically mimicked the firm's domestic operations. Eventually, then, these firms moved toward the global integration of their international operations.

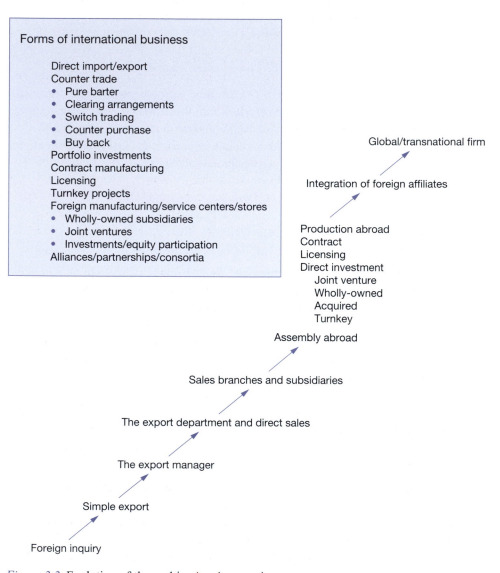

*Figure 2.2* Evolution of the multinational enterprise

In some ways this is a simplistic view of the development of international firms, as IHRM in Action 2.1 illustrates, describing the early years of Ford Motor Company's international operations and how it is now having to adapt its structure to fit new realities. In recent years, new patterns have developed. Some firms have used complete assembly or manufacturing plants as their means of initial entry to certain countries, normally to take advantage of cheap labor or sources of materiel, manufacturing products for export, such as is often the case for American and Asian firms in the *maquiladora* sector of the Mexican economy. Others have internationalized through subcontracting or licensing their manufacturing. Still others have used franchising or joint ventures or partnerships to internationalize. And, of course, as soon as firms put up web sites to offer (or even just to describe) their products or services, they become international immediately as they receive foreign inquiries and orders online. Many firms, of course, end up relying on some combination of these entry strategies.

The pattern of development experienced in different industries also varies widely. Businesses in extraction industries, such as oil and mining, set up foreign subsidiaries to manage their extraction (and sometimes processing) operations. Banks, such as Citibank, or insurance companies, such as Lloyd's, may initially locate in a foreign country in order to provide services to home-country clients who are active in the foreign country. Firms such as McDonald's typically sell franchises to local individuals, but often have to first prepare an infrastructure in foreign locations in order to provide their foreign businesses with the quality and types of inputs needed before they establish their local outlets. And department store or grocery store chains, such as Wal-Mart, CarreFour, Toys 'R' Us, IKEA, or Safeway, may acquire existing similar businesses or enter foreign markets by building new stores similar to those in their home countries.

Each of these stages of involvement and forms of international business creates different requirements for HRM policies and practices. In the simplest stage of international business, that is, *export*, few employees are sent on international business trips and none on expatriate (longer-term) assignments. The overall impact on the HR department is very limited. But as firms move to larger sales offices overseas and even to *assembly* and *production* (in the case of manufacturing) or *complete offices* or *stores* (in the case of service businesses) or joint ventures and alliances, the HR implications increase steadily. Such firms will send parent-country sales representatives to market products overseas, managers to negotiate contracts and customer deals, technical experts to transfer technology to overseas production and service sites, and managing directors and financial officers to control and manage overseas operations.

Often, in the early stages of internationalization, foreign operations are viewed as sites for replicating what has already been done at home. Thus parent-company management style, corporate culture, and HR practices are usually transferred to the foreign locations. The international operations can be viewed as secondary to the success of the firm, but the impact on HRM can still be quite significant. For example, in recent years, some firms, such as in telecoms (e.g., Nortel and AT&T)

have ramped up their international operations quite rapidly as the telecommunication industry became global seemingly overnight and within a few years had hundreds of employees on short and long-term international assignments. The HR functions in these firms have had to develop their international expertise quite rapidly.

Over a period of time, further development brings the international operations to greater responsibility for revenue and profit generation and thus for the overall success of the firm. Firms will begin to select and prepare the best employees for foreign assignments and they will begin to develop an international management pool with a common language and culture, drawing on managers from all of its operations. Often these more "advanced" stages of international involvement are achieved through acquisition of existing foreign operations or merger with such. International mergers and acquisitions are discussed in some detail in Chapter 4. In these stages of development, HR has to develop much more sophisticated international expertise and capability.

## International orientation

One aspect of international business strategy that has been relatively well discussed and studied involves the orientation of senior executives, usually referred to in terms such as ethnocentrism, regio-centrism, polycentrism, and geocentrism.[24] The key strategic issue in these orientations is the degree of domination of the MNE headquarters over subsidiary management and HR practices as compared with the degree of integration of subsidiary practices and cultures into those of headquarters and other subsidiaries. Normally these orientations are explained in the context of progressive development over time from one mind-set to another, as a firm develops greater international experience and sophistication.

### Ethnocentrism

The initial orientation of many managers, especially those from a more homogeneous national population and culture or from a country with a strong patriotic culture, is one of *ethnocentrism*. In this orientation, managers use a home-country standard as a reference in managing international activities. The outlook is one of centralized decision making and high control over operations. Managers with such a mind-set are likely to follow an international strategy of maintaining control from the home-country and parent-firm headquarters, and replicating home-country systems and procedures and structure abroad.[25]

### Polycentrism or regio-centrism

The next level of development or evolution of the managerial orientation is referred to as *polycentrism* or *regio-centrism*. Here, as international investment and involvement increase, the host-country culture and practices assume increased salience. This may be extended to include a number of similar countries in a region, and host-country standards are increasingly used as a reference point in managing company operations. The strategies typically followed are likely to be multinational (or multi-domestic) strategies that emphasize decentralized and autonomous operations of wholly-owned subsidiaries.

### Geocentrism

When a firm reaches the level of global orientation, a *geocentric* mind-set will have developed and been adopted. Here the managerial outlook is one of creating a global network and a preference for following a transnational strategy that is integrative and interdependent among various elements of the global organization.

It would be expected that HR policies and practices would be as centralized or decentralized as the overall strategic mind-set of the firm. Indeed, in one study relating these concepts to IHR practices, it was found that IHR practices do indeed correlate with these mind-sets.[26] That is, in firms with an ethnocentric orientation, HR practices for international operations tend to copy parent company practices and are very centralized. In firms with a polycentric mind-set, HR practices tend to be decentralized and local subsidiaries tend to be much more likely to be left alone to follow local HR practice. And in firms with a geocentric orientation, HR practices tend to be more eclectic, borrowing best practices from around the world, rather than giving preference necessarily to either headquarters or local practices.

## A model for Strategic IHRM

The following paragraphs describe a model (see Figure 2.3) for Strategic IHRM that links (1) international business strategy; (2) types of international employees used to implement international strategy; and (3) International HRM policy and practice. This model illustrates the relationships between the major components of Strategic IHRM and suggests the gaps in our understanding of many of those relationships.

## The model: international business strategy

The right-side axis of Figure 2.3 presents the set of strategic IB choices that a firm might make to determine its entry into international business and its evolution in pursuit of international business objectives, as explained earlier in this chapter. Since the whole point for HR in terms of strategic IB should be one of matching its functional strategies and efforts to the company's strategy, it seems apparent that one of the most important variables to be considered in an analysis of strategic IHR should be the set of options a business has for "going international." Ultimately, IHR must develop its practices to support and to implement these strategies. As described

Human resource policies and practices

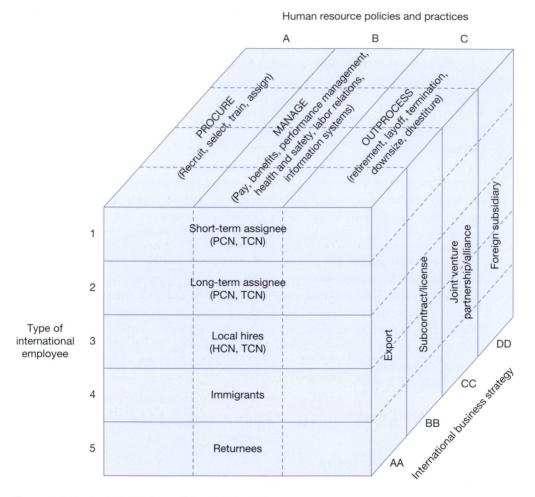

*Figure 2.3* Strategic IHRM: matching HRM to IB strategy

in the first part of this chapter, IHR activities and responsibilities vary considerably, depending on the form of international business activity chosen by the firm.

## The model: type of international employee

A critical component of IHR responsibility involves making decisions about who is to work in the MNE. There are a number of terms used to describe the various types of employees utilized by MNEs, but the most commonly used general categories for international employees includes PCNs (parent-country nationals or expatriates), HCNs (host-country nationals), TCNs (third-country nationals), immigrants, and returnees. Chapter 8 provides an extensive introduction to the many types of international employees. Figure 2.3 illustrates these five general categories; but there are many types of employees with international responsibilities, all of which need to be considered in strategic decisions about staffing IB activities. As the numbers and types of employees and employment relationships expand for firms conducting international business, any model of SIHRM must also expand to accommodate the many choices and options as described in Chapter 8.

## The model: HR policy and practice

The top axis on Figure 2.3 displays HR policies and practices grouped by areas of the HR responsibilities that are important in the international arena, whether managing the international assignee population or managing local workforces in foreign subsidiaries and joint ventures. The three areas of core HR responsibility presented in Figure 2.3 include:

- Procurement (recruit, select, acquire the best possible talent; align, partner, orient, train, develop, assign).
- Management (compensate, set expectations, manage performance, monitor and enhance health and safety, employee relations, information systems).
- Outprocessing (retirement, layoff, termination, downsize, divestiture).

Each of these three areas of HR policy and practice vary dramatically from country to country and from type of employee to type of employee, and may well also vary according to the international strategy chosen by the business. Thus a major benefit of this model is its ability to isolate the specific intersections of these three variables: the form of IB activity and strategy, the type of IB employee, and the IHR policy and practice that combines the first two together.

## The model: organizational outcomes – integrating IHRM and IB strategy

It is at the intersection of the three components of this model that Strategic IHRM can gain its greatest value. It is at this intersection that IHR must begin to assess the desired organizational outcomes for the interactions of these three components of IHR. The intersection of any two of the components provides the type of information that has been historically focused on by HR managers in MNEs, for example, the particular type of employee used to implement each form of IB strategy, the specific nature of the IHR activities needed to procure, manage, and outplace each type of international employee, or the specific IHR policies and practices that are most appropriate and necessary for each form of IB strategy. But a focus on the intersection of the three components can provide a new level of understanding for strategic IHR. The chapters in this book offer insights, examples, and suggestions for what MNEs do or can do under different strategic conditions. None the less further research needs to be done. For example, the type of questions that IHR practitioners and academics could address that would help to determine more effective IHRM practice for MNEs might include:

- In each three-dimensional cell: what is currently being done? What works? When? What should be done?
- What is an "exemplary practice" at each intersection? That is, what are the most successful MNEs doing?
- What difference does national and corporate culture make? When must national culture override corporate culture and when can corporate culture take precedence?

## *Organizational objectives*

In answering these questions, there are a number of specific organizational and individual objectives that can be considered in each cell, particularly as research and experience are used to assess the above questions. These might include the following organizational objectives that are used to achieve the internationalization strategies. (These are consistent with the objectives of the multiple stakeholders described in Chapter 1.) The degree of importance of each of these objectives will vary according to the particular strategy, and the needs of the multiple stakeholders, as presented on the right-hand side of Figure 2.3.

- Technology transfer.
- Organizational learning and knowledge transfer.
- Marketing/sales.
- Control: accounting/finance/operations.
- Management/supervision.
- Competitiveness.
- Training of locals.
- Career development; development of international experience and perspective.
- Cost control.
- Customer/vendor/regulator/community satisfaction.
- Performance enhancement; improved productivity.
- ROI (return on investment).
- Revitalization (innovation) and renewal.
- Union–management relations.
- Societal contribution and environmental impact.

An illustration of the use of these outcomes in response to possible interactions of the three components of the model might include consideration of this sort of question: If technology transfer is important for use of a joint venture, which type of international employee will best achieve this transfer of technology and what will be the best ways to recruit, hire, prepare, and manage such international employees?

Federal Express, as it has opened operations at airports around the world, has found that its original focus on trying to accommodate national cultures but within the context of its strong corporate culture has needed to focus more on the ability of its site managers to get the business job done, that is, to establish the offices and to solicit business and to then manage the operations. Les Real, Federal Express's early director of International HR and key member of the teams that established many of its overseas operations, says initially the balance of attention to culture versus the business need was about 80–20.[27] But experience eventually taught them that the business outcomes were more important, such that the priority changed to something more like a 60–40 emphasis on achieving the business need.

## Individual employee outcomes

There are also a number of individual outcomes or objectives that can be considered. These might include:

- Performance/productivity (efficiency and effectiveness).
- Job satisfaction and motivation.
- Retention and commitment.

Here, the type of question that can be researched is: Which type of international employee assigned to which international organizational strategy will produce the best performance, highest job satisfaction, and best retention?

In addition to these organizational and individual-level outcomes at the intersection of the three components of interest to SIHRM, the model also suggests that there are some issues (or concerns) that "cut across" all three components and influence the content of every cell. These include:

- The degree of organizational centralization versus localization (introduced earlier and discussed at some length at the end of this chapter).
- Culture (national and organizational) (discussed in detail in the next chapter).
- Organizational concerns for cost and effectiveness and the concerns for all the multiple stakeholders of the MNE.

All three of these considerations can influence all three components as well as the content of the cells. That is, they influence choice and implementation of international strategy, choice and management of type of international employee, and priority and assessment of various organizational and employee outcomes. All of these need to be taken into consideration in research into and observation about the interactions of these variables.

A number of questions for IHR practice and Strategic IHR are raised by this model including:

- What type of employee is most appropriate for each IB strategy?
- What is the best way to recruit/select/train/assign each type of employee in each particular IB strategy?
- What is the best way to manage each type of employee in each particular IB strategy? What do we now know? And what do we still need to determine?

For example, a researcher (or practitioner, for that matter) might focus on a particular cell, and try to understand best practice in that area in an attempt to prescribe IHR practices for any organization for whom that particular situation applies. Any given business enterprise with international business can locate itself on the axis of IB strategy; it probably can draw adequate conclusions from the IHR literature and from its own and other, similar organizations', experiences about the best type(s) of employees to hire or assign to staff that form of business; and it then can seek guidance about how best to staff and manage such an international workforce. For example, an organization developing a joint venture in a foreign locale might focus on the types of international assignees (it may need to consider both short and long-term assignees) and local hires it needs; and then it can begin to assess how to best go about staffing and managing such a workforce, given concerns about culture, cost, and organizational structure. The desired outcomes such as technology transfer, control, and return on investment will influence the types of employees sought. And national and corporate cultures will influence methods for such staffing and managing.

## IHRM strategy

As HRM becomes more involved with helping organizations to be successful in their international endeavors, it must develop a strategic focus. That is, it needs to develop its own strategies to hire, manage, and retain the best employees throughout the organization's international business activities, as well as contribute to the firm's overall international strategic planning. This section has presented a model to help guide IHR as it develops its own implementing strategies for successful achievement of international vision and objectives. And it has suggested a way for researchers and practitioners to begin to develop the knowledge and understanding needed for designing and implementing such IHR strategies.

Often, the limited integration of HR with a firm's international strategic planning takes place in the context of discussions concerning a very limited set of global issues of importance to the firm, such as acquisitions or divestitures of overseas facilities, entering or withdrawing from foreign markets, proposed corporate structures and management systems to accommodate different nations and cultures, the means for controlling relationships between overseas subsidiaries and the parent firm, and procedures for effectively managing the fundamental elements of the HRM system (e.g., staffing policies and practices in multiple countries, compensation and benefits systems, labor relations, etc.).[28] Even these discussions are likely to take place only when there is a close personal relationship between the senior HR executive and the firm's CEO. It is still not as common as it needs to be for firms to engage HR in these types of discussions.[29]

### Critical issue: centralization versus localization

Historically, basic trade-offs have come into play when managers have considered where in the organization certain decisions should be made. The central trade-off pits pressures for centralization against the need for decentralization. Centralization is the concentration of authority and decision making toward the top (HQ) of an organization. Decentralization is the dispersion of authority and decision making to operating units throughout the organization. In the international context, this involves the degree of centralization or decentralization of corporate authority and decision making throughout a firm's global operations.

This tension between integration (centralization) and differentiation (localization) is becoming a major dilemma for IHRM and large global firms. Firms must become simultaneously more highly differentiated and more integrated or coordinated. Local nationals may feel that they can run operations in their own countries, even though their firms now require a global perspective and global qualifications. And local laws and practices may dictate certain HR practices and yet an international perspective may require different approaches to routine HR responsibilities.

As Percy Barnevik, former CEO of the merged Swedish-Swiss firm ABB Asea Brown Boveri, puts this issue:

> You want to be able to optimize a business globally – to specialize in the production of components, to drive economies of scale as far as you can, to rotate managers and technologists around the world to share expertise and solve problems. But you also want to have deep local roots everywhere you operate – building products in the countries where you sell them, recruiting the best local talent from the universities, working with the local government to increase exports. If you build such an organization, you create a business advantage that's damn difficult to copy.[30]

MNEs are frequently both praised and criticized for being tools of global integration.[31] There are many forces for "convergence," or the use of parent-company policies and procedures throughout a firm's global operations. MNEs face strong incentives to maximize economies of scale in research and development, purchasing, production, and markets, and encounter relatively low barriers to the dissemination of technologies and best practices. These incentives and low barriers encourage the continued use in foreign locales of practices and procedures found to work well "at home." Of course, all of this is supported by overall firm strategies to internationalize and country cultures that encourage the view that our (company and country) way is best.

On the other hand, many firms in the past evolved in such a way in their international operations that their local and regional offices became, in many ways, independent organizations. IHRM in Action 2.1, makes the point that the days are past for most MNEs in which subsidiaries in various countries could effectively operate as quasi-independent companies (as in a multi-domestic or, even, regional strategy), optimally adapted to local circumstances and markets with very little interference from headquarters. Even in markets where adaptation to local circumstances is mandatory, MNEs work hard to bridge the gap between global and local and to identify ways of reconciling global integration, e.g., in production, with the required extent of local responsiveness, e.g., in marketing and product design and in management and personnel practices. Thus MNEs function as motors of a process of international convergence that may ultimately make national differences rooted in institutional and cultural characteristics less relevant or even disappear.

In addition to convergence due to company-wide policies, though, there are also enduring sources of divergence, such as attempts by local subsidiaries to become centers of excellence. Furthermore, there is considerable evidence demonstrating that cultural and institutional differences play a role in the manner in which seemingly universal techniques and procedures (globally applied) are implemented (in varying ways) within differing countries.

In the end, however, the critical strategic decision for the IHRM department (as well as for the business as a whole) is the resolution of the dilemma created by the conflict between centralization for control and international (internal) control of policies and practices and decentralization to meet local requirements (localization). As was expressed in the first chapter, there is no easy answer to this choice. Should the MNE superimpose (HRM) practices on its international subsidiaries and other forms of operations (with the local HR office run by an HR manager from the parent firm), or should it allow subsidiaries to follow local customs, laws, and practices as much as possible (with the local HR office usually run by a local national HR manager)?

The experiences of long-term multinational firms suggest that the trend is to move toward more local control and management over time, which is consistent with the pattern described in the first part of this chapter. And yet, as is discussed in greater detail later in the book, successful multinational firms have found ways (such as cross-national management training, cross-national assignments for management development and promotions, and cross-national project teams) to develop a common set of values and culture to ensure worldwide pursuit of a common corporate vision and objectives. Indeed, some firms are seeking ways to develop globally consistent HR practices throughout all of their operations as a way to reinforce a common corporate culture.

Limited research has been made of the extent to which multinational firms involve their HRM functions with their strategic decisions related to integration versus decentralization:

> An important management issue is the design of the international human resource management (IHRM) system, yet there has been little research on what determines the type of human resource management system an MNE chooses for its overseas subsidiaries. A key choice the MNE must make regarding the type of HRM system it institutes in its overseas subsidiary is whether it will allow each subsidiary to create its own HRM system, attempt to create a consistent HRM system between HQ and subsidiaries, or develop a global HRM system that is created from practices developed in both the HQ and subsidiaries. Typical ways of achieving consistency are to transfer the HQ's own HRM system to overseas subsidiaries, or to transfer HRM practices between overseas subsidiaries themselves.[32]

# Research on Strategic IHRM

It has only been recently that a number of authors have focused their research and writing on the issue of Strategic IHRM.[33] Their articles have extended our understanding of SIHRM, yet there is still much that is not known about the factors involved with Strategic IHRM. The following provides a short summary of the variables focused on and the subsequent findings of this research:

- The degree of centralization or localization of HR practices in foreign subsidiaries was found to be linked with country and cultural differences and with the form of international business strategy and the nature of the local affiliate.[34]
- The form of coordination between headquarters and subsidiary. Specific aspects of HR practice, such as management development and reward systems, were found to be linked with a firm's particular international business strategy, such that, for example, global firms were more likely to rely on internally designed programs.[35]
- The variables (such as type of international business, nature of competition, extent and pace of change, and flexibility of host country culture) that influence the nature of subsidiary HR policies.[36]
- The link between managerial orientation and IHR practices, e.g., a geocentric mind-set was found to be linked with the broad geographic scope of a firm's strategy and with the use of globalized IHR policy and practice.[37]
- The link of IHR practice with country culture. HR practices were found to differ by country, and MNEs from different countries did indeed vary in their likelihood of adapting their subsidiary practices to those of the host country.[38]
- A strategic concern for both fit (between HQ and subsidiaries, between HR functions, and with the cross-national environment) and flexibility in IHRM policy and practice was hypothesized to increase in later stages of the organizational life cycle (as an MNE matures).[39]
- The identification of IHR principles for policy and practice that are associated with improved organizational results in international business. For example, it was found that following the most appropriate global HR practice rather than using only the parent-firm's HR practices was associated with better organizational performance.[40]
- Large global Japanese and European MNEs were found to be more likely to pursue global IHR strategies than was the case for similar American firms.[41]

In general, all of this research has dealt with some form of linkage between corporate international focus (degree of ethnocentrism or geocentrism, for example) and HR policy and practice in foreign subsidiaries. If HR strategy must implement corporate strategy, then the extent to which HR practice in foreign subsidiaries reflects corporate international business strategy is an important consideration. But as is typically observed by these authors, the examination of IHR strategy is in its infancy. Even though a number of models and variables are put forth in these articles, there is still much more to examine to understand the complexities of SIHRM. Both the responses and the choices are more complex and numerous in practice than the models presented in these articles have yet demonstrated.

## Conclusion

This chapter has been about Strategic International Human Resource Management. It provided the context by describing international business strategy and how it has evolved and then showing how the international strategy of a business impacts and is impacted by Human Resources. The components of IB strategy and IHR strategy were then used to develop a three-dimensional model of SIHRM. The three components of this model include the three primary areas of HR responsibility, the many types of international employees, and the entry strategies for firms to "go international." The intersections of the three components in this model help to provide ways to understand the relationships between these components and point toward the large job still left to describe, explain, and understand the nature and role of Strategic International Human Resource Management.

The chapter then described the academic research that has been pursued to better understand the nature of Strategic IHRM and closed with a discussion of the critical HQ concern with centralization (of IHR policy and practice) versus the local concern with the ability to differentiate such policy and practice according to local custom and culture.

## Points for further discussion

1 Consider the case of Lincoln Electric in China. Is it a good example of strategic international human resource management?
2 What type of business strategy did Lincoln Electric pursue in China?
3 What are the pros and cons of centralization and decentralization for Lincoln Electric?

# 3

# Organizational structure and design of the multinational enterprise

## Learning objectives

After considering Chapter 3, the reader will be able to describe:

- The basic characteristics associated with different organizational structures for the conduct of international business
- The implications for IHRM of the different structures
- The role of IHRM in the design of the MNE
- The importance of teams and networking in the MNE
- The need for learning in MNEs and implications for IHRM

## Key terms

- Organizational structure, integration, and coordination
- International, geographic, product, functional, and matrix structures
- Organizational design
- Networks, teams, learning

One of the challenges for HR in global firms is to become an organizational architect. Global organizations need appropriate structure in order to effectively conduct business in the chaotic yet interconnected global economy. The only clear source of sustainable global competitive advantage is designing organizations for knowledge creation and sharing across borders and, thus, learning and innovation on a global basis. The traditional needs for control and integration, combined with their need for learning and creativity, when applied across national borders in the highly complex global economy make the problems of organizational design especially difficult.

Accordingly, this chapter is about organizational design and structure for the successful conduct of international business. It deals with organization charts, management expertise, and organizational experimentation in the global arena. The development and complexity of international business are forcing firms to create new forms of organization and new applications of old forms and these efforts are creating new challenges for management in general and IHR in particular. Firms are having to cope with a greater number of countries (and their politics, governments, and cultures), protect a greater level of foreign investment, deal with greater overall political uncertainties, develop new mental mind-sets, and manage an increasing number of sites and partnerships in order to learn faster and better than their competitors and, thus, to grapple effectively with today's global economy.[1]

For virtually all companies in both developed as well as developing countries, market opportunities, critical resources, cutting-edge ideas, and competitors lurk not only just around the corner in the home market but increasingly also in distant and often little understood regions of the world as well.[2] How successful an enterprise is at exploiting emerging opportunities and at tackling the accompanying challenges and new global competitive pressures depends essentially on how intelligent it is at observing and interpreting the dynamic world in which it operates and figuring out how to deal with it, capitalizing on all the available global resources. Designing effective global organization structures is key to dealing with these challenges and pressures and thus competing effectively in this new environment. And IHRM is expected to help provide key strategic advice in this design effort.

## Global organization design: an introduction

This chapter is about organizing for complex international business operations and the contribution that IHRM can and should make to that organizing. How an MNE organizes for global business is essentially based on four factors:[3]

- The firm's forms and stages of international development (see Figure 2.2).
- The amount of cross-border coordination required by the firm's strategy (that is, the degree of desired centralization and integration versus the degree of acceptable and/or necessary localization) (Chapters 2 and 4).
- The nature of host governments' activity in the economic process.
- The diversity and complexity of the MNE's business operations.

To a large degree, this concerns the form of development and interconnectedness of an MNE's various subsidiaries and alliances. Such subsidiaries and alliances can range in structure from simple sales offices to complete, stand-alone operations (wholly or partially owned), formal joint ventures, and less formal partnerships of various kinds, as introduced in Chapters 2 and 4. More specifically they can take on one or more of the following three forms:[4]

- The subsidiary or partnership can be a start-up (initially, probably a sales office) that can be used to establish the firm's international business; in such cases it usually will take the structural form of reporting directly to an executive in the domestic structure or to the head of an international and/or geographic division. The primary concern will be transferring technology, products, and management from headquarters to the foreign subsidiaries.

- Once the firm has a well established international business, it will use its subsidiaries and alliances to operate its international strategy. In such cases the firm is likely to develop a structure using a multidimensional network of business centers. In the case of a single-product or service business, there will usually be a network of traditional business functions (e.g., marketing and finance with sub-offices devoted to the international business) and autonomous country subsidiaries (generally self-contained mini-versions of the business "at home"). In the case of a multi-business enterprise, there will likely be a network of business functions, country subsidiaries and alliances, and global product-line coordination, creating a three-way matrix of global responsibilities and reporting structures. The primary concerns will be twofold: learning by the parent firm about and from local (foreign) interests as it figures out how to make money in the global environment and figuring out how to control and integrate the far-flung operations of this newly international firm.

- When the firm reaches the level of having a high proportion of assets/sales/ employees outside of its home country, the subsidiaries become leaders in creating new market share and competitive advantages which are then transferred to the global network, and even back into the home country. In this case, the structure will be an even more complex network of multiple business centers with a strong focus on the integration of these many centers (see IHRM in Action 3.1).[5] The primary concern here will be the ability of all the diverse components of the organization to learn from and support each other within the context of global integration.

In all circumstances, the structure necessary to conduct international business is more complex than is the case for a purely domestic firm. The more assets and employees a firm has in its foreign subsidiaries and partnerships and the more languages, cultures, and time zones it has to cope with (and the more it relies on international joint ventures and alliances, in addition to its traditional wholly-owned subsidiaries), the more complex that structure will need to be.

These three levels of structural development for overseas operations create the basic underpinning for this chapter. Each creates its own challenges for the firm and for IHRM. All three can be implemented through acquisition, joint venture, or alliance and rely increasingly on cross-border and virtual teams for the integration necessary to conduct effective international business, which is discussed in some detail in the next chapter. IHR professionals are being asked to advise on the design and implementation of these approaches. So the objective of this chapter is to provide the necessary knowledge and understanding of the basic design approaches to enable IHR professionals to provide that advice.

In the past, MNEs have dealt with the complexity of international business by trying to simplify their operations and organizations. This has often led to development of

# The effective global firm of the future

The limits to a firm's handling of the challenges of globalization are set by its ability to handle the complementary challenge of integration of the parent firm with its widespread global operations. This challenge of integration has at least four elements: direction (goals, visions, targets), control, coordination, and the sharing of learning and innovation.

A jump into the future might reveal the following glimpse into how the global firm of the year 2005 (or later) handles this integration, taking business planning as one example, but this would also be true for product lines, marketing, finance, human resources, training, advertising, customer service, etc.

The enterprise will be organized into multiple centers or units. If it is a fairly large firm, it might have, let's say, 600 strategic business units (to handle separate product lines and applications), geographic units (to manufacture for and market to local and regional customers), centers of technical and functional competence (such as R&D, finance, marketing research, HR), global customer centers, and some centers at the boundary of the firm (e.g., outsourced manufacturing and development and IT partnerships with other firms). In addition, the firm is likely to have a number of alliances and joint ventures, helping it to gain access to new markets and technology. Many of the centers of competence are probably not located in the mother country, even though they serve the whole firm. They are located where they can best develop their competence – e.g., in China if that is the source of qualified manufacturing labor, in India if that is the location for the best IT professionals, and in Europe if that is a major customer base.

One of top management's tasks is to specify or identify who has to work with whom. This specification of linkages is a formal process, guided by the strategy for the future. There is of course a structure (e.g., global product divisions) which reflects the dominant linkages, and a majority – but far from all – of these interdependencies lie within the structural units. As the strategy and industry make-up and competitive situation change, so the specification of who-has-to-collaborate-with-whom will change.

Thus the business manager for a particular center (let's call him Jacques Dupont in Lyon, France) may be formally interdependent with, say, twenty-five other centers. Jacques prepares his business plan, which he sends to these centers, including one headed by Margaret Smith in Milwaukee, US. Margaret reads the plan. If it does not meet her needs, if she feels that there is an interest in pooling resources or exploring an unidentified opportunity, she gives Jacques a call. They resolve the matter on the phone, or they meet, or they set up a task force, and they revise their plans accordingly.

It is only if they cannot sort things out that the matter is referred to the formal hierarchy. The hierarchy exists, but as a court of contentions. If Margaret and

Jacques cannot sort things out, it is probably because the issue raises a basic question of strategy, structure, or principle, which should indeed be referred up the hierarchy.

It is this informal networking (the firm must facilitate the development of these networks and the skills to work effectively within them) and formal/centralized strategy that will mark the structure and functioning of the global firm of the future. And it is the managing of this complexity that will mark the major challenge of the global firm.

What is learned within the business centers and in the interactions between them must also be coordinated, made explicit, and shared in ways that everyone within the global firm can access that knowledge and use it to better serve and solve problems for their existing and potential customers.

common policy and practice throughout their global operations and to simple forms of organization, typically copying their domestic organizational structures, such as the use of global product divisions or independent country subsidiaries, reporting through the traditional marketing or manufacturing chains of command. This has minimized the problem of management and control in the global context, since the assumption was that if managers could handle domestic organizations, then they could also manage effectively the structures and systems duplicated to handle international commerce, transferring parent-company products, technology, and management style to foreign operations.

Major multinational enterprises (ones with longer-term experience and with greater foreign investment and number of employees) are discovering (have discovered) that this doesn't work very well. The global economy is too complex and unpredictable. Other countries and cultures don't always accommodate the parent-company products, styles, and culture. MNEs have often needed to develop more complex structures to deal with this complexity and to develop new managerial skills to deal with multiple cultures, languages, and ways of conducting business. Many new forms of organization and more complex forms of management have been developed in order to handle the complexities. This has created new challenges to develop coordination mechanisms and to train and develop managers that can manage these more complex forms of structure and systems.[6] Organizational systems are needed which are as complex as the challenges global firms confront and their managers need to have the ability to manage that complexity.

Given this context, this chapter discusses the ever-increasing importance and use of various organizational structures (and this builds on Chapter 2) that have been developed to control and manage this complexity. All are discussed in the context of the critical role that IHR plays in the design, implementation, and success of these business arrangements. As these forms of organizational structure have become more prevalent, senior executives have increasingly asked their senior HR managers for advice and help in the design, implementation, and management of the MNE.

## IHRM and organizational design

Even though the conduct of business everywhere is becoming internationalized, not all aspects of business are internationalizing at the same pace. Many of the challenges encountered by the multinational or global firm are associated with international human resource management. Learning to conduct business and to manage workforces in multiple countries with multiple political and governmental systems is a major challenge.

International firms are doing business in and employing people from increasing numbers of countries and cultures. Interactions between these people are increasing, as these firms sell, purchase, and outsource in an increasing number of countries, acquire more firms in other countries, and use more international joint ventures and alliances and cross-border teams and task forces. Indeed, the use of these organizational strategies and the problems associated with them have become so important that the subjects have earned themselves their own chapters in this edition of this book. As this and the next chapter point out, designing the multinational enterprise is increasingly complex and to a large degree presents mostly people issues of cross-border coordination, control, teamwork, learning, and integration. Thus senior executives of these firms expect to get help from their human resource managers in this critical endeavor.

IHRM in Action 3.1 provides a vision of what one of these complex firms might look like and what its managers must be prepared to do in order to deal with it. Later sections provide more depth of explanation of the issues presented by such a vision.

## Designing the multinational enterprise

Just because a firm has built or acquired or negotiated operations in multiple countries, does not mean that it has learned how to conduct international business effectively. To move to the next step, that is, to convert their global presence into global competitive advantage, firms must take advantage of five opportunities.[7] These include being able to: (1) adapt to local market differences; (2) exploit global economies of scale; (3) exploit economies of global scope; (4) tap into the best locations for activities and resources; and (5) maximize knowledge and experience transfer between locations. That is, the major challenge is both to effectively take advantage of local differences and to facilitate integration across the firm's many locations and operations of what is learned from those differences. These are all, at their core, international human resource issues.

The basic problem that underlies the ability of firms to organize in such a way in their international operations as to be able to exploit these advantages is the challenge of figuring out how to coordinate and balance the opposing forces of integrating their foreign operations with each other and with the parent firm while at the same time allowing the necessary autonomy and local control needed to meet unique national and cultural interests.[8] This is what has been referred to in earlier chapters as the centralization–decentralization (or globalization–localization) problem. Firms have dealt with this issue by first creating simplicity of structure and then, when that didn't suffice, developing ever-increasing formality and structure. But, as stated above, they are now realizing there are limits to the formal tools (structures and systems) of organization.

MNEs need integration and sharing of learning and experience, and they typically seek common policies in a number of areas related to overall performance, such as financial objectives, yet they need to allow localized adaptation to cultural differences. The emphasis on increased layers and size of formal structure and more sophisticated systems has in fact slowed down communication, learning, and decision making, and limited international firms' abilities to adapt effectively to local differences. Thus MNEs are turning increasingly to reduced size of business units, increased numbers of smaller business centers, and informal networks for improved communication, control, and coordination, as described later in the chapter.[9] As Jay Galbraith, one of the foremost researchers on issues related to the design of the global corporation, says, "Organizing a company to do business on a global scale remains one of the most complex organizational responsibilities."[10] And coping with the challenge of combining centralized control and integration with localized product and managerial adaptation creates one of the most significant of those complexities.

MNE managers reconcile these potentially conflicting imperatives in several ways. One way, sometimes celebrated as "think global, act local," is to encourage local initiatives, but then globalize information about these activities. Typically, the corporate headquarters has some form of scoreboard monitoring its operations around the world. Any local success could have global implications and might be applicable worldwide. More usually, local adaptations stay local. For example, Shell gave help to pig farmers in the Philippines, which protected its pipelines from sabotage by insurgents. Such a strategy did not find adherents in other locales.

Another way of integrating cultural diversity is to decentralize "centers of excellence" to those cultures that do the job best and most cheaply. Hence Motorola has made Bangalore in India its software headquarters, drawing on the skills of some of the world's best software engineers. Sony sources its software in the US. Apple found Singaporeans so good at high-quality computer assembly that they now manage Apple's factories around the world. The automobile of the future may be designed in Italy, with engines made in Germany, safety systems from Japan, and so on. In this strategy, global excellence becomes a synthesis of approaches taken in many places.[11]

> No doubt leaders of all companies face such dilemmas. So what is so special about global
> companies? The answer is that worldwide operations render these dilemmas more acute,
> since the values of whole cultures may put varying priorities on one or the other side of a
> dilemma. In some cultures, for example, stock markets dominate the supply side,

shareholders own and can dispose of under-performing assets, in others cross-shareholdings makes this much more difficult.[12]

Through a variety of studies and interviews with, among others, twenty-one chief executives, researchers at the Judge Institute, Anglia Business School, and the Trompenaars–Hampton–Turner Group discovered that "trans-cultural competence," the capacity to integrate seemingly opposed values, was among the most important skills of the MNE chief executives.[13] Such managers scored significantly higher on this criterion than a general sample. This, then, creates one of the most important opportunities for IHR, i.e., to plan and implement the systems for developing such competencies among the global management team.

It should be obvious that no one type of international organization structure embodies the right system for all firms. Rather, the multinational enterprise needs to be a multidimensional network of businesses, countries, and functions. Global customers are demanding single points of business contact and global strategies seek simplified reporting structures. In response, firms are being forced into four- and five-dimensional networks, as discussed through the rest of this chapter. Global firms (and individuals) which can develop and build global networks, including global electronic networks, will be best positioned to meet these challenges. The virtual teams that will be formed from these networks (and developed to do the research and development work of the global firm) will allow companies to continue to organize and reorganize along whatever new dimensions may yet be needed.[14] And global managers will need to be trained and developed to operate effectively with multidimensional structures as well as multiple types of structures.

The next section of this chapter provides an overview of the design options that international firms have utilized as they have evolved in their conduct of international business.

## Global organizational structure

The basic organizational challenge to MNEs has always been the integration of activities that take place in different countries and coordination of foreign subsidiaries with headquarters.[15] This has been the primary task of managers with global responsibility for product lines and for functions like finance and research and development. The basic global structure, then, of every MNE, has been a blend at least of (1) product lines, (2) country subsidiaries and alliances, and (3) business functions. (In recent years, as will be illustrated, even more organizational responsibilities have been added to this mix.) Varying international strategies, as described in Chapter 2, have led to various combinations and foci across these three dimensions. And, now, increased foreign direct investment and new technologies are causing the convergence and realignment of industries in such a way as to blur the traditional boundaries between these three dimensions and making the design and management of MNEs even more complex than before.

The rest of this chapter discusses the traditional choices firms have made to combine these three dimensions in their efforts to effectively manage their global operations.[16] In addition, it focuses on the ways in which IHRM can contribute to these decisions. The next chapter describes the HRM implications from the use of cross-border acquisitions, joint ventures, alliances, and teams in the implementation of these structural choices.

## International, geographic, and product divisions

The earliest structure created by most MNEs to manage their international operations (other than for simple export) was a simple headquarters and subsidiary model, as shown in Figure 3.1. Subsidiaries either reported directly to the CEO or the vice-president (VP) of operations or to marketing or manufacturing. Eventually, as the international business developed, the subsidiaries reported to an international division, established to manage the international business as illustrated in Figure 3.2, Bausch & Lomb's original organizational structure for its international business.[17] Each of the product lines contained all of the business functions, while its international division was responsible for all of its overseas activities, with each country and region handling all the product lines sold in that country or region and being relatively self-contained.

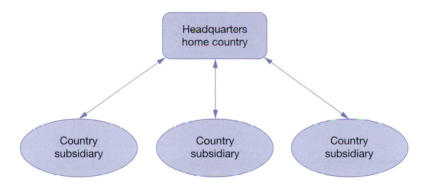

Figure 3.1 Simple headquarters – subsidiary model

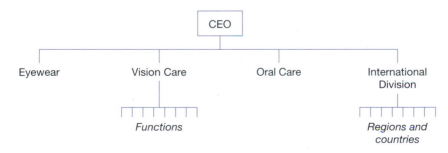

Figure 3.2 Bausch & Lomb's international division structure c. 1984

As international sales increased, the international division typically gave way to a geographic structure, with each region becoming an independent division reporting directly to the CEO (see Figure 3.3, Bausch & Lomb's later structure). In multiple product-line firms, a product-line focus was often added to this regional focus, with country subsidiaries taking on specific product responsibilities (see, for example, Figure 3.4, Black & Decker), as firms added formal structure in order to cope with increasing product and political complexity (such as with the development of the European Union).

This simple hierarchical model, however, turns out to be inadequate to handle the complexities of the needs of today's multinationals, which often have multiple organizational forms and networks. The organizational needs of the modern multinational must be configurable into business unit dimensions – in order to handle the creation and dissemination of new products – and into geographical and regional

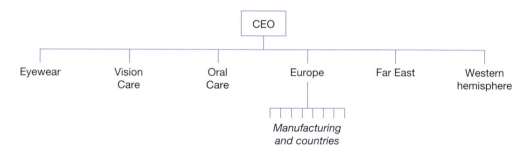

*Figure 3.3* Bausch & Lomb's international geographic structure *c.* 1992

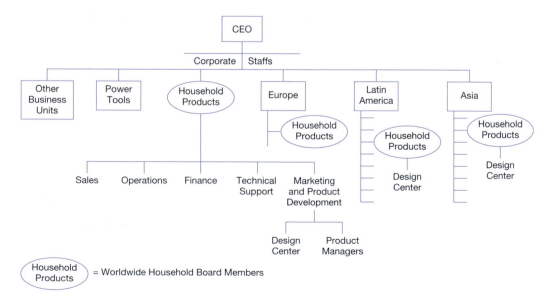

*Figure 3.4* Black & Decker's international structure, with both product and regional focus

units able to speak with one voice to political units such as the European Union or the Chinese government. Some of the units need to be able to be integrated into a single research unit while others must be configured to serve global customers across countries and across businesses.

## Multidimension network

As the needs for more business centers increases, for example to accommodate additional countries and for additional research and development centers to adapt products to local customers, global firms look for ways to create a network of centers around the world, in order to better coordinate, control, and learn from them. These structures tend to vary in form, depending on whether the firm is a single- or multiple-product business.

### *Single-business organization*

If the business is a single-business firm, and its global business was primarily developing into what was for it new areas with heterogeneous markets and active local governments, yet it has a fairly simple business model, then the firm is likely to develop a strong geographical dimension to its structure (see Figure 3.5), in order to deal effectively with these markets and governments. This type of business (such as Coca-Cola or McDonald's) tends to have regional headquarters servicing the country subsidiaries in that region.

These regions typically include North America, Latin America (prior to the advent of NAFTA, most firms included Mexico in the Latin America region, now some choose to include it in their North America region), Europe (for firms with limited business

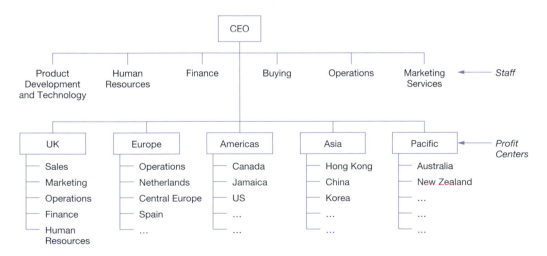

*Figure 3.5* Single-business geographic structure

in the Middle East and/or Africa, these areas were often included with their European regional headquarters, while those with extensive business in either the Mid-East or Africa tend to have regional headquarters servicing each or both of these additional areas), and Asia/Pacific. In the Asia region, firms with extensive business in the Asian subcontinent, for example, India and/or Pakistan, and in Southeast Asia (Thailand, Malaysia, Indonesia, the Philippines, Singapore, Australia, etc.), often create regional headquarters for both South or Southeast Asia and Pacific Asia (China, South Korea, Japan, Taiwan, Hong Kong, etc.). For example, Colgate-Palmolive, with operations in almost 200 countries, divides the world into six international divisions: North America (not including Mexico), Latin America (including Mexico), Africa, Eastern Europe and the Middle East (including Russia), Europe, and Asia Pacific (including every country from Australia to India to China to Korea to Japan).[18]

In some global firms, the countries with the largest operations often have their own separate division, reporting direct to the CEO, as illustrated by the UK in Figure 3.5. As firms expand their businesses to an increasing number of countries and regions (many companies are now represented in over 150 countries around the world), obviously the structure that is necessary to coordinate and integrate these many locations becomes increasingly complex, even if the business model is fairly simple.

## Multi-business enterprises

If the international business portfolio is quite diverse, with multiple products and a number of business logics or models, and the markets for each product line are relatively homogeneous and well known, served by standardized products, then there is likely to develop a strong strategic business unit (international product line) structure (see Figure 3.6). In this case, the firm will have multiple international product lines and is likely to use a multi-domestic structure, with relatively autonomous subsidiaries responsible for each product line operating in each country. Concerns for overlap and lack of coordination/integration often lead to the development of regional headquarters and complex reporting mechanisms.

3M's structure, as illustrated in Figure 3.6, shows the complexity of combining product lines (sectors) with country businesses (RSOs, regional subsidiary organizations) with business functions (HRM, Finance, Sales and Marketing, Manufacturing and R&D). The number of specific units (e.g., ten RSOs in Europe with eighteen business centers in Europe with dozens of sales and marketing units and manufacturing centers and labs) shows how complex the problems of coordination, integration, and cross-border and cross-unit learning can become.

## Global matrix structure

As concerns for cost control compete with concerns for integration and cross-fertilization across national borders, firms tend to look for ways to coordinate all the

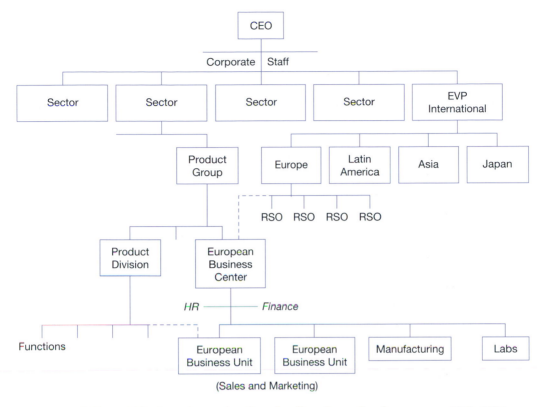

*Figure 3.6* 3M's multi-business international product line plus regional structure *c.* 1992–1993

many critical components of the firm: country subsidiaries, product lines, local and global customers, business functions, research and development, regional and central headquarters, etc. Thus, other combinations of the critical variables are developed to include structures to integrate the traditional business functions with country and product (see Figures 3.7 and 3.8). Often these organizational designs have evolved as the firm has increased its global presence and tried to cope more effectively with the complexities it encounters.

These matrix structures involve two or more lines of reporting.[19] Typically there will be a country "leg" to the matrix with managers reporting to a local national boss plus reporting to a product group or regional or headquarters functional office, as well. Sometimes there are three or more legs and they may be given equal importance (solid line reporting) or may have different levels of priority, with a solid line for direct reporting and dotted line for more indirect reporting relationships.

These structures cause a new set of dilemmas and require a new set of skills. The many diverse demands of global business require the global firm to give management focus to both the local and the corporate levels. The matrix doesn't resolve this dilemma, it just makes it a permanent part of the management environment. At best, the matrix structure allows local and global realities to be reconciled; at its worst,

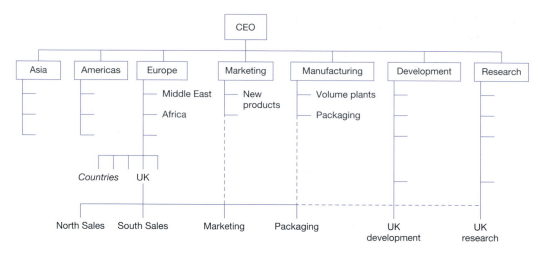

*Figure 3.7* MNE structure combining traditional business functions with geographic/country focus

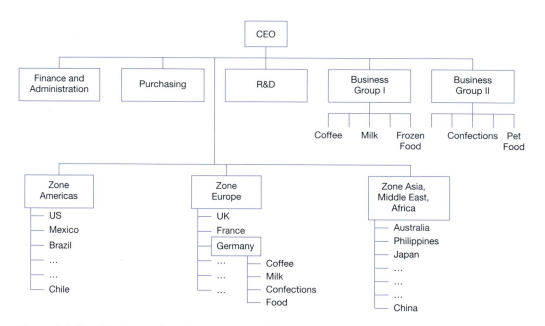

*Figure 3.8* Nestlé's international structure combining geographic, business, and functional units

it allows individual managers to pursue narrow objectives without regard to their impact on the other legs of the matrix, that is, on the other parts of the organization. Problems with divided loyalties and multiple bosses have to be resolved. Ultimately, managers working in a global matrix organization, must learn to think more broadly and, as stated earlier, to develop network skills to negotiate resources, resolve trade-offs, and to manage through influence and persuasion, not necessarily direct authority.

At the level of the individual, the central dilemma that many managers face in this organizational need for integration is that of divided loyalties.[20] Loyalty is local, that is, people are more loyal to the colleagues they socialize with, see daily, and spend time with. If the formal organizational structure requires interaction with strangers (particularly strangers in another country), it is only to be expected that priority attention will flow to the local colleagues, unless significant effort is put into developing the relationships across borders. Interestingly, attitudes about loyalty vary according to country culture and to functional specialty. For example, managers in Spain and France prefer loyalty to the remote (normally central) part of the organization while managers in the UK, Ireland, and China prefer loyalty to local colleagues. HRM was one of the functions that most preferred loyalty to local colleagues. But, clearly, HR must get involved with training managers in the need to foster both local and central relationships and must foster such relationships themselves.

## Transnational organization

One of the more complex business structures has been developed by ABB Asea Brown Boveri, the Swiss-Swedish global firm. ABB is often used as an example of a transnational firm, that is, one with a truly global focus, making resource decisions without reference to national origins, sharing its ideas and technology with all of its units on a global scale, while cultivating a local character in all of its individual businesses. ABB has 150,000 employees worldwide, divided into 150 business lines and 5,000 profit centers. Figure 3.9 illustrates its business–geography organizational structure.

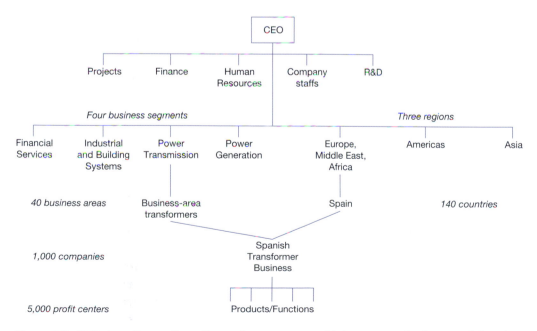

*Figure 3.9* ABB Asea Brown Boveri's matrix structure combining country, business, and function

## It's more than formal structure

All of these organizational structures, from the simpler Bausch & Lomb design to the complex designs of Black & Decker, 3M, Nestlé, and ABB, illustrate how complex the typical organizational structure of the modern multinational enterprise often becomes.

As an MNE develops, it must find a way to coordinate its business functions (such as finance, manufacturing, and marketing), its strategic business units, its R&D activities, its country subsidiaries and local and regional operations, its strategic alliances, its global customers, with its headquarters' orientation, vision and values, and balance sheet. Thus simple global business structures are focused on function, country, and product lines. And as the businesses of the MNE become more complex, dealing with increased numbers of countries, customers, products, and development issues, the necessary structures evolve into more complex forms. Indeed, the structures may get too complex to draw (and as previously described, global firms such as ABB begin to lean more heavily on informal networks and relationships to make them work).

As described in IHRM in Action 3.1, the glimpse into an effective global firm demonstrates how managers of the near future might be able to find solutions to their needs for integrating the types of far-flung operations just discussed.[21] Hopefully, such managers will find the networking skills they need enhanced and developed by skilled IHR professionals who understand the importance of the linkages, how to create the skills to use the linkages, and how to make sure the linkages provide the "glue" necessary to hold these far-flung and complex operations together.

## Networks

The firm in IHRM in Action 3.1 is highly differentiated; but it is held together by a network of relationships (managerial and otherwise). Firms have tried a number of strategies, described in this and the previous chapter, to hold these complex global businesses together with increasingly complex formal structures – including multiple dimension matrixes, with formal reporting structures that include product lines, functional responsibilities, country business units, regional and parent-country headquarters, multiple specialty centers such as R&D and product development and global training and development, and cross-border acquisitions, IJVs, partnerships, and virtual teams, described in the next chapter.

Because of these multiple and complex layers, informal networks of relationships develop in order to handle the practical components of day-to-day business activity, such as business planning, again as illustrated in IHRM in Action 3.1. Such informal networks work only if Jacques and Margaret in the example know and trust each other well enough to work out their different purposes. They work if the people that need to interact and coordinate have a shared superordinate vision of the direction of the overall firm and their parts in it, high capacity for self-control and willingness to collaborate, and capacity to negotiate their differences.[22] This requires constant attention to the application of what Evans calls "glue technology," or the management development technology of integration, that is, management development practices that have as a primary purpose the integration of the management and executive workforce of the firm and the building of the necessary competencies to use the resulting networks in an effective way.[23] Such global management development programs are discussed more fully in Chapter 10 on training and executive development.

## Use and management of cross-border teams

Given the increasing complexity of organizations as described so far in this book and in this and the prior chapter, much of the work that needs to get done in a global enterprise requires a high degree of interaction and interdependence between globally dispersed organizations and between people in various, globally dispersed sections of those organizations. This interaction is often relegated to a work group, or team.[24] And, increasingly, these teams are made up of people from multiple and varying organizations (or parts of the same organization), geographic locations, countries, cultures, languages, ways of thinking and working, and time zones. Often they have the characteristics of "virtual" teams, that is, they don't meet face to face and are not co-located, they are widely geographically dispersed.

These cross-border teams come with many different names: global teams, multinational, multicultural, transnational, trans-cultural, geographically distributed or geographically dispersed, non-co-located or out-of-sight teams. All of these terms refer to the phenomenon of people working together in teams, with common goals, who are not physically located in the same place and often do not meet but rather conduct their "business" via electronic means. In this book, such teams will generally be referred to by the term cross-border teams, since this is the primary structure of interest in this chapter and the phrasing that seems to be most commonly used.

These cross-border teams represent a dramatic change in the way managers function and they present two major new challenges.[25] Both of these challenges stem from issues related to the physical separation of workers and managers made necessary by globalization[26] and possible by technology:[27]

The first challenge has to do with managing people you can't see. Managers must make the transition from managing which activities get done when to managing projects and their results.

The second managerial challenge is to redefine the role of management, itself, since the "virtual" nature of cross-border teams creates much uncertainty as to whether managers still have a role to play in managing employees who are no longer present in the same locale. In addition, these teams tend to be largely self-managing, with the members working very interdependently via the internet.

The goal in this discussion of cross-border teams is to provide enough understanding of the problems and their solutions that are involved in their use so that IHR managers can provide the necessary advice, training, and facilitation to ensure their global firms can gain their intended and possible benefits. (More detail is available in Schuler *et al.*, *Managing Human Resources in Cross-border Alliances*, in this series.[28]) This will become more important because virtual teams will become more prevalent because:

- The complexity of global business requires the interaction and networking of people with multiple competencies from many different locations.
- Virtual teams save the money involved in travel for teams to meet or to relocate team members so they can be together. Indeed, some global firms, such as Glaxo-Wellcome, find that extensive travel can be disruptive and hard on team members.[29]
- Technology such as the internet and audio and video teleconferencing makes it much easier for cross-border teams to meet in a virtual fashion. These teams can function in one or both of two different modes:[30] (1) they can do everything face to face, which requires extensive travel to get team members together (and which eliminates one of the reasons for using such teams in the first place, that is their ability to meet electronically); or (2) they can do most of their work in virtual mode, relying on electronic technology to facilitate their interaction.

Many problems arise with over reliance on virtual teams and on teams meeting in virtual mode, although one unanswered question is whether younger people who "grow up" using the computer and are much more used to interaction with others via a computer monitor might well be better able to interact effectively without the need for face-to-face, cocktail, time in order to trust out-of-sight team members well enough to overcome these problems. The use of e-mail may increase the quantity of interaction, but some studies suggest the quality decreases.[31]

Most studies, in fact, suggest that the critical variable in the successful functioning of virtual teams is the level of trust between team members. And this seems to be a function of the amount of time the team has spent in "face-to-face" time, particularly at the beginnings of the life of the team.[32] Some experience with virtual teams also suggests that the "half life" of trust in virtual teams, i.e., the time it takes before the level of trust falls below some dangerous threshold, is less than three months.[33] What this indicates is that virtual teams, in order to maintain healthy working relationships, probably need to meet face to face every three months, or so.

Managers supervising the physically remote legs of the global firm have the additional challenge of managing these "virtual" teams. As already indicated, these teams operate across barriers of distance, culture, time zones, and technology. Most management training still assumes that management skills are applied face to face and in the manager's own culture, which is no longer the reality for many of these managers. Using the old skills to manage these new remote operations results in too much travel, inappropriate attempts to micro-manage (since trust and relationships have not been developed), and concerns about personal visibility with remote staffs.

Managers in these new organizations need to gain the skills of relationship building and teamwork from long distance.

Some of the lessons learned about the effective management of cross-border and virtual teams include the following:[34]

- Develop an e-mail protocol, to include appropriate topics, frequency and time of use, definition of urgency, who should participate and when, the importance of respect in use of titles, etc., speed of response, attitudes about jokes, profanity, and intimacies, and guidelines for use of voice-to-voice communication.
- Select the appropriate people for virtual team membership, including people who are self-starters, have strong communication skills, and have good virtual team skills (can use e-mail well, etc.).
- Identify from the beginning the team member who will have the team leadership role.
- Keep virtual team projects focused on the task, with clear goals, targets, and deadlines.
- Provide adequate face-to-face, social time to build the trust necessary to work well in a virtual format.
- Celebrate the reaching of targets and completion of projects.
- Identify the barriers to collaboration that you want to overcome and work together to resolve them.
- Provide cultural mentors to the team to deal with cross-cultural problems and misunderstanding.
- Identify what people should do when a crisis occurs, including whom to contact and the decision-making hierarchy within the group.
- And identify the ground rules for virtual teamwork, including establishing regular times for group interaction, setting up firm rules for communication, using visual forms of communication whenever possible, ensuring regular and consistent communication, agreeing on standard technology to ease communication, encouraging informal, off-line conversation between team members, and helping team members make the transition from the virtual team to their next assignments.

## The global learning organization: the tie that binds

Ultimately, the "tie" that binds (glues) the global firm together is the intellectual and social capital it has in the knowledge and skills held by its employees (around the world) and its abilities to create, share, and use that knowledge on a global basis. In today's world, where the only sustainable competitive advantage any firm has is its ability to learn faster than its competitors, creating a culture of learning and nurturing and facilitating learning across borders may be the only avenue to success.[35] In today's global economy, "change is complex and messy, [so] many stick with the known for fear of the unknown. . . . It is much more reassuring to stay as you are . . . than to try to make a fundamental change when you cannot be certain that the effort will succeed."[36] Yet a firm has to do it, in today's chaotic, global environment. It has to take the risk to find ways to facilitate learning so that change is possible. As John Browne, CEO of BP Amoco, puts it, "Learning is at the heart of a company's ability to adapt to a rapidly changing environment."[37] From a global perspective, this means a firm must facilitate learning on a global basis – across borders, across parts of the organization in different country locales, in cross-border teams, with people on foreign assignments, and in international joint ventures and cross-border partnerships and alliances.

As Peter Senge says, "Perhaps for the first time in history, humankind has the capacity to create far more information than anyone can absorb, to foster far greater interdependency than anyone can manage, and to accelerate change far faster than anyone's ability to keep pace."[38] Thus this challenge to firms of learning on a global basis must become a central focus. And technology alone (such as creating IT data bases and repositories of knowledge and experience) will not solve the challenge. People must want to use such knowledge sources and must be willing to contribute their own "learnings" to them. In the end, people must be committed to: (1) the importance of learning; and (2) the need to share and use information. In turn, the MNE needs to create the organizational culture and structure and the HRM policies and practices to encourage and facilitate such attitudes and behaviors. This is the essence of learning organizations and knowledge management.[39]

The attention in the next chapter to cross-border acquisitions, IJVs, and partnerships stresses that one of the key objectives of such organizational strategies is always to learn from the foreign firms and/or partners. For many reasons, this is often quite difficult and, indeed, often is not done to the satisfaction of the firms involved.

The global firm must use its people who have international experience and who have been posted to international assignments, spreading them throughout the organization. It must ensure that individuals coming back from overseas assignments are provided new jobs that use the knowledge and skills learned overseas and are given opportunities to share that learning. In order for a firm to reap the benefits of learning, it is imperative that its valuable expatriate employees remain with the organization long enough to willingly share their experiences. A failed assignment (early return) by an expatriate, or early exit by a repatriate, limits the ability of the firm to capitalize on their learning. And, as is discussed in Chapters 8 and 9, whether or not expatriates stay appears to be related to the extent to which their international skills and knowledge are used after they return. Since learning is so important, and learning across borders (taking advantage of the global experience and multinational learning of a global firm's global workforce) is so necessary, then managing foreign assignments to ensure successful expatriation and repatriation would seem essential.

Special efforts also need to be made to expose employees and managers "at home" to the products and processes of foreign subsidiaries and foreign acquisitions and partners, and vice versa, including visits to each other's operations to observe and learn through direct interaction. The firm must spread employees and managers from the countries of its operations throughout its operations, including at the very highest levels of the executive team and the board of directors, itself. Only in these ways can the global firm make effective use of any technology that has been adopted to facilitate learning on a global scale, such as talent directories, intranets for sharing information, etc.

## Conclusion

This chapter has discussed the difficult task of designing organizational structure for the complexities of the modern global enterprise. The evolution of the global firm from a simple headquarters–subsidiary model to very complex matrix structures that try to link hundreds of centers located in dozens of countries was described, with the goal of providing some guidance on options for designing an effective architecture for firms trying to integrate and control their far-flung, and often locally centered operations. In the end, as the chapter discusses, individual managers in such firms must learn how to utilize extensive networks of contacts throughout (and outside) their firms in order to make such complex systems work effectively. And it is up to IHR to implement the development programs that will enable their global managers to learn the competencies needed to lead such networks.

## Points for further discussion

1 Using materials from Chapters 2 and 3, describe the structure, stage, and form of entry being used in Lincoln Electric, globally, as well as in China.
2 What would you consider some of the biggest challenges facing Lincoln Electric today?
3 Are there key informal networks and relationships in Lincoln Electric? Where are they?

# Cross-border mergers and acquisitions, international joint ventures, and alliances

**4**

## Learning objectives

After considering Chapter 4, the reader will be able to describe:

- The basic nature of cross-border acquisitions, international joint ventures and partnerships
- The major HRM implications from cross-border mergers and acquisitions, joint ventures and alliances
- The HR professional's role in implementing effective cross-border mergers and acquisitions, and international joint ventures

## Key terms

- Cross-border mergers and acquisitions
- International joint ventures
- Due diligence
- Alliances and partnerships

This chapter examines the ways in which organizations "go international," besides starting a foreign operation "from scratch" or just expanding internally. This includes the use of cross-border acquisitions, international joint ventures and alliances. Increasingly, these strategies are the "methods of choice" used by enterprises as they internationalize for many reasons. So this chapter looks at the important role IHRM performs in the implementation of these internationalization strategies.

The previous chapter described the options available to global enterprises as they seek ways to structure their international operations. The strategies discussed in this chapter provide the means by which global enterprises build their organizations. They can be fitted into any of the complex organizational structures described in the previous chapter. Because of these global business-building realities, and the many problems and complexities they present, IHR professionals are being asked to advise on the design and to assist in the implementation of these approaches. So, the objective of this chapter is to provide the basic knowledge and understanding of these approaches to enable IHRM to provide that advice and assistance.

## Cross-border M&As, international joint ventures and alliances

This chapter discusses cross-border mergers and acquisitions, international joint ventures, and cross-border alliances or partnerships. All of these forms of international combination create major coordination and integration challenges, and thus are areas of international business that HRM professionals must thoroughly understand in order to provide senior managers with the advice they need for designing the effective global business.

First, the discussion addresses some general issues related to the importance of these organizational strategies. International mergers and acquisitions and alliances of various types are increasingly used by firms to gain access to new global markets and global resources, such as technology and skilled people. The number and value of such cross-border deals continue to increase dramatically.[1] According to the United Nations, in the first half of the year 2000, alone, there were 1,660 cross-border acquisitions worth some US$5.285 trillion.[2] According to the Canadian research firm Thomson Financial, in numbers that differ slightly from those of the United Nations, a new record was set in the year 2000. Its data indicate that there were 38,292 cross-border transactions worldwide, totaling nearly US$3.5 trillion.[3] Since then, the numbers have leveled off, owing to the global economic slow-down. Even so, such transactions still continue at a high level. And just as important as these alliances are to the ongoing internationalization of US firms, they are also increasingly used by the firms of other countries, as well. Examples of significant cross-border M&A deals include Daimler–Chrysler, BMW–Rover, Ford–Jaguar–Volvo–Mazda, Renault–Nissan, SKB–Glaxo–Beecham–SmithKline–Beckman, CIBA–Sandoz, Nestlé–Purina, Deutsche Telekom–Voice Stream, Vodaphone–Airtouch, Japan Tobacco–RJR Nabisco Tobacco, Unilever–Best Foods–Ben & Jerry's, and Credit Suisse group's purchase of US investment firm Donaldson Lufkin & Jenrette. Firms of every size and type are using cross-border acquisitions to access global business.[4]

There appear to be a number of pressures causing this huge wave of cross-border mergers and acquisitions, including either a felt need to constantly grow the business to compete more successfully with other large global firms and to achieve world-class and industry leadership (e.g., Daimler–Chrysler) or to acquire assets and resources (usually technological and knowledge-based in nature, e.g., the many acquisitions of smaller technology firms by Cisco Systems) needed to compete and that would otherwise be too expensive, take too long, or would just be impossible to develop internally (see IHRM in Action 4.1, "The acquisition strategy of Germany's Siemens").[5] When acquisition is the choice for entry into a new market, it is often seen as a quicker and more effective way to develop a presence in a local market than to build such capability from scratch.

There are also a number of forms of international alliances or partnerships. In some cultures or countries, alliances or partnerships are, if not the only way to enter the marketplace, at least the "smartest" way, either because foreigners can, for practical purposes, do business in the country only through local partnerships (because relationships are of primary importance to doing business in that culture) or because the government requires such local partnering. Rosabeth Moss Kanter provides one way to view the variety of options for alliances or partnerships.[6] Kanter's model includes the following forms of combination:

- Pooled (or cooperatives, usually research-based).
- Alliances (or joint ventures).
- Linkages (or partnerships, along the value chain, with customers and suppliers, e.g., subcontracting and long-term buyer–vendor relationships as in *keiretsus* and *chaebols)*.

In addition, there are other forms of international combinations, such as "foreign participation" or partial ownership (as is often used in Central and Eastern Europe, Russia and the former Soviet republics, and China, where firms typically from the developed countries contribute financial, people, and/or technological resources to foreign firms, often without equity participation or with significantly less than majority ownership). This can provide a major way for the "foreign" firms to gain access to the markets of such countries and for the local firms to gain access to the resources, expertise, and technology of the foreign firms.

## Record of success and failure

Some surveys suggest that 40 percent or more of international combinations fall short of their objectives and one-third are dissolved within a few months or years.[7] A study of alliances (as contrasted to mergers and acquisitions) through interviews of top financial services leaders by the management and technology consulting firm Accenture found that 90 percent of alliance negotiations fail to reach agreement and that only 2 percent create deals that last more than four years.[8] At least half of all alliances fall well short of expectations. The report says that is an "astonishingly high failure rate," considering that as many as one-fourth of all companies will derive more than 40 percent of their total market value from related activities by 2004, representing at least US$25 trillion in market value. A similar record of failure appears to be the case for cross-border mergers and acquisitions, as well. Table 4.1 illustrates the results over the last few years of changes in shareholder wealth after ten of the biggest acquisitions of all time. Only two of the ten, as of July 1, 2002, could show an increase in shareholder value.

# The acquisition strategy of Germany's Siemens

The 150-year-old German firm Siemens is a world leader in electrical engineering and electronics, with 480,000 employees in over 190 countries. The company spends some €6.8 billion (US$6 billion) per year on R&D out of its US$70 billion in annual sales and has over US$80 billion in assets spread across a wide range of businesses making products from light bulbs and consumer electronics to x-ray equipment, trains, and power stations.

In recent years Siemens has invested heavily to expand its overseas operations, particularly in the US. Its strategy for these acquisitions has been to primarily favor smaller, targeted transactions, rather than mega-acquisitions. The US has been a major target for acquisitions because it is the company's biggest single market, with annual sales of about €20 billion (a larger share than from Germany) with about 70,000 employees, more than Coca-Cola or Microsoft have within the US. Says Kenneth C. Cornelius, a senior US executive and 25-year Siemens veteran: "We [the US] have gone from being an outpost to being the strategy."

Siemens's primary objective in its international acquisitions is to be able to fully integrate the firms that they take over into their existing portfolio of businesses. Integration teams with members from both sides of the transaction start developing the transition programs even prior to the actual acquisition. The real work starts during the post-merger period. According to CEO von Pierer, "I think it's important that the buying company doesn't try to overrun and completely change the corporate culture in the acquired company. We at Siemens always strive to establish ourselves as good corporate citizens in all our local markets. That includes forming a trusting relationship with our colleagues and partners. While a rigorous, success-oriented culture throughout the company is important for big corporations like us, it's equally important to give the individual units entrepreneurial freedom in their daily operations. That's what we practice at Siemens, and it's also how we integrate newly acquired companies."

Siemens' integration strategies

Interview with Dr Kai Lucks, Vice-president and Head of Department Cooperation Strategies, M&A Integration, Siemens AG

*What does the integration process look like?* Integration is one of the key processes in mergers and acquisitions. It begins in the preparatory stage of an M&A project. During the transaction phase, the integration plan has to be developed in order to be ready for action directly after closing. The post-merger integration measures are to be based on the pre-closing integration plan.

continued

*Is there usually an integration manager in charge of the integration process, or are business unit managers automatically in charge of their related integration activities?* The relevant business unit is the owner of the M&A project. They have to nominate an integration manager at the beginning of the transaction phase. The integration manager has to follow the rules for integration determined by our Center of Competence for M&A integration. These rules have been developed together with specialists and experienced M&A integration people worldwide.

*What are your integration priorities?* Priorities for the individual M&A project are consistency with overall strategic goals (achievement of competitive leading positions), value generation (EVA), and realization of measures (integration performance).

*In your experience, have you faced any important issues in cross-border mergers caused by cultural differences between the two companies? If so, can you give an example?* The cultural differences between different company types and value-added steps (e.g., big global player versus specialized software house) are by far bigger than cultural differences between different regions. The cultural similarities in global industries are very high. This was one of the favorable conditions, for example, for the integration of Siemens fossil-fuel power generation with the Westinghouse Power Generation Business Unit.

*What advice do you have for other senior executives contemplating cross-border mergers?* Identify your rivals and tell your people why you can beat them only by joining forces.

Nevertheless, cultural clashes threaten Siemens's US prospects. Like many foreign companies, Siemens has traditionally run its US operations from Germany, under a cadre of German-born executives. This top-down management style leaves little room for local adaptation and innovation. And it tends to tie the hands of local managers, keeping the company's many units from collaborating and learning from each other. The German deliberateness and structure directly conflict with the American fast pace and intense competition. In the end, Siemens is having to learn a new way of doing business, with a new organizational and managerial structure.

"Most organizations do not have the knowledge, experience, or capability to manage alliances to maximize returns on all sides," according to the report.[9] "Unlike a merger or acquisition, an alliance is ongoing and needs to be governed throughout as a relationship." But many of the same problems of integration exist for acquisitions, as well, as the rest of this section describes. Indeed, many top executives have not

*Table 4.1* The numbers don't lie: ten of the biggest mergers of all time and their effect on shareholder wealth as of July 1, 2002

| Deal | Year | Value since acquisition (US$ billion) | |
| | | Created | Destroyed |
| --- | --- | --- | --- |
| AOL/Time Warner | 2001 | – | 148 |
| Vodaphone/Mannesmann | 2000 | – | 299 |
| Pfizer/Warner-Lambert | 2000 | – | 78 |
| Glaxo/SmithKline | 2000 | – | 40 |
| Chase/J.P. Morgan | 2000 | – | 26 |
| Exxon/Mobil | 1999 | 8 | – |
| SBC/Ameritech | 1999 | – | 68 |
| WorldCom/MCI | 1998 | – | 94 |
| Travelers/Citicorp | 1998 | 109 | – |
| Daimler/Chrysler | 1998 | – | 36 |

Source: Hammonds, K.H. (2002), "Size is not a strategy," *Fast Company*, September, p. 80.

changed their "mental models" from the command-and-control approach often used in the past for mergers or acquisitions to the necessarily participatory, relation-building nature of a successful cross-border joint venture or alliance (or, even, for that matter, merger or acquisition).

Typically the reasons for pursuing an acquisition or alliance are financial or strategic in nature due to perceived compatibility of or synergism in operations, products, services, markets, or technologies. Firms usually decide that a cross-border merger or acquisition (or, for that matter, a divestiture) will yield increased value and profits or improved market position for any one of five different reasons:[10]

- It enhances industry consolidation (thus helping to eliminate expensive overcapacity) which is typically the situation when the overall market is mature and where market opportunities are flat or shrinking.
- It enables geographic expansion into neighboring regions for a newly internationalizing, heretofore local, firm.
- It enhances expansion into new markets, for revenue growth, in which the opportunities will not wait for internal development.
- It involves acquisition of new technology or products or knowledge when the firm doesn't have the resources to develop the product or technology, internally.
- It involves combining with one or more other firms in order to realize a synergy that will form a preeminent firm with superior market advantages or economies of scale, often when new industry configurations are being created by new technologies.

## Due diligence

In order to achieve these objectives (which, as pointed out above, happens all too rarely) firms must conduct thorough preliminary "due diligence" to assess carefully the "real" values to be gained. However, in the typical situation, "People often just jump into the deal and then comes the realization that you have to work at it. . . . There are no easy mergers or acquisitions. Mergers need to be more thoughtful, more precise with regard to their objectives, more deliberate with regard to their people and processes and yet be done in a rapid time."[11]

As a result, the typical due diligence review of the target firm during the pre-combination phase of partnering rarely considers the critical people, organizational, and HR issues that may well provide the eventual reasons for the success or failure of the combination. The reasons for failure usually have more to do with the incompatibility of people, cultures, and/or HR systems than with problems with the originally perceived financial or strategic benefits. These HR complications often include issues such as overestimation of the abilities of the partner firm, an exaggerated assumption of the synergies available from the combination, inadequate attention to the incompatibilities of the firms' programs, ways of conducting business, and cultures, and unwillingness to prepare for the frequently experienced loss of productivity and staff after the merger is completed. Add to these problems the typical differences experienced between legal and cultural systems in different countries, and it becomes easier to understand the necessity of HR due diligence prior to any international acquisition or alliance and of paying attention to the necessary post-merger people integration issues, as illustrated by Siemens in IHRM in Action 4.1.

And yet "globalization mandates alliances [and cross-border acquisitions], makes them absolutely essential to strategy. . . . Like it or not, the simultaneous developments that go under the name of globalization make alliances – *entente* – necessary."[12]

## Managing the cross-border merger or acquisition

This section outlines the typical process followed by firms as they proceed through acquisition planning and implementation. This description sets the stage for explanation of the HR-oriented due diligence that firms should carry out that are considering such international combinations. Examination of target firms is so important that it provides a critical opportunity for HR academics, consultants, and practitioners to provide a very significant assistance and advice in the ultimate success of firms looking into joint international endeavors. In the best of circumstances, HR plays a major part in the planning for and implementation of cross-border acquisitions and alliances.

# Process of combination

The actual process of combination usually proceeds through three stages.[13] Each stage has its special problems and considerations. These stages are pretty much the same for the establishment of cross-border M&As as for IJVs and alliances, although there are enough unique characteristics for both IJVs and alliances, that those differences will be addressed in separate sections of the chapter. The stages of combination include the following phases:

- *Phase 1 Pre-combination.* This first phase involves the initial target screening and pre-bid courtship of the potential target firm, the "due diligence" review of the target company, the price setting and negotiation of the approach the partners will take to the combination, and the agreement on the contract wording of the deal. HR should be closely involved with each of these steps, particularly the due diligence process, since many aspects of the integration will involve issues of primary concern to HR. This process of due diligence is discussed in more detail in the next section.
- *Phase 2 Combination planning and signing of the agreement.* Once the deal has been negotiated, this second phase involves deciding how to implement the deal, discovering and working through differences and different ideas about the deal, and actually signing the agreement. Here, too, HR should play a major role in providing advice on how to implement the deal and anticipating problems that will occur during the implementation.
- *Phase 3 Post-combination and implementation of the deal.* Once the deal has been consummated, the hard work of implementation must be executed. In this third phase, HR has a key role in helping to facilitate the integration with the merged firm or between the partners in an alliance or joint venture. One critical aspect of HR's role will be in creating and providing employee communication about the nature of the merger or alliance and about the vision for the business that will result after the merger/alliance has been consummated. In addition, HR will perform a critical role in training employees to accept and to fit into the new situation, in developing new assignments and staffing, in designing the new compensation and benefits systems, etc.

Problems that will be encountered in Phase 3 implementation should be addressed during the thorough due diligence in Phase 1 and implementation planning in Phase 2. Since this is often not done, it is little wonder that many combinations across national boundaries come unwound in a relatively short period of time.

# Due diligence and the role of HRM

As mentioned above, one of the key reasons for the high failure rate in acquisitions involves the lack of attention prior to "signing the agreement" and during the implementation phase to issues related to the organization and to people, in general, and to Human Resource Management, in particular.[14] "Increasingly . . . the people and organization fit is coming to be seen as the main factor why businesses fail to reap the benefits of mergers [and acquisitions and alliances]. The people issues revolve around the way the merger [and alliance] process is handled, the impact of the merger on individuals and the way they react to what is happening."[15]

One of the critical functions for ensuring the success of cross-border acquisitions or alliances is effective due diligence prior to the eventual "marriage" of the firms.[16] It also tends to be one of the most underrated phases of the process of creating and managing a cross-border M&A, IJV, or alliance. Many global ventures have fallen prey to failure or reduced levels of success because this crucial research effort doesn't reveal the weaknesses or incompatibilities of a prospective foreign business partner.

Often, the only due diligence that is performed involves a detailed audit of financial and legal issues and possibly product and market compatibilities or synergies. This will normally include review of things like annual reports, financial reports, product brochures, corporate legal documents, and other documents relating to the prospective partner's business practices. General information consisting of credential and certification confirmation (such as ISO certification) concerning principals, activities, and other requirements significant to the potential venture are also audited. Additionally, capability identification and verification may require individual meetings with employees, substantiation of facts with principals, locale inspections, bank references, customer interviews and references, existing partner conversations, and competitor interviews.

Regrettably, many of the aspects of the potential partner that often determine success or failure are ignored or minimized during the due diligence process. Many of these relate to HRM practices and people issues, such as the compatibilities or differences in the corporate cultures and in likely employee losses and the effect on later executive succession. These are the issues discussed in some depth in the next section of this chapter, providing an approach that can increase the likelihood of success in such ventures. The actual due diligence process as it involves HRM issues can be quite complex. The following describes both the process itself and suggested content for any foreign-combination due diligence activity related to HRM.

## Preparation (items to determine ahead of time)

The whole point of due diligence from an HRM perspective, is that HRM professionals should help their firm prepare for potential liabilities and incompatibilities in the merger of HRM practices and programs prior to the signing of the agreement and to establish the likelihood of achieving strategic and financial objectives. This should include the development of a checklist of critical issues to be assessed and the identification of a task force membership that can be called into use as soon as a target firm is identified (or even before). HRM professionals can take the initiative to ensure that critical HRM and people issues are considered before the combination becomes a "done deal." This should ensure, at a minimum, that there are HRM professionals on the due diligence task force and that the task force does indeed examine HR and people/organizational culture issues. This checklist should be evaluated after each acquisition and adjusted and updated to fit the firm's needs. The following paragraphs describe some of the important components of such a due diligence process. All of these issues should be addressed as early as possible and the actual due diligence activity should be given adequate time for a good evaluation and for planning the implementation of any subsequent combination. This activity can include:

- *Making a predetermined action plan and checklist of items to evaluate.* HR should determine ahead of time the data and information that it will want to evaluate (this is discussed in more detail in a later section) as well as trying to establish from whom that information should come (both internal and external to the target firm). This action plan should include a schedule for action, that is, determining when this plan would be called into action and what is its position in the pre-combination evaluation (ideally at the very beginning of deliberations and consideration). The last part of this action plan should include determining what will be the deliverables or outcomes, such as a report, recommendations, etc.
- *Creating a SWAT team.* Part of the early planning should include planning the team, that is, identifying the key people that would be called into action as soon as senior executives begin to consider even the possibility of a foreign combination. The desired characteristics of the members of such a team (in an international context) should include personal traits such as being inquisitive, having non-directive interviewing skills, ability to "read" people, and the ability to recognize when they are not getting the full story, as well, of course, as their necessary cross-cultural, language, and technical business expertise. In addition, the planning for this team should include determining when and how the SWAT team would operate. From an HRM point of view, these individuals should have the technical and professional ability to know what (of an HR nature) to look for and how to find it, familiarity with compensation and benefits financial data, differing accounting systems, sensitivity to cultural and language differences, awareness of possible union and labor differences, and objectivity.
- *Forming and communicating the new culture.* Since HR is the department that ultimately has responsibility for people issues, it usually is up to it to deal with concerns for the nature of the new firm and its culture that can be expected or is desired to be created from the firm that results after the combination is completed. What is expected needs to be addressed and communicated clearly and carefully to the workforces in both the acquired and the acquiring firms (or in the case of a partnership, to the workforces in the newly formed joint venture or partnership). This is discussed in some detail in the following section on acquisition integration. IHRM in Action 4.2 describes how BCE handled the difficult many-country communications in the acquisition of Teleglobe International.[17]

## Continual two-way communication in BCE's acquisition of Teleglobe International

Lance Richards, at the time Teleglobe's international director of HR, has been through a number of major international acquisitions and alliances. These included British Telecom with MCI and GTE with Bell Atlantic and then with BCE and Teleglobe. Lance has found through this experience that ensuring that employees know what is going on, who is in charge, and where the combined organization is heading needs to be in the front of HR initiatives. Some of the vital lessons he has learned include:

- The CEO must be visible to the employees and continuously interact with them.
- The company must communicate – clearly, constantly, and quickly.
- The dialogue must be two-way. Employees must have a way to feed questions and concerns back to the business and people in charge, then get answers.

As Lance puts it, in many mergers and alliances the corporate heads roll out a well crafted vision of the new entity, how it will lead its market, and how it will now be able to leap ahead of its competitors. But for the average employee, all they want to hear is what is going to happen to their particular jobs. In M&A activity, where the intellectual capital that resides in the employees is often (or should be) the overriding concern, it is important, at the end of the day, to remember that employees are concerned about things like making their next car payments or paying the next term's tuition for their child.

The BCE acquisition of Teleglobe provides a great example of how to handle employee expectations and concerns with professionalism and candor. Simultaneously with the after-market-hours announcement to the public, all employees received an e-mail with a link to a pre-recorded streaming video, with messages from the chairmen of both firms. They clearly outlined the reasons for the acquisition, as well as the benefits, and then committed to maintain clear communications throughout the process of merging the two firms.

A Q&A board was established on the companies' intranets, accessible in all forty-three countries where the firms have employees, with most questions answered within five business days. Within a month, BCE had appointed a new CEO. Within a week of his arrival he held the first of several meetings with employees. Initially, he made presentations in person in all of the firms' primary employment cities, then changed to a live, multi-country broadcast format, followed by conference calls for outlying countries. Simultaneously, he launched a series of breakfast and lunch meetings with fifteen to twenty employees, which continued for months, wherever his travels took him. In consequence, the new CEO won much favor with employees for his candor and style. The key was that Teleglobe International (and BCE) immediately opened a variety of one- and two-way communication venues for all employees, and ensured that there was a steady flow of information to everyone.

## Content (or specific issues to assess ahead of time during the due diligence phase)

There are many forms of HR information that should be assessed during the early due diligence. The following sections describe some of the key issues including:

- *General "people" issues.* There are a number of issues that might be referred to as general people issues that need to be addressed during the due diligence phase. These are issues that impact the whole organization and all employees and include the following:
  - The national and corporate cultures of the acquired firm. As will be discussed in more detail later, differences (incompatibilities) in national and/or corporate cultures is often the leading cause of failure in mergers and acquisitions. A survey by Watson Wyatt reported that 90 percent of businesses concentrate on hard assets during their due diligence while just 46 percent pay attention beforehand to organizational culture, even though 78 percent report that aligning the corporate cultures is the key to a successful merger/acquisition.[18]
  - Approaches of key executives to strategy, management, and decision making. A second major problem in acquisition integration is the incompatibilities of executive and management styles.
  - Skeletons in the closet (any issues of concern that are not immediately obvious, such as pending lawsuits, scandals involving executives, secret executive compensation promises, labor problems, etc.).
  - Managerial succession plans (or lack thereof). Identifying key people in both firms early on is vital, as is devising plans to hold on to them (or replacing them if they leave). Losing up to 60 percent of an acquisition's top managers is quite common.[19] Indeed, focusing on the retention of long-tenure executives relates directly to post-acquisition success.[20]
  - Management capabilities (that is, the general quality and depth of management).
  - Quality and depth of employee skills.
- *Language skills/concerns.* Since it is a cross-border acquisition, the language abilities of the management and employees of the acquired firm need to be assessed: are there possible problems in the integration of the firms and their customers due to too few people in the acquired (or the acquiring, for that matter) firm having the necessary language skills?
- *Specific IHR issues.* In addition to the above issues, there are many issues that are specific to HR administration. When specific HR practices and programs are being assessed, overriding attention needs to be paid to compatibilities and differences between the parent company's and acquired company's country cultures and legal environments. Many differences will be due to these concerns and the team assessing the HR practices must have enhanced sensitivity to the extent to which national cultural and legal differences can impact HR.

The next few paragraphs only introduce what some of these differences might be. But experience suggests they can indeed be the issues most critical to the eventual achievement of the financial and/or strategic objectives of the international combination. Potentially, there can be significant incompatibilities and thus liabilities in every area of HR practice.

Initially, due diligence that focuses on specific IHR issues needs to examine four general concerns that can potentially impact all the specific considerations. These include:

- Adequate funding of obligations, such as pension and health care plans.
- Foreign employment regulations, both legal requirements and enforcement practices.
- HR department status, practices, policies, and organization.
- Merger of corporate cultures.

Once these issues are assessed, the team must focus its attention on the many specific areas of HR policies and practices, such as the following.

*Staffing*   Staffing practices vary dramatically from country to country and firm to firm. Thus these need to be among the first things assessed. In various countries, HR selection may rely on connections, family relationships, schooling, or merit, any of which may vary from the practices in the acquiring firm. Recruiting practices may vary significantly. Local law and custom may make it difficult or even impossible to terminate or lay off employees once hired, at least not without major termination indemnity, which can run into tens of thousands of dollars per employee. In some countries, a firm cannot terminate for any excuse or cannot close facilities without approval from unions or works councils, as well. This may be very different from the "management rights" the firm is used to. What the acquiring firm is used to may not at all be available, due to either law or culture, in the acquired firm.

Since a common assumption in acquisition is that the resulting firm will cut costs through downsizing (usually the acquired firm) in order to help pay for the cost of the acquisition, this area needs to be assessed carefully. In order to achieve strategic post-acquisition staffing targets, the new firm may face significant liabilities.

In many countries, as well, all employees when hired receive extensive written employment contracts, detailing their employment rights. These need to be carefully assessed for promises that may greatly increase the financial obligations of the acquiring firm. This will be particularly important for all key executives and technical personnel, but will apply to all employees.

The overall workforce also needs to be evaluated in terms of what the law and culture requires for full and part-time employees, how many and specifically who must be retained at what compensation and benefit package. Some personnel may be located in remote locations and not initially be obvious. And of course the level of employee – and management – skill and training must also be carefully scrutinized.

*Compensation*   Everything about compensation needs to be evaluated. This includes the general level, form, and delivery practices of employees' pay. Country and firm pay levels, pay scales, and methods of payment all tend to vary significantly from country to country. In addition, these may vary significantly from what the acquiring firm practices and what is normal in the acquiring firm's country. For example, the treatment of incentive plans, stock options, and employee ownership may be treated by law very differently, may not be desired culturally, or even not be allowed by law. In addition, the accounting system may handle employee compensation very differently than the acquiring firm's system and thus even be difficult to assess.

*Benefits*     Benefit programs provide one of the most important areas for examination during the pre-combination due diligence. Retirement and savings programs, employee health and welfare programs, and other supplemental benefits can all create significant financial, administrative, and employee qualification problems. Potential buyers or initiators of a merger or joint venture should ask the following types of questions: which benefit plans does country law require of all employers? Will or can the plans be terminated, continued, or merged? What do the tax laws require in each country? Are there any problems or violations in the seller's plans that would taint the buyer's plans if there were a merger or consolidation of the plans? Will vesting schedules with the seller be recognized by the buyer? How different are the benefits, rights, and features of the seller's plans from those of the buyer?

Often laws in other countries require that employee benefits be protected and thus can't be taken away. This may require the buyer to modify its plans in order to include the seller's benefits, rights, and features. Do the seller's plans contain investment options that are not allowed under the buyer's plans? What are the ongoing funding and fiduciary requirements? How will the financial status of the seller's plans affect the financial statements of the buyer? If the plans are to be terminated and employees of the seller are to be absorbed into the plans of the buyer, what will be the cost? Are there sufficient assets to cover the termination liabilities?

Some specific forms of employee "benefits" that will vary dramatically between countries, requiring close attention to merger of separate company's practices, include items such as health care, holidays, vacations, medical and family leave, and pensions. The amount, form (defined benefit/defined contribution), type of funding, and relation to social security and government-provided pensions or retirement plans can all cause problems for merger or partnership.

*Training and management/career development programs*     Acquiring firms need to ask these types of questions about skill training and management or career development programs: How important is training to the firm being acquired (related to its importance in the acquiring firm)? How much time and money is devoted to it? How is it delivered? Is it largely online or delivered primarily in a classroom setting? Is it delivered on or off-site? How much of the support for training or management development (or lack of it) is due to cultural differences? Does that make a difference? Does the firm support outside education? To what extent? Does the firm invest in career or management development? What form does it take? A focus (or not) on training and development can be a result of very different cultural and national values about such concerns. And major differences here can result in significant operational conflicts and unmet expectations.

*HR information systems*   The information system can cause major problems for HR as it tries to merge workforces and data about employees. Legal constraints may cause problems (some countries protect the privacy of employee data more stringently than others, for example, not allowing the transfer of employee data out of the country), the forms of data maintained may be significantly different from country to country, and the computer software and hardware may be so radically different as to make the chore of developing a common HR data base and information system very difficult. This impacts every area of HR, such as compensation and benefits, but also impacts general management concerns, such as performance management, etc.

*Unionization/nature of labor relations/labor contracts*   This is another area that may cause significant incompatibilities. The nature of labor relations, in general, the presence of unions (and the form they take), the role of government, unions, and firms in labor relations, and the nature of collective bargaining and resulting labor contracts may all be significantly different between the acquiring and acquired firm. Major conflict (with unions, government, and employees) can result when acquiring firms ignore this issue and/or presume that practices "at home" can continue in the new locale.

*Employee involvement/works councils*   In many countries, law requires firms to formalize employee involvement in the management of the firm through elected "works councils." Acquiring firms from countries like the US, where these types of provision do not exist, may find they face major new complexities and complications if they don't realize ahead of time the importance of these councils and incorporate into their post-acquisition planning their accommodation.

## Process of integration

Once the due diligence is completed, and the formal merger/acquisition process of combination is completed, the firms must plan and implement the integration of the firms. Yet, organizational integration in the aftermath of mergers or acquisitions is often reported as being problematic.[21] As discussed earlier, surveys and studies indicate many acquisitions do not meet financial or organizational targets. And the underlying reasons are not always clear. One frequently mentioned cause of integration problems is a general resistance to change. It is assumed that people seek stability and that any major change to one's employer such as an acquisition is anxiety-provoking. Employees in both the acquired and the acquiring firms feel frustration, shock and apathy, and insecurity. This can hamper the day-to-day operating of both companies, among other things because teamwork can break down and people may start behaving destructively. Stress can become a common feature. Often employees lose faith in their organizations' willingness to live up to expectations, promises, and legitimate demands. A lack of commitment, loyalty, and enthusiasm can often result. Employees may lose their sense of identity and membership while the acquiring firm is viewed as being obsessed with controlling the acquired firm. Indeed, the most mobile of employees (in both firms, but for sure in the acquired firm) are likely to leave, making later recovery and integration even more difficult.

One of the sources of this resistance to change involves employees' sense of (or worry about) loss of their corporate (and, in this international context, national) culture and values. The process of acculturation (individuals and organizations adapting and reacting to each others' cultures) can take place in a number of different ways, not all of them healthy.[22] As much as both parties typically state the merger or acquisition is a combination of equals, in practice one group always dominates in the acculturation process. Thus the process of acculturation can result in any of the following:

- *Assimilation*: the non-dominant group relinquishes its identity.
- *Integration*: the non-dominant group maintains its cultural integrity but becomes at the same time an integral part of the dominant culture.
- *Rejection*: the non-dominant group withdraws from the dominant culture.
- *Deculturation*: the non-dominant group loses cultural and psychological contact with both its own original culture and the dominant culture.

The point is that assimilation is not always the result of the merger or acquisition of one firm by another. When there is a lack of agreement on the preferred adaptation process by the acquired and acquiring firms (due to things like the attractiveness of the acquirer to the acquired or the degree of similarity of the firms or the degree of existing multiculturalism of the acquiring firm), problems will occur and integration may not happen.

> How organizational combinations are handled affects the bottom line. Specifically, revenue is impacted by unrealized potential in sharing of synergies and best practices, improved market position, etc. The cost impact of a merger can be seen in lower productivity, loss of key talent, and an emergence of organizational cynicism and negative cultural effects. In some notable cases, such as the proposed merger between Renault and Volvo several years ago, the deal was called off due to cited cultural difficulties. Perhaps the most difficult aspect to manage is cultural integration.[23]

Since cultural integration is often so problematic, how is it managed effectively? IHRM in Action 4.1 (Siemens) and 4.3 (General Electric)[24] illustrate how two major MNEs have learned to address particularly this issue. In general, in order to assess the possibilities, HRM professionals might want to ask the following questions:

- Have cultural gaps and differences been identified and addressed?
- Is there an executive leadership group, including participants from the acquired partner's senior leadership team, visibly leading the change process?
- Has the shared vision of the new organization been created and communicated to all employees with clearly defined goals, roles, and responsibilities?
- Has a link been made between the business strategy and the quality, skills, and number of people to achieve the business plan?
- Has a decision to consolidate the processes and procedures around compensation, incentives, and recognition programs been made?

## Acquisition integration: GE lessons learned

Over the years and as the result of experience with many, many acquisitions, GE Capital Services' acquisition integration process has been discussed, debated, tested, changed, and refined. It is now well established and codified. The following are some of the lessons they have learned about how to ensure the success of any acquisition.

- Acquisition integration is not a discrete phase of a deal and does not begin when the documents are signed. Rather, it is a process that begins with due diligence and runs through the ongoing management of the new enterprise.
- Integration management is a full-time job and needs to be recognized as a distinct business function, just like operations, marketing, or finance.
- Decisions about management structure, key roles, reporting relationships, layoffs, restructuring, and other career-affecting aspects of the integration should be made, announced, and implemented as soon as possible after the deal is signed – within days, if possible. Creeping changes, uncertainty, and anxiety that last for months are debilitating and immediately start to drain value from an acquisition.
- A successful integration melds not only various technical aspects of the business but also the different cultures. The best way to do so is to get people working together quickly to solve business problems and accomplish results that could not have been achieved before.

Even with the ten and more years spent on refining the acquisition integration process and making "best practices" available via the intranet, including things like communication plans, 100-day plans, functional integration checklists, workshop agendas, consulting resources, and human resource department support, the process remains an ongoing challenge. Every acquisition is unique, with its own business strategy, personality, and culture. Thus, GE Capital continues to strive to make every new acquisition integration better than the last. Maybe the most important lesson that GE Capital has learned is that the competence to make the integration process work must always be worked on – it is never fully attained.

- Is there a plan to consolidate or maintain existing retirement benefits and health and welfare benefits?
- Are measures and rewards established, communicated, and aligned with the organization's desired state?

## The separation process

Interestingly, the separation process (divestiture) is very similar to the acquisition process. Most of the issues of concern to IHR during a divestiture can be viewed as being quite similar to those examined during the acquisition process, except they are from the other side of the transaction, whenever the firm being purchased is a part of another, larger firm. The parent of the firm being sold needs to also be careful to do thorough due diligence to assess issues such as the impact on union contracts and pension liabilities (as well as other promises and liabilities) and the impact on the parent firm, which is trying to improve its own financial and operational situation. Dissolution, or divestiture, or demerging, or spinning off, or selling off parts of an existing enterprise is often the result of a merger or acquisition that didn't work out well because the original planning was inadequate.[25]

## Summary

In the process of international M&A, IHR professionals need to make sure they are prepared to provide procedural and content advice to their executives in all three phases of planning, signing, and implementing, especially for issues related to due diligence, impact of culture, and specific IHR program integration issues. The degree to which all of these items need to be assessed and addressed and the nature of the solutions that will be required will depend on:[26]

- The firm's strategic purpose and desired results.
- The degree of planned operational integration of the resulting firm.
- Management's orientation and intention for the resulting firm.
- Cultural environment factors.

Ultimately, the success of the acquisition may well depend on the abilities that the IHR team bring to the discussion, preparation, and implementation.

## International joint ventures

The above discussion of IHR in cross-border mergers and acquisitions was based on relatively extensive literature. Similar literature is not as extensive, however, for the last subjects in this chapter: international joint ventures, partnerships and alliances. Nevertheless, as indicated early in the chapter, these forms of international combination are increasingly important and need to be understood by IHRM students and practitioners. Schuler *et al.*, *Managing Human Resources in Cross-border Alliances*, in this series was specifically written in part to help address this very reality.[27]

When a firm acquires an existing entity in another country, the central problem is to integrate an existing firm and its culture and practices into the parent firm. In an international joint venture (IJV), a new legal entity is created. Although there are a number of definitions of an IJV, a typical definition is: "A separate legal organizational entity representing the partial holdings of two or more parent firms, in which the headquarters of at least one is located outside the country of operation of the joint venture. This entity is subject to the joint control of its parent firms, each of which is economically and legally independent of the other."[28]

Thus the central challenge in an IJV is always to create a new firm, with all its dimensions, culture, and practices. This new entity can emulate one or more of the partners; that is, it can be some form of integrated entity, drawing on the culture and practices of the partners. Or it can be designed to be an entirely new organization, separate from the cultures or practices of the partners.[29] One of the keys to success of an IJV is for the partners to be clear about and to agree on which one of these choices is being pursued. Lack of clarity on this issue can lead to conflicting expectations for the performance of the resulting organization and will typically lead to unmet expectations and eventual dissolution of the venture.

This section describes HR responsibilities related to international joint ventures. The aim is to describe the HR practices and policies that influence the success of IJVs, drawing on the studies that have focused on HR and IJVs.[30] As far back as the mid-1970s, IJVs replaced wholly-owned subsidiaries as the most widespread form of US multinational investment.[31] In general, IJVs have become a major (if not, the major) form of entry into new global markets.[32]

## Reasons for international joint ventures

Reasons for entering into IJV agreements (not so different from the reasons for cross-border acquisitions, except for the reduced risk, since it is shared in a new, separate entity) include the following:[33]

- To gain knowledge about local markets, culture, and local ways of doing business in order to transfer that knowledge back to the parent firm, i.e., to learn from the joint venture partner.
- To gain access to the partner's product technology, product knowledge, or methods of manufacturing.
- To satisfy host-government requirements and insistence.
- To gain increased economies of scale.
- To gain local market image and channel access.
- To obtain vital raw materials or technology.
- To spread the risks.
- To improve competitive advantage in the face of increasing global competition.
- To become more cost-effective and efficient in the face of increased globalization or markets.

The overriding motive in most joint ventures seems to be the desire by one or all parties to gain knowledge and learn from their partner(s). Obviously, for a firm to learn from a partner, the partner must have some level of willingness to share what they know. If all partners wish to learn from the others, then, to be successful, all the partners must be willing to share. This is often a source of conflict, in itself, particularly where there is not a sufficient level of trust among the partners. In this case, sharing will tend to be minimized and the original objective will be stymied. Often, the central strategy for learning from the IJV has to do with the choices for staffing. "Transfer of staff between the JV and the parent firms can provide a mechanism for sharing information, for learning from each other's abilities and expertise, and for the creation of synergies related to product development."[34] But if the wrong people are chosen to staff the IJV, that is people with poor interpersonal or cross-cultural skills or limited technical ability, this objective of the partners may be difficult to achieve.

## Track record

The prior section of this chapter spent considerable space on the importance of HRM due diligence to the eventual success of cross-border mergers and acquisitions. Everything said there also applies to the development of international joint ventures. The compatibilities of the partners' cultures (both corporate and country), styles of management and decision-making, HR practices, etc., are critical to the development of a successful IJV, as well.[35]

As with M&As, the high failure rate and managerial complexity of IJVs also suggest that particular examination of the human resource issues is required.[36] As far back as 1987, Shenkar and Zeira pointed out that even though IJVs had become the "most widespread form of . . . multinational involvement, the substantial failure rate and managerial complexity suggest that a closer examination of human resource issues is required."[37] The reasons for failure are many and complex, but for any particular situation will include one or more of the following, many of which are directly or indirectly within the responsibility of HR:[38]

- Poor selection of partner(s).
- Partners don't clarify each others' goals and objectives or have differing goals.
- The negotiating teams lack joint venture experience.
- The parties do not conduct adequate or realistic feasibility studies.
- The parties lack clarity about the real capabilities of their partners.
- The partners fail to do adequate due diligence and thus don't learn enough about each other, which can be particularly true for cultural issues.
- The parties fail to judge realistically the impact of the venture on the parent organizations, particularly the loss of control and possibly profits, at least in the short run.
- There is too little thought during the design phase of the new venture about organizational and managerial issues.
- The partners fail to adequately integrate their activities.
- There is unequal commitment to the partnership or unequal contribution (real or perceived) to the joint venture.
- The partners do not trust each other.
- The parties to the venture make a poor selection of personnel to staff the venture.
- The managers from the parent firms do not get along.

- The established local partner does not assign its best people to the venture.
- One of the partners is a government, so that there is a built-in variance in objectives (profit versus possible political goals, for example).
- There are divergent national interests.
- There is "bad faith" on the part of one or more of the partners, that is, one or more of the partners has always planned on only extracting something of value from the partnership without giving anything in return, even though they claim otherwise during negotiations.
- The loyalty and commitment of the assigned managers are unclear (or are only to their assigning firm).
- The local employees resent the privileged position of assigned expatriate managers, particularly if they are only assigned to the venture on a temporary basis.
- The new entity cannot decide which parents' rules to follow (or which ones to establish, if there are to be new rules).
- There is a failure to adapt the business practices of the new venture to the local culture.

If the partners to an IJV can't cope with the demands of managing a joint venture (that is, dealing effectively with a partner), then it may be better for the partners to use non-equity forms of cooperation, such as partnerships and alliances (as addressed in the next section), which can take the form of agreements for cross-marketing, cross-production, licensing, or research and development consortia.[39]

Those who have studied IJVs find that some of the keys to creating a successful joint venture require the partners to seek complementary strategies and technical skills and resources among prospective partners, accept their mutual dependence, resolve issues related to differences in size of the partners, ensure the compatibility of the partners' operating policies and practices, work to eliminate communication barriers between the partners and between the new IJV management team and the IJV employees, and take strong steps to develop trust and commitment among the partners.[40]

## Role of HRM in international joint ventures

From a human resource management point of view, the lessons learned from successful joint ventures include:[41]

- When national and corporate cultures are blended, the partners need to spend time building trust; understanding and accommodating each others' interests.
- Job design can be enhanced when the partners are willing to learn from one another.
- Recruitment and staffing policies should be well defined in the early stages of the venture.
- Orientation and training of employees should focus on preparing employees to deal with the social context of their jobs, as well as the development of technical skills, for the new organization.

- Performance appraisals need clear objectives and clearly assigned accountabilities, liberal time frames in which to achieve results, and built-in flexibility related to changing market and environmental demands of the new venture.
- Compensation and benefit policies should be uniform to avoid employee feelings of inequity.
- Career opportunities must be ensured for local managers relative to managers assigned to the joint venture from the parents.
- In the early stages of the venture, the partners must agree on suitable terms for relations with any unions.
- The partners must establish the specific role of HR within the new venture (since the partners' HR policies and practices are likely to differ).
- HR managers in the joint venture must become process experts, managing issues like communication with employees about the new organization, expected nature of the integration of the partners in the venture.
- HR must implement the necessary training (e.g., cultural – both corporate and national, and technical), integrated and consistent compensation and benefit systems, and performance management systems that will give the IJV its own identity.

## Alliances and partnerships

Alliances and partnerships (both formal and informal) have become much more common and popular in recent years.[42] They provide ways to increase capabilities and to enter new markets in relatively low-risk and low-cost ways. As important as cross-border acquisitions have become, the use of strategic alliances and partnerships may have become even more important.[43] They take many forms, for example, outsourcing, information sharing, web consortia, joint marketing, and research projects. The most radical take the form of corporate partnerships, like Coca-Cola's and Procter & Gamble's alliance to market their non-fizzy beverages and snacks. Technology companies like IBM, pharmaceutical firms like Pfizer, and diversified manufacturers like Siemens and General Electric have partnering built into their operating plans, both for joint research partnerships and for joint marketing efforts. BEA Systems, an infrastructure software company, spent US$200 million in 2000 to develop partner programs. Eli Lilly hosts partnership training classes for its managers and for its partners (since managing a partnership is not like managing a business you own).

According to Thomson Financial, the number of new strategic alliances grew from 5,200 per year in 1996 to double that number by the year 2000, almost equaling the number of mergers and acquisitions.[44] M&As get much of the press, but strategic partnerships and alliances are just as numerous and may be even more important for fueling growth. Accenture, the giant consulting firm, estimates that US companies with at least $2 billion in annual revenues formed an average of 138 alliances from 1996 to 1999[45] and 177 between 1997 and 2000,[46] illustrating how rapidly firms are moving to reliance on partnerships. One study suggested that, by 2002, 35 percent of corporate revenues (at least in the US) would result directly from alliances.[47] And the trend is no less significant for European and Asian firms. Indeed, the *keiretsus* of Japanese firms, the *chaebols* of Korean firms, and the overseas Chinese conglomerates have formalized business networks and partnerships in ways that contribute incredibly powerfully to the success of their members.[48]

In most modern partnerships, the three most important reasons their members form alliances are growth, access to competencies like technology and research capability, and expansion into new markets. E-mail, file sharing, and web-based conferencing and collaboration tools make alliances across corporate and national boundaries workable. In the past, the route to growth was paved with mergers and acquisitions. What firms lacked they could acquire. This is still a popular approach. But as indicated in the previous section, trying to create a competency your firm lacks is costly, time-consuming, and often fails.[49] Too often, the best of the acquired assets (the acquired firm's people) leave for other firms (often the competition). In the 1990s, M&As were often ruinously expensive (with the inflated stock market) in terms of debt accrued, cash depleted, equity diluted, and key employees lost through subsequent downsizings. Partnerships have become the solution to the problem. Partnerships are the cheapest and least risky way to grow and build – or acquire – technology and resources: no dilution of stock, no dangerous leveraging of the balance sheet, and if managed well, no loss of talent. If the deal doesn't work, it can be dissolved. IHRM in Action 4.4 provides an example of one such partnership that has helped both partners increase their capabilities and enter successfully into each others' markets.[50]

## Options for managing alliances

As with cross-border acquisitions and IJVs, there are a number of choices for design of an alliance or partnership. These include the following:[51]

- The operator model, where there is one dominant partner.
- The shared model, where the organization draws on culture and practices from both partners.
- The autonomous model, where a new organization culture and management structure is purposely developed.

The partners need to discuss and agree on which model for the alliance they wish to pursue in order to forestall subsequent misunderstandings and conflict.

## General people issues

There are a number of concerns that might be referred to as simply "people and general management issues" in alliances for which HR might be expected to be the source of expertise and attention. If they are not addressed by HR, they are likely to not be addressed at all.[52] Most of these issues are similar to those faced by

## Links between Bombay and Manhattan firms open doors for two architects

A few years ago, a mutual friend introduced Manhattan architect William Leeds to Indian architect Bobby Mukherji. Mukherji, founder of a five-person firm in Bombay, was interested in entering the US market. Leeds was also eager to tap into India's thriving economy. Since then, the two architects have designed a variety of projects, including a fabric showroom, a trendy Chicago restaurant, and a major Indian government office opening in New York. They enjoy sharing their talents and views.

"To be working with somebody from a place as far away as India gives us a new perspective on architecture and a new approach to planning," said Leeds, who has about half a dozen employees. "Bobby brings in new ideas that we wouldn't necessarily have at our fingertips."

Besides new ideas, Mukherji provides Leeds and his US clients with access to unique Indian building materials and a team of twenty-five Indian craftsmen and artisans on his payroll in Bombay. Many Mukherji projects, especially at his night clubs, feature original artwork and hand-carved details.

Although they live thousands of miles apart, Leeds and Mukherji communicate frequently by phone, fax, and modem. They have added the ability to communicate via videoconferencing.

The firms work together project by project, based on a handshake, not a written agreement. They split the expenses and profits depending on who does what. Projects with Mukherji now make up about 10 percent to 15 percent of Leeds's total billings. Leeds says that eventually he hopes 25 percent of his total projects will be with Mukherji's firm. Both say one of the great benefits of the relationship is acting as each other's marketing representative in the US and India.

"We look out for his interests and for him to grow," Leeds said. "In India, Bobby helps us because he can determine who is real and who is not. Between the two of us, we can accurately target the right clients."

"India is extremely friendly," Mukherji said. "Personal relationships are very important. There is a lot of weight given to word-of-mouth agreements, and people respect that." Obviously, this is one partnership that was built on relationship and has helped both parties achieve business objectives in each other's countries.

cross-border acquisitions and IJVs, as well. All of the following need to be assessed and addressed by the partners prior to establishing the alliance:

- Organizational structure and reporting relationships: a clear managerial structure is often non-existent in a partnership, and staff members – including HR professionals – tend to report to many people.[53] Partnerships tend to not have the traditional pyramidal management structure of the partner firms. They are usually established as projects, with typical project structure and with project members assigned temporarily from other areas of the partner firms, possibly even as part-time assignees, with employees having multiple responsibilities, some in the partnership and some in the parent firms. So, in order to establish and manage performance expectations and outcomes, the partners need to be clear about who is responsible for what and to whom.

- Culture: as with all other forms of cross-border organization, both national and corporate cultures need to be assessed for in-compatibilities. This is important for all interactions within the partnership and between the partnership and the parent firms. To the extent that people from all the partners must work together, they will need cultural awareness and competency in both their own organizational and national cultures as well as those of their partner counterparts.

- Pre-alliance due diligence requires that the parties be aware of any "skeletons in the closet" of their potential partners, e.g., scandals involving senior executives, recent negative media stories, nepotism (employment of family members), etc. Any of these sort of hidden problems or issues can doom an alliance to failure when they become centers of media attention or hindrances to management after the alliance begins to function.

- Since the alliance will involve employees and managers from more than one culture, the cross-cultural skills of involved executives also need to be assessed, both of those executives that will be assigned to the alliance and those who must work with the alliance.

- Even if the partnership is intended to have a limited life, succession plans need to be developed to determine what is to be done if people leave, for any reason: resign, termination, promotion, or retire. In terms of employee skills, who will be assigned to the alliance and who will make these decisions? Will overall assignments be a joint decision or will each partner have the freedom to make the employee reassignment. How are they to be replaced? Will new people from outside the partnership be assigned to replace those who leave? Will original employees assigned to the alliance be developed to take over managerial positions that open? What preparation will replacements from the outside receive to integrate into the ongoing partnership organization?

- What management capabilities do the partners have and what managerial capabilities will they assign to the alliance? Will the alliance get high priority for assignment of top talent by all partners? If the latter is the case, assessing the quality of the talent to be assigned becomes particularly important, if the partners are truly committed to the success of the partnership.

- In cross-border alliances (particularly where the partners speak different languages), close consideration must be given to the language skills of the people who will be working in the partnership. This is important both for interaction involving the work of the partnership as well as for interactions between the partners and between the partners and the management of the partnership.

- And – maybe the most important people and management issue – putting together the right team of people to start up and implement the alliance.[54] Often, the members of this team are chosen for the wrong reasons, e.g., because they are available, are strong negotiators, or are familiar with or expert on the product or technology that is to be the focus of the partnership. Often, too, the intention of the partner is that these individuals will not manage the alliance beyond getting the deal under way. But experience shows that putting the right team together to get the alliance through its start-up is critical. Such individuals must have functional and technical expertise, but also the interpersonal competencies and requisite partnering mind-set necessary to work collaboratively.

## Role of IHRM in alliances

Depending on the size of the alliance itself, there well may be IHR professionals assigned to it. But "The differences between practicing IHR in a partnership versus in a corporation are both subtle and profound, and being an IHR professional in a partnership takes extraordinary patience, creativity, and political skills," says David Kuhlman, a senior international consultant, with experience in partnerships, both as an IHR practitioner and as a consultant.[55] Typically, the IHR professional assigned to an international partnership or alliance has not only to deal with many more decision makers (from all of the partners), thus having to exercise much greater negotiation skills, but also tends to have to take on more extensive responsibilities, combining those of a local nature and those of an international nature.

Different rules often apply. For example, people who work in partnerships are still employees of the separate partners, thus may not only be difficult to "supervise" but in terms of legal status may also not fall under employment protection statutes of the locale of the alliance. This may give the partnership greater flexibility with respect to compensation and job assignments, but may also create significant liability when "employees" are covered by the laws of their parent employer, such as under sexual harassment claims. Under tax laws, employees – from various partner parents – assigned to a partnership may not be entitled to the same benefit plans, thus causing problems of perceived unfairness and inequity.

## Conclusion

International mergers and acquisitions and alliances of various types have become very popular in recent years. Yet a high percentage of these combinations fail to achieve financial or strategic objectives. This is often due to inadequate attention to issues of concern to the human resource function. This chapter examined the process of combination and provided a framework and content for performing a thorough due diligence review of the human resource policies and practices and programs of firms being considered for cross-border alliances. Such review is explained as critical to the success of such cross-border combinations. These combinations include cross-border acquisitions, international joint ventures and partnerships, and cross-border teams. Much of the chapter describes the role of IHRM and the IHR professional in designing, facilitating, and implementing these four specific types of cross-border combinations. All four types of these combinations are increasingly used and IHRM can and should play a major role in helping ensure the success of their design and implementation.

## Points for further discussion

1 What forms of international combination does Lincoln Electric in China represent?
2 What other famous MNEs use international combinations? What forms are they? Why do they use them?
3 What are the advantages and disadvantages of working for an IJV?

# 5 | Country culture and MNE culture

## Learning objectives

After considering Chapter 5, the reader will be able to describe:

- The concept of culture, using a number of different models
- Research on national cultures, characteristics on which they have been found to differ, and ways in which they have been found to cluster on similar characteristics
- Examples of cultural constraints in managerial and HR practices and processes
- The impact of culture on IHRM
- A general model for developing personal cultural competency
- The basic interactions between MNE culture and country culture
- The nature of research in IHRM and how the concept of culture impacts it

## Key terms

- Culture, national and country culture, and MNE culture
- Cultural competency and adaptation
- Universal, situational, convergent

Many of the most important and difficult challenges to the conduct of international human resource management stem from the differences encountered in various countries' (and MNEs') cultures. The cultural characteristics found in different countries, and, indeed, in different MNEs, vary significantly from each other.

Often these differences clash. The situation is made even more complex because business people often lack knowledge about or sensitivity to these differences, resulting in frequent mistakes in both business and personal interactions. Even when they understand the differences, they often mistakenly assume that their own country or company way of doing things provides the best way to conduct business. Thus they make decisions and behave in ways that alienate their foreign counterparts, the people with whom they interact from other countries or companies, or they make mistakes that lead to business and/or personal failure.

It is also true that often other countries and companies have developed not only different ways of doing things, but better ways. Thus a major part of the challenge of interacting with other countries and other cultures is to not assume that just because they are different they are somehow inferior. That is, the challenge is to learn from them and to apply that learning throughout one's own organization and experience.

## The most important issue: culture

Knowledge about and competency in working with country and company cultures is the most important issue impacting the success of international business activity. And possibly the area of business that is most impacted by cultural differences is the human resource function. That is, the most important issue in the successful conduct of both international business and international HRM is: *culture*. Accordingly, this chapter provides an introduction to the concept of culture as it impacts the conduct of international business, in general, as well as ways in which cultural differences impact the responsibilities of international human resource management, in specific. Because it is so closely linked with the issue of culture (both in its focus and in how it is conducted), this chapter also discusses research in IHRM and the importance of research in helping to understand the impact of culture on the international organization and on IHRM.

Every country has at least some differences from all others, e.g., its history, government, and laws. The more countries with which a firm interacts (sells, sources, hires or transfers employees, develops joint ventures, etc.), the more complex and difficult conducting business becomes. The primary cause of this complexity and high level of difficulty has to do with the importance and critical nature of the differences between various countries' cultures. And increasingly, businesses of all types are involved with an ever-growing variety of countries and cultures.

People's varying values, beliefs, and behavior patterns are critically important to the success of every aspect of international business, including such activities as cross-national negotiations, sales interactions between people from different countries, management of the performance of employees from different countries, the understanding and treatment of contracts between firms from different countries, and all HR responsibilities, such as staffing, compensation, training, labor relations, and performance appraisal.

Often, business people – particularly those with limited international experience – operate with the expectation that the business methods and models to which they are accustomed will work just as well in business interactions in other countries. People and companies with long experience in the international arena suggest that such positive overlap is rarely the case. IHRM in Action 5.1, drawn from a survey of executives from around the world, reports on their perceptions of how well "intercultural understanding" is developed in the communities in which they operate.[1] Evidently, at least in these executives' perceptions, people from some countries exhibit a much greater degree of such expertise than do people from other countries. And presumably, therefore, business people from such countries have an advantage in the conduct of international business.

MNEs need to learn to cope internationally with issues like selecting and preparing people for working and managing in other countries, negotiating and conducting business in foreign locales, and capitalizing on and absorbing that learning throughout their international operations, including at home. At the core of success in these endeavors is the need for cultural awareness and understanding of effects of culture on day-to-day business operations.

## Intercultural understanding

A survey of more than 3,292 executives from around the globe rated countries from 1 to 10 on how well developed "intercultural understanding" is in their business communities. The higher the score, the more highly developed the "cross-cultural competency" in that country.

| | | | | | |
|---|---|---|---|---|---|
| Switzerland | 8.02 | Thailand | 6.13 | Peru | 5.32 |
| Singapore | 7.45 | Germany | 5.95 | Ireland | 5.30 |
| Netherlands | 7.39 | Argentina | 5.92 | US | 5.22 |
| Hong Kong | 7.37 | Israel | 5.89 | Portugal | 5.20 |
| Malaysia | 7.30 | Turkey | 5.89 | Hungary | 5.18 |
| Belgium/Luxembourg | 7.12 | Iceland | 5.79 | France | 5.08 |
| Denmark | 6.94 | Finland | 5.78 | Japan | 5.08 |
| Sweden | 6.75 | Brazil | 5.71 | Colombia | 5.04 |
| Chile | 6.72 | Jordan | 5.67 | Italy | 5.04 |
| Canada | 6.63 | Greece | 5.64 | UK | 5.03 |
| Egypt | 6.48 | New Zealand | 5.59 | Mexico | 4.65 |
| Austria | 6.44 | Indonesia | 5.56 | Poland | 4.57 |
| Taiwan | 6.44 | Venezuela | 5.44 | Czech Republic | 4.06 |
| Philippines | 6.31 | Spain | 5.42 | South Africa | 3.98 |
| India | 6.23 | Norway | 5.39 | China | 3.42 |
| Australia | 6.15 | Korea | 5.35 | Russia | 3.10 |

IHRM IN ACTION 5.1

Stories abound about mistakes with cultures (from mistakes in activities as wide-ranging – yet as important – as translation of advertising campaigns and integrating cross-border acquisitions), showing that people need extensive training and experience in order to reach the skill levels (cross-cultural competency) needed to function effectively in international business. Although simple things such as gift giving or introductions can create problems and destroy an international business opportunity, the real challenges are found in the importance of – and methods for developing – relationships and the patience to spend the time to develop them with counterparts in other countries.

As two long-time participants in the international business environment put it:

> More than any other aspect of the business experience, our knowledge and understanding of culture affects the outcome of business ventures. Without insight into the ways of others, we can't expect to develop credibility, nurture goodwill, inspire a workforce, or develop marketable products. And that directly translates to bottom-line results. Culture affects the way we develop and maintain relationships. It plays a significant role in determining success with colleagues and partners, and helps us grasp how to evolve into respected leaders around the world. Understanding culture fundamentally affects how we run our business, what characteristics to look for in selecting people, how to develop global talent, how to conduct meetings, and how to manage employees and work with teams.[2]

Business people who operate in the international arena, including HR executives, need a context into which they can place the culture(s) they know and the new ones they do or might encounter, so they can modify their own behaviors and their approach to organization to be more effective in both business and social situations. They need a way to cope with the significant constraints imposed by cultural differences between countries. Indeed, dealing with these cultural differences may well provide the most important variable in whether or not their international ventures succeed or fail.

The next few pages present a model for developing this awareness and understanding so as to enable IHR managers to more effectively cope with their international responsibilities, to interact more effectively with their international colleagues, and to enhance their learning from their exposure to and experience with HR practice in other countries.

# The concept of culture

## An introduction

There have been many definitions of the concept of culture offered over the years. For the purposes of this text the following definition is used: *Culture is the characteristic way of behaving and believing that a group of people in a country or region (or firm) have evolved over time and share.* Thus a people's culture:

- Gives them a sense of who they are, of belonging, of how they should behave.
- Provides them the capacity to adapt to circumstances (because the culture defines what is the appropriate behavior in that circumstance) and to transmit this knowledge to succeeding generations (in the case of countries) or to new employees (in the case of organizations).
- Affects every aspect of the management process – how people think, solve problems, and make decisions (for a country or a firm).

As Schell and Solomon phrase it:

> Learned and absorbed during the earliest stages of childhood, reinforced by literature, history, and religion, embodied by . . . heroes, and expressed in . . . instinctive values and views, culture is a powerful force that shapes our thoughts and perceptions. It affects the way we perceive and judge events [and other people], how we respond to and interpret them, and how we communicate to one another in both spoken and unspoken language. Culture, with all of its implications [and forms], differs in every society. These differences might be profound or subtle; they might be obvious or invisible. Ever present yet constantly changing, culture permeates the world we know and molds the way we construct or define reality.[3]

For just one example of importance to IHRM, when staffing foreign operations, local culture and environment can have a major effect on the definition of jobs and job candidates – and candidates' qualifications for positions. What appears by name to be a job that is similar to what an IHR manager is familiar with from her or his home country may in fact be a job that requires very different skills in another country or be filled based on entirely different qualifications. In some locations, such as Africa, for instance, hiring on the basis of being a member of a person's family group may take precedence over a candidate's technical expertise or, even, experience. And in other locations, such as India, Japan, the Middle East, and Latin America, personal and/or family connections may provide the most important considerations for hiring or job assignments. When a firm enters a new country and performs activities such as hiring, using its home-country practices, it can cause significant lack of trust and alienation in the local country, which can have further ramifications, for example, in attaining a quality workforce.

## Culture as layers

One of the complexities that makes "culture" so difficult to deal with is its multiple layers. There are many readily observable things about the culture of a country, a region, or a firm that differ quite obviously from that of other countries, regions, and firms. These characteristics, including such things as food, art, clothing, greetings, and historical landmarks, are clearly visible. Sometimes these are referred to as artifacts, or manifestations, of underlying values and assumptions.[4] These underlying values and assumptions are much less obvious.

One way to understand this is to think about the concept as if culture were an iceberg, with only part of its "reality" visible.[5] Only limited aspects of the values and beliefs held by a group of people are visible, those which manifest themselves in things like architecture, food, clothing, greetings, ways of working and managing, importance of the family or group, even language. But many of the underlying attitudes and history, tradition, and religion that provide the foundations of the visible values and behaviors are not as obvious or even as well understood; they are "below the waterline," and thus not easily visible. An awareness of and appreciation for these underlying factors is often critical to being able to operate effectively in or with people from another culture.

Another approach which is often used to understand this concept is illustrated in Figure 5.1, which presents culture as a series of concentric circles with multiple layers.[6] The layers of culture, or onion, model provides a way to understand culture as a series of layers, with each layer, moving from the outside to the inside, representing less and less visible, or explicit, values and assumptions, but correspondingly more and more important values and beliefs for determining attitudes and behaviors. These layers include:

- *Surface culture* (the outside layer): things that are readily visible, such as dress, food, architecture, customs, body language, gestures, etiquette, greetings, gift giving.
- *Hidden culture* (the middle layer): values, religions, and philosophies about things like child rearing, views of what is right and wrong.
- *Invisible culture* (the core): the culture's universal truths.

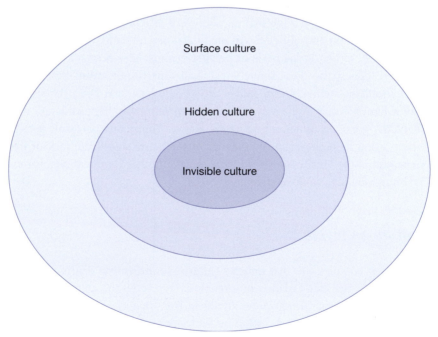

*Figure 5.1* The three layers of culture. Outer layer or *surface culture:* dress, food, architecture, customs. Middle layer or *hidden culture:* values, religions, and philosophies about child rearing, views of right and wrong. Core or *invisible culture:* the culture's universal truths

This approach to an understanding of culture (as multiple layers, with some aspects of culture readily visible and other, maybe more important aspects, hidden from immediate view) are used throughout this book as various business and IHR practices, such as preparing employees for international assignments or developing compensation and motivation practices for application in foreign operations, are described and evaluated.

As people develop an ability to work successfully with differing cultures, they typically must go through a process such as that illustrated in Figure 5.2, "Development of cross-cultural competence." This approach to building knowledge

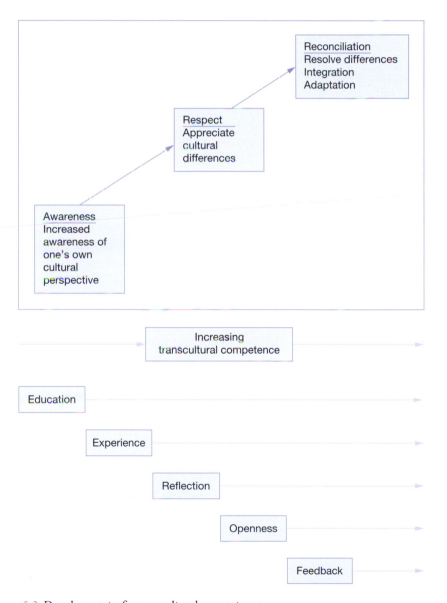

*Figure 5.2* Development of cross-cultural competence

about another person or group's behavior and values and eventually adapting to or being able to integrate with that other person's or group's behaviors and attitudes assumes that a person must first understand her or his own cultural values and beliefs before s/he can develop an appreciation and respect for cultural differences, which precedes the eventual movement toward reconciliation and integration with differing national and organizational cultures.

All three stages are challenging. All three stages require progressing from basic education and training about one's own and others' cultures through gaining experience with other cultures to reflecting on and then developing an openness about and finally a willingness to seek feedback about one's own values and behaviors in relation to the foreign culture(s). Ultimately, as McCall and Hollenbeck found in an extensive study of the development of global executives, one learns best to deal with the complexities of culture by living in a different culture.[7] But these other steps are also important in developing what is referred to here as "cultural competency." The issue of preparation and training for learning to accept and adapt to one or more "foreign" cultures is dealt with in much more depth in Chapter 10, on training and development.

## National and regional cultures

An increasing number of researchers are assessing whether or not the wide variety of cultures around the world can be reduced to a more limited set of cultures with similar characteristics. If so, it would greatly reduce the number of problems associated with determining management and HR practices in various countries.

### The research of Geert Hofstede

The best known of these studies (and the first major study of cultural values in a large sample of countries) was performed by Geert Hofstede, in the subsidiaries (in fifty-three countries) of one of the major multinational corporations, now known to have been IBM.[8] In particular, this study focused on identifying country differences and regional similarities on the basis of a series of work-related factors. The following provides a short summary of the factors identified in this research:

- Degree of acceptance of *power distance* between bosses and subordinates.
- Degree of individualism or collectivism.
- Degree of masculinity or femininity in social values.
- Degree of *uncertainty avoidance* or tolerance for ambiguity.

Hofstede found not only that certain countries consistently show similarities based on the presence of these characteristics but also that there are clearly major differences between the various groupings of countries. The significant conclusion for MNEs was that the idea was wrong that managerial and organizational systems as developed and practiced in the parent country and parent company of an MNE should be – or could be – imposed upon the MNE's foreign subsidiaries.[9] As is discussed in more detail toward the end of this chapter, such large-scale research is difficult and expensive. And, not surprisingly, such research has been very difficult to replicate, although ongoing research in the original firm of Hofstede's research (IBM) is confirming both the cultural characteristics and the country profiles.[10] An update of this research is discussed later in this chapter.

## *The research of Fons Trompenaars*

Fons Trompenaars has more recently published results of a similar large-scale study (over 15,000 employees from over fifty countries).[11] Even though Trompenaars focused on different aspects of culture – such as how different cultures accord status to members of their cultures, the varying attitudes toward time and nature, and differing attitudes toward individuals and groups and resulting relationships between members of society – his overall conclusions are quite similar to those of Hofstede. Trompenaars identified five distinct cultural factors into which the countries in his study could be categorized. These include the following:

- Universal versus particular (emphasis on rules versus relationships).
- Collectivism versus individualism.
- Range of emotions expressed (neutral versus emotional).
- Range of involvement with other people (diffuse versus specific).
- Method of according status to other people (based on achievement or ascription).

In the words of Trompenaars:

> These five value orientations greatly influence our ways of doing business and managing, as well as our responses in the face of moral dilemmas. Our relative position along these dimensions guides our beliefs and actions through life. For example, we all confront situations in which the established rules do not quite fit a particular circumstance. Do we do what is deemed right, or do we adapt to the circumstances of the situation?
>
> If we are in a difficult meeting, do we show how strongly we feel and risk the consequences, or do we show admirable restraint? When we encounter a difficult problem, do we break it apart into pieces to understand it, or do we see everything as related to everything else? On what grounds do we show respect for someone's status or power, because they have achieved it or because other circumstances (like age, education, or lineage) define it?[12]

Since the reporting of these studies, other researchers and consultants have reported similar findings or developed alternative ways to categorize cultural values. For example, the Globe Leadership and Organizational Behavior Effectiveness (GLOBE) research project categorizes countries on nine cultural dimensions including assertiveness, future orientation, gender differentiation, uncertainty avoidance, power distance, institutional collectivism, in-group collectivism, performance orientation and humane orientation.[13]

## *Update of the IBM research*

Researchers at IBM (reported by Saari and Schneider) have been conducting
employee surveys with at least a partial intention to re-examine Hofstede's results.[14]
The recent research confirms Hofstede's original country and cross-cultural dimension
findings. Interestingly, Saari and Schneider's research also confirms that, in spite of
the importance of globalization (increased interactions between employees and
customers in increasing numbers of countries) and the strong IBM corporate culture,
country culture still provides the most important impact on individual attitudes and
behaviors.[15] And, consistent with most research, the dimension of individualism–
collectivism appears to be the most dominant characteristic of country culture.

## National cultural clusters

Because the potential number of different national and ethnic cultures is so great, the
efforts by Hofstede, Trompenaars, and others, to cluster countries with similar
cultural profiles and to identify a limited set of variables with which one can
understand cultural differences, have of course been welcomed by firms working in
the international arena. The hope and expectation for these efforts would be that they
would simplify the problems encountered in adjusting to varying national cultures by
limiting the number of significantly different countries for the purpose of facilitating
international management. The results of several studies suggest cultural groupings of
the following cultures:[16]

- *Anglo*. Australia, Canada, Ireland, New Zealand, South Africa, United Kingdom,
  United States.
- *Arab*. Abu-Dhabi, Bahrain, Kuwait, Oman, Saudi Arabia, United Arab Emirates.
- *Far Eastern*. Hong Kong, China, Indonesia, Malaysia, Philippines, Singapore,
  South Vietnam, Taiwan, Thailand.
- *Germanic*. Austria, Germany, Switzerland.
- *Latin American*. Argentina, Chile, Colombia, Mexico, Peru, Venezuela.
- *Latin European*. Belgium, France, Italy, Portugal, Spain.
- *Near Eastern*: Greece, Iran, Turkey.
- *Nordic*. Denmark, Finland, Norway, Sweden.
- *Independent*. Brazil, India, Israel, Japan, South Korea.

People with extensive international experience will probably suggest that many of
these groupings hide some significant within-group (between countries that are in the
same group) differences.[17] But the various research efforts to identify countries with
similar cultural characteristics suggest that the countries in each group do indeed
exhibit significant similarities in their cultural profiles.

These kinds of studies – even if they only confirm managers' assumptions about
certain country characteristics – can provide some guidance to general managers and
HR managers as they structure policies and practices in foreign operations and

activities. At a minimum, these studies provide support for decentralizing many aspects of organizational structure and management and offer a suggestion for creating regional divisions for managing at least some aspects of the highly complex multinational firm.

## Generalized national cultural characteristics

A related effort to consolidate these studies has resulted in development of a set of variables that "pulls together" the various approaches to describing the critical characteristics of cultures. It is probably impossible to make a totally inclusive list, but the following includes most of the variables that various researchers and practitioners have found to be valuable in conducting successful international business.[18] For each of these particular characteristics that have been found to be important, managers and employees involved with international business need to gain knowledge and awareness of the underlying values and norms, beliefs and attitudes, and motivations that create the specific behaviors that are observed. (No attempt is made here to thoroughly explain all of these variables: that would require a book; most have already been explained or can be easily determined or found in the references.)

- *Time/relationship cluster*: attitudes toward time and time sensitivity; relationships (both their importance and the appropriate behaviors for developing and maintaining them); communication and language.
- *Power cluster*: hierarchy; status attainment; physical space at work; importance of work.
- *Social interdependence cluster*: group dependence; diversity receptivity; change tolerance.
- *Social interaction*: degree of formality; dress and appearance; food and eating habits; greetings (kiss, bow, or shake hands); gift giving; physical touching (e.g., same gender holding hands or embracing).[19]

Learning to exhibit culture-appropriate, specific behaviors as in gift giving, punctuality, greetings, introductions, physical touching (such as holding hands or embracing in public), speaking patterns (for example, with more than one person talking at a time), and physical space between people during conversation are behaviors that can be learned (at least one can develop a sensitivity to country or culture-specific differences).[20] An unwillingness to do so or assumptions that what a person is familiar with is adequate will inevitably lead to the unsuccessful conduct of international business and IHR.

## The observations and experience of Richard Gesteland

An interesting and practical approach to understanding cultural differences is based on the observations and experiences of Richard Gesteland over a thirty-year career as expatriate manager and international negotiator in many countries.[21] Gesteland has observed that variances in four general patterns of cross-cultural business behavior provide critical help in understanding international marketing, negotiating, and managing. These four patterns include:

- *Deal focus versus relationship focus.* Gesteland states that this focus on "making or doing the deal" rather than "building relationships" provides the "Great Divide" between business cultures, with differences in this focus often proving to be exceedingly difficult to bridge.
- *Informal versus formal cultures.* Problems occur here when informal business travelers from relatively egalitarian cultures cross paths with more formal counterparts from hierarchical societies.
- *Rigid-time (monochronic) versus fluid-time (polychronic) cultures.* One group of the world's cultures worships the clock while another group is more relaxed about time and scheduling, focusing instead on the people around them.
- *Expressive versus reserved cultures.* Expressive people communicate – verbally, nonverbally, and in writing – in radically different ways from their more reserved counterparts, which often causes great confusion that can spoil the best efforts to market, sell, source, negotiate, or manage people across cultures.

Table 5.1 presents the way Gesteland observes countries grouping on the basis of combinations of these four patterns of cross-cultural business behavior. Here, again, the groupings are quite similar to those presented above. Each of these approaches provide the practitioner and researcher with enough similarity to inform managerial and organizational decisions and practices. But, as the following section suggests, there may also be some reasons to question whether the similarity is as real as at first appears.

## The danger of oversimplification

The attempts to isolate country variances and then to group countries or regions with similar profiles and to minimize the variables with which we try to understand cultural differences can simplify the management (and IHR management) task of figuring out how to interact effectively in various countries. But this may oversimplify the understanding of cultural differences.[22] For example, Brannen expresses the concern that this focus on country differences falls short on two levels: (1) that it provides little explanation of within-group differences, that is, it treats countries or cultures as monolithic wholes, that everyone within the country or culture is alike; and (2) it provides little understanding of how cultures change, that is, it tends to treat cultures as a given – impermeable and static.[23] Brannen suggests that experience shows that cultures are not nearly as monolithic nor as static as these studies suggest. There are considerable differences within cultures and they do, in fact, change over time.

*Table 5.1* International cross-cultural country profiles

| Group | Culture | Countries |
|---|---|---|
| 1 | Relationship-focused<br>Formal<br>Polychronic<br>Reserved | India<br>Bangladesh<br>Indonesia<br>Malaysia<br>Vietnam<br>Thailand<br>Philippines |
| 2 | Relationship-focused<br>Formal<br>Monochronic<br>Reserved | Japan<br>China<br>South Korea<br>Singapore |
| 3 | Relationship-focused<br>Formal<br>Polychronic<br>Expressive | Saudi Arabia<br>Egypt<br>Greece<br>Brazil<br>Mexico |
| 4 | Relationship-focused<br>Formal<br>Polychronic<br>Variably expressive | Russia<br>Poland<br>Romania |
| 5 | Moderately deal-focused<br>Formal<br>Variably-monochronic<br>Expressive | France<br>Belgium<br>Italy<br>Spain<br>Hungary |
| 6 | Moderately deal-focused<br>Formal<br>Variably-monochronic<br>Reserved | The Baltic States |
| 7 | Deal-focused<br>Moderately formal<br>Monochronic<br>Reserved | Britain<br>Denmark<br>Finland<br>Germany<br>The Netherlands<br>Czech Republic |
| 8 | Deal-focused<br>Informal<br>Monochronic<br>Variably expressive | Australia<br>Canada<br>US |

Source: adapted from Gesteland, R.R. (1999), *Cross-cultural Business Behavior: Marketing, Negotiating and Managing across Cultures*, Copenhagen: Copenhagen Business School Press.

## Cultural attitudes and values and management practices

In terms of sociological and educational issues, which derive from a country's underlying culture and history, cultural attitudes and values such as those listed in Box 5.1 illustrate the variety of topics that are relevant to MNEs and International HRM. In particular, varying attitudes and values about the role of business and management and related values as well as the level of development of and attitudes about education can either facilitate or hinder the transfer of products, services, and business practices and technology to overseas locations. The farther away from the values of the parent country and company are those found in the foreign location, the more difficult it may be to transfer products, technology, and management systems (including HR practices). Although, having said this, the improving state of education in many "developing" countries, the growing numbers of people from developing countries that travel abroad to work or to get higher education, and the availability of global communications (print, radio and television, and the internet), are making it easier to recruit and develop local foreign workforces that readily accept the foreign (to them) organizational technologies and management systems.

When examining the variances in management practices around the world, one encounters a significant level of cultural differences that is important to MNEs and to IHRM. There is clearly more than "one best way" to manage successful enterprises,

---

### Box 5.1 Cultural attitudes and values relevant to MNEs and IHRM

#### Sociological

- View toward business and its managers
- View toward authority and subordinates
- Inter-organizational cooperation – between business, unions, government, education
- View of "achievement"
- Class structure and possibility of individual upper mobility
- View toward wealth and material gain
- View toward scientific method for problem solving and decision making
- View toward risk taking
- View toward change

#### Educational

- Literacy level and extent of primary education (for both boys and girls)
- Specialized vocational and technical training and general secondary education
- Higher and advanced education
- Special management training programs (not run by firms)
- Attitude toward education and training in general
- Education match with requirements of firms
- Availability of business education

although many authors have focused on aspects of organizations which are presumed to be present in all "excellent" firms[24] and although there is some research evidence to suggest that there is a fairly high degree of consistency among managers around the world.[25] This reality makes it necessary for multinational firms to understand the major differences in management style practiced in different countries and to find ways to accommodate those differences while holding on to those practices of their own managerial and corporate structures that are necessary or desired for worldwide coordination.

The difficulties encountered with merging corporate and management styles in cross-border joint ventures, mergers, or acquisitions and the resistance encountered when trying to impose a parent-company style or culture on a foreign subsidiary demonstrate how important this problem can become (indeed, this issue is so important, this edition of this book now includes a complete chapter – Chapter 4 – on the IHR aspects of these cross-border and multinational organizational problems). A survey conducted a few years ago (more support for this issue appears in Chapter 4) by the *International Herald Tribune* of firms involved with cross-border acquisitions found that "cultural differences among senior managers are one of the major obstacles to making an acquisition work."[26] Only slightly over half of cross-border acquisitions in the survey (52 percent) succeeded, with 35 percent of executives in the survey ranking cultural differences as the most important problem and an additional 20 percent ranking unrealistic expectations as the most important.[27]

In terms of particular management activities, there are a number of practices that are impacted directly by the type of cultural attitudes and values discussed in the previous paragraphs. Box 5.2 illustrates a number of these, showing many of the practices of management that can be influenced by cultural values. Most of these specific practices are important to the development of human resource practices in a multinational environment, including issues such as methods and criteria for selecting employees, nature of benefits provided employees, importance of family linkages in employee selection and placement, and the nature of education and job preparation for host-country nationals.

## Impact of culture on IHRM

The discussion in this chapter illustrates just how important the concept of culture is in the conduct of international business and International HRM. Indeed, every aspect of IB and IHRM are impacted by culture. Every topic throughout the rest of this book is influenced by the realities of varying country and company cultures. This will be true for the HR management of international assignees as well as the HR management of local workforces in subsidiaries and joint ventures.

This chapter has provided an introduction and a frame of reference. The concepts and ideas will be utilized the rest of the way through the text to help describe the complexities of IHR. For example, some of the responsibilities in IHR that are strongly impacted by cultural differences (and where they are discussed in the book):

## Box 5.2 Management practices impacted by cultural values

- Planning methods, tools
- Time horizon of plans
- Degree to which organization is bureaucratic and dominated by rules
- Types of performance and control standards used
- Degrees of specialization
- Degree of centralization or decentralization
- Spans of control
- Grouping of activities and departmentation
- Extent and use of committees or task forces
- Selection and promotion criteria used
- Nature and extent of training programs
- Degree of participative versus authoritarian management
- Communication structure and techniques
- Techniques for motivating personnel
- Nature and extent of employee benefits, welfare services, facilities
- The ease or difficulty of obtaining employees with the desired skills and abilities
- The ease or difficulty of motivating employees – both managers and workers – to perform their jobs efficiently and effectively, and to improve performance
- The degree to which individuals identify with their departments and the overall firm
- The degree of frustration, high morale, absenteeism, and turnover among employees
- The degree of cooperation and conflict common among employees
- The degree of information distortion and ineffective communication in the organization
- The degree of unproductive time spent in unmeaningful bargaining, restrictive practices, and socializing
- The ease or difficulty of introducing changes, the attitude toward innovation and improvement
- The attitude toward customer service
- The degree to which the "scientific method" is used to deal with problems, both in terms of understanding causation and in decision making
- The degree of organizational flexibility to cause or adapt to changing conditions

- Mergers and acquisitions (Chapter 4).
- Ethics (Chapter 7).
- Personnel assessment (in Chapter 9 on the management of expatriates).
- Staffing (Chapters 8 and 9).
- Training and management development (Chapter 10).
- Compensation (Chapter 11).
- Performance management (Chapter 12).

## Developing cultural competency and cultural adaptation

As indicated earlier in this chapter, learning to conduct business effectively in one or more foreign cultures involves a process of learning in order to develop cultural competency and the ability to adapt to the foreign culture. This topic will be covered in some detail in Chapter 10, on training, but it is important to be reminded of the steps involved, as illustrated earlier in Figure 5.2 ("Development of cross-cultural competence"):

- Knowledge (training, education).
- Experience.
- Reflection.
- Openness.
- Feedback.

## MNE culture versus country culture

Just as countries develop unique patterns of values, norms, beliefs, and acceptable behavior, so also do companies. Most MNEs take great pride in their "enterprise cultures," which reflect, at least initially, the values of their founders and evolve to create corporate personalities that give employees a template for how to behave, including in areas like the making of decisions, the acceptance of continual improvement, and the treatment of customers.

For many MNEs, these values take precedence over country cultures, particularly when there is a conflict between them. For example, many large MNEs that originate in the US or the UK may feel very strongly about the assignment of women to senior management positions and will do this even in cultures where it is rare (and not supported by cultural norms) for women to have these types of appointments. Or MNEs from Western countries may feel strongly in favor of egalitarian and participative management styles and compensation practices and may decide that this value is so important that they will pursue a strategy to implement these practices in their foreign operations, even though local culture supports a very different set of values (and often even in the face of resistance from the local cultural – even legal – norms). Or Asian MNEs may emphasize strong group loyalty and discussion, with deference to senior employees, in the ways they operate, even in their foreign subsidiaries, even when this is not an accepted or understood way to operate by local employees and managers.

It was mentioned in the first two chapters how pervasive the conflict was between the pressures for centralized policies and practices (for example, to ensure brand recognition or to equalize and simplify compensation systems) and the need for local adaptation (due to cultural differences). This dilemma may never be fully resolved and will be touched on throughout this text when explaining how it impacts IHR policy and practice. IHRM in Action 5.2 describes how this issue plays itself out in one well known global company, McDonald's.[28]

One additional example that illustrates when this becomes important is in the circumstance of cross-border acquisition or merger, where the company cultures (as well as the country cultures) are very different (this issue is discussed in more detail in Chapter 4, and Schuler *et al.* in this series, *Managing Human Resources in Cross-border Alliances*[29]). Because it can be very difficult to merge different cultures (company or country), cross-border partnerships of various kinds often fail, as has already been discussed.

## McDonald's

An example of how even mass-market suppliers are heeding cultural diversity is illustrated by McDonald's. The Big Mac is so quintessentially American that "McWorld" has become an epithet for the homogenization of world tastes by the US. But the chairman of McDonald's discovered that the global popularity of the McDonald's product was increasingly qualified by exceptions.

The international division sustained McDonald's throughout much of the 1990s. Domestic sales were in trouble and it was the company's local adaptations, introduced by franchisees and national coordinators, which showed the most sales success, registering fifteen years of sustained revenue growth. More important, the autonomy first ceded to foreign operators now has become the policy of the whole corporation.

When the Indonesian currency collapsed in 1998, potato imports became too expensive. Rice was substituted and later maintained. In Korea, roast pork was substituted for beef, while soy sauce and garlic were added to the bun in much of Southeast Asia. Austria introduced "McCafes", a variety of local coffee blends. And there are many other adaptations, as well, such as beer in Germany and soy- and lamb-based burgers in India.

Yet in key respects of quality, cleanliness, speed, and branding, McDonald's will remain uniform. "Decentralization does not mean anarchy," says Greenberg. "Those things aren't negotiable."

IHRM IN ACTION 5.2

# Research in IHRM

One of the reasons for the apparent lack of development in International HRM stems from the problems inherent in studying international organizational issues. This is one of the most important areas in the study and management of international business in which the significance and complexity of culture makes itself manifest.

International business research began to develop in the 1970s (along with the expansion of IB).[30] Cross-cultural management research, however, remained quite limited throughout the 1970s and 1980s and, even now, represents only a small percentage of management and organizational published research.[31] Much of the published research has been from an American perspective, performed by American (or American-trained) researchers,[32] and mostly done in the top industrialized or developed countries.[33] Research published by non-Western scholars (or published in non-English sources) has gone largely unnoticed in the US, in particular, and in Western Europe and Japan to a lesser extent.[34] And among the business disciplines, management, organization, and HRM have been among those topics receiving the least attention.[35] All of this has contributed to the lack of research contribution to the development of IHRM.

The limited research that has been published on international and comparative management and organization in general, and IHRM in particular, has been criticized as lacking in analytical rigor, relying too heavily on description of organizational practices (as opposed to critically evaluating such practices), being expedient in research design and planning, and lacking the sustained effort needed to develop case material and other types of longitudinal studies.[36]

There are numerous reasons for this. Multinational – or cross-border or cross-cultural – research is expensive, takes more time and typically involves more travel than domestic research, and often requires skills in multiple languages, sensitivity to multiple cultures, and cooperation among numerous individuals from different countries, companies, and, often, governments. All of this combines to make such research quite difficult, if not impossible. Throw in problems with cultural differences among researchers and at research sites, translation problems (see the next few paragraphs), interpretation variances among multinational research teams, and difficulties with research designs such as the use of control groups and the creation of equivalent groups for comparison purposes, and one can see some of the reasons for the lack of rigorous research in International HRM in particular, and to a lesser extent, international management in general.[37]

Even though the amount of research into topics of relevance to IHRM continues to be quite limited, the quantity and quality are growing.[38] As described above, and as with all research into topics related to international business (if not all forms of international research), there are a number of issues that make such research difficult to perform, difficult to describe, and difficult to get published.[39] The following is a short introduction to issues related to the conduct of research into IHRM which should help those interested in both the conduct and the reporting of such research as well as help people to evaluate the research that is reported, both of an empirical and of a more general, anecdotal, nature.

## General frustrations

International management researchers have reported frustration with four particular problems:

- Inconsistent and vague definitions of terms like *culture*.
- Inaccurate translation of key terminology (the next few paragraphs).
- Difficulty in obtaining representative or equivalent samples. It is very hard to isolate in different cultures the variables of interest.
- Difficulty in isolating cultural differences – versus identifying cultural characteristics which might be common across varying cultures – amid national economic and political realities (such as stage of development of the country or culture and nature of the political system).

## Forms of IHRM research

IHRM research has basically taken one of three forms. These are:

- Cross-cultural, i.e., the study of issues or practices, comparing one country to another.
- Multicultural, i.e., the study of a practice or issue in a number of countries.
- HR practices in other countries, i.e., describing HR practices in one or more countries that are "foreign" to the researcher.

However, the majority of the published research has been of the first variety, primarily due to the many problems with conducting cross-border studies, as described earlier.

## *The special case of employee surveys[40]*

Although most IHRM research – such as the types mentioned above – is conducted by academic researchers (although some of the research reported earlier, for example, by Hofstede, Trompenaars, and Gesteland, was conducted by consultants and/or practitioners), some is conducted by in-house scientists. Saari (Director, IBM Global Employee Research) and Schneider (industrial/organizational psychology professor emeritus from the University of Maryland) reported on work being done in-house at IBM through global employee surveys.[41] One of the functions of IHRM research is to help a firm evaluate its own IHRM practices. One of the common methods used for such research is employee surveys. Even though surveys may be relatively simple in terms of research design, they are still impacted by all of the issues that have been discussed in this section as those hampering cross-national and cross-cultural research, in general. Every issue, from translation and item equivalence to union or works council reviews to length of time to administer to varying privacy guidelines or attitudes to methods for administration, to problems in working with multinational teams, can cause problems.

## Basic assumptions

The basic models and/or assumptions that underlie such research have been described as falling into one of the following three "camps." The perspective of a particular researcher will obviously influence the approach taken:[42]

- *Universal*. A researcher with a universalist assumption has the attitude that there exist some universal cultural characteristics; his or her research task is to identify them and thus demonstrate that certain management and HR practices will work anywhere.
- *Situational*. A researcher with this perspective maintains that there are different management practices for different situations; thus his or her task is to identify the cultural situations in which HR or management practices differ or which practices differ based on which cultural variables.
- *Convergent*. A researcher with this perspective begins with a view (and tries to verify) that countries with similar industrial and cultural backgrounds will converge to a common set of management practices as they approach similar levels of economic maturity.

The particular perspective can have a significant impact on the researcher's approach, the types of questions researched, and the type of data or information sought.[43]

## Specific difficulties

Some of the specific reasons for the difficulties in doing international/comparative management and HR research and getting it published include the following.

*The particular focus of the researcher(s)*   There are often the following two foci described:[44]

- *Emic*. Trying to identify culture-specific aspects of concepts/behavior, i.e., different across cultures.
- *Etic*. Trying to identify culture-common aspects, i.e., the same across cultures.

These terms have been borrowed from linguistics: a phon*emic* system documents meaningful sounds specific to a given language, and a phon*etic* system organizes all sounds that have meaning in any language. Both approaches provide legitimate research orientations, but if a researcher uses an etic approach (i.e., assumes universality across cultures) when there is little or no evidence for doing so, or vice versa, it makes the results difficult to interpret – or leads to errors in interpretation – and will cause problems with review and publishing.

These approaches obviously interact with the universalist versus situational perspectives described in the previous paragraphs. A universalist approach can look for evidence to suggest that there is really only "one best way" and that countries that have practices that diverge will eventually converge to the best way. For example, in the 1950s, authors predicted that Japanese management practices would have to evolve toward Western (American) practices, or the country would be "destined to fall behind in the ranks of modern industrialized nations."[45] The perspective of the 1960s, 1970s, and 1980s – as Japan became one of the world's great economic powers – shows how greatly wrong this prediction was (as much of the rest of the world thought pretty hard about how to adopt the perceived successful Japanese practices). But this also suggests one of the important issues and difficulties in cross-cultural and cross-national research: the time horizon of one's perspective is quite important. Most cultural research is pretty static – that is it doesn't take into account a long-enough perspective to show that pressures within cultures (or broader, global environments) can lead to significant change and adaptation. The point here is that if the distinction between the *emic* and *etic* approaches is ignored in research design or if unwarranted universality assumptions are made, major methodological difficulties can arise.

*Language problems*   Language problems are at the root of many of the problems encountered in conducting cross-national research (this is discussed in more detail later).

*Measurement and/or methodological problems*   Such problems can occur when conducting research in multiple cultures and/or languages (attempting to get equivalence in various languages, particularly in questionnaire and interview research).[46] "Measurement error occurs when the measure or scale employed fails to reflect the correct extent to which the subject possesses the attribute being measured."[47] These errors can arise because of flaws in scale design or mathematical properties, problems with instrument validity, or because of incorrect application of the scale. These are general methodological problems and can occur in any type of research. However, the complexities of cross-national research add additional problems involving issues such as the reliability of the measures in terms of equivalence of language in different versions of the instrument and equivalence in various versions of the instruments, themselves.[48] In addition, the cross-cultural researcher needs to be aware of the need for equivalence of administration of research and of response to the research in different national or cultural locales.

## Equivalence problems in cross-cultural research

The three critical equivalence issues that arise in conducting cross-cultural and cross-national research include:[49]

- *Metric* (stimulus) equivalence. This deals with trying to ensure that the psychometric properties of various forms of the research instruments, such as questionnaires or interviews, which have to be translated into languages different from the original form, are the same; this is usually accomplished through back translation, i.e., having translators convert the translated forms back into the original language to see if this "back translation" gets the same words as were present in the original. Most cross-cultural research focuses here, and this step is pretty much required of all such research, in order to get published. But, as is demonstrated in the next few paragraphs, more is needed than this.

- *Conceptual* equivalence. The concern here is to ensure that not only do the words translate the same, but that they have the same meaning in different cultures and produce the same level of consistency in the results, i.e., are the measurement results similar? For example, in a cross-cultural survey administered in China, South Korea, Japan, and the US, researchers found significant effects attributable not only to country differences but also to the type of scale used, e.g., Likert or semantic differentials.[50] The authors' conclusion was that attitude scales are culturally bound and need to be matched to country situations.

- *Functional* equivalence. This form of equivalence is concerned with ensuring that the terms used and the translations developed are viewed in each culture in similar ways, which requires having "insider" knowledge about the culture, adequate to determine what the various cultures value and what the concepts really mean in each culture so as to produce "functional" similarity. In addition, functional equivalence is concerned with ensuring that the concepts work the same way and are implemented the same way in each culture.

The point here is that the results achieved through the research may be due to problems with the research itself (the scales, the language, the wording, the translations, etc.) rather than with any "real" differences in the variables being studied. In addition, there are two other issues including:

- *Subjectivity of the topics themselves*. There can be differences in cultures in how cultures approach the very concept of doing research. The emphasis in Western research is on objectivity and specificity. But there are potentially a number of points at which people from non-Western (and, even, some or what would be normally labeled "Western") cultures would view research differently. For example, the choice of topics to research, that is, what is seen as most important to research, is likely to vary from country to country. And topics, themselves, are likely to be viewed very differently and approached very differently in different cultures. For example, US business (males) have traditionally shown a bias for action but French business (males) prefer thought before action. Whether action or thought comes first could well be researched using objective measurement; but which is the "correct" managerial bias is subjective.

- *Factors other than culture*. Lastly, there may also be factors other than culture that make interpreting the results of cross-cultural and cross-national research very problematic. For example, a review of research published in Arabic showed conflicting results over preferences for various leadership or management styles in

Arab countries.[51] The author concluded that management styles in these countries varied with situational factors other than culture.

## Research content in IHRM

Traditionally, the majority of IHRM research and writing has been related to the selection and preparation of expatriates. Gradually that shifted to research related to international assignees more generally (such as local country and third-country nationals – these terms will be explained in more detail in Chapter 8). But clearly, there are many practices of importance such as compensation and training and development in IHRM in MNEs that are getting attention from researchers.[52] Many of these practices and the research are reflected in the chapters throughout this book.

## Conclusion

This chapter has described the concept of national and MNE culture and discussed its importance to the successful conduct of international business and international human resource management. Cultural differences impact international business and IHRM in ways that make both much more challenging and complex. MNEs and managers need understanding and appreciation for these differences as well as competencies in working within these varying cultural contexts. This chapter has only provided an introduction to the issues of national and MNE culture and research in IHRM. But it has provided a framework within which the rest of IHRM and this book can be understood.

## Points for further discussion

1 Discuss the culture of Lincoln Electric. Did Lincoln Electric have to change its culture as it expanded internationally?
2 Describe the country culture of China. Is that country culture compatible with the culture of Lincoln Electric?
3 How did the various country cultures impact the business and human resource management practice of Lincoln Electric?

# Global employment law, and labor relations

## 6

### Learning objectives

After considering this chapter, the reader will be able to describe:

- Several important regional and global organizations that can impact MNEs
- Several important global employment laws and their impact on MNEs
- Some aspects of comparative employment law
- Labor relations around the world
- Elements of immigration law

### Key terms

- ILO, EU, UN, OECD, NAFTA, Mercosur, ASEAN, WTO, GATT, ALO
- Safe harbor
- Immigration laws

One of the most important areas of global context for IHR is the area of employment law. Even though there is only limited employment regulation developed by international organizations, that is, employment law developed by bodies with global reach and/or jurisdiction, and what international development there has been involves quite limited ability of enforcement, every firm that operates in the global economy must contend with the varying employment laws in every country in which they operate, as well as abiding by whatever international standards also exist.[1] Typically, these foreign laws and practices differ drastically from what MNEs are familiar with at home. Thus there can be considerable risk of making mistakes, pursuing risky strategies, and putting the enterprise at considerable potential liability for not understanding adequately what these laws, standards, and codes require of the MNE.

Every country's employment laws vary significantly from every other country's employment laws, making this area of the IHRM environment very complex. In addition, as more and more firms operate in countries outside their original "home" borders, judicial systems within many countries are beginning to take into consideration laws from the parent countries of the MNEs that now operate within their jurisdictions, in addition to their own laws, making it increasingly difficult for MNEs to ignore either their own home-country laws in their foreign operations or the laws in their host countries.

When an employee is in Japan one day and Mexico the next, subject to different cultural and social norms as well as contrasting laws and regulations, or an employee in the US meets with a colleague from Sweden to finalize a project in Spain, today's MNE must make sure that any number of standards that apply in the different jurisdictions are not violated. And compounding the complexity is the fact that the legal statutes and regulations not only vary from country to country, but they are also continually being revised and updated.

The purpose of this chapter, therefore, is to provide an overview of the critical issues of international employment law for the global enterprise. Global HR ethics, codes of conduct, and related labor standards are specifically addressed in the next chapter. Whether an MNE establishes new foreign offices, expands across borders through acquisition, or develops cross-border joint ventures or partnerships, and whether it operates through wholly-owned subsidiaries, partial equity arrangements, joint ventures, partnerships, or subcontractors, licensees, or franchisees, it must acquaint itself and comply with all local employment laws and any regional or international employment standards that apply to its international operations. As suggested above, failure to do so can carry liabilities at many levels, including, of course, legal and financial liabilities, but also including the potential consequences of negative public opinion, consumer dissatisfaction, and hostile local governments.

IHR managers with responsibility for labor and employment relations issues for MNEs typically approach these issues in one or more of the following ways:

- *Understanding international regulations* that apply to the labor and employee relations of enterprises that operate in more than one country, such as those developed by the European Union (EU), the International Labour Organization (ILO, a body of the United Nations), or the Organization for Economic Cooperation and Development (OECD, an agency established by twenty-eight major industrial powers to develop common trade policies).
- *Analyzing labor and employment issues that are common to all MNEs*, such as problems with adaptation to local culture.
- *Conducting an analysis of the labor and employment laws and practices in each of the countries* within which the MNE operates, such as rules related to discrimination and worker terminations.

Obviously these approaches overlap. The strategic IHR manager will try to understand international employee relations from all three perspectives. For many IHR managers, their responsibilities usually allow them relative autonomy to develop IHR policy and make decisions that can be applied in all countries. But this is not so true for decisions and practices related to employment and labor issues. Complying with local, regional, and international laws and regulations adds an extra layer of concern that requires local input and involvement.

Six general areas are discussed in this chapter: (1) international employment law and enforcement; (2) comparative employment law; (3) extraterritorial application of national law (with particular attention to the US); (4) enforcement of national law to local foreign-owned enterprises (with particular attention to the US); (5) labor/union relations around the world; and (6) immigration law (with particular attention to the US).

## Global employment law and enforcement

This section describes the basic organizations that are involved in the global arena with establishing employment law or standards that apply to most (or many) countries and to all organizations that conduct business across borders. The next section provides some detail about specific areas of employment relations that have been regulated by these bodies and the impact of such regulation on MNEs.[2] Gradually there is developing a certain level of consensus on basic employment rights among all of the groups described, here. Box 6.1 provides a list of these general standards.[3] These standards are now becoming not only the basis for standards for various international groups, but regional affiliations and national legislatures are also beginning to incorporate these standards in local law and jurisprudence.

### Box 6.1 General statement of equivalent employment standards stated by various international organizations

- Freedom of association (i.e., the right to organize and to bargain collectively)
- Equal employment opportunity and non-discrimination
- Prohibitions against child labor and forced (prison or slave) labor
- Basic principles concerning occupational safety and health
- Consultation with workers' groups prior to carrying out substantial changes such as workforce reductions and plant closures
- Grievance or dispute resolution procedures
- Use of monitors (internal or external) to audit employment practices

## United Nations

The United Nations plays a relatively insignificant direct role in employment law or standards. Until quite recently, the United Nations operated in this domain only through related agencies, such as the International Labour Organization, discussed in the next section. The United Nations had mostly focused on the social dimensions of international trade through its Conference on Trade and Development (UNCTAD), its focus on the transnational corporation, within the work of UNCTAD,[4] and through regional economic commissions (such as the Economic and Social Commission for Asia and the Pacific), primarily through convening conferences and commissioning studies to focus on the social impacts of liberalized trade and the increased importance of transnational corporations.

However, the United Nations is beginning to take on a more active role, within the context of developing and giving visibility to its Statement of Universal Human Rights. In July 2000 the UN General Assembly adopted the Global Compact that calls on businesses around the world to embrace nine universal principles in the areas of human rights, labor standards, and the environment.[5] The Global Compact is a voluntary initiative that purports to provide a global framework to promote sustainable growth and good citizenship through committed and creative corporate leadership. These are enumerated in Box 6.2.

## Financial institutions

The World Bank and the International Monetary Fund have both undertaken extensive research on the relation between labor markets (wages, unemployment, etc.) and trade policy reform. Their primary interest has been in protecting "social safety nets" in the phasing and sequencing of their programs, and, for example, where structural reforms (such as privatization of government-owned sectors of the economy or reductions in protective tariffs) have led to significant retrenchment of jobs (such as in the public sector), programs including severance payments and worker retraining schemes have been introduced.

## International Labour Organization

The ILO was established in 1919 at the end of World War I, by delegates to the Paris Peace Conference, who had formed a fifteen-member Commission on International Labor Legislation.[6] That commission was composed of representatives of governments, employers, and employees (unions) from the US, the UK, France, Italy, Japan, Belgium, Cuba, Czechoslovakia, and Poland. This tripartite structure has remained as the mechanism through which the ILO carries on its work. In 1946 it became the first and only specialized tripartite agency within the United Nations. Its primary goal is the improvement of working conditions, living standards, and the fair and equitable treatment of workers in all countries. It carries out its objectives by

## Box 6.2 The United Nations global compact

### Human rights

- Businesses should support and respect the protection of internationally proclaimed human rights
- Businesses should make sure they are not complicit in human rights abuses

### Labor standards

- Businesses should uphold the freedom of association and the effective recognition of the right of collective bargaining
- Businesses should uphold the elimination of all forms of forced and compulsory labor
- Businesses should uphold the effective abolition of child labor
- Businesses should eliminate discrimination in respect of employment and occupation

### Environment

- Businesses should support a precautionary approach to environmental challenges
- Businesses should undertake initiatives to promote greater environmental responsibility
- Businesses should encourage the development and diffusion of environmentally friendly technologies

issuing recommended labor standards (providing non-binding guidelines for national legislation in member countries), by organizing conferences to draft international labor conventions (for ratification as binding treaties with member countries), by monitoring compliance with its recommendations and its conventions, and by providing technical assistance to member states. The ILO currently has 175 member countries and is the only really global organization that deals with labor issues, including setting standards and stating generally accepted employment standards that apply to all members.

In June 1998, the ILO adopted the Declaration on Fundamental Principles and Rights at Work and Follow-up Mechanisms with the collective understanding that these principles are accepted by all members by virtue of their being members of the organization. That is, they do not need to be verified independently by national legislatures in order to set minimum standards for every member's firms' employment relations. The declaration provides, in part:

> [A]ll members, *even if they have not ratified the Conventions in question*, have an obligation arising from the very fact of membership in the Organization to respect, to promote and to realize, in good faith in accordance with the Constitution, the Principles concerning the fundamental rights which are the subject of those Conventions, namely:
>
> (a) freedom of association and the effective recognition of the right of collective bargaining;
> (b) the elimination of all forms of forced or compulsory labor;
> (c) the effective abolition of child labor; and
> (d) the elimination of discrimination in respect of employment and occupation.

## Organization for Economic Cooperation and Development

The OECD evolved from the Organization for European Economic Cooperation (OEEC) that was formed by a number of European nations to administer the US Marshall plan to rebuild the war-ravaged economies of Europe at the end of World War II. The OECD was formed in 1960 after the US and Canada were asked to join a reformulated organization that would coordinate economic policy among the Western industrialized countries. Over the years the OECD membership has continued to gradually expand to its current twenty-eight members – including most of the countries of Western Europe plus Mexico, Canada, the US, South Korea, Japan, and Australia, that is, most of the countries of the world that meet a defined level of national development (*per capita* GDP of approximately US$28,000 per year).

In June 2000, the OECD issued the Revised Guidelines for Multinational Enterprises. These guidelines are recommendations on responsible business conduct for MNEs operating in or from adhering countries. They provide voluntary principles and standards for responsible business conduct consistent with applicable laws. The guidelines address numerous areas of business, including employment and industrial relations, including:

- Respecting the right of employees to be represented by trade unions.
- Abolishing child labor, forced labor, and discrimination.
- Providing pertinent information to employees and representatives.
- Ensuring standards of occupational safety and health.
- Employing local personnel.
- Providing notice of collective lay offs and dismissals and similar adverse affects on employees.

## World Trade Organization

The WTO is the international body in which multilateral tariff reductions are negotiated, non-tariff trade barriers are reduced, and international trade disputes are reviewed and adjudicated.[7] It replaced the earlier General Agreement on Trade and Tariffs (GATT). To this point in time, the WTO has not taken any direct action to define labor standards. But it is under constant pressure, primarily from the developed countries, and among them, primarily the US and the EU, to examine ways to link labor codes with tariff reductions.

Some industrial nations and labor advocates think the WTO should use trade sanctions as a means of pressuring countries that, in their opinion, are violating "core labor rights," a term that covers such matters as the use of child labor and forced labor and the right to organize trade unions. Advocates of such WTO sanctions argue that a country with lower standards for labor rights has an unfair advantage for its exports. Thus, they argue, it is an appropriate topic for consideration by the WTO.

There has been considerable discussion within the WTO about ways to be involved with labor issues, such as linking with the ILO. But thus far, there is no consensus to do so. Indeed, the general consensus appears, for now at least, to be for the WTO to defer to the ILO in the pursuit of global labor standards.

## Regional trade treaties

There are a number of regional trade treaties that are pursuing, to greater and lesser extents, common labor standards throughout their areas of treaty. The best known (and most fully developed) of these is the European Union (EU), but also includes the North American Free Trade Agreement (NAFTA), Mercosur, and ASEAN, among other less developed regional agreements. The following provides a short overview of the key treaties' efforts in the arena of labor and employment standards.

### *European Union*

The European Union is a body of states from Western Europe that began as a "free trade" agreement (the Treaty of Rome, signed in 1957) to, over time, integrate the economies of Western Europe to better enable them to compete in a global economy and to remove ongoing excuses for conflict between the member states. Every few years since 1959, the European Community has met to expand the areas of the economies of the member countries that are integrated, add additional countries to the treaty, and to perfect the political mechanisms for developing rules to implement the basic accords and ways to enforce those rules. As of 2003, there are fifteen member countries in the EU. Procedures are under way for that number to increase to twenty-five by 2004 (essentially adding countries from Central and Eastern Europe) with another three actively trying to gain admittance. As the number of countries increases, so also does the size of the population covered by the treaty, such that by 2004 the EU became the largest single integrated market in the world, although there continue to be a number of areas of disagreement among the members.

The particular issue of interest here for the EU is what is referred to within the EU as the social dimension.[8] The Social Charter of the EU, first adopted in 1989 and finalized in the Maastricht accords in 1992, sets out twelve principles of fundamental rights of workers. These are summarized in Box 6.3.

Since the adoption of these principles, the EU has been translating them into practice through directives and standards, with the intent of defining a minimum set of basic rules to be observed in every member country. The intent is to raise the standards in the poorer countries, while encouraging countries that want to do so, to move to even higher levels of worker protections or to, at least, maintain their already higher standards. Of course, these principles and standards apply to all firms, locally owned or foreign-owned, that operate within the EU.

Under the Maastricht Treaty of 1991, the following protocols for EU-wide adoption with regard to the various areas of social policy were agreed to:

- Require unanimous agreement by all member states: social security, social protections, individual terminations, representation/collective defense including co-determination, third-country national employment conditions, and financial aid for employment promotion.
- Requiring a qualified majority vote: issues related to the environment, safety and health, working conditions, information and consultation, equal opportunity – labor market opportunities/treatment at work, and integration of persons excluded from the labor market.
- Exempted (i.e., left to the discretion of individual states): levels of pay, the right of association, and the right to strike or lockout.

Under the Treaty of Amsterdam in 1998, the EU included an employment "chapter" (section) in the basic treaty, with the purpose of promoting throughout all member

## Box 6.3 Fundamental social rights of EU workers

- The right to work in the EU country of one's choice
- The freedom to choose an occupation and the right to a fair wage
- The right to improved living and working conditions
- The right to social protection under prevailing national systems
- The right to freedom of association and collective bargaining
- The right to vocational training
- The right of men and women to equal treatment
- The right of workers to information, consultation, and participation
- The right to health protection and safety at work
- The protection of children and adolescents
- A decent standard of living for older people
- Improved social and professional integration for disabled people

states a high level of employment and social protection. Employment policy remains the responsibility of individual member states, but the new chapter on employment policy has the intention of providing a common and central focus on employment policy, including improving the employability of the labor force (particularly young workers and long-term unemployed), encouraging and facilitating entrepreneurship, encouraging greater adaptability of businesses and their employees (by modernizing work arrangements, such as flexible work arrangements and tax incentives for in-house training), and strengthening the policies for equal opportunity (tackling gender gaps in some economic sectors, reconciling conflicts between work and family life, facilitating reintegration into the labor market, and promoting integration of people with disabilities).

The EU has passed many directives that address specific areas of concern with the overall objectives of the Social Charter. It is necessary for IHR managers in any enterprise doing business within the EU to understand these regulations and to ensure that their firm's policies and practices abide by them. It is no longer possible to locate an MNE's operations in any specific country with the strategy of hoping to find "softer" employment standards and regulations. Now they apply to all member states and as the number of member countries increases over the next few years to twenty-five or more countries, the task of ensuring compliance within the EU will become even more extensive (and complicated).

The Social Charter also established the European Social Fund, whose purpose is to promote the geographical and occupational mobility of workers by focusing development funds on training and retraining schemes, particularly for younger workers and women, migrants, workers threatened with unemployment in restructuring industries, workers with disabilities, and workers in small and medium-sized enterprises.

## North American Free Trade Agreement

NAFTA signed in 1992 by Canada, the United States, and Mexico, aims at promoting more trade and closer economic ties between the three member countries. The treaty provoked considerable protests from groups, such as labor unions, concerned about possible negative consequences that such freer trade might have on employment, wages, and working conditions. It was then decided to negotiate a supplemental agreement on labor issues. This agreement (NAALC – North American Agreement on Labor Cooperation) was concluded in 1993. Under this agreement, all countries are committed to respect and enforce their own labor laws but, in addition, the NAALC provides mechanisms for problem-solving consultations and evaluations of patterns of practice by independent committees of experts.

Since 2000, the US has negotiated three bilateral trade agreements which, for the first time, have incorporated within the body of the trade treaties (not as a side agreement, as with NAALC) a linkage between labor standards and the liberalization of trade.

These treaties provide that the parties to the agreements will "strive to ensure" that internationally recognized standards on specific labor matters (those stated by the ILO) are "recognized and protected by domestic law." These bilateral agreements have been signed with Jordan, Chile, and Singapore.

For the last ten years, pretty much out of the scrutiny of the public or the media, every country in the western hemisphere (thirty-four countries) has been meeting to negotiate a free-trade agreement for the hemisphere (referred to as FTAA, or the Free Trade Agreement of the Americas).[9] The FTAA will include labor standards that will be more inclusive than those enumerated in the Social Charter of the EU or any other existing free-trade agreement. The last meeting of the negotiations is 2004 and the signing is planned for 2005.

## Mercosur

Mercosur is the free-trade agreement in Latin America. This common market agreement for the free circulation of goods and services and the adoption of common trade and tariff policies was signed in 1991 by Argentina, Brazil, Paraguay, and Uruguay. Shortly after conclusion of the treaty, the Ministers of Labor of the four countries issued a declaration noting the need to take into account labor issues to ensure that the process of integration of the members' economies would be accompanied by real improvement and relative equality in the conditions of work in the four member countries. In 1994, the Presidents of the states issued a joint statement stressing the relevance, for the establishment of a common market, of issues related to employment, migration, workers' protection and the harmonization of the labor legislation of the four countries. A tripartite (labor, management, and government) working subgroup was set up to deal with labor relations, employment, and social security issues. In the final structure established in 1994, an Economic and Social Consultative Forum was established to make recommendations to the central commission about labor and social issues. Thus, labor and social issues form a part of the institutional structure of Mercosur, but it remains an advisory role.

## Association of South East Asian Nations

ASEAN has undertaken a number of studies concerning the social dimensions and impacts of the liberalization of trade within the member states. So far, the members have not developed standards for member states, although it is to be expected that this will happen in the near future.

## Arab Labour Organization

The ALO has studied carefully the Free Trade Agreements of GATT and WTO and their consequences for the economies of the Arab countries, especially as regards labor. They are particularly interested in the work of the ILO, but as of 2003 there is no formal mechanism to incorporate international labor standards in the national laws of the Arab states.

## The Delhi Declaration

The Labor Ministers of the Nonaligned and Other Developing Countries, meeting in New Delhi, India, in 1995, condemned the practice of child labor and committed themselves to implementing the United Nations Convention on the Rights of the Child. And the Ministers affirmed the importance of promoting, at the national and international levels, the implementation of measures to improve the working and living conditions of workers. However, they remained opposed to efforts to link the development and enforcement of labor standards to the liberalization of trade.

# Comparative employment law

There is not enough space in this introduction to international employment law to provide very much detail about the employment laws in separate countries. Other books in this series will provide regional information about employment laws and the book by Gary Florkowski, *Managing Global Legal Systems*, will provide additional information about the global employment-related legal system. The intention here is to provide a short overview of particular important areas of concern to the MNE IHR director, including works councils, terminations – including reductions in force and work transfers, acquired rights, employment contracts, and privacy protections. Many of these areas overlap, making it important for IHR managers (and their firms' legal advisors) to know these connections and to consider them as firms make decisions that affect their workforces in the countries in which they operate.

# Works councils

Works councils are a critical component of worker relations in many countries, particularly in Europe.[10] In many countries in Europe, particularly the Netherlands, Germany, France, Hungary, and Italy, there is a long tradition of worker rights to participation in decision making relevant to the operation of their employers. These rights are in addition to rights of organization and collective bargaining. Many other countries, such as the US, Japan, China, Australia, Mexico, and the UK, do not have such histories and do not have built into their industrial relations systems the concept or practice of works councils. This makes it essential that IHR managers from such countries gain an understanding of what is involved in these works council requirements.

Essentially, these works councils (which are made up of elected representatives of the firm's workforce) have the right to receive information and consultation relative to many decisions a firm makes (particularly, to ease the social consequences of restructurings by companies and within industries). The extent to which the councils have authority to approve employment-related (or, even, more broadly, enterprise) decisions varies from country to country. For example, since many countries in Europe have long involvement with works councils, the EU has gradually been passing directives that require employers with more than fifty employees in all member countries (or twenty in any single country) to inform and consult with their workforces – through works councils or other, equivalent forums – on employment-related matters such as job security, work organization, and terms and conditions of employment.[11] Under the most recent directive, member countries have until March 2005 (2008 for smaller employers in the UK and Ireland) to pass legislation requiring works councils in every employer with more than fifty employees and establishing the obligation to inform and consult. Once the legislation is passed, employers – if they don't do it on their own – can be compelled to set up an "inform and consult" arrangement if workers request it. IHRM in Action 6.1 describes the efforts of the first American firm (Hewlett Packard) to establish an IC framework in the UK.[12]

---

## Works councils and "inform and consult" at the merged Hewlett Packard/Compaq in Europe

IHRM IN ACTION 6.1

The merger of Hewlett Packard and Compaq in May 2002 triggered extensive consultation with workers in Europe. Under EU requirements, such corporate mergers require companies with 1,000 or more employees in the EU, with at least 150 of those in each of two or more member states, to consult with their employee representatives (through their works councils) on any business decisions contemplated as a result of the merger, such as layoffs, restructuring, and changed work arrangements (all of which were triggered by the merger).

Because of that experience, Hewlett Packard took the initiative under the new EU Inform and Consult directive and the pending UK enabling legislation to become the first US firm in the UK to announce an "Inform and Consult" framework which was approved by its workforce. At quarterly meetings, HP's management will consult with and inform their employee representatives on matters such as HP UK business strategies, financial and operational performance, investment plans, organizational changes and critical employment decisions, such as layoffs, outsourcing, workforce agreements, and health and safety.

Key UK HP managers plus HP employee representatives elected to the HP consultative forum from each of the four UK business units meet on a quarterly basis. Wally Russell, HP's European employee relations director, says, "My own preference is that we be the master of our own destiny. So let's work together now to [develop] a model that suits HP's culture. . . ."

In addition, an earlier directive required all employers with more than 1,000 employees throughout the EU and with at least 150 employees in each of two countries to establish a Europe-wide works council to receive information and consultation on all decisions that cut across country boundaries. This is one important and key effort by the EU to establish standards that cut across national borders. Under this directive, larger employers not only need to establish country-required works councils (which under the new directive, all countries must require), but must also establish a Europe-wide council. Firms that operate in Europe, but that come from countries where the concept of a works council does not exist, must learn to adapt to the EU requirements. This means that any decisions such as plant or office closings, work restructuring or movement from one country to another – including outsourcing and subcontracting, and employment downsizings – all require firms to inform and consult with their councils prior to implementation of such decisions. In some countries, such as Germany, the council must agree with the nature of the decision and its planned implementation; in other countries, such as the UK, extensive consultation about the impact and planned efforts to mitigate them, is required.

In October 2001, the EU adopted legislation giving companies operating in the EU the possibility of forming a single European company, also known as a *Societas Europeae* (SE), instead of having to form a number of companies under the laws of each of the individual member countries. This way MNEs operating in Europe can form an SE to avoid the complexities of the different regulations in each of the countries in which they operate a business. The critical issue here is that, relative to employee involvement, the MNE does not need to establish an employee involvement mechanism where none already exists and this gives them, then, a way to establish a single, Europe-wide, employee involvement procedure.

## Terminations and reductions in force

In most countries, employment is protected by a contract that defines the terms and conditions of employment and that cannot be ended unilaterally by the employer. The concept of "employment at will," as practiced in the US (where the employer, with a few exceptions, has the right to terminate an employee for any, or no, excuse) does not exist in most countries. Therefore, in most countries, an employer's rights to terminate, lay off, reduce, restructure, move, outsource, or subcontract work (and, therefore, workers) is highly constrained. In most countries, even the US, employees (or work) cannot be terminated on grounds of health and safety, pregnancy or maternity, asserting a statutory right, union activity, or on the basis of gender, race, religion, or disability. In general, though, firms need to search for alternative employment (within the firm, or with assistance if nothing is available internally) and consult with their unions, works councils, and the individuals affected (at least thirty days prior to taking action, if twenty to 100 people will be involved, and ninety days prior if 100 or more people are to be made redundant). This includes any outsourcing, work transfers to other countries, and subcontracting. In terms of pure reductions in force, only three situations are seen as possible excuses: (1) business closure; (2)

workplace closure; and (3) diminishing need for the work. And all of these would involve the notice and consult requirements described above.

Most countries require payments to terminated employees. Indeed, in most countries it is very difficult to terminate any employee for any reason, even with notice and consultation. Particularly when the termination involves a number of employees (that is, involves a downsizing, relocation, or significant layoff), notice and consultation are both necessary. Even so, when terminations are possible and done, it usually requires significant compensation. Such compensation is often required even when the termination is for disciplinary or poor performance reasons, as well as for the normal reasons of economic necessity. Table 6.1 summarizes separation practices in a number of countries, illustrating both the legal requirements for dismissal and the severance payment formula.[13] In most countries, the amount of severance pay is pro-rated by the employee's age, years of service, and last rate of pay or salary. For example, as of a few years ago, a terminated forty-five-year-old employee with twenty years' service and a salary of US$50,000 in Belgium would have been owed US$94,000 in severance pay.[14] A similar employee terminated in Ireland would have been owed US$13,000 and in Venezuela US$106,000. These figures would, of course, be higher, today. It is not unusual for termination pay for longer-term employees to equal as much as eighteen months' pay.

In some countries, employees will find it difficult to terminate employees at all. In Portugal, for example, all terminations are legal actions defended in court, while in countries such as Germany, where there is a strong tradition of reliance on works councils, terminations are topics for mandatory consultation. Also, in many countries, all employer-paid benefits become what are referred to as acquired rights, that is, once offered they cannot be taken away, even in the case of redundancies of any type, e.g., in acquisitions, employee transfers, work transfers, or closing of offices. Employers cannot move work or workers to new countries or locales and, in the process, create new compensation, benefits, or work design that are less than in the previous location. In many countries, particularly in Europe, and in EU law more generally, the employee has "acquired rights" to his or her existing levels of compensation and benefits and to the nature of his or her work that cannot be reduced by either moving the employee or the work to another location. After notification and consultation, often MNEs "buy" their way out of these liabilities by negotiating settlements with affected workers to compensate them for their acquired rights. But they cannot just unilaterally reduce the benefits. The section in this chapter that deals with union relations describes a number of situations where multinational firms have tried to make workforce changes without abiding by local law and the consequences of such efforts.

One additional consideration, particularly in firms with highly specialized technology or other forms of intellectual property that is critical to their ability to compete, involves different countries' attitudes about non-compete agreements, that is agreements signed by employees to restrict their going to work within some particular time period for a competitor, setting up on their own a new competing business, or taking competitive-critical information with them to their new (former competitor)

*Table 6.1* Global termination practices

| Country | Legal requirements | Severance payment formula |
| --- | --- | --- |
| Argentina | Fifteen days to two months' notice, depending on length of service | One-twelfth of highest monthly salary for each month of service longer than ten days |
| Australia | One to three weeks' notice, depending on service | Up to eight weeks' pay, depending on length of service |
| Belgium | Large-scale dismissals must involve the Labor Office and works councils | Payment varies by age, salary, position, length of service; minimum payment three months' salary |
| Brazil | At least one month's notice | Accumulated contributions to special unemployment fund plus 40% |
| Canada | Varies by province | Payment varies by age, length of service, position, and location; minimum payment of one month's salary for each year of service |
| Finland | One to three months' notice | Minimum one month's salary for low-level employee to ten months' minimum for executives |
| France | Labor inspector must approve layoffs involving more than ten employees | Payments to executives usually exceed minimum required three months' salary |
| Germany | Dismissals must be discussed with executive board and union | Three to six months' salary |
| Hong Kong | Payment required for employees with at least two years of service | Two-thirds of one month's salary for each year of service; maximum payment of HK$270,000 per employee |
| Japan | One month's notice | Payment varies by financial condition of firm |
| Korea | All dismissed employees are legally entitled to severance pay | Payment varies by salary and length of service |
| Mexico | No notice required | Twenty days' salary for each year of service, plus seniority premium and accrued benefits; minimum three months' salary |
| Netherlands | Companies must present valid reasons in a court of law | Payment varies by age and length of service; minimum one month's salary for each year of service |

*Table 6.1* continued

| Country | Legal requirements | Severance payment formula |
|---|---|---|
| New Zealand | Consultation period is required; one month customary | Four weeks' salary for first year of employment and two weeks for each additional year; no legal minimum or maximum |
| Singapore | Few restrictions | Mandated payments are modest |
| Sweden | Notice must be provided to Labor Office and union | Receive unemployment benefits for up to 300 days |
| Switzerland | One to three months' notice | Two weeks' to one month's salary for every year worked; maximum payment of one to one and a half years' salary |
| UK | For large-scale layoffs, companies must notify Department for Education and Employment | Payments are age and service-related; maximum payment is £220 per week for thirty weeks |
| US | Required thirty-day notice for large-scale plant closings | No mandatory severance pay; minimum one week's pay for each year of service is customary |
| Venezuela | Severance pay due on both voluntary and involuntary separation | Thirty days' pay for each year of service; maximum payment of 150 days' pay in cases of involuntary termination |

employer.[15] As labor markets become global, and firms develop new forms of relations with workers in foreign locales (such as IT workers or call centers in overseas locations), it becomes increasingly difficult to control the movement of workers from one employer to another and their taking of intellectual property (such as, product or process technology or customer lists and preferences) from their current employer to their new one. Because the rules (and cultures) are so different from one country to another, it becomes very difficult to enforce any non-compete agreements in employment contracts.

For example, as Wanda Holloway, associate general counsel for global human resources at Compaq (now a part of Hewlett Packard) in Houston, Texas, says, Compaq does not generally enter into non-compete agreements with its staff, but

> we do use intellectual property assignment agreements and confidentiality restrictions which mitigate the impact of loss of key personnel. We take protection of our intellectual property very seriously and have been increasingly aggressive in putting a halt to predatory hiring tactics [pirating away of key staff by competitors] and in addressing situations where there would be inevitable disclosure of our intellectual property.[16]

IHRM in Action 6.2 discusses the case of Value Partners, an Italian management consulting company, and its loss of personnel to an American competitor in Brazil.[17] This situation shows how difficult it can be to enforce covenants, like non-compete agreements, particularly in situations involving firms from outside countries. The more reasonable a restrictive covenant is, the more likely it is that courts worldwide will enforce it. But in some regions, such as Latin America and the US state of California, non-compete clauses in employment contracts are illegal. However, generally speaking, the shorter the time period of the restraint and the more narrowly defined the people covered, the more likely it is to be enforced across borders.

Table 6.2 provides the enforceability of non-compete agreements in a selection of countries.[18] Obviously the requirements are not the same everywhere. And in cases where MNEs use compensation systems like stock option plans which build over a period of years as an incentive to employees to sign non-compete agreements (or, alternatively, to encourage longevity and loyalty, particularly among key foreign employees), employers should include a clause about employees not being able to exercise their stock option gains if they engage in disloyal activity or go to work for a competitor. Indeed, a US federal court held in 1999 that an IBM employee forfeited around US$900,000 in stock option value on joining a rival, violating his stock option agreement non-competition restrictions.

## Non-compete agreements and *Value Partners v. Bain International*

Value Partners, headquartered in Italy, opened its Brazilian subsidiary in 1994. By the end of 1997, its São Paolo office had twenty employees producing annual revenues of about US$5 million. Rival Bain International consultancy established their São Paolo office in October 1997 and by early November had hired away almost all of Value Partner's staff.

Value filed criminal charges in Brazil and New York against many of the staff, alleging breach of trust and loyalty, and theft of confidential information. The US courts ruled that the case would be more conveniently and efficiently dealt with in Brazil under the doctrine that the US was not the most convenient place to hear the case. Unfortunately for Value Partners, Brazilian law offered none of the US's significant compensatory and punitive damages for employee disloyalty.

Many US and UK legal consultants advise their MNE clients to consider specifying that litigation should take place wherever the headquarters are located. This means that local courts in places where the foreign firm may not get favorable treatment cannot act. But if the employer is fighting another multinational, it can mean going against the competitor directly and taking advantage of the UK and US's broad "unfair competition" laws. This would have made all the difference for a firm like Value Partners in its competition over its human capital and intellectual property in Brazil.

*Table 6.2* Enforceability of non-compete covenants around the world

| Geographical area | Enforceable? | Maximum time period for restraint | Additional information |
|---|---|---|---|
| US | Yes | One to two years | Unenforceable in Georgia, Hawaii, and California |
| Canada | Yes | Six months to one year | |
| Australia | Yes | Six months to one year | |
| Latin America | No | | Employees cannot be legally bound by non-compete agreements under right-to-work premise |
| UK | Yes | One to two years | No obligation to pay ex-employee in specified time period |
| Belgium | Yes | One year | Must pay 50% of ex-employee's gross remuneration, including benefits for said period |
| Germany | Yes | Two years | For regular employees only. Must pay 50% of gross remuneration |
| Italy | Yes | Three years | Enforceable only in Italy. Some 30–40% of remuneration payable |
| Holland | Yes | One year | 50% of remuneration payable |
| France | Yes | Twelve to eighteen months | Payment not obligatory but expected in some industries |

## Discrimination, harassment, and victimization

Around the world, countries are passing legislation to protect the rights of employees and job candidates to be free from discrimination and harassment based on their gender, race, color, religion, age, or disability. The laws in place, in some countries, such as the US and now in the EU, are pretty well developed, although, within the EU, there has been a distinct lack of uniformity in many of these areas, with the possible exception of sex discrimination. However, in 2003, directives went into effect requiring all member states to pass legislation prohibiting discrimination on the basis of race, gender, disability, age, sexual orientation, and religion or belief. The countries have not yet moved beyond maybe approving the ILO accords. But this is clearly an area of international labor standards to which every MNE must pay close attention.[19] And because of national and regional cultures that in the past may have allowed practices which are now being prohibited, making sure that all managers and employees of the global firm abide by these new standards presents a major challenge to IHR.

Table 6.3 presents the legal regulations related to various aspects of discrimination for five countries (and regions): the US, the EU, Japan, the UK, and Mexico.[20] What this comparative table demonstrates is that even though there is considerable convergence developing, there are still also some significant variances. Since courts in some countries are beginning to refer to the laws of parent countries in cases involving MNEs in their jurisdictions, it certainly suggests that IHR and their MNEs must pay close attention to these differences.

## Privacy protection

With the advent of the internet and the ease of global communication, allowing information to be shared and distributed quite readily, concern over the protection of information about individuals (for example, employees and customers) has become of increasing concern in many countries.[21] Often, that concern is based in those countries' constitutional guarantees of protection of individual privacy.

In Europe, these protections are particularly strong.[22] Because of this, in 1998 the EU issued a directive on the protection of employee privacy. Of particular interest to MNEs operating in Europe, under the terms of the directive, personal data on European employees, including expatriates working in Europe, cannot be transferred out of the EU unless the country in which the data recipient resides has acceptable privacy protection standards in place. In any case, any firm transferring employee data from Europe to the US (or anywhere else outside Europe) must pay close attention to how such information is managed and shared with third parties.

This has been of particular concern to American MNEs in Europe, since there is no consensus in the US on how to provide adequate privacy protections. As of now, the US wants to rely more on self-regulation and laws applying to only particular sectors, such as health care and financial institutions. In late 2000, the EU agreed to a "safe harbor" principle from the US in which American firms which agree to abide by the basic European privacy standards will certify to the US Department of Commerce that they are in compliance, which will be reviewed by the EU. Such certified firms will be able to transfer data on European and expatriate employees from Europe to the US. The potential liability for American firms that do not certify compliance with basic European privacy laws through this "safe harbor" procedure is to lose their right to do business anywhere in the EU.

Table 6.3 Comparative international labor laws

| US | European Union | Japan | UK | Mexico |
|---|---|---|---|---|
| **Title VII of the Civil Rights Act of 1964** Prohibits discrimination and harassment based on race, color, sex, religion, and national origin; retaliation for exercising rights under the statute prohibited | **Charter of Fundamental Social Rights** Provides for equal treatment for men and women in working life<br><br>**Equal Treatment in Working Life Directive** Prohibits discrimination based on sex or marital or family status<br><br>**Directive 2000/43/EC** Prohibits discrimination based on race and ethnic origin<br><br>**Directive 2000/78/EC** Requires prohibitions of discrimination based on religion or belief, or sexual orientation by December 2003 | **Art. 14 of Constitution** Prohibits discrimination in political, economic, or social relations because of race, creed, sex, social status, or family origin<br><br>**Equal Employment Opportunity Law and Labor Standards Law** Prohibits discrimination against women workers | **Race Relations Act 1976, as amended by Race Relations (Amendment) Act 2000** Prohibits discrimination based on race, color, nationality (including citizenship), or ethnic or national origin<br><br>**Sex Discrimination Act 1975** Prohibits discrimination in employment and working conditions based on sex | **Constitution** Provides for equal rights for women and men<br><br>**Federal Labor Law** Prohibits discrimination based on race, sex, religious creed, political doctrine, or social condition |
| **Pregnancy Discrimination Act (PDA)** Prohibits discrimination based on pregnancy | *No comparable directive* | **Equal Employment Opportunity Law** Prohibits dismissal of female employees because of marriage, pregnancy, or childbirth | **Sex Discrimination Act 1975, amended in 1986** Includes pregnancy discrimination as form of sex discrimination | **Federal Labor Law** Requires removal of pregnant women from heavy or dangerous work or work with toxic substances |

| Americans with Disabilities Act (ADA) | Directive 2000/78/EC | Law for Employment Promotion of the Disabled (Law No. 123 of 1960) | Disability Discrimination Act 1995 | National Public Access Program of 2001 |
|---|---|---|---|---|
| Prohibits discrimination and harassment based on disability; requires reasonable accommodation to allow an employee to perform the essential functions of the job | Requires prohibitions of discrimination based on disability by December 2006 | Promotes employment of physically and mentally disabled persons; establishes quota for employment of disabled employees; provides adjustment allowance to employers who hire disabled workers | Prohibits discrimination in employment based on physical or mental disability; requires employers to make reasonable adjustments to working arrangements or conditions | Promotes equal access and rights for individuals with disabilities. Discrimination is prohibited by some state laws |
| **Age Discrimination in Employment Act (ADEA)** | **Directive 2000/78/EC** | **Stabilization of Employment for Older Persons (Law No. 68 of 1971)** | *No comparable law* | **Federal Labor Law** |
| Prohibits discrimination and harassment based on age (forty and above) | Requires prohibitions of discrimination based on age by December 2006 | Encourages employers to employ older workers; promotes employment of older workers | | Prohibits discrimination based on age |
| **Equal Pay Act (EPA)** | **Equal Pay Directive** | **Equal Employment Opportunity Law and Labor Standards Law (Article 4)** | **Equal Pay Act 1970 (Chapter 41)** | **Constitution** |
| Requires equal pay for men and women for equal work | Requires equal pay for equal work; directive includes all terms and conditions of employment | Prohibit discrimination in wages based on sex | Prohibits discrimination in terms and conditions of employment based on gender | Requires equal pay for equal work, regardless of sex or nationality |

*Table 6.3* continued

| US | European Union | Japan | UK | Mexico |
|---|---|---|---|---|
| **Family and Medical Leave Act (FMLA)** Requires employers to provide up to twelve weeks of unpaid leave for employees to care for themselves or family members | **Parental Leave Directive** Allows time off from work for family emergencies; allows parental leave from three months to eight years after the birth or adoption of a child | **Child Care Leave Law (Law No. 76 of 1991)** Provides one year of unpaid leave to either mother or father after the birth of a child. National Personnel Authority regulation No. 15–14 and 10–7 provides fourteen weeks' maternity leave before the birth of a child | **Employment Relations Act 1999** Provides a minimum eighteen weeks' maternity leave, three months' parental leave, and job reinstatement at the end of parental leave | **Federal Labor Law** Provides six weeks of leave before and after childbirth and time off for breast feeding in appropriate employer-provided facilities |

Source: Paskoff, S.M. (2003), "Around the world without the daze: Communicating international codes of conduct," paper presented at the fourth annual Program on International Labor and Employment Law, Dallas, TX, September 30–October 1.

Several challenges face American firms in implementing the principles of the EU directive. These include logistical difficulties in getting consent in companies with large numbers of employees; limited power to persuade employees to consent to data releases, since employers cannot use consent in hiring decisions and thus will have to find different ways, such as the use of pseudonyms, for transferring data without compromising the privacy of the employee; and a risk of public exposure from a number of privacy rights groups that have threatened to draw public attention to firms that they consider to employ substandard privacy practices.

Box 6.4 summarizes the privacy rights as protected under the EU's Data Protection Directive. A reading of these rights (which are well established, accepted, and protected in European firms but not so well established or accepted in the US) helps to understand both why the Europeans are so concerned about their enforcement and why American firms (and presumably firms from other countries, such as Japan and South Korea, that also have extensive operations in Europe and also may not have such extensive privacy protections in place) are concerned about their implications and implementation.

## Box 6.4 EU privacy rights

- *Notice.* Organizations must inform individuals about the purpose for which they collect and use information about them and how to place inquiries or complaints and to make changes.
- *Choice.* Organizations must give individuals the opportunity to deny permissions to transfer their data.
- *Onward Transfer.* Before transferring employee data, employers must ensure that the third-party recipient adheres to the safe harbor principles.
- *Security.* Organizations that create, maintain, use, or disseminate personal information must take reasonable precautions to protect it from loss, misuse, unauthorized access, disclosure, alteration, or destruction.
- *Data Integrity.* Organizations must take reasonable steps to ensure that personal data is reliable for its intended use, accurate, complete, and current.
- *Access.* Individuals must have access to all of the personal information about them that an organization holds and be able to correct, amend, or delete any information where it is inaccurate.
- *Enforcement.* Organizations must develop mechanisms for assuring compliance with the principles and recourse for individuals affected by non-compliance. In addition there should be an external mechanism for enforcement of the principles.

## Extraterritorial application of national law (with special attention to the US)

Every multinational enterprise must consider the application of its parent-country laws to its overseas operations (referred to as the extraterritorial application of national law). In general, international jurisprudence holds that MNEs are accountable to the laws in the countries where they operate. However, there are some exceptions to this general rule.

US multinationals, in particular, must comply with the extraterritorial application of three specific US anti-discrimination statutes. In 1991, the US Congress amended the Americans with Disabilities Act (ADA) and Title VII of the Civil Rights Act of 1964 to give extraterritorial effect to those laws. Earlier, in 1984, the Age Discrimination in Employment Act of 1967 (ADEA) was also given extraterritorial effect. Title VII prohibits discrimination and harassment on the basis of sex, race, national origin, color and religion. The ADA prohibits discrimination against disabled individuals, and requires employers to make reasonable accommodation for those disabilities. And the ADEA prohibits discrimination on the basis of age against individuals age forty and older. The effect of these amendments was to grant American citizens working anywhere in the world, for a US-owned or controlled company, the right to sue in a US court for alleged violations of these Acts, wherever they occur. Hence, an employee of an American firm (who is a US citizen) who believes she has been subjected to sexual harassment in Japan or who believes he has been terminated because of his age in Germany, may bring a lawsuit in the US to pursue these alleged claims. In any circumstance, the law of the foreign country in which a firm operates takes precedence, although, in US courts the viability of the defense of an otherwise-in-the-US illegal action on the basis of the foreign law restriction is still unsettled.

## Application of national law to local foreign-owned enterprises (with special attention to the US)

Every firm that operates businesses in other countries confronts issues related to this, that is, their need to abide by the laws of the countries in which they do business. The issue can be viewed from the perspective of the country in terms of how it applies its laws to foreign-owned and operated firms in its country. Or it can be viewed from the perspective of the firm, as it tries to understand how it must operate its foreign subsidiaries and joint ventures. At a minimum, the MNE must understand that the local laws apply, not its home laws, although, as described above, MNEs from some countries, such as the US, may also find themselves subject to their home laws, at least in terms of treatment of their home-citizen employees in their foreign operations. And this may well apply to the firm's parent-country expatriates in the foreign locales as well as to how they manage their local employees. So, for example, giving preference in job assignments or promotions to a firm's expatriates over qualified local employees may run afoul of local laws.

Since the end of World War II, the US has negotiated with some twenty countries treaties that are referred to as Friendship, Commerce, and Navigation (FCN). Treaties that, among other things, provide that companies from each country can make employment decisions within the territories of the other party, with regard to key personnel of their choice.[23] A number of foreign companies that have been sued in US courts for national origin discrimination (i.e., giving preference in employment decisions in their local subsidiaries to their parent-country nationals) have used a defense that their FCN treaties give them the right to do so. US courts and legal experts have not developed a consensus as to whether or not such treaties provide that type of protection.

There are other complexities in US law that often require each specific situation involving treatment of US employees and parent-country nationals in foreign-owned subsidiaries in the US to be interpreted separately. The bottom line is that IHR managers in MNEs that operate in foreign countries need to make sure they understand the local legal landscape before establishing employment policy and practice in those foreign operations.

## Union and labor relations

## The international situation

Multinational enterprises usually must share decision-making power with unions (and/or other representatives of employees, such as works councils) and, often, agencies of government, to greater or lesser degrees throughout the world but almost always to some degree. For many businesses, what they confront in their foreign operations is often quite different than what they deal with at home. So, responsibility for labor relations is frequently left to the HR manager at the level of the local subsidiary or joint venture.

MNEs usually develop worldwide approaches to issues such as executive compensation, but such a worldwide approach to labor and employee relations is quite rare. IHR departments within MNEs often follow one of these seven approaches to labor/employee relations in the global context:

- *Hands off* (by headquarters of the parent firm). In this approach, responsibility for labor/employee relations is left totally in the hands of local managers.
- *Monitor*. In this approach, headquarters IHR managers will try to forestall major problems for the parent company by asking intelligent and insightful questions about labor and employment responsibilities at each of their foreign locations. But primary responsibility still stays in the hands of local managers.
- *Guide and advise*. This approach is a step beyond mere monitoring. Here IHR managers from headquarters will provide ongoing advice and guidance to subsidiary managers on how to conduct labor and employee relations, usually based on policies of headquarters. Of course, this requires a higher degree of

knowledge about local labor relations regulations and practices. Still, overall control stays in the hands of local staff.

- *Strategic planning*. At this level of involvement, international labor relations issues are fully incorporated into the MNE's strategic planning. Management of all aspects of the global firm, including labor and employee relations, are integrated into a centralized program, particularly for policy purposes. Local control may still exist, but all labor relations practices will follow this global strategy.
- *Set limits and approve exceptions*. MNEs that follow this approach to their international labor/employee relations provide even more specific centralized control over local practices. Subsidiaries are allowed freedom of action only within quite narrowly defined limits, and any efforts to try different approaches must be approved by headquarters.
- *Manage totally from headquarters*. In this scenario, local subsidiary staffs have no freedom of policy or practice in their labor/employee relations activities. Indeed, all labor relations actions are directed by staff from headquarters.
- *Integration of headquarters IHR and line management in the field*. In this final approach, labor and employee relations in the field, as managed by local HR and management, are fully integrated with IHR assistance from headquarters.

Firms that operate at the level of the last three options tend to be American (and, sometimes, Asian) firms that have strong anti-union or, at least, very adversarial, approaches to labor relations and which try to ensure that this approach is followed as much as possible in their overseas operations. Of course, in many countries (e.g., where there are works councils or union negotiations are mandated), even these firms must deal with third parties, whether they want to or not. For example, IBM, which is basically a non-union firm in the US, must deal with unions in many of its overseas operations. In its French subsidiary, if even a single employee claims to belong to a union, IBM must negotiate with that union. There are five national unions in France. In addition, IBM France has its own, company, union, as well. As a consequence, under French labor law, IBM France must negotiate with six different unions.

Still, much autonomy is often possible, even when the law requires dealing with third parties, such as works councils or unions. And because each country is so different in its evolution of labor relations law and practice, leaving primary responsibility for labor and employee relations to the local level is often the only workable approach (maybe with certain overlying strategic objectives providing some guidance).

The global economy places many stresses on industrial relations. In all countries, union relations are carried on only within that country, even though the exact form of negotiations or union relations will vary considerably from country to country. However, multinational enterprises (with operations largely decentralized in order to operate as local actors in the many countries in which they operate around the globe) and transnational, or global, firms (with operations throughout the world and decisions made about employees, sourcing, financing, technology, and location of manufacturing and services without regard to national boundaries) tend to dwarf the power and influence of the country-specific unions. This leads to a concern (primarily from unions) about an imbalance of power between unions (representing the rights of workers) and firms (representing the rights of managers and owners).

In any case, MNEs must cope with very different labor relations systems in each of the countries in which they operate.[24] It is not the intention of this book to provide in-depth coverage of union relations in various countries. Rather, a very limited sampling of the variations of the law and practice of labor relations is provided to provide the IHR manager with a sense of the importance of understanding the impact of those variations on their operations around the globe. IHRM in Action 6.3 describes some of the global labor relations scene for Ford Motor Company, a firm that has had global operations for over 100 years.[25] Obviously, for a firm like Ford, global labor relations is indeed quite complex.

As mentioned above, unions (and, therefore, labor relations) exist and operate mostly at the local, firm, regional (within a country), or national level, even though a few unions have the term *international* in their names. The increase in global trade and in the number of MNEs has led to concern by trade unions about this primarily local

## Ford Motor Company's global industrial relations

Ford Motor Company manufactures cars, trucks, and parts in thirty countries, with 275,000 hourly employees worldwide. It negotiates contracts with fifty-six different unions in every country where it manufactures, except six (where there are no unions). But, in some countries, such as Italy, it must also negotiate with salaried staff and managers, who are also unionized.

Because of this great variety of unions to deal with, bargaining takes on a very different form in each country. For example, in Australia, all major issues are first discussed by subcommittees at the local level, which, after agreement is reached, are taken to the full national bargaining committee for Ford Motor of Australia. In contrast, in Germany, negotiation is done through the national employers' association (for all of the auto companies) and the national metalworkers' union (for employees).

Even with this complicated bargaining reality, or maybe because of it, bargaining is handled almost exclusively at the local level, with minimal coordination on a global level. As can be imagined, this causes coordination problems not only for the many unions involved, but also for Ford Motor Company itself. In spite of this, the office of the Director of International Labor Affairs Planning and Employee Relations in Ford's headquarters in Dearborn, Michigan, is literally only one person. As David Killinger, the Director of International Labor Affairs, says, "because I work in so many countries, one of my primary roles is to educate all the parts of the business in the US about what is going on around the world and how that affects the total business."

IHRM IN ACTION 6.3

and national influence. Their major concern is that multinational firms can manipulate local unions in collective bargaining by having the ability to move work to areas of the world that either have no unions or where unions are weak or where, in general, wages and benefits are less and working conditions are less protected. And because unions are not organized on a global basis, and there are no international laws requiring bargaining on a cross-border basis, and because unions tend to be primarily focused on local and national concerns of their members (and thus sometimes find it difficult to work together with unions in other countries who often have different concerns), they perceive that the power balance between unions and MNEs is totally skewed toward the MNEs. MNEs operate in many countries and often in many industries. In contrast, unions almost always have membership in only one country and normally in only one industry. And thus they can typically bring pressure to bear on only a small segment of an MNE – one industry (or even one firm within one industry) within one country.

For example, a number of years ago, Hyster, an American manufacturer of forklifts, with facilities in both Scotland and Holland, sought pay cuts from the workers in each locale in exchange for locating its reorganized manufacturing there.[26] In essence, Hyster was playing off the benefit of new jobs in one location against the willingness in that location to take significant pay cuts beyond what was being agreed to in the other location. The local unions had no communication with each other nor any way to "force" Hyster to negotiate together with Scotland and Holland. But Dutch law called for consultation about such things and the plant union took Hyster to court in the Netherlands. There, a judge ordered Hyster to discuss its strategy with members of the factory works council. It did, but it only revealed the small part of its global strategy that applied to them. This was unsatisfactory to the Dutch union, which maintained its suit. Eventually a deal was struck to postpone transferring production to Scotland (where the workers had agreed under this pressure to a significant pay cut). But, for its part, Hyster maintained that it had to reduce costs throughout its operations (not just Holland and Scotland) to compete with the Japanese, who had captured a large share of the European market. And the unions were stuck with national bargaining that could not cope with the larger, multi-country issues.

There has been very little cooperation between unions across national borders, and there is no union structure similar to that of the multinational enterprise, so that, for example, an international union might be able to negotiate a global agreement with an MNE that would apply to all of its operations around the world (although some recent collective bargaining agreements in the airline industry – which by its very nature is international – have moved in that direction). In practical terms, what this means is that unions view MNEs as being able to:

- Locate work in countries with lower social protections and lower wages and benefits (often this means countries with no unions or very weak unions), staying away from countries with stronger unions and stronger protections and higher wages and benefits.
- Force workers in one country, faced by competition from workers in other countries, to "bid down" their wages and benefits in order to keep their jobs.

- Take advantage of differences in legally mandated benefits for workers by restructuring the operations in countries where the costs of workforce adjustments are lowest and thus force excessive dislocation burdens on workers in these low-benefit countries.
- Outlast workers in the event of a labor dispute in one country because cash flows (and the ability to maintain business) are at least partially maintained by operations in countries where there are no disputes.

One result is that, gradually, unions are beginning to look for ways to exercise influence over labor relations on a cross-border and multinational scale. National trade union federations and more recently established international federations and trade secretariats are providing assistance to national unions in dealing with MNEs (described in the last part of this section) and have become closely involved with bodies like the ILO and the OECD, working with them to develop, enhance, and enforce their covenants and declarations on labor standards. Their ultimate goal is to develop transnational bargaining, although right now there are no laws or regulations that require it. As described above, the ILO and OECD guidelines are trying to go beyond merely suggesting that MNEs abide by the industrial relations statutes in force in each of the countries in which they operate. And local courts are beginning to defer to or consider these international standards or a firm's parent-country laws. This has been accomplished at least partially because of the pressures of these international union federations.

Nevertheless, these guidelines and standards are only as effective as individual firms and governments are willing to allow them to be. Adherence to them is essentially voluntary. For example, a few years ago, the Badger Company, a subsidiary of Raytheon, a US MNE, closed its Belgian subsidiary without paying required termination payments for its displaced workers. Badger (Belgium) had declared bankruptcy, but Belgian labor unions argued that Raytheon should assume the subsidiary's financial obligations. Raytheon initially refused, but under intense pressure from the Belgian government and American and Belgian labor unions – and a "finding" by the OECD that their guidelines implied a shared responsibility by subsidiaries and their parents – Badger executives and Belgian officials eventually agreed to a scaled-down settlement.[27]

But in similar types of situations, many international firms ignore local union contracts and country regulations in countries such as Korea, where in recent years there have been a number of illegal plant closings by foreign-owned subsidiaries of MNEs without the legally required notice and without their paying owed wages and other required compensation due in cases of plant closures. But neither has the Korean government been willing to put pressure on the US (or other involved foreign governments) to take these employers to court (there are no laws in either country that would mandate such action) nor has the US government been willing to take action on its own. A few years ago, El Al, the Israeli airline (owned by the state of Israel) faced a strike from its US employees at its American operations in New York City. Rather than negotiate with the union, El Al brought in workers from Israel.

The union sued for unfair labor practices (refusal to bargain, among other charges), but the US government was not willing to force Israel to abide by American labor laws, even within its operations in the US. In result, there was no way for the union to force El Al to a settlement.

The result is that there remain a number of barriers to multinational bargaining. In addition to the global power of MNEs and the fractured nature of unions, and the unwillingness of nations to get involved under the existing lack of international governing covenants, other obstacles also will need to be overcome in order for progress to occur in movement toward multinational bargaining:[28]

- The widely varying industrial relations laws and practices among different countries.
- The lack of any central, international authority for labor relations or global labor law.
- Major economic and cultural differences among different countries.
- Employer opposition.
- Union reluctance at the national level, because the national leadership often fears that multinational bargaining will transfer power from them to an international leadership.
- Absence of a centralized decision-making authority for unions.
- Lack of coordination of activities by unions across national boundaries.
- Differing national priorities.
- Employee unwillingness to subordinate local concerns to concerns of workers in other countries.

Over the last fifty years, or so, national trade unions have created the beginnings of an international trade union structure in an attempt to develop some international focus and capabilities to deal more effectively with multinational enterprises. At the same time, employers have also created equivalent trade associations to provide a cross-border and cross-industry voice for global labor relations. These organizations include the following:

- *International Confederation of Free Trade Unions.* Founded in 1949, the ICFTU is the major global confederation of national labor unions. Its main purposes are to further the purposes of trade unions throughout the world and to work with international bodies, such as the ILO and the United Nations, to protect the rights of workers.
- *International Trade Secretariats.* The ITS has eleven member unions from worldwide industries, such as the chemical workers, metalworkers, building and woodworkers, educators, and clerical and professional employees. (There used to be eighteen members, but industrial unions are consolidating, just as are their industries and firms in their industries.) The ITS exists to provide a forum for pursuing the global interests of the industrial trade unions.
- There are also similar international employer organizations, some organized as confederations of country organizations and some as confederations of industry and trade associations.[29] Some of these confederations exist to provide services to

their members (e.g., the ASEAN Confederation of Employers, the Union of Industrial and Employers' Confederations of Europe, and the Confederation of Latin American Employers' Organizations), such as education and training to upgrade members' skills, promotion of social responsibility in environmental protections, and planning for increasing cross-border trade and globalization. And some exist to work with international organizations, such as the ILO (e.g., the International Organization of Employers) and the OECD (e.g., the Business and Industry Advisory Committee to the OECD), in their tripartite discussions and negotiations of international business and employment standards.

Before global labor relations evolve very far, however, the following types of questions will need to be addressed:

- What rules will apply to the resolution of disputes?
- What rules will apply to the process of negotiations?
- What law will cover the negotiations, e.g., between companies in two or more countries?

As companies become more global and more connected across borders, it is inevitable that multi-country, maybe even multi-employer and multi-union negotiations involving employers and unions from multiple countries will develop. Business global issues are already part of the "relevant facts" for negotiations in many MNEs. And this will only increase in prevalence and importance. For a more detailed discussion see the book in this series by Morley and Gunnigle entitled *Global Industrial Relations*. Now the challenge is to develop mechanisms to accommodate the reality.

## Global labor relations for MNEs

The above section described elements of the international situation for unions and MNEs. This section describes some of the important characteristics of industrial relations within at least some countries. Even though the practice of industrial relations has some common elements in countries around the world, every individual country has its own unique approach to the relationships among the industrial relations actors – labor, management, government, and the public – and their various organizations. While the laws and practices may be tightly and specifically stated in some countries, other countries provide ample opportunity for improvisation. The percentage of the workforce and the nature of employees who belong to unions varies dramatically from country to country; but this alone may not indicate the power of unions or employers within their respective countries. For example, even though a relatively low percentage of workers belong to unions in France (about 12 percent), the unions play a very important role in determining government policy toward workers and toward general industrial policy, and employers are required by law to negotiate with any union present (represented by as few as one employee) and to implement national policies on wage rates, and so on. In fact, about 85 percent of all workers in France are covered by the contracts negotiated by unions, even though their actual membership is quite low.

One difficulty in assessing the power or importance of unions in various countries arises from the inconsistencies between countries in how they count membership. For example, retired workers are still union members in most Scandinavian countries but not usually elsewhere and professionals such as teachers and members of professional associations, such as engineers, are sometimes included and sometimes not. Changes in labor relations are also occurring so rapidly in many countries that data only a few years old can be out of date by significant amounts. Nevertheless, relative differences remain quite obvious. For example, only 16 percent of the labor force are union members in Spain (yet 50 percent of the labor force are covered by union contracts) while in Japan, about 25 percent belong to unions, with approximately 60 percent of the labor force covered by union contracts. As illustrated, some countries have quite low union membership (which doesn't necessarily indicate how many workers are covered by the contracts negotiated), while other countries have much higher union membership, such as Denmark with about 75 percent union membership and Sweden with about 85 percent membership.

In terms of the patterns of labor relations practices themselves, some countries have developed industrial relations systems patterned after the laws and traditions of other countries. And yet others have pursued relatively unique avenues to labor relations. Within this milieu, each country has developed a tradition and legal framework that reflects its own special history and political experience. As a consequence, firms that conduct business on a multinational or transnational basis must understand and cope with a great deal of diversity in the performance of industrial relations around the world. This typically leads to decentralizing the labor relations function (much as is also true of the general HRM function), providing subsidiaries with considerable autonomy in managing employee relations.

George McCullough, former industrial relations executive at Exxon Corporation, illustrated this point with the following statement about Exxon's view of local autonomy for labor relations:[30]

> My company operates in 137 countries. The variations in our labor relations processes, the manner in which we go about collective bargaining, and the differences in items included in collective agreements are staggering. Even in two countries like Holland and Belgium, where the proximity between Rotterdam and Antwerp has caused us to consolidate some management functions, the labor relations processes are totally independent of each other and the contracts bear little resemblance.

In some countries (e.g., Canada, the US, Germany, and Japan), union activity is basically economic. That is, unions involve themselves primarily with economic issues of concern to their members, such as wage rates, hours of work, and job security; and this is usually manifested through some form of union–management collective bargaining. In other countries, particularly England, France, Italy, and those in Latin America, unions tend to be very political and often try to achieve their objectives through political action rather than through direct collective bargaining. This is not to say that "business-focused" unions don't try to influence government to achieve legislation favorable to their members and that "politically focused" unions don't participate in collective bargaining. But their historical pattern has been the former forms of activity, respectively, rather than the latter.

In some countries, union activity is focused on industry-wide or even national bargaining while in other countries union relations are very decentralized, taking place almost exclusively at the local firm level. Thus, even in industrialized (and usually heavily unionized) countries, major differences in labor relations can be found relative to issues such as (1) the level at which bargaining takes place (national, regional, industry, or workplace); (2) the types of workers involved (craft, industrial, professional); (3) degree of centralization of union–management relations; (4) the scope of bargaining, that is, the topics which are usually included in negotiations and contracts; (5) the degree to which the government is involved or can intervene; and (6) the degree of unionization. In order to be effective in labor relations throughout the operations of an MNE, IHR managers need to understand these issues and differences in each of the countries in which they conduct business.

In addition, economic and political issues of concern to management and unions are not static. They are constantly changing. And globalization, technological and job changes, and changing demographics are also heavily impacting the role and importance of unions (and companies, for that matter) in most countries, as well.

American multinationals may face an even more difficult problem in understanding and coping with industrial relations around the world, since American labor relations are quite different in many respects from those practiced in other countries. The primary features of the American labor relations scene include the following:

- Only non-supervisorial and non-managerial employees have the right to organize or join unions.
- Typically, professional and technical workers also do not form or join unions.
- The only employees who belong to unions (that can thus bargain with the employer) work for employers where a majority of those employees have voted in free but secret elections for union representation.
- Contracts between such unions and employers are negotiated primarily at the local level between a single union and a single employer.
- Such collectively bargained contracts are legally enforceable and typically last for three years.
- The only mandatory subjects for bargaining are wages, hours, and working conditions.
- Both unions and employers are restricted in their behavior toward each other by a considerable amount of regulation.
- Disagreements over the meaning of contracts are handled through established grievance procedures (not by renegotiating the contract), settled by union and management acting together and settled in the case of impasse by a privately hired, neutral arbitrator.

This highly decentralized, "business" unionism (although extensively regulated) is significantly different from the form of unionism present in most other countries (which is often referred to as "political" unionism).[31] In most countries, labor relations practices are very different, even opposite, to these characteristics. Thus the American MNE may have even more difficulty coping with the diversity of labor relations practices, because its experience and familiarity may well not provide adequate guidance in other countries. Of course, every MNE will experience differences in labor relations practices, although they may not be as great.

So, in summary, multinational enterprises will need to seek answers to the following types of questions regarding global labor relations practices wherever they operate:

- What are the nature and role of the employers' associations in each country? Because there is very little multi-employer bargaining in some countries (such as the US) and most bargaining takes this form in other countries, MNEs need to learn as much as possible about the role of these associations in each country. Sometimes the multi-employer bargaining is regional (within an industry), sometimes industry-wide, and sometimes national, covering all or most industries. The questions an MNE needs to address relative to employers' associations include: Which associations exist? Should the MNE belong (why, why not)? What does membership entail, do most employers join, and can the firm avoid joining? With the weakening of unions which is happening in many countries, is most bargaining still being conducted on a national and/or industry-wide level, applying to all or most employers and employees?
- What is the nature of the unions in each particular country? Are they associated with political parties and, if so, which ones? Are they related to the Church? How are they organized: by firm, region, industry, national, craft? Who belongs? Who is covered by the contracts? Who does the firm have to negotiate with? What is the role of government in bargaining?
- Is it possible to operate union-free? (It is often impossible.)
- Is there multi-unionism within firms, so that the MNE must negotiate with multiple, often competing unions, within the same subsidiary or organization?
- Are there "closed shop" requirements or practices? That is, is the situation such that employees *must* belong to the union(s)?
- Is there white-collar unionization? Do managers belong to unions, such as the *dirigenti* in Italy?
- What is the nature of the plant or site-level role of unions? Are there shop stewards? Are there works councils that are essentially arms of the unions?
- What is the nature of the contracts or agreements with unions? Are the contracts enforceable? Are they breakable for any reasons? When and under what circumstances are contracts renegotiated? For what reasons can and do unions go on strike? What topics are contained in the contracts? Are they specific or general in nature?

All of these questions illustrate potentially significant differences between labor relations practices in differing countries. This is just one more area of complexity with which IHR managers and MNEs must learn to cope.

# Immigration law

Every country exercises control over its definition of citizenship and the immigration that it allows into its territory. Some countries, such as Japan, allow very limited immigration. Others like the US, even though they may exercise control over who is granted immigration rights, admits large numbers of immigrants every year. Indeed, in many years, the US admits more immigrants (legal and illegal) than the rest of the countries of the world combined. Most other countries fall somewhere in between these two extremes. As was suggested in Chapter 8 on global workforce planning, a country's attitudes about immigration vary according to its particular employment needs at any point in time. And these change over time, as attitudes and needs change.

Virtually every country requires a work visa whenever a person is transferred to a job in their country for a period of six months or more. But there are also usually many other situations that can trigger the requirement for some other form of visa, even if the work will only last a couple of days. The activities that will trigger the need for such special visas and the amount of time required to process such a visa vary from country to country and from situation to situation. Because of this, IHR managers must be sure, when decisions are being made about sending employees on everything from short-term business trips to longer-term relocations for a number of months or years, that the necessary visas are applied for and that an adequate amount of time is allowed to be able to gain the necessary approvals for such travel and transfers. Immigration law firms that specialize in helping firms acquire the necessary visas and work permits can provide the information needed to make such judgments.

The destruction of the World Trade towers in New York City on September 11, 2001 by individuals who had been living in the US, legally and illegally, on student and tourist visas, led to a major tightening of immigration rules and procedures and increased scrutiny of visa applicants of all types in the US. For example, the Immigration and Naturalization Service (INS) that held the responsibility for customs, border control, and immigration and citizenship issues was closed and its responsibilities taken over by the new Department of Homeland Security, with the mandate to tighten scrutiny of visa applications and immigration. Nevertheless, most of the forms and procedures of the INS will remain in force.

The events of Nine-eleven led to increased scrutiny of legal immigration issues in other areas of the world, as well, partially due to pressure from the US. This is especially true for certain countries and areas of the world that are perceived to be involved with international terrorism, as the US has pressured them to tighten their own procedures and to aid the US in its tightened procedures.

As an example, Box 6.5 provides a short summary of the types of visa categories used by the US. Many countries follow similar procedures. Gaining approval of these various visas can be very time-consuming, expensive, and difficult, as the countries tighten their procedures for even business-related and tourist visas. This list of US visas also points out how complicated the area of immigration law is. Firms that hire immigrants, move people around the globe, and seek talent all over the world must manage this complexity in order to effectively staff their global operations.

## Box 6.5 US immigrant and non-immigrant visas

### Non-immigrant visa categories

B  Business (not involving gainful employment in the US) and pleasure visitors

E  Treaty traders and treaty investors (renewable visa for individuals from treaty countries to set up and direct an investment in the US that is less than the $1 million investment required by the fifth preference category immigrant visa described below)

F  Academic students (*bona fide* student at approved school with continuing foreign residence)

H  Temporary workers:
  ○ H-1B Specialty occupations, requiring college education or equivalent and all professional licenses (primarily for shortage occupations)
  ○ H-1C Professional nurses
  ○ H-2 Unskilled (mostly used for skilled manufacturing)
  ○ H-3 Trainee

J  Exchange visitors (designated by US Information Agency)

K  Fiancés and their minor children; spouses and unmarried minor children of US citizens while waiting for permanent residence

L-1 Intra-company transferees (executives and high-tech engineers for up to seven years)

M  Vocational students (at vocational or non-academic institution)

O  Aliens of extraordinary ability

P  Athletes and entertainers for up to five years

Q  International exchange to share the history and culture of the person's country for up to fifteen months

R  Religious workers for up to five years

TN status  Certain Canadian and Mexican business travelers (under NAFTA)

### Immigrant visas

- First preference immigrant visa categories: "priority workers":
  ○ Aliens of extraordinary ability in the arts, sciences, business, or athletics
  ○ Outstanding professors or researchers (with international recognition)
  ○ Certain multinational managers and executives (moving from branch office or subsidiary to US company)
- Second preference immigrant visa categories:
  ○ Aliens of exceptional ability and professionals with advanced degrees
  ○ Aliens whose work is in the national interest

- Third preference immigrant visa categories:
  - Professionals holding basic degrees, skilled workers, and other workers
- Fourth and fifth preference immigrant visa categories:
  - Religious workers
  - Employment creation investor (invest US$1 million in a new US business and create jobs for ten US workers or bail out an existing troubled business or increase the net worth of an existing business by at least 40 percent)

## MNE employment policy and practice

One of the most visible and important pressures for IHRM and MNEs to pay attention to the international employment law aspect of the global environment is the increased pressure of litigation risks. As described in this chapter, these risks focus on activities in foreign jurisdictions and in dealing with overseas employees. In recent years there has been a significant trend toward holding MNEs accountable in litigation forums for their human rights and employee protections in foreign countries. Increasingly, enterprises are being sued in their home jurisdictions on the basis of allegations of breaches arising from the firm's activities in a foreign jurisdiction. In the past, MNEs have been able to block such actions on the basis that the home courts were not the appropriate jurisdictions in which to litigate the dispute. However, recent cases are illustrating that this defense may not be sufficient as courts are increasingly willing to hold parent firms accountable under both their parent-country laws and those of the foreign country in which such litigations are initiated.

The implication of all of this complexity in global labor and employment law and regulation is that the MNE needs to develop the strategic policy for itself that establishes a code of conduct that defines the acceptable behavior in terms of employee and labor relations for its far-reaching managerial and employee workforce.[32] This code of conduct should be defended as the "company culture," a culture that insists on abiding by all national and international employee relations regulations and, further, defines what is seen as legal and ethical behavior when dealing with these regulations. Without this, the firm and its managers and employees can face any or all of criminal liability, damaged individual careers, damaged firm global reputation, lowered share prices, and even possible risk of loss of organizational viability. The point is, top leadership must insist that this is the "way they want to run their business," that, for example, sexual or racial discrimination (or, even, just banter) is not wanted because it limits the firm's ability to work together, to be a team, such behavior is divisive, and it is just not wanted. This removes the possibility of disagreement with certain practices, a disagreement which may be based on perceived local or national cultural practices that vary from those in an MNE's parent country. The decision to abide by certain labor standards is based on the defined company culture, not on any given country's cultural practices.

## Conclusion

This chapter has examined the broad nature of international labor law and standards and the development of regional and national employment regulations that impact IHR and the MNE. Every MNE must work to understand this very complex legal environment and work to comply with all relevant codes, laws, and guidelines. Failure to do so can lead to significant liabilities. The chapter described efforts to develop international labor standards by groups like the International Labour Organization and the Organization for Economic Cooperation and Development, some of the areas of HR law that are being passed in most countries and that IHR and the MNE needs to abide by, the extraterritorial application of national law outside a country's national borders and the application of national employment law to foreign-owned subsidiaries within a nation's borders, concerns about international labor and union relations and activities, and finally immigration, as it is constrained and implemented by national rules about the control of cross-border movement of people.

## Points for further discussion

1 Describe some of the regional and global organizations that can impact Lincoln Electric in China. What is the nature of their impact?
2 What labor laws are relevant to the global operations of Lincoln Electric?
3 Describe some immigration laws that may be relevant to Lincoln Electric in Cleveland, Ohio.

# 7 Global ethics and labor standards

## Learning objectives

After considering this chapter, the reader will be able to describe:

- The role of ethics in IHRM
- Numerous agencies that play important parts developing roles in labor standards
- Various rules and standards developed by agencies that impact IHRM
- How some MNEs are responding to the various agencies and their rules and standards

## Key terms

- Ethical relativism, ethical absolutism, cosmopolitanism
- ILO, WTO, ICC, OECD
- Caux Round Table

The conduct of international business increasingly involves concerns about the values and practices of multinational enterprises when they conduct business outside their countries of origin. International governing bodies, such as the United Nations and the International Labour Organization (ILO), non-governmental organizations, such as Amnesty International and the Organization for Economic Cooperation and Development (OECD), labor organizations, such as the US AFL-CIO and the International Confederation of Free Trade Unions (ICFTU), and special interest groups, such as the Interfaith Center on Corporate Responsibility and environmental, consumer, and student activist groups, increasingly raise questions about the "ethical" nature of business practices of many MNEs, often particularly as they relate to employment-related practices. As businesses look outside their country borders for business opportunities, they claim many benefits derive from this global business activity. At the same time, however, they are charged with exploitation and being the cause of increasing inequities in the countries in which they do business, particularly in the less developed countries. Because of this, the possibility of confusion about business rules, ethics, and HR policies and practices has intensified, often because of results from business practices that are seen by some as highly beneficial and, yet, by others as both tragic and costly.[1]

Chapter 5 discussed in some detail the concern with and impact of country and company variances in culture. In this specific area of ethics applied to business practice in foreign settings, even the best-informed, best-intentioned executives must often rethink their assumptions. What works in an enterprise's home country can be viewed very differently in a country with different standards or perceptions of what is ethical conduct.[2] Evidence even suggests that not only is there variance among countries and cultures, but even among different industries.[3] And often one's national perspective clouds one's view of another country or culture's way of doing things. For example, the traditional development of long-term business linkages, which are central to the conduct of business in certain countries – such as the *keiretsu* in Japan or *chaebol* in Korea – is often viewed as collusion from an American perspective. Difficulties in understanding and working with another country's often very different practices are unavoidable for business people who live and work outside their home countries.

Many of the issues and/or practices that are seen as raising concerns about ethics fall within the managerial and administrative responsibilities of human resources. Because these concerns appear to be increasing, as more firms operate outside their countries of origin, and as more groups such as labor unions, groups of activists and college students, and the international media give attention to these issues, more firms are finding it in their best interests (both in terms of public and customer opinion and ultimately in terms of competitive advantage) to pay closer attention to the ethical conduct of their foreign operations.[4]

Even if there is relative agreement on basic human values and ethical principles around the world (although some would even disagree with this premise), clearly there is considerable variance in what might be referred to as the ethical climate within different countries.[5] That is, differing country cultures view various issues, such as bribery, gifts or favors, tax evasion, or child labor, differently. Thomas Donaldson, one of the US's top experts on international ethics, tells the story of a manager of a large US company operating in China who fired an employee caught stealing and turned him over to local authorities, according to company policy.[6] Later, the manager was horrified to learn that the employee had been summarily executed. Obviously, the cultural context in which the policy was formulated was vastly different from the cultural context in which the manager carried out the policy. In the US, no firm would expect an employee caught stealing from the company and turned in to local police for prosecution to be executed. And yet in the Chinese culture, such acts seen as important enough to "turn in" the employee, are clearly viewed with a much greater degree of finality.

# The ethics of HR decision making in foreign operations: a general perspective

The basic ethical dilemma for human resource management in a multinational firm involves what the international HR manager should do when an employment practice that is illegal or viewed as wrong in the home country is legal and acceptable in the host country, that is, the foreign attitudes or standards are viewed as lower than those held in the home country.[7] Examples might include sex or race discrimination in hiring, job placement, or compensation; use of child labor; or providing unsafe working conditions.

Ethicists describe two opposing approaches to questions of this type. One approach is *ethical relativism*, which suggests that what is right is whatever a society defines as right. There are no absolute rights or wrongs. In this perspective, if a society says that women shall not be paid the same as men for the same work or that child labor is all right, those rules are right for that society at that point in time. Under ethical relativism, there can be no external frame of reference for judging that one society's set of rules is better – or worse – than another's. So, under ethical relativism, IHR managers who try to impose their values on human resource practices in a host country are guilty of what is often referred to as ethical imperialism, or ethical chauvinism. Under the philosophy of ethical relativism, it is entirely appropriate to follow local practices regarding the treatment of employees. Though appearing on the surface to be a liberal, open-minded approach, this view may result in actions that home-country constituencies (at least from the Western industrialized countries) would find entirely unacceptable, such as child labor or gross inequality.

The opposite position is called *ethical absolutism*. This is the view that there is a single set of universal ethical principles, which apply at all times, in all circumstances, in all cultures. This approach might be very useful to an IHR manager, as it would suggest which local practices – though they be quite different from those of the parent country – are morally acceptable because they do not violate universal principles and those which are not morally acceptable and must not be followed, because they do violate such universal principles. The problem with this view is specifying what the universal principles are and developing a logical case for why these, and only these, principles are truly universal. In adopting the values of a single culture or religion as universal one again runs the risk of ethical imperialism.

Thus both of these philosophies create potential problems for the IHR manager and for expatriates being posted to foreign subsidiaries. In order to deal with these extremes, some have suggested that situations often compel the MNE, through collaboration and/or imagination, to develop a unique response to a cross-cultural ethical dilemma, one that tries to find the common ground among disparate moral views. This has been referred to as *cosmopolitanism*.[8] Later in this chapter, a number of such solutions are illustrated.

Thomas Donaldson has tried to provide a framework for decision making in a multinational environment that tries to resolve these possible ethical dilemmas.[9]

Donaldson states that the task is to "tolerate cultural diversity while drawing the line at moral recklessness."[10] In some ways, his approach is absolutist because it relies on a statement of thirty fundamental international rights (which have been recognized by international bodies, such as the United Nations, in the Universal Declaration of Human Rights), maybe ten or so that apply directly to issues of concern to IHRM. These include the rights to freedom of physical movement; ownership of property; freedom from torture; a fair trial; nondiscriminatory treatment; physical security; freedom of speech and association; a minimal education; political participation; freedom to work in fair and safe conditions and to earn a decent standard of living. Organizations need to avoid depriving individuals of these rights wherever they do business (even though, in some countries, some of these "rights" are not very well recognized or agreed to).

However, these rights alone are not sufficient guidelines. When IHR managers are trying to decide if their corporations can follow a practice that is legal and morally acceptable in the host country but not in the parent country, Donaldson suggests they ask themselves a series of questions. First, ask *why* the practice is acceptable in the host country but not at home. Answers to this question fall into two categories: (1) because of the host country's relative level of economic development; or (2) for reasons unrelated to economic development. If the answer is 1, the next question is whether the parent country would have accepted the practice when (or if) it was at that same level of economic development. If it would have, the practice is permissible. An example might be the building of a fertilizer plant that provides a product necessary for the feeding of the population of the country, despite the fact that there is a risk of occupational disease for employees working in the plant. If the parent firm (or the parent country) were willing to accept this risk for itself under similar circumstances, then the building of such a plant would be all right within Donaldson's framework.

The second answer, that the difference is not based on economic considerations, requires a more complicated decision process. The manager must ask two additional questions: (1) Is it possible to conduct business successfully in the host country without undertaking the practice? (2) Is the practice a clear violation of a fundamental right?[11] The practice is permissible *only if* the answer to both questions is no. That is, the practice is acceptable if it is critical to doing business in the country *and* it does not violate a fundamental right. Otherwise, the organization should refuse to follow the local practice.

For example, in Singapore it is common to see "help wanted" ads for "Chinese women, age 21–28." This type of advertisement violates US (and other countries') laws and *mores* regarding age, sex, and ethnic discrimination. Would it be permissible for a US subsidiary in Singapore to run an ad like that? According to Donaldson, the answer is "no" because the discrimination is not tied to the level of economic development, is not necessary for doing business in Singapore, and violates the fundamental international right to nondiscriminatory treatment (a right which is codified in the resolutions of a number of international bodies, such as the United Nations and the International Labour Organization). There can be many difficulties when discussing issues of ethical attitudes and practices in various countries.

Obviously, the gap between policy and practice can often be quite wide. Solutions to the problem of child labor, for example, are not necessarily easy to develop in a way that really benefits the parties involved. This point is discussed in more detail later in the chapter when solutions to such problems are described.

## Specific ethical problems

There are a number of general issues that must be dealt with when MNEs endeavor to develop ethics policies or codes of conduct for their international employees and business units.[12] In general terms, these include at least the following:

- The meaning of rules. Are they to be obeyed without question or exception or merely be ideal guides that sometimes can be honored only in the abstract, such as in the situation described earlier of the American firm in China?
- Special treatment of any kind of "elite" class, which may be acceptable or even necessary in a foreign locale (for example, based on a person's social, economic, religious, or job class).
- Whom to hire (such as friends and relatives, children, only the young and/or attractive, from certain schools or locales, or hiring based on merit?).
- How to deal with local government bureaucrats, for example, use of bribes to ease delivery of services, such as acquisition of work permits or handling of customs paperwork.
- Use of facilitators (e.g., to stand in lines or push required paperwork).
- Attitude toward gifts and bribes, particularly to acquire business. Clearly there are major differences in attitudes and traditions related to this topic.
- Role of (that is, degree of deference to) local "simpatico" leaders or managers (who, within the local culture, can set the ethical tone for everyone).
- Approach to the protection of group confidentiality and loyalty, which in some cultures can be a more important value than respect for company trade secrets or proprietary/intellectual property.
- Rules relating to office gender roles, that is, the treatment of women (since there may be significant differences around the world).
- Standards for working conditions, since local practice and regulations may either not be as strict as home-country practice, or potentially even more restrictive.

The rest of this chapter considers specific areas of ethical dilemma for International HRM as well as some of the solutions being suggested. A number of these issues have become of top concern to executives of multinational enterprises as well as of governments and nongovernmental organizations (NGOs) that would like to find approaches to these issues that would both provide protection for the rights of employees worldwide as well as provide guidelines for organizations that enable them to conduct business in ways that benefit all of their constituencies: customers, employees, owners/shareholders, suppliers, and communities in which they conduct business. For at least these particular issues, the international HR manager will be looked to for guidance.

## Historical perspective

The need for international labor standards has long been recognized.[13] The International Labour Organization (ILO) was formed in 1919 to, in part, raise labor standards and improve working conditions throughout the world. The ILO has over the years drafted a number of conventions addressing labor standards, but it lacks an effective enforcement mechanism. In addition, depending on the standard, there can be difficulty experienced in getting member countries to ratify the conventions. At the 2000 conference of the ILO, member nations finally voted overwhelmingly to adopt the ILO Declaration of Fundamental Principles and Rights at work.[14] This commits all members to work towards:

- Freedom of association and the right to collective bargaining.
- The elimination of forced labor.
- The effective abolition of child labor.
- The ending of discrimination in employment.

The declaration incorporates a follow-up mechanism to monitor observance of these principles, which means that for the first time even countries which have not yet ratified the conventions covering these topics will see their legislation and practices subjected to ILO monitoring. The ILO will compile an annual report examining global trends towards compliance with each of these principles.

In addition, the US and the EU have proposed inclusion of a "social clause" in the World Trade Organization (WTO) that would promulgate minimum international labor standards and provide a mechanism for their enforcement. This proposal continues to be opposed by many developing nations, although there appears to be growing agreement on at least some of these issues.

Today, there appear to be four forces driving the move toward adoption of international labor standards: pressure from social advocacy groups, labor union activities, resentment of multinational corporations in developing countries, and US and European proposals to link trade policy and human rights. Each of these will be addressed in the remainder of this chapter. But first, the primary problems addressed by proposed standards are examined.

## Corruption/bribery

The level of corruption present in any culture (which often originates within government, itself) is one of the major factors that make consideration of solutions to ethical problems difficult.[15] Corruption may, in fact, be illegal. But that doesn't keep it from being present.

One of the major reasons for the complexity in this area is due to this: what is called corruption in one country may be merely seen as actions to sustain relationships in another. Even so, there is typically agreement on at least the extremes. Most people will agree that payment of hundreds of thousands of dollars to line a military general's pockets is wrong; but payments to people who take goods off the docks to expedite service is often considered necessary and all right, given the level of pay of the dock workers and the prevailing cultural norms which see this as a normal way of conducting business.

However, even among developed countries, there are considerable disagreements over what is acceptable behavior. Firms from countries such as the US complain about the disadvantages they sustain, since their laws preclude them from being able to give bribes, while some of their competitors for global business from countries such as Germany, France, and the Netherlands can take tax deductions for such bribes. Studies suggest that US firms lose at least US$45 billion a year in foreign contracts due to American laws that preclude, upon penalty of fine and jail time, the payment of bribes in order to acquire foreign sales or projects.[16] Indeed, it is estimated that 80 percent of the deals available for major contracts in foreign countries are received by firms that pay bribes.

A number of organizations make estimates of the level of corruption present in various countries. The one that has received the most media attention, Transparency International in Berlin, Germany, measures "bribery, graft, extortion, and all their slimy cousins" in fifty-two countries, as perceived by business people. In this organization's most recent rankings, Denmark ranked first, followed by Finland, Sweden, New Zealand, and Canada. The US lands in fifteenth place, behind Britain, Germany, and Chile, but ahead of Hong Kong, France, and Japan. The bottom five included Nigeria, Bolivia, Colombia, Russia, and Pakistan.[17]

The range of possible actions that might be undertaken by any particular country to combat corruption is quite broad.[18] These actions could include changing everything from the civil service system and the country's laws and regulations governing procurement of goods and services to reform of the accounting and auditing requirements to reform of the country's criminal law and tax systems. But these types of reforms are long term and require a level of political will and agreement that is rarely present.

In order to address concerns about the levels of bribery and corruption on a global level, international groups have begun to try to develop guidelines for ethical conduct.[19] In 1999, the UN General Assembly finally passed (after a number of earlier unsuccessful attempts) a forceful Declaration against Corruption and Bribery in International Commercial Transactions which, in addition, called on several other UN organizations, such as the ILO, to take complementary action. Both the International Chamber of Commerce (ICC) and the Organization for Economic Cooperation and Development (OECD) have developed policies intended to end the practice of payment of bribes in order to gain foreign contracts by getting their member countries to stop allowing companies to deduct foreign bribe payments from tax payments.[20] The new rules of conduct being pursued under these arrangements include banning extortion, bribes, kickbacks, "off the books" and secret accounts, and ensuring that intermediary business agents only be paid "appropriate remuneration for legitimate services rendered." The measure adopted in 1997 by the ministers of the members of the OECD (the world's thirty-two leading industrial and most developed nations) aims to make it illegal to bribe foreign public officials to obtain or maintain a contract, such as has been the case in the US since the passage of the Foreign Corrupt Practices Act in 1977.

The World Trade Organization, since its first summit meeting in Singapore in 1996, has had a working group on corruption. In addition, the World Bank, the International Monetary Fund, and most regional development banks have also adopted formal anti-corruption policies. In recent years, the World Bank and the International Monetary Fund have withdrawn or postponed development projects because of refusal of receiving countries to deal adequately with problems of corruption. And regional groups, such as the Organization of African Unity and the Organization of American States, have also adopted conventions against corruption. All of this suggests that the issue of corruption and bribery has finally reached the level of concern that most countries are now at least trying to take action to stop it and to change the circumstances that allow it to exist.

## Culture and ethics

A particularly difficult question for ethical values, as they relate in particular to corruption, involves whether there are cultural differences in attitudes and values related to specific areas of behavior, such as the demand for or the payment of bribes in order to get contracts or to get things done.[21] In lists compiled of the most corrupt countries in the world, one variable stands out as common among the most corrupt: poverty. Even though the poorest and most corrupt countries typically have laws against bribery, it is still often a common practice of government and business officials. Besides being poor, economies perceived as relatively corrupt also tend to be overregulated, that is, tangled in red tape, and less controlled by the rule of law. Bureaucrats usually are given much discretionary authority to arbitrarily determine issues for or against companies, particularly foreign firms, and this often leads to the request for bribes to expedite decisions and/or to land contracts for major work projects.

Studies also suggest that societies in which illegal payments are common share a number of specific cultural traits. These include:

- They are relationship-focused; personal connections are crucial.
- They are strongly hierarchical, valuing wide status differences, and thus giving strong power and authority to high-level officials (with governments usually run by royalty or military or people with strong links to royalty and/or the military).
- They are polychronic, that is, they have a relaxed attitude toward time and scheduling.

It is important to note that these three characteristics *per se* do not guarantee that there will be official corruption; it is just that the countries identified as the most corrupt share these values. What may be most important for business people is that these values can suggest ways to avoid making illegal payments and possibly getting caught in either local or parent-country legal problems for doing so. For example, in countries with these types of cultural values, research and experience shows that carefully taking the time to develop contacts and to build relationships are crucial in conducting successful foreign business.

## Staffing

A second area of HR responsibility that often confronts charges of unethical business behavior involves activities related to the staffing of international operations. These include transferring work from higher-paid employees in the parent country to lower-wage foreign workers, use of child labor, poorer working conditions in foreign operations, use of unpaid prison or indentured workers, etc. The following paragraphs introduce some of these concerns and discuss various approaches taken by MNEs and governmental and nongovernmental organizations to address them.

A charge which is often levied against employers in the developed countries is one of taking advantage of "unfair competition from low-wage foreign workers" – a charge which is not only made against employers in the developed countries, but which has a counterpart in just about every country of the world. Yes, US and European unions and politicians complain about American and European firms moving operations "offshore," e.g., to the Far East, such as to the Philippines or to Thailand or to Indonesia, or in recent years, under the North American Free Trade Agreement, to Mexico. But Mexican unions and industrial leaders have also worried about losing jobs, particularly during the Asian financial crisis of 1997–1999, to Asian countries which, because of their currency devaluations, gained a wage advantage over Latin American countries. And Asian countries that have been recipients of foreign investment, and thus jobs, during the 1980s and 1990s have been complaining in recent years about losing jobs and investment to even lower-wage countries such as China and Vietnam. No matter the country, there always seems to be another country with even lower wages.

The issues raised in this movement of jobs seeking low wages is one of fairness to parent-country workforces, of exploitation of foreign, low-wage labor forces, of motives for moving operations (such as escaping difficult and costly regulations and cultural demands – and, therefore, presumably, seeking less regulation and less costly management and HR practices), and of "lower" working conditions provided in foreign locales. Key to the charges is that foreign trade and investment both causes a loss of jobs in the home country as well as causing a reduction in wages, as employees have to take cuts in wages in order to remain competitive with their lower-wage foreign counterparts.[22]

For example, one of the major charges against many firms from developed countries that outsource work or establish foreign operations seeking lower costs for manufacturing or assembly is that these foreign operations often employ very cheap child labor in working conditions that would be labeled "sweat shop," or even slavery, in the firms' home countries. There is much disagreement over the validity of this charge. The charge is made and often pursued by the media and special interest groups (and, even, politicians and legislatures) who have an anti-business or anti-globalization agenda.

First of all, not all child labor is in the employment of subsidiaries of foreign or foreign-owned firms. In fact, most is not. The ILO reported in 1997 (using figures from major surveys conducted by the UN Children's Emergency Fund, UNICEF) that approximately 250 million five to fourteen-year-olds are employed, 50 percent of them full-time, and most of them in family or locally owned agricultural or small-business enterprises.[23] This figure breaks down to 153 million children working in Asia, 80 million in Africa, and 17.5 million in Latin America. And as bad as the situation depicted by these figures is, countries like Pakistan are now losing jobs to even lower-cost locales such as China.

And yet most people around the world agree that mistreating children is wrong. The difficulty arises in that they may disagree as to what constitutes mistreatment. For instance, most Americans and Europeans, today, consider child labor mistreatment (although in both places, the elimination of child labor as a fairly common practice is probably only fifty years or so old). But in countries in which economic conditions warrant child labor (e.g., it may be the only income in the family or the family works together in a shop or in agriculture), and laws and definitions of the family unit support it, it isn't regarded as cruel, but rather as a fact of life[24] (refer to IHRM in Action 7.1, "Child labor at Levi Strauss").[25]

At about the same time that Levi Strauss was developing its policies for its overseas suppliers, so also was Nike, although Nike was possibly being driven by lots of adverse publicity about the working conditions in many of its overseas subcontractors. Nike introduced a code of practice in 1992, but in May of 1998 put in place a major revision to its rules.[26] The company, which directly or indirectly employs around 500,000 people across the world, announced that the minimum age of footwear factory workers worldwide was to be eighteen; in apparel, meanwhile, no one under the age of sixteen was to be taken on, although existing under-age employees would not be dismissed.

The company also expanded its independent monitoring system to include nongovernmental organizations, such as Amnesty International, which were empowered to make spot checks on Nike subcontractors. In addition, Nike decreed that it would order only from footwear factories which offer some form of after-hours education to qualified workers, and extended its micro-credit program for employees wanting to branch out into self-employment projects.

Nike pays the locally mandated minimum wage or more, and in April, 1998, all twelve of its footwear factories in Indonesia hiked salaries by up to 15 percent to protect staff from the worst effects of the Asian financial crisis and the major Indonesian currency devaluation and the resulting economic downturn. In October of 1998, Nike announced the pay increase would equal a 25 percent increase over the

# Child labor at Levi Strauss

Levi Strauss has global sourcing and operating guidelines that address workplace issues. The company uses these guidelines to select business partners who will manufacture its products. Established in 1992, its guidelines were (among) the first created by a multinational company for its business partners. The terms of engagement detail everything from environmental requirements to health and safety issues. Among them: wages, discrimination, child labor, and forced- or prison-labor issues. To create these guidelines, the company used the Principled Reasoning Approach (a decision-making tool that Levi Strauss uses to teach its employees how to translate ethical principles into behavior). And to launch them, it conducted audits of contractors it was using worldwide.

Levi Strauss discovered that in Bangladesh it had two contractors using workers in the factories who appeared to be under-age. International standards have set a reasonable working age for factories at fourteen. When the company brought it to the attention of the factory owners, the owners asked the company what it wanted the factory to do. There were no birth certificates, so there was no way to know exactly how old the children were. Also, even if the children were younger than fourteen, they would very likely be a significant contributor to the family income and probably would be forced into other ways for making a living that would be more inhumane than working in a factory – such as prostitution or begging.

"So, we were faced on the one hand with a set of principles that were very clear, and on the other with the reality of under-age workers and severely impacting their family incomes," says Richard Woo, senior manager for global communications at Levi Strauss. The solution? "The contractor agreed not to hire any more under-age workers," he says. They also hired a physician to examine children who seemed to be less than fourteen years old, using growth charts identified by the World Health Organization. Although not hiring young workers may force them to find work elsewhere, Levi Strauss's position is to be ethically responsible for business issues it can control – such as responsible child labor conditions – as opposed to social conditions in a country that it has no control over.

Levi Strauss also negotiated for the contractors to remove the under-fourteen workers they already had from the production line and continue to pay them wages as if they were still working. In exchange, Levi Strauss covered the cost of the children's uniforms, tuition, and books so they could go to school. When the under-age workers reach the age of fourteen, they will be offered their original factory jobs back. The contractors complied with all this, "to maintain the contracts with us," says Woo.

government minimum wage.[27] And in March, 1999, Nike again raised its workers' wages in Indonesia to stay ahead of new government raises in the minimum wage.[28] Nike said the new package includes bonuses, housing, health care, transportation and meal allowances, and is designed to cover all the workers' individual needs. (Of course, some people, such as John Sweeney, president of the AFL-CIO, continue to think that much of what Nike has announced is merely "window dressing," and, in any case, does not represent serious effort to treat their foreign workforces with dignity.)[29] Additional information about Nike and other apparel manufacturers is provided in the section later in the chapter on United Students Against Sweatshops.

The attention given by the media and special interest groups to these plants in the Far East has also impacted other major firms with similar plants. For example, earlier in 1998, Reebok had announced a similar 20 percent increase over the Indonesian minimum wage for its workers in Indonesia. IHRM in Action 7.2 presents excerpts from Reebok International's code of conduct, adopted in the mid-1990s, under pressure from activist groups similar to that faced by Nike. Since firms like Nike and Reebok primarily use subcontractors in their overseas manufacturing, not wholly-owned subsidiaries or joint ventures, these codes of conduct address their relationships with their business partners, or subcontractors. As the Reebok code indicates, these codes address many human resource issues.[30]

As great as this sounds, particularly to Western customers and the public in general, it is not without controversy. Some experts suggest that this type of wage setting by large multinationals can cause significant disruption in the local labor market as local firms often cannot successfully compete for workers given this form of wage pressure.[31] As is so often the case with these types of international issues, the firm may look good at home in trying to meet the concerns of local activists, but not be seen as a good corporate citizen in the foreign locale because of what may be seen as unfair wage pressure put on local employers. And the experience in many locales has been that the underage employees let go under pressure from the parent firms have ended up in lower-paying and/or worse situations, such as begging or prostitution.[32] Their families need the income and there often are no other employment opportunities available.

The pressure on businesses to monitor the employment practices of their overseas partners is growing and no company is immune.[33] Firms as different as Nestlé, Starbucks Coffee, Reebok athletic shoes, Shell Oil, Wal-Mart stores, and Levi Strauss have come under fire in recent years for employment practices in their overseas subsidiaries or subcontractors.

In late 1998, a number of apparel manufacturers joined a new organization, the Fair Labor Standards Association, formed to monitor foreign contractors for sweatshop conditions.[34] But by 1999, many college student groups were organizing to get their schools to be even more strict in the investment of their pension and endowment funds and to require their store purchasers to buy apparel only from firms that met strict monitoring standards, including disclosure of locations for their subcontractors, monitoring by what they consider neutral parties, and payment of a living wage

# Excerpts from Reebok International's human rights production standards

1 *Non-discrimination*. Reebok will seek business partners that do not discriminate in hiring and employment on grounds of race, color, national origin, gender, religion, or political or other opinion.

2 *Working hours/overtime*. Reebok will seek business partners who do not require more than sixty-hour work weeks on a regularly scheduled basis, except for appropriately compensated overtime in compliance with local laws, and we will favor business partners who use forty-eight-hour work weeks in their maximum normal requirement.

3 *Forced or compulsory labor*. Reebok will not work with business partners that use forced or other compulsory labor, including labor that is required as a means of political coercion or as punishment for holding or for peacefully expressing political views, in the manufacture of its products. Reebok will not purchase materials that were produced by forced prison or other compulsory labor and will terminate business relationships with any sources found to utilize such labor.

4 *Fair wages*. Reebok will seek business partners who share our commitment to the betterment of wage and benefit levels that address the basic needs of workers and their families so far as possible and appropriate in light of national practices and conditions. Reebok will not select business partners that pay less than the minimum wage required by local law or that pay less than prevailing local industry practices (whichever is higher).

5 *Child labor*. Reebok will not work with business partners that use child labor. The term "child" generally refers to a person who is less than fourteen years of age, or younger than the age for completing compulsory education, if that age is higher than fourteen. In countries where the law defines "child" to include individuals who are older than fourteen, Reebok will apply that definition.

6 *Freedom of association*. Reebok will seek business partners that share its commitment to the right of employees to establish and join organizations of their own choosing. Reebok will seek to assure that no employee is penalized because of his or her non-violent exercise of this right. Reebok recognizes and respects the right of all employees to organize and bargain collectively.

7 *Safe and healthy work environment*. Reebok will seek business partners that strive to assure employees a safe and healthy workplace and that do not expose workers to hazardous conditions.

8 *Application of standards*. Reebok will apply the Reebok Human Rights Production Standards in our selection of business partners. Reebok will seek compliance with these standards by our contractors, subcontractors, suppliers and other business partners. To assure proper implementation of this policy, Reebok will seek business partners that allow Reebok full knowledge of their production facilities and will undertake affirmative measures, such as on-site inspection of production facilities, to implement and monitor these standards. Reebok takes strong objection to the use of force to suppress any of these standards and will take any such actions into account when evaluating facility compliance with these standards.

(see the section on United Students Against Sweatshops later in this chapter). Interestingly, leaders of some low-wage countries do not necessarily see enforcement of a "living wage" standard as to their benefit. They argue that they will lose jobs to lower-wage countries, hurting the local economy and the workers the standards are intended to help.

There are issues to be resolved in all of this, of course, such as defining "living wage" in countries where no government or even private data are available for the purpose. And the level of profits of the parent firms is also of concern. They have benefited from the cheap foreign labor, as have consumers, with lower-cost products, but global competition – which puts constant pressure on costs and thus product prices – also makes necessary the constant search for the cheapest possible labor.

There are many stakeholders in this discussion. And the nature of the eventual resolution of protection of all of their often opposing values and interests is not yet resolved. Further, the nature of the acceptable resolution of the ethical values related to this aspect of global business and global industry is not clear. Some suggest that it is in the self-interest of both MNEs and their customers in developed countries to actively support improvements in wages and working conditions and the elimination of child labor in the developing world,[35] while, as has been discussed already, others, often from the affected developing countries themselves, suggest caution as to method and implementation of such efforts. Later sections of this chapter present some of the solutions being proposed and implemented.

One interesting effort in the anti-sweatshop crusade is being supplied by Ben Cohen, one of the founders of Ben & Jerry's homemade ice cream, which was founded on principles of social responsibility (and which was recently sold to the Dutch-British multinational, Unilever).[36] Ben is founding in Los Angeles (where thousands of workers make less than the legal minimum wage and routinely work twelve hours a day cutting, sewing, packaging, and shipping clothes in dark, dangerous warehouses) the US's first high-profile "sweat-free" clothing manufacturer. While such clothes will cost slightly more than those produced in sweatshops, Ben Cohen is hopeful that college stores and others will be willing to market their output (and consumers will be willing to purchase at a slight price premium), specifically because it comes from verified "sweat-free" manufacturing shops.

## Labor relations

A number of issues related to labor/union relations can arise that present potential problems of ethics. Most of these are related to the degree to which an MNE accepts host-country attitudes toward unions, particularly if those attitudes and/or laws are different than those in the MNE's home country (or are different than those desired by the MNE's directors). For example, the MNE may come from a country where it can be union-free, yet now it wants to do business in a country where local law and history require employees to belong to one or more unions. Or the MNE may come from a country where it has a very adversarial relationship with its union(s), but may now be doing business in a country where unions are a highly supported and positive part of the employment relations landscape. How the MNE operates in this situation can be viewed as an ethical problem – does the MNE try to continue to operate union-free (or with a very adversarial attitude) or does it accept local practice? There have been many examples of MNEs operating in their foreign subsidiaries (or encouraging such in their foreign subcontractors) in a way as to frustrate the operation of local unions, even when in the local situation unions are accepted or even mandated.

## International standards

Official organizations, such as the United Nations and the International Labour Organization, and private groups are all working to develop standards for international economic conduct. This section describes a number of those efforts.

One of the earliest of these efforts, the Caux Round Table, was created in 1986 by Frederick Philips (former president of Philips Electronics) and Olivier Giscard d'Estaing (at the time, vice-chairman of INSEAD, the major French international business school) to bring together leaders from Europe, Japan, and the US, in order to focus attention on global corporate responsibility.[37] Including such major MNEs as Siemens, Chase Manhattan Bank, ITT, World Bank (France), Minnesota Mining & Manufacturing (3M Co.), Canon, and Matsushita, the group has developed world standards to measure ethical behavior. The standards are based on two principles: the concept of human dignity, and the Japanese doctrine of *kyosei* – the idea of living and working together for the common good to enable mutual prosperity.

The Round Table lays out seven general principles that range from the general edict to protect (and, where possible, to improve) the environment, to more specific ideas, such as supporting the multilateral trade systems of the world. Underlying these ideals is the assumption that respect for cultural differences requires sensitivity and some flexibility. The members of the Round Table agree to work to implement the agreed-upon standards throughout their global operations. IHRM in Action 7.3 presents excerpts from the Caux Round Table's "Principles for Business," as they relate to human resource issues.[38] These principles illustrate the results of one of the earlier efforts at finding common ground for internationally acceptable labor standards. However, because it is a private effort, there is no mechanism, other than public pressure and the moral force of members' attitudes, to enforce these principles.

## Interfaith declaration

From 1989 to 1994, representatives of Islam, Judaism, and Christianity met under the auspices of HRH the Duke of Edinburgh, HRH Crown Prince Hassan of Jordan, and Evelyn de Rothschild, to see if it would be possible and useful to draw up a set of guidelines on business ethics which would be applicable wherever economic activity

# Excerpts from the Caux Round Table principles for business

## Section 3 Stakeholder Principles

### *Employees*

We believe in the dignity of every employee and in taking employee interests seriously. We therefore have a responsibility to:

- provide jobs and compensation that improve workers' living conditions;
- provide working conditions that respect each employee's health and dignity;
- be honest in communications with employees and open in sharing information, limited only by legal and competitive restraints;
- listen to and, where possible, act on employee suggestions, ideas, requests and complaints;
- engage in good faith negotiation when conflict arises;
- avoid discriminatory practices and guarantee equal treatment and opportunity in areas such as gender, age, race, and religion;
- promote in the business itself the employment of differently abled people in places of work where they can be genuinely useful;
- protect employees from avoidable injury and illness in the workplace;
- encourage and assist employees in developing relevant and transferable skills and knowledge; and
- be sensitive to serious unemployment problems frequently associated with business decisions, and work with governments, employee groups, other agencies and each other in addressing these dislocations.

### *Communities*

We believe that as global corporate citizens, we can contribute to such forces of reform and human rights as are at work in the communities in which we operate. We therefore have a responsibility in those communities to:

- respect human rights and democratic institutions and promote them wherever practicable;
- recognize government's legitimate obligation to the society at large and support public policies and practices that promote human development through harmonious relations between business and other segments of society;
- collaborate with those forces in the community dedicated to raising standards of health, education, workplace safety and economic well-being;
- promote and stimulate sustainable development and play a leading role in preserving and enhancing the physical environment and conserving the earth's resources;
- support peace, security, diversity and social integration;
- respect the integrity of local cultures; and
- be a good corporate citizen through charitable donations, educational and cultural contributions and employee participation in community and civic affairs.

involving adherents of their religions took place.[39] The purpose of the resulting Declaration of International Business Ethics was to provide:

- A moral basis for international business activity.
- Some principles of ethical practice to help business people, traders, and investors identify the role they and their organizations perform in the communities in which they operate.
- Guidance in resolving genuine dilemmas which arise in the course of day-to-day business.

The principles upon which the declaration was based (which recur in the literature of the three faiths as the basis of human interaction and which were deemed to be applicable to business relationships) included justice (fairness), mutual respect (love and consideration), stewardship (trusteeship), and honesty (truthfulness). The declaration, then, proceeds to outline a code of ethical conduct that, among other concerns, includes a requirement to follow best practice relative to employees, particularly involving working conditions that are safe and healthy and conducive to high standards of work, levels of remuneration that are fair and just, and respect for the individual (whether male or female) in their beliefs, their family responsibilities, and their need to grow as human beings (which, by necessity, therefore, must include equal opportunities for training and promotion and nondiscrimination on the basis of race, color, creed, or gender).

The code has been translated and fairly extensively distributed throughout the regions of the world most represented by these three religions. The developers of the code are now trying to develop a dialogue to determine if the doctrines and business practices of other of the world's major value systems can be accommodated within such a code of ethics. And, again, there is no enforcement mechanism for such a privately developed code.

## International Labour Organization

As discussed earlier, the International Labour Organization (ILO) has long been involved with trying to establish basic codes of conduct for enterprises operating abroad.[40] These included:

- Employment: creating and promoting jobs, job security, eliminating discrimination in the workplace.
- Vocational training.
- Conditions of work and life: wages, benefits, and job safety and health.
- Industrial relations: freedom of association, right to collective industrial dispute resolution.

The goals of these principles were to:

- Inspire MNEs to make positive contributions to economic and social progress.
- Minimize and resolve difficulties that MNEs may cause as they operate worldwide.

In recent years the ILO has worked with a number of other groups to establish widely acceptable guidelines for MNEs. For example, the efforts of the OECD on banking and corruption as described earlier. Other guidelines are discussed in the following paragraphs.

# SA (Social Accountability) 8000[41]

In 1997, the Council on Economic Priorities Accreditation Agency (CEPAA) was founded by the Council on Economic Priorities (CEP, based in New York) in order to develop and manage a set of standards for "social accountability," i.e., a set of standards for treatment of employees that would be applied throughout a firm's worldwide operations (the standards are outlined in Box 7.1). The name for this set of standards is SA (Social Accountability) 8000. The intent is that these standards be viewed as comparable to the ISO 9000 quality and ISO 14000 ecological guidelines.

The SA 8000 certification process requires companies to meet uniform standards in the following areas: child labor, forced labor, health and safety, collective bargaining, discrimination, disciplinary practices, working hours, and compensation. The standards are derived from ILO treaties, the Universal Declaration of Human Rights, and the UN Convention on the Rights of the Child. The process was developed at the urging of the ILO and monitoring is accomplished by independent auditing firms.

The standards were designed by a group of representatives from diverse firms and countries/regions of the world in order to bring multiple perspectives to a discussion of these issues. These organizations included Toys 'R' Us, Amnesty International, Avon Products, OTTO-Versand (which owns Eddie Bauer), KPMG Peat Marwick, the Body Shop, National Child Labor Committee, Sainsbury's, the University of Texas, Abrinq, the International Textile Garment and Leather Workers' Federation, Eileen Fisher, Grupo MSA, Amalgamated Bank, Reebok, SGS-ICS, and CEP. SGS-ICS (an international firm focused entirely on independent verification of processes such as ISO 9000 and which has been in business since 1878) was chosen as the first organization to do certification auditing and granting of SA 8000.

While this approach to setting standards for social/employment policy remains controversial, many firms are interested in ways such as this to guide them in their approaches to employee relations and working conditions around the world and to defuse the public and political charges of unfairness and exploitation in their overseas operations.

One of the factors working against the SA 8000 approach is the competition from other organizations which are also developing social and labor standards for international business. The ILO passed such a set of standards in 1999 (Declaration of Principles and Rights at Work) and in early 1999 US President Bill Clinton announced intentions to seek funding for a multilateral program at the ILO to put basic labor protections in place in developing economies and to provide technical assistance to developing nations for the development of such labor standards. In

## Box 7.1 SA 8000 requirements

Social Accountability 8000 standards are based on international conventions of the International Labour Organization and related international human rights documents, including the Universal Declaration of Human Rights and the UN Convention on the Rights of the Child. The standard also requires compliance with prevailing laws, regulations, and other applicable requirements (such as contractual agreements). SA 8000 is a consensus standard specifying minimum requirements in the following areas.

- *Child labor.* The company must abide by laws governing minimum age, young workers, school attendance, working hours, and safe areas of work.
- *Discrimination.* The company must not permit discrimination on basis of race, caste, national origin, religion, disabilitiy, gender, sexual orientation, union membership, or political affiliation.
- *Disciplinary practices.* Corporal punishment, mental/physical coercion, and verbal abuse are not permitted.
- *Working hours.* The company must be in accordance with applicable laws: employees must not work more than sixty hours per week; overtime (over forty-eight hours) must be voluntary; and employees must be given at least one day off in seven.
- *Compensation.* Wages must be legal/industry minimum and must cover basic needs plus discretionary income; employers must provide benefits, handle deductions and not avoid labor laws through false apprentice schemes.
- *Forced labor.* The company must not engage in or support the use of forced labor or hiring with bribes or deposits required; it must allow employees to leave at the end of a shift and allow employees to quit.
- *Health and safety.* The company must provide a healthy and safe working environment, prevention of accidents and injury, health and safety training, clean and sanitary support facilities and access to potable water.
- *Freedom of association and the right to collective bargaining.* The company respects the right of all personnel to form and join trade unions of their choice and to bargain collectively.
- *Management systems.* The company must agree to: create a publicly available policy committed to compliance with applicable laws and other requirements; ensure management review; assign company representatives to oversee compliance; plan and implement controls; select suppliers based on compliance; establish a means to address concerns and provide corrective actions; communicate openly with auditors; provide access for verification of compliance; and show supporting documentation and records.

Source: CEPAA.

addition, there have been private interest-group initiatives, such as the Fair Labor Association (see the next section), which have also been developed to provide firms with guidelines in the area of employment policy for firms with operations in foreign countries.

Many large US employers who buy products from subcontractors overseas have been accused of major workers' rights abuses (such as Wal-Mart, Target, Kohles, Nike, Reebok, Levi Strauss, Sears, the Gap, Tommy Hilfiger, and J. Crew). These firms are seeking publicly acceptable ways to demonstrate the quality and fairness of their overseas operations. For them, as well as the thousands of smaller firms that operate affiliates in other countries or are subcontractors to the big firms, being certified as fulfilling the standards such as those set by SA 8000 or by the ILO provide just such demonstration.

## Fair Labor Association

The Fair Labor Association (FLA) was set up by Nike, Liz Claiborne, Reebok, and Phillips-Van Heusen along with human rights groups, under the auspices of a US presidential task force, to monitor a sample of a company's factories. The White House and the founding members have been unable to recruit additional corporate members, although about fifty colleges and universities have signed on to buy apparel from the founding firms. This particular effort was described earlier in the section on staffing.

## United Students Against Sweatshops

On April 15, 1999, student representatives from 100 colleges formed this organization to demand that universities get involved with creating a more rigorous monitoring plan than that available in either the FLA or the SA 8000 plan.[42] They want companies to publicly disclose the locations of their foreign factories so that human rights and labor groups can independently verify any monitoring and to independently monitor treatment in these facilities. And they want employers to pay a so-called living wage that meets workers' basic needs in different countries. This effort was also described earlier in the section on staffing. In July, 1999, this group took its efforts to strengthen conduct codes to Washington, DC, in a protest on the steps of the US Department of Labor.[43]

In spring, 2000, Nike agreed, under pressure from student activists and the USAS, to disclose fully the audits of all 600 of its subcontractors, so that they can be independently monitored. Indeed, the USAS has recruited about fifty universities and colleges to join its efforts to strengthen independent monitoring and has persuaded some to quit the FLA and join their efforts instead.[44] The FLA has been working diligently to develop an effective monitoring system and to hire competent auditors. But the USAS efforts may end the FLA approach and require redeveloping the methods and abilities for independent monitoring.

As mentioned earlier, many people question these efforts. They argue that forcing these types of standards on countries that are struggling to industrialize will likely cause the loss of the few jobs that exist, resulting in increased unemployment and poverty and forcing workers, particularly children, into other work with even lower pay and worse working conditions.

The approach suggested by Donaldson, described in the first part of this chapter, offers the point of view to compare these conditions with those present at similar levels of development in the now developed countries. Child labor and "sweatshop" conditions have only fairly recently been eliminated in developed countries (and in most there are still pockets of such conditions, although typically illegal), suggesting that this may be a necessary (albeit unpleasant) stage in development. These efforts to force the current standards of developed countries on to countries trying to develop may be a very ethnocentric approach to a difficult problem. Individual efforts like those of Levi Straus (IHRM in Action 7.1) and Reebok (IHRM in Action 7.2) may offer the best solution to this difficult ethical dilemma.

## Trade treaties

A number of regional trade treaties have incorporated some aspects of common practice in areas related to employment. These policies apply to all employers within the confines of these treaties. The most advanced – that is, incorporating the broadest coverage of issues – can be found within what is called the social policy of the European Union (EU), most of which was established under the Maastricht Treaty of the European Union in 1992. The North American Free Trade Agreement contains a "side agreement" that addresses labor issues, while other regional trade agreements (such as Mercosur in South America) typically do not yet incorporate employment issues. But it might be expected that, as the country signees of these agreements gain experience with such regional treaties, they might seek ways to codify many aspects of employment policy throughout the region covered by the treaty, so as to eliminate country advantages/disadvantages within the region and to, thus, eliminate internal disadvantages relative to foreign competitors.

## Ethics and international employees

In the end, the assurance of ethical behavior and conduct of firms that conduct business outside their home borders depends on the attitudes and behaviors of their managers, at home and abroad. Accordingly, it is suggested that businesses can take three steps to help ensure that their employees (managers at home, expatriates abroad, and their foreign employees) behave not only appropriately, but also ethically:[45]

- Develop a clearly articulated set of core values as the basis for global policies and decision making.

- Train international employees to ask questions that will help them make business decisions that are both culturally sensitive and flexible within the context of those core values.
- Balance the need for policy with the need for flexibility or imagination.

Given these three points as general guidelines for an overall approach, the following list of steps provides some guidance on how an MNE might ensure an effective implementation of ethical standards for worldwide operations.[46]

- Be clear about your reasons for developing a global ethics program. Is it for compliance reasons (at home or abroad)? Or is it an opportunity to build bridges across varying cultures and constituencies, a way to instill a common set of corporate principles and values in order to unite the firm and its customers and suppliers around the world? Within that purpose for an ethics code, design and implement conditions of engagement for suppliers and customers that fit it.
- Treat corporate values and formal standards of conduct as absolutes. That is, once the program is developed, do not allow local variations (except within the standards established in the program – see the rest of these guidelines).
- Consult broadly with people who are affected, including international personnel who will need to implement the program and junior-level managers who may be the people implementing the program in the future. Allow foreign business units to help formulate ethical standards and interpret ethical issues.
- Choose your words carefully. Many terms do not translate effectively into other languages, as was discussed in Chapters 1 and 5. Even the term (or concept of) "ethics" does not translate well into many other languages and cultures. Alternatives, such as managerial responsibility, corporate integrity, or business practices are less culturally loaded and easier to translate.
- Translate the code carefully. When communicating the code to operations in other countries, the firm must be careful to translate the meanings and to screen for parent-country biases, language, and examples.
- Translate your "ethics code" training materials. The same thing, of course, is true for training materials and practices. The training materials and activities also need to be carefully translated and carefully presented. For example, John Sweeney of the AFL-CIO, says that even though Nike claims that its code of conduct is translated and distributed to all the employees in its foreign contractors, independent monitoring in countries such as China finds that employees say they have never seen it.[47]
- Designate an ethics officer for your overseas operations. For all regions where there are a large number of employees, a local ethics officer should be appointed, preferably a native who knows the language and customs of the region.
- Speak of international law, not just US (or parent-country) law. Acceptance is greater when the reference is to "the law in many countries," or the codes of the United Nations, or the ILO, or even the OECD.
- Recognize the business case. In host countries, support efforts to decrease institutional corruption. And exercise moral imagination in dealing with cultural

differences that conflict with your ethical standards. Be identified as the international firm with strong integrity but one that cares about local conditions. Companies with such reputations often gain a competitive edge with consumers and employees, as well as with government agencies.

- Recognize the common threads. While it is important to understand and be aware of the significant cultural differences that do exist, fundamentally, people around the globe are more alike than they are different. They share many of the same priorities, interests, and basic ethical principles. Most of the time, the real challenge is how to communicate these principles effectively.

## Balancing the extremes: suggested guiding principles[48]

The preceding discussion in this chapter has pointed out the difficulties for MNEs in both adopting a host country's ethics and in extending their home country's standards. Even the traditional test suggested in the US – what would people think of your actions if they were written on the front page of the newspaper – is an unreliable guide, since there is no set of agreed-to standards for business conduct. Kidder says,[49] "the very toughest choices people face [in international ethics situations] are not questions of right versus wrong, but questions of right versus right."

Therefore, it might be suggested that companies need to help managers distinguish between practices that are merely different from those that are wrong. For relativists, nothing is sacred and, therefore, no practice is wrong. For absolutists, many things that are different are, because of that, wrong. Neither extreme provides much guidance in the real world of business decision making. Donaldson[50] suggests that the best solution to this dichotomy must lie somewhere in between.

Donaldson[51] recommends that, when it comes to shaping ethical behavior in their international operations, companies should be guided by three principles:

- Respect for core human values, which determine the absolute moral threshold for all business activities. These are generally found in all moral and religious traditions and include the following: individuals must recognize a person's value as a human being (respect for human dignity); individuals and communities must treat people in ways that respect their basic rights (respect for basic rights); and members of a community must work together to support and improve the institutions on which the community depends (good citizenship). Kidder[52] says his research reveals five core human values to be common across cultures: compassion, fairness, honesty, responsibility, and respect for others. These are quite similar to the core values reported by Donaldson.
- Respect for local traditions.
- The belief that context matters when deciding what is right and what is wrong.

## Conclusion

This chapter has discussed the issue of ethical conduct for IHR managers in the conduct of their enterprises around the globe. There are many issues that confront IHR, such as corruption, cheap foreign labor, sweatshops, and codes of conduct for managers and employees. A number of organizations have developed guidelines for international ethical behavior, particularly as it impacts these interests of IHR, and even others continue to put pressure of MNEs to improve their operations in their overseas subsidiaries and subcontractors. This chapter has provided some guidance for evaluating IHR policy and practice, but ultimately IHR managers must continue to be sensitive to country and cultural differences while seeking ethical approaches that fit their company as well as international standards.

## Points for further discussion

1 What international rules and standards are most relevant to Lincoln Electric operating globally?
2 Does Lincoln Electric currently follow international rules and standards?
3 Who is most responsible in an MNE for how it behaves in the global arena?

**Part II**

# International Human Resource Management in the multinational enterprise: policies and practices

# Global workforce planning, forecasting, and staffing the multinational enterprise

**8**

## Learning objectives

After considering Chapter 8, the reader will be able to describe:

- The components of the global labor market and the global labor force
- Differences among the traditional categories of international assignees such as PCNs, HCNs and TCNs
- The many other types of international employees that MNEs use in staffing their global operations
- How MNEs can decide which international employee to use in their global staffing decisions

## Key terms

- Global labor force, global labor market
- PCNs, expatriates, inpatriates, HCNs and TCNs, international assignees, international employees

Part I of this book laid the groundwork, that is, it described the environment for understanding the policies and practices of International Human Resource Management, as practiced in global enterprises. This second part describes those policies and practices.

The first chapter of this part introduces the nature of and problems associated with the planning and staffing of global enterprises' international operations. As the approaches to and strategies for conducting international business have become more complex and difficult, so also have the staffing options for such firms. The chapter begins by describing the challenges involved in planning the global workforce for an MNE. And then it describes the many options now being reviewed by MNEs for staffing their operations around the world. And it presents some of the problems presented in trying to evaluate which approach works best when.

## Global workforce planning and forecasting

As with employment planning in a purely domestic firm the objective of global workforce planning is to estimate employment needs and to develop plans for meeting those needs from the available global labor force. The term "workforce" applies to any enterprise's employees. The term "labor force" applies to the pool of potential employees, the labor market, from which a firm hires its workforce. The size of the labor force – and whether or not it is global – from which a firm seeks employees varies according to many variables, such as the participation rate of men and women in various locations, whether only local people would be expected to apply for a particular job, whether the education or skills required for a particular job would require a firm to seek job candidates from all over the world, etc. The first part of the chapter addresses these types of variables.

One of the key complexities added by operating in the global environment is that an enterprise's activities are potentially spread all over the world, in dozens or hundreds of locations, languages, and cultures. And the labor pool from which they draw staff is also located in all of those places, languages, and cultures (and, possibly and potentially, in all others, as well).

This chapter, therefore, provides a short overview of issues related to the global labor market (from which global firms draw their employees) and to global workforce forecasting and planning. Difficulties in preparing both the MNE's workforce demand on a global basis as well as the gathering of data for the labor force supply around the world are stressed. Many factors define the dynamics of global labor markets, including the quantity and quality of employment in a country, the levels of employment and unemployment (i.e., the labor force participation rates of various segments of a country's population), the quality and extent of education for various components of a country's population, and the occupational and industrial structures of employment in a country.[1]

Once workforce forecasting and planning are described, the chapter then describes the many options that MNEs are examining today in their actual staffing of their international operations.

## The global labor market and the global workforce

Enterprises that develop international operations must deal with the issue of finding staff in whatever location(s) the enterprise decides to operate. HR professionals can be asked to provide information about the adequacy of the local labor markets prior to the making of decisions about where to locate such operations or whether to participate in any cross-border acquisition, joint venture, or alliance. Then HR professionals are asked to ensure adequate staffing of these operations. Of course, in the case of ongoing operations, HR professionals plan for and implement their staffing on an ongoing basis.

The first part of this chapter looks at a number of issues related to an understanding of labor markets around the world. The intent is to provide some basic information that can help an MNE carry out its workforce planning, forecasting, and implementation.

## Availability of data

One of the major constraints for MNE workforce planning – particularly on a global scale – is the lack of accurate data about the nature of the labor force in most countries, particularly in less developed countries. Ideally, data such as labor force participation rates, levels of education and literacy, availability of skill training, and unemployment rates, by country and metropolitan areas within countries would be available to help IHR plan for local workforces. Usually these data are developed by an agency of the national government, or sometimes by international agencies, such as the International Labour Organization (ILO) or the Organization for Economic Cooperation and Development (OECD). For example, Table 8.1 shows the female participation rates (defined as the female labor force divided by the female population aged fifteen to sixty-four), according to data developed by the OECD. This table illustrates the range of female participation rates to be in the high 70 percent and 80 percent level for Scandinavian countries down to 34 percent in Turkey and 42 percent in Mexico. Such data can inform IHR departments of the possibilities for tapping into the female labor force in any particular locale, although the table also shows how rapidly the female participation rates are changing. And this type of data tells nothing about the types of jobs women perform in an economy or culture or their general levels of education and training.

But government agencies don't always exist or the data they provide are inadequate, inaccurate, and/or politically motivated. In any case, they often do not provide specific or adequate enough data for an IHRM department to be able to assess whether the people with the necessary skills and education are available or can be developed in any particular location to be able to staff planned operations.

This usually implies that IHR professionals must develop these data from independent sources. There are a few efforts, by national or local consultants, to provide such information.[2] And, often, basic data can be accessed from sources such as chambers of commerce, embassies, firms that aid foreign companies in local employee sourcing, etc. In addition, IHRM staff can often acquire some of the perspective, if not specific information, they need from other foreign companies that have prior experience in the particular foreign locale.

*Table 8.1* Female participation rates in selected countries, defined as the female labor force divided by the female population aged 15–64 (%)

| Country | 2000 | 1990 |
|---|---|---|
| Iceland | 83.1 | 66.2 |
| Norway | 76.3 | 71.2 |
| Denmark | 75.8 | 77.3 |
| Sweden | 74.6 | 80.6 |
| US | 71.7 | 68.3 |
| Finland | 71.3 | 74.2 |
| Switzerland | 70.3 | 63.2 |
| Canada | 69.6 | 67.0 |
| New Zealand | 67.7 | 61.4 |
| UK | 67.5 | 66.0 |
| Czech Republic | 64.9 | N/A |
| Luxembourg | 64.6 | 49.2 |
| Netherlands | 64.5 | 51.0 |
| Australia | 64.4 | 60.8 |
| Japan | 63.8 | 59.2 |
| Germany | 62.8 | 55.5 |
| Austria | 62.2 | 54.3 |
| France | 60.8 | 57.4 |
| Poland | 59.0 | N/A |
| Belgium | 57.8 | 51.6 |
| Ireland | 54.9 | 41.9 |
| Korea | 53.1 | 50.6 |
| Hungary | 52.1 | N/A |
| Slovak Republic | 52.0 | N/A |
| Greece | 49.0 | 43.5 |
| Spain | 48.9 | 40.2 |
| Italy | 46.0 | 43.8 |
| Mexico | 42.1 | N/A |
| Turkey | 34.0 | 38.2 |

Source: estimate based on OECD data available at www.oecd.org.

## Developed countries: aging populations and labor shortages

Probably the most important labor force issue for developed countries is the significance of their reduced birth rates, extending from at least the early 1960s, and their resultant aging populations.[3] In virtually all developed countries (and even some less developed ones, particularly in Central and Eastern Europe), there are more people retiring than there are available to fill the resulting open positions, let alone provide workers for any expansion of these economies. Table 8.2 demonstrates what this means for a select set of countries, comparing the extent of elderly populations for four developed countries and three less developed countries. At one end, Japan has almost a third of its population beyond their retirement age, and at the other end, South Africa has fewer than 8 percent over their retirement age.

The direct result of this is a labor shortage in the developed countries. Such labor shortages are particularly acute for positions that require high levels of education and expertise, such as in all areas of "high" technology, e.g., computers and their many applications, computer software, telecommunication, biotechnology, and in virtually all industries where application of technology is changing the way business is done. This leads to long lead times, often months or even years, to fill open positions. But, as IHRM in Action 8.1 shows, it is also an issue in developed countries for jobs at the low end of the economy, as well, such as in agriculture, restaurants, hotels, house and yard work, and construction.

Employers have reacted to this shortage in many ways, e.g., increasing their hiring of foreign immigrants and their recruitment of foreign employees, moving jobs "offshore," outsourcing work, subcontracting to retirees, hiring workers "in place" in other countries and using the internet and telecommunications for management and control, greater use of robots and computers to perform work, etc. IHRM in Action 8.1 illustrates how a hotel in Colorado Springs, in the US, found a way to access foreign workers to help meet its shortage of staff.[4]

Table 8.2 Share of population aged over sixty (%)

| Country | 1996 | 2010 |
|---|---|---|
| Japan | 21.0 | 29.8 |
| Germany | 21.0 | 25.1 |
| UK | 20.7 | 23.3 |
| US | 16.4 | 18.8 |
| India | 7.3 | 8.6 |
| Mexico | 6.2 | 8.1 |
| South Africa | 6.5 | 7.3 |
| World | 9.6 | 10.8 |

Source: estimates adapted from data from World Bank, *World Development Indicators*, 1998.

## The Broadmoor Hotel finds a new way to fill jobs

At a time when workers were scarce and the Broadmoor Hotel in Colorado Springs found its premier service and five-star resort ranking at risk, the hotel had to find a new way to fill jobs. Despite trying every conventional way to fill its jobs, the hotel still had at least 300 positions it couldn't fill.

The answer that the HR department came up with was to recruit staff from all over the world. Now, nearly a fourth of the Broadmoor's peak-of-season workforce of 1,700 workers are foreign citizens on temporary visas through various government programs. Broadmoor president Steve Bartolin thinks every country in the world is represented (obviously an overstatement), but also says, "We are still understaffed – we still have 100 openings, but that compares favorably with 200 to 300 positions we had three or four years ago."

Because of a general labor shortage in the Colorado Springs area, many other employers, ranging from high-tech giants to restaurants and construction firms, are using foreign workers to fill their labor needs. No single strategy solves the worker shortages for individual employers, but the Broadmoor's example shows that recruiting foreign employees can help employers cope.

IHRM in Action 8.2 illustrates another example of how firms are coping with the labor shortage, in this case how the Dutch have dealt with it by hiring the retired.[5] Indeed, all of these responses to labor shortages are intertwined as countries seek new ways to deal with the shortages. Various countries and firms are discussing the preferences of using various hiring options, ranging from immigrants to retirees to working mothers to robots and computers. Not all options are equally desired in different cultures and countries. And these shortages suggest to MNEs that are pursuing strategies to extend their global operations into developed countries that they must take into consideration the possible lack of availability of the types of employees they may need to staff those operations.

### Less developed countries: young populations and labor surpluses

The labor markets in less developed countries tend to be almost the opposite of those in developed countries. In most developing countries, the populations are very young (as sampled in Table 8.2) with resultant labor surpluses and high unemployment levels, particularly of people with limited education and job skills. Even so, in many such countries, particularly the highly populated ones, there are large numbers of individuals with higher education who are attractive to global firms from developed countries. IHRM in Action 8.3 discusses one way MNEs, particularly in high technology, are taking advantage of just such labor markets.[6]

## In the Netherlands, labor shortages are dealt with by hiring the retired

Frans Tuijntjes, a former pilot who has flown all over the world, is now selling men's clothing and loving it. Recruiting the elderly – men and women who are either bored in retirement or need to supplement their pensions – is a new Dutch strategy to combat their labor shortage. In a program referred to as 65+ the Dutch created an employment agency designed specifically for recruiting of the elderly.

Dutch companies find that their older employees are unusually motivated, experienced, and loyal. A short time ago, the Dutch welfare state was subsidizing retirement and encouraging people to retire early. Many people opted out. But now, with a labor shortage due to low birth rates over the last forty years and fast economic growth, firms are finding the tight labor market is hampering growth because they can no longer fill vacancies.

Interestingly, the labor shortage is prompting a national debate (in the Netherlands as elsewhere) on some sensitive issues: How many more immigrants should be let into the country? Can the government force people to retrain? Should the government raise the retirement age and if so by how much?

At any rate, the retired Dutch who have gone back to work are finding it a rewarding experience. Frans Tuijntjes, the retired pilot, says, for example, "I've sold airplanes, so I figured I could sell a suit." He says his part-time job at Marks & Spencer is a lot of fun because he gets to meet a lot of people and he can use his many skills, such as practicing his multiple languages.

For firms that want to set up shop in a developing country, IHRM's role in ensuring a good local workforce can be critical.[7] For example, when the Edinburgh-based marine service company BUE Marine moved into Azerbaijan's capital Baku to take advantage of its natural resources, it faced a catalogue of HR challenges from nepotism and theft to low skills and overstaffing and deceitful résumés. "When companies want a foothold in a developing country, they need to research labor costs, cultural differences, benefits, legal jurisdiction, and how to hire people locally."[8] In addition, firms need to carefully examine the role of government in contracts and enforcement. It falls upon IHRM to forestall labor problems and to provide information to senior executives on the costs of dealing with any issues, such as those identified above.

### Increasing diversity

One of the results of increased globalization and readily available technology and global communication on the global labor market is that education and skills are

## A world marketplace for jobs

It used to be necessary to bring workers to where the work was. But with the advent of the world wide web and the internet, it is now possible to send work to wherever workers are by putting together multinational project teams. This new style of employment is arising particularly in response to the computer and information industries' chronically desperate labor needs.

For example, one firm from Silicon Valley recruited from the web a group of doctorates in discrete mathematics and graph theory from as far away as Belarus, India, Israel, and Ireland, for a semiconductor design project. Team members never left their home countries and the team leader never left his home office. And the task group beat its deadline.

In industry after industry, as customers expect quicker service and competition forces shrinking product life cycles, employers are being driven to apply a "Hollywood model" to their tasks. They assemble the best talent available at the moment from anywhere in the world. When the project is complete, the team breaks up and the members move on to new projects. The end result is a new and highly efficient global labor market unlike any seen before.

increasingly available from almost everywhere, making potential employees available from all racial, ethnic, and nationality origins. This has the impact of dramatically increasing the level of diversity with which global firms must cope. In addition, employees for the global firm will come from groups that in the past and in many countries were not participating in the labor pool: young and old, male and female, disabled, married and single, any type of religious affiliation or none, etc.

### Labor mobility: emigration and immigration

The world is experiencing emigration and immigration on an unprecedented scale. Some of it is voluntary and some of it is forced. In either case, it is creating mobility of workers in such large numbers that it has to be taken into consideration as MNEs examine their options in hiring their global workforce.

Millions of people work outside their home countries, either as traditional expatriates (on assignment from their employers) or hired to emigrate to fill vacant positions in other countries. In addition, millions leave home to find work in other countries, either because they need better jobs or they seek international experience – and many never return. Millions are forced from their homes because of civil unrest or natural disasters and become permanent refugees. And treaties such as those signed within the European Union to facilitate regional trade can include provisions to facilitate movement of workers between member countries, in order to allow people to seek the best possible work opportunities, facilitate putting together high-quality workforces by drawing on talent from throughout the EU, and to eventually level the wage and benefit "playing field" across the member states of the treaty area.[9] Other treaties such as NAFTA and Mercosur do not yet include such labor mobility provisions, but if the European Union is developing the model for such regional trade treaties, it may only be a matter of time before other regions of the world also begin to look at ways to facilitate such labor mobility, as well.

One aspect of labor mobility that must be taken into account by IHRM workforce planning has to do with whether people want to move away from their towns or countries. Some people would argue that this is happening in unprecedented numbers. And others would argue that most people still want to grow up, work, and die in the same village or town in which their parents lived. In either case, in the global workforce planning MNEs need to be aware of where the talent is (or is willing to relocate to). IHRM in Action 8.4 discusses some of the issues MNEs face as they try to figure out where the talent lives or wants to live, so as to figure out where to locate their business operations.[10]

## Location, location, location

Today, it is still important to be located near your customers. But in the war for talent, it may be equally important to be located in the best place to attract the high performers and specialists your business needs. Over the last few years, specific locations have arisen as preferred places to live and work. High-talent employees can establish themselves in locales that enable them to create the life–work balance that meets their current needs.

So, where are such places?

As it turns out, people don't look so much at countries as they do at cities, and often it is small cities that provide the lifestyles they are looking for. For example, it includes Groningen, a small, obscure town in the north of the Netherlands, and Eindhoven, another small town – but major business location – in the Netherlands. Of course, the traditional, popular big cities continue to have appeal, but there are also new areas that are attracting the talent that today's MNEs need.

In Europe, this would include an area marked on the map by a gentle curve drawn from Barcelona, across southern France, northern Italy, Switzerland, and southern Germany, an area that already boasts the highest *per capita* income level in the world. The big cities of interest in Europe still include Amsterdam, Brussels, London, Paris, Nice, Berlin, Milan, Dublin, and Zurich. In Asia, these cities would include Sydney and Brisbane, Auckland, Singapore, Kuala Lumpur, Tokyo, Seoul, and Shanghai. If a global firm cannot find talent where its customers want them to locate, then maybe it needs to figure out where the talent is and go there.

IHRM IN ACTION 8.4

### Brain drain and job exporting

One of the major problems in the increasingly mobile labor pool is what many, particularly developing countries, refer to as a brain drain, as their educated and skilled workers leave for better paying jobs in developed countries. From the point of view of the developing country, they have expended many resources on the education and development of these people, who are seen as important to the continuing development of their parent countries, and it is therefore seen as wrong for developed countries to take advantage of their higher salaries and living standards to "pirate away" these valuable and irreplaceable human resources.

An alternative to this brain drain, and one that is increasingly pursued by many global firms, is to export the work and jobs of the firms of the developed countries to the foreign employee in his or her home country, rather than export the employee to the work or position in the developed country. Both sides can benefit from this arrangement: the firm gets top talent at a lower cost and the developing country gets to hold on to its top talent.

In summary, today's typical MNE, with operations in dozens of countries, has a workforce that spans the globe. The task of IHRM professionals in these firms is to facilitate the hiring of a competent, high-performing workforce that enables sustainable, competitive advantage throughout the global marketplace. As the above paragraphs illustrate, planning for and hiring such a workforce is a complex activity. It involves determining what education and skills are needed and figuring out where to find that talent and how to recruit and hire it. This is difficult enough for local hires for local operations. But it is even more difficult for talent that is in short supply and must be recruited from a global labor market. Technology may make this easier to accommodate, but no less easy to plan and manage.

The global marketplace for labor and the need for human resource planning on a global scale by global enterprises can be exceedingly complex. And yet the health of today's MNEs is a function of IHRM's ability to match their firms' workforce forecast with the supply of global talent. Indeed, "In a fast-changing global economy, world-class workforce planning is the key to success."[11] With global workforce forecasts and plans in place, MNEs next move to fulfill those plans through staffing.

## Staffing the multinational enterprise: an introduction

Staffing of multinational enterprises has typically been simplistically described as involving only three different types of international employee: parent-country nationals (PCNs), host-country nationals (HCNs), or third-country nationals (TCNs), the last of which can be either permanent or temporary immigrants into the countries in which they are hired, although this distinction is seldom made.[12] These terms appear to have first been introduced into the IHRM literature by Patrick Morgan, at that time director of international HR at Bechtel, in 1986.[13]

# Categories of international employees

Most of the attention of IHR (professionals and academics) has concerned itself with PCNs, who are typically defined as citizens of the country of the headquarters of the multinational firm and employed by the firm in the country of its headquarters. When such employees are transferred (posted/assigned) to another country, to work in a foreign subsidiary or other type of operation (such as a joint venture or alliance) of the MNE for more than one year, they are generally referred to as expatriates. When they return home, they are referred to as repatriates. Indeed, the management of the traditional expatriate has historically provided the primary time-consuming responsibility of the IHR manager (and the primary research focus of academics). Managing the expatriate is specifically the focus of the next chapter and the primary focus of the rest of the chapters in Part II.

Most of the literature in IHRM that deals with expatriates (individuals who are or have been on foreign assignment) assumes that all international "assignees" fit into this generic category. Studies have invariably referred to "international assignment experience" or "expatriate" to simply refer to someone who has been on a foreign assignment for more than one year. As will be illustrated in this chapter, there is a need to differentiate types of assignments and assignees, since they are not all the same and should not be managed in the same ways.

For example in a recent study on the impact of international assignment experience on MNE CEOs, the definition of "international assignment experience" was having been on a foreign assignment for more than one year.[14] In another study designed to determine reasons for MNEs' use of PCNs versus HCNs in their subsidiary staffing practices, the term PCN was undefined but assumed to refer to a person posted to a longer-than-one-year foreign assignment.[15] Indeed, almost all articles about "international assignment experience" reflect the same limited definition. In both a study of American expatriates,[16] and in a similar study of German expatriates,[17] only the (undefined) typical expatriate is discussed, one who is assumed to be on a foreign assignment of more than one year, with no differentiation of various types of assignment or experience or various types of assignees.

The second "generic" type of international employees are HCNs, defined as citizens of the country of a foreign subsidiary or joint venture who are hired to work in the subsidiary located in their home country. If they are relocated to the headquarters of the parent firm, they are generally referred to as inpatriates (although they are probably viewed by themselves and their home-country family, colleagues, and friends as expatriates from their home country). And when an MNE hires a citizen of a country other than the parent country or the country of the subsidiary to work in one of its foreign subsidiaries, this person is referred to as a TCN (third-country national). In contrast to the literature on PCNs and expatriates, there has been very little published literature on local nationals (HCNs) or TCNs, with the exceptions of short discussions in books about expatriates or IHRM.[18] Interestingly, MNEs are starting to devote more time to the strategic role of HCNs. A significant amount of time at HR professional conferences deals with HCNs and TCNs,[19] since they continue to be of importance to the staffing of MNE foreign operations. In addition, MNEs such as Microsoft, Siemens and Morgan Stanley are deciding to move more work from their domestic operations to locations such as India, China, Russia, and the Philippines. In these locations MNEs can find highly skilled and educated employees at wage levels far less than their domestic counterparts. This process of moving work from one's domestic location to one's international location is referred to as "offshoring".[20]

The almost exclusive focus in the HR literature on PCNs and expatriates has meant that IHR managers (and MNE executives) have had to implement their global staffing plans without all the information they need to make fully informed decisions about their employment options. One of the early reactions in IHRM and among various MNEs to the increasing complexity of global staffing was to seek a more generic term to describe the variety of expatriates. Thus terms such as "international assignee," or "transpatriate," or, even, "transnational" were developed, in an attempt to come up with a term that might describe anyone on a foreign assignment. Today, most businesses and consulting firms use the general term "international assignee" to refer to anyone posted to a foreign assignment. Yet, still, an international assignee is assumed to be a PCN on a typical expatriate assignment. Thus, even this term does not fill the need for a term that refers to all types of international employees. This chapter tries to fill that void by describing the many different options from which MNEs now select employees for various types of global assignments.

The literature described above places international assignees essentially into categories based on the employee's country of origin (parent-country, host-country, third-country). There has been, however, some literature that describes international assignees based on the nature of the assignment rather than on the category of the employee. The following paragraphs summarize these efforts.

## Task roles or purpose of assignment

The earliest article on the purpose of the assignment was published in 1974.[21] The categories described included the following:

- CEO – director or general manager of a foreign subsidiary.
- Structure reproducer – sent abroad to duplicate (start up) the domestic operation in a foreign locale.
- Troubleshooter – sent abroad to solve business or personnel problems.
- Operative – sent abroad to perform functional tasks, such as accounting, sales, or manufacturing, usually as a supervisor.

Others have used these or similar categories in subsequent research, also based on the purpose or role of the international assignee. For example, these general purposes have been described:[22]

- Top managers (e.g., general manager, director generale).
- Middle managers (e.g., chief accountant, sales manager, manufacturing manager).

- Business establishers (e.g., technology transfer, business start-up).
- Project employees (e.g., roll out new product, establish new procedures).
- Research and development (e.g., new product design).

A slightly different approach to the use of expatriate managers was published in 1977.[23] This article identified three motives for transferring executives abroad, including (1) to fill positions, involving the transfer of technology; (2) management development, to develop international and managerial expertise; and (3) organization development, involving, in the authors' view, the use of managerial transferees to coordinate and/or control foreign subsidiaries. This model has been most thoroughly studied in Germany, by Harzing[24] and many others, and reflects what many authors have reported: German firms seem to be more reliant on the use of expatriates than is the case for other European or American MNEs.

Harzing examined the control role of expatriates.[25] Specifically, she identified three control roles: (1) the *bear*, to implement HQ-dominated decision making and surveillance; (2) the *bumble-bee*, to socialize local employees and to effect cross-pollination between HQs and the subsidiary; and (3) the *spider*, to weave an informal communication network within the subsidiary, between subsidiaries, and between subsidiaries and home.

Another article has provided a different approach to the categorization of types of international assignments, also based on the purposes for the assignments.[26] These authors' research into the practices of primarily larger and more mature multinational firms found concerns about three issues: deploying employees effectively in the global arena, disseminating knowledge and innovation throughout global operations, and identifying and developing talent on a global basis. This led to the authors' categorization and analysis of four types of international assignments: aspatial careers (the traditional, long-term expatriate), awareness-building assignments (relatively short-term assignments to develop global perspectives and international management ability), SWAT teams (short-term projects to transfer technical processes and systems), and virtual solutions (electronically connected teams). This article provides an important step forward in our understanding of the variety of purposes for which international assignees are used and builds on the earlier efforts.

## Diversity in international assignees

An early article about the management of diversity in organizations discussed the similarities between managing cross-national workforces (expatriates posted from parent country to host country and inpatriates sent from subsidiary to parent country, with no attempt to differentiate different types of expatriate assignments or different types of expatriates) and intranational workforces (various ethnicities within a particular country), suggesting that many of the issues related to the adjustment and management of expatriates have application even within local workforces, due to the national origin, ethnic, and even language diversity found within many countries' labor forces.[27] This chapter suggests the same, but also expands the notion to focus on the many types and varieties of employees with international responsibilities beyond the traditional category of expatriate and inpatriate, which not only increases the diversity of assignees that must be managed but also the diversity of assignments, as well.

In addition to these articles, and a few short articles in the professional literature as cited throughout the rest of this chapter in describing particular nontraditional types of assignments, there have been few other published attempts to identify and analyze the wide variety of international assignees actually being deployed in various firms. Many researchers and writers on the subject of international assignees continue to use the terminology of expatriates and PCNs/HCNs/TCNs. Some researchers, however, are beginning to describe this subject using the term global staffing. Both descriptions are used in this chapter and the next.

With this in mind, the purposes of the rest of the chapter are to: (1) describe many other different forms of international employee now being utilized by various MNEs; (2) suggest some research questions about the strategic and effective utilization of these various types of these employees; and (3) provide some help for IHR professionals to identify when and where it is appropriate to utilize the various types of global staff and how best to select, prepare, compensate, and manage them. This introduction then feeds into the rest of the chapters in Part II, which provide more details for selecting and managing the international employee.

## Further options for global staffing

MNEs have particular concern for the global staffing and development of their employees and, through that, their ability to disseminate knowledge and innovation throughout their global operations.[28] This has led IHRM professionals to seek as many options as possible for international staffing.

Even though the use of expatriates has seemed to be a logical choice for staffing international operations – after all, the use of parent-country nationals seems to be most appropriate for the control and managerial tasks assigned them, particularly maintaining the policies and culture of the parent firm (as true for Philips as for Matsushita and Procter & Gamble) – several issues have arisen that have persuaded MNEs to seek other options.[29] Some of the issues (described in more detail in the next chapter) include the high cost of foreign assignments, difficulties in providing adequate training for foreign assignments and thus problems with adjustment of expatriates and their families, local countries' desires for hiring of local employees and managers, problems encountered in dealing with repatriates, and a growing suspicion that local hires may actually perform better.[30]

One result of this is that an approach to global staffing that continues to give the only priority to expatriates is coming to be a thing of the past.[31] "This arrangement was adequate in yesterday's international organization because leadership, decision-making authority, and organizational power flowed from the parent site to the foreign subsidiaries. Today, however, new technologies, new markets, innovation, and new talent no longer solely emanate from headquarters but are found cross-nationally, making the expatriate model obsolete."[32] Indeed, international managers can and do come from just about everywhere, not just the homes of the traditional large MNEs, as illustrated in the next section.[33]

The following is a list and description of other types of international employees that have been identified through observation of multiple MNEs, review of the literature, and through interaction with IHR professionals at many IHRM conferences and at their companies. Here, the term "international employee" (IE) is used (rather than international assignee, PCN, HCN, or TCN) to refer to the broadest possible characterization of employees who have international responsibilities in their jobs. All of these do play a role in the staffing of today's MNE.

## Domestic internationalists

These are domestic employees whose jobs entail frequent interaction with people in other countries (via telephone, e-mail, fax, or even snail mail) but who never leave home. These contacts could involve sales, procurement, or banking with people or businesses that are located outside the home country of the firm. These types of employees may be present in any firm with business in more than one country, even if the businesses do not export or import anything nor have operations in other countries.[34]

## International commuters[35]

These are people who typically live (and do most of their work) in their home countries but who regularly commute to specific foreign locales to perform some aspect of their work (e.g., sales people who work with specific customers, members of teams of various types, or managers who visit specific foreign locales on a regular basis). Such foreign visits are always very short term but are frequent. Or, conversely, the commuter may stay at the foreign locale for extended visits (probably staying in a hotel or company-owned or -rented apartment) but commute home frequently, even every weekend. Living next to a border with business on the other side (such as in San Diego with business in Tijuana, Mexico, or in Windsor, Canada, with business in Detroit) provides obvious opportunities for this type of international commuting, possibly on a daily basis. Another example is provided by managers or sales people who live at home, for example in one country in Europe, but whose business responsibilities take them regularly – even daily – to other countries in Europe.

## Employees on long-term business trips[36]

These IEs take international trips that last a few weeks or months at a time. They involve, for example, trips for negotiations (say, of a licensing agreement, a subcontract, a sale, a purchase arrangement, or an alliance), to check up on deals, to work with development teams, to work with staff in multiple countries, etc. These trips are *ad hoc* in that they involve nonrecurring business needs and typically involve parent-company managers and technicians, but could involve employees from regional headquarters or even foreign subsidiaries.

## Assignees on short-term foreign postings[37]

These are assignments that last less than one year (but more than a few weeks) and are increasingly used as a substitute for more expensive longer-term international assignments.[38] Employees on these types of assignments can be HCNs, PCNs, or TCNs and could be referred to as expatriates, inpatriates, or international transferees, depending on which direction, relative to the parent firm, they are relocating, although normally the term "expatriate" is used for individuals who relocate for a period longer than one year. These assignments are usually used for technology transfer or to establish new operations, but are also being increasingly considered as a tool for management development, to leverage this form of business travel to help increase the global mind-set among firm employees or to teach the global culture of the firm.[39] Short-term assignments are concentrated in the high-tech sector and in the pharmaceutical, diagnostics, and healthcare sectors.[40] Normally these short-term assignments do not involve the relocation of the employee's family. This international employee will probably live in a company-owned or -rented apartment or hotel room and will not be paid the traditional "rich" expatriate compensation package.

Increasingly, the term "extended business traveler" (EBT) is being used for this category of international employee.[41] Many firms have allowed this form of foreign assignment to take place without IHR becoming involved. It is often viewed as "just another business trip" and is used for the purpose of reducing the cost of overseas assignments. However, firms are beginning to realize that there can be hidden liabilities for country-specific noncompliance of tax and/or immigration regulations that need to be monitored. In addition, there can also be strategic policy and cultural issues that need to be addressed when substituting EBTs for longer-term international assignments, particularly when they are used in countries where the building of long-term relationships or critical cultural sensitivities are a cornerstone to business success.

## Assignees on intermediate-term (twelve to thirty-six months) foreign postings[42]

This is the traditional expatriate (normally considered a PCN, at least in US firms, where assignments have tended to be for this duration). Surveys find that 58 percent of assignments are up to three years in length, while 42 percent are for over three years.[43] Most of the IHR literature concerns itself with the selection, preparation, compensation, and management of this type of expatriate (both going to – expatriate

– and returning from – repatriate – foreign assignment). These IEs are usually used either to manage foreign operations or for control purposes (e.g., accountants or financial comptrollers) and are typically concentrated in the machinery, shipbuilding, manufacturing, chemicals and agricultural, and consumer products and retailing sectors.[44] Increasingly, as well, these types of assignments are used for developmental assignments for managers earlier in their careers in firms that are concerned about developing a more globally savvy management team.[45] These relocations normally include the IE's family and involve an incentive-based compensation package. Sometimes these employees are referred to as "permanent outbounds."

## Assignees on long-term (greater than thirty-six months, e.g., up to five years) foreign postings

These types of assignments tend to be used more by firms from countries, such as Japan, or in Western Europe, than, say, by US multinationals. But some US MNEs, such as PepsiCo, which use such long-term assignments, differentiate the long-term from the short or intermediate-term assignments.[46] These types of assignments obviously involve major commitments by the parent firm and would normally be managing director assignments for major foreign subsidiaries or to regional headquarters. They include major relocation incentives and involve the relocation of and support for the whole family.

## Permanent transferees

Often referred to as localization, this normally refers to the situation where a person in the previous category (long-term assignment) is converted to permanent local status.[47] These people stay in that one locale, usually for the rest of their career with that firm. They become permanent residents of the foreign country. The major reason for converting assignees to local status is to remove them from the typical, very expensive, expatriate compensation and benefit package, which is meant to keep the expatriate "whole" until they return to their home country. Since it is usually the individual's choice to stay in the foreign locale, fairness to local employees and to the firm dictate that the person be treated as other local employees, thus they are "localized," although many firms find it difficult to remove all the expatriate differentials. In reality, the typical expatriate who has stayed this long in a foreign assignment is living like a local, anyway, and has made the decision to become "localized" (even if they usually want to hold on to their expatriate support package).

## Permanent cadre[48]

Some organizations with lengthy international experience (such as Royal Dutch Shell, Nestlé, Unilever, the United Nations, CitiBank, and many countries' foreign diplomatic offices), employ international employees who spend their whole careers in overseas assignments. They move from one foreign assignment to another. They may maintain citizenship in a particular country, but in many ways could be viewed as employees with no home country (except of course, for diplomats). These employees are referred to as permanent cadre or globalists, and often receive some form of global compensation and benefit package. Most of the time this term is used to describe individuals who make their full careers with a particular MNE, such as a German who works for Siemens and for much of his or her career moves from one Siemens subsidiary to another. Infrequently, this term is used to refer to individuals who make their careers moving from one foreign assignment to another, but who work for many different employers. Many problems related to compensation and benefits (such as the portability and coverage of insurance and pensions) arise for IHR in the management of these employees, as they move from one country to another.

## Local hires

These are the traditional HCNs.[49] There is increasing focus on preparing and relying on local employees (referred to as a "localization strategy"). Generally the foreign country wants the foreign investor to employ local citizens as much as possible and the MNE often accepts the many business reasons for relying on local hires, as well.[50] Recruiting, selecting, training, and compensating such a "foreign" workforce can create major complexities for IHR, as will be discussed in the following chapters.

## International transferees

This category refers to people who are moved from one foreign subsidiary to another, but who maintain their home bases (in a foreign subsidiary) and usually return after such assignments to their home offices. This is usually done for development purposes (of foreign employees), but not seen as in the permanent cadre category. Large, mature MNEs, such as Unilever and Nestlé, use these types of assignments for their local employees to internationalize them and to teach them about the international operations and culture of the firm.

## Immigrants (a)

The traditional TCNs, employees hired either in the country of a subsidiary or as immigrants to that country but who are from a country other than that of the parent firm or of the country of the subsidiary and are employed by the subsidiary. When critical skills are short in a foreign locale, firms often recruit from anywhere and everywhere in order to staff their foreign operations.[51] Country immigration policies and how they affect companies can pose a major constraint for this strategy and are examined in Chapter 6.

## Immigrants (b)

People hired by the parent firm (either in-country or as new immigrants) to work in the parent country. (This is not typically the type of employee for whom the TCN term has been used.) Such people could be hired either as short-term hires or as permanent residents. These types of employees, particularly those with technical skills, are of increasing interest in many countries and MNEs and involve many issues for recruiting, selecting, compensating, managing, and relocating of "foreign" employees and are usually closely controlled by governmental visa requirements. This type of employee is also discussed in Chapter 6.

## Internships (temporary immigrants)

Some employers who are having a hard time finding employees during a tight labor market are resorting to recruiting workers from outside the firm's home country, for six-month to two-year internships.[52] Such a tactic is viewed as a way to recruit highly skilled workers (usually college students) and to screen them for potential full-time employment (and, of course, to fill a job need, at least on a temporary basis).

## Returnees[53]

These are emigrants who are hired (or selected) to return to their home countries (they could be hired in a number of places, e.g., the country of the parent firm or some other country and could be current employees or not). These types of assignees are possibly recent college graduates who have attended college in the country of the parent firm and who are recruited while going to school or shortly after graduation but are recruited solely for the purpose of assigning them to a position in their home countries. Sometimes these individuals are longer-term immigrants (usually they have become naturalized citizens of the country of the parent company) who are recruited because of an assumption that their familiarity with their country of origin coupled with experience after emigration with business practices in the country of the hiring firm will make them well suited to establish or manage subsidiary operations back in their countries of origin. Sometimes such emigrants seek the opportunity to return, e.g., to be involved in the development of their home countries. For example, in a highly successful strategy, KFC employed a first-generation Chinese American to return to China to establish its chicken restaurants.

These international employees may not be placed on a full expatriate compensation package, but rather may receive a form of hybrid compensation, with some aspects of the package received by a traditional expatriate and some aspects of local employees, although the typical form of compensation for this category needs to be further researched. During the 1990s, firms opening subsidiaries or joint ventures in Central Europe and China often sought emigrants from these locales to return "home" to manage or start up these new operations, such as GE's selection of an experienced Hungarian-American on its staff to be the initial managing director on its acquisition of Tungsram lighting company in Hungary.

## Boomerangs[54]

This term is similar in some ways to the previous term, "returnees," since its initial use evidently is in application to Japanese who are returning home to work in new career opportunities as well as to foreigners who have been on assignment in Japan and who desire to return, particularly for job opportunities in high technology sectors. Obviously, those who are most successful are those who have the language and cultural skills to maneuver through the complex Japanese business environment. Gradually, this term is being applied to equivalent individuals in other countries, as well.

## Second-generation expatriates

This term is being applied to naturalized citizens (immigrants) who are sent on foreign assignments, but to other than their countries of origin. They are seen as having had the "expatriate" experience so they may be more culturally competent and, thus, be more likely to adapt effectively to a new culture.[55] That is, they are seen as being "experienced" expatriates – having experienced the move from their countries of origin to their new countries – and thus may be more effective in a foreign assignment than people who have not had such experiences.

## Just-in-time

*Ad hoc*, or *contract*, expatriates.[56] These people are recruited from inside or outside the company. They are recruited only (and just) when the need arises, are hired because they possess the specific skills needed by the foreign assignment, and are placed on a contract just for the duration of that assignment. They receive no preparation and get no long-term commitment from the firm. They are strategically needed only for (typically) one to three years and are used only for that particular foreign assignment. Typically the need for this type of IE would involve some form of technology transfer, as exhibited by GTE in its use of just-in-time expatriates in order to fairly quickly recruit enough staff to start up its many telecommunication projects overseas during the 1990s. There is no long-term need for the individual's international skills, the firm doesn't want to worry about any career issues, and no ongoing employment relationship is inferred or promised.

## "Reward" or "punishment" assignees

A reward assignment is one in which an individual who is fairly late in his or her career and approaching retirement is sent on a desirable foreign assignment as a way to end his/her career in an enjoyable position and to add to his/her pension basis because of the increased expatriate salary. These types of assignees have been used by large MNEs, such as Unilever and Shell, with many years of overseas operations.

A punishment assignment is used to get rid of an individual for a while. This can be done by sending the individual to a hardship assignment or locale or just to a foreign location, away from the parent firm. This may be done for individuals who are for some reason "protected" or vested in the firm and cannot be terminated (or the firm just doesn't want to terminate them or it is too expensive to terminate them) yet for some reason they cannot be retained in their present position. This may be done, also, in firms that do not value highly their foreign operations, in general, or the specific locale to which the "punished" employee is being sent.

## *Outsourced employees*

This is a situation where the MNE decides to pay someone else for the services of an "employee" or group of employees. These people could be traditional "temporaries" hired from an agency, leased or rented managers or specialists, or a whole task or project outsourced to an external firm.

In recent years, global employment companies (GECs) have evolved, similar to domestic employee leasing firms, that can provide a few employees or staff a whole operation in an overseas location. This type of arrangement is used by firms establishing *maquiladoras*, staffing their cross-border plants in Mexico through employee "brokerages." Japan Tobacco International refers to its internally developed GEC as an "Overseas Payroll Company," which, the vision is, will eventually manage a large cadre of globally mobile employees. This source of IEs simplifies compensation and benefits issues, since all the employees (from the GEC) receive the same pay and benefits, no matter where they work within the firm, possibly with cost-of-living adjustments. Another use of outsourced employees is the practice of MNEs to have another company, such as Wipro in India, take over some of their operations. Typical work that is outsourced by MNEs to other firms, e.g. in Eastern Europe, India, and the Philippines, includes call centers and back office operations. Increasingly MNEs in the US and Europe are outsourcing more technical and professional work such as x-ray reading, software development, and research.[57]

## *Virtual IEs*[58]

This is a situation where all or most of the work is performed across borders via electronic media: tele-conferences, e-mail, telephone, video-conferences, fax, etc. The parties don't meet face to face (at least, not on a regular basis). In this context, it refers to situations where the parties who work together are located in two or more countries. Cross-border and virtual teams are described in some detail in Chapter 4.

These "virtual" international employees are often found in multinational (cross-border) project teams (e.g., R&D, product development, software development), management teams, control/audit teams, consulting teams, research teams. Some of the specific forms of business structure in which the virtual work relationships are found include: (1) shared partnerships across borders, such as in airline alliances; (2) core business with foreign satellites, such as with an MNE's local consumer product manufacturers; (3) virtual value chains (suppliers, vendors, financial, etc., such as high-tech or apparel firms where all the manufacturing is outsourced to foreign manufacturers); (4) integrated but not co-located firms, such as is true for the many global companies that make up ABB; and (5) electronic markets, such as B2B (business-to-business). Other terms that are often used here include "out of sight" employees and geographically dispersed or non-co-located teams, as well as electronic immigrants and cross-border telecommuters. Working across borders in this virtual form creates numerous problems with coordination (such as dealing with numerous time zones and varying holiday schedules), communication, language, and culture, and are clearly not appropriate or effective in every situation or with all employees or supervisors. Even so, increasing numbers of firms in the US and Europe are employing such virtual IEs.

## Individuals on self-initiated foreign work experience (SFE)[59]

This term refers to individuals who travel abroad (usually primarily to be tourists) but who may seek work as they travel, and it may involve a large (although unstudied) number of people.[60] The reasons for such travel may differ from region to region and such SFEs may be similar to – yet significantly different from – traditional expatriates, in nature of their assignments and in their treatment on normal IHR issues, such as compensation and benefits. To some extent, these individuals might often be what are referred to earlier as TCNs, although they are typically hired as locals.

## Retirees[61]

Some firms are tapping into their retirees for short-term foreign assignments, which can provide a new source of experienced employees for international projects and who may be willing to accept foreign assignments with reduced expatriate compensation packages. When retirees are not available or affordable, sometimes the International Executive Service Corps (IESC – not connected with Service Corps of Retired Executives or SCORE, which is a domestic US entity) can provide staff. This is an organization of retired executives, "volunteers," who accept assignments to foreign locales to aid in the establishment of businesses, usually in developing countries.

# Purposes of the various types of international employees

There are two issues that appear to have led to this use of these different types of IEs. One has to do with increased needs that firms experience as they increase their level of international commerce. And the second has to do with the problems they experience as they cope with these increased needs.

As new firms become engaged in global commerce and experienced firms become engaged in new and unfamiliar countries, both seek help from employees who before might not have been closely considered for international assignments. In addition, technology has made it possible (even necessary) to conduct global business in new ways. Thus firms are more likely to use domestic internationalists, virtual assignments, returnees and second-generation expatriates, and outsourced and just-in-time IEs.

When problems with the high cost of traditional expatriates, retention of repatriates, and increasing resistance from employees and their families to foreign assignments continue to go unresolved, firms rely more heavily on short-term assignments, extended business trips, commuters, local hires, returnees, and retirees. As firms recognize their need to internationalize their workforces and management ranks, they gradually place more emphasis on developmental assignments, such as shorter-term international assignments and international transferees. And problems with transfer of learning among units of global businesses (HQs, subsidiaries, joint ventures, partnerships) lead MNEs to pay more attention to the management of all their global staffs.

In summary, the above descriptions demonstrate the many different types of international employees, beyond the traditional PCN, HCN, and TCN categories. Many of these types, however, can be placed into the original categories (see Box 8.1), but most of them do not fit the "traditional" characteristics of those traditional categories, such as the length of assignment (three to five years) or incentive-based compensation and benefit packages. In addition, some IE types fit into two or all three of the categories, such as the international commuter or the employees on "virtual" assignments, who could come from any of the source countries, parent, host, or third. Thus the tradition of referring to all international employees as expatriates – or even international assignees – falls short of the need of IHR practitioners (and academics) to understand the options available for international staffing and to manage those various options and fit them to evolving international business strategies.

As this list of staffing options illustrates, the types of people being sent on foreign assignments are expanding – and in many enterprises, particularly the global firm as focused on in this book, almost all employees have some connection with the international work of the organization. Indeed, most of the workforces in today's MNEs are being "internationalized." This internationalizing appears to be occurring in all sizes and types of firms, in all industries, and in all forms of business, including the traditional forms of MNE using cross-border wholly-owned subsidiaries, licensees, subcontractors, franchisees, etc., as well as in such newer forms of business as cross-border alliances and international joint ventures.

## Box 8.1 International employee types linked with traditional categories

### Parent-country nationals

- Domestic internationalists
- Short-term foreign assignees
- Intermediate-term foreign assignees
- Long-term foreign assignees
- Permanent transfers
- Permanent cadre
- Returnees
- Second-generation expatriates
- Reward or punishment assignees

### Third-country nationals

- Immigrants (a)
- Immigrants (b)
- Internships
- Self-initiated foreign work experience

### Host-country nationals

- Local hires
- International transferees

### Multiple categories

- International commuters
- Long-term business trips
- Boomerangs
- Just-in-time assignees
- Outsourced
- Virtual "expatriates"
- Retirees

From a strategic IHR point of view, then, IHR must consider in its global workforce planning that the number of "regular" employees who have international components in their jobs are also increasing. This includes sales and service people who deal with foreign customers, purchasing agents who buy materials or products in the international marketplace, financial managers who deal with foreign investors and bankers, etc., but who never leave home to visit foreign locales. These types of employees need to be included as IHR plans its staffing, training, compensation, and benefits programs in this new global context.

## Global staffing choices: implications for multinational enterprises

IHRM professionals need to develop an appreciation for the fact that their responsibilities related to their international employees has become very complex. That is, they vary according to the particular form of international employee and their country of operation, the type of foreign operation (for example, wholly-owned subsidiary or international joint venture), or phase of globalization.[62]

This increased variety of employees presents all sorts of new challenges for the selection, preparation, deployment, and management of a global workforce. Not the least of these is the increased need by all managers – and for IHR managers in particular – for increasing their cross-cultural awareness, knowledge, and skills, their foreign language ability, and their overall management competency within this new international setting.

For example, firms have much to learn about how to manage the performance of a global workforce. The performance management of traditional expatriates, themselves, is not always handled well (this is discussed in Chapter 12), even though many global enterprises have many years of experience dealing with them. But the cross-national interaction among all the many different types of international employees described in this chapter and between global managers and IEs creates many new performance management problems, which become even more difficult as the variety of employees expands. All of these become critical concerns: the impact of national culture on performance and how it is defined, on standards for performance, on the review-ability of reviewers, on who reviews (their cultural experience and savvy), etc.[63]

Pay and support services are also likely to be structured differently for a short-term business traveler sent on an assignment for six months to finalize the start-up of a new foreign subsidiary than for a manager sent for three, four, or five years to run such a subsidiary. Differences would also be pretty important between the pay and support services of the immigrant or foreign student (and each of these would be different from each other) hired to return home to work in a foreign subsidiary in comparison with a person who makes a career out of moving from one foreign assignment to another. Compensation issues are discussed in more depth in Chapter 11.

The rest of the chapters in Part II will discuss the many problems of selecting, training, compensating, and managing this complex and varied global workforce. To the extent that it is possible, exemplary practices around the world will be described. And where such examples are lacking, the chapters will provide what information is available to aid IHRM in its strategic management of the global workforce.

Some of the types of questions that IHR and the global enterprise need to address in order to better manage their global workforces are suggested here to help guide the reader as she or he reads the rest of the chapters in this book. Some of these types of questions, providing descriptions of exemplary practices relative to the selection, preparation, and management of traditional expatriates, are finally being addressed.[64] But, as the rest of the chapters will demonstrate, there is still a strong need for additional research and observation. Indeed, even the traditional focus on three basic reasons for the use of international employees (to fill positions for technology transfer, for management development to develop international business competency, and to coordinate and control foreign operations) is no longer adequate.[65] The questions include the following:

- What is the extent of the use of each of these types of IE?
- How do the preparation and support for each of these types of IE vary? What form do the preparation and support take for each?
- Does the international strategy or structure of the firm influence the type of IE employed? Or, stated from the other direction, which type of IE tends to be used under which strategy (international, multi-domestic, global) or structure (subsidiary, joint venture, alliance, subcontract) or managerial orientation (ethnocentric, region-centric, geocentric)?
- Which IB or cross-cultural competency is required by which type of international employee? For example, does every type of international employee require full cross-cultural preparation, training, and support? Does every type need full knowledge of how to conduct international business?
- Which performance management problems arise for which type of international employee? And which solutions are most appropriate?
- Are there specific management, organizational, and IHR outcomes that differ according to the type of international employee? For example, do difficulties with performance or retention vary with type of international assignment? Do the staffing, training, compensation, and management solutions also vary with the type of international assignment?
- For which type of work and business purposes – management, sales, control, technology transfer, business development, product development, management development – are the various types of international employees used? Why? Which is most effective? Will the outsourcing and offshoring of this type of work continue? What will be the impact on the domestic workforces of MNEs that do this?

Purposes for these various employment or assignment situations will vary significantly. For example, these purposes could include any of the following: an ongoing assignment, a project team, a short-term negotiation of a deal, intermediate-term transfer of technology, longer-term managerial and control assignments, personal developmental assignments, or assignments to start new operations. Obviously the end result that is sought in each situation is different and the skills and competencies sought by the employing organization should also vary according to the purpose of the assignment. At the same time, the need for cross-cultural understanding and competency may be similar.

- Which types of international employee are most cost-effective? Which provide the best business results? The extent of the cost variances and the ability of IHRM to measure and to manage these differences (and the extent to which IE choices are made on the basis of these differences) needs to be examined. In the authors' experience, even though the costs of IE assignments are rarely measured, the benefits are almost never measured, making any assessment of return on investment (ROI) of foreign assignments almost always impossible. Since MNEs are under constant and strong cost pressures, it would seem that this should be an area for major attention (and for payoff from results of such attention).
- What are the best practices among various types of international firms in terms of the utilization of various types of international employees?

- Do varying types of IE experience differential amounts of stress or other forms of personal problems? Researchers have begun to look at issues such as stress as associated with varying forms of international activity, seeking, for example, to identify the extent and nature of particular problems associated with different types of international assignments.[66]

The UK's Cranfield School of Management has provided some clarification of uses for four basic types of assignments (short-term, long-term, international commuter, and frequent flyer) and the types of problems associated with each.[67] The types of problems examined included dual career/family issues, work/life balance, cost of assignment and administration, repatriation/career, tax management, cultural differences, stress and burnout, inconsistent policy and practice, and compensation packages.

The answers to the types of questions suggested here and the analysis of the problems can go a long way toward helping to fill the business need for ensuring the best (most effective, productive/profitable, and cost efficient) utilization of employees in this increasingly complex global business environment. In order for IHR to adequately fulfill its mission in support of the MNE's staffing, it needs to clarify which type of international employee works best when and for which purpose.

## Conclusion

This chapter first described the nature of the global labor market and the global labor force in the context of the multinational enterprise. The labor markets in developed countries were contrasted to those in developing countries, illustrating issues surrounding decisions as to where to locate international operations and where to seek skills that may be in short supply in an enterprise's home country.

The chapter also discussed workforce forecasting and planning for MNEs and provided a short, comprehensive, description of more than twenty types of international employees that have been identified as currently being used in various settings by today's multinational enterprises, in order to fill their strategic business needs and their subsequent workforce requirements on a global scale. The terminology that has been extensively used in the past to describe the traditional forms of international assignees was discussed and was shown to be inadequate, given the many types of international employees outlined in this chapter. Next the chapter discussed some of the implications of the complexity that surrounds the management of this expanded view of the international employee. The chapter ended with some questions that still need to be addressed about the most effective ways to develop, motivate, and compensate these many types of international employees and thus lead to better contribution by IHRM to the strategic management of the international enterprise. The following chapters address many of the issues, challenges, and practices in developing, motivating, and compensating international employees of MNEs. But first the next chapter further extends our discussion of global staffing.

## Points for further discussion

1 What types of international employees does Lincoln Electric use in China? In other parts of the world?
2 Did Lincoln Electric do a good job in planning and forecasting its human resource needs in China? In other parts of the world?
3 What are the trends over the next ten years in global staffing for Lincoln Electric in China and in other parts of the world?

# 9

# Staffing the global enterprise
## Selection of international assignees

## Learning objectives

After considering this chapter, the reader will be able to:

- Describe the general process of selection of international assignees (IAs) for international assignments
- Explain the major criteria used for selecting IAs
- Discuss the issue of failure in an IA assignment and reasons for it
- Describe many challenges to the effective selection of IAs
- Explain the essential nature of repatriation and inpatriation
- Describe the characteristics of successful IA selection programs and exemplary practices

## Key terms

- Repatriation, inpatriation
- Expatriate failures, expatriate success
- Cultural translator

## International assignees and international assignments

The staffing responsibilities for firms that operate in a multinational environment are very complex. In addition to normal domestic hiring responsibilities – which in today's global economy often involve the selection of employees from numerous nationalities and cultures – the international HR staffing manager takes on a number of new responsibilities.

Chapter 8 introduced the topic of MNE staffing, providing a description of global workforce planning as well as the traditional description of types of employees utilized by international businesses: PCNs (parent-country nationals), HCNs (host-country nationals), and TCNs (third-country nationals). And then the chapter provided a description of a much larger set of types of international employees that are being seen in today's MNE, only some of which fall into the traditional categories. This chapter focuses primarily on the issue of selecting traditional PCNs, or expatriates, although some of the chapter discusses the selection of the other traditional types of international employees (HCNs and TCNs) for international assignments. It also examines other common types of international employees, particularly as they relate to the discussion of PCNs, HCNs, and TCNs, such as inpatriates and transferees. Most of the time and effort of IHRM is spent in the management and administration of expatriates. Accordingly, most of this chapter and the rest of the chapters in Part II deal primarily with expatriates, although this is just one of several international employees that are referred to throughout this text as international assignees. The central concern in this chapter is the process of identification and selection of the best candidates for international assignments. Later chapters also deal with training and development, compensation, performance management, and the health and safety of international assignees in their international assignments.

Staffing for the multinational firm within its home country as well as hiring by its foreign subsidiaries can involve seeking employees from any of the above three traditional sources, as well as other, less traditional sources, as described in Chapter 8. But typical employment practices for managerial and often marketing and technical positions in foreign subsidiaries place heavy emphasis on the use of expatriates, particularly of the traditional type, i.e., employees on assignment for more than one year from the parent firm.[1] There are many reasons that MNE's transfer personnel from one country (the home country) to another.[2] These usually include the need to establish a new facility or operation; transfer technology to a foreign operation, solve particular problems or to use a particular expatriate's technical or functional expertise; ensure control of the foreign subsidiary by the parent firm, enhancing employees' career development; developing managers with global perspectives; helping to develop a common, worldwide organizational culture; and the training and development of local managers and technicians.[3] Research and observation suggest that there can be numerous reasons for the use of expatriates, but the key reasons still appear to be for their technical or functional expertise, for control, to start a new operation, and for managerial development purposes.[4] As the following quote suggests, increasingly, at least large MNEs are recognizing the importance of overseas experience for higher-level managerial positions (although as will be shown later in this chapter, the rhetoric may be stronger than the reality).

> What seems clearly true is that at many big companies – Ford, Coca-Cola, and Dow, for example – putting in time abroad is increasingly a required, and critical, step in an executive's progress up the ladder. To run a global enterprise, the reasoning goes, you need the ability to psych out the foreigner as a consumer, as well as a sense of how to get things done offshore. What better training for this than a tour of duty overseas?

Another, more subtle consideration may also be at work. A number of companies report finding that the personal qualities that enable an executive to negotiate his way through a job over there – an ability to think himself into the shoes of someone else, a capacity to make decisions even in the face of thoroughgoing ambiguity – are precisely those qualities increasingly needed at the top back here.[5]

But not all employees on foreign assignment, these days, are traditional expatriates, as explained in the previous chapter. Michigan-based Dow Chemical Company, a $16.7 billion diversified chemical manufacturer with facilities in thirty-one countries and 250 sales offices worldwide, illustrates how complex the movement of personnel from country to country can become. Dow has about 62,000 employees around the world, with at any point in time about 1,000 of them on assignment outside their country of origin.[6] Only 175 of these are US employees based abroad. Another 175 or so are non-US nationals now in the US (these are what is referred to later in the chapter as inpatriates). The remaining 650 expatriates are non-US employees based in other international locations, different from their home countries. (These are what was referred to in the last chapter as transferees.)

In addition, global businesses are also increasingly interested in staffing their foreign operations with local employees, including managers and technical staff. Pressure for the development of host-country nationals stems at least partially from governmental attitudes in many host countries (and in many large multinationals, as well), preferring the development of local personnel and managers. The need for large numbers of highly qualified personnel has also made it increasingly necessary to use larger numbers of foreign (host-country/local) nationals.[7]

> Most multinational firms favor hiring local nationals for foreign subsidiaries, home-country nationals at headquarters, and, where a regional organization exists, a mix of foreign and home-country managers for regional positions. Within this general approach, however, the nationality mix will vary with the nature of a firm's business and its product strategy. Where area expertise plays a major role, as in the case of consumer goods and/or a limited product line, the use of home-country personnel for overseas assignments will be minimal. Where product expertise is highly important and/or industrial markets are being served, home-country personnel will be used more extensively for foreign assignments because they generally have quick access to the home-country sources of supply and technical information. Service industries also tend to have more home-country personnel in foreign posts, particularly where the firm is serving home-country multinationals in foreign areas, as has been the case in banking.[8]

Thus, in the typical MNE of any size (and, for international businesses in total), there are divergent forces operating relative to the use of expatriates. Larger MNEs use a greater number of HCNs but also need international experience among their management team. So to develop this experience, they are increasingly likely to move managers from the parent company, as well as their foreign managers, to assignments in countries other than their countries of origin. Firms which are newly developing their international business, of which there are a constantly increasing number, typically early in that development rely heavily on expatriates from the home office (or parent-country managers and technicians) for the development of their international business, but also then need the assistance of local nationals to effectively expand their foreign activities.

However, in that situation where the multinational firm needs or wants to hire host-country nationals, the availability of local nationals with the necessary education and skills often becomes a major problem. Sometimes, there is simply a shortage of the needed local nationals, particularly with technical skills and in developing countries (although, with global communications and hundreds of thousands – if not millions – of students from the developing world getting higher education in developed countries, this is rapidly becoming less of a concern). This can result in the heavy use of PCNs in some countries and the ability to function almost without them in other countries.

> Among US multinational enterprises, for example, about 60 percent of their employees in Saudi Arabia are expatriates, but less than 1 percent in Western Europe. Although US firms have the bulk of their investments in industrial countries, more than 70 percent of the American expatriates that they employ are in the developing countries.[9]

Nevertheless, multinational firms throughout the world are increasingly concerned about hiring, developing, and retaining managers with international experience and global perspectives, as described pretty thoroughly in the next chapter on training and management development.[10] IHRM in Action 9.1 describes one such manager, Adel Zakaria, an Egyptian-born, naturalized US citizen, who is head of the world's largest manufacturing plant, the Waterloo, Iowa, plant of John Deere, America's second oldest company, founded in 1837.[11] John Deere is a diversified manufacturer of farm equipment and appliances and has a significant worldwide presence in more than eighty countries. As the insert indicates, Adel Zakaria fits the mold of the new, global manager – one who can do more than one job, in more than one language, in more than one country or culture.

The transfer of personnel from one country to another appears to be necessary, for a multitude of different reasons. But it is rarely an easy process. And it has always been a very expensive process yet critically important to the success of an MNE's overseas operations. Most of the rest of this chapter deals with problems associated with the expatriation process. However, some of the issues associated with the hiring of local and third-country nationals will also be discussed.

## Staffing with international assignees

The rest of this chapter describes and discusses the general topic of staffing with international assignees. This includes expatriates, repatriates, inpatriates, host-country nationals, and third-country nationals but mostly it refers to expatriates. And it includes procedures and criteria for selection and the many challenges that MNEs

# John Deere's competitive advantage

Adel Zakaria, an Egyptian-born naturalized American, is an example of a new breed of manager for global firms like John Deere. He's extremely well qualified technically – an industrial engineer with postgraduate work and several degrees. But best of all, he fits the multicultural, multilingual, multifunctional criteria of the global manager. He's a manager who can do more than one job, in more than one language, in more than one country.

Zakaria is very aware of the process that's put him where he is today – at the head of the largest plant in the world, the Waterloo Works, owned by the second oldest company in the US, John Deere, the diversified manufacturer of farm equipment and appliances founded in 1837.

The John Deere Company sees its foreign-born employees as an integral part of its worldwide organization. They're implanted and integrated into the global workforce. They broaden the company's perspective, enabling it to see beyond the dominant cultures wherever they have operations. The company is convinced that this helps it to maintain a competitive advantage as the diversity of its customer base continues to grow, worldwide.

Zakaria was born into a minority status in his own country. A Coptic Christian, in the overwhelmingly Muslim country of Egypt, he has been dealing with issues of prejudice and persecution since grade school and has evolved an effective world view. "I came to this country [the US] in 1968 when I was nineteen years old. I had a mechanical engineering degree from Ain Shams (Eye of the Sun) University in Cairo, and a desire to pursue my graduate studies." Zakaria is an early example of the "gold-collar worker" of today, highly skilled and highly sought after employees with advanced degrees from other countries who've done research in technical fields.

Zakaria says, "Those of us from smaller countries are usually more international in outlook. We have to be to survive. Some people I meet may unconsciously label me as a foreigner. But I refuse to be alienated. I'm a fully naturalized American with great respect for the rights and privileges I enjoy here. People make assumptions when they hear my accent and ask me, 'Where are you from?' And when I say, 'Waterloo, Iowa,' they say, 'Before that?' Then I say, 'Quad Cities' and they start showing signs of frustration. 'No, I mean before that!' and I answer, 'Buffalo, NY,' before I finally tell them I was born in Egypt. . . . We [foreign-born employees] must not allow others to alienate us."

He implies that if native-born Americans paid closer attention to the overall process of acculturation (which one can learn from the foreigners and recent immigrants who live and study in the US – we don't necessarily have to travel abroad to acquire this sensitivity) we could learn more about the specifics of what works and what doesn't

continued

and what products are desirable, with which groups, and why. And then, when we needed to do the adapting – for example, to the different preferences of customers in other countries – we'd already have some practice.

Zakaria went to work for John Deere at a time when they were going through major expansion of the firm into global markets and he had opportunities to work with some of the early global visionaries of the firm. The corporate engineering staff of which he was a part traveled to projects throughout the world, modernizing and expanding facilities in many manufacturing locations. And now Zakaria is one of the firm's executives who carries that vision forward. Whether speaking to business school students in Iowa universities, or visiting John Deere plants in Europe and Asia, or dealing with the Taiwanese, Indian, Mexican, and other foreign-born employees in the US, Zakaria works with the many levels of diversity in a completely natural way. He's internalized it to the point that it is second nature to him.

It is managers and employees like Adel Zakaria that will continue to give John Deere a competitive advantage in its global marketplace.

confront in their efforts to ensure the staffing of their global operations with effective and successful IAs.

## Expatriates

Expatriation has been historically viewed as the process of moving from the parent company or headquarters to foreign subsidiaries or "overseas" operations. But expatriation might better be viewed as the process of moving from one country to another while staying in the employment of the same firm. Thus this process can take many forms. At any particular location in the global firm, an individual manager may be a TCN and still be an expatriate from another country who is employed by and represents the parent company. Or she or he may be a transferee from one subsidiary to another. The last chapter provided even more possibilities. For these reasons, and others, most large MNEs, today, refer to their traditional expatriates as "international assignees." This chapter focuses primarily on the traditional expatriate, or IA, meaning someone on an international assignment for longer than one year. When it is necessary in this chapter to distinguish the traditional expatriate from some other form, other terminology will be used.

Expatriation continues to be a major concern for MNEs, even while it may be taking on new forms, particularly with large, global firms (refer to the previous chapter for a discussion of the many different forms that "international employees" are taking). For example, some firms, such as Unilever Corporation, the large Anglo-Dutch global consumer-products firm, move managers from company to company and country to country to help build global relationships and a common corporate identity and business culture among their management ranks.[12] More will be said about this in the next chapter. Nevertheless, it is clear that there still are many firms using expatriates to develop and manage their foreign operations.[13]

This is particularly true for firms that are new to operating parts of their business outside their home country. Expatriates are used to beef up the skill levels in the international subsidiaries. In many firms, international experience is seen as important for executive promotion. It helps managers shake off the assumption that products or methods that work at home will automatically work in foreign lands. Tours of duty offshore are seen as necessary to understand the increasingly important international components of these businesses. The foreign duty also helps the expatriate gain insights into how foreign competitors operate. And the same skills needed to work in different cultures and markets in foreign assignments and to make decisions in the face of the type of ambiguity often faced in an unfamiliar culture are often seen as precisely those skills needed at the top of multinational corporations. The international experience is often a way to give "fast track" managers experience in running good-sized operations without close oversight from headquarters.

But all of this takes time. In many big companies, globalization is being developed division by division. The firms want to develop a culture that values the international experience. So they try to produce role models, individuals who have gone overseas and returned and subsequently done quite well in their careers.

There is also a counter concern. Good business practice and local government pressures often dictate the use and development of local nationals. This conflicts with the ongoing desire by most MNEs to continue to use parent-company expatriates in their overseas operations, e.g., to help market their products, to transfer technology, for management development purposes, to reward long-time employees, and/or for control purposes. This places ongoing stress on the ability of firms to carefully select and prepare individuals for overseas assignments who will enhance the probability of the firm achieving its foreign-market objectives.

As suggested already, the roles and purposes for expatriation may well be changing. As MNEs increasingly develop (or hire) local nationals to run their overseas operations, it might be suggested that the numbers of expatriates may actually be on the decrease. Countering this possibility, though, is the increased use of expatriation for individual and organizational development purposes coupled with the obvious increase in the number of firms operating internationally. And as historical experience shows, firms that are early in the evolution of their international activity tend to use more PCN expatriates to manage and develop their international sales and operations than do more internationally mature firms.

As would be expected, there are no counts of the numbers of expatriates, either in the US or in other countries. But some estimates can be made. The Internal Revenue Service in the US reports increasing numbers of tax returns from US expatriates.[14] Surveys by differing consulting firms find varying results: some find a reduction in the numbers, some find an increase.[15] The explanation for the different findings, though, is probably found in the pattern of evolution of multinational firms: the number of expatriates for the first couple of years after international start-up is high, grows for a short time, and then tapers off to the minimum number necessary to ensure effective continuity of the international business. The survey results from most consulting firms come primarily from larger, more experienced MNEs. Thus they tend to show declining use of expatriates.

The use of expatriates is high during the initial stages of foreign operations in order to accomplish technology transfer, including production and management technologies, product-knowledge transfer, and staffing and implementing a start-up.[16] The number of expatriates will usually then decline as the firm's local managers and technical staff assimilate this knowledge. The number expands again as local operations become increasingly integrated into a global operational framework. In addition, as the firm becomes more global, it develops a need for international managers with more international experience as it develops its worldwide competitive advantages. But at this stage, these international managers may well come from any country, not necessarily, or even primarily, from the country of the parent company.

## Selection decisions

The selection decision is important. It needs to receive full management attention and support. Errors in selection can have major negative impact on the success of overseas operations.

In terms of the parent company, it is most important that potential expatriates be seen as able to perform both the specific tasks to which they will be assigned as well as to perform well in a different cultural environment. Thus, the first consideration for international firms is to fully understand the requirements in both technical and cultural terms of the jobs to which expatriates will be assigned as well as of the country of assignment. (Refer to Figure 9.1, "Successful expatriate experience.")[17] As with all HRM activities, a thorough job analysis of the foreign assignment (including an examination of the work environment) is necessary in order to make correct expatriate selection decisions.

Because of the nature of most overseas assignments, selections for international transfer are most successful when based on factors such as the following:[18]

- The maturity of the candidate (i.e., being a self-starter, able to make independent decisions, having emotional stability, sensitive to others who are different, and having a well-rounded knowledge of on- and off-the-job subjects to facilitate discussion with foreign colleagues and contacts who are often quite knowledgeable and interested in such topics).
- Ability to handle foreign language(s) (see discussion below).
- Possession of a favorable outlook on the international assignment by the expatriate and his or her family (i.e., s/he wants to go overseas).

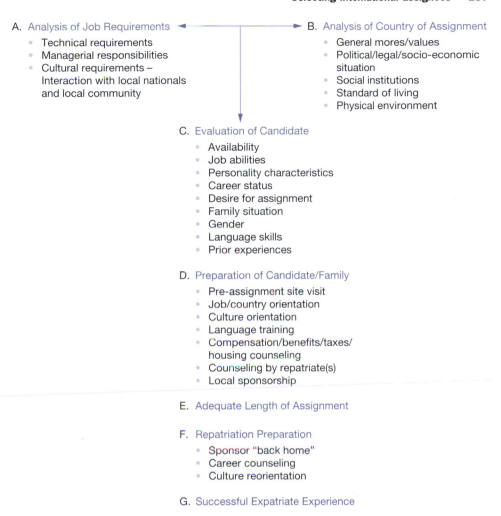

A. Analysis of Job Requirements
- Technical requirements
- Managerial responsibilities
- Cultural requirements – Interaction with local nationals and local community

B. Analysis of Country of Assignment
- General mores/values
- Political/legal/socio-economic situation
- Social institutions
- Standard of living
- Physical environment

C. Evaluation of Candidate
- Availability
- Job abilities
- Personality characteristics
- Career status
- Desire for assignment
- Family situation
- Gender
- Language skills
- Prior experiences

D. Preparation of Candidate/Family
- Pre-assignment site visit
- Job/country orientation
- Culture orientation
- Language training
- Compensation/benefits/taxes/ housing counseling
- Counseling by repatriate(s)
- Local sponsorship

E. Adequate Length of Assignment

F. Repatriation Preparation
- Sponsor "back home"
- Career counseling
- Culture reorientation

G. Successful Expatriate Experience

*Figure 9.1* Successful expatriate experience

- Possessing appropriate personal characteristics (excellent health, desire for the assignment, this is an appropriate time in the individual's career and family, individual resourcefulness, adaptability).

From the viewpoint of the persons being considered for transfer, studies suggest that two specific factors – in addition to a strong personal interest in the foreign experience, usually based on having previously enjoyed living overseas – are primary in their decisions to take on such an assignment: increased pay and improved career mobility.[19] This suggests the importance of paying close attention to these factors when making the selections for overseas positions. Both of these factors are discussed in later chapters.

From the company side, increasingly the problem of selection of expatriates involves finding managers with the necessary skills to function successfully in the new "global" environment. Table 9.1 lists the skills that are being cited as important for the twenty-first-century expatriate manager.[20] In the words of two MNE executives:[21]

"The top twenty-first-century manager should have multi-environment, multicountry, multifunctional, multicompany, multi-industry experience," according to Ed Dunn, corporate vice president of Whirlpool Corporation. Michael Angus, chairman of

*Table 9.1* The twenty-first-century expatriate manager profile

| Core skills | Managerial implications |
|---|---|
| Multidimensional perspective | Extensive multi-product, multi-industry, multifunctional, multi-company, multi-country, and multi-environment experience |
| Proficiency in line management | Track record in successfully operating a strategic business unit(s) and/or a series of major overseas projects |
| Prudent decision-making skills | Competence and proven track record in making the right strategic decisions |
| Resourcefulness | Skillful in getting him/herself known and accepted in the host country's political hierarchy. |
| Cultural adaptability | Quick and easy adaptability into the foreign culture – individual with as much cultural mix, diversity, and experience as possible |
| Cultural sensitivity | Effective people skills in dealing with a variety of cultures, races, nationalities, genders, religions. Also sensitive to cultural difference |
| Ability as a team builder | Adept in bringing a culturally diverse working group together to accomplish the major mission and objective of the organization |
| Physical fitness and mental maturity | Endurance for the rigorous demands of an overseas assignment |
| *Augmented skills* | *Managerial implications* |
| Computer literacy | Comfortable exchanging strategic information electronically |
| Prudent negotiating skills | Proven track record in conducting successful strategic business negotiations in multicultural environment |
| Ability as a change agent | Proven track record in successfully initiating and implementing strategic organizational changes |
| Visionary skills | Quick to recognize and respond to strategic business opportunities and potential political and economic upheavals in the host country |
| Effective delegatory skills | Proven track record in participative management style and ability to delegate |

Source: adapted from Howard, C.G. (1992) "Profile of the 21st-Century Expatriate Manager," *HR Magazine*, June, p. 96.

Unilever, adds, "Most people who rise toward the top of our business will have worked in at least two countries, probably three. They will probably speak another language and they most certainly will have worked in different product areas."

Selection decisions that are aligned with corporate strategy and goals is becoming more common.[22] As more firms go global, IHR faces increasing complexities in their role of identifying and developing talent, including those sent on international assignments. Although the strategies of different MNEs vary, successful global firms link their global staffing decisions with their global business goals. The more important the international strategy and the more complex the structure developed to implement that strategy, the more critical are the choices that the enterprise makes to staff its international operations.

Selection decisions also need to consider the receiving manager and location. Successful international assignments make demands not only on the IA but on the sending manager and company as well as the receiving manager and company.[23] Often the sending manager has never lived or worked outside his or her own country and, therefore, does not have a clear idea of what it takes to handle an international assignment. Receiving managers may have the same problem – they have not worked at headquarters or elsewhere outside their home countries and they do not know what strengths it takes for a successful expatriate assignment. The sending company, itself, can negatively impact the chances for IA success, as well, through its insistence on specific forms and timing of results that are drawn from the domestic experience and may not fit the overseas situation. These issues are discussed in more detail in Chapter 12 on performance management.

## Criteria for selection

The specific criteria an MNE uses to select its IAs has a lot to do with their future success in the foreign assignment. First, this section takes a look at a number of criteria that are used by various firms to select their IAs. Then the section examines the consequences of making mistakes in either choosing IAs or in preparing and supporting them in their assignments or helping them make a successful return to home.

- *Job suitability*. Most firms base their choices for international assignments on the candidates' technical expertise.[24] That is, the primary focus is on their ability to perform the target job requirements. Experience suggests, however, that all the other topics discussed in this text are at least as important as the individual's job competencies. Nevertheless, at least in smaller and medium-sized American firms, the supervisor usually makes the choice of individual to be sent on an international assignment and that choice is usually based on the individual's perceived ability to fill a perceived (and usually immediate) functional or technical need in the foreign operation.
- *Cultural adaptability*. Experience in MNEs suggests that cultural adaptability is at least as important to the successful completion of an overseas assignment as is the

individual's technical ability. Expatriates must be able to adjust to their new and often alien environments while effectively delivering their technical and managerial expertise. They must graciously accept their new cultures but not at the expense of not getting their jobs done. While technical expertise is usually important (and the primary reason most firms send a particular expatriate to a foreign assignment), the principle difficulty faced by most expatriates lies in the inabilities of the manager and his/her family to adapt to the foreign culture. American firms tend to be more likely to place the emphasis on the individual's work expertise.

● *Desire for foreign assignment (candidate and family).* Since adaptation to the foreign culture is so important to an IA's performance, his or her desire for that foreign assignment is critical to their willingness to make the necessary effort to adjust. This needs to be assessed in the early stages of candidate review.

● *Profiles of a successful international assignee.* Some companies and consultants have composed profiles of a successful IA. These profiles are then used to screen potential IA candidates, on the generally valid assumption that candidates with similar profiles are more likely to do well in the international assignment. These profiles usually include factors such as experience, education, personal interests and activities, signs of flexibility, family situation, and desire for such an assignment.

When an organization first begins to develop international business, it normally doesn't have the luxury of developing its own expatriate managers in-house. And it may not have employees who already have the necessary experience or cultural and language competencies. It will need to recruit such people from the outside or acquire the expertise from consulting firms. (Of course, many firms pursue international business with their own inexperienced managers and sales people, but this inevitably leads to months, and often years, of frustration while these managers "learn the [international] business.") And, then, such expertise can also sometimes be recruited from the overseas countries, themselves. And, over the long term, future foreign managers can often be recruited from local universities of either the country of the parent firm or the countries in which the firm plans to operate.

The primary purpose of the selection process is to choose individuals who will stay for the duration of their global assignments and who will accomplish the tasks for which they were sent overseas. Executives who make these choices should, therefore, consider both enterprise-based as well as individual- and family-based factors to enhance the probability that the international assignment will be successful.

## Process of selection

Different organizations rely on differing procedures in their selection of individuals for international assignments. They rely on varying criteria, as summarized above. And they use one or more of the following in application of those criteria. This is just a short summary of selection methods and illustrates that methods used in selection for international assignments is probably not much different than the methods used in domestic staffing decisions. As with everything international, however, the differences lie in the impact of culture in how these procedures are applied and in the focus in each procedure.

- *Interviews (IA and spouse/partner)* may be best done with a representative of the home office (representing the technical requirements of the position), a representative of the foreign office (possibly the host manager), and an interculturalist, i.e., someone with the ability to assess the candidate's and family's ability to adjust to the foreign culture.
- *Formal assessment.* There are a number of formal assessment instruments designed by industrial psychologists that primarily evaluate a candidate's personal traits that have been found to be important to successful foreign cultural adjustment, such as adaptability, flexibility, proclivity for new experiences, and good interpersonal skills. Critical here is whether or not any such instrument has been validated for predicting expatriate success. IHR or other managers who seek to use such instruments need to make sure they get evidence of their validity from any consultant or manager that is requesting their use.
- *Committee decision.* In many large MNEs, the process of selecting individuals for overseas assignments is a committee decision, a committee made up of someone from corporate HR, country HR, country manager, director of development, functional manager with a decision based on the individual's preferences, assessment of past performance and future potential, needs of the foreign assignment, and developmental needs of the individual candidate.
- *Career planning.* The choice of IA may be made as one step in the individual's career plan with the MNE.
- *Self-selection.* Many MNEs use some combination of the above procedures but rely, in the end, on self-selection by the candidate. In particular, the MNE is interested in candidates taking the time (and usually using some formal self-assessment instrument) to look at the issues involved with relocation to a foreign country and culture and assessing whether they think they are ready or have the necessary skills, experience, or attitudes to be successful in the overseas assignment.
- *Internal job posting and individual bid*, usually then combined with interviews and/or other assessment instruments.
- *Recommendations* from senior executives or line managers with overseas human resource needs.
- *Assessment centers.* A few organizations have used assessment centers as a tool for evaluating candidates for suitability for foreign assignments.[25] But it is rare for MNEs that use assessment centers to adequately think through the impact of culture on everything from the nature of the exercises used to the cultural sensitivities of the evaluators used, in order to be able to assess an IA candidate for an international assignment.

The actual techniques used are probably an extension of procedures used for domestic staffing decisions. Thus, there may be an *ad hoc* nature to this, using whatever technique seems easiest and quickest given the circumstances surrounding any particular need for an IA. Smaller firms are likely to use less formal and *ad hoc* procedures while larger, more experienced firms are likely to have developed more formal and standardized procedures.

## Failure in assignment

The firm must select managers who, with their families, will be most able to adapt overseas and who also possess the necessary expertise to get the job done in that foreign environment. Many firms that lack experience in international operations, as they try to increase their foreign sales, overlook the importance of the cultural variations in other countries. This attitude, combined with firms' inclinations to choose employees for the expatriate experience because of their technical abilities, generally leads to international assignments being made without the benefit of training or help in acculturation.[26] This may – and all too often does – lead to failure in the foreign assignment with premature return to the parent company and country, or even dismissal in the foreign locale.[27]

Success or failure for expatriates is usually defined in terms of early return to the home country. But success or failure is a more complex issue than this.[28] It might also be defined in terms of poor overall performance in the foreign assignment, personal dissatisfaction with the experience, lack of adjustment to local conditions, lack of acceptance by local nationals, or the inability to identify and train a local successor (see Box 9.1). All of these can be important to IHRM in planning the selection, preparation, and placement of expatriates.

In addition, a number of factors seem to influence the severity of expatriate failure rates (and help to explain why Japanese and European firms don't experience the high rates of expatriate failure experienced by many American firms). These include length of assignment (longer assignments appear to be based on the employer's willingness to provide the expatriate with more time to adjust and to "get up to speed" in terms of performance, which is more common among Japanese and European multinationals), receipt of training and orientation (with training and orientation about the new country and culture being associated with more successful adaptation), the lack of participation by HR in the selection process, too much emphasis placed in expatriate selection on the expatriates' technical expertise to the exclusion of attention to his or her other attributes that might aid in adaptation to the new foreign assignment, and lack of support provided by home office for IA and family while on assignment.

A number of surveys and studies have found the most important factors in the early return of expatriates to lie in the inability of their families (and/or themselves) to adjust to the foreign environment.[29] To the extent that preparation is provided, often the parent company will typically provide that preparation for the new assignment only to the relocating expatriate, not to his or her family. In addition, after arrival in the foreign location, the individual expatriates have the advantage of personal

## Box 9.1 Definition of expatriate failure

- Usually defined in terms of *early return home or termination*
- But could also be defined in terms of:
  - Poor quality of performance in foreign assignment
  - Employee not fully utilized during assignment
  - Personal dissatisfaction with experience (by expatriate or family)
  - Lack of adjustment to local conditions
  - No acceptance by local nationals
  - Damage to overseas business relationships
  - Not recognizing or missing overseas business opportunities
  - Inability to identify and/or train a local successor
  - Leave soon after repatriation
  - Not use foreign experience in assignment after repatriation
- *Compounding factors*
  - Length of assignment
  - Concern about repatriation
  - Overemphasis in selection on technical competence to disregard of other necessary attributes
  - Lack of training for overseas assignment

contacts with their colleagues at work, while their spouses and families are often left on their own to "figure out" their new surroundings and to develop local relationships, often with little understanding of the culture and an inability to speak the language. Thus the individual expatriate often finds adjustment easier and less "lonely" than does his or her spouse and family. Box 9.2 lists the most common reasons for expatriate failure, when defined as early return or termination from foreign assignment.

The expatriate's own ability to adjust and/or difficulty in merging with the new culture can also be a major handicap. Too often, expatriates bring stereotypes and prejudices – as well as strongly felt biases in favor of their own culture's way of doing things – that keep them from feeling comfortable in their new foreign assignments. And, lastly, when the employer makes a mistake by assigning an employee who lacks the necessary technical abilities or motivation to perform the foreign requirements, the expatriate may be sent home early.

The rate of early return for American expatriates varies in different companies (and in different surveys) from 10 percent to 80 percent (with a common failure rate in the 30–40 percent range) with the average cost per failure to the parent company ranging from US$500,000 to US$1,000,000 or more.[30] These figures don't include the cost to the overseas operations of the loss of such key personnel, or the costs associated with

## Box 9.2 Reasons for expatriate failure

- Inability of spouse/partner to adjust or spouse/partner dissatisfaction
- Inability of expatriate to adjust
- Other family-related problems
- Mistake in candidate/expatriate selection or just does not meet expectations
- Expatriate's personality or lack of emotional maturity
- Expatriate's inability to cope with larger responsibilities of overseas work
- Expatriate's lack of technical competence
- Expatriate's lack of motivation to work overseas
- Dissatisfaction with quality of life in foreign assignment
- Dissatisfaction with compensation and benefits
- Inadequate cultural and language preparation
- Inadequate support for IA and family while on overseas assignment

Sources: adapted from GMAC Global Relocation Services/Windham International, National Foreign Trade Council, and SHRM Global Forum, *Global Relocation Trends Annual Survey* Reports; Tung, R.L. (1987), "Expatriate assignments: Enhancing success and minimizing failure," *Academy of Management Executive*, 1 (2): 117–126.

the other forms of failed assignments. On the other hand, European and Japanese multinationals rarely experience failure rates over 10 percent, which seems to have to do with, in the case of the Europeans, more exposure to differing cultures and languages, and, in the case of the Japanese, the generally longer adjustment periods accommodated with the longer assignments (and, possibly, to the unwillingness in the culture to offend someone by cutting their assignment short due to performance or adjustment problems).[31]

## MNE mistakes in IA selection

Multinational firms typically do a number of things that lead to choosing the wrong IA, an IA that is likely to fail in his or her overseas assignment.[32] These include:

- Decision to relocate someone made with too little lead time.
- The spouse or partner is not included in the decision to relocate.
- Spouse/partner and kids not allowed on pre-assignment visit.
- Spouse/partner and kids not allowed language lessons.
- Spouse/partner and kids don't receive cultural training.
- Spouse/partner receives no counseling on jobs and other options.
- Spouse has no home office contact.

## Challenges to the successful selection of IAs

There are many challenges to MNEs in their quests to select the best employees for international assignments. The following paragraphs introduce eight issues: language, gender, family, lifestyle, localization (or "going native"), career development, costs, and candidate pools.

*Language*    One of the continuing issues with both IAs and foreign workforces concerns the issue of language. Do IAs on foreign assignment need to learn the language of the country to which they are posted? And to what extent do local workforces need to know or learn the language of the parent firm? These issues are discussed at some length in Chapter 5 on culture and in Chapter 10 on training and development. Like concern with cultural differences, concern with language differences also impacts most of international business. And it certainly is an issue with the selection of IAs.

Even though English has become the international language of business, it is just as important for expatriates to have a working knowledge of the language of the countries to which they are assigned. They need to speak their customers' languages – if their business relationships are going to flourish.[33] IHRM in Action 9.2 describes two American firms that have taken different approaches to providing language instruction, but both of which have found the increased numbers of employees who can speak foreign languages an asset in the development of their global businesses.

Language training, on a wide scale, can be quite expensive, in both employee time and in money. For example, Siemens, with over 400,000 employees around the world, spends millions of Euros a year for language training.[34] It offers ten languages, with training divided into eight stages all requiring eighty to 100 hours each. Lower-level executives are told that one and preferably two extra languages are necessary for continued success in the company. Siemens sees this as critical to its ongoing success as one of the most important electronics enterprises in the world.

In surveys of expatriates, language is often mentioned as the most important personal or professional challenge in their assignments.[35] An expatriate living in Germany says, "Speaking only English during an assignment is a big mistake. You can be a friend and a colleague speaking English, but to be 'one of them,' you must speak their language."[36] An expatriate in Brazil offers the advice: "Persevere with the language at all costs."[37] Often, one major factor in the inability of MNEs to fill key expatriate assignments is the lack of language expertise and preparation. And as is discussed in this section, many firms do not provide any opportunities for language training. Interestingly, some countries seem to understand this problem better than others. Maybe only a third of American MNEs provide language training, while, in comparison, almost all Japanese MNEs offer both language and cultural training.[38]

English has become the international language of business for a number of reasons.[39] These include the fact that English is the major language spoken in the home country of many of the major MNEs, e.g., MNEs which come from England and the US, as

# Language skills improve global business

Two American firms have found different ways to provide foreign language skills for their employees. At ARCO Products Company the downstream refinery and marketing arm for ARCO, now a division of BP Amoco, a pilot language training program was established after the firm began to explore business opportunities in China. When their technical team visited China all discussions had to be translated, and when the Chinese delegation visited the US to tour the Los Angeles refinery, again translators were necessary. Paula Johnson, ARCO Products' human resources consultant for international projects, thought that since they were still in the exploratory stages, the time could be well spent offering Mandarin classes.

After looking at a number of possible vendors, ARCO eventually decided on a national language training firm that could provide flexibility in beginning classes in LA, immersion for anyone being sent on assignment to China, and in-country follow-up training. Classes were offered during work hours, both at the company's LA refinery and at the firm's engineering and technology facility in Anaheim and were offered to anyone who was interested. The first classes began with twenty-eight employees but ultimately dwindled to ten. Learning Mandarin, with its tonal characteristics, is quite difficult. But ARCO now figures it has some employees who are positioned to help it develop its business opportunities in China.

The 3M Company has taken a very different approach. Thirty-five years ago at its company headquarters in St Paul, Minnesota, a group of employees used to gather at lunchtime to practice their German. Now this has become a well loved employee tradition and a unique company asset. It is called the "Language Society" and has over 1,000 members who are current or retired 3M employees or immediate family members, studying and practicing seventeen languages, taught by a cadre of seventy volunteer teachers from within the company. Participation in the language lunches has no official connection with employees' jobs, but over the years the lunches have produced a large number of employees, now dispersed throughout the firm's global operations, who speak a significant number of foreign languages. Of course, this training and practice has been quite helpful at corporate headquarters, as well, in areas like customer service, international sales, global sourcing, etc., where employees regularly interact with people from other countries. One additional benefit of this program at 3M has been that it has produced a large number of employees who are available to act as language tutors for both outbound IAs and inbound inpatriates. All of this has helped enhance 3M's global outreach and its reputation for being very focused on customer satisfaction.

well as the fact that English is also the first or second language in many other important countries, such as Canada, South Africa, Nigeria, India, Australia, Malaysia, the Netherlands, New Zealand, etc. In addition, many companies from countries whose languages are not widely known internationally, such as Japan, Korea, Hong Kong, Sweden, Norway, and the newly opened Eastern and Central European countries of Hungary, the Czech and Slovak republics, Poland, the Baltics, and the Commonwealth of Independent States, have found it necessary for their managers to speak English in order to be able to interact in international markets. Indeed, China even claims that today more people are studying English in China than speak it as a first language in the rest of the world. This may be an overstatement, but there are some 350 million Chinese now studying English!

Not all interactions are likely to take place in English, particularly within the host country. As stated above, dealing with customers, suppliers, and employees is often best done in the local language. But transnational exchanges are more and more expected to take place in English. When the top worldwide staff of Swiss-Swedish ABB Asea Brown Boveri meet, the one common language for their joint sessions is English. And when the Italian middle manager for the Milan, Italy, branch of Commerz Bank of Germany phones to headquarters in Frankfurt – which she must do many times a day – the conversation takes place in English. Of course, all the worldwide managers above a particular level for firms like Unilever (a Dutch-British firm), ABB Asea Brown Boveri, or IBM, or Toyota Motor Car Company, all of which operate in seventy or more countries, must speak English. And, even though it was controversial, when Euro-Disney opened in April, 1992, all of the 12,000 employees were required to be able to speak English, French, and, of course, the language of their home countries, if it wasn't French or English.

It is in fact now estimated that English is spoken worldwide by more people than any other language, by at least one billion persons.[40] One result of this may be that employing local nationals that are fluent in English may be as important as requiring expatriates to be fluent in the local language(s). Even so, it is clear that an ability to speak the local language is still quite important – for expatriates to deal with local nationals and local customers and suppliers, as well as to adapt to the host culture (and be accepted into that culture), both of which are major keys to successful expatriate experiences.

*Cultural translator*   One last issue involves the issue of separate languages being spoken by a parent firm and its subsidiaries and international joint ventures. In any situation where there is frequent interaction between headquarters and its foreign operations, the opportunity for mistakes, misunderstandings, and disagreements can be huge. This can occur in situations where contracts are being negotiated, the setting up of a new office, transferring technology to host-country workers and engineers, or even just in day-to-day communications between home office and host operations. Partially there is a need for a language translator. And partially, since language is so related to culture, there is a need for a "cultural translator," someone who can not only translate the words in such interactions, but who can also help both sides understand the cultural implications and nuances in meaning of the written and spoken words.[41] Such cultural translators can prevent conflicts from arising and smooth over conflicts that do arise and keep them from becoming major, costly, crises. In many countries where context is so important to understanding meaning, such as Japan, China, India, and Saudi Arabia, having such a person available can make the difference between success and failure of the foreign endeavor. Usually this is an expatriate who speaks (or learns) the foreign language and stays in the assignment long enough to learn the culture, as well. Again, the need to focus on IA candidates' skills and interests are so important. Becoming a cultural translator requires someone with the ability to learn the language and the willingness and interest to learn the culture.

*Gender* Most expatriates are men. Gradually, over the last twenty-five years or so, the percentage of women on international assignments, as determined by surveys, has increased from about 5–6 percent to 16 percent, or so, today.[42] This low percentage may have been as much due to stereotypes about foreign acceptance of women in professional or managerial roles as to the realities in the host countries.[43] Early research showed that one of the key factors in women not receiving overseas assignments was that selecting executives generally assumed that women would not be accepted in the foreign culture.[44] Other barriers to women receiving international assignments included their dual-career marriages, domestic managers not choosing them, perceptions that women were not interested in such assignments, etc.[45] In recent years the number of women who have successfully taken on foreign assignments, even to countries such as Japan, Brazil, and China, has risen considerably, although it still is a relatively small proportion of the total expatriate population, except in some industries, such as banking.[46] Of course the use of women expatriates, except in very specialized professional positions, is likely to remain very limited in some countries such as Saudi Arabia.[47]

The evidence, though, suggests that the fact that there are only a limited number of women working overseas for MNEs may be due more to bias and stereotyping in the parent country and company than to prejudice in the host country or foreign subsidiary.[48] Women not only welcome such opportunities (for the same reasons their male counterparts seek them), but often perform better than their male colleagues, even in traditionally male-dominated cultures, such as in Asia and the Middle East.[49] As an American professional woman on assignment in China put it,

> I feel more respected as a manager in China than I do in the United States. The Chinese value two qualities in their leaders: competence and *ren* [warmheartedness, benevolence, and readiness to care for others]. If a leader is *ren*, he or she will receive subordinates' loyalty in turn. Adopting *ren* behavior is more common by American female assignees than by American males.[50]

Typically, female expatriates are treated first as representatives of their parent firms or as professionals, and rarely experience the prejudice that the stereotypes from their home firms presume. This isn't meant to imply that women never experience stereotyping and treatment in line with cultural norms that may not accept women in the workplace, except in very menial tasks. This does happen.[51] But the evidence suggests that women are frequently quite successful in international assignments.[52]

In addition, women expatriates also have trailing spouses and families to consider, and thus need to be given the same considerations received by their male counterparts. Women are clearly interested in international positions and have demonstrated that they can perform well in global assignments.[53] Increased global competition pressures MNEs to make the best use of all of their resources, including their women employees.[54]

*Family*   Increasingly, multinational firms are confronted with new issues when assessing employees for potential expatriate positions – based on the new types of workforces they must draw from at home. Many of these issues deal with family problems. These new diverse workforces include managers in dual-career couples (which create special family needs and which involve problems with "trailing spouses" who have career concerns of their own and who follow their husbands/wives to the foreign assignments);[55] potential expatriates with unresolved problems with their adolescent children, health, dependent parents, or psychological difficulties (such as a flying phobia); male expatriates with wives who are trying to re-enter the labor force (which will be difficult to do in the foreign location); special education requirements for children (such as gifted children or children looking for colleges to attend); or individuals with unmarried partners (homosexual or otherwise). Ultimately, potential expatriate choices (or members of their families) with medical problems like AIDS, substance abuse or even alcohol abuse, or problems like multiple sclerosis, can cause what may seem like insurmountable problems for IHRM. These types of individual or family problems are both a problem in expatriate selection and a problem for acceptance into and adaptation to foreign cultures. And yet firms, in order to find the numbers of expatriates they need and to stay away from possible charges of illegal discrimination, must accept and find ways to accommodate IA candidates with these types of problems.

Many of these concerns make a health screening of the expatriate and his or her spouse and family members advisable, both to determine if a health problem exists that might either preclude relocation or be aggravated by a relocation. Often even minor health problems are not treatable in the foreign country because qualified health professionals or facilities are not available.

*Lifestyle*   Increasingly MNEs are having to deal with employees who either seek foreign assignments or who are eligible for such postings who live what might be referred to as "alternative" lifestyles that may not be acceptable in target foreign locations. This could involve "gay" or unmarried couples or single (unmarried) employees who may live with their parents or employees who are taking care of elderly parents. Or it might just concern employees involved in outside-of-work activities that are very important to the individual and they may not be able to pursue them in the host location. All of these situations create challenges for IHR to find ways to accommodate.

*Localization or "going native"*   One challenge with IAs that has been confronted by many more mature MNEs involves the expatriate that stays for an extended period (usually at the firm's request, but sometimes at the IA's request) in a foreign assignment (refer to the last chapter for more description of this issue).[56] They may be critical to the success of the foreign operation, but they have learned to live like locals, possibly have married one and are raising a family in the foreign locale, yet are still receiving an expensive expatriate compensation package. Many firms have developed policies (such as the IA having to "convert" to a local compensation package after some period of time, usually five years) to deal with this; but it still creates specific problems for dealing with this particular situation.

*Career development*   Since often it is expected that an overseas assignment is highly developmental, and since many firms now expect managers above some level in the organization to have international assignment experience, it is becoming more common to make a posting to a foreign assignment a critical part of an individual's career plan.[57] The challenge is to manage this process, both from the standpoint of the organization (where key managers may have their own ideas as to who they want to fill an open foreign position) and the individual, who may not see the career advantages. The firm may state the importance to one's career advancement; but observation suggests that expatriates on return to the parent firm are not always given assignments that use or take advantage of the foreign experience.

*Costs of international assignments*   This will be discussed in more detail in Chapter 11 on compensation and benefits, but the challenge is to contain the costs. Expatriates are expensive, both their direct remuneration (compensation and benefits) and the administration of their relocation. MNEs are dealing with these high costs with more short-term assignments and extended business trips. They are outsourcing the administrative aspects of managing IAs.[58] They are looking for ways to reduce the compensation incentives and add-ons that make international assignments so expensive.[59] And at least some MNEs are recognizing they can minimize the costs of failed assignments through developing better selection processes (that consider cultural adaptation as well as IA candidates' technical expertise), better preparation and orientation, better support services, and offering of language training, for both IAs and their families.

*Developing a pool of IA candidates*   One way that MNEs can develop more lead time to manage the IA selection process is to develop a pool of potential candidates.[60] This will involve early assessment, self-identification of interest and self-assessment for readiness, and possible early preparation, in terms of language training, cultural training, and other cultural awareness activities and training in international business. With such a pool of interested and qualified candidates available, when needs are recognized, IHR can refer to this pool of qualified candidates and can encourage (insist?) line managers to rely on the pool for identifying candidates for their open positions. And over time this will encourage line managers to get involved with earlier planning and identification of potential candidates for the pool.

# Repatriation

Repatriation is the opposite of expatriation: it involves the move of the IA back to the parent company and country from the foreign assignment. For many expatriates, the move "back home" is even more difficult than the original move overseas – and is a concern that is generally overlooked in the total expatriation process.[61] Because repatriation is often so difficult, it is just as important to manage the repatriation process as it is to manage the expatriation process.[62]

The overseas experience is generally challenging, exciting, highly developmental, and full of visibility and exposure for the expatriate. The expatriate is the representative of the parent company (i.e., headquarters) and is therefore looked to for perspective, help, and favors. In addition, because the compensation practices of most MNEs reward their expatriates quite well, the expatriate and family typically live quite well in the overseas location, often better than they do "at home." Thus expatriates usually return from such experiences quite "charged." They expect their employers to use their new experiences and excitement.

But if an MNE is to reap the benefits of its expatriates' learning while on foreign assignment, it is imperative that these valuable employees stay with the organization long enough to share their experiences. This should encourage MNEs to place a strong emphasis on the repatriation experiences of their IAs.

But the reality is more likely to be: "out of sight, out of mind." Firms often fail to use the experience or knowledge gained in the foreign assignment and most likely have not thought about the career implications of this experience. Typically, the repatriate is reassigned to a position similar to the one he or she left two or three years before. Repatriates often find it difficult to relate the value of their global experience to managers with a domestic focus.[63] Domestic managers, themselves usually without any international experience, cannot relate. For the repatriate, this makes the job search within the company upon return quite difficult.

The global experience may be viewed as helpful to the specific foreign situation; but the domestic manager usually views domestic experience as more important. To many domestic line managers, developing international experience and a global mind-set to operate internationally is the CEO's problem. Globalization is often not a concern to the line manager trying to achieve a specific set of local objectives.

For these reasons, career planning for expatriates needs to begin prior to an overseas assignment and be updated regularly during the assignment. The assignment needs to be part of a larger plan for the firm so that the repatriate returns to a specific position and expectation for using the international learning and experience. One of the programs used by some firms, such as Motorola, is a back-home mentor or sponsor, who is both a contact in the home office for the expatriate who is at least partially responsible for looking after the interests and prospects for the expatriate while on assignment, but who is also an avenue for keeping the expatriate informed about what is going on back home. In Motorola, this person is more than a mentor, being an at-home contact to keep the expatriate informed about what is happening in the parent firm, but is a sponsor, responsible for the expatriate's career back home and responsible for helping the repatriate locate that next position upon return.[64]

In addition, the repatriate and his/her family often also have trouble readjusting to the home lifestyle. Most people are changed by the foreign experience and not only must relearn their original culture and lifestyle, but probably view it very differently than when they left. Indeed, time does not stand still while the expatriate is abroad. While changes at home may be all but invisible to those who experience them gradually (those at home), to the repatriating expatriate, they can be overwhelming.[65] Just as MNEs need to provide their expatriates with preparation for the move abroad, so must they prepare their expatriates for the move back home and prepare themselves to use these individuals' overseas experiences in their home assignments. This preparation can make the difference between an overall favorable attitude by the repatriates about the whole experience and a failed expatriate experience. Ultimately, an unfavorable attitude will likely lead to the individual resigning and seeking a position with another employer that will utilize that individual's foreign experiences and skills.

The kinds of practices that MNEs have used to ensure a successful expatriation and repatriation experience include assigning a "sponsor" back home to look after the expatriate while s/he is away (including keeping the expatriate informed about significant events and changes back home and looking after the expatriate's career interests, including putting the expatriate's name into consideration for key openings when the expatriate is ready to return home), providing career counseling to ensure job assignments upon return that meet the needs of the repatriate, orientation for the expatriate and his/her family for adjustment back into the home culture, use of the skills acquired overseas in special task forces and projects, and special support networks for the repatriate and her/his family both during the overseas assignment and upon return home.[66] These steps go a long way toward ensuring a successful readjustment. IHRM in Action 9.3 describes how Monsanto Corporation has redesigned its repatriation efforts in order to more effectively use its expatriates and their international experiences, integrating them with their domestic operations.[67]

# Inpatriation

An inpatriate is an employee (HCN or TCN) who is relocated from a foreign subsidiary or joint venture to the parent company. This posting is usually for a relatively short period of time (one to two years) and is for the purpose of teaching the subsidiary or IJV employee about the products and culture of the firm from the perspective of headquarters.[68] Or, increasingly it could be to fill a functional or technical need for a limited period of time or to serve on a multinational team for a specified period of time. The challenges of selecting and managing inpatriates are basically the same as those for expatriates, except in reverse. Now all the issues are from the receiving end. Yet all the same issues are still present, such as effectively

## Repatriation at Monsanto

In 1992, Monsanto Corporation undertook a detailed change of its repatriation policy, concentrating on the logistical planning for returning its expatriates home, the kinds of skills and cultural development the company wanted its expatriates to learn, and the placing of its repatriates, after their return, in projects where their recent overseas experience was needed. John Amato, the manager of international assignments in human resources, says there was growing concern about the firm gaining from the personal and cultural development that expatriates were assumed to experience while on their foreign assignments.

Amato says that the repatriation process now begins six to eighteen months prior to return in both the host and the home countries. This primarily involves identifying a position for the expatriate to return to for which the operating unit is responsible. An extensive orientation program is also run for the employees and their families.

The repatriate orientation is exceptionally thorough: he or she is debriefed with peers and managers in the new job and is expected to provide recommendations about global development and to provide a view other than that of domestic Monsanto. Peers are expected to discuss the differences and changes in the organization that occurred while the expatriate was abroad. Managers are encouraged to free up repatriates for committees, work groups, and demonstrations where their new global knowledge is needed, over and above the employee's regular job. Repatriates are counseled to be aware of how much they and the organization have changed when they come back.

screening candidates, assessing cultural adjustment ability and technical skills, screening for family problems, schooling for children, housing needs, language, etc. And support services and cultural orientation and preparation are just as important to the inpatriate's successful adjustment as they are for the outbound IA.

## Host-country nationals

In general, MNEs staff their subsidiaries – at least below the top management levels – with local nationals (host-country nationals, HCNs).[69] At times, these workers may be supplanted by TCNs, described in the next section. Of course, whether or not there are enough potential employees with adequate training, education, and skills is always of utmost importance to an IHR strategy of staffing with HCNs. In the case where the strategic decision has been made to locate a subsidiary in a country where the local population lacks the necessary education or training, then IHR must find other ways to staff the necessary workforce, for example by training locals or hiring TCNs.

## *Relying on local managerial talent*

The expensive expatriate failure problem and a general trend toward geocentrism (a truly global approach to resources, customers, and employees) in recent years have resulted in a greater reliance on local managers in foreign operations.[70] Foreign nationals already know the language and culture and do not require huge relocation expenditures. In addition, host-country governments tend to look favorably on a greater degree of local control and the development and use of local personnel. Indeed, some countries require that most staff come from the local labor force. On the negative side, however, local managers may have an inadequate knowledge of home-office goals and procedures and have difficulty with the parent-company language. Thus the staffing of foreign positions – particularly key managerial and technical ones – is necessarily decided on a case-by-case basis.

In some ways this strategy may not be as easy as is sometimes suggested, either by the firms that want to follow it or the governments that encourage it. For example, in some countries with their own successful multinational firms, such as Japan, the best candidates take positions with their own country's companies. This leaves the foreign MNEs with having to rely on the "rejects" or the more risk-oriented local nationals, often those who have gone to school overseas. Two other categories of possible local candidates include young women graduates who prefer working for an MNE because they find more career opportunities than may be possible in local firms (owing to cultural attitudes about the role of women in the workplace) and individuals who are fluent in the language of the multinational. However, one problem that sometimes arises with the bilingual candidates is that they may get hired for their language skills rather than because of a thorough screening of their technical skills. Nevertheless, MNEs are increasingly likely to compete locally for managerial and technical talent at a time when local firms are increasing their own demands for these employees.

## Third-country nationals

TCNs tend to be used particularly in areas where there is either a shortage of the necessary type of workers, e.g., the use of Koreans in Saudi Arabia for construction projects by Western oil companies or Turks in Germany for unskilled jobs, or where there is relatively free movement of people from one country to another, e.g., within the EU. In recent years, with the global shortage of people with skills in information and computer technology, many firms have relied on the hiring of people from third countries with these skills to fill positions in their foreign subsidiaries, just as they do at home, as well.

Of course, the movement of workers will be driven by the growing gap between the world's supplies of labor and the demand for it (as described in the previous chapter). While much of the world's skilled and unskilled human resources are being produced in the developing world, most of the well paid jobs are being generated in the cities of the industrialized world – although this is beginning to change as more firms subcontract to firms in developing countries, hire employees offshore to work via telecommunications, and invest directly in operations in the developing world. The mismatch between where the potential employees are and where the jobs are has several important implications:

- It will trigger massive relocations of people, including immigrants, temporary workers, retirees, and visitors. The greatest relocations will involve young, well educated workers flocking to the cities of the developed world.
- It will lead some industrialized nations to reconsider their protectionist immigration policies as they come to rely on and compete for foreign-born workers.
- It may boost the fortunes of nations with "surplus" human capital. Specifically, it could help well educated but economically underdeveloped countries such as the Philippines, India, Egypt, Cuba, Poland, Hungary, Brazil, Argentina, South Africa, and, maybe, Mexico.
- It will compel labor-short, immigrant-poor nations like Japan to improve labor productivity dramatically to avoid slower economic growth.
- It will lead to a gradual standardization of labor practices among industrialized countries. By the end of the century, European standards of vacation time (five weeks) will likely be common in the US. The forty-hour work week will have been accepted in Japan. And world standards governing workplace safety and employee rights will emerge.[71]

Much attention has focused on the current or looming labor shortages in the industrialized world, particularly in the US, Europe, and Japan, due to the aging of the populations in these areas.[72] Yet the overall world labor supply continues to grow (primarily in the developing world). In addition, the growth in the labor force in the developing world is magnified by the entrance of women into the labor force, a phenomenon which has pretty well worked itself out in much of the developed world (although not all of it, as participation rates for women in the labor force are still quite low in some developed countries, such as Germany and Japan). When these demographic differences are combined with the different rates of economic growth between the developed and developing world, it becomes likely that firms in the developed world will increasingly seek workers among the excess in the developing world. Just as product and service markets have become or are becoming global, such will also happen to the labor market. In one sense, this may alleviate the labor surpluses among the developing countries of the world; but in another sense it may well exacerbate the economic differences between the countries of the developed world and those of the developing world as MNEs hire the educated and trained citizens of the developing countries, lessening those countries' available human resources for their own needs.

An extension of the focus on local managers, as described at the end of the previous section on HCNs, involves an increasing willingness to look for managers from all countries for assignment to any country. These TCNs are often the solution to overseas staffing problems. IHRM in Action 9.4 shows how a number of American MNEs have increased their use of TCNs.[73]

## Firms woo executives from "third countries"

Multinational firms are tapping more "third-country nationals" for overseas posts. Nationality matters less as businesses race to enlarge their ranks of global managers. So-called third-country nationals – neither Americans nor local nationals – often win jobs because they speak several languages and know an industry or foreign country well. The average number of third-country nationals (TCNs) per US company continues to rise from year to year, say consultants Organization Resources Counselors.

Pioneer Hi-Bred International employs twenty-nine TCNs in key jobs abroad, triple the number five years ago, partly because they accept difficult living conditions in Africa and the Middle East. Raychem has a dozen such foreigners in top European posts, up from eight a few years ago. "The numbers are going to increase" as Europe's falling trade barriers ease relocation, suggests Edward Keible, a senior vice-president. A Frenchman runs the company's Italian subsidiary, a Belgian is a sales manager in France, while a Cuban heads the unit in Spain.

Scott Paper, whose ranks of TCN managers have leaped to thirteen from two a couple of years ago, will step up recruitment of young foreigners "willing to move around Europe or around the Pacific," says Barbara Rice, HR chief.

## Successful expatriation

Expatriation success is the flip side of the issue of expatriate failure. Typically, expatriate success is defined as: (1) completion of the foreign assignment (as defined at the beginning); (2) cross-cultural adjustment while on assignment; and (3) good performance of the job while on the foreign assignment.[74] Sometimes these factors are viewed as a unitary construct, that is, they are seen as a package of issues that go together to define a successful assignment. But research shows them to be separate constructs, meaning that each needs attention.[75] And this demonstrates that the foreign environment (company and national culture and practices), local management, technical skills, and expatriate personal characteristics, as discussed throughout this chapter, all ultimately play a role in expatriate success.

Recent research by ORC (Organization Resources Counselors, a major IHRM consulting firm) found that international HR managers believe that dual-career-couple overseas assignments are one of the top five challenges they face.[76] According to a survey by Bennett Associates of accompanying career spouses, worldwide, active involvement in the career of the accompanying spouse is the type of assistance preferred by dual-career couples above all other possible interventions.[77]

According to surveys by Runzheimer International and ORC, nearly 50 percent of firms offer some form of spouse assistance for dual-career international assignees.[78] Of those firms, 87 percent provide *ad hoc* interventions (helping as and in ways that seem necessary) but only 13 percent have formal policies. Programs fall into three broad categories: personal adjustment; career maintenance; and offset of loss of income. Types of interventions – as appropriate – found in these surveys included the following:

- Pre-acceptance assessment sessions and site visits.
- Career and life planning counseling.
- Pre-departure and re-entry job hunting trips.
- Couple/family counseling.
- Specially adapted cross-cultural/language training.
- Relocation assistance to help spouse settle in and network quickly.
- Search firm retained.
- Company employment or consulting opportunities.
- Intra and intercompany networking and job search assistance.
- Visa and work permit assistance.
- Shorter-term assignments for expatriate employee.
- Commuter marriage support.
- Tuition and/or training reimbursement.
- Professional development trips.
- Child care provision.
- Partial compensation replacement for spouse.
- Increased employee compensation, bonus, and non-cash benefits.
- Re-entry outplacement.
- Tax equalization for second income.
- Spouse "inconvenience" or incentive payment.
- Set allowance to be applied to a "cafeteria" selection of assistance programs.

## Exemplary practices

A number of IHR consulting practices, surveys, and research projects have identified what might be considered "exemplary practices" in the selection of IAs.[79] In general, these reports suggest the following to maximize the effectiveness of international assignments:

- Involve HR in global strategic planning.
- Link each assignment to corporate strategies.
- Help assignees and their families make the smoothest transition into, during, and out of assignments.
- Utilize an assessment process that promotes the selection of the correct employees for international positions.
- Administer consistent international assignments through comprehensive programs that cover each step from design of the assignment to return of the employee and family.

More specifically, these reports suggest the following:

- Periodically review relocation policies and practices to ensure fit with current business and strategic situation.
- Train home office staff well in dealing with international assignees.
- Be honest about the job and location.
- Provide adequate lead time for relocation.
- Involve spouse/partner/family at the outset of the expatriation process.
- Provide language and cultural training for IA and family.
- Recognize the importance of dual-career and trailing spouse/partner issues, financially and otherwise (pre-departure job counseling, networking contacts, education or training, job hunting assistance, legal assistance for work permits, career assistance upon repatriation, etc.).
- Provide pre-assignment site visit for whole family,
- Don't neglect repatriation issues.

## Complying with local laws and culture

Because of the potential conflict between foreign and local practices in many MNE situations, the general practice that has evolved is for foreigners (such as expatriates and their families) to comply with the laws and mores of the countries to which they are assigned, whether or not they conflict with the individual's home-country laws or mores. Thus, for example, women expatriates (or female family members) while in Saudi Arabia, are expected to cover their arms and legs at all times, avoid wearing shorts, driving vehicles, walking unescorted, or chatting casually in public with men who are not their husbands. Women in Saudi Arabia can be expected to ride in the back of public transportation, and may be excluded from some stores. In addition, they may well be restricted in terms of the professional or work roles they can occupy. The local workforce should also be recruited and managed in accordance with local laws and practices, although not all MNEs have historically followed this approach.

## Support services

All surveys of IAs find that the quality of an MNE's support services for their IAs and their families are crucial to the adjustment process and ultimately to the feelings of satisfaction with the assignment. These support services are discussed in more detail in Chapter 14, but are also mentioned in the above list of exemplary practices and are discussed in the other chapters in Part II.

# Immigration law

A last topic of concern to IHRM staffing is the nature and application of immigration law. This issue becomes important to HR managers as they hire new immigrants, acquire visas for inpatriates, and work with HR managers and government officials in other countries as they get work visas for the managers and technicians they send abroad as expatriates. It is beyond the scope of this book to examine the wide variety of immigration regulations found in varying countries. Basic US immigration law (and its many categories of entry visas) is summarized in Chapter 6 on international employment law. But to be effective in the management of IAs, IHR managers of US MNEs have to gain some knowledge of the laws of each of the countries to which they plan to send expatriates. Because this area of responsibility is so complex, the typical IHR manager, though, will retain external expertise, e.g., a local law firm or one of the large, international, law firms, or, potentially, one of the law firms that specializes in immigration law (although they normally specialize in one country), to help with this.

## Conclusion

This chapter focused on the IHRM responsibility for staffing, but primarily on the issue of expatriation and repatriation, the movement of employees of multinational firms from either the parent company to a foreign subsidiary or from a foreign subsidiary to another subsidiary or to the parent firm. In the development of their early international activities, typical MNEs rely heavily on the use of PCNs. As they mature, they rely more heavily on the use of HCNs and eventually evolve toward staffing with employees and managers hired worldwide for worldwide needs.

This chapter examined the difficulties experienced in the selection and management of expatriates and repatriates and suggested some of the approaches successful MNEs use to ensure positive experiences with those expatriates and repatriates. In addition, the chapter discussed problems that MNEs experience with non-traditional expatriates, such as women.

The biggest issue for most MNEs in the management of their IA system, is the alignment of the competing interests of the firm, IHRM, and the IA and family. The business is concerned about its globalization and needs quick action, to generate new revenues, and to manage the costs and risk involved with doing that. IHR needs adequate lead time to find and select effective IAs; they need a low enough case load of IAs to be able to provide good service; they want to be able to apply an effective process for selecting and developing quality IA candidates; and they desire to be able to apply a consistent policy of treatment of IAs. And IAs themselves, and their families, desire adequate compensation for the personal and career sacrifice they make in relocating; they want their family concerns to be given central priority; and they expect the be able to come back to a career promotion that will take advantage of their overseas experience.

MNE experience suggests a number of steps that can be taken to ensure the success of international assignments. And when the steps are followed, experience suggests that MNEs will enjoy greater success in the global operations.

## Points for further discussion

1 Does Lincoln Electric do a good job in selecting its international assignees in China? In other parts of the world?
2 What can Lincoln Electric do to help ensure that its international assignees are successful in China and other parts of the world?
3 Should Lincoln Electric require that all its senior managers have at least five years of international experience? Why?

# Training and management development in the global enterprise

**10**

## Learning objectives

After considering this chapter, the reader will be able to describe:

- The role and importance of training in the MNE
- The nature of and problems with training of foreign workforces
- Issues of language and culture in the training of foreign workforces
- The training and preparation of international assignees
- The development of global executives in the global enterprise
- The nature and development of a global mind-set

## Key terms

- Cross-cultural adjustment, culture shock
- International assignees
- Global mind-set, global competencies, global leadership

Firms that operate in the global arena confront a number of special problems related to the training and development of their global workforces and managers. Responsibility for training and development is traditionally one of HR's core functions. So when an enterprise's international business reaches a significant level, when it is involved with multiple subsidiaries and partnerships in other countries, with the transfer of its technology to other countries, with developing and pursuing a global strategy, and with the assignment of a number of employees to international positions, the training and management development function takes on a new and more complex nature.

In this chapter, training and development is examined from the perspective of the MNE, including exporting training to foreign worksites and host-country employees, the special training needs of people on international assignments, and the design and delivery of global management development programs and the development of a management group with global perspective. All of these issues are critical to the success of the MNE; thus the MNE's IHR managers need to be prepared to develop and deliver training and development programs that will help the MNE achieve a competitive advantage in its global operations. It is the objective of this chapter to provide the basics for that responsibility.

## Training in the global enterprise

When enterprises operate subsidiaries and partnerships overseas, the training of the members of their global workforce takes on special importance and difficulty. Many IHR professionals simply try to apply successful training programs from headquarters. But often this doesn't work, as General Electric found out when it purchased a French medical equipment manufacturing firm, Cie Générale de Radiologie (CGR), in a bid to solidify GE's place as the leader in this industry.[1] Essentially, GE attempted to "Americanize" the French firm by establishing its successful, American, management systems. GE executives planned seminars for the French managers to socialize their new French counterparts into the "GE culture." The French managers were given T-shirts to wear at the seminars with the slogan, "Go for one," meaning "Our goal as GE managers is to be number one in the industry." The French managers wore the T-shirts but were highly insulted and humiliated, feeling they were being forced to wear uniforms, something which is anathema to the French. Needless to say, the seminar did not achieve its goal of building cohesion among the French managers and their new employer, GE.

In addition, GE posted English-language posters, tried to adapt the accounting system without understanding French accounting standards, shut plants and laid workers off, American-style, when it lost money the first year, resulting in 1,500 key employees quitting and creating a recruiting nightmare. In essence, GE lost a significant portion of its competitive advantage in Europe in this industry due to its cross-cultural misunderstandings, its lack of respect for anything French, and a poor HR strategy.

Under the best of circumstances, the provision of training programs, particularly programs so seemingly nebulous as cross-cultural training, are controversial among top executives. When competition is strong and there is heavy pressure to cut costs, as is generally the case with international competition, training budgets are often among the first areas that get cut. Even though executive rhetoric usually expresses the importance of maintaining a highly trained workforce, particularly in today's high-tech environment, many firms don't give training the priority the executives and their annual reports suggest is necessary. This low priority assigned to training and development turns out to be just as true in the international arena as it is on the domestic level.

Nevertheless, since a global enterprise's human capital may be its most important source of competitive advantage, a well trained and educated global workforce is critical to success in the global marketplace. Therefore, the following seven imperatives have been suggested as key to global organizational learning and training and development.[2] Further, these imperatives provide a statement of the values which underlie this chapter's discussion of training and management development for the successful MNE.

- *Think and act globally.* That is, a global enterprise must think about and prepare for a presence in all the critical markets in the world, not just its home region.
- *Become an equidistant global learning organization.* That is, learning from all cultures, anytime, in any manner possible, must be facilitated.[3] As Kenichi Ohmae, head of the Tokyo office for the global management consulting firm McKinsey & Co., says: "It may be unfamiliar and awkward, but the primary rule of equidistance is to see – and to think – global first. Honda, for example, has manufacturing divisions in Japan, North America, and Europe – all three legs of the [major markets of the world] – but its managers do not think or act as if the company were divided between Japanese and overseas operations. In fact, the very word 'overseas' has no place in Honda's vocabulary, because the corporation sees itself as equidistant from all its key customers."[4]
- *Focus on the global system, not its parts.* That is, development programs need to focus on breaking down the silos of departments and even the boundaries between countries and those that separate customers and suppliers and focus on the "big picture" global organizational system.
- *Develop global leadership skills.* Global leadership requires competencies different from those needed in the domestic marketplace. These should be the focus of global training and development programs.
- *Empower teams to create a global future.* Multinational and cross-border teams should be increasingly used and empowered to perform critical organizational projects and problem-solving activities. In addition, multinational teams can, themselves, be a major tool in the development of cross-cultural competencies.
- *Make learning a core competence for the global organization.* That is, the global organization needs to become a global learning organization, where learning and development permeates all that the organization does.[5] As Arie de Geus, former head of strategic planning at Royal Dutch Shell, puts it, "Over the long term, the only sustainable competitive advantage may be an organization's ability to learn faster than its competitors."[6]
- *Regularly reinvent yourself and the global organization.* That is, constant self-development must become the cornerstone of strategies for success for both individuals and organizations in today's highly competitive global economy.

The challenge of mastering the ever and rapidly changing and expanding global needs of individuals and organizations may be overwhelming. But it is exactly this challenge for IHRM which is addressed in this chapter on global training and management development.

## Training in foreign subsidiaries and joint ventures

The types of problems confronting the MNE when it begins to discuss the need for training of its local workforces around the world include the following:[7]

- Who should deliver training in the foreign subsidiaries and joint ventures? Trainers from headquarters? Local trainers? Independent trainers?
- How should the training be delivered? Are there local cultural differences that need to be considered?
- What are the effects of language differences? Will there be translation problems (for both written and orally presented materials)? Are there differences in the meanings of words? Are there terms and phrases that don't exist in the "foreign" language(s)? Who should take responsibility for translation? Headquarters personnel or host-country specialists?
- Should training programs be exported from headquarters? Or should overseas employees be brought to centralized or regional training facilities? Can training programs be developed in various locations and made available to everyone? What are the effects of the various options?
- Should courses for management development be handled differently than training for host-country and third-country employees?
- To ensure respect for each host country's culture, should each subsidiary or joint venture develop its own training? Do they have the capability? Or are there strong reasons to insist on centrally developed training programs?
- How does an MNE adapt a training program (in terms of both the content and the process of the training) to different countries and cultures?

Of course, part of the challenge for MNE trainers and IHR is that there are no easy answers to these questions. Because of that, many firms develop international training practices to fit their particular needs, resources, and assumptions about what should work best. IHRM in Action 10.1 presents the global training practices of a number of different major American MNEs (Johnson Wax, IBM, 3M, McGraw-Hill, and Merck) and illustrates both the variety of approaches and also some of the types of problems confronted and some of the complexities in designing and delivering such international training.[8]

### *Cross-cultural issues*

The approaches taken by differing MNEs to training of local workforces in their foreign subsidiaries and joint ventures range from total localization, with all training designed and managed at the subsidiary level, to total integration, with all training directed from headquarters and with the goal of full integration with the culture and perspectives of the parent firm, as described in the General Electric acquisition of Cie Générale de Radiologie. IBM's establishment of a subsidiary in Japan, where its goal was to run the company just like a Japanese company provides an example of the localization strategy.[9] IBM-Japan's compensation, training, reward, selection, and

# International training at Johnson Wax, IBM, 3M, McGraw-Hill, and Merck

Managing and delivering workforce training on a global basis can be a highly complex responsibility. Here are the approaches of five very different global firms.

Johnson Wax, of Racine, Wisconsin, designs and often delivers training for forty-five different subsidiaries around the world. The director of training indicates that they do not ordinarily adapt their courses to fit the cultures of the various countries in which the subsidiaries are located, since Johnson Wax wants to maintain a strong corporate culture and believes this is one way to cultivate it. Still, there are differences among countries that sometimes make some changes necessary. For instance, a team-building course that has been delivered at Johnson Wax locations around the world has not been delivered in Brazil. Brazilian advisors indicated that the country's culture is so imbued with the idea of teamwork that asking Brazilian employees to take a team-building course would be redundant and probably viewed as insulting.

In other cases, corporate imperatives have sometimes indicated the need to counter a country's culture – albeit maybe slowly – in order to achieve Johnson Wax's goals. For instance, in its Chinese operations the firm has found that the concept of destiny is so strong that the corporate attitude about self-development often seems pointless. After all, if you are destined to be a supervisor, it's fruitless to try to develop yourself into a middle manager or top executive. Setting objectives and doing performance appraisals are other concepts common in the US but uncommon – and sometimes considered inappropriate – in other countries.

Johnson Wax expects its HR directors around the world to advise the corporate director of training on whether, when, and how a training program should be delivered. It is their task to ensure that culture is taken into account when necessary. In addition, of course, the local general manager will be consulted to make sure that the corporate training agenda is appropriate for the local workforce. Ideally, the corporate director of training would like to have a full-time trainer in each subsidiary who could deliver all the training in the native language. But many of the subsidiaries are too small to afford such a luxury.

Most companies probably would like to emulate IBM, which has an education department in each of its worldwide locations. But that's expensive. IBM organizes its education functions from 132 countries into five geographic units (although, increasingly, for technology firms like IBM – and others that are extensively using technology – training courses are available online for all employees anywhere in the world). In each geographic unit, there is an education organization that acts as the coordinating hub. Then, within each country, there is an organization that is responsible for education. Some countries have only a few trainers, while the US

continued

education division employs about 2,000 people. The director of education for IBM worldwide coordinates the regional education directors, whose job it is to establish an overall education strategy. Each director is responsible for implementing that strategy within their regions and delivering whatever courses are needed.

3M is even more decentralized in its approach than IBM. 3M has subsidiaries in fifty-two countries, each of which is responsible for its own training, although regional offices, such as the European headquarters in Düsseldorf, Germany, coordinate educational offerings for all of Europe. Usually the subsidiaries develop and deliver their own courses, although sometimes they ask corporate headquarters for consulting help. They might need training connected with a new product developed in the US. Or they might ask for a particular type of generic course, with the understanding it will be adapted to the country. Indeed, 3M's director of global training sees no reason that training can't be developed in the field and imported to the US. A number of top executives traveled from corporate headquarters in St Paul, Minnesota, to Düsseldorf to participate in a management development course prepared in Europe for delivery in Europe.

Some companies take a more centralized approach, sending headquarters trainers around the world to deliver training. But they typically try to adapt the instruction as much as possible. For example, the vice-president at McGraw-Hill who is in charge of international training often delivers training in the firm's seventeen locations, largely in Asia and Europe. A while back, McGraw-Hill merged its US and international operations. Shortly after that, corporate executives decided that all employees needed training that, if done properly, could bind the two divisions together and help to nurture a common corporate culture. Prior to this, very little training had been done in McGraw-Hill's overseas locations. Now the units request whatever training they need and it's usually delivered by a trainer from corporate headquarters.

However, the ultimate goal is to develop people in each unit as instructors. In the meantime, headquarters trainers try not to be too American ethnocentric in their delivery of training at foreign locales. They network extensively with other international trainers and with their own general managers about the needs for their divisions and how they prefer to have the training delivered. Then they arrive several days in advance to get a feel for the location and to spend time with participants prior to delivery of the training.

Some global firms that don't maintain training departments in each subsidiary, but still believe in the importance of training delivered locally, sometimes cultivate independent local trainers in various countries (if they are available). That is one of the approaches taken by MSD Agvet, a division of Merck pharmaceuticals, which produces and markets livestock and agricultural products. It does business in more than 100 countries and has subsidiaries in more than twenty. Agvet's manager of training and conference services says that most of Agvet's training is developed centrally and pilot tested in the US. But Agvet uses a variety of ways to deliver the programs in the subsidiaries. Marketing and sales managers come together for their training in each of the regions in which Agvet operates. But to train salespeople in the subsidiaries, Agvet uses three different approaches.

In subsidiaries with at least twenty-five people, it will often train a line manager to deliver the training. Local managers are seen as having the advantage of knowing the trainees and being able to adapt the courses to mesh with the local culture. In smaller subsidiaries, in which there is no one available to deliver training but the subsidiary's general manager wants the training delivered by a local person, a local, independent trainer is hired, someone who has been worked with before who can deliver the course in the local language and is able to make the necessary adaptations (and who can do a good job of delivering the training) is used.

The third approach used by Agvet is to send someone from headquarters in New Jersey, an approach often used for new-product releases because local trainers lack the knowledge of the new product and corporate trainers don't have the time to train them. Sometimes this requires simultaneous translation during the course, but since most trainees know English as a second (or more) language, this doesn't create a major obstacle. If trainees' language skills are weak, the trainer will usually break them into small groups to discuss the product(s) in their native tongues.

career development systems parallel those in other large Japanese firms. Consequently, its employees regard IBM-Japan as a Japanese company, rather than an American one. This approach has paid great dividends over the years in terms of IBM's competitive strength in the Japanese marketplace and has allowed IBM-Japan to compete with major Japanese firms in hiring new college graduates from the best Japanese universities and in retaining their best workers.

There is no general road map for adjusting training programs to local conditions and cultures, but, at a minimum, IHR professionals must make the effort to understand local laws, practice, and employer obligations in order to improve the probability of reproducing the IBM-Japan type experience as opposed to the GE–CGR experience.

An American multinational spent several million dollars on upgrading its IT systems in all of its plants around the world, as well as on training initiatives to make sure that everyone understood the new system.[10] Yet its HR director couldn't understand why months after the training had taken place, some subsidiaries were still using the old procedures. Although the Scandinavians and the British welcomed the new ideas, the French, Italians, and Latin Americans were reluctant to accept another *Diktat* from US headquarters. And although the Asians didn't complain during the training sessions, they, too, failed to implement the new system.

It's a common scenario, says Richard Harlow, senior development consultant at global training consultancy TMA in the UK[11]

> Time and time again, I hear similar stories of global training initiatives not having the desired effect. And it boils down to a number of reasons. Sometimes badly interpreted material is to blame, other times internal politics may be at play, or perhaps employees in a particular location are just not accustomed to the way the briefing/training is delivered. And companies end up digging deeper in their pockets to retrain or troubleshoot.

Sometimes, firms face such disappointments because they simply transfer a program devised at HQ straight to another country, without taking cultural norms into account. It goes much deeper than just translating the training material into another language; trainers have to work around the cultural nuances as well. In many cases, the "global" training falls flat because it is just completely inappropriate for the particular culture.

The next few paragraphs discuss a number of reasons that training often does not transfer smoothly to other cultures or countries.

## Language

There are a number of issues in multinational training that involve language. One has to do with whether to provide training for the global workforce in a single, common language, or to translate training programs into varying languages for the global workforce. Another has to do with providing language classes, themselves, in order to enable employees to be able to interact more effectively both within the enterprise as well as to interact effectively with external constituencies, such as suppliers, subcontractors, and customers.

In today's shrinking world, the ability to communicate accurately and effectively takes on increasing importance. Even though English has become the primary language in which global business is conducted, it is clear that being able to sell, negotiate, discuss, and manage in the language of one's neighbors, customers, and employees can improve the probabilities of successful communication and, therefore, successful business transactions. Firms such as Coca-Cola have learned how important foreign-language skills are. The ability to speak another language is seen as so important it has become a major plus when recruiting new employees. Mike Semrau, assistant vice-president and director of international human resources for Atlanta-based Coca-Cola, says, "If I'm out recruiting somebody and they speak Spanish, that facilitates our ability to move them into certain areas where Spanish is critical. We increasingly are hiring people who are broader-based."[12] He further indicates that increasingly within at least Coca-Cola, internationalists having multilingual and multicultural capabilities will be the norm.

The importance of being multilingual is well stated by George Gourlay, vice-president of corporate manufacturing operations for Coca-Cola Company: "Understanding how to function in different cultures and different languages is fundamental to our success. Knowing how to give our customers what they expect – consistently, wherever we operate, regardless of local conditions – is our challenge."[13] He sees language study as opening the door to deeper cultural understanding, that speech patterns, thought patterns, and behavior patterns (for example, of customers) are interlinked. And, therefore, language study is a link to better understanding (and interacting with) the customer.

Indeed, the ability to speak two or more languages (a skill held by many Europeans, for example), is finally being seen as important enough, in at least some American firms, that some chief executives are even working on learning a second language. For example, Du Pont chief executive Edgar S. Woolard, Jr, took a crash course in Japanese and a number of his executive colleagues (at Du Pont and at other firms such as Eastman Kodak, Citicorp, and General Electric) are also taking cram courses in second languages. French, German, and Japanese still appear to be the favorites among Americans attending major language schools, but Spanish probably maintains a lead in secondary school and university-level language courses and in the number of Americans that speak it as a second language (and probably second in number of Americans who speak it as a first language). In addition, Chinese (particularly Mandarin) has become more popular as firms send increasing numbers of employees on assignment to China.

John Reed, former CEO of Citicorp, explains this issue from the perspective of Citicorp, one of the most successful global banks:

> There are few companies in the world that are truly global . . . Our most important advantage is our globality. Our global human capital may be as important a resource, if not more important, than our financial capital. Look at the Policy Committee, the top thirty or so officers in the bank. Almost seventy-five percent have worked outside the United States; more than twenty-five percent have worked in three or more countries. Half speak two or more languages other than English. Seven were born outside the United States.[14]

Training everyone in a common language, usually English, has also become popular, at least in some firms. Such programs (usually referred to as ESL, English as a Second Language, or ESOL, English for Speakers of Other Languages, programs) not only help new employees adapt (in the case of recent immigrants into an English-speaking country, for example) but also help others do their jobs better and increase worker loyalty and improve customer relations.[15] To the extent possible, language lessons should be presented in terms of workplace situations, which enhances the training's immediate usefulness.

Another area of primary concern relates to the language of the training itself. Global enterprises must make difficult decisions about whether to translate training materials into the languages of the local (foreign) workforces and whether to provide the training, itself, in the language of the local workforce (either through the use of local trainers or through translators, if the trainers come from regional or corporate headquarters training groups and they don't speak the local language). If the decision is taken to provide the training through translators, then the selection of interpreters and translators needs to be given special attention, since being good at interpretation and translation requires more than training in the original and the foreign language. It also requires close familiarity with the nature of the business and any technical and special managerial terminology that may not translate easily into the foreign language or back into the original language.

## Transfer of learning issues

There are a number of practical problems in training in the global arena with achieving what is referred to as "transfer of learning." This has to do with the extent to which people in training programs are able to (and/or actually do) apply what they learn in training programs to their day-to-day jobs. Many of these issues are related to the types of cultural issues that have been discussed throughout this book, since cultural issues impact every area of IHR and global business, including training. The next few paragraphs provide only a summary of these issues.

*Culture (both national and corporate)*    National (and even professional and corporate) culture influences training in a number of ways. Before they set up a training program in a foreign subsidiary, IHR professionals must understand how that culture views the educational process. For instance, in many Asian cultures, education is considered to be a very authoritarian phenomenon. The teacher is seen as the expert, as someone students should respect. Teachers impart knowledge through one-way conversation: the teacher tells, the student listens. Students do not ask questions, and teachers do not solicit students' opinions. The atmosphere is formal and respectful toward authority. US educational techniques, for example, which are less formal and encourage student participation, can be ineffective in an Asian environment.

The degree of deference to instructors influences the extent to which a participative style can be used and the extent to which participants will ask questions or offer opinions and become involved in open discussion. Culture will influence adherence to a hierarchy among students, such as deference to the most senior member of a training group in discussion and stating of opinions. Culture influences all forms of interactions with instructors and influences what a training group will accept in terms of behavior of instructors, e.g., degree of formality and appearance. Culture influences the roles of students, e.g., based on their gender and positions, in ways that may be different from that which is familiar to the trainer or to those who developed the training. Training which is delivered to employees from cultures which are foreign to that of the people who designed the training or delivered by people from different cultures must take into account these and other issues related to culture or the success of the training may be limited.

Table 10.1 illustrates one attempt to match training pedagogies with the cultural characteristics of a number of countries, particularly the degree of power distance and uncertainty avoidance, since they impact trainees' experiences with participation in the learning process.[15] As the table suggests, people from high power distance

*Table 10.1* The match of training techniques to country culture

| Country | High PDI/Strong UAI | Didactic | Training technique |
|---|---|---|---|
| Guatemala | ↑ | ↑ | Readings |
| Greece | | | |
| Portugal | | | |
| Mexico | | | Panel |
| El Salvador | | | |
| Belgium | | | |
| Venezuela | | | Lecture |
| France | | | |
| Turkey | | | |
| Peru | | | |
| Chile | | | Demonstration |
| Arab Region | | | |
| Japan | | | Programmed instruction |
| S. Korea | | | |
| Brazil | | | Instruments |
| Spain | | | |
| Malaysia | | | |
| Philippines | | | |
| Argentina | | | Discussion groups |
| West Africa | | | |
| Thailand | | | |
| Taiwan | | | Brainstorm |
| Indonesia | | | |
| Pakistan | | | |
| Italy | | | |
| Costa Rica | | | Case studies |
| Iran | | | |
| India | | | |
| East Africa | | | Round robins |
| South Africa | | | |
| Hong Kong | | | |
| Israel | | | Role plays |
| Switzerland | | | |
| Finland | | | |
| The Netherlands | | | Simulations |
| Canada | | | |
| Australia | | | |
| US | | | Structured exercises |
| Singapore | | | |
| Norway | | | |
| Austria | | | |
| New Zealand | | | Fishbowl |
| Great Britain | | | |
| Ireland | | | |
| Sweden | | | T-groups |
| Denmark | ↓ | ↓ | |

*Weak UA/Low PD*      *Experiential*

(acceptance of status differences between students and instructors) and strong
uncertainty avoidance (unwillingness to take risks and to try new things) cultures are
likely to desire and perform better in training programs that rely more heavily on
structured and passive learning techniques, such as reading assignments and lectures
versus those who come from weak uncertainty avoidance and low power distance
countries, who will probably do better with experiential training techniques. Refer to
the discussion of national cultures in Chapter 5 for a thorough discussion of the
impact of culture differences. Of course, individuals within a culture may vary from
these guidelines and any particular country subsidiary may have developed a
company culture that supports the use of training techniques that are different from
the norm for the particular culture.

*Learning styles*    This issue is related to culture. It is clear that people from differing
cultures and countries are used to differing training and teaching styles. And thus
their most comfortable learning approach needs to be considered in the design and
delivery of training. IHRM in Action 10.2 illustrates how culture and learning styles
issues impact the effectiveness of training programs in subsidiaries in Malawi, a
Southeast African country and a former British colony.[17]

*Education levels and forms*    One of the reasons that the provision of training to
multiple subsidiaries around the world is so complex is because the basic educational
infrastructure varies so much from country to country. The basic level of literacy
varies dramatically; the nature of the educational system and the type of education it
provides varies significantly (e.g., whether theoretical or practical in orientation); the
level, nature, and availability of higher education varies; the availability of vocational
education varies considerably; and teaching and, therefore, learning styles, used in
any country's school system, vary from culture to culture as well. In addition,
familiarity with various teaching techniques and media as well as relationships
between students and instructors also vary so much that it is often impossible to
transfer directly either the content or the method of instruction from one place to
another.


Transfer of learning issues are not trivial. Not only do they need to be understood
by the multinational enterprise providing training, for example, to its foreign
ventures, but, as firms go to more and more countries, training itself becomes an
increasingly complex responsibility. Trainers have to consider not only the nature of
cross-border training but also must pay closer attention to who needs to receive
training, for example, maybe an otherwise well educated workforce, say in a
developing country, that may need training in things like new technologies. All of the
above problems, plus additional cultural problems (such as arise in the merging of
various company and national cultures in cross-border acquisitions, coping with
increased cross-national diversity due to increased numbers of cross-border
acquisitions and partnerships, and the many problems of cross-cultural work teams)
make the management of international training programs a very complex
responsibility, indeed.

# Training managers in Malawi

Malawi was once a British colony. Thus it inherited a British administrative tradition, which is very Western and very bureaucratic. However, traditional Malawi cultural values, which emphasize family membership and attention to status, are also superimposed on to business administrative systems, mostly imported from Europe and the US.

*The Malawian culture.* Workers in Malawi view employers as an extension of their families. They expect to be provided with a broad array of benefits from their employer, such as housing and transportation.

Malawi society places great importance on status differences. The relationship between managers and subordinates is viewed as authoritative: workers give deference and expect managers to act paternally. Malawians view proper protocol as very important. Managers often resist accepting individual blame for their own mistakes and do not directly criticize their subordinates. Malawian managers rarely delegate authority because the culture believes that delegation strips managers of their authority and thus lowers their status in the eyes of their subordinates.

*Development of training programs by MNEs in Malawi.* MNEs setting up local operations in Malawi must consider the following three realities when developing training programs:

- American models of innovation, motivation, leadership, etc., will not work well in Malawi. For example, most US management experts believe that proper leader behavior depends on the situation: there is no one right way to lead. However, the Malawian culture believes that leaders should always be authoritative. Consequently, HR professionals must first learn how these issues apply in Malawian culture and then train the Malawian workers accordingly.
- Status-conscious Malawian managers will resent being ordered to attend a training program. They will interpret this gesture as an indication that they are considered "below average" performers. A company must thus carefully prepare a strategy to solicit trainee attendance in a way that will not cause managers to "lose face" with their peers or subordinates.
- Training methods must be congruent with employee learning styles. Malawians learn best in "process-oriented" educational settings. Consequently, training methods that use small-group techniques and other "supportive learning" techniques should be used in lieu of those that focus on lectures and rote learning.

## Training and preparation of international assignees

The first international training responsibility for an HR manager usually involves the training and preparation of international assignees and their families. Indeed, for many enterprises that have recently "gone international," this may well be the only international training issue looked at for some time after the enterprise begins developing its international operations. And, as indicated in the previous chapter, even this area of training responsibility often receives little attention. Management development programs will typically not involve any international considerations and the training of local workforces stays primarily the concern of local national HR managers. Yet, at some point, the global enterprise usually comes to recognize the importance of training and preparing its expatriates. That is the subject of this section of the chapter.

As discussed in Chapter 9, the preparation of international assignees prior to going overseas (and after arrival) is at least as important to their successful performance as selecting the right candidate and family in the first place. A lot of evidence suggests that firms still do not do a very good job of selecting or preparing their IAs. Indeed, surveys find that only about 35 percent of US firms offer any pre-departure cross-cultural or language training for their expatriate managers.[18] The percentage is not much different for Asian or European firms.[19] And yet the inability to adjust or to perform the expected role – both of which can be improved through training and orientation – generally provide the major reasons for "failure" in an overseas assignment. According to Roger Herod, who at the time was vice-president of international human resources at Campbell Soup Company, "There is too much emphasis on executives' technical abilities and too little on their cultural skills and family situation. When international executive relocations fail, they generally fail either because expatriates can't fathom the customs of the new country or because their families can't deal with the emotional stress that accompanies relocation."[20] In both cases, orientation to the "culture shock" they will experience in their new environments seems particularly important.

## Cross-cultural adjustment

Many international assignees and their families experience difficulties adjusting to their new, foreign situations.[21] Most of the time, the spouse (usually a wife, since most IAs are men, although this is gradually changing) has to give up a job, house, friends, and family to accompany her husband on his foreign assignment. The husband may also give up house, friends, and family, but he still has his job and relationships from work at the new assignment. Consequently, the wife typically has more difficulty adapting to the foreign environment. The following summarizes some of the adjustment problems faced by people as they move to a new, unfamiliar, foreign assignment:

- *Routines*. Many of life's established routines have to change in a foreign locale. This includes everything from eating habits and favorite foods to initiating and developing relationships. This disruption takes significant energy and time to combat. And the greater the scope, magnitude, and criticality of the disruptions the more draining and, depending on one's success in dealing with them, the more depressing they can be.

- *Culture shock.* This is the set of psychological and emotional responses people experience when they are overwhelmed by their lack of knowledge and understanding of the new, foreign culture and the negative consequences that often accompany their inadequate and inexperienced behavior. The psychological and emotional symptoms of culture shock include frustration, anxiety, anger, and depression. Disruption of one's routines leads to these consequences. But culture shock often leads to reactions that go beyond even this.

Most people don't experience culture shock at the beginning. There is usually a form of euphoria and excitement about the new experiences in the early stages of the assignment. The IA and family usually don't even know enough at this stage to understand they are breaking local cultural taboos. But after a while, the IA and her/his family will begin to realize they don't know or understand many of the basic cultural ground rules, and this creates a major blow to their egos. The more significant the ground rules being broken, the more significant the blow to one's ego, and the greater the subsequent feelings of culture shock and depression. Some never recover from this culture shock and many of these return home early. Yet others stay and eventually work their way through culture shock, learn to understand and accept the local culture, and gradually adjust to living and working in the foreign locale.

The pain of mistakes is the primary cause of culture shock but it is the learning to which these mistakes lead that shows the way out of it. Once a cultural mistake is made and, more importantly recognized, it is less likely to be repeated or to become an ongoing source of frustration, anger, or embarrassment. Gradually, by making mistakes, recognizing them, and observing how others in the culture behave (and putting forth the effort to understand the deeper values that underlie local cultural behavior), people learn what to do and say and what not to do and say.[22]


## Preparation for the international assignment

Experienced IHR managers think it is absolutely essential for success in international assignments to first, provide both an international assignee (IA) and his or her family enough adequate and accurate information about the assignment and location for them to be able to make informed decisions about the desirability of such an assignment (beyond the self-assessment discussed in the prior chapter).[23] This needs to be more than a short familiarization trip to the proposed location, even though this is important and should be seen as a necessary part of the preparation and orientation process. Both the employee and spouse should be well briefed on the new assignment's responsibilities, as well as on the firm's policies regarding IA compensation, benefits, taxes, security procedures, and repatriation.

In addition, the employee and family need to be provided with all the information, skills, and attitudes which they will need to be comfortable, effective, and productive in the overseas assignment. Much of this orientation and training must be focused on the cultural values and norms of the new country and their contrast with those of their home country. Box 10.1 illustrates how many of these concerns might be sequenced and delivered in the preparation of an IA for an overseas assignment.[24] Given a number of different types of problems that IAs and their families might face plus a number of possible development objectives, the particular methods chosen for training and orientation should vary as well.

First, in the development of such an IA preparation and training program, IHR must recognize the various types of problems that exist for IAs. These range from difficulties with business relationships (either within or external to the firm or with headquarters), difficulties within the IA's family, or difficulties with either the host- or home-country governments. Each of these potential sources of difficulty has its own particular solutions with its own specific objectives that will help overcome the problems. For example, developing a working knowledge of the host-country language can lead to improvements in a number of the possible relationship concerns. And the particular development methods chosen should be matched to specific development needs (see Table 10.2).[25] As the differences between the culture of the IA and his or her family become greater relative to that of the new foreign location, the length and rigor of the training should also become greater.[26] Ultimately, the objective is for the IA to be successful in his or her assignment, to remain in the foreign locale for the duration of that assignment, and to return to the parent firm to an assignment that effectively uses the IA's new skills and motivation.

In terms of design for training for international assignees, research and writing about training, in general, have suggested a number of guidelines that seem appropriate, here.[27] For example, training needs to take into account the influence of the environment, which seems particularly relevant in cross-cultural training. And it ought to progress in terms of content and pedagogy in relation to the knowledge, experience, and competencies of the trainees. Lastly, it has been suggested that IA training most comprehensively should focus on all of these competencies:[28]

- *Cognitive competency:* the acquisition of knowledge and facts about cultures, including such factors as history, economics, politics, business practices, sensitive areas, and family relations.
- *Behavioral competency:* the ability to adapt to diverse conditions, to communicate in other cultures, to scan the country environment capably, to show skill at human relations in another culture, and to manage stress effectively.
- *Performance competency:* the ability to perform well in the assigned business or organizational tasks in another culture, including the appropriate technical and managerial skills, the ability to be creative at adaptation while engaging in critical thinking, positional understanding and learning on the job, and the ability to develop networks and support systems for accomplishing the tasks at hand.

## Box 10.1 Preparation and training for international assignees

### Establishing and maintaining relationships

- Internal within the firm
- External with the community
- Family
- Host government
- Home government
- Headquarters

### Preparation objectives

- Review terms and conditions of assignment
- Increase cultural awareness
- Increase knowledge of host country
- Impart working knowledge of the foreign language
- Increase conflict management skills
- Minimize re-entry problems

### Forms of training

- Pre-departure
  - Cultural orientation
  - Area study
  - Language instruction
  - Cross-cultural T-group
- Behavioral simulations
- Case studies
- Post-arrival training
  - Cultural orientation and training
  - Inter-group problem solving
- Re-entry training and orientation

### Training outcomes

- Knowledge about cultural, political, economic, business, legal, and social factors of the host country
- Awareness of the needs and expectations of the different parties interested in the international operation
- Awareness of the problems of family relationships in the host country

*Table 10.2* Preparing and training the international assignee

| Method | Technique | Purpose |
|---|---|---|
| Passive/Information | Lectures<br>Reading material<br>Transfer of training<br>Videotapes/DVD<br>Movies | Area studies, company operation,<br>parent-country institutions |
| Intercultural<br>experiential workshops | Cultural assimilators<br>Simulations<br>Role playing<br>Action learning | Culture-general, culture-specific<br>negotiation skills, reduce<br>ethnocentrism |
| Sensitivity training | Communication workshops<br>T-groups<br>Outward bound trips | Self-awareness, communication<br>style, empathy, listening skills,<br>non-judgmentalism |
| Field experiences | Pre site visit<br>Meetings with ex-IAs<br>Minicultures<br>Host-family mentors<br>Culture coaches | Customs, values, beliefs,<br>non-verbal behavior,<br>etiquette, protocol |
| Language skills | Classes<br>Cassettes | Interpersonal communication, job<br>requirements, survival necessities |

At a minimum, training and preparing IAs for international assignments should cover the following *topics* to facilitate the ever crucial adjustment process:[29]

- Intercultural business skills (e.g., negotiation styles in different countries and cultures).
- Culture shock management (e.g., what to expect and how to deal with the stress of adaptation)
- Lifestyle adjustment (e.g., how to deal with different shopping and transportation systems and the different availability of familiar foods and entertainment).
- Host-country daily living issues (e.g., any unfamiliar problems with water or electricity).
- Local customs and etiquette (e.g., what to wear and different behavior patterns and gestures for men and women).
- Area studies (e.g., the political and religious environment and the local geography).
- Repatriation planning (e.g., how to stay in touch with the home office and how to identify an appropriate assignment prior to repatriating back home).
- Language learning strategies, both before leaving for the new assignment as well as after arrival.

In the broader picture, many firms divide their preparation of IAs into two categories: counseling and training. The counseling component deals primarily with the mechanics of a move abroad while the training tries to develop skills and sensitivities to national and cultural issues that will better enable the IA and family to adapt to and enjoy their new situation. Increasingly, firms are realizing how important such preparation is to the international business success of their IAs. Novartis, the Switzerland-based global pharmaceutical firm, does a particularly good job of this type of preparation.[30] The types of topics covered by its normal counseling and training sessions for people going on a foreign assignment include the following:

- *Counseling*: compensation, benefits, and taxes; travel; shipping and storage of household goods; housing and property management; local transportation; allowances; vacations and home leaves; language training and orientation; and children's educational expenses and options.
- *Training*: local customs, politics, religions, attitudes; local laws; safety, health, and security; cultural sensitivity, food, water, and so on; and background briefing on company: history, policies, individuals.

And lastly, another firm recommends that a thorough preparation program should include all of the following:[31]

- A pre-visit to the new site.
- Language training.
- Intensive area study.
- Country-specific handbooks that include both country and company facts and where to get additional information.
- In-company counseling on issues such as taxes, legal matters, compensation, the move, and the like.
- Meetings with repatriates who have recently returned home from the location to which the IA is moving.
- Local sponsorship and assistance for arrival and orientation to the new locale and assignment.

Such an extensive program of preparation can minimize the high level of premature returns and bad experiences due to maladjustment to foreign assignments by IAs and their families and the consequent inadequate levels of performance in the foreign assignment.

Even though there is much controversy as to the ability of people to learn about other cultures through training programs (some authors suggest one must experience a culture first-hand in order to gain a real understanding and/or adaptation to it – this is discussed in more detail in the section on developing global executives), at least some evidence suggests that these sorts of training programs do help.[32] Indeed, the experience of the American university-based Business Council for International Understanding in its work with Shell Oil Company in the US shows that pre-departure training can reduce dramatically the IA failure rate (as described in the previous chapter).[33] Prior to providing any training to their employees being sent to Saudi Arabia, Shell was experiencing a 60 percent early return rate. With three days of training, that rate dropped to 5 percent. With a six-day pre-departure program, the figure dropped to 1.5 percent! It is estimated that without any pre-departure cross-cultural training, only about 20 percent of Americans sent overseas do well.[34]

As stated in the discussion of culture shock, IAs and their families must learn to cope with – depending on the country – a varying number, importance, and criticality of disruptions to their normal routines and ways of living. Accordingly, effective pre-departure training must vary its content and intensity according to the distance between what is normal and familiar and what will be experienced in the new assignment. The greater the distance between the home culture and the host culture, the more extensive and lengthy the training should be. And, whenever possible, both pre-departure and post-arrival training should be provided, with the post-arrival training focusing on the more complicated aspects of the new culture, since the typical IA and family is not ready for the more detailed cultural training until they have experienced the culture first-hand.[35]

## The design and delivery of cross-cultural training

Training for cross-cultural adjustment should focus on helping IAs and their families do three things: (1) become aware that behaviors vary across cultures, including being different than what they are used to, and work at observing these differences quite carefully; (2) build a mental map of the new culture so they can understand why the local people value certain behaviors and ideas and how those behaviors and ideas may be appropriately reproduced; and (3) practice the behaviors they will need to be effective in their overseas assignments. Without training of this sort, most people will not be successful in learning how to adapt to their new cultures.[36]

When the training and preparation of IAs and their families is done well, the IHR department will have completed a checklist that looks something like this for each IA and his or her family:

- Develop an overseas compensation and benefits plan, taking into account cost-of-living differences and any special needs.
- Provide tax advice and financial counseling.
- Supervise the sometimes extensive paperwork involved with making an international move, such as arranging work visas.
- Assist with housing and the selection of good schools for any children.
- Help the IA set up banking accounts and make cash transfers.
- Transfer medical, dental, and school records, and assist with inoculations.
- Help with absentee ballots and international drivers' licenses.
- Organize and provide cross-cultural training to be delivered both pre-departure and post-arrival to both the IA and the family.
- Provide language training, often through "immersion" courses.
- Assist with moves of household furniture and goods abroad and living arrangements in the foreign locale.
- Helping the trailing spouse get work permit and/or job abroad, if possible.

The more effort and time both trainers and trainees put into such training and preparation, that is, the more rigorous is the training, the more likely the IA and family members will be to learn the behaviors and attitudes they will need for success in the foreign assignment. And matching rigor to the needs of the IA and family and to the degree of "differentness" of the new country and culture is the key to the design of a valid cross-culture training and preparation program.

The previous paragraphs in this section have focused on the training and preparation of international assignees and their families. But some form of training and/or orientation would also seem appropriate for other international employees, as introduced in Chapter 8. This would include domestic internationalists, international commuters, business travelers, and virtual internationalists, as well as traditional short-term and long-term international assignees. If the global enterprise really wants to expand its workforce's global business capabilities, then it seems essential that it provide cross-cultural training and orientation to everyone.

## Global executives: developing managers in the global enterprise

There also comes a time in the development of global enterprises when they begin to examine the development of their managers from an international perspective. At this point, they will begin to realize that not only is international experience necessary for their parent-country managers, but they will also begin to realize the importance of developing their managerial talent from throughout their global enterprise. Indeed, probably the most formidable task in the human resource area facing many global firms today is the development of a cadre of managers and executives who have a deep understanding of the global marketplace, have the capability to transfer this knowledge into resolute global action, and who expect to see their rewards and personal and professional growth linked to opportunities for global careers in which to exercise this understanding.[37] Global companies need executives (and, probably, other employees as well) who can easily switch from one culture to another, people who are fluent in several cultures and languages, and who can work effectively as part of an international team, keeping misunderstandings to a minimum.[38] They are the keys to global business success.

But it's not easy. To date, too many companies have been slow to become truly culturally aware simply because their key decision makers lack the necessary international experience and exposure, and, therefore, global vision.

Many global firms have invested well in the development of their local staffs (in both their parent-country and host-country operations) and can thus identify competent managers who are well qualified to handle local operations in most of their principle markets. At the same time, though, they are short of seasoned executives with broad international skills who are closely attuned to the firm's global strategy.

Too much localization has often resulted in insufficient globalization of the managerial ranks. But reversing this reality is not easy, in terms of both the cost and complexity of developing a new breed of global executives and the challenge this creates for the established process of management development.

Often, the business environments that international firms experience are radically different than what they are used to. In such situations, IHR must tailor its policies and practices to local conditions while at the same time modifying the mind-set and technical skills of local managers and employees to accept and match world-class standards. To facilitate and manage this globalization, it becomes critical for firms to identify and develop leaders who are capable of functioning effectively on a global scale and with a global perspective. In a global economy, this strategic preparation of global leaders has become a major component of IHR's contribution. In essence, IHR must design HR processes, including global training and management development programs, which encourage and facilitate the organization so as to ensure that its "global whole" is greater than the sum of its domestic parts.

## Patterns of global management development

As important as management development with an international focus is for today's MNEs, the reality is that there has not been much research into patterns or methods employed by major firms. Nevertheless, the following few paragraphs summarize what has been identified.[39]

The most important of these common elements for the major MNEs is the priority placed on identifying and developing management talent. At firms such as IBM, Shell, Philips, and Unilever, responsibility for international executive development is so important that it is specifically a board concern and the executive in charge of this activity reports directly to the CEO. These firms have found that the lack of globally savvy management talent has been a major inhibitor in setting up overseas businesses or developing new global projects, even in some cases preventing them from staffing projects which have been technically feasible. Even smaller firms have come to understand the importance of having a cadre of global managers. In the words of Graham Corbett, who a few years ago was senior partner for KPMG's Continental European practice: "We are on a fast growth track, and our major task is to attract and develop enough professional talent to enable us to support the [global] growth rates we are experiencing."[40]

Firms from different countries appear to have evolved varying approaches to management development. Yet there are some common elements among them. These include practices such as (1) the early identification of individuals with executive potential, either through early-in-career assessment procedures and close monitoring of job performance or recruiting at only elite universities and *grandes écoles* or the use of in-house apprenticeships that lead to increasing levels of management responsibility; and (2) the close monitoring of those individuals identified through whichever procedure(s) to be candidates for positions of executive leadership.[41]

The primary purpose of the close monitoring is to manage the careers and job assignments of these high-potential employees. The movement (or mobility) of these individuals is controlled so as to ensure that they experience job assignments, including overseas assignments, of adequate variety, challenge, and appropriate responsibility (to include multiple functional, product, and country experiences, and important developmental content, often away from the individual's area of proven expertise) and length, so as to ensure the individuals learn how to achieve results in new settings and through associates, particularly colleagues from other countries and cultures. A number of observers have also noticed that this mobility among international locations creates informal networks that enable information and problem solving to be shared worldwide in a more effective way than the formal, traditional, hierarchical structures appear to provide (as discussed in Chapter 3, on the structure of the global organization).

For example, Unilever Corporation, the very large global consumer products firm with joint Anglo-Dutch ownership, has long been committed to the development of its human resources as a means of attaining durable competitive advantage. As early as the 1930s, the company was recruiting and developing local employees to replace the parent-company managers who had been running most of its overseas subsidiaries.[42] Although Unilever was delighted with the talent that began working its way up the organization, it soon realized that by reducing the transfer of parent-company managers abroad, it had diluted the powerful "glue" that had bound its diverse organizational groups together and had linked its dispersed operations.

In order to address this problem, Unilever began to increase, again, its cross-border assignments for high-achieving managers, this time without as much attention to their countries of origin. And it developed a major, global, management development and training center near London (referred to as "Four Acres"), to which high-potential managers from around the world were sent for management training and networking. The ultimate aim of these actions was to facilitate the development of contacts and relationships among its managers worldwide. In the words of a senior HR manager at Unilever:

> By bringing managers from different countries and businesses together at Four Acres, we build contacts and create bonds that we could never achieve by other means. The company spends as much on training as it does on R&D not only because of the direct effect it has on upgrading skills and knowledge but also because it plays a central role in indoctrinating managers into a Unilever club where personal relationships and informal contacts are much more powerful than the formal systems and structures.[43]

Senior executives from Europe, Asia, and the US indicate that their firms have a shortage of managers with the necessary competencies to operate effectively in a global marketplace.[44] They indicate that this is a major constraint on their abilities to expand their operations and to compete well in that global marketplace. In this context, then, IHR managers must ask themselves the following questions: If global enterprises do indeed have such shortages, then what does a global executive "look like"? That is, what are their characteristics? And how can an MNE develop them? Or is it possible to just copy in the international arena that which is done on the domestic front? This section of the chapter addresses these types of questions.

Box 10.2 summarizes actions found among major American firms to globalize their management teams.[45] These "tips" show the importance of international mobility and experience for individual managers and the necessity to integrate those who gain this international experience into the rest of the firm. This list of actions does not include the more traditional "classroom" type of courses and other action-oriented learning programs that most firms also provide as part of their management and executive development programs.[46]

## Development of a global mind-set, global competencies, and global leadership

First, this section takes a look at the concept of a global mind-set.[47] One of the goals of many management development programs in the global arena is to develop a cadre of managers who have what is referred to as a global mind-set.[48] As will be discussed, an international management development program alone may not achieve this objective. This global perspective includes sensitivity to multiple cultures and their differences, work experience in more than one country, and knowledge about how and willingness to seek customers, financial resources and supplies, technology, innovations, and employees throughout the world.

### Box 10.2 Tips on how to "globalize" management

- Select a small number of rising "superstars" and send them on meaningful overseas assignments. Repatriate them after two or three years.
- Bring the best overseas talent into headquarters for meaningful interim assignments followed by repatriation.
- Recruit staff out of universities worldwide and place them in entry-level positions overseas early in their careers. Pay these recruits as close to local hiring rates as possible – do not give them standard IA pay packages.
- Reserve one or more positions in your international HR activity for returning expatriates. Too many international HR departments lack credibility on international perspectives.
- Move some of the best talent of all nationalities, including HR professionals, internationally.
- Develop a longer-range view of management development, including overseas assignments.
- Consider moving certain businesses, units, or functions to another country for more effective global interaction.

The internationalization of jobs, companies, technology, products, money, and neighborhoods has caught many people and firms off guard. As indicated in previous chapters, people's thinking has not caught up with the reality: business and life, in general, have been and are being globalized. Few people have much long-term experience working or living with people from other cultures. The result is that few people are familiar with the rules to follow when engaging in business across international borders. And most people assume that the rules they are familiar with and that work well "at home" should be adequate when they work abroad. But, as has been emphasized throughout this book, this is seldom the case. Thus, the opportunities for being embarrassed and making mistakes are ever present. Often, the reaction of managers and employees, in their interactions with colleagues, customers, and suppliers from other countries, is "Why can't they be like us?" But they aren't, and their ways of behaving and conducting business too often seem strange and difficult. Because of this, businesses are increasingly concerned about how to develop managers and employees that exhibit a global mind-set, that is, an ability to think and function effectively in a multiculture world.

Whirlpool Corporation, when it significantly increased its international presence by purchasing the US$2-billion appliance division of Philips of the Netherlands in 1989, realized it needed a way to develop a global perspective for both its US managers and its new European associates.[49] One of the solutions for Whirlpool was to organize a conference in Montreux, Switzerland, for its top 140 executives from sixteen different countries of North America and Europe. The conference was designed to achieve four objectives:

- Advance a unified vision of the company's future.
- Instill the idea of embracing the future as one global company.
- Establish a keen sense of responsibility within the leadership group for creating the company's future.
- Identify and initiate explicit steps toward integrating various activities and ideas throughout Whirlpool's worldwide operations into a unified whole.

The conference architects determined that the first goal of the conference was to encourage managers to think of each other not as *foreigners*, but rather as business partners.[50] The second goal was to give them the amount of time and tools they needed to identify the company's challenges and create solutions to move Whirlpool's worldwide businesses forward. The conference was so successful, it has become an annual event.

In the words of Ed Dunn, then Whirlpool's corporate vice-president of HR, "The first day these were 140 strangers, but by the last day they were 140 very close colleagues."[51] Dunn continues, "You can't globalize your company unless you first globalize your people. To be effective, employees need to know and understand each other before they can work together."

David Whitwan, CEO of Whirlpool, declared that the key to globalizing the firm was to get everyone in the organization to think and act globally, not just a few.[52]

Developing a global mind-set in which people have the ability to exchange ideas and implement activities easily across cultural and personal boundaries, to accept other cultural perspectives, and to break down natural provincial ways of thinking was essential. The rest of the chapter describes many of the organizations that are trying to do this and the methods they are using.

IHRM in Action 10.3 provides an example of the development of an international perspective by a manager in a much smaller business.[53] It illustrates that even for smaller and medium-sized businesses, having an international perspective is critical to success.

People try to make sense out of the confusing effects of globalization with their existing *mind-sets.* Essentially people's mind-sets are the interpretive frameworks that come from their experiences and cultures and that guide how they classify and discriminate events and people in ways that help them to understand what they observe and perceive. These mind-sets determine people's perceptions of and reactions to international experiences and observations of people from other countries and cultures. But their lack of international experience and exposure often limits their abilities to be successful in their international experiences (except maybe as travelers, although a domestic mind-set can cause problems even while traveling).

## The global CEO

Dick Rubin decided in 1990 to take his firm, Boston Metal Products, global. So he and his wife picked up and moved – to the Hague. "I could have delegated the job to someone else," he says, "but what would I be delegating? I didn't know *anything* about doing business in Europe. All I knew was that we belonged there, that there was a market for our products." Within three years, international sales were accounting for 20 percent of the company's profits and revenues, the latter of which totaled more than US$20 million.

Along the way, Rubin made a surprising discovery about what he calls "the power of the presidency" and what might be referred to as the cultural ignorance of many American business people. He says, "Everywhere I go, I run into middle managers of US companies. I've yet to meet an American CEO. Evidently, people just don't realize the respect accorded presidents in Europe. It opens doors; it instills confidence that promises will be kept."

Rubin thinks he has benefited as much as his company has from going global. "I took over my father's business in 1967. Today I feel as if my personal clock has gone back twenty-five years; I'm building something from scratch again, and I'm thriving on it. I feel revitalized." So when does he intend to come home? He doesn't. He says he is having too much fun. He says the move is permanent.

IHRM IN ACTION 10.3

Given the globalization of business, the success of employees' and managers' interactions with global customers, suppliers, and colleagues often is dependent on their abilities to think and act with a global frame of mind and reference, even though they work and live at a time when national pride and focus is as strong as ever. Indeed, the ability to cope with this conflict between a global focus and a local/national focus is one of the critical competencies in today's business world.[54]

This global mind-set predisposes people to cope constructively with these competing priorities (global versus local), rather than advocating one set of cultural values (most likely to be the individual's home-country values) at the expense of all others. This mind-set involves being able to form and sustain a holistic global outlook, that is, a completely different way of looking at the world and being able to synthesize the many complex and conflicting forces.[55] In the words of Catherine Scherer, who has studied those whom she calls *internationalists*, a global mind-set is characterized by tolerance, flexibility, curiosity (inquisitiveness), and the ability to deal with ambiguity.[56] Shirley Gaufin, vice-president of HR for Bechtel Group, a global engineering firm, says, "Global awareness is a subtle characteristic, but it's absolutely essential for expatriate success. It's part of someone being a good leader, part of someone being flexible and adaptable."[57] The next few pages describe a number of more specific qualities of the global mind-set.

## Definition of a global mind-set

Knowing how to live and work across cultures is the essential competency of people with a global mind-set. For most people, developing this mind-set is both an emotional education as well as an intellectual one. The lessons are both professional and personal – often profoundly personal.[58] It is the complexity of the professional lessons and the transformational quality of the personal lessons that leads to the broader perspective of those with a global mind-set. It is in fact this unique perspective that underlies this quality called a *global mind-set.*

One author, with extensive international business experience and writing for the American Society for Training and Development, says, this global mind-set "is a way of being rather than a set of skills. It is an orientation to the world that allows one to see certain things that others do not. A global mind-set means the ability to scan the world from a broad perspective, always looking for unexpected trends and opportunities that may constitute a threat or an opportunity to achieve personal, professional, or organizational objectives."[59]

Another set of authors, who are European academics and consultants, define the global mind-set in terms of both its psychological (personal) and its strategic (professional) perspectives.[60] That is, they see it as "the ability to accept and work with cultural diversity" as well as involving "a set of attitudes that predispose individuals to balance competing business, country, and functional priorities which emerge in international [situations] rather than to advocate any of these dimensions at the expense of the others."

Ultimately, the global manager must become the facilitator of personal and organizational change and development on a global scale. To achieve this, the global manager must not only be attentive to and a developer of organizational cultures, values, and beliefs that reach well beyond the manager's own cultural, technical, and managerial background, but s/he must also be a consummate reframer of the boundaries of the world in which s/he works.[61] This global mind-set is about balancing perspectives, not just about being global. The global manager needs to continue to understand, appreciate, and accommodate local, cross-cultural differences and variations while at the same time maintaining a global view. As a precaution, however,

> academics and others writing from a normative perspective sometimes have the tendency to see global or cosmopolitan as superior to local, calling for a "universal way that transcends the particular of places." What is "'local" is seen as parochial and narrow-minded. However, in our view, global mind-set requires an approach that may be seen as the opposite to such one-dimensional universalism – it calls for a dualistic perspective, an immersion in the local "particulars" while at the same time retaining a wider cross-border orientation.[62]

## Characteristics of a global mind-set

Learning a global mind-set requires the developing of a new set of competencies. Even though there is much disagreement over exactly what are the characteristics of those who possess this global mind-set, the following is a synthesis of the efforts to describe these characteristics.[63] In the end, there is considerable agreement over the following. Those with a global mind-set exhibit the ability to:

- *Manage global competitiveness.* They have broader business skills, exhibiting the ability to conduct business on a global scale as well as to design and manage complex international structures and strategies.[64] They demonstrate awareness of national differences, global trends and options, and the global impact of their decisions and choices. These technical and business skills provide them with credibility in their various international assignments.
- *Work and communicate with multiple cultures.* They show the ability to interact with people (employees, customers, suppliers, colleagues) from many cultures with sensitivity to their cultural and language differences. They understand differing cultural contexts and incorporate that understanding in their work and communication styles. And they understand the impact of cultural factors on communication and work relationships and are willing to revise and expand their understanding as part of their personal and professional growth and development.
- *Manage global complexity, contradiction, and conflict.* They show the ability to manage the complexity, contradictions, and conflict which are experienced when dealing with multiple countries and cultures. They develop a sensitivity to different cultures and cultural values; they function effectively in different cultural environments;[65] and they show the ability to handle more complexity and

uncertainty than is experienced by their domestic counterparts.[66] They consider more variables when solving problems and are not discouraged by adversity.

- *Manage organizational adaptability*. They demonstrate the ability to manage organizational change in response to new situations (that is, they are able to manage the global corporate culture and adapt it to multiple cultural environments). They show the ability to reframe their fields of reference, to be flexible, changing their organizational culture when necessary.[67] And they possess extensive curiosity and openness toward other ways of living and speaking, from which they draw ideas for organizational adaptation.
- *Manage multicultural teams*. They are able to effectively manage (and manage effective) cross-border and multicultural teams. They value the diversity present in such teams and are able to be a cross-border coach, coordinator, and mediator of conflict for such teams.[68] They relate well with diverse groups of people and are able to develop the necessary cross-border trust and teamwork that is important to the effective performance of such teams.[69]
- *Manage uncertainty and chaos,* which is so characteristic of global experience. They are comfortable with ambiguity and patient with evolving issues; they can make decisions in the face of uncertainty and can see patterns and connections within the chaos of global events. They show extensive curiosity about other cultures and the people who live in them.
- *Manage personal and organizational global learning*, both for themselves and for others with whom they work.

## Characteristics of organizations with a global mind-set

An organization with a global mind-set is often referred to as geocentric. That is, its ultimate goal is to create an organization with a globally integrated business system with a leadership team and workforce that have a worldwide perspective and approach. It recruits employees for their global and expatriate potential, because its perspective is that all employees must contribute to the global success of the firm. The whole workforce needs to be globally aware and support the enterprise's global strategy.

For example, at Tetra Pak (an MNE based in Lund, Sweden), global interaction is common, and employees with multiple-language skills and multiple-culture experience are in high demand.[70] "It seems every day we're searching the office for someone who speaks Swedish or German or Spanish to translate a fax or interpret during a phone call," says Barbara Shimkus, personnel manager in Tetra Pak's Chicago office.

At Bechtel, the American global engineering firm, restructuring has given the 25,000 employees who work on projects in more than seventy countries more regional authority.[71] Instead of managing from above, the firm is focusing more on multinational awareness and cultivation of its global talent. As Shirley Gaufin, vice-president of HR for Bechtel Group, puts it, "In the past, we were more of a

US firm doing business internationally. We are now becoming more 'global.' As part of that, we're working to develop a stronger global workforce." Bechtel is placing more emphasis than ever on global competencies, assuring that every member can contribute to future multinational growth.

It is, thus, not just members, e.g., of multinational product development or sales teams, that must interact daily with people in other countries, but in firms like Bechtel and Tetra Pak, everyone, including receptionists and secretaries, must answer daily phone calls and correspondence from overseas. The firm with a global mind-set understands this and all its managerial and IHR practices reflect this.

## Transformation: acquisition of a global mind-set

The bottom-line experience that is required for developing a global mind-set is living in another culture and going through the culture shock that is necessary to learning how to accept and to enjoy living in the foreign culture. A number of people have argued that in the end people who seem able to operate effectively in a global environment are not just described by a list of attributes that are largely extensions of the knowledge, skills, and abilities needed by those who are effective in a purely domestic environment. Indeed, the evidence is accumulating that at some point a fundamental transformation takes place for globally successful people – a transformation that can be described in shorthand as the acquisition of a global mind-set.[72] Such transformed people become more cosmopolitan, they extend their perspectives, they change their cognitive maps of the world:

> Out of this deep change, the individual develops a *new perspective or mind-set.* This is not just a new view of oneself but also a new view of one's organizational and professional role. This change goes far beyond a change in the skill-set – it is a change in the *person.* We know that these deep changes in personal identity occur as a result of being confronted with a higher level of complexity in the environment . . . and that is precisely what happens in an international assignment. . . . Not only does the person develop new perspectives, but he or she also *develops skills in the taking of new perspectives, and developing and holding multiple perspectives.* This ability to acquire and hold multiple, perhaps competing, perspectives (i.e., the ability to see a situation through another person's eyes) is a quality of a more "evolved" identity.[73]

As studies are now finding, the lessons of cultural adaptability are pretty much *only* learned with expatriation, that is, through living in another culture.[74] As with most learning experiences, global executives report learning from challenging assignments, significant other people, perspective-changing events, etc. But, when these experiences take place in different cultures, they take on a decidedly different tone; they are decidedly more complex. Functioning in a country significantly different from their own was an experience for which there was no substitute. And then doing it a second time, in a substantially different culture, again, was transformational. The key experience seemed to be "culture shock," the result of entering and learning to live in a radically different culture. Global executives report that one cannot learn cultural adaptability and the competencies associated with it (the development of a global mind-set) without actually living and working in another culture.

As John Pepper, former CEO and then Chairman of the board of directors of Proctor & Gamble puts it, "There are a few things that totally change your life, and taking my first international assignment in Italy was just that kind of experience. Of all the career changes that I have had, the international assignment was the most important and developmental. It changed me as a person."[75]

However, people don't necessarily learn about others or develop this global mind-set purely through being in close proximity or through osmosis. Proximity doesn't necessarily lead to better communication or understanding. Nor do common sense and goodwill take the place of deliberate education. That is, one must work at it, one must want to learn from their new cultural experiences and must let go of the attitude that what is familiar is necessarily best.[76]

To develop cultural literacy or competency, one must take deliberate steps to learn about another country's or culture's practices and values. One must make a concerted effort to learn about the deep values that motivate people and provide the context for their actions. One must experience the culture shock of coping with a new culture in order to begin to fully understand it so as to function effectively within it. And it is this that IHRM and MNEs must facilitate and encourage.

Many multinational enterprises, learning from both their own and others' experiences, now make overseas experience a necessity for the development of executives.[77] Indeed, all high-potential managers in these firms are required to have significant international experience as part of their career development. These international assignments, of course, work best when the expectations of the organization and the individual are aligned. That is, the real (and psychological) contract between the firm and the individual assignee need to be in agreement and both sides need to live up to their obligations and to the other sides' expectations.[78] And this requires constant vigilance by both sides as well as regular discussions about both expected consequences from the assignment and how the assignment is to unfold and how it actually does unfold.

## Management development in the global enterprise

In the last few years, a number of management researchers have reported on studies of global executives. These studies have reported what was found both in terms of what are the characteristics, or competencies, of these global executives and in terms of what it takes to develop these competencies. This last section in this chapter summarizes these studies. As will be demonstrated, the task of developing these global competencies is daunting, but IHR executives responsible for just this task can learn from these studies exactly what is required and, hopefully, move their organizations closer to creating development programs that can produce global executives.

## Global managerial competencies

The following presents the various studies that have identified the essential competencies of global executives in alphabetical order by name of the major author. As you will notice, there is overlap in concepts; yet there is also richness of diversity among these various studies. A composite profile would be difficult to draft, since the differences between the various studies are so great.

### Nancy Adler[79]

Adler focuses on the skills and competencies required by managers working for transnational firms. As she indicates, transnationally competent managers require a broader range of skills than traditional international managers. First, transnational managers must understand the worldwide business environment from a global perspective. And they must develop a series of skills for working with businesses and people from multiple countries and cultures. Table 10.3 summarizes the skills of a transnational manager and contrasts them to those required of the traditional international manager.

### Stewart Black, Allen Morrison, and Hal Gregersen[80]

This group of professors have written extensively about the management of expatriates. They reported on a three-year study of what they referred to as the "global explorers." Their in-depth interviews of 130 global executives from some fifty companies throughout North America, Europe, and Asia provided them with the finding that every global leader must have a core set of global characteristics. They found that global leaders are consistently competent in four important areas:

- *Inquisitiveness*. The characteristic of inquisitiveness and curiosity was the glue that held the other characteristics together. Effective global leaders are unceasingly curious. Far from being overwhelmed by all the differences in language, culture, government regulations, and so on that exist from one country to another, they are invigorated by the diversity. They love to learn and are driven to understand and master the complexities of the global business environment.
- *Perspective*. Global leaders also have a unique perspective on the world. While most managers have learned to avoid uncertainty and structure their environments to get rid of it, global leaders view uncertainty as an invigorating and natural aspect of international business.
- *Character*. Character is defined in this study as the leader's ability to connect emotionally with people of different backgrounds and cultures through the

*Table 10.3* The skills of the transnationally competent manager versus those of the traditional international manager

| Transnational skills | Transnationally competent managers | Traditional international managers |
| --- | --- | --- |
| Global perspective | Understand worldwide business environment from a global perspective | Focus on a single foreign country and on managing relationships between HQs and that country |
| Local responsiveness | Learn about many cultures | Become an expert on one culture |
| Synergistic learning | Work with and learn from people of many cultures simultaneously | Work with and coach people in each foreign culture separately or sequentially |
|  | Create a culturally synergistic organizational environment | Integrate foreigners into the headquarters' national organizational culture |
| Transition and adaptation | Adapt to living in many foreign cultures | Adapt to living in a foreign culture |
| Cross-cultural interaction | Use cross-cultural interaction skills on a daily basis throughout one's career | Use cross-cultural interaction skills primarily on foreign assignments |
| Collaboration | Interact with foreign colleagues as equals | Interact within clearly defined hierarchies of structural and cultural dominance |
| Foreign experience | Transpatriation for career and organization development | Expatriation or inpatriation primarily to get the job done |

consistent demonstration of personal integrity. This is essential for engendering trust and goodwill in a global workforce and with a global firm's many partners.

- *Savvy.* This is demonstrated by the ability to recognize global business opportunities and then to mobilize organizational global resources in order to capitalize on them. Global leaders are highly skilled at both identifying market opportunities and applying organizational resources to make the most of those opportunities.

### Maxine Dalton, Chris Ernst, Jennifer Deal, and Jean Leslie of the Center for Creative Leadership[81]

This team from the Center for Creative Leadership (CCL), through their interactions with hundreds of managers from around the world, identified five essential managerial capabilities that are important in both a domestic and an international environment, although their application in the global context requires significant adaptation. These core capabilities include the abilities to manage people, action, and information, the ability to cope with pressure, and a strong fundamental understanding of how business works. But being good at these skills in the domestic context does not mean that the individual manager will also be good at them in the global context. In order to adapt these skills to the global environment, CCL has found that the global manager is able to understand their use across geographic distance, different country infrastructures (everything from phones to banking and transportation systems), and differing cultural expectations.

In addition, CCL found that global managers had to learn to see the world through the eyes of others – at least to understand that what others are seeing is different from what they are seeing. Global managers have to allow their way of viewing the world to coexist with others' ways of viewing the world. To do this, global managers, in addition to being able to use and adapt the core capabilities, also develop four pivotal global capabilities:

- International business knowledge.
- Cultural adaptability.
- Perspective-taking (listening well and taking into account others' views).
- Ability to play the role of innovator (seeing problems in new ways and willing to try new approaches and to seize new opportunities).

These pivotal capabilities are critical to the manager when the work is global, but not when the work is domestic. These capabilities represent the knowledge and motivation to make the adaptations of the domestic skills to the global context and the specific skills needed to be successful internationally.

### Morgan McCall and George Hollenbeck[82]

McCall and Hollenbeck interviewed 101 executives in thirty-four cities and on three continents who were identified by their employers as their "global executives" in an effort to see if it might be possible to identify and develop such global executives. In the midst of studying the stories they uncovered through their interviews, McCall and Hollenbeck were able to identify what their interviewers related to them as the key competencies of the global executive. These are summarized in Box 10.3, and like the other lists here, include cultural, personal, and business competencies.

### Robert Rosen[83]

Rosen, a leading consultant to global firms, interviewed the CEOs of seventy-five global companies from twenty-eight countries, surveyed over 1,000 CEOs from companies in eighteen countries, and researched dozens of national cultures in his effort to identify the skills and competencies required for global leadership now and into the future. The result was four global literacies that Rosen describes as essential

## Box 10.3 Competencies of the global executive

### Open-minded and flexible in thought and tactics

The person is able to live and work in a variety of settings with different types of people and is willing and able to listen to other people, approaches, and ideas.

### Cultural interest and sensitivity

The person respects other cultures, people, and points of view; is not arrogant or judgmental; is curious about other people and how they live and work; is interested in differences; enjoys social competency; gets along well with others; is empathetic.

### Able to deal with complexity

The person considers many variables in solving a problem; is comfortable with ambiguity and patient in evolving issues; can make decisions in the face of uncertainty; can see patterns and connections; and is willing to take risks.

### Resilient, resourceful, optimistic, and energetic

The person responds to a challenge; is not discouraged by adversity; is self-reliant and creative; sees the positive side of things; has a high level of physical and emotional energy; is able to deal with stress.

### Honesty and integrity

Authentic, consistent, the person engenders trust.

### Stable personal life

The person has developed and maintains stress-resistant personal arrangements, usually family, that support a commitment to work.

### Value-added technical or business skills

The person has technical, managerial, or other expertise sufficient to provide his or her credibility.

to success in the new global marketplace. As Rosen says, "What's needed in this new, increasingly complex world is a new language of global business, a language where leaders see the world's business challenges as opportunities, think with an international mind-set, act with fresh global-centric leadership behaviors, and mobilize world-class companies."[84]

Rosen's global literacies include:

- *Personal literacy*: understanding and valuing oneself.
- *Social literacy*: working with, engaging, and challenging others.
- *Business literacy*: focusing and mobilizing your organization.
- *Cultural literacy*: valuing and leveraging cultural differences.

These four global literacies have to be implemented within the context of the global firm, helping the global leader answer the universal business questions of purpose, plan, teamwork, resources, and results in the global context.

## *Michael Marquardt*[85]

In terms of purely global business competencies, Marquardt's framing is among the best. It illustrates the difficulty of the task of development, which Marquardt suggests can best be done through multinational teams, especially teams that use action learning to solve global business problems. As is discussed throughout this chapter, many also argue that international assignments are also critical. According to Marquardt, global leaders should seek to develop a variety of "globable" competencies, such as the abilities to:

- Describe clearly the forces behind the globalization of business.
- Recognize and connect global market trends, technological innovation, and business strategy.
- Outline issues essential to effective strategic alliances.
- Frame day-to-day management issues, problems, and goals in a global context.
- Think and plan beyond historical, cultural, and political boundaries, structures, systems, and processes.
- Create and effectively lead worldwide business teams.
- Help one's company adopt a functional global organization structure.

Of course, many companies have also developed their own list of global competencies, a task which is often completed in conjunction with developing a global management development strategy. These range from a list of 150 competencies at Citicorp to twelve at 3M.[86] The 3M competencies are grouped under the following categories: *Fundamental* (ethics and integrity, intellectual capacity, maturity and judgment), *Essential* (customer orientation, developing people, inspiring others, business health and results), and *Visionary* (global perspective, vision and strategy, nurturing innovation, building alliances, and organizational agility). Each of these has a set of behaviors which define specifically what is expected. For example, the global perspective competency involves these behaviors:

- Respects, values, and leverages other customs, cultures, and values. Uses a global management team to better understand and grow the total business; able to leverage the benefits from working in multicultural environments.
- Optimizes and integrates resources on a global basis, including manufacturing, research, and businesses across countries, and functions to increase 3M's growth and profitability.
- Satisfies global customers and markets from anywhere in the world.
- Actively stays current on world economies, trade issues, international market trends, and opportunities.

This competency model is now used to evaluate the top executives at 3M and their direct reports, the behaviors are used to set expectations for development for executives throughout the organization, and, lastly, it is used for succession planning. 3M leadership believe this approach is critical to the deepening of their "bench strength" and to the development of a stronger pool of global leaders. Ultimately, the belief is that this will result in improved and measurable business success.

In the global business environment, each firm has its own challenges and each country grapples with its own world view. What is similar and different among people, firms, and countries is what the globally competent manager learns to appreciate and use. To use these similarities and differences, global managers have to learn to read cultures and to not underestimate their influences. They know well that a superficial understanding can have a tremendous negative impact on business. They understand the impact of culture on management strategy and style, and they know how to bring diverse people and businesses from different cultures together. This is what these various studies have demonstrated and illustrated.

Now the question is, what can organizations (and IHR) do to enhance the development of these characteristics, competencies, and literacies? That is, what should the management development program for a global firm look like?

## Management development of global competencies

This chapter has related the stories of multiple firms as they strive to develop their global workforces and their global managers. And it has described the work of many researchers and organizational observers about those strivings. There is variance in findings and foci. For example, one level of focus is about what the firm can do to enhance its overall level of international cultural and business savvy. And a second level of concern has to do with how to develop the individual manager's level of international cultural and business savvy. This last section offers a summary of the examples and research findings on these two points.

Box 10.4 summarizes a number of steps that IHR might take to increase cross-cultural skills within the organization.[87] In general, these involve ways to more fully integrate people from multiple countries and with cross-cultural experience into the firm in all functional and business areas.

## Box 10.4 The development of organizational cross-cultural savvy

- *Make globalization an integral part of the company's mission.* Increase global awareness among employees by communicating the firm's global strategy and by educating employees about international suppliers, customers, and competitors. Provide access to international business and news publications (newspapers, magazines, books). Help employees to understand global interdependence, particularly as it relates to the business.
- *Know your own culture.* An in-depth knowledge of the firm's corporate and national culture is a prerequisite to identifying and eliminating stereotypes about other cultures.
- *Do not stereotype others.* Having a global mind-set requires employees to be flexible and adaptable to change. Do not base assumptions about others on stereotypes, but on an understanding of their culture's various values and how business is conducted.
- *Recruit staff with cross-cultural and language skills.* An increasing number of potential employees already have an international background, education, and experience. It's easier to teach new recruits about your business practices and products than it is to develop non-existent cultural and language skills. At a minimum, seek recruits with a strong and active interest in "going international."
- *Promote people from different cultural backgrounds to management positions.* By diversifying the cultural and national backgrounds of your managers, your company will be less likely to view the world solely from a domestic perspective.
- *Utilize your global workforce.* Assign your high-potential employees from foreign locations to headquarters and to other countries. Assign your best home-grown talent to foreign assignments. And then use these people in critical assignments (during and after the initial assignments) to utilize their international perspectives and experiences.
- *Provide opportunities for cross-cultural learning and languages.* Consider the acquisition of cross-cultural and language skills as a part of employees' personal and professional development. Provide them with learning opportunities through education, training, and international assignments. Working in a global environment requires people to become proficient in at least one additional language. Language acquisition is the basis of socialization into a culture, and a competitive advantage for conducting business better in that new environment.
- *Learn from your international experiences.* Share the knowledge of your international successes and failures with everyone so that everyone may learn.

- *Shift your emphasis from short-term task accomplishment to long-term relationship building.* This will make it easier to conduct business in countries in Asia and Latin America.
- *Remember the global rule:* treat people from other cultures as they would like to be treated. That is, it is up to the visitor/guest to adapt to the host, not expect the host to adapt to the visitor.

But in addition to this, the observation must be made that all the studies reported in this chapter pretty much agree that the most important aspects of global management development occur primarily on the job, that is they occur through specific experiences that have the capacity to teach the lessons that are necessary for success as a manager. In the global context, then, those experiences must also include jobs in other countries. One must go through a number of critical learning experiences, such as being responsible for a foreign start-up, solving some significant problem, and a significant jump in responsibility, specifically in a foreign assignment.

This is not to imply that most global firms don't also provide extensive management training in many forms.[88] Cross-border teams, action learning teams with global membership and global projects, case studies, simulations, even reading assignments and lectures contribute to the knowledge, and to a lesser extent, to the skills, that managers must develop for competency in the global marketplace. But, in the end, foreign work experiences must be an integral component of any successful global management development program.

In addition, as mentioned in earlier sections, such a program must also include early identification of management potential (and, in the global context, assessment of cross-cultural potential, as well), self- and organizational-assessment for global assignment potential and interest, be accessible to all members of the firm around the world, and, again, provide as much training as is possible, prior to actual foreign posting.

Bestfoods, formerly CPC International, and now owned by Unilever Corporation, provides an example of how such an inclusive development program can pay off. Bestfoods, with over 60 percent of its business outside the US, its home country, and with operations in sixty countries and products marketed in 110, has made a corporate commitment to reflect total inclusiveness throughout its workforce, beginning at the top.[89] Half of its corporate officers come from outside the US, with eight nationalities represented. Similarly, members of the board of directors hold five different passports. Two-thirds of its 44,000 employees work outside the US, and by 1997, 14 percent of its board, 16 percent of its corporate officers, and 13 percent of all of its directors and vice-presidents were women. Indeed, experience and observation suggest that women in fact can and do make major contributions around the world, as individual contributors at all levels, as international assignees, as members of global teams, and in most countries.[90]

IHRM in Action 10.4 describes Colgate's global management development program.[91] It provides a good synthesis of many of the ideas presented here and it seems to have paid off well for Colgate, making it one of the most successful of global firms. This chapter has mentioned many other firms that implement significant and successful global management development programs, such as Unilever and 3M. Others that have developed programs similar to Colgate's and to the others mentioned and also benefit from them in terms of their competitive stature throughout their global operations include Gillette, Rhône-Poulenc Rorer, and JTI (Japan Tobacco International).[92] All involve high-potential employees from throughout their global operations, all involve extensive formal training as well as required multiple international assignments, and all have benefited both from globalizing their firm's operations as well as globalizing their executive ranks.

## Cross-national career advancement

One aspect of global management development that has not been dealt with directly in this chapter, but which needs to be incorporated into any global firm's management development program, is the development and promotion of foreign employees through assignment to higher positions in third countries. This is called "cross-national career advancement."[93] It is a widespread practice among Continental European firms. Electrolux, a Swedish firm, had a French director in its Singapore factory.[94] Some American firms practice it also. A manager of Hyatt Hotel in Jakarta was Danish, who subsequently was transferred to Egypt. Michelin (the head of Michelin-Okamoto in Japan was a German who was fluent in Japanese) and Thomson of France (German, Irish, and Japanese engineers work together in its laboratory in Singapore) practice it.

In contrast, until recently Scandinavian Airline System (SAS) did not practice it in its Tokyo office. But it has begun to practice it as it has worked to develop a global development program. The effect for SAS has been considerable. In a small local office of twenty employees, one cannot advance very far if there is no cross-national career advancement. Therefore it will not attract young ambitious applicants. But establishment of cross-national career advancement opens wider and higher opportunities and makes the firm much more attractive to top Japanese graduates.

Those who are cross-nationally promoted are usually at managerial, technical, or professional levels, since those at lower levels have some room for advancement inside the country (even in small offices). Therefore, cross-nationally promoted employees usually assume a managerial position in a culture that is foreign to them. They must be capable of management adaptation to the host-country culture, primarily meaning how to interact and how to organize.

# Colgate takes its management development global

Mary Beth Robles, a New York native, is director of marketing for Colgate-Palmolive in Brazil. Fluent in English, Spanish, and Portuguese, in addition to a little French, she is a product of Colgate's global management development program. Robles epitomizes their international cadre of employees, the people behind their global sales, almost 70 percent of which come from outside the US. She's lived in Madrid and DC and her stints for the company include Mexico, Uruguay, and Atlanta, in addition to her current position in Sao Paolo.

Colgate-Palmolive has been operating internationally for more than sixty years. Its products, such as Colgate toothpaste, Palmolive soap, Fab clothes detergent, and Ajax cleanser, are household names in more than 170 countries. Colgate understands global complexities, having been in the global arena for decades. It doesn't underestimate the importance of HR and staffing needs for bottom-line results. However, it wasn't until quite recently that Colgate looked to HR to design a strategy that would directly affect its global staffing.

In the 1980s, as Colgate-Palmolive greatly expanded its overseas reach, it began to focus more clearly on its need for a global workforce. It became clear that HR's ability to identify and develop global talent to meet business goals would directly impact the bottom line. As HR addressed this issue, it became clear that certain decisions were going to have to be made, decisions that were complicated by the size and scope of the global business. For example, how were they going to staff their overseas operations? When was it most effective to rely on expatriates versus local nationals? Who is it best to send abroad? What personal and professional qualities lead to success? What about host-country employees? How could they develop a team of global managers?

In 1991 a global team of twenty-five Colgate HR leaders and senior line managers began a year-long quest to develop a global staffing plan. The group met to develop global criteria for selection, succession planning, coaching, and performance management. Brian Smith, director of global staffing and HR strategy, said, "This global business strategy requires identifying a certain type of manager who not only understands the particular niche and communities in which we operate locally, but who also has that global perspective and understands the tremendous benefits of a global product line. It allows managers to move quicker and be more competitive internationally, while it demands that they wear a global hat and take the global perspective."

One direct result of this planning was the Global Marketing Program. It takes approximately fifteen high-potential recent MBA graduates per year and rotates them through various departments for eighteen to twenty-four months. Recruits learn about the sales process, experience the global-business development group, and

continued

get exposed to manufacturing and technology. After their stint at company headquarters, they're deployed overseas. The program is seen as such a powerful tool for creating the international cadre of global management that Colgate needs, that more than 15,000 people stand in line for the slots every year. Typically, participants have a master's degree, speak at least one foreign language, and either through past experience or personal travel, demonstrate an interest in living abroad.

As Colgate moves these people up the global ladder, it looks for individuals who have developed functional competencies, who have developed sensitivity to diverse cultures, and who understand their own expectations of living abroad. The fact that Colgate rotates the individuals early in their careers helps people figure out early on if they can handle this kind of responsibility. If they can, it is common in this program for someone to move functionally from finance to marketing to human resources, and move from Ivory Coast to Panama to Thailand before returning to New York headquarters some dozen years later. And it isn't just about recruiting US nationals, it attracts people from around the world.

Building on the success of the Global Marketing Program, the company has replicated it in other functional areas, as well, such as in finance and human resources. In addition to recent grads, other high-potential people early in their careers already in the company are also encouraged to apply. It gives them exposure and perspective.

As a part of these programs, and for other business needs, Colgate offers an array of overseas assignments to its employees: long-term, short-term, and stop-gap for particular expertise needs. Because of the firm's reputation, it attracts people who want to become globalites – those who want global skills so that they can have international careers anywhere in the world. Colgate makes possible a diverse and fluid environment in which people frequently move in and out of US headquarters. The result is that fully 60 percent of the company's international assignees are from places other than the US. And since 1960, half its CEOs have not been US nationals. In addition, all of the top executives speak at least two languages. Colgate is a global company for which management development on a global scale has certainly paid off.

## Global trends in training and development

This chapter has demonstrated the important role of IHR in its delivery of training and management development to the global enterprise. Indeed, even major international development bodies, such as the International Labour Organization, the World Bank, the International Monetary Fund, and the United Nations have focused on the importance of training and development, both for their own organizations and for transnational firms, in general.[95] It is helpful at the end of this discussion to summarize what these organizations are saying about the importance into the future of training and development activities and to combine that with some suggestions about how IHR and MNEs can continue to use training and development to ensure their global success. These trends are summarized in Box 10.5.

## Box 10.5 Global trends in training and development

- Training will continue as a highly valued activity for building and enhancing the skills required by enterprises and individuals. The progress of the evolution of work requirements from agriculture to manufacturing to service to information is still evident at all stages in most countries. Many important skills will survive, but they will be in new forms and in new environments.
- Training and development will continue to be essential for enhancing competitive advantage. Enhancing workforce capabilities and capacities will make it possible to be competitive anywhere in world markets. Multinational enterprises will increasingly understand the importance of training and development and seek to enhance their performance through more sophisticated training and development programs.
- Training in soft skills will grow in importance, including cultural training, customer relations, safety and security, management skills, etc.
- Training in working in new ways and in venues will continue to gain in importance.
- Training will grow in importance in mega-corporations spanning the globe as workforce development will increasingly become a global undertaking.
- Training will increasingly become re-training as skill sets deteriorate and are reconstituted in new forms and as young workforces in developing countries make up an ever-growing portion of the global firm's workforce. This will also be driven partly by the increasingly rapid technological change and by other factors inherent in the globalization of business.
- Systems of training will have to become increasingly flexible and fluid, responding to the needs of a global economy demanding rapid workforce responses to changing circumstances and product innovations.
- Distance learning technologies will become more common and implemented globally.
- Human capital investment and knowledge management will become the centers of global business strategy. Training and development are cornerstones of this strategy.
- New categories of workers will increasingly enter the workforce and need to be trained. Training will have to respond to the aging and the diversification of the workforce.

## Conclusion

This chapter has focused on the training and development of the MNE's global workforce. This included training of host-country workforces, training and preparation of international assignees, and global management development, including the nature and development of a global mind-set, the competencies of global managers, and the nature of management development programs in a global context.

Since a highly trained and competent global workforce and management team is so crucial to the building and retaining of competitive advantage in the global marketplace, the effective design and implementation of global training and development programs becomes a central responsibility of IHRM in today's MNE. A key ingredient in creating competitive advantage through a high-performing and fast-learning workforce is an effective program both to train local workforces and to prepare employees and managers for successful overseas assignments and to then ensure the integration of that training and development into the ongoing global operations of the firm.

The most important theme for design of training for local workforces was the importance of sensitivity to local language and culture. And the most important theme for management development was the importance of international assignments. The effective IHR department understands both of these issues and works to ensure that both are handled well and with sophistication. This chapter has provided both many examples and research and writing of what firms from around the world are doing to offer successful global training and development programs. It is now up to IHR managers in other firms to use what was described here to develop successful global training and development programs in their own organizations.

## Points for further discussion

1 What type of training and management development did Lincoln Electric use for its employees in China?
2 Did Lincoln Electric do a good job of preparing its managers for their expatriate assignments?
3 Who should be responsible for development of global competencies in an MNE?

# 11

# Global compensation, benefits, and taxes

## Learning objectives

After considering this chapter, the reader will be able to describe or explain:

- The basic objectives of global compensation
- The seven options available for design of a compensation system for expatriates
- The most commonly used system for expatriate compensation: the balance sheet approach
- The two major components of the balance sheet approach: incentives and adjustments
- The major approaches to managing taxes
- Major problem areas with managing compensation and taxes
- Design of a global compensation system
- A number of critical components of compensation and benefits for the global workforce

## Key terms

- Balance sheet approach, localization, lump sum
- Cost of living allowance (COLA)
- Stock options, employee ownership

The design and maintenance of an enterprise's compensation system is always a critical responsibility for human resource managers. The conduct of international business makes this responsibility much more complex and difficult. The determination of individual and organizational pay and benefits on an international basis becomes extremely complicated because of considerations such as pay and benefits for international assignees, subsidiary workforces in multiple countries, employees from many different countries (such as inpatriates, HCNs, and TCNs), varying country approaches to and levels of pay and benefits, and problems such as dealing with multiple currencies, exchange rates, inflation rates, tax systems and rates, and differing standards and costs of living.

Even though much space in this text has already been devoted to many other IHRM responsibilities, the majority of the time of headquarters-based international HR managers is spent creating and managing compensation packages for expatriates.[1] When development of compensation systems for subsidiaries and determining pay for a global workforce is added to IHRM responsibilities, it is easy to see why this area of concern is so important.

One of the reasons that this area of IHRM responsibility is so complex is that salary levels and benefit provisions invariably differ significantly among the various countries in which an MNE operates.[2] Employees performing essentially similar jobs in different countries will receive varying amounts and forms of compensation. This is due to differing costs of living and general pay levels throughout these economies and varying traditions and values for particular jobs. Thus, it is increasingly difficult to develop and maintain a compensation package that attracts and retains qualified expatriates and local managers, copes successfully with changing exchange rates and varying inflation rates, and is consistent yet fair to both expatriates and local employees. In addition, the cost of attracting and maintaining expatriates and an international cadre of managers and technicians in the traditional ways has become so expensive that MNEs are now looking for new ways to handle international compensation.[3] But the effective design of just such a compensation philosophy and package is absolutely necessary for successful human resource management in the multinational enterprise.

How an MNE copes with these issues tends to at least partially be a function of its level of international development. In the early stages of development, the firm's primary international involvement will be with a limited number of expatriates sent abroad to market its products, transfer its technology, and manage relatively small operations. At this stage of development, compensation concerns are largely limited to providing adequate remuneration and incentives for expatriates. But as the firm's international involvement develops even further, concerns about compensation programs for employees from multiple countries moving around the world for the firm as well as equity among workforces in many different global locations present many new problems.

Therefore, the main objectives for the typical MNE global compensation program include:

- Attraction and retention of employees who are qualified for foreign assignments (from the perspective of the parent company, but includes the perspectives of the PCNs, HCNs, and TCNs).

- Facilitation of transfers between foreign affiliates, between foreign affiliates and the parent company (usually headquarters), and between parent-company and foreign locations.
- Establishment and maintenance of a consistent and reasonable relationship between the compensation of employees of all affiliates, both at home and abroad.
- Maintenance of compensation that is reasonable in relation to the practices of competitors yet minimizes costs to the extent possible.

One of the most important considerations for multinational enterprises in the design of their compensation programs is the problem of comparability (although cost is probably a very close additional and primary consideration). Indeed, in at least one survey, 77 percent of the expatriates surveyed were dissatisfied with their salaries and benefits and their international compensation packages in general.[4] (Not all surveys show this level of dissatisfaction, but these results suggest that at least some samples of expatriates are unhappy with their compensation.) And a significant portion of this dissatisfaction was due to feelings of inequity in their salaries and benefits.

This problem of comparability has at least two significant components: (1) maintaining comparability in salaries and benefits (to similar employees in other firms and to peers within the firm) for employees who transfer from one country to another (either from the parent company to foreign subsidiaries or from one subsidiary to another or to headquarters); and (2) maintaining competitive and equitable salaries and benefits among the various operations of the organization.

Until recently, most MNEs felt it was necessary for expatriates to receive a salary and benefit package at least comparable to what they were receiving in their countries of origin.[5] (Because of the high cost of expatriates and because of changing attitudes about and approaches to international assignments – such as the use of shorter assignments, more business trips, and more people willing to work at local salaries – this view about expatriate compensation is being questioned. This is discussed in more detail later in the chapter.) But comparisons between local nationals and expatriates (and between local nationals in different locales of the multinational firm) are inevitably made. In a globally competitive economy (or, even, a regionally competitive one, such as within Europe), recruiting and holding on to the best employees requires developing a compensation strategy and policy that will minimize problems associated with such comparisons. This chapter discusses both of these issues: wage determination and comparability for expatriates and compensation program design and comparability for subsidiaries in multiple countries.

For firms that are newly developing their international presence, the answers to these three questions may help establish their overall compensation policies:

- Who (which other companies) are their competition for people (local firms or international firms)?
- How much should their compensation and benefits conform to headquarters goals and practice versus practice at the overseas location?
- To what extent does the firm want to set precedent for its future presence in the international arena. (Does the firm want any particular practice or policy to be its

program for all future situations or does it want to customize compensation packages for each international assignee and subsidiary?)

IHRM in Action 11.1 illustrates how difficult these issues can be for one multinational high-tech firm headquartered in San José, California.[6] Even though there seem to be many reasons to maintain company-wide pay scales and comparable benefit packages so that, for example, all marketing managers for consumer products worldwide are paid on the same pay scale, not adapting wage scales to local markets presents numerous problems.[7] In the first case, such marketing managers are less likely to feel inequities among themselves around the world and the problems associated with keeping track of disparate country-by-country wage rates is simplified.

In the second case, problems are created because it is much more expensive to live in some countries (such as Japan) than others (like Greece). If these cost-of-living differences aren't considered it may be almost impossible to get expatriates to accept postings to high cost locales. But paying marketing managers in different countries different salaries based on the local cost of living won't solve all problems either. New problems are thus created by, for example, moving a highly remunerated marketing manager from, say, Tokyo, to Athens. (In all cases, an assumption underlying the approach is that the firm can determine fairly accurately what the community pay levels are within each of the countries of its subsidiaries – an assumption that is clearly not always correct.)

First the chapter looks at the problems associated with compensation for expatriates. Because of the extreme complexity of this subject (MNEs universally contract with specialists to administer the details of expatriate compensation, benefits, and taxes), this chapter can provide only a short overview of many of the issues. Second, the chapter looks at the design of global compensation programs. And last, the chapter examines the problems associated with the design of worldwide benefit and taxation programs and policies.

## Compensation and benefits for expatriates

Just as there are objectives for an overall international compensation program, the component that involves expatriates (expats) must also meet certain objectives in order to be effective. These include (1) providing an incentive to leave the home country for a foreign assignment; (2) maintaining a given standard of living (although this is being questioned by many MNEs as the cost of sustaining expatriates overseas gets too high); (3) taking into consideration career and family needs; and (4) facilitating re-entry into the home country at the end of the foreign assignment.[8] To achieve these objectives, MNEs typically pay a high premium over and beyond base salaries to induce managers to accept overseas assignments. The costs to firms often range from two to two and a half times to four to four and a half times the cost of maintaining the manager in a comparable position at home.[9]

# Compensation problems with a global workforce

Expanding the international workforce to include non-US employees has brought increased capabilities and decreased costs – along with a new set of compensation problems. For example, the director of international HR for a large multinational company, faced just such a dilemma. "It seems as though our international compensation program has gotten out of hand. I have US expatriates, third-country nationals, and inpatriates yelling at me about their allowances. [In addition] headquarters is yelling at me because the costs are too high. Quite frankly, I can't seem to get any answers from our consultant, and no one else in the industry seems to know how to approach the problem."

This San José-based multinational has forty US expatriates working as field engineers and marketing managers in fourteen countries. But it also has foreign national employees from the Philippines, Japan, and Bolivia working alongside the US employees in eight locations worldwide. And, finally, it has foreign nationals from Thailand and the Philippines working with US nationals at the organization's San José, California, headquarters. In all cases, it is the firm's policy to send such employees out on foreign assignments for less than five years and then return them to their home countries. An example of the type of complaints that were being received from the expats involves the following problem concerning inpatriate employees working at the San José headquarters.

The firm has a field engineer from the Philippines who's earning the equivalent of US$25,000 in Manila. It has another field engineer from Thailand who's earning the equivalent of US$30,000 in Bangkok. And they've both been relocated to the San José facility and are working side by side with American field engineers who earn $60,000 for the same job. Not only do they work side by side, but they live near each other, shop at the same stores, and eat at the same restaurants. The problem the IHR director has is that he's spending a lot of money on cost-of-living adjustment data for expats from two different home countries, both going to San José, and yet their current standard of living is the same, and the same as that of their local peers. They're angry because their allowances don't reflect how they live in San José. Their allowances also don't reflect how they lived in their home countries, either.

"So what we have are two employees, one earning $25,000 and the other earning $30,000 (plus cost-of-living adjustments), working and living side by side with US counterparts who are earning $60,000. The solution that most companies have tried is to simply raise the foreign nationals' salaries to the $60,000 US level, thereby creating a host-country pay system for a home-country employee.

"Unfortunately, there's nothing more pathetic than the tears of your foreign nationals when it's time to return home, and you have to tell them you're cutting their salary to the pre-US assignment level. What you . . . are looking for is a pay system that will compensate your foreign nationals either by pay or by provided benefits [including, e.g., housing and local transportation], in a consistent, fair and equitable manner, and will allow you to repatriate them with minimal trauma."

## Types of expatriates for purposes of compensation

In the past, most MNEs (particularly from the US), compensated all expats with standard incentives and adjustments. As described in Chapter 8, however, firms are realizing that not all expats are alike and do not need to be compensated as though they were all the same. This has led to the development of different programs for different groups and even greater administrative complexity.

For the purposes of compensation, there appear to be at least five distinct types of expats. These include (1) temporaries (employees who are on short-term assignments, typically less than six months); (2) young, relatively inexperienced expats (with assignments from six months to five years) who can be compensated and managed similar to local hires; (3) older, experienced expats (relocated for their technical or managerial skills) who are compensated with incentives, add-ons, and adjustments; (4) international cadre (expats from throughout the firm) who move from one foreign assignment to another and need to be compensated with a global salary and benefits; and (5) permanent expats (posted to a foreign country but who stay there for an extended period – beyond the normal five-year limit for expats) who need to be reclassified as locals.

Each of these types of expats has different needs and can be compensated on different programs. Many MNEs are beginning to recognize these options and are looking for more flexible expat compensation systems. The next section describes the differing approaches now being used by various MNEs.

## Approaches to compensation for expats

There are seven basic approaches followed by global enterprises to compensate their expats.

### *Negotiation/*ad hoc

When firms first start sending employees on international assignments, and while their number of assignees is still relatively low, the common approach to determining pay and benefits for those expats is *ad hoc*, or negotiation of a separate (and usually unique) compensation package for each individual considered for an overseas posting. At the early stages of "going international" the firm sends its best expert overseas. There usually isn't much of a search; and the firm does whatever it takes to get the person relocated and pays whatever costs arise. Because the person and the assignment are so important, the firm tends to take care of all of their concerns. This approach is quite simple initially, and, given the inexperience of HR managers at this stage, the limited amount of information available about how to design a compensation system for expatriates, and the many complexities in such a compensation package compared with domestic compensation and benefits, it is easy to see why IHR managers follow this approach.

## *Balance sheet*

The approach followed by most multinationals when their international business expands to the point where the firm has a larger number of expats (in the vicinity of twenty or so) is what is referred to as the *balance sheet* approach. At this stage, the negotiation, or *ad hoc*, approach will have led to too many inconsistencies between the compensation packages of its many expats and the firm will realize it needs to develop policy and practice that will apply to all expatriates. (In addition, the *ad hoc* approach will now be viewed as taking too much time – and cost – to negotiate, develop, and manage such a unique package for each expat.) The firm will seek a more standard approach and will begin to make policy about what will and what will not be covered (although the actual application of all the possibilities in a balance sheet approach can still be quiet cumbersome and administratively expensive).

In essence, the balance sheet approach involves an effort by the multinational to ensure that its expatriates are "made whole." That is, at a minimum, expats should be no worse off for accepting an overseas assignment. Ideally, the compensation package not only should make the expatriate whole but also should provide incentive to take the foreign assignment, to remove any worry about compensation issues while on that assignment, and to ensure that the individual and his or her family feel good about having been on the assignment. Making all of this even more complicated, of course, is that it takes place in an environment that increasingly asks IHRM to control all employment costs, including the costs of expatriation.

Figure 11.1 provides a model that helps to understand the balance sheet approach to expatriate compensation. This has particularly been the approach of MNEs with significant international activity but prior to becoming what was referred to earlier as a global or transnational firm. This approach is primarily used when the MNE is sending expats from the parent firm to its foreign subsidiaries. The approach becomes much more complex as the firm evolves to moving individuals between foreign subsidiaries and from its foreign subsidiaries back to its headquarters or other home country locations (as illustrated in IHRM in Action 11.1). Firms that are also developing an international cadre of managers who move from foreign assignment to foreign assignment add even another level of complexity to expat compensation and difficulty in application of the balance sheet approach.

Box 11.1 lists most of the components that a complete balance sheet program could provide. Box 11.1 expands on the items listed in Figure 11.1. As in Figure 11.1, these items are listed separately for incentive components and equalization components. What this illustrates and confirms is that an MNE that is seriously trying to make its expats whole does indeed provide an expensive package of support. Refer to Table 11.2 for an example of the costs associated with an hypothetical expat relocation from the US to France.

The balance sheet approach is particularly used for experienced senior and mid-level expats and keeps them whole compared with their home-country peers and with their lifestyles while at home while encouraging and facilitating their movement abroad

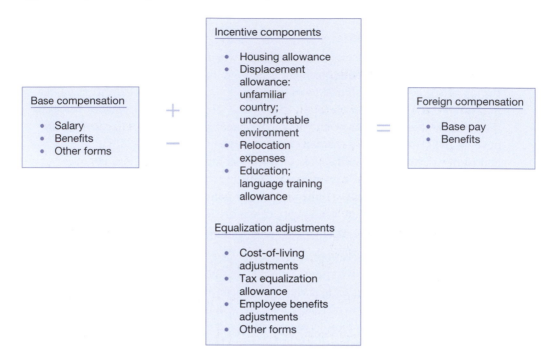

*Figure 11.1* International compensation: balance sheet approach

and return home at the end of their assignments, meeting many of the objectives for expat compensation. But with a large number of expats, this can become as complex to administer as the *ad hoc* negotiated packages. Some firms have found that this approach begins to lead managers to view the incentives and adjustments as entitlements that are sometimes difficult to change (indeed, in some countries, they are mandated as entitlements, once offered, as described in the chapter on employment law). And some expats have complained that this approach to determining their overseas compensation (for example, defining their spending patterns to determine the cost-of-living adjustments) is much more intrusive into their personal lives (basically determining their appropriate standards of living, etc.) than is true for the traditional domestic compensation package.

The balance sheet approach to determination of an expat's compensation (which is still pretty much customized, in most firms, for each expatriate, although there will be standardized options) begins with the employee's existing parent-company compensation (salary, benefits, and any other forms of monetary or non-monetary remuneration). To this is added two other components: a series of incentives to accept and enjoy the foreign posting and a series of equalization components that ensure the expatriate does not suffer from foreign-country differences in salary or benefits. Interestingly, today, even with pressure to reduce the high cost of expat compensation, most MNEs still find it necessary to provide significant incentives to encourage potential assignees to accept foreign postings.

## Box 11.1 Salary differentials for foreign assignments

### Incentive components

- Overseas/foreign service premiums
- Compensation for life adjustments (displacement allowances: unfamiliar country, uncomfortable/harsh/dangerous environment)
- Relocation/travel expenses; house-hunting expenses; shipment and storage of household goods; furnishings for foreign housing; home sale protection or rental assistance; automobile shipping or sale protection
- Temporary living expenses
- Housing allowance: comparable to original home; comparable to foreign peers; utilities allowance
- Education allowance for self, children, spouse; language and cultural training allowance
- Spousal support: education, income replacement, employment services and career planning
- Perquisites, e.g., club memberships, home leave, R&R leave, company car and driver
- Tax preparation assistance
- Financial advice
- Expatriation counseling
- Home-country career support and counseling
- Repatriation assistance and planning

### Equalization adjustments

- Cost-of-living adjustment (COLA)
- Reimbursement for payments into host-country welfare plans
- Income taxes – withheld for home taxes, pay local taxes; equalization and protection
- Protection for fluctuation in exchange rates; inflation
- Employee benefits adjustments (pension, retirement savings plans, health care)

One of the key complications in this balance sheet approach is the determination of the base upon which to add incentives and adjustments.[10] A number of possibilities exist, including basing the expatriate's salary on:

- Home-country salaries (this is the most common base for the balance sheet approach).
- International (usually based on headquarters) standard.
- Regional standard (e.g., the EU, US and Canada, Latin America, South East Asia).

- Host-country (or destination) salaries; or the salaries of other expatriates while on assignment – peers and/or colleagues – in the host location.
- Better of home or host approach.

The choice of base to use may be best related to the nature of the firm and its international business strategy.[11] That is, if the international assignment is long (three to five years) and assignees often go from one foreign-country assignment to another, then an international standard is probably most appropriate (but it will still probably be based on the parent-country/company base, particularly if the MNE is from a high-wage, developed country). If assignees go to foreign postings for relatively short assignments and then return to the parent country, then a home country base makes more sense. For truly global firms, such as Coca-Cola, it may make sense to use regional bases (although these may in reality be some percentage of the home country base, with the intent of eventually merging the regional bases with the parent-country base).

To date, most companies compensate their expatriates based on either a home- or host-country philosophy (or some combination).[12] The home-based balance sheet approach is used by most firms, particularly in situations where the expat is opening new markets and new operations, transferring technology, and training local staff.[13] These are clearly not jobs similar to those performed by locals. Thus the need to maintain equity is greatly lessened. But where the operations are ongoing and in developed countries, the expat assignments are likely to be alongside locals performing similar jobs and the need for equity is high and a host-country base makes more sense. In addition, an MNE with operations in many foreign countries may opt for a home-country or headquarters (international) approach because of the sheer size of the administrative paperwork involved. On the other hand, if the firm only operates in one or two countries, a host-country approach may be necessary because of local legal or cultural differences.

The better of home or host approach compares the net pay under the home-country compensation system to a local (location of assignment) net salary. The expat then receives the higher of the two. The philosophy underlying this system is that an expatriate will never have to live at a lower standard than a local counterpart, but that the expat will also be protected when the home-country package requires a higher standard than the local counterpart receives.

Interestingly, in contrast to the earlier survey referred to, with all the attention given to designing these compensation packages for expatriates, other surveys show that expatriate managers tend to be pretty satisfied with their financial packages but dissatisfied with the limited career planning, lifestyle support, and cultural training that is provided.[14] This suggests, as discussed in previous chapters, that more attention ought to be paid to these non-compensation factors. There are, however, other issues in the balance sheet approach that MNEs need to decide:

*Determining the type and amount of incentives*   Once the base salary has been determined, then the firm must decide which incentives it feels are necessary to convince its employees that it will be to their financial advantage (or, at least as is being increasingly maintained, not to their disadvantage),[15] to take the foreign assignment. One of the key issues that has arisen, here, at least for more experienced MNEs, is the high cost of expatriation. In the past (and still normally for less developed multinational firms), many incentives were offered, often with sizable monetary benefit to the expatriate.

For example, one of the most common incentives has been a large "overseas premium," used to (1) compensate the expatriate for all the adjustments that s/he will need to make; (2) compensate the expatriate and her/his family for the "dislocation" of having to move to an unfamiliar country and to live in what might be seen as an uncomfortable (i.e., different) environment; (3) provide an incentive to take the foreign assignment; and (4) keep up with the practices of other MNEs. These premiums used to average about 25 percent of the expatriate's base pay. Today, it is more common for this premium to be about 15 percent of base pay. Also, these premiums were higher for high cost-of-living postings, such as Tokyo, Geneva, or Brussels (see Table 11.1, State Department indexes). As an example of the disparities from one city to another, the annual cost of living for a family of four from New York City having a US salary of $75,000 in 2002 was $63,750 in Johannesburg, $90,000 in Moscow, $108,000 in Stockholm and London, and $137,250 in Tokyo![16] A few years ago (as, for example, reported in the first edition of this book) the range was much wider, from $64,000 in Mexico City to over $200,000 in Tokyo. Surveys by consulting firms are finding a gradual reduction in cost-of-living extremes across the world.[17] Obviously, exchange rates at any point of time and a merging of living standards have a strong influence on these numbers.

Increasingly, firms are questioning whether it is necessary to pay this premium for an overseas assignment (or, at least, for most overseas assignments).[18] Critics argue that in a truly global economy with improved communication and transportation, general availability of global consumer products, and accepted international business norms, there is no longer as much trauma and dislocation associated with an overseas transfer. Still, a large number (although declining) of MNEs continue to pay such premiums.[19]

Additional forms of incentive include premiums for "hardship" postings and dangerous postings, which could include many assignments to developing countries, locations where the threat of kidnapping or terrorist activity is high, or to remote locations (such as the outback in Indonesia or on an ocean oil drilling platform) or locations with primitive conditions. The three broad areas typically considered in evaluating the extent of hardship include physical threat, level of discomfort, and inconvenience.[20] The physical threat category includes potential or actual violence, hostility to foreigners from the local population, prevalence of disease, and the adequacy of local medical facilities and services. The discomfort category evaluates the physical environment and climate, as well as geographical, cultural, and psychological isolation. And the inconvenience category rates the local education system, the availability and quality of local housing, access to recreational and community facilities, and the availability, quality, and variety of consumer goods and services.

*Table 11.1* US State Department indexes for cost-of-living and housing allowances for selected cities

| Location | COL index (DC = 100) | Maximum annual housing allowance ($) | Hardship (%) | Danger (%) |
|---|---|---|---|---|
| Canberra, Australia | 105 | | | |
| Brussels, Belgium | 121 | 30,700 | | |
| Rio de Janeiro, Brazil | 127 | | | |
| Beijing, China | 122 | | 20 | |
| Cairo, Egypt | 87 | | 15 | |
| Paris, France | 136 | 55,700 | | |
| Munich, Germany | 126 | 25,000 | | |
| Hong Kong | 176 | | 5 | |
| New Delhi, India | 95 | | 15 | |
| Jakarta, Indonesia | 100 | | 20 | |
| Tel Aviv, Israel | 146 | | 10 | 20 |
| Tokyo, Japan | 183 | 80,000 | | |
| Nairobi, Kenya | 121 | | 25 | |
| Seoul, Korea | 121 | 46,300 | | |
| Kuwait City, Kuwait | 117 | | 15 | 15 |
| Mexico City, Mexico | 120 | 37,500 | 15 | |
| Moscow, Russia | 130 | | 15 | |
| Riyadh, Saudi Arabia | 116 | | 25 | |
| Singapore | 129 | 35,900 | | |
| Johannesburg, S. Africa | 85 | | | |
| Madrid, Spain | 105 | 29,700 | | |
| Stockholm, Sweden | 144 | | | |
| Geneva, Switzerland | 164 | 64,000 | | |
| Istanbul, Turkey | 132 | | 10 | |
| London, UK | 144 | 64,800 | | |
| Caracas, Venezuela | 120 | 52,000 | 15 | |

Source: "US Department of State Indexes of Living Costs Abroad, Quarters Allowances, and Hardship Differentials: January, April, July, October, 2003," http://www.state.gov/m/a/als/qtrpt/.

Note: Indexes for living costs in foreign locale compared to Washington, DC, weighted by US purchase pattern, excluding housing and education, for a family, with salary above US$72,381 as of the year 2003.

Hardship allowances typically range from 5 percent to 25 percent of base pay with danger pay maybe adding another 15–20 percent to base pay. Many US MNEs use the US State Department tables for determining these amounts. Table 11.1 shows cost-of-living indexes, housing costs, and hardship and danger pay for a few locations as determined by the US State Department. Depending on the location (such as Kuwait City, Kuwait), hardship and danger-pay incentives could add as much as 30 percent to an expatriate's income.

An example of what corporations provide for hardship pay is provided by these results of a survey of MNEs from a few years ago in the Middle East for the percentages of base pay added to expatriate compensation for assignments to the area:[21] United Arab Emirates (12.5 percent), Bahrain (20 percent), Egypt (20 percent), Saudi Arabia (25 percent), and Israel (42.5 percent). Given recent events in the Middle East, these percentages are probably even higher, today.

Additional incentives usually (or may) include housing allowances, either to ensure the expatriate lives as well as her/his foreign peers or to make her/his housing comparable to what s/he had "back at home" – and to take care of her/his home in the parent country and the storage of household goods (again, the State Department also provides reports quarterly of maximum housing allowances for foreign locations, see Table 11.1); settling-in allowances; education allowances for the expatriate (e.g., for language courses), her/his spouse, and any other dependants (e.g., for private schools for the expatriate's school-age children); all travel and relocation expenses necessary to go to and return from the foreign assignment; local transportation in the foreign locale; any language training expenses prior to leaving for the assignment; and special perquisites, such as club memberships in the foreign assignment and special R&R (rest and relaxation) and home leaves, for the expatriate and her/his family (refer to Box 11.1).

*Determining the type and amount of adjustments*   In addition to the many incentives that firms offer their expats, MNEs also often provide a number of what are referred to as equalization adjustments. These are payments whose purpose is to adjust for differences (generally in a higher direction) in mandated payments that expats have no control over – some of which are paid by the expat and some of which are paid to the expat. These have included compensation for any items like fluctuations in exchange rates between the expatriate's parent-country currency and that of the foreign assignment; all locally mandated payments, such as payment of salary for additional days or weeks per year (in many countries, firms must pay employees for thirteen to fourteen months every year, or as in Saudi Arabia, must pay for seven days work per week, i.e., must pay for rest days as well as work days); an agreement to adjust for decreases in the value of the expatriate's compensation due to high inflation in the foreign country; similarly, an allowance to adjust for differences in (higher) costs of living (see Table 11.1, data provided by the US Department of State); reimbursement for any mandatory payments into the host country's welfare plans, such as health insurance or social security; and ensuring that the expatriate will not have to pay more in income taxes while on the foreign assignment than he or she would have to pay while at home.

The most common and probably significant of these adjustments is the cost-of-living adjustment (COLA). A number of consulting firms can provide data to help companies determine local costs of living around the world, comparing such costs with either particular US locations or an average of US cities, or to many other source cities. Of course, such data is available for most countries as base countries to most other countries as receiving countries.

The purpose of the COLA is to enable expatriates to maintain as closely as possible the same standard of living in the foreign assignment that he or she would have had at home (or better, if coming from a low-cost-of-living city or country). The COLA is determined by calculating the costs for typical goods and services in the home location as well as in the foreign location and adjusting accordingly. Since the typical expatriate resides in a major city where costs of living tend to be quite high (particularly the costs of transportation and housing, which may not be available – except at very high cost – in forms comparable to what the expatriate family experienced at home), COLAs of 50 percent or more are relatively common.

The ratios vary according to family size and income, and the consulting firms that provide this type of data will alter the estimates based on these factors. Fluctuating exchange rates and local rates of inflation (which are often quite high in developing countries, for example) will also alter the figures and may require frequent updating. As an example, a manager with spouse and two children posted to Paris, France (refer to Table 11.2) would receive a COLA of about 80 percent above what they had needed to spend in their hometown for basic goods and services, excluding housing and transportation. If the dollar weakened relative to the euro, the expatriate would receive more, and vice versa if the euro weakened against the dollar.

These adjustments also vary according to the technology that the consulting firm uses to determine the cost of living in various foreign locations.[22] There are at least two common techniques used. One of these uses staff of the consulting firm that are located in the particular foreign cities to estimate the cost of living in those locations based on their surveys of costs in a standardized (typical expenditures from the home location) market "basket" of goods and services. A second technique involves the surveying of existing and former expatriates of the clients of the particular consulting firm for their typical spending in the particular foreign locale. Often this second technique – which arguably assesses the actual items that expatriates typically buy, as opposed to a theoretical market basket of goods and services – results in a lower cost of living than that arrived at by the first technique. This second technique is referred to as the Efficient Purchaser Index (EPI). Obviously, MNEs have an interest in trying to minimize the level of this adjustment, which as shown above can often be a significant amount of money. Even the US State Department now offers an EPI-equivalent index alongside its traditional comparison to a standard basket of goods and services purchased in Washington, DC.

Depending on the location, these incentives and adjustments typically cost the MNE more than US$150,000 per expatriate relocation. Indeed, for some locations, where

*Table 11.2* Compensation for expat relocation from New Jersey to Paris, first year (US$)

*Basic compensation*

| | |
|---|---:|
| Salary | 100,000 |
| Bonuses | 20,000 |
| Stock options | 0 |
| Miscellaneous salary adjustments | 0 |
| Employer pension contribution | 20,000 |
| Total compensation | 140,000 |

*Allowances*

| | |
|---|---:|
| Cost-of-living allowance | 35,000 |
| Net housing allowance | 35,000 |
| Automobile | 4,500 |
| Moving expense reimbursement | 10,000 |
| Home leave | 15,000 |
| Children (two)/Spouse education allowance | 25,000 |
| Cultural/Language training allowance | 5,000 |
| Expatriate premium | 12,000 |
| Hardship premium | 0 |
| Danger premium | 0 |
| Home management/maintenance | 0 |
| Club membership/fees | 5,000 |
| Tax services provided | 0 |
| Other allowances | 0 |
| Mobility premium | 0 |
| Relocation allowance, first year only | 5,000 |
| Other earned income | 0 |
| Loan bonus interest | 0 |
| Nontaxable assignment costs | 0 |
| Other adjustments to salary/allowance detail | 0 |
| Total allowances | 151,500 |

*Tax costs*

| | |
|---|---:|
| Actual tax liabilities | |
| US federal | 3,713 |
| US FICA | 8,034 |
| New Jersey | 552 |
| France income | 101,150 |
| France social insurance | 0 |
| Total actual tax | 113,449 |

*Table 11.2* continued

| | |
|---|---|
| Less hypothetical tax | |
| US federal | (23,834) |
| US FICA | (5,580) |
| New Jersey | (3,374) |
| Total hypothetical tax | (31,788) |
| | |
| Employer's social insurance, US | 8,034 |
| Employer's social insurance, France | 0 |
| Other corporate taxes | 0 |
| Tax cost to company | 89,695 |
| | |
| Total costs | 361,195 |

the cost of living and cost of housing are particularly high, the figure can reach US$500,000 or more annually. This is in addition to base salary and benefits. For example, in Tokyo, the rent for an expatriate family often exceeds US$300,000 per year.[23] It is no wonder that the cost of expatriate failure is so high (often figured to be in the neighborhood of US$1 million). And it is no wonder that large multinationals are beginning to reconsider their approaches to expatriate compensation. Table 11.2 illustrates what the compensation package might look like for the first year for an American relocating from New Jersey to Paris.[24] The US$360,000 cost of this package is not unusual and explains the assumption of US$1 million cost for a three-year posting.

One of the consequences of these increasing costs is that firms are increasingly looking to provide the higher overseas salaries through various forms of incentive pay based on performance (either individual or organizational, even though this may be difficult to assess, as discussed in the chapter on performance management) for at least part of the pay package for expatriates, just as they are using such programs in their domestic operations.[25] In order to minimize costs, firms are designing bonus deferrals (paid at the end of the assignment), in-kind benefits, and equity-based plans for expatriates as well as HCN and TCN executives (for globalized stock option and equity participation plans, see the next section), tied to achievement of long-term strategic objectives in the subsidiaries (such as growth in subsidiary revenues and profits or return on capital employed at the subsidiary level).

## Localization

A relatively new approach to expat compensation is referred to as localization. This approach is being used to address problems of high cost and perceived inequity among staff in foreign subsidiaries. Under localization, expatriates (usually individuals who are early in their career and who are being posted overseas for relatively long-term assignments or are TCNs or are returnees) are paid comparably to local nationals. This can be relatively simple to administer, but since expatriates may come from different standards of living than that experienced by local nationals, special supplements for expats may still have to be negotiated.

## Lump sum[26]

Another approach that some MNEs are trying, particularly in response to concern over the perception that the balance sheet intrudes too heavily into expatriates' lifestyle decisions, is the lump sum approach. In this approach the firm determines (sometimes in negotiation with the expat candidate) a total salary for the expat, to cover all the major incentives and adjustments, and then lets the expat determine how to spend it, for example, on housing, transportation, travel, home visits, education, lifestyle, and so forth. This lump sum allowance is a single payment, made at the start of the relocation process, to the transferring expat to cover all of the above, or only the costs associated with the relocation, itself. Or, sometimes, the lump sum payment is split between payment at the outset of the assignment and the remainder paid upon successful completion of the assignment (as an incentive to perform successfully and to stay with the firm until the end of the assignment).

## Cafeteria

An approach which is increasingly being used for very highly salaried expat executives is to provide a set of "cafeteria" choices of benefits, up to a predetermined monetary limit in value. The advantages accrue to both the firm and to the individual and are primarily related to the tax coverage of benefits and perquisites as compared to cash income (pay check). Since the individual doesn't need as much cash (since most expenses are paid for by the firm), this approach enables the expat to gain benefits such as a company car, insurance, company-provided housing, and the like that do not increase the expat's income for tax purposes.

## Regional systems

For expats who make a commitment to job assignments within a particular region of the world, some firms are developing a regional compensation and benefits system to maintain equity within that region. This is usually seen as a complement to the other approaches. And if such individuals are later moved to another region, their pay will be transferred to one of the other regional systems, depending on what is used there, such as the balance sheet approach.

## Global

A final approach being followed, at least for expats above a certain pay level (i.e., therefore, for professional/technical/managerial employees), is to implement a common global pay and benefits package for each covered job classification applied to everyone in that classification, worldwide. This is often done in recognition of the fact that for many specialized occupations, there is in fact a global labor market, with qualified specialists from anywhere and everywhere in the world all applying for the same jobs. In this approach, MNEs will have two general pay classifications: local employees below a defined level and international. The international level will almost always include a performance-based component. The standard used is usually the level paid for those occupations at the firm's headquarters.

Once the amount of the expatriate's compensation has been determined, the firm must decide whether the expatriate will be paid in local currency or in parent-country currency. Where there is limited convertibility between the parent-country currency and that of the foreign locale, or there is rapid inflation, it is probably better for the firm to take care of providing the expatriate's salary in local currency (of course, with guarantees against loss of purchasing power if there is rampant inflation).

It is typical for US MNEs to pay their expatriates based on a US scale plus incentives and adjustments. This is paid partly in US and partly in local currency (with the amount in local currency pegged to ordinary living expenses and the amount in dollars usually left in a US savings account, while bonuses are also paid in dollars and typically left in the US, as well). This is referred to as a split payroll or split currency approach and helps to maintain an expat's purchasing power in their foreign assignment in the face of varying currency exchange rates and inflation. For expats from other than parent-country homes, similar arrangements are made, using their home country and home currency as the base.

## Flexibility in expatriate compensation

Current methods for paying expats are being criticized for many different reasons. There is concern that all of these approaches don't adequately take into account the nature of the assignment or the country of assignment and often actually discourage expatriates from assimilating into the local culture.[27] The housing differentials, for example, frequently serve to pay for host-country housing which is likely to be better than that enjoyed by their host-country counterparts, although, as mentioned above, whether or not that is appropriate will depend on the nature of the expat's assignment. Even the continuation of home-based consumption patterns for goods and services does not encourage the cultural awareness so critical to the expatriate's success in the host country.

In addition, critics argue, it seems as though the expat compensation systems ought to pay more attention to the differences in perceptions by expatriates and by host-country nationals about issues like the value of money compensation versus other types of perquisites or forms of motivation.[28] A flexible menu of perquisites, traditional incentives and adjustments, and tax reimbursement schedules might well meet some of the criticisms while actually reducing overall costs to the firm. Such an approach might even enable an MNE to replace the traditional cost-of-living concerns with a quality of life or a quality of career opportunity focus.

## Taxes on expatriate income

A major determinant of an expatriate's lifestyle abroad can be the amount of money the expatriate must pay in taxes. Employees who move from one country to another are confronted with widely disparate tax systems, philosophies, and rates. And to make things even more difficult, tax systems and rates are constantly changing, often every year. For an example of differences, even for countries right next to each other, a US manager earning $100,000 in Canada would pay nearly $40,000 in taxes, in excess of $10,000 more than in the US.

Thus, taxes create one of the most complicated compensation issues for IHRM. This includes both income taxes and social security taxes. Table 11.3 shows the widely varying income tax rates for a number of countries.[29] Of course, social insurance rates

*Table 11.3* National income tax rates: approximations, ranked from high to low (annual salary US$150,000, married filing jointly

| Country | Total tax liability (US$) | Effective tax rate (%) |
| --- | --- | --- |
| Sweden | 79,076 | 54.02 |
| Netherlands | 69,304 | 46.20 |
| Japan | 47,908 | 45.00 |
| Australia | 66,287 | 44.19 |
| South Africa | 64,061 | 42.71 |
| Germany | 53,844 | 35.35 |
| UK | 48,810 | 34.13 |
| Mexico | 48,954 | 32.66 |
| France | 46,815 | 32.00 |
| Thailand | 43,094 | 29.32 |
| Brazil | 37,209 | 24.96 |
| US | 34,051 | 24.76 |
| Argentina | 32,093 | 19.39 |
| Singapore | 27,136 | 18.56 |
| Hong Kong | 22,500 | 15.00 |

and benefits vary dramatically from country to country, even more than income tax rates. Expatriates (or their firms) are responsible for taxes on their (expatriates') incomes. (This can mean in both their home countries and their host countries.) Since typical MNE policies establish that the firm will cover these costs for their expatriates (at least any differential over what the expatriate would pay in her or his home country), the use of parent-country expats can be very expensive. The multinational firm must therefore determine a strategy for dealing with these variances and potentially heavy costs. (In countries with lower tax rates, the expatriate's compensation is typically adjusted to reflect that fact, so that a manager, for example, being posted to Singapore – with high tax rates – would still receive comparable overall compensation to a colleague who is posted to Hong Kong – with lower tax rates.)

In general, MNEs follow one of four strategies: *laissez-faire*, tax equalization, tax protection, or an *ad hoc* policy.[30] The following paragraphs describe and evaluate these alternatives.

## Laissez-faire

This approach is uncommon, but smaller employers and those employers just beginning to conduct international business may fall into this category with their taxation policies. In essence, under this approach the expatriate is expected to take care of his or her own taxation, even if it means tax obligations in both home and host countries.

## Tax equalization

This is the most common approach, since tax rates and obligations vary so much from country to country. Under this strategy, the firm withholds from the expatriate's income the tax obligation in the home country (that they would otherwise have to pay, anyway) and then pays the taxes in the host country. In essence, the taxes that the expatriate must pay are equalized between home and host countries, with the expatriate obligated only for their home-country taxes. This can be quite expensive if the expatriate is posted to a high-tax country, such as many European countries.

## Tax protection

Under the tax protection strategy, the employee pays his or her taxes up to the amount that would be owed in the home country, with the employer paying the difference. In essence, the employer pays the expatriate any excess of foreign income tax over the home-country income tax. If the tax rate is less in the foreign assignment, then the employee receives the difference. The employer protects the expatriate against higher foreign taxes.

## Ad hoc

Under this strategy, each expatriate is handled differently depending on the individual package she or he has been able to negotiate with her or his employer.

In addition, the typical allowances paid to expatriates are often viewed as taxable income. So the resulting tax bill – in both the home and host country – can negate the financial incentives provided the expatriate. To compensate, companies usually reimburse their expatriates for the global tax costs in excess of the tax they would have been responsible for if they had remained at home. The purpose is – as with other components in the expatriate compensation package – to keep the employee whole. Indeed, surveys find that at least 75 percent of responding firms provide the following benefits tax-free to their employees on foreign assignment (usually by adding to the pay check the costs of the taxes for these items – referred to as "grossing up" the salary):[31]

- Tax reimbursement payments.
- International premium.
- Cost-of-living adjustment.
- Housing allowances.
- Automobile reimbursements (for business use).
- Emergency leave.
- Moving expenses.
- Dependent education.

In addition, many firms provide tax-free a car for personal use (48.3 percent) or club memberships (62 percent).

MNEs that operate in many countries are subject to widely disparate tax rates (see Table 11.3). Because of this and the complex systems of taxation, with differing attitudes toward what is and what is not taxed in various countries (i.e., what is counted as income), MNEs must use international accounting firms for advice and for preparation of expatriate tax returns.

An additional factor involves the varying country-specific practices related to social security taxes and government-provided or mandated social services, ranging from health care to retirement programs. These can add considerably to the foreign taxation burden.

## Taxation of US expatriates

US citizens are taxed on their income, regardless of where it is earned or where they live.[32] Fortunately, special rules can limit the US tax liability of US expatriates. As of the time of this writing, Internal Revenue rules allow US employees to exclude up to $70,000 of foreign-earned income (and certain foreign housing costs above a particular amount) provided the expatriate meets one of two tests: (1) 330 days' presence in foreign countries in any consecutive twelve-month period or (2) foreign residence for any period that includes an entire taxable year. The income and foreign housing exclusions are both prorated on the basis of the number of days in the year in which the expatriate qualified under one of the tests. In addition, US tax laws provide a "foreign tax credit" that US citizens may use to reduce their US tax liabilities (limited to 90 percent of minimum tax, and only applicable to US income tax on foreign income). This is a dollar-for-dollar reduction against US taxes. The bottom line in terms of the amount of tax owed, however, is dependent on the level of tax rate in the foreign country compared with the tax rates in the US.[33]

One thing the US has done to help simplify tax obligations for MNEs is to negotiate income tax and social security treaties with a number of America's major trading partners – referred to as totalization agreements. There are totalization agreements for income taxes with approximately forty countries and for social security taxes with seventeen countries (Austria, Belgium, Canada, Finland, France, Germany, Greece, the Republic of Ireland, Italy, Luxembourg, the Netherlands, Norway, Portugal, Spain, Sweden, Switzerland, and the UK).[34] These treaties generally provide tax exemption to residents of one treaty country on short-term assignment – typically 183 days' presence in a year – to the other country.

IHRM in Action 11.2 provides some practical advice to MNEs for saving money in their complicated tax obligations around the world.[35] Some of these ideas will work in some countries. That is, there are no approaches that will work everywhere. Nevertheless, the following precautions and advice make good general sense:[36]

- Get professional tax advice for all international assignees.
- Don't leave tax affairs to the responsibility of expats. Mistakes can impact an organization's corporate reputation and relations with the host government (and potentially create legal liabilities).
- Tax agreements between most developed nations mean that with openness and good planning, employees should not lose.
- Tax havens are a great way to avoid paying tax only so long as that is where the firm or the individual is doing business and nowhere else. In other words, it is best to stay away from suggested ways to dodge taxes.

Because taxes on expatriate compensation coupled with provided incentives and adjustments make expatriates so expensive, firms are increasingly looking for ways to reduce these expenses without eliminating the attractions of overseas service. Because managing this area of international compensation is so complex, most MNEs have had to develop strategies that involve the use of outside assistance. IHRM in Action 11.3 describes how Physical Acoustics Corporation, a specialty computer manufacturer from New Jersey, deals with this complexity.[37]

## The price of an expatriate

To illustrate, in generic terms, what this typically means for a firm sending an expatriate and family abroad, Table 11.2 illustrates why the common cost for an

# Tax savings to help the global bottom line

Foreign governments are becoming more aware of tax loopholes, so many MNEs claim that it is getting increasingly difficult to avoid paying taxes in the host countries where they operate. However, there are a number of legitimate ways to avoid paying some of the tax and reduce the costs of operation; but tax laws everywhere in the world continue to evolve. So it makes sense to plan ahead. Generally, international accounting firms and human resource consultants specializing in international business can often save MNEs money if the MNEs will consult with them before any action is taken. Here are some ways to save that apply in some countries:

*Provide employees with in-kind assistance that doesn't show up as income.* For example, provide housing, rather than pay a housing allowance. Make contributions to schools or buy scholarships for employees' dependent children instead of paying educational allowances. Reimbursement of employees' actual home-leave expenses may be treated favorably (i.e., non-taxable) in some countries. A loan often isn't taxable or is taxed at a lower rate. A loan can be given to the expat later with which to pay off the loan.

*Provide some of the expat's income in the home country (what was referred to earlier as split pay).* Some countries' tax laws allow corporations to split the payroll with the home country, as long as a certain amount is paid in local currency. The firm may also be able to pay for such remaining home-country expenses as benefits, pension, social security, or mortgage payments on employees' permanent residence, as non-taxable expenses.

*Provide part of the compensation before or after the assignment.* An employee may receive a large bonus before departure and another after returning home. Such payments often are taxed at a lower rate because they are outside his or her period of residence in the host country.

*Time the assignment to take advantage of residence laws.* One company used this strategy to negotiate a savings of $170,000 in taxes for two employees, earning annual salaries of $57,000 and $48,000, who were sent to Italy. The negotiated savings applied as long as they were non-residents and lived in the country nine months or less. In some countries, residence depends on whether the expatriate is living in leased or purchased housing.

The US has tax treaties with many countries and is negotiating such arrangements with others. US citizens or residents may be exempt from taxation in those countries – for example, provided the assignment doesn't exceed a certain number of days (often 183 days in one tax year), the employer isn't a host-country company and the income earned isn't used as a deduction in computing the profits of any home-country company. Obviously, such treaties are only useful for short-term assignments.

continued

The assignment might be spread out over more tax periods, requiring a lower tax on partial years. For example, a two-year assignment might be spread over three tax periods by sending the employee to the foreign country in the middle of the tax year, thereby reducing earnings on the first and last tax years. But the MNE must be careful, since tax years vary. In the UK the tax year begins April 5, but in Australia the date is June 30.

*Take advantage of incentives offered in the host country.* Many countries provide tax advantages to employees of industries they're trying to attract. These advantages may vary from one area to another within the same country, or there may be other strings attached. Companies that provide workers having specific skills needed in the host country often can receive tax incentives.

If the company provides a needed service, it may be able to negotiate a *tax holiday* with the host country. This may be especially true in Eastern/Central Europe or the new countries of the former Soviet Union. An accounting firm or international management firm can help to negotiate this.

In some countries it's possible to establish a foreign subsidiary that's considered a local, rather than a foreign, company. Usually this requires staffing the company with enough locals to give credibility as a local company.

The ways multinational corporations can save money on expatriate taxes are complex and continue to change. But with the help of specialist advice, the typical MNE can indeed find ways to save on the expense of their international assignees.

expatriate can exceed US$300,000 in the first year. Even though some of these expenses – such as the relocation costs – will only occur the first and last years of the foreign assignment, the costs of maintaining an expatriate in a foreign operation obviously greatly exceed those of maintaining the same person in a domestic assignment.

## Major problem areas in expatriate compensation

It should be obvious by now that international compensation management is more complex than its domestic counterpart. This is at least partially due to the following problem areas not confronted in domestic HRM. First, the collection of data about pay rates, benefit packages, government practices, and taxation systems in different countries, and in different languages and cultures, from unfamiliar sources, makes it very difficult to design comparable pay packages for expatriates or for consistency among various overseas operations. Second, pay systems, particularly for expatriates, must contend with government currency controls (for instance, limiting amounts that can be taken out of the country) and constantly changing exchange rates, making it

# How Physical Acoustics manages its international taxes

With major subsidiaries in the UK, France, Germany, and Japan, and a number of competitors close on its heels, Physical Acoustics Corporation (PAC), a manufacturer of computers based in Lawrenceville, New Jersey, is committed to finding the best international tax strategies it can. PAC's chief financial officer, John C. Heenan, suggests this blueprint for success:

*Use local tax advisors.* "Every country has a different set of tax laws on everything from income taxes to duties," warns Heenan. When PAC's US office bills its Japanese subsidiary for consulting work, for example, the fees are taxed by both Japan and the US; a similar transaction with the company's UK subsidiary, on the other hand, is taxed only by the US government. Rather than expecting his US tax advisors to keep current on all international tax minutiae, Heenan uses his American contacts – including CPA and law firms, bankers, and industry sources – to help find qualified tax experts overseas.

*Appoint a US executive to coordinate international tax policy.* At PAC, Heenan is point man on international taxes, keeping the company's overall financial interests in mind while consulting regularly with local tax experts. He relies on his foreign advisors to keep him informed of key changes by telephone and written reports. Having local tax policies and updates trickle up to one US office makes it easier to plan corporate activities to maximize overall tax advantages.

*Look for tax-advantaged opportunities that don't exist in the US.* PAC's CFO has found especially valuable ones on the employee benefits front. "As you get to know the tax laws of different countries, you see many ways to motivate and reward key employees that aren't permitted in the United States." PAC, for example, can give European managers trips and company cars without subjecting those employees to the tax liabilities they'd face in the States. "In the United Kingdom, if one of my managers spends enough time outside the country working on sales, he can qualify for a fairly significant income-tax break because he is seen as working to enhance the export market," Heenan says.

*Keep international taxes in perspective.* Heenan stresses that international tax regulations should not direct a corporation's overall business activities. "International taxes are just another financial factor we have to keep in balance to achieve our most important goal, which is to manage a growing and profitable international business."

necessary to constantly adjust expatriates' incomes in local currencies. A third issue that adds to the complexity is the varying rates of inflation encountered in foreign locations, that may also require frequent re-establishment of expatriates' pay rates to counteract the effects of sometimes high inflation rates. Add to this the desire to export compensation concepts such as incentive pay, bonuses based on firm performance, equity ownership plans, and the desire to create a common global data base to keep track of all the variances, etc., and international compensation gets complicated indeed. When all of this combines with variances in legal systems and in country practices in compensation and benefits, it may be a miracle that MNEs ever satisfy either expats or local workforces.

As IHRM in Action 11.1 hinted, it is often very difficult for MNEs to get country-specific compensation data that have much reliability. Very few governments (at least in developing countries) collect or publish adequate data. And there exist in only a few locations local trade associations that collect and publish such information (as is available in most developed countries). Therefore, MNEs must rely on the information provided by accounting firms with international practices, consulting firms that specialize in developing such data, US State Department data, or developing their own data through local MNE "compensation clubs" that share such information. None of these options provides necessarily reliable data, particularly in less developed countries, illustrating the difficulties encountered by international HR managers as they try to develop cost- and managerially effective compensation packages for their expatriates and equitable compensation programs for their foreign subsidiaries.

An additional problem with international compensation programs involves the maintenance of payroll files on international personnel. (Refer to the last chapter for additional discussion of international HR information systems, including systems for handling payroll and benefits.)[38] The normal (i.e., domestic) HRM information system will not be designed to handle all the additional pieces of information that are common, particularly for expatriates, such as foreign service premiums, language training expenses, education allowances for dependants, storage of household goods, currency conversion, etc. Compounding the problems associated with maintaining these files is that typically the compensation package for each expatriate is unique, developed specifically for that expatriate and her or his family. And, of course, tax and withholding requirements are different in every country, as well. Keeping these files up to date and using the information in them for employee decision making, such as pay increases or adjustments or career and job assignment decisions, gets even more difficult as many countries maintain laws against the transfer of "private" employee information out-of-country. (There is a discussion of privacy laws in Chapter 6 on global employment laws.) There are no easy answers to these problems, short of designing a computer program specifically to handle the problems of your international employees or hiring a firm to handle them for you, but for sure they must be considered when tackling the issue of creating and managing a compensation program for an international workforce.[39]

One last area of concern for the development of global compensation systems involves efforts by MNEs to include IHR issues in the strategic management of the enterprise. Global compensation systems are affected at a number of points, including the following:

- Decisions to downsize often include expatriates because of their high expense, but then it becomes more difficult to convince new people to accept foreign postings.
- Pressuring IHRM to control costs.
- Fitting IHR compensation systems into the firm's efforts to localize while globalizing.
- Merging compensation systems in cross-border acquisitions.
- Designing or negotiating new compensation systems in international joint ventures and cross-border partnerships and alliances.
- Trying to simplify the design and administration of the international compensation system.
- Coping with the new types of expats, including dual-career couples.
- Figuring out how to apply US antidiscrimination laws in the global context to compensation issues, such as those that "protect" the disabled, employees over forty years of age, and employees on the basis of their religion, gender, race, or national origin.

## The special problem of "bandits"

Many mature MNEs have a special problem with expatriates who have stayed overseas for many years and continue to receive many or all of the special incentives and adjustments that they received when they went abroad initially.[40] Often these individuals occupy important positions within the foreign operations of the firm, are located in highly desirable locations, such as Switzerland, and refuse to be reclassified as locals. Obviously this can be very expensive for the MNE and, thus, must be dealt with in a way that hopefully holds on to the expertise of the employee while reducing costs. What many firms are now doing is establishing a policy that requires that such "bandits" reclassify after some period of years, usually five, to local status.

## Benchmarking global international assignee compensation practices

Many firms are now trying to determine what successful MNEs are doing in terms of design and implementation of their international compensation systems.[41] Often this attempt to benchmark the best practices seems like an exercise in "codification of ignorance," since there is so little research to identify what works best when.[42] Surveys of practices of MNEs may be doing nothing more than identifying what is currently being done. But as the above discussion indicates, many practices have evolved over time, without much knowledge or research to indicate which practices are best and under which circumstances. Over time this may result in many firms following what are totally wrong, costly, or inappropriate practices. There is clearly a need for more and better research on international compensation and benefits practices.

### Compensation by foreign multinationals in the US

Just as American firms have recognized the need to pay their international assignees at least as well as their local colleagues (in countries where the locals make more than their US counterparts), such is also true for foreign firms that operate in the US. Foreign owners of US companies – and of US subsidiaries – are realizing that they must match US executive compensation practices to stay competitive and to retain their top US executives.[43]

In most countries, executive compensation is not a subject that receives much attention, either outside firms or within them. This is clearly not the case in the US. Besides, overall executive salaries tend to be much higher (with maybe fewer perquisites) in the US.[44] Thus, foreign firms with operations in the US, particularly those that have acquired US firms, have had to adapt their policies and practices to fit US practices. For example, foreign firms have relied more heavily on base salaries and less on annual bonuses and long-term incentives than is common in the US.[45] Since this can lead to problems with retention of their US executives, foreign-owned firms in the US are increasingly adapting their compensation practices.

The same issues are present when enterprises from any country operate in any other country. The end result is that there is increasing conversion of compensation practices, at least at the top executive level (although there is also a countervailing pressure to localize practice, as well).[46]

### Compensation and taxation of foreign nationals working in the US

A last issue of concern is compensation and taxation for foreign nationals on assignment to the US. (These employees are usually referred to as inpatriates.) This issue, of course, has a counterpart in foreign nationals who move from a subsidiary in any country to the country of the parent, no matter the country of ownership of the enterprise. A discussion of the treatment of immigrants into the US is beyond the purposes of this text. Immigration laws are quiet complex and are constantly changing. (There is a short discussion of US and other countries' immigration laws in Chapter 6, global employment law.) So what is provided here is only a summary statement about issues related to short-term immigrants, called inpatriates, brought to headquarters for a relatively short period of time – usually two years or less – for the purpose of learning about the firm.

First, US MNEs that bring inpatriates into the US are increasingly realizing that they need to adapt these employees' compensation programs just as they must do for their expats that are sent abroad.[47] At a minimum, trying to keep inpatriates in as many of their home-country benefit programs as possible and pegging their compensation to their home-country structures appear to help minimize many of the problems discussed at the beginning of the chapter in IHRM in Action 11.1. As with US expatriates, such foreign employees in the US can typically be removed from extra premiums and adjustments after they have been in the US for a period of time, such as after four or five years.

For US tax purposes, foreign individuals living and working in the US may be considered either "resident aliens" or "nonresident aliens." The US resident is subject to US tax on all worldwide income, in the same manner as a US citizen, while the nonresident generally is taxed only on certain income connected with a US business or from US sources. Other variables adding complexity to the classification of foreign nationals concerns whether they are entering the US on immigrant or nonimmigrant visas and whether their country of origin has negotiated a tax equalization treaty with the US. As US-based MNEs (US or foreign-owned) expand their use of foreign staff in their US operations, considerations such as tax treatment of these employees become just as important as the tax treatment of US assignees sent abroad.

## Designing a compensation strategy for multinationals

In addition to the problems associated with compensation and benefit packages for expatriates, sooner or later the MNE must begin to examine its compensation and benefit programs among its foreign employees at each and all of its foreign operations. The greater the number of foreign subsidiaries and joint ventures and the greater the number of countries within which the MNE operates, the greater will be the problems associated with establishing, monitoring, and controlling compensation programs on a worldwide basis.

The stage of the MNE's evolution or development makes a big difference in how it handles compensation of all of its global employees. If it is still in stage 1 (export) or 2 (sales subsidiaries), it will differentiate between parent-country (PCN), host-country (HCN), and third-country (TCN) employees and most IHRM attention from headquarters will be given to compensation packages for expatriates (PCNs). Later, when in stages 3 (international), 4 (multinational), or 5 (global), i.e., becoming more global in emphasis and attention, the compensation package will be more likely to be designed for all employees worldwide.

The MNE's efforts to design a global compensation program will have to address these types of questions:[48]

- Under which country's benefit and compensation programs should employees be covered – home country, host country (for those who relocate), or some specially designed program for everyone?
- How should potential gaps or inequities in pension and health care coverage be bridged? Can employees be covered under a single plan throughout their careers?
- Is benefits coverage adequate for all employees? What's more, is the benefits package equitable when compared with the benefits of peers in other countries, both within and without the parent firm? Should employees be covered under the provisions of selected home *and* foreign programs?

- How can the cost of providing social benefits be minimized? Can coverage under employees' home-country social programs be maintained, even as they move around? Should there be a global umbrella program to provide equitable coverage for everyone?
- What are the tax effects to employers and employees of special benefit arrangements for all global employees?

A number of different options (for establishing a worldwide compensation system) have been used by various MNEs. These include basing global employees' compensation on:

- *Headquarters scale*, a worldwide scale based on salary levels in the parent company with differentials established for each affiliate according to their differing costs of living.
- *Citizenship*, a scale based on employees' countries of citizenship.
- *Global*, determining a global base per position for everyone (possibly with affiliate differentials). This then becomes a form of equal pay for equal work on a worldwide basis. The global approach is usually followed only for employees above a particular job or salary classification.

One approach to a global compensation program suggests that the MNE develop both qualitative parity and quantitative parity.[49] Qualitative parity is a commitment to offer something from each core category of benefit to every employee worldwide. This would include:

- *Core benefits*, a basic item that the company commits to making available to all employees worldwide, such as a certain level of health care.
- *Required benefits*, a compensation item or non-cash benefit required by local law.
- *Recommended benefits*, a less essential compensation or benefit program to be made available wherever cost considerations permit, such as life insurance.
- *Optional benefits*, a non-essential compensation item to be made available if it is a competitive practice in the local marketplace, such as local transportation or meal support.

The use of qualitative parity is one component of a firm's global compensation approach that provides a means of making a commitment to the entire workforce while still preserving local variations in pay for the less skilled and less mobile employees.

Implementing a program of quantitative equity is usually done only for key global executives. After the elimination of all justifiable differences, any remaining variations are, by exclusion, vestiges of the old system that should be methodically smoothed out. Through eliminating over time the differences that came from different countries' approaches and from the uncoordinated approach to compensation, what is left is a process that assures executives that they are being compensated for their skills, abilities, and contributions – rather than for their choice of address.

However, even the best global compensation program will not eliminate future claims by employees of perceived continued inequity. That is because variations in local labor laws, tax systems, and the cost of living will ensure that dissimilar programs and varying gross pay levels will continue to be a fact of life in a global organization. The goal, though, of a global compensation system is not to eliminate employees' questions about compensation, but rather to remove the demotivational impact of inexplicable variations in compensation across borders. Designing a global compensation program in this way can enable IHR to create a working environment that hopefully will retain good employees and keep them focused on performance. IHRM in Action 11.4 summarizes the approach taken by a major consumer products firm – Colgate-Palmolive – to develop its global compensation programs.[50] Colgate-Palmolive has found ways to globalize its compensation programs and, thus, to attract and retain the best talent available throughout the world.

One major problem that arises is the establishment of host-country nationals' salaries on some form of consistent yet global basis.[51] The solution often is to create two classifications – local and international. All local nationals above a certain classification level are placed on the headquarters scale, with salaries that are then performance-based. And yet, even here, practices can vary enough so as to make this

---

## Global compensation programs do work

IHRM IN ACTION 11.4

Colgate-Palmolive is a US$9 billion global company with operations in over eighty countries and 50 percent of its executives are US nationals stationed in other countries. They use global expatriates for many of their key management positions around the world. Because of this, Colgate-Palmolive has developed a global compensation program in order to attract and retain the best talent to help the firm achieve its vision of becoming "the best truly global consumer products company." Colgate benchmarks its salaries and benefits against the best in its industry and then tries to improve on them.

Their global compensation plan consists of three parts: a base salary program, that varies significantly from country to country; annual incentives, that cover all key managers worldwide, based on sales and profit targets, adjusted for local conditions; and a long-term incentive plan, for all global senior executives and managers, made up of global stock options and bonuses based on achievement of significant global business objectives.

Colgate struggles with the willingness of employees to accept overseas assignments, even though it is clearly identified and communicated that such experience is an integral part of the career track for all employees. There are many reasons for the resistance, but this global compensation plan often provides the necessary response to those concerns. The firm has clearly found that the role of the expatriate has proven invaluable for the success of the company as a global player in the consumer products industry.

strategy difficult to implement. In the US (and most developed countries), there is typically a fairly constant differential between job classifications, i.e., there is typically about a 15 percent increase in salary from job class to job class, and this tends to be the case across all job classifications. In many developing countries, where there tend to be many people with low levels of education and training and few with high levels of education, it is common to have low pay at all of the lower job classifications, with very little differential between them and then a major jump in compensation only at the upper few classifications. This creates a situation where there can be a much greater ratio between top management and lower-level employees, such as between the top manager and his/her secretary, than would be the case in the typical US-based, or other developed country, parent-country MNE workforce. For example, in Mexico, in 1996 a secretary made US$821 per month and her office manager boss made US$1,812, while in the US a secretary made $2,735 and her office manager made $3,325.[52]

Not only is there great disparity between wage rates and salary levels in different countries, but it is also difficult to get reliable data on what those rates and levels are. Nevertheless, international banks (e.g., the Union Bank of Switzerland), consulting firms (e.g., Hay International), and the US Department of Labor research and publish comparative wage rate data on at least some common locations for MNEs. (See Table 11.4 for comparison of hourly manufacturing labor costs for a select few countries.)[53]

Another important aspect of this problem of comparisons of salaries among various countries concerns pay at different levels, particularly when related to relevant costs of living. Table 11.5 shows the average pay for chief executives in firms with annual

*Table 11.4* Hourly compensation costs for production workers in manufacturing, selected countries (US$)

| Country | Cost |
| --- | --- |
| West Germany | 21.53 |
| Norway | 20.24 |
| Japan | 15.42 |
| US | 14.77 |
| France | 14.33 |
| UK | 13.64 |
| Former East Germany | 13.23 |
| Italy | 12.78 |
| Spain | 11.46 |
| Portugal | 5.26 |

*Table 11.5* Average pay for chief executives in firms with annual sales of more than US$25 billion

| Country | Annual remuneration (US$) | % based on merit |
|---|---|---|
| South Africa | 295,000 | 12 |
| Canada | 426,000 | 36 |
| Netherlands | 429,000 | 14 |
| Australia | 430,000 | 19 |
| Japan | 442,000 | 12 |
| Italy | 472,000 | 18 |
| UK | 479,000 | 25 |
| Germany | 482,000 | 16 |
| Belgium | 496,000 | 13 |
| Singapore | 560,000 | 32 |
| France | 570,000 | 24 |
| US | 908,000 | 49 |

Source: Towers Perrin (1996) reported in *Argus*, February, 1997, p. 4.

sales over US$25 billion (in other words, large firms), including the percentage of salary based on merit.[54] Since the date of these figures, CEO pay has risen dramatically around the world, particularly in the US. A more recent survey (2000) by Towers Perrin shows a range of CEO salaries (excluding bonuses) from a low of under US$200,000 in countries like Thailand and China to mid-range salaries (from US$400,000 to US$600,000) in countries like Singapore, Japan, Germany, and Brazil, to US$1,400,000 in the US![55] Expenditures for taxes, savings, cars and commuting vary considerably from country to country, as do annual and long-term incentives, and need to be taken into consideration when trying to determine appropriate salary structures for staff in foreign subsidiaries.

## Compensation of third-country nationals

As the number of TCNs in MNEs increases, their compensation often approaches that of their expatriate colleagues. However, firms often have problems in defining TCNs for compensation purposes as it is difficult to decide which base to use to determine their salaries. In the past they were typically defined in terms of their home countries, but as they move around, this makes less and less sense. The increasing trend is to define them in terms of a region of the world, usually tied to their parent language and culture. Many multinationals establish cultural zones, for example, Western

Europe might be considered one zone, with Africa considered to be another, and so on. Other firms use a combination of geographic and language zones. Thus, a manager might be defined as a national as long as he or she is within his or her parent region. This manager is treated as a traditional TCN only when he or she moves to a different zone.

## International benefits and related taxes

The design of a comprehensive compensation program for all worldwide employees must, of course, include non-salary benefits. The major concern that MNE's have for designing their benefit packages is the widely varying approaches to employee benefits as approached by each country.[56] The problems this creates cannot be overstated. In the US, for example, benefits make up a significant portion of the cost of payroll, averaging about 40 percent of payroll expenses. In the US, many benefits that, in other countries, are provided by the government and paid for through employer taxes or are mandated by the government are provided on a private and voluntary basis by each firm. This includes significant benefits such as health care, retirement pensions, vacations, and holidays.

An important example involves the handling of health care. In some countries, such as the US, health care is basically a private system paid for either by individuals or their employers. In most other countries, though, health care is provided by a tax-supported system of government-controlled medicine. In yet other countries, such as Great Britain and Mexico, in addition to the government-sponsored, tax-supported system of health care there is also a competing private medical system, mostly paid for by insurance, with premiums paid by some employers, particularly for higher-level managers.

In every area of benefits, the variance from country to country in terms of what is normally provided, what is paid by the government from tax revenues, and what employees expect of their employers is quite wide. The benefits manager in the MNE is faced with such tremendous complexity that it is very difficult for any such manager to be knowledgeable about more than a few countries. As with taxes, the MNE must typically seek advice and assistance from international accounting and HR consulting firms.

## Vacation requirements

Table 11.6 illustrates an example of the wide variances among countries in a benefit that is mandated in some countries and voluntarily provided in others. It shows the vacation requirements, holidays, and hours of work (weekly) in a number of different countries.[57] Among the countries listed, vacation provisions range from six days for employees with one year of service in Mexico to thirty days for such employees in Austria and Denmark. A US worker must often stay at a job for thirty years to match

*Table 11.6* Vacations, holidays, and working hours around the world

| Country | Mandated vacation days | Holidays | Work week |
|---|---|---|---|
| Mexico | 6–12+ | 7–10 | ? |
| Russia | ? | 10 | 40 |
| China | ? | No mandatory | 37.5 |
| Singapore | 7–14 | 11 | 44 |
| Hong Kong | 7–14 | 12–18 | 48 |
| US[a] | 10 | 10 | 40 |
| Japan | 10–20 | 12–14 | 40 |
| Canada | 10–15 | 9+ | 40 |
| New Zealand | 15 | 11 | 40 |
| UK | 20 | 10 | 40 |
| Switzerland | 20 | Variable | 40 |
| Netherlands | 20–24 | 10 | 40 |
| Ireland | 20 | ? | ? |
| Belgium | 20 | ? | 39 |
| Australia | 20 | 9+ | 38 |
| Spain[b] | 22 | 10 | 40 |
| Brazil[b] | 22 | 13 | ? |
| Germany | 24 | Up to 15 | 40 |
| Sweden | 25 | 13 | 40 |
| Norway | 21 | 11 | 40 |
| France[c] | 25–30 | 11 | 35 |
| Austria | 30 | ? | ? |
| Denmark | 31 | ? | 37 |

Notes

a No statutory minimum; 82 percent of companies provide from two weeks (ten days) to fourteen days.

b Thirty total calendar days.

c Based on six-day work week.

(and most never reach that level, even in thirty years) the level of paid vacation time that is commonly provided to beginning workers in many European countries. The US, Canada, New Zealand, and Japan are the developed countries that provide the shortest paid vacation time for employees – each granting an average of only ten to fifteen days a year.

In the US, paid vacation time is left to the discretion of each company, a situation which is true for most benefits. Most firms base the amount of time provided to employees on the employee's length of service. The average received by American employees in their first years at a firm is eleven days. After five years of service, they earn fifteen days, on the average. Ten years of service result in seventeen days, and thirty years earn employees twenty-four days of paid vacation.

In contrast, most European countries (and others, as well) mandate paid vacation for workers. Denmark mandates thirty-one days of paid vacation, while Austria requires companies to give their employees thirty days of vacation; France requires five weeks; and Germany mandates twenty-four days. In addition, most European employers actually extend employee vacation time to six weeks. In the UK, employees average twenty-two days off with pay.

Because of these widely varying practices, corporate policy on establishing and changing benefits must be monitored in such a way as to minimize unnecessary differences among subsidiaries while maintaining parent-company concern for costs, competitiveness, and comparability from locale to locale.[58] Since a foreign subsidiary's benefits program may be more difficult to monitor or control than the parent company's domestic counterpart, it often makes sense to appoint an effective local manager in each country to act as that country's benefits coordinator, responsible for coordination and liaison with headquarters. And yet there must also be global or, at least, regional coordination, as well. When managers transfer from one country to another, they will expect to at least retain benefits, such as vacation time comparable to that from their home country. For expatriates moving from countries with relatively low levels of such benefits, this will not create a problem. But for managers moving in the other direction, it can be the source of significant concerns.

## Pension plans

Pension plans provided by MNEs create their own special set of complexities.[59] For example, when Johnson & Johnson examined its pension system, it "discovered" that it not only had a US defined benefit pension plan covering some 20,000 participants with $1.2 billion in assets, but that it also had another fifteen plans with 15,000 participants worldwide and another $700 million in assets.[60] IHRM in Action 11.5 shows how complex managing their pension program is. And this is only one of the many benefit programs with which MNEs must concern themselves.

## Stock options, equity participation plans, and employee ownership

In recent years there has been a trend in global firms to look for ways to internationalize their employee equity participation schemes.[61] In particular, this has

# International pensions at Johnson & Johnson

In 1988, Johnson & Johnson formed a task force to look at its US pension plan's actuarial assumptions and funding strategy. After completing the study for the domestic plan, the task force turned to the international companies and their pension plans. According to Eugene Barron, assistant treasurer, there were a lot of questions. What were the foreign subsidiaries doing with their investments and what were their funding patterns? Why were they funded in a particular way? Why did they use certain assumptions? Was there any special tax or regulatory item that would impact funding or investments? The study examined all their major international plans, ranging in asset size from US$2 million up to US$250 million.

The first task was to gather information that was not at the time available at corporate headquarters, such as: How's their asset management doing? What are the returns? How are the funds invested? Who manages the funds? What was found was a lot of money sitting out there and no consistently applied philosophy as to why it was there in those amounts and what should be done with it. With one exception. As on the domestic side, the philosophy that was handed down was to fund generously. The task force began to question that philosophy in light of the environment of pressure on costs.

There were a few places where the firm didn't fund because it didn't make sense, such as Germany, Italy, and France. In Germany there was a benefit to not funding, and there is a tax cost to fund. In Italy, there is a severance obligation upon retirement and no vehicle to fund it. And on the other hand, it was found that J&J had funded pension plans in thirteen countries that had more than one company in each country, usually even more than four. Some countries had two plans; some had countrywide arrangements; in some countries, every company in the country had its own plan. Every country was different.

In each location, the task force first determined who the key pension contact was and then tried to figure out who else was on the local pension committee. Thus one of the results of the study was to create a living document on who all the players were – something that hadn't existed at corporate headquarters previously.

The results were fascinating. Worldwide, the results fell into certain categories: first, everyone understood that the requirement was to fund adequately, not generously, and they understood the dangers of overfunding. Second, increased coordination between local and corporate people was established. Third, professional staff from headquarters are now directly involved with foreign subsidiaries in advising on pension investments in order to improve what was a spotty investment performance.

continued

The process of studying the international pension plans took much longer than the year that had been expected. But when it was done, headquarters IHR finally had a good idea of what was happening in each location. IHR knew what was going on in the UK, Japan, Australia, Mexico, Brazil, Belgium, Italy, Germany, and Canada. The firm finally knows where it is, and it has told each country to do a number of things to improve the management of J&J pensions on a more consistent and globalized basis – such as combine plans, try and create a countrywide plan, look for ways to separate employer and employee funds.

included experimenting with ways to grant stock options and restricted stock to their overseas employees.[62] And since US companies have developed the most sophisticated structures for providing equity (shares of stock) to employees in various forms of pay-for-performance and employee ownership schemes, many global firms have looked to US MNEs for concepts and techniques for achieving the objective of improving the ability of their global workforces – particularly their managers – to share in the success and rewards of their global efforts. Of particular interest has been the use of US-style stock-based executive compensation programs. As stated by William M. Mercer International:

> These plans are seen as a means of more closely identifying executives with their companies' business objectives. Such plans focus executive attention on the company's long-term growth and profitability, and align the financial interests of executives with those of the stockholders. And they can provide a mechanism for setting performance standards and rewarding their achievement.[63]

But the design of such programs is not easy. Every country has its own laws and regulations related to the use of such practices and their tax treatment. And not all foreign employees understand the concept of firm ownership or necessarily agree with it when they do.

IHRM in Action 11.6 highlights Canon, a Japanese MNE that has adopted decidedly non-Japanese incentive schemes to support its global competitiveness,[64] and IHRM in Action 11.7 illustrates the difficult experiences of some American MNEs as they have tried to extend their employee stock ownership plans overseas.[65] Both US firms (using these plans overseas) and foreign firms operating in the US with such plans for their American employees are affected by the accepted accounting rules that govern the balance sheet and tax treatments of these programs. IHR must be vigilant in its monitoring of the use of these programs. But even though there are many difficulties in establishing these stock sharing schemes, at least one international consulting firm has found "how great the welcome has been by local management in a number of countries for an ability to participate in a share option or share scheme providing parent company shares."[66]

# Canon uses incentive compensation – a Japanese exception

As multinational firms open more and more operations in more and more countries, they must make basic decisions about what structure they want for their compensation system in each country. Trying to use a centralized system everywhere can cause problems in countries that may utilize different compensation systems. And, yet, trying to localize the compensation system may also run up against cultural assumptions about what might or might not work, as the following example shows.

At the end of 1995, Canon ranked forty-third in market value on the Tokyo stock exchange. By the end of 2001 it had shot up to eighth. Canon's performance is driven by a competitive company culture that sets it apart in Japan. Canon has long based compensation on performance instead of seniority, creating significant wage differentials, greater than at other Japanese companies. For example, in March of 2002, twenty-one of its best assembly workers were each awarded a bonus and the title "Meister." This clearly goes against the traditional Japanese culture of group performance and recognition and seniority-based pay.

Canon's R&D also runs on competitive principles. Cash-flow management reduces development time and cost. Unprofitable products are cut mercilessly. Patents protect newly developed technology. Researchers can receive unlimited rewards for big patents, and such incentives have spurred epoch-making products like the laser beam printer and bubble jet printer.

CEO Fujio Mitarai says, "Canon works on competitive principles. It does not treat people equally – but it does treat them fairly." Clearly, MNEs must assess carefully what will work best where.

## Share ownership/equity bonuses

Many multinational firms are seeking ways to provide equity ownership in their firms for their employees around the world.[67] The concept of employee ownership is not new, nor is it a concept limited to a few countries. Over the years, numerous approaches to employee ownership have been tried in various countries, with varying degrees of success.[68] Now, newly democratizing and newly industrializing countries are looking afresh at the idea of employee ownership as one approach to converting their state-owned enterprises to privately owned firms. Multinational firms with an interest in providing employee ownership can try to follow the patterns that have evolved in the countries of their foreign subsidiaries or they can export concepts from their home countries, to the extent that local laws allow such innovations.

## US employee equity plans run into foreign snags

Unexpected hurdles arise as US companies begin offering stock plans to staff members worldwide. Such programs, designed to increase loyalty and productivity, sometimes run into problems because share ownership is unknown or restricted in numerous foreign countries. In July 1989, PepsiCo rolled out a stock option plan called Share Power for about 140,000 of its 308,000 employees. But 21 percent of those eligible have yet to receive options, worth 10 percent of annual compensation.

"We had to develop a customized approach in every country we operate in," said Charles Rogers, Pepsi vice-president, compensation and benefits. In certain locales, such as Greece, poorly educated staffers didn't even know what stock was. In Mexico, Brazil, and Japan, Pepsi had to switch from large-scale videotape presentations to flip charts for small groups because "videotapes are a relatively foreign form of communication" for businesses there, Rogers adds.

Du Pont, while planning a similar program, discovered that it couldn't give stock options in twenty-five of fifty-three nations – primarily because laws ban stock options or limit ownership of foreign shares. The chemical concern substituted stock appreciation rights, giving cash for any appreciation in its stock price without enlarging the pool of employee shareholders. Legal hurdles kept Du Pont from giving either stock options or appreciation rights in Ecuador.

To avoid such stumbling blocks, Reader's Digest Association and Colgate-Palmolive designed global stock programs country by country. Reader's Digest employees in the US have been able to buy shares at a 10 percent discount, but a UK unit instead uses a modified stock option arrangement. "It would be almost impossible to have a plain-vanilla plan that would apply in all countries," said Joseph Grecky, vice-president, human resources.

Colgate wanted to extend its US stock grants to permanent employees worldwide, starting with Britain. Tailoring plans for all sixty-two countries where it operates "will take a long time," says Reuben Mark, chairman and chief executive.

In the US, tax law provides incentives to employers to establish Employee Stock Ownership Plans (ESOPs). Money used to purchase shares in a firm that are distributed to employees is tax deductible. By 1990, over 10,000 firms had ESOPs in the US, covering over 10 million employees. Many American multinational firms have ESOPs in the US and are now extending this opportunity to their foreign employees. In addition, many countries, particularly in Europe and the developed countries in the Asia-Pacific region, are now passing laws to accommodate employee ownership.[69] But the tax laws in most countries still do not provide any incentive to do so. The following is a short summary of the employee ownership practices in a number of countries.

## Central America

Firms in Latin America are primarily owned by foreign companies, governments, or wealthy families. Nevertheless, there has been some experimentation with employee ownership. Approximately 20 percent of LACSA, the national airline of Costa Rica, is owned by employees. And about 30 percent of La Gloria (a large chain of department stores) is owned by its employees. In both cases the firms are selling stock to employee associations that are distributing the shares to employees. In Guatamala there are now about fifty firms with employee associations that are purchasing shares for their members.

## Europe

Except for the UK, there are no tax-advantaged, US-style ESOPs in Europe. Many countries have developed various approaches to employee share ownership, and many are now examining the US experience to see if it might be adopted there. In the UK, there have been forms of employee ownership since the nineteenth century. Examples include the John Lewis Partnership, which has an employee trust which owns all shares in the company and distributes profits to employees as bonuses, and Imperial Chemical Industries (ICI), which allows employees to buy shares on preferential terms and has a profit-sharing scheme that distributes shares of stock to employees. In 1989, the UK parliament passed legislation providing tax deductibility for employer contributions to US-style employee share ownership plans.

In most other countries in Europe, the tax laws provide tax deductions (usually limited in scope) to individuals for income used to purchase shares in their employers' firms. This is true for example in France, Sweden, Belgium, Denmark, and Switzerland. In other countries, such as Germany, Italy, and the Netherlands, shares distributed to employees by the firms are not counted by the tax authorities as income. In Spain, the Mondragon group has provided experience with worker-owned cooperatives for many years. Included in this group are now more than 160 individual cooperatives with over 20,000 members and US$1 billion in sales with exports of more than US$230 million.

Even with these limited advantages for employee share ownership, European MNEs are looking for ways to provide this opportunity throughout their operations. For example, Asea Brown Boveri (ABB) put shares in the company worth over US$600 million on offer to its employees in over twenty-five countries, available in some twenty local currencies.

## Japan

As is generally the case, the interest within any particular country in employee ownership is based on local factors. In Japan, there is increasing interest in employee share ownership as an additional strategy for helping to deal with problems associated with a rapidly aging population in a country where there is no private or public retirement income support. ESOPs are seen as a possible way to provide a source of economic relief (to provide income after retirement and to enhance employee motivation – for higher productivity which will increase the values of their firms and thus their shares). At present, these schemes in Japan are essentially employee savings plans contributed to by both employees and employers.

## Australia

Australia has a long history of interest in worker ownership, originally as an alternative to classical capitalism, or, more recently, as a way to establish economic democracy. That is, there were political reasons to pursue worker ownership. This primarily took the form of cooperatives. But now there are a number of firms with employee ownership, as well, but still often founded out of religious, paternalistic, or egalitarian motives.

The trend in Australia has been that when certain firms became quite successful, they were converted into cooperatives or employee-owned ventures. In addition, a number of smaller firms were converted to employee ownership upon the death or retirement of the founder or owner. And many firms which are today owned by the employees were originally cooperatives that were restructured, often because of financial problems.

There is now some limited support in the tax system for ESOP-style share ownership. But Australian legislators continue to be concerned over the economic, political, and social effects of ESOPs. Thus there is a strong feeling that they need to know more before providing additional tax incentives to encourage the establishment of US-style ESOPs.

## Egypt

Even in countries such as Egypt, firms are experimenting with employee ownership. A tire company has been formed in Cairo with a major portion of its initial capitalization coming from an employee shareholders' association. This ESA was created to substitute for a legal trust, a device which does not exist in Egyptian law. This ESA borrows the money to purchase shares for the 750 employees. This loan is repaid out of the dividends on the shares. No employee payroll deductions are required. And the workers' shares are pledged as the only source of security for the loan.

## Central and Eastern Europe

Most of the countries in the former Soviet bloc are examining the use of various forms of employee ownership as one way to privatize enterprises that were formerly all state-owned. Sometimes employees must purchase the shares, in other situations they are receiving the shares in a "free" distribution from the state, or they receive vouchers that can be turned in for shares, etc. Philosophically, the idea of employee (worker) ownership fits the social values of many people in these countries. But practically, there is no experience anywhere in the world for converting economies from state-owned and operated to market-based and private ownership on these scales. Only time and experimentation will provide evidence of what will work in these economies.

## Insurance

Insurance is another area of benefits that can add complexity to the design of compensation programs for expatriates. Most big firms provide their managers and senior technicians with life insurance as part of their employees' benefit packages. But many life insurance policies have clauses that in case of declared or undeclared war the insurance is null and void (which may be more likely to happen in a foreign assignment). Thus the firm may need to purchase special coverage while the expatriate is overseas.

In addition, the typical travel coverage (such as that provided when buying airline tickets through a credit card) may not be valid if going abroad for an extended period of time. Again, the firm may want to consider purchasing special travel insurance for its expatriates and their families.

Depending on the location of the overseas assignment, the firm may also have to provide special "work risk" insurance, for more dangerous or remote locations and, possibly, other forms of special insurance, e.g., kidnapping insurance (discussed in Chapter 13 on health, safety, and security).

## Maternity and family leave

An area of employee benefits that has been receiving increasing attention from state and federal legislators in the US involves the provision of leave for reasons related to family need (e.g., maternity leave, paternity leave, family leave, etc., with or without pay, with guarantee of getting one's job back at the end of the leave). This is a benefit provided by most countries, but is still not fully provided in the US. It has been a long time coming in the US (and is still not there at the level experienced by most workers around the world). Almost immediately after Bill Clinton became President in 1993, Congress passed the Family Medical Leave Act, providing unpaid leave for employees who need to take care of family emergencies, a bill which the new President signed. A number of states have also now passed similar legislation.

Other countries tend to be further advanced in the provision of this particular benefit. Approximately two-thirds of all nations, including most industrialized countries, have provision for paid and job-protected maternity leave of four to twelve months prenatal and three to twenty-nine months postnatal.[70] The leave may be paid by the employer or by the government, or both. In some countries, including Norway, the Netherlands, Belgium, and Germany, up to 100 percent of salary is reimbursed during maternity leave. Leave in Sweden is available to either parent at 90 percent of wages during the first twelve months, and less thereafter. Table 11.7 illustrates the maternity leave provided in selected countries.[71] Even though the EU is trying to develop common practices on these types of social policies, this table shows the diversity that exists even within these close-proximity countries.

## Flexible benefits

Flexible benefits are the approach to benefits in an increasing number of American organizations. In essence, employees are typically given choices, up to a certain dollar limit, among a series of options for their benefits, including such things as pension contributions, health insurance options, dental insurance, life insurance, etc. MNEs are beginning to examine flex benefits for their global operations, designing global flex-benefit plans similar to what has been tried within the US.[72] This is happening because:

- Flex benefits have been successful in the US, so employers in other countries are beginning to take a look at the idea.
- MNEs have a need to attract and retain more diversified workforces (in terms of age, marital status, family situation), thus they are looking at flex benefits as a way to attract workers with diverse benefit needs.
- Foreign firms are investing in American health care companies and are thus being exposed to how important flex benefits are in the US for controlling rising health care costs.
- The increased aging of the labor force around the world is leading MNEs to look at flex benefits as a way to provide diverse benefits to all workers with a single benefits program.

Issues such as tax treatment of benefits, private versus state health care, employee expectations and culture, non-standardized social benefits from country to country, and varying company structures will need to be addressed in order to design flexible benefit packages that might be used throughout an MNE. Nevertheless, such an approach may help simplify worldwide complete compensation systems for multinational firms.

## Continuing global compensation concerns

The following is a list of ten major concerns that IHR managers identified in a survey as the most important issues in developing a system of global compensation.[73] These continue to be the major concerns:

*Table 11.7* Statutory maternity leave in EU and selected other countries

| Country | Maternity leave | Pay |
| --- | --- | --- |
| Belgium | 14 weeks (6 before birth) | 100% for 1–4 weeks, thereafter 80% |
| Denmark | 28 weeks (4 before birth) | 90% of salary |
| Germany | 14 weeks (6 before birth) | 100% of salary or fixed sum |
| Greece | 15 weeks (6 before birth) | 100% of salary |
| Spain | 16 weeks | 75% of salary |
| France | 16 weeks (6 before birth) | 84% of salary |
| Ireland | 14 weeks (6 before birth) | 70% of salary |
| Italy | 20 weeks (8 before birth) | 80% of salary |
| Luxembourg | 16 weeks (8 before birth) | 100% of salary |
| Netherlands | 16 weeks (6 before birth) | 100% of salary up to ceiling |
| Portugal | 90 days (6 weeks before birth) | 100% of salary |
| UK | 18 weeks | 6 weeks at 90% of salary and 12 weeks at a fixed reduced sum |
| Australia | 6 weeks | Unpaid |
| Hong Kong | 10 weeks | 80% of salary |
| India | Up to 12 weeks | 100% of salary |
| Japan | 14 weeks | 60% of covered pay |
| Singapore | 8 weeks | 100% of salary |
| Brazil | 120 days | 100% of salary |
| Canada | 25 weeks | 55% of covered pay |
| Chile | 126 days | 100% of pay up to ceiling |
| Mexico | 12 weeks | 100% of pay up to ceiling |
| US | Up to 12 weeks | Unpaid |

Sources: adapted from Kaplan, C.Y., and Bernstein, Z.S. (2000), "Other benefits," in Reynolds, C. (ed.), *2000 Guide to Global Compensation and Benefits*, San Diego, CA: Harcourt; Keller, W.L. (ed.), *International Labor and Employment Laws*, I, 1997; II, 2001; and updates, International Labor Law Committee Section of Labor and Employment Law, American Bar Association, Washington DC: Bureau of National Affairs.

- Managing expatriate (and all global employee) compensation expectations.
- Adding "appropriate" value to expatriate and subsidiary compensation packages.
- "Localization" of expatriate compensation.
- Cost containment for compensation worldwide.
- Global pension and other benefit schemes.

- Integration of global business and HR planning with expatriate and subsidiary compensation.
- Management development as a crucial factor in expatriate compensation planning.
- Regionalization of compensation and benefit programs.
- Revisiting the "balance sheet" concept.
- Centralizing and decentralizing assignment policy.

## Conclusion

This chapter has presented IHRM practices related to the development of compensation and benefit programs among MNEs. The discussion followed three primary foci: compensation and benefits for expatriates; compensation and benefit programs for MNEs among the various locations of their overseas workforces, i.e., at their various subsidiaries; and issues related to the wide diversity among compensation and benefit approaches in various countries around the world.

The chapter described seven alternative approaches to compensation for expatriates, with extensive discussion of the balance sheet approach, which adds numerous incentives and adjustments to a parent-country base and is the most commonly used method for paying expats. But the complexity of the balance sheet approach and the necessity for firms to get deeply involved with their expats' lives when using this approach (as well as the high cost of expat compensation and administration of the balance sheet) have led many firms to begin experimenting with one of the other possible approaches.

The issue which adds most of the complexity to the compensation of expats involves taxation practices and taxation rates in different countries. In an effort to ensure that their expats don't need to pay double taxation (for both their countries of origin and their countries of residence while on foreign assignment), MNEs use one of three methods: *laissez-faire*, tax equalization, or tax protection. In the latter two cases, the purpose is to limit the tax liability of the expatriate. Compensation and taxation issues are also discussed for foreign multinationals operating in the US.

Next, the chapter discussed the many problems that MNEs confront as they try to design and implement global compensation and benefit programs throughout their global operations. Country differences in laws and practice make this hard to do. But headquarters pressure for equity and ease of administration provides the motivation to IHR to work on development of such global programs.

Lastly, the chapter described and discussed many of the various approaches taken to compensation and benefits, such as vacation and pension practices, in a number of different countries. For MNEs that operate in multiple countries with local subsidiary workforces, having an understanding of these country-specific variances becomes critical to designing rational HRM practices for the total firm.

The design and management of compensation programs for international assignees and for multiple workforces around the world are indeed a complex and difficult function. This chapter has made it clear why compensation and benefits absorb the bulk of the typical international HR manager's time and energy.

## Points for further discussion

1 What issues of global compensation are most relevant to Lincoln Electric in China?
2 Can Lincoln Electric use all the components of its incentive system in all the other countries in which it operates?
3 What components of the incentive system work in China? Which ones might work in China but not in the US?

# International performance management for international assignees and foreign managers

**12**

## Learning objectives

After considering this chapter, the reader will be able to:

- Describe the nature and purposes of international performance management (IPM) for international assignees (IAs) and foreign managers (FMs)
- Describe the characteristics of and provide guidelines for effective IPM systems
- Explain the major challenges and their solutions to international performance management in MNEs
- Discuss the typical senior managers' attitudes toward IPM

## Key terms

- IAs, FMs, PM, IPM
- Criteria, relevance, acceptability, sensitivity, practicality
- Rater competence, rater bias

Foreign subsidiaries and joint ventures tend to be structured and managed much like their parent firms, except that they usually have both expatriate and local managers. As with everything else in the global arena, managing the management of international operations is therefore more complex and difficult than is the case with domestic operations.

A critical component in the development of international management is the system of performance management (PM) used by an MNE. The word "system" is used because there are many inter-related aspects to performance management. For example, some of the critical yet connected aspects involved in the PM system include the context of the appraisal process, the raters of performance, and the performance appraisal form and format, itself.[1]

The PM system used in the international arena relates to many areas of IHRM responsibility, such as evaluating international assignees (i.e. expatriates) and foreign managers (FM, i.e. TCNs and HCN managers) for pay increases. Although all of these employee groups are all described as international assignees in Chapters 8 and 9, for our discussion on international performance management and compensation they are distinguished as IAs (expatriates) and FMs (TCN and HCN managers) because each has unique characteristics relevant to performance and compensation. The IPM system also plays a particularly important role in performance feedback, individual job assignments, development planning, and identification of training needs. The performance of international assignees and other managers in global firms is critical to the success of the multinational enterprise. However, one of the most serious stumbling blocks to the effective management and development of these managers and IAs is the frequent lack of recognition of the value of their foreign experience and expatriation, in general, and the informality with which firms often evaluate these IA/FMs' overseas performance. That is, one of the most serious stumbling blocks to effective global management and management development derives from problems with the performance management system for international assignees and foreign managers.

Indeed, large MNEs with many overseas assignees and many foreign subsidiaries report that most (83 percent) do not use performance management to measure IAs' success. And many (35 percent) don't use any type of measurement at all.[2]

A firm's performance appraisal system can greatly impact the performance of its workers. Yet conducting valid performance appraisals, even in the home environment, is quite a difficult task. Appraising performance and conducting effective performance appraisals is even more challenging in the international HR arena.[3]

For one thing, the types of skills developed and used in an overseas job are different from those developed and used in the domestic environment. The international assignee and other foreign managers must, of course, develop and use the competencies necessary for any managerial assignment. But, in addition to these capabilities, they must also develop the following:[4]

- Being able to manage an international business and all the complexities that entails.
- Being able to manage a workforce with cultural and subcultural differences.
- Being able to plan for, and conceptualize, the dynamics of a complex, multinational environment.
- Being more open-minded about alternative methods for solving problems.
- Being more flexible in dealing with people and systems.
- Understanding and managing the interdependences among the firm's domestic and foreign operations.

These skills are a natural outgrowth of the increased autonomy that IAs and their foreign manager colleagues experience in the international environment. In addition, this autonomy results in a greater impact on the subsidiary's performance than would be possible at that level in the home-country situation. With increased decision-making responsibilities in the foreign environment, IAs and foreign managers are typically subjected to a more intense working environment to which they have to adjust fairly completely and quickly. But the often distant evaluators seldom understand these difficulties and tend to not take them into consideration when evaluating IA/FMs.

In order for the individual contributor and his/her organization to benefit, however, from this enhanced learning and performance, the organization must have a way to track and evaluate it. The reality usually is, though – as stated above – that this doesn't happen, either very well or at all.

There are many reasons that the international performance evaluation system doesn't work very well, including:

- Problems with the choice of evaluator (e.g., local or parent company) and that person's amount of contact with the expatriate.
- Host-country management's perceptions of performance. (There are often considerable differences between headquarters and foreign locales in what is valued in terms of performance and in terms of perceptions of the actual behavior.)[5]
- Difficulties with long-distance communication with headquarters (for example, in the time and the timeliness of the communications and the understanding of the communications, particularly as this relates to performance evaluations, but also as a major component in the expatriate's and foreign manager's job activities, themselves).
- Inadequate contact between parent-company rater and subsidiary ratee.
- Inadequate establishment of performance objectives for the foreign operations (unclear, contradictory) and means for recording levels of individual and organizational performance.
- Parent-country ethnocentrism and lack of understanding of the foreign environment and culture.
- Frequent indifference to the foreign experience of the expatriate and to the importance of the international business, in general.

## Purposes and roles of international performance management

Organizations develop performance management systems for a number of reasons, but primarily for evaluation and for development.[6] These purposes are much the same for domestic and international operations. The major difference is that implementation of these goals is much more difficult in the global arena, as this chapter will make quite clear.

*Evaluation goals* for performance appraisals in the international environment include:

- To provide feedback to managers so they will know where they stand.
- To develop valid data for pay, promotion, and job assignment decisions, and to provide a means of communicating these decisions.
- To help management in making discharge and retention decisions, and to provide a means of warning employees about unsatisfactory performance.

*Development goals* for performance appraisals in the international environment include:

- To help managers improve their performance and develop future potential.
- To develop commitment to the company through discussion of career opportunities and career planning with the manager.
- To motivate managers via recognition of their efforts.
- To diagnose individual and organizational problems.
- To identify individual training and development needs.

Of course, the nature of the overseas job, the degree of support from and interaction with the parent company, the nature of the overseas environment in which the performance occurs, and the degree of expatriate and family adjustment all impact the ability of any global organization to achieve these objectives.[7]

## Challenges to the effectiveness of the IPM system

Given the major differences between the domestic and international PM environments, it is probably to be expected that there will be a number of challenges in implementing the IPM system. The following paragraphs describe in more detail the most important of these issues involved with an IPM system.

## Invalid performance criteria

International assignees often receive inappropriate performance appraisals because the performance criteria common in their home countries are often superimposed on to an IA/FM even though those criteria might not make sense in the foreign culture. For instance, in American MNEs, the job performance of American managers is often measured in terms of profits, rate of return on investment, cash flows, efficiency or input–output ratios, market share, and the like. In addition, many performance appraisal forms use trait-based formats, evaluating items like initiative, judgment, timeliness, friendliness, etc. These sorts of criteria for evaluation may not be as relevant in the foreign setting, or, if they are important, given the remoteness of most evaluators and infrequent contact with the expatriate/FM, they are certainly much more difficult to assess. They are probably less applicable in many foreign cultures, as well. Even in terms of the business-related criteria, there are problems. For instance, IAs and foreign managers may have less control over profit levels, because their profits are so heavily influenced by such external factors as exchange rate fluctuations, price controls, depreciation allowances, general overhead charges, and differences in established accounting practices.

An American assigned to a mine in Chile who almost single-handed stopped a strike that would have shut down the mine for months, where such action was seen as a major accomplishment, especially for an American, nevertheless received an evaluation as an only mediocre performer.[8] Exchange rate fluctuations with its primary trading partner in South America depressed demand for their ore temporarily by some 30 percent. So this reduction in sales is what the home office saw, not the external factors influencing the IA's performance nor the superb negotiation skills he demonstrated to avert the strike.

MNEs cannot simply use standard appraisal criteria – developed in the domestic context – overseas and expect valid results. External factors usually influence the financial and operational results much more so in the overseas environment than they do domestically. Items like severe inflation, currency devaluations, local leave and holiday requirements and thirteenth-month pay norms just are not issues in the domestic context for many MNEs. Thus, MNEs need to construct criteria for evaluation according to each subsidiary's unique situation. And executives from the home office who are responsible for IA/FM performance review need to be helped to understand the working of these local issues. More appropriate criteria (at least in addition to traditional business measures and tempering them) for evaluating expatriate managers might include such dimensions as relationships with union leaders and individuals in local government, local market share (if the subsidiary services a local market), public image of the firm, negotiation skills, cross-cultural skills, relationships with the local workforce, community involvement, speed and quality of local adaptation, and employee morale.[9]

Many of these factors of a global manager's job are not easily quantified or measured, and are not within the observation limits of the reviewer (see the next two sections). If they are not measured and thus not evaluated, the expatriate/FM soon learns that it doesn't pay (literally) to pay close attention to them. But it also means that critical (to performance) issues are not assessed and included in the expatriate/FM evaluation.

## Rater competence

When it comes to evaluating an IA/FM's job performance, the key question is "Who should conduct the appraisals?" In the home-country setting, managers are evaluated by bosses with whom they have significant amount of interaction and with whom they work pretty closely. This is typically not the case in the overseas work environment. Surveys suggest that 75 percent of top executives in multinational firms have had no overseas experience, nor have any top executives in about 80 percent of MNEs.[10] Parent-company executives who have never worked or lived overseas often complete expatriates' appraisals. Lacking an understanding of the social and business contexts in which the work is performed, these managers have no feel for the unique challenges faced by IAs or other overseas managers. Under these circumstances, the chance of rater error increases significantly.

The experience of this high-potential manager who was assigned to the Tokyo office of his semiconductor company provides an example of exactly this issue.[11] Because of the difficulties of cracking a nearly impossible market, his stateside boss gave him a very low appraisal. On returning to the US, he was physically and mentally exhausted from the battle. He sought a much less challenging position and got it because top management believed it had overestimated his potential. In fact, top management never did understand what the expatriate was up against in the foreign market.

IHRM in Action 12.1 illustrates the kinds of problems that can be encountered in the evaluation of overseas managers, in this case an English manager working for a Swiss chemical company in Thailand and trying to evaluate a key Thai subordinate within the local context, but while trying to follow corporate guidelines.[12] It shows how difficult it can be to develop consistent criteria across locations within an MNE, how important the level of international experience is in the role of the evaluator, and how important context is in the implementation of any cross-cultural performance evaluation system. The parent-company general manager in Bangkok finds it impossible to apply parent-company standards within the Thai context.

International assignees and foreign managers often indicate that their home office deals with them from an "out of sight, out of mind" perspective and that the home office does not understand what sorts of problems they encounter overseas. Because of this the IA/FMs are often left pretty much alone, isolating them from activities in the parent company and from their home office superiors.[13]

A competent or internationally experienced rater who understands the realities of the global business situation can compensate for a poorly designed performance appraisal system that either measures the wrong things or doesn't have a way to take into account the external factors. The combination of a poorly designed system and a rater who does not understand the international business situation and/or the cultural context of the ratee will almost inevitably lead to invalid performance evaluations. When top management does not understand overseas business realities, mistakes in IA/FM evaluations, whether done formally or informally, are likely to occur.

## Rater bias

Even when performance evaluations are made by a host-country manager (or home-country executive) who better understands the IA and foreign manager's challenges, its validity will not be assured. Individuals from different cultures consistently misinterpret each others' behaviors, possibly biasing the appraisals.[14] At times, these misinterpretations will be based on a preconceived (prior to the evaluation) attitude on the part of the rater, that is, based on some characteristic of the IA/FM that is not directly related to the performance under review. For an example of this problem, consider the following situation.[15]

In France, women are allowed six months of maternity leave, and during that time, they are not legally allowed to do any work related to their jobs. An American expatriate manager in France had two secretaries taking maternity leave. The

# Evaluation of local national by Richard Evans, expatriate managing director

Richard Evans was managing director of Siam Chemicals Company (SCC) in Thailand, a division of Chimique Helvétique Ltd (CHL), a Swiss chemicals group headquartered in Basle. He had only been in this position eighteen months, but dealing with the evaluation of Mr Somsak, one of his local mainstays, was about ready to drive him back to Switzerland or to England, from where he originally came. This was Richard's first assignment outside Europe, and he had not found it an easy adjustment. Between the long commutes from home to the plant, due to the terrible traffic, the lack of sidewalks for taking his young son out in his pram, and the incredibly strong attitude of deference the Thai employees exhibited toward him, most of his first eighteen months had been spent trying to get used to the locale and the culture. It was his first time in Asia and the culture shock for himself and his family (wife and three young children) had been harsh. To move from international schools and skiing in clean, dry air in Switzerland to hot, humid, dirty, and polluted Thailand, where they spoke not a word of the local language and had no idea of the local customs, was indeed quite a shock.

It was shortly after arrival that he had had his first encounter with Mr Somsak, considered one of the senior and longer-established employees after three years on the job. Somsak worked both for Richard and for James Brown, the regional marketing manager, in the firm's regional offices in Singapore. Somsak had resigned right after a meeting that Richard had had with him to try to counsel him on how to function better within the matrix organizational structure of CHL. Somsak had explained to Richard that Thai people found the concept of two bosses impossible to reconcile with their strong sense of hierarchy. They preferred to know exactly who was their senior boss so they would know whose approval to seek. Richard had seized on the opportunity to counsel Somsak in a style that had always worked with his European managers. He had been stunned when Somsak had reacted with these words: "I realize from what you have said that I am not doing a good job. I am not suitable for my post and so the only thing I can do is to resign." Only through the strenuous efforts of Somsak's other boss, James Brown, to whom he owed a strong sense of allegiance, had he been persuaded to stay.

But now, eighteen months later, Richard was trying to figure out how to reconcile a major dilemma in how to complete the corporate evaluation form on Mr Somsak. During the last eighteen months, Mr Somsak had maintained a very polite and correct but by no means warm attitude towards his managing director. For his part, Richard had come to appreciate that Somsak was a very hard-working and meticulous manager. He was willing to work every hour of the day, was highly intelligent, and spoke excellent English, since he had been dealing with European firms for many years. Richard had made every effort to convey his appreciation of Somsak's efforts and recently had been heartened by signs of a more trusting, comfortable relationship. Now the evaluation problem threatened all the gains Richard felt he had so carefully made.

Richard knew that corporate headquarters (both his own direct supervisor and the corporate HR director) wanted all subsidiaries to adopt a more consistent form. The annual evaluation process was imposed on all CHL's subsidiaries and had been in use in Thailand ever since the company's foundation, seven years ago. The same format was used company-wide for all management grades. The basis of the form was a set of six to seven key objectives to be achieved by a certain point in time during the coming year. The actual process involved two one-on-one meetings between the supervisor and the subordinate managers. The first meeting was to go over that year's performance and the second was to set objectives for the next year.

Richard found that his local managers found the very idea of sitting down with their boss to discuss their performance a threatening and alien concept. Even the most senior, who had a good command of English and had been with the company for some time, found it difficult both to meet with Richard for their own evaluations, and also to carry out the process with their own staffs. It was not for them to make any judgment about their performance, that was the job of the boss.

The most difficult part of the process involved the assigning of a letter grade. The chemical group used a standard A–E grading in which a normal distribution was to be applied, with an A grade being applied to the top 3–4 percent of really outstanding managers and the C category, into which 60–70 percent of managers usually fell, implying a good, standard performance with all requirements fulfilled. Looking through the records, Richard found that his predecessors had decided it was best to not disturb the relationships with local staff and had been awarding A grades to over 90 percent of the local managers.

Richard thought it was part of his obligation as managing director and as representative of the parent company, to move the local evaluation system to reflect the international standards. In addition, the corporate HR director was championing the idea of developing an international cadre of managers who could help to staff the rapidly growing expansion of CHL's global operations. He had indicated how important a role the performance evaluation system was in that effort to identify the best managers within the local subsidiaries to begin developing them for other assignments.

In terms of achievement of objectives for the regional office, Somsak had done an A job. But in terms of meeting other objectives that Richard had set for him, such as dealing with better integrating his team with the broader firm, Richard felt that he had not done what was expected. He had built up his team but had only succeeded in forming an isolated clique. The team acted like a family centered on Somsak. In his own mind, Richard thought an overall C grade was totally appropriate. But the reality was that Somsak (and probably James Brown) would not understand and would again resign, and Richard would lose a very important contributor. And it was entirely possible in this culture that he would lose the whole team.

He had no idea how to proceed.

American asked them to work at home, unaware that such a request was illegal. Feeling sorry for her boss, one of the women complied with his request. When the American's French boss found out that the secretary was working at home, he became very angry and intolerant of the American's actions. As a result, the American was given a lower overall performance evaluation than he deserved.

Because people who work in foreign environments often have preconceived (and often unfounded) notions (call them prejudices or stereotypes) about the nature of the attitudes and behaviors of the "foreigners" with whom they work, it is too frequent that they will base their evaluations on these biases. In the above situation, the American had preconceived notions about what commitment from employees meant. And the French manager had preconceived notions about the level of knowledge an expatriate should have about legal working requirements in France.

In Chapter 10, the importance of cross-cultural training and orientation for IAs was discussed in some detail. It should be clear that some level of this type of training is also appropriate for their bosses. If cross-cultural misunderstandings remain unresolved, they can affect performance evaluations quite negatively.

## Host environment

The environment in the foreign setting is of primary importance. The international context, with its differing societal, legal, economic, technical, and physical demands, is a major determinant of IS/FM performance.[16] Consequently, IA/FM performance and performance expectations need to be placed within its international as well as its organizational contexts. The type of structure in the foreign setting adds another dimension to this concern over the host environment. In many locales, for example, working in a wholly-owned subsidiary will probably be much easier than working in a joint venture with a local partner. Similarly, overseeing the opening of a new office or facility in a foreign country, especially in a developing country or emerging market, will be different than the challenges faced in a more mature operation.

## Cultural adjustment

This issue has been discussed in prior chapters, such as Chapter 5 on culture and Chapter 10 on training and development. But it also relevant to consider here. The process of cultural adjustment is a critical determinant of IA job performance and needs to be taken into consideration when evaluating that performance. One of the dilemmas, in terms of IPM, is that adjustment to a foreign culture is multifaceted with individual reactions and coping behaviors varying according to a number of difficult to assess factors, such as prior experience, local assistance, and degree of preparation and orientation. Thus, determining the relevance of adjustment to the new environment when evaluating IA work performance may be problematical.

# Managing the IPM system

Multinational enterprises can do a number of things to ensure that valid performance evaluations are made in their global operations, or, at least, to increase the likelihood of good results from the PM system. The following puts these actions into categories related to the above challenges.

# What criteria should be used for evaluation (i.e., what should be evaluated)?

The answer to the question of what should be evaluated for IA/FMs is indeed complex. They need to meet parent-company standards and they need to do it within the international and local-culture contexts. So the evaluation system needs to take both sets of standards into account. The problem is, criteria, roles, and performance expectations are typically defined in the home country but performed in the host country. The cultural norms that define performance in the parent country may not be the same as those considered appropriate in the foreign locale.

For the IA and/or FM, this can cause significant role conflict.[17] If the IA or FM adapts his or her behavior according to the role behavior expected in the host environment, it may well conflict with that predetermined at headquarters. This type of role conflict is likely to result in situations where the IA/FM has an understanding of the host-country culture and realizes that the use of headquarters procedures or actions may lead to ineffective management. Evidently, the higher the degree of intercultural interaction, the more problems the IA or FM are likely to have with role conflict. Such role conflict is also compounded by the lack of autonomy in many foreign assignments (more structure and defined protocols), allowing less space to deal with the conflicting expectations.[18] And this concern over conflicting role expectations is even more pronounced for third-country nationals than it will be for host-country nationals (FMs) or parent-country nationals (IAs).[19]

Each criterion is composed of a number of sub-categories. One attempt to suggest a set of criteria and sub-categories for international appraisals is found in Box 12.1.[20] The first category refers to Qualifications, meaning the criteria used to select the IA (and FM) for the foreign assignment. These are included under the understanding that IA/FMs' performance should be a function of the original assessment of their qualifications for the assignments and their ongoing evaluations should continue to assess whether the original qualifications were accurate. The other categories take into account the variety and complexity of criteria that have been suggested are so necessary in this environment. Normally, a variety of factors are applied, depending on the IA/FMs' job descriptions and local circumstances. However, observation of common practice suggests that use of detailed criteria such as listed in Box 12.1 is not really so common as the presence of this table suggests. And broader standards and more general evaluations are probably more the norm.

## Box 12.1 Criteria for appraisal of international assignees and foreign managers

### Qualifications

- Training
- Experience
- Technical skills
- Social and language skills
- Education

### Targets

- Directly derived from the parent company's objectives
- Directly derived from the subsidiary's objectives
- Directly derived from local objectives
- Individually dictated, e.g., developmental goals

### Attitude for

- Flexibility
- Interpersonal understanding and communication skills
- Ability to cope with the stress (culture shock) of the assignment
- Openness to change

### Job performance

- Result areas; development of local team
- Communication and decision making
- Personal growth and development
- Application of (newly gained) expertise

Obviously, business strategy largely dictates the overall expectations for IA/FM performance in any specific country. For example, it might not make sense to focus heavily on profits as a standard for success for a global manager in the early years of a subsidiary in the People's Republic of China. Efforts in the early years are most likely to be concentrated on development of relationships and on building a base of customers. To expect your IAs or FMs to produce profits equal to those generated in a similar kind of operation at home is unrealistic and will cause heavy frustration and possibly lead to wrongly destroying a manager's career. There needs to be alignment between parent-company strategy and the realities of the local situation.

In order to ensure this type of alignment, the home office will have to spend adequate time and attention to understand the local/foreign situation. Executives must travel to the foreign locale to observe and ask a lot of questions in order to gain understanding and insight into the local culture and operating situation. At the home office, outside experts from universities and consulting firms, as well as former expatriates (i.e., repatriates) from that country, should be brought in to help provide the information upon which executives can best judge the factors for success in the foreign locations in question. Interestingly, research finds that transnational corporations are more likely to use the same basic performance criteria throughout their operations, with some variance in criteria importance depending on country situations.[21]

> Ideally, a manager who has returned to the home office from an overseas site should be a permanent part of the team that updates performance criteria for overseas assignments. Reevaluating the criteria and their prioritization periodically will ensure that the performance criteria will remain current with the reality of the overseas situation.[22]

## Who should do the evaluation?

Given all the problems in implementing an effective IPM, the issue of who should conduct performance appraisals of expatriates and foreign managers also becomes quite complex. How can the MNE and IHRM compensate for the many problems described above? The answer developed by most MNEs is found in the use of multiple reviewers.[23] These additional reviewers may not all be as directly familiar with the work of the IA/FM (although some may actually be more familiar, given the problems of time and distance discussed above), but they may be able to add necessary perspective: peers, subordinates, customers or clients. This is an application of what is referred to as the 360 degree review process, i.e., using reviews from above, below, and beside the candidate reviewee, and even using self-review.

In the domestic context, the 360 degree review process is relatively complex (certainly more complex and messy, at least, than the traditional superior-only review process). In the overseas context, it is even messier. In the overseas context, associates of the rated IA/FM are located many miles and time zones away from the parent firm, but who come into contact with the IA/FM's work and can render a valuable evaluation of the individual's performance. Most IA/FM jobs include direct supervision from someone in the home country plus usually a direct supervisor in the host country, as well. In addition, the IA/FM will entertain regular visits from home-country staff and line employees, people on missions to check in on the foreign operation and will also have frequent direct contacts in the foreign location with local customers, suppliers, banks, and government and community officials, the nature of which will be difficult to assess from home. Table 12.1 illustrates what one survey of MNEs found in terms of the percentages of usage of various types of potential evaluators.[24] Clearly home-country and host-country supervisors are the most common, although other home-country and host-country and regional executives also get involved frequently. Interestingly, a high percentage of firms also use self-evaluation.

*Table 12.1* Raters of international assignee performance

| Inside host country | | Outside host country | |
|---|---|---|---|
| *Rater* | *%* | *Rater* | *%* |
| Customers | 1 | Sponsor | 7 |
| Subordinates | 7 | Corporate HR professional | 17 |
| Peers | 10 | Regional executive | 23 |
| HR professionals | 12 | Supervisor | 41 |
| Self | 39 | | |
| Supervisor | 75 | | |

Note: Percentages refer to average percentage in which each type of rater is involved in evaluations across sample MNEs.

But some typical raters in 360 degree evaluation systems, such as customers and peers, turned out to not be used very much, at all.

To illustrate how this might work, here is a list of potential reviewers for an expatriate manager of sales and marketing for the subsidiary of an American firm in Paris: her immediate manager, the director of sales and marketing (located at product headquarters in Atlanta in the US); the country manager, France; the HR director, Paris; the marketing director, European region, located in regional headquarters in Brussels; the corporate head of marketing, located at corporate headquarters in Chicago; her expatriate and Paris staff peers, including the manager of sales, France; the entire team of subordinates in the Paris operation working for her; and selected clients and customers in the French market. Granted, the use of such multiple ratings is complicated; but the difficulties involved with overseas operations indicates the need to collect multiple perspectives to enhance the accuracy and completeness of expatriate/FM performance evaluation.

Multinational firms participating in a survey by a large global consulting firm gave the following responses to their use of various forms of expatriate performance review:[25]

| Type of review | % |
|---|---|
| Performance review in host country | 71 |
| Performance review in home country | 56 |
| Regular expatriate visits to home office | 44 |
| Regular manager visits to host office | 39 |
| Annual expatriate surveys (self-reports) | 19 |

Obviously, as was suggested earlier, often the expatriate evaluation process is a pretty informal process. The survey found that companies with fewer than 100 expatriates favored home-country reviews, while companies with more than 100 expatriates favored host-country appraisals. Apparently, once the foreign operations reach a certain size, the preference is to delegate the appraisal process to the local level where, presumably, managers with a more direct contact with the IA/FM are able to provide more accurate and complete evaluations, although there is no direct research to verify that local managers do any better job at IA/FM performance appraisal than do home-country or regional office managers. Indeed, given the many perceptual issues stemming from differences in cultural values and norms and from problems with cultural adaptation, there is some reason to question the assumption that local managers are better equipped to perform these evaluations than are home-country managers.

One additional result of the previous survey that relates to who does the assessments is that firms reported that on average IA/FMs are evaluated by an average of three individuals, while the same firms reported an average of six raters for their home-country positions.[26] So even here, the international situation, even though admittedly much more complex and difficult, does not receive the same level of management attention and involvement as happens in the purely domestic environment.

- *Home-country managers*. In many cases, the final appraisal is done in the parent country, where the appraisers typically have little knowledge of local circumstances or of local culture and their impacts on the overall unit performance or on the expatriate or local manager's performance. Achieving results equivalent to a comparable unit or manager in the home country may well require larger efforts in terms of flexibility and creativity, to say nothing of interpersonal and managerial skills, all of which are difficult to quantify or measure, and, therefore, aren't taken into consideration.
- *Host-country managers*. In view of the geographical, communicative, and cultural, distance between the foreign subsidiary or joint venture and the home-country appraiser, local management are often called in to give their opinion. In the case of mid-level managers and expatriates, the immediate supervisor responsible for the evaluation is probably a local manager. The assumption is that they are familiar with the expatriate's performance and are, therefore, in the best position to evaluate and explain it within the local situation and environmental factors. However, their perceptions and, therefore, their evaluations will be governed by their own cultural backgrounds and biases. Thus, for example, a parent-company manager, who is used to guiding and managing with a high degree of involvement and participation, might at least initially find resistance from local team members, who expect strong leadership and ideas and initiative from their bosses, and thus not get the desired level of team performance, resulting in a negative (or lower than expected) evaluation.[27]

## How should evaluations for IA/FMs be done?

There are a number of issues presented in answering the question of how international performance evaluations should be done. These include concerns about the specific form of the appraisal, the frequency of the appraisal, and the nature of feedback provided to the IA/FM as a part of the evaluation process.

## Form

There continues much controversy over the specific form to be used in any performance review process, although this is not an area that has received any attention specifically focused on the international setting. So, presumably, all of the concerns over evaluation based on achievement of objectives versus trait-based reviews, or other approaches, such as critical-incident methods, that have been researched in the domestic context would also apply to the international context. In addition, however, the international context must also take into account issues over language and translation or interpretation of terms and phrasing as well as the cultural context, such as the nature of relationships between subordinates and superiors, etc. Refer to IHRM in Action 12.1 for an example of a particular situation that points out some of these problems.

It is typical for firms to develop standard forms for their appraisal processes.[28] And there are valid reasons to retain such forms, including the importance of experience, comparative data for extended usage, costs, etc. These reasons remain valid, as long as the context of the performance doesn't change. However, for IA/FMs the context most obviously does change. Thus, using standard forms, developed for the domestic situation, can be problematical. Despite this, surveys find that US firms, at least, tend to use the same standardized forms developed for the home-country environment for their expatriate, and, presumably, their FM populations.[29] This makes the problems associated with consideration of cultural context in the actual assessment of performance that much more important, but probably results in even less attention being paid to these contextual issues.

## Frequency

This is one area where, at least in terms of general performance appraisals, some basic guidelines can be established. According to Wayne Cascio, a major contributor to knowledge about the performance appraisal process, "Research over the past twenty years has indicated that once or twice a year is too infrequent. Considerable difficulties face a rater who is asked to remember what several employees did over the previous six to twelve months. . . . People often forget the details of what they have observed and they reconstruct the details on the basis of their existing mental categories."[30] Supervisors tend to evaluate what they remember from the last few weeks or days, rather than over the six to twelve-month period. Even if they have maintained good records of events and performance, they are likely to be most persuaded and influenced by recent events. Ultimately, of course, to the extent the purpose of the evaluation is to provide feedback to the ratee for development purposes, the more frequent the evaluation and feedback, the better.

It is also true that the frequency of evaluation should also vary according to the role of the evaluator.[31] On-site superiors should rate their subordinate IA/FMs after the completion of all significant projects or tasks. This helps the superior to focus clearly on the specific context of the particular performance being assessed. These can then be reviewed at the time of the annual or semi-annual official reviews. Other reviewers, such as peers, subordinates, and customers are probably best to be asked for reviews that fit the schedule of the formal review.

## Feedback

Usually, an important component of any effective IPM system would include the provision of timely feedback of the results of the evaluation. As IHRM in Action 12.1 points out, however, this may prove to be problematic in many cultural settings. And, in addition, given time and distance issues separating many reviewers and their ratees, provision of this feedback is also likely to not take place in a timely manner, if at all. And evaluation by a distant manager probably only has face validity against hard criteria, adding another obstacle to effective PM.

## International assignee and foreign manager development

One of the most important functions of global executives is developing and grooming IAs and foreign managers for promotion and for higher-level responsibility. Given the nature of IPM as discussed above, this can be a difficult task. Cultural differences can have a major impact on evaluation for these purposes because the underlying assumptions that executives make about an employee's potential may not take such differences into account.[32]

To determine an IA's or foreign manager's promotion potential, executives are likely to consider such questions as: How is initiative demonstrated? What behaviors show commitment? How much is high potential determined by accomplishing the task and how much is determined by good interpersonal skills and general intelligence? How do employees get to use and showcase their unique talents? In the international context, the answers to every one of these questions must take into account the affect of culture. Initiative and commitment are defined differently in different cultures. The importance and role of task accomplishment versus interpersonal skills also varies from culture to culture, to say nothing of methods of task accomplishment and the definition of "task" itself. And the executive must as well be aware of the impact of cultural issues such as time orientation, hierarchy, group orientation, and communication styles on all of these questions in order to make accurate assessments of promotion potential. And it is the performance management system, in order to effectively contribute to such judgments, which must be designed and implemented in such a way as to take into account these cultural issues.

# Senior managers' attitudes about international performance management

The end result all too often of the problems described is that the senior managers in the parent-company/headquarters either ignore performance evaluation all together for their individual IAs and overseas managers or they pay attention only to overall financial results of the subsidiary or joint venture with little or no sensitivity to the impact of local culture or to individual behaviors that were (or had to be) exhibited in order to achieve those results (refer back to the example of the American expatriate manager in Chile.) The individual may have performed under extremely difficult circumstances and achieved highly favorable and unexpected results, given the situation, but the bottom line doesn't show it. Without headquarters appreciating that results would have been much worse except for these efforts of the IA, what gets evaluated are the resulting less than satisfactory (based on parent-country standards) financial figures.

From the standpoint of the expatriate, his or her performance is based on his or her mostly independent (and, usually, isolated) overseas judgment, technical know-how, and various relevant environmental factors, such as the quality of local relationships and ability to function within the local culture. His or her actual performance, though, tends to be evaluated in terms of perceived performance (either locally or from the parent company, or both), which is based on a set of fairly complex variables usually below the evaluator's level of awareness. Depending on whether the manager (local or parent-company) who is assessing the IA's performance has had personal overseas experience or is otherwise sensitive to problems associated with overseas work, the performance appraisal will be more or less valid.

> *The bottom line for the expatriate is that the performance appraisal will influence the promotion potential and type of position the expatriate receives on returning* [*home*]. Because expatriates generally return from their experience with valuable managerial skills, especially for firms pursuing an international or global market path, it behooves organizations to carefully review their process of appraising expatriates and the evaluation criteria themselves.[33]

# Overcoming IPM challenges

As has been described in this chapter, it is extremely difficult to appraise performance accurately in cross-cultural environments. The potential for misunderstandings and for inaccurate assessments is great. At a minimum, the likelihood of cross-border evaluations not taking into account important information based on the impact of culture and the problems of working in the international environment are significant. Working in an overseas situation is just not the same as working in the domestic environment and, thus, different criteria for evaluation must be considered.

Unfortunately, there are no easy solutions. Companies should use multiple raters and make sure that some of those raters have lived and worked in the country in which the expatriate and other managers being evaluated are working. In addition, however, IAs must also understand that their performance may be misunderstood and go unappreciated. They, too, have some responsibility to ensure the accurate understanding of the problems they confront in getting their jobs done. This should include frequent interaction with their evaluators with discussion of expectations, of problems encountered, of solutions implemented, and of adaptation experiences and successes. Armed with this input, it would be hoped that evaluators would be able to make better and more accurate assessments.

Because the appraisal will have a major impact on the expatriate's promotions and other career decisions, type of assignment upon repatriation back home, training and development opportunities, and probably on compensation bonuses and pay increases, it is of major concern to him or her. Expatriates usually return home from their overseas experiences having learned and exercised valuable managerial and international business skills. Therefore, it behoves multinational enterprises to carefully review their procedures for evaluating their expatriates and foreign managers and their evaluation criteria, themselves, or they risk losing these valuable managerial resources.

In establishing performance criteria, issues should be considered such as the operating language of the foreign assignment (and how fluent the IA is or needs to be), the cultural "distance" to be experienced (refer back to the discussion of cultural adaptation and preparation and training in Chapter 10), and the stability and controllability of major performance factors such as the nature of the workforce, rates of inflation and currency exchange rates. The local manager ought to have major input into the evaluation, but if the evaluation is actually developed by the parent-company manager, the assistance of a former expatriate from the foreign location under consideration can be quite valuable in developing an understanding of the local factors that are significant in the expatriate's performance.

Evidently, those multinational firms that use appraisal systems in their global operations rely on a wide variety of actual appraisal techniques, ranging from a mix of formal and informal procedures, visits to and from headquarters, and examination of operating and financial statistics. In most firms, considerable weight is given to the "gut feel" of specialist IHRM or senior line executives from headquarters.[34]

## Characteristics of effective IPM systems: guidelines

There are a number of things that can be done to improve the effectiveness of an MNE's IPM system. These include the following:

- *Relevance.* IHR needs to ensure that the criteria and process for evaluation are relevant to the content and requirements of the job. This involves IHR and reviewers having a clear understanding of the unique situation of the foreign job requirements.

- *Acceptability*. The criteria and process used also need to be acceptable to those using it, i.e., both evaluators and ratees. One aspect of this is that the criteria being rated need to be in control of the ratee. The rater needs to objectify the evaluation as much as possible, while considering the realities of the foreign assignment, using input from as many sources as possible, including from the IA/FMs themselves. In addition, the rater needs to follow standard procedures and the appraisal results need to be seen, particularly by the ratee, as fair and accurate. The appraisal form, itself, needs to accommodate special or unique circumstances; the ratee needs to receive timely feedback, the rater should suggest how the ratee can improve, and the ratee should get the necessary resources to improve, such as training programs. All of this is to say that the process needs to be seen as having "face" validity, i.e., it needs to be seen as fair, reasonable, and accurate.

- *Sensitivity*. An effective IPM system takes into consideration cultural and international business realities. It will include input from people with experience in the particular foreign setting, such as former expatriates. It needs to take into account issues like the operational language of the foreign organization, the cultural distance between the foreign firm and the parent, and the importance of issues like the power of local unions and stability of exchange rates. IHR can build into the evaluation process a numerical factor based on the difficulty of the foreign location, freeing the home evaluator from having to directly assess this, him or herself.

- *Practicality*. The last guideline here is that the performance evaluation system needs to easy to use. If it is either too complex or too difficult to administer, managers will not use it. Or they will only give it surface attention, shortcutting a serious evaluation and thus abrogating any potential value from the assessment process and making it impossible to achieve the objectives set out for an effective IPM system.

All of these characteristics illustrate how important it is for IA/FM evaluators to be trained in the use of international evaluation systems. The effectiveness of an IPM system can be improved, but it requires IHR to get involved and to work on implementing the types of characteristics described here.

"Regardless of the effectiveness or availability of Performance Management (PM) tools, expatriate PM success depends largely on the manager and expatriate in question: how well they both understand, internalize, and accept PM, and how skillful they are in its implementation. To this end, appropriate PM training should be available for all expatriates, including their superiors."[35]

IHRM in Action 12.2 illustrates how Nokia has developed an effective performance appraisal system for its expatriates, that utilizes many of the approaches described in this chapter.[36] This system uses multiple raters, multiple criteria for evaluation, and multiple ratings in terms of types of ratings, forms for ratings, and frequency of ratings.

As stated by Cascio, "Performance appraisal has many facets. It is an exercise in observation and judgment, it is a feedback process, it is an organizational

# Nokia tackles expatriate performance management

Nokia, the Finnish-based world leader in the telecommunications industry, has extensive experience of sending and receiving people on foreign assignments, with about 1,200 expatriates on foreign assignment at any one time. Because of this, Nokia has had to learn how to manage the performance of this large group of employees who are so key to the success of the firm's global business. Nokia has developed a comprehensive performance management program that includes goal setting, performance appraisal and feedback, continuous training and development, and performance-related compensation. One thing that Nokia has learned is that the performance of its various types of expatriates, who are in varying types of assignments and situations, should be managed dissimilarly, even within the context of trying to apply a standard approach throughout its global operations.

Nokia has put in place what looks, on the surface, like a global, standardized performance management system, with the objective that all employees' performance is managed (to a great extent) the same. In terms of expatriates, however, it turns out that there are at least five different types of expatriates, including top managers, middle managers, business establishers, customer project employees, and R&D project personnel. For each of these groups, there are some common practices. For example, all expatriates know what is expected of them, how well they are performing, and what the opportunities are for them to develop new competencies in order to meet present and future job requirements.

However, the various expatriate groups also experience some differences in how their performance is managed. These differences revolve around the following:

- Whether and how performance goals are set, who sets them, and what types of goals are set.
- How performance is evaluated and who conducts the evaluation.
- Whether training and development plans are agreed upon with the expatriate.
- Whether expatriates have the opportunity to attend training while on their foreign assignments.
- What type and how clear the linkage is between expatriate performance and pay.

For example, as might be expected, the higher the expatriate's level the more independent their position and the more distant their performance management. In addition, they and their bosses are more likely to have a longer-term focus, both for their present international position and in terms of their careers and developmental concerns.

Middle manager expatriates reported typically to a local manager and had local, relatively short-term, goals and focus. Feedback was given by the local manager, and the local manager determined financial incentive rewards. Performance goals for

continued

business establisher expatriates and for customer project expatriates were tied to the nature of their assignments, more so than the earlier two categories, with start-up objectives for the former and deadlines for network operation common in the latter. Indeed, in all four areas tracked (goal setting, performance evaluation, training and development, and performance-related pay), performance management criteria were implemented differently for the five different groups of expatriates, even though all expatriates were managed in some form or another on all four areas.

This major global firm illustrates the high degree of importance that contingency factors play when managing expatriate performance. Even though Nokia has put in place a standard performance management system intended for global use, the reality is that expatriate performance was managed differently in the five categories of expatriate assignments. Evidently, off-the-shelf solutions may not produce the desired improvements in expatriate and company performance.

intervention. It is a measurement process as well as an intensely emotional process. Above all, it is an inexact, human process."[37] And when an organization has to add cultural and international dimensions to the process, it is even more difficult on every one of these characteristics. It is up to IHRM in the multinational enterprise to ensure that the IPM process makes the important contribution that it can and should.

## Conclusion

This chapter has addressed the crucial issue of performance evaluation and performance management for international assignees and managers in foreign operations. It has described the many difficulties encountered in trying to implement an effective IPM system in the international arena, not the least of which is figuring out how to accommodate in the evaluation process factors stemming from the nature of the local cultural environment. It is clear that it is inadequate to simply apply a PM process designed at the home-country level for domestic use to the international setting. It is necessary to make some accommodations for problems with cultural adaptation and associated with the complexities of conducting international business. The chapter ended with a discussion of a number of suggestions and guidelines for improving the process of implementing an effective IPM system. Appropriately assessing an IA/FM's performance is a question of fairness to the IA/FM; but it is also a question of ensuring that the MNE receives full value from its managers and international assignees and the best subsidiary or joint venture performance possible. Ultimately, an MNE's objectives relative to an effective IPM system are to retain their IAs and FMs and effectively develop and position them within the organization so that the firm's global business strategy will be increasingly guided by those who have experienced and understand the firm's worldwide operations and markets.[38]

## Points for further discussion

1  How does Lincoln Electric in China evaluate the performance of its managers?
2  Should the senior managers at Lincoln Electric headquarters in Cleveland, Ohio, be interested in the performance appraisal of the IAs and FMs in China? Why?
3  Who should evaluate and how should the performance of the local Chinese workers be evaluated?

# Health, safety, and crisis management in the global enterprise

**13**

## Learning objectives

After considering this chapter, the reader will be able to:

- Explain the importance of health and safety concerns for the global enterprise
- Describe the most significant issues related to occupational health and safety in MNE subsidiaries and IJVs in various countries around the world
- Describe a number of critical issues for health, safety, and security for international business travelers and IAs and their families
- Explain the recommended programs and policies governing health, safety, and security for business travelers and IAs
- Describe a crisis management plan and program to deal with emergencies and crises for an MNE's global workforce

## Key terms

- AIDS, SARS
- Crisis management plan
- Crisis management

This is one of the most challenging topics to write about in IHRM. There has been relatively little written about this issue (or any of the specific aspects of it) in either the "popular" press or the academic or practitioner press. Periodically, events occur that put certain aspects of the topic on the front page. But this is fairly rare. Still it is an increasingly important topic for MNEs, for the following reasons:

- Increasing attention to employee well-being around the world.
- Increasing numbers of employees at potential risk because of increased global trade:
  - Increasing number of business travelers in general.
  - Increasing number of people on short- and longer-term international assignments to an increasing number of countries.
  - Increasing number of offices and plants overseas in an increasing number of locations and forms (subsidiaries, licensees, joint ventures, alliances, subcontractors).
- Increase in risk factors.

All of these factors create increasing concerns for the health and safety of an MNE's global workforce – and potentially for the safe and continuing operation of the global business. Although it is not always the case, in most countries health and safety is one of the responsibilities of HR, and, therefore, in the global enterprise, of IHR.

Even though not much has been written about this subject (it does show up at most international HR practitioner conferences as a popular presentation and is an important topic at local IHR discussion groups around the US and presumably elsewhere, as well), a number of specific aspects of this topic can be identified and discussed. These include (1) the establishment of health and safety policies on a global basis for all employees of the MNE; (2) coping with health and safety practices and regulations that vary from country to country; (3) dealing with specific health and safety concerns of business travelers and international assignees and their families as they travel on business trips around the world or are posted to foreign assignments; (4) and the very specific threat of issues like kidnapping and/or terrorist acts against foreign operations and international assignees and their families; (5) and dealing with real and potential, natural and man-made, threats and disasters. Given the scarcity of information on these concerns, the following tries to at least introduce some of the factors which the IHR manager in an MNE might need to consider when dealing with international health and safety issues. The chapter first discusses issues related to health and safety programs at the country or region level. Then the chapter discusses issues related to health and safety for business travelers and employees on international assignments. The chapter closes with proposals for creating crisis management programs for preparing for and dealing with various health and safety contingencies.

## Employee health and safety around the world

In most large firms, even though responsibility for employee health and safety resides in the HR department, the HR manager responsible for international HR in the headquarters of an MNE does not often deal with health and safety issues among foreign subsidiaries or joint ventures. Responsibility for health and safety issues is normally left to the local subsidiary or IJV HR manager within the constraints of local custom, culture, and regulation. Clearly, attention to these concerns varies dramatically from country to country.[1]

## Health and safety statistics

It is even difficult to compare business health and safety statistics across countries in order to assess the results of the varying practices.[2] For example, different countries follow different reporting standards regarding what constitutes an injury and whether it must be reported. Even for workplace fatalities, variation in methods makes cross-national comparisons difficult. For example, some countries (but not all) include deaths that occur when an employee is traveling to or from work, whereas others exclude deaths from occupational disease.

In the US, occupational fatalities are reported in relation to the number of person hours worked. In 1987, the rate was 0.027 deaths per million person hours. Japan uses the same method and reports a fatality rate of 0.010. Most other countries report fatalities per 1,000 people employed per year. Data for a sample of these countries from 1987 are shown below. (Remember that the data are not directly comparable to the rates for the US and Japan.)

| | | | |
|---|---|---|---|
| Austria | 0.097 | Hong Kong | 0.075 |
| Canada | 0.075 | New Zealand | 0.072 |
| Cuba | 0.112 | Norway | 0.040 |
| Denmark | 0.030 | Poland | 0.107 |
| Egypt | 0.160 | Spain | 0.120 |
| France | 0.075 | UK | 0.017 |
| Greece | 0.058 | | |

(Given the range and disparity of these figures, it is likely that even these data are not exactly comparable.)

A more recent study from the International Labour Office reports the following fatality rates for a number of regions of the world, figured as fatalities per 100,000 people employed.[3]

| | |
|---|---|
| Established market economies | 5.3 |
| Formerly socialist economies of Europe | 11.1 |
| India | 11.0 |
| China | 11.1 |
| Other Asia and islands | 23.1 |
| Sub-Saharan Africa | 21.0 |
| Latin America and the Caribbean | 13.5 |
| Middle Eastern crescent | 22.5 |

The most important point is that the rates vary widely for a number of reasons, including the mix of industries present in each country. Some industries are inherently more dangerous than others. For instance, the logging, mining, and quarrying industries tend to have the highest fatality rates in most countries, while construction, transportation, utilities, and agriculture have moderately high rates. World Health Organization data suggest that, worldwide, approximately half the world's workers are employed in hazardous jobs, both from risk of injury or illness and from death.[4] The retail trade, banking, and social service industries generally have many fewer fatalities, or even injuries and illnesses. Thus those countries which have a mix of industries that favors those with lower fatalities will have more favorable country-wide statistics.

## Health and safety laws and standards

A country's occupational safety and health laws and enforcement procedures may also influence fatality rates. A comparative study in 1986 of five European countries and the US concluded that the US is the weakest in terms of law and enforcement mechanisms. Sweden, the former East Germany, and Finland were the highest ranked (although with what is now known about the levels of pollution, the age and maintenance of equipment, and the poor quality of labor and health statistics in many former East German factories and factory towns, the conclusions about the former East Germany might well be called into question), followed by the former West Germany and the UK. The study concluded that a strong national union movement facilitated the passage and active implementation of effective health and safety measures. In Sweden, union-run safety committees may order production stopped if they believe that a hazard exists, and keep it stopped until the hazard is remedied. These committees also have a great deal of control over the hiring and firing of industrial physicians and safety engineers. Because these types of practices and emphases vary so much from country to country, it is important for HR managers in MNEs to be sensitive to these differences as they develop health and safety policies and react to various health and safety actions by employees, unions, and works councils throughout their firms' global operations.

In general, unions and the philosophy of industrial democracy are stronger in Europe (and Australia) than in the US. In recent years, these factors have led to the passage of laws giving European employees or their elected worker representatives (in works councils) a stronger role in monitoring and enforcing workplace safety. Legally mandated works councils or workers' safety committees in Germany, the Netherlands, Luxembourg, France, Belgium, and Denmark give workers substantially more control over occupational safety than US workers have (although US workers, under the Occupational Safety and Health Act, do have considerable protection of their workplace health and safety).

The European Union has adopted a common framework for occupational health and safety, and as the EU expands its membership additional countries will come under this framework. Pursuant to this framework, member nations are modifying their workplace safety laws to achieve common standards, with some resistance from countries such as Great Britain that have a tradition of greater independence of their firms. The intent is to retain the high safety standards set in the more progressive countries, while minimizing the competitive advantage that might otherwise flow to nations with less stringent standards.

At the opposite end of the spectrum, the setting and enforcement of occupational safety standards in developing countries (to say nothing of the more difficult to define and monitor occupational health standards) often leaves much to be desired. Most developing countries have only rudimentary employment safety laws on the books and very limited funds for enforcing such laws. Concern over this issue indeed became one of the stumbling blocks in Congressional approval of the North American Free Trade Agreement (NAFTA) with Mexico. Many people were concerned that American firms were moving operations to Mexico to take advantage of cost differentials due to lower health and safety standards and lax enforcement of existing laws. Even though many of the *maquiladoras* (twin-plant operations, typically assembling products from parts manufactured in the US or elsewhere and then exported under favorable tariff conditions to the US) maintain facilities and operations as clean and safe as their counterparts in the US, American unionists and environmentalists sustained a concern that American firms not take advantage of Mexico's limited resources for enforcement of health and safety regulations.

As discussed in Chapters 6 and 7, efforts by developing countries to attract foreign investment are often enhanced by offering a business environment relatively free of government regulation. Typically unions are weak or are primarily focused on issues such as politics, wages, and fair treatment of employees, so they aren't focused on workplace safety concerns. In addition, the tendency to rely on labor-intensive enterprises, the preponderance of dated equipment, pressure for production and jobs, and lack of safety training for specialists as well as for workers, in general, also contribute to the poor safety record in many developing countries. The point of this for MNEs (typically from countries with more highly developed health and safety concerns) is whether or not to export these concerns, standards, and internal monitoring and enforcement, to their foreign subsidiaries. And, if so, how to do that, in an environment where such has not been the practice.

Additional areas of concern to multinational IHR managers within this topic of employee safety include the differences in medical systems in various countries (both in the form and quality of the delivery of medical services and in access to high-quality health care); the coverage of the health care system in different countries and who pays for health care; and the form and level of support systems for various forms of disabilities.

All of the above issues will have an impact on employment practices for both international assignees and for local nationals. Attention to fitness, employee stress, use of drugs, awareness of problems with major health issues such as AIDS, and problems with inadequate nutrition are all issues which can also influence IHR practices in international locations.

## Acquired Immune Deficiency Syndrome

AIDS is a special situation in a number of countries, particularly in Central and Southern Africa and South and South East Asia, and a concern to all countries.[5]

"AIDS, so often regarded as a public health or humanitarian issue, casts a looming shadow over global business and already has begun causing bottom-line losses."[6]

In 1999, 2.6 million people died from AIDS/HIV and an estimated 5.6 million people worldwide contracted HIV, the virus that causes AIDS. According to UNAIDS, the UN program on HIV/AIDS, the total number of people estimated to have HIV as of December, 1999, was 33.6 million. This group obviously includes employees, family members on employee benefit plans, the future hiring pool, customers, and policy and decision makers. Death in any of these groups affects an organization's performance and bottom line. When it hits key personnel, it can put business activity on hold. IHRM in Action 13.1 describes one such situation in which a key executive died of AIDS and left no one to continue a crucial negotiation.[7] The negotiations were put on hold as new people were trained and brought up to date in order to carry on.

In the worst-affected areas, HIV/AIDS affects one in four urban-based adults. In such areas, health care systems are overwhelmed and organizations now experience staffing shortages and productivity interruptions. UNAIDS reports, "AIDS . . . is decimating a limited pool of skilled workers and managers and eating away at the economy. . . . Businesses are already beginning to suffer."[8]

Clearly, every area of business for the multinational enterprise is affected. Every business program from sales (effect on customers) to employee education (about HIV/AIDS) to employee benefit plans (providing medical care for employees and/or family members with HIV/AIDS) to business operations to visas for business travelers and IAs is affected and must be considered as multinational enterprises plan their global businesses.

## AIDS threatens global organizations

Recently, negotiations for a loan between an East African government and the World Bank were suspended when the high-ranking negotiator for the government died of AIDS. No one else in the country's government could take over the negotiations. No one had the necessary training or experience.

The official's death resulted in significant unanticipated delays and suspension of the loan negotiations until other officials could be briefed and readied to continue the discussions with the World Bank. Critical national business and public sector issues and projects were put on hold.

In Africa, as well as elsewhere, organizations must start planning for workforce disruptions due to the worldwide AIDS epidemic. All parties need to start understanding HIV and AIDS as a business and HR issue – one that is local, yes, but also cuts across borders, as this case illustrates, and one that can, indeed, impact the "bottom line."

IHRM IN ACTION 13.1

# Health and safety for international assignees

Many of the above issues overlap with concerns for the health and safety of business travelers and IAs and their families. Some are standard concerns for employees while traveling and some after their arrival at their new assignments. Under any circumstance, these concerns are usually left up to the IHR department to worry about and resolve (if, indeed, anyone has been given such responsibilities).

# Nature of the situation

The following is a list of possible situations in which IHR can find itself (all are real events):

- A visiting manager in Colombia is kidnapped; the first the headquarters hears about it is when a journalist contacts the manager's family to inquire about the US$3 million ransom.
- An international assignee employee is in an automobile accident near Ayres Rock in the middle of Australia; the local medical care is not adequate to take care of the individual's injuries.
- An international assignee on holiday in Greece is in jail for overcharging on a credit card.
- Monsoon flooding in Thailand has ruined a major subcontractor's plants; there is currently no work being done and the MNE needs the product supplied by this facility; as far as can be ascertained, all of the employees are fine, but it is hard to be sure since the communication system has been disrupted.
- Two members of an international assignee's family in Nairobi, Kenya, are very ill with some unknown exotic/tropical illness; the manager wants some help.
- A manager who has been hand-picked by his boss and IHR for an overseas assignment informs IHR that he has tested HIV positive; he insists on confidentiality; the country to which he was to be sent does not allow visas to anyone who is HIV positive or has AIDS.[9]
- A young buyer has recently returned from a trip to India to visit subcontractors and is very upset over the perceived unsafe working conditions she found.
- An international assignee in Rio has been mugged – and lost his passport and travelers' checks and credit cards.
- A sales manager in Singapore has had a heart attack and died.
- An international assignee's family in London was shopping near by when an IRA or terrorist bomb exploded; they were not injured but are very traumatized: they want to come home, *now*.

This is only a short list of possible emergency and safety situations in which a firm with overseas activities can find itself: crime, arrest, illness, fire, natural disasters, terrorist acts, civic disturbances and civil wars, political unrest, accidents, local safety and health problems, bad food or water, unfamiliar medical systems, kidnappings, etc.

And all of these can be made worse because of inability to speak the local language, lack of familiarity with and/or distrust of local medical or emergency services, and problems of time and distance when trying to help or deal with emergencies. The simple act of calling for help in the location of the problem can pose a major obstacle, e.g., not speaking the local language (or not speaking it well enough to describe the emergency), not knowing whom to call for help, problems with the local phone system, and problems with the competency of local police and emergency workers and hospitals/clinics.

International business travelers and IAs and their families need to be briefed on and prepared to deal with problems of health and safety while traveling and in their new countries. They should be given an orientation to the different medical systems in their new country, how to take care of prescriptions and any special medical conditions, the identification of doctors and hospitals to provide for health care in their new location, and usually the acquisition of medical evacuation insurance to cover possible contingencies. IHR should be prepared to deal with crises in the MNE's foreign locations. And much more.

The following is an introduction to specific issues of concern to business travelers and IAs and their families.

## Specific health and safety concerns

### Terrorism

One aspect of the topic of health and safety for IHRM that has received a small amount of attention, but is probably the least important (unless, of course, it happens to you!), is the problem of terrorism and/or kidnapping (the subject of a separate heading).[10] International terrorists have at times targeted the facilities and executives of MNEs (and/or their families). Even though the news media attention to these acts when they occur makes it seem as though they happen all the time, everywhere, to all expatriates and their families, the frequency of and danger involved with terrorist acts demonstrates that people are more likely to drown in their own bathtubs than to be killed by terrorists![11] This is not to say that expatriates and their families don't need to be briefed on such concerns and oriented to a constant awareness of the potential risks.

Of course, some countries present greater risks than others. And when expatriates are being asked to serve in locales of greater risk, greater precautions need to be taken. Various corporate reactions have ranged from essentially trying to ignore such terrorism to abandoning certain markets where such terrorism is seen as more likely. Some firms have tried to protect their managers and their families in various ways, such as fortifying their homes, providing trained chauffeurs and guards, and using local-sounding names for their subsidiaries to try to hide the identities of the MNE parents of their local operations. In addition, some firms have purchased kidnap and other kinds of insurance to cover their key executives; but, of course, information about the extent and amounts of this are not typically made public.

The events of September 11, 2001, and the subsequent focus of the US government on what it calls a "war on terrorism" have potentially increased the problems in this area. Much pressure is being applied worldwide to counter the efforts of "terrorists" and, seemingly, the efforts of terrorists are being increased to counter that pressure. In many ways, this makes the world a more dangerous place to do business. And to the extent that such is the case, the task of IHRM to keep their MNE workforces safe is made more difficult and complex.

## Crime

Actually, the biggest threat to international travelers is not terrorism but old-fashioned crime, such as theft and pickpocketing.[12] In addition, the arrest and incarceration of traveling employees who either knowingly or innocently break local laws can be a major concern. "Travelers have been thrown in jail for exceeding a credit card limit, buying artifacts from an unlicensed dealer, entering an Islamic country with alcohol, or failing to meet a contract deadline."[13] Indeed, in some countries, even false arrest of American personnel can be a problem, particularly where this is a practice of local, low-paid government officials or police to earn extra income.

And, then, while some expatriates end up in jail because they unknowingly commit what may seem (at least in their home countries) not very serious crimes, others may commit quite serious crimes while on foreign assignment (such as extortion or drug trafficking). And yet others get involved with less serious but still quite illegal activities, such as drug and alcohol use, use of illegal prostitution, taking illegal pictures, or black market money exchange.

Here, as with the other areas described, IHR needs to prepare policies and procedures for dealing with such contingencies. And it needs to brief IAs and families on the seriousness of local law and how to access the support that the employer can provide.

## Kidnapping

The US State Department calls kidnapping a "cottage industry" in Latin America. Every year, some 15,000 people are kidnapped throughout Latin America. Granted, most of the victims are local managers and officials or members of their families, yet a significant number of them are foreigners or travelers on assignment to countries in Latin America. It has got to the point where local gangs are using kidnapping as a way to raise money. And this does not just occur in Latin America; there are an estimated 20,000–30,000 such kidnappings worldwide.[14]

For IHR this poses a significant issue that must be addressed. Employee advising, special kidnap insurance, security for IA living quarters and for foreign offices and plants, special trained drivers, response plans, etc., all need to be addressed ahead of time by IHR. For any MNE with employees traveling to or residing in a country where there is a risk of terrorism, extortion, or kidnapping, IHR needs to do a thorough analysis of the risk and to employ security professionals to provide security briefings and protection for executives and other employees traveling to and/or residing in high risk cities and countries.[15]

## Other traumatic events

Other kinds of emergency while traveling abroad are much more likely to occur than terrorism or kidnapping. These include sudden illness, serious accidents, major problems with transportation – such as bad weather or a strike on the traveler's airline, hotel fires, and natural disasters – such as floods or volcanic eruptions. The trauma experienced by such problems when in another country can be greatly compounded due to distance from home and normal support systems, language difficulties, cultural misunderstandings, and different laws and different medical or criminal justice systems.

## Health problems

Business travelers and IAs and their families frequently (if not usually) suffer from health complaints ranging from intestinal disorders due to exposure to new bacteria that the immune system is not used to to major exotic illnesses.[16] Some publications even suggest that health problems abroad are on the increase. Key reasons include:[17]

- Increasing poverty in developing countries.
- Increasing failure of the health infrastructure in many parts of the world, following political or economic instability.
- A changing pattern of disease, with increasing drug resistance.
- Increased accessibility of destinations that were previously remote.
- Increasing global competition for business opportunities in developing countries, so more travel to them and more people assigned to them.
- Relaxation of health formalities on entry, resulting in reduced "need" to seek medical advice prior to travel.
- Increased global travel, particularly by air, which enables new infectious diseases to spread quickly, such as was experienced in 2003 with SARS, a virus that spread from China across the world almost over night, certainly before it was recognized and could be isolated and countered.

Under all circumstances, business travelers and expatriates need to be briefed as to what to expect, how to prepare for conditions in the country or countries to which they are going, and how to react when confronted with any health or safety problem. IHRM in Action 13.2 describes what may be a too common problem of lack of preparation for a person sent on foreign assignment and the consequences, both for the individual involved and her organization.[18]

## Truth and consequences: expatriate health abroad

This is the true story of Kate Cawthorn, a twenty-five-year-old London-based trainee solicitor (attorney), sent on a very short-notice (three days) traineeship assignment to Ghana. On her very first day she contracted a severe dose of shigella dysentery. She continued to try to do her job for five weeks, with no medical tests or treatment, but finally decided to fly home. Her symptoms got worse, which left her unable to complete her internship and thus unable to qualify as a solicitor. She has never recovered well enough to go back to work. Kate Cawthorn claimed that her employers negligently failed to provide an adequate standard of immunization and pre-travel health advice for her trip. She was given just three days to prepare for departure and was referred to a local clinic that provided her with gravely inadequate travel advice – even failing to mention the high risk of malaria, for example. So, eventually, she sued her employer, asking for £633,000 for loss of her career as a lawyer, personal injury, and distress. The case was settled for a "high" six-figure sum.

The case attracted widespread publicity in the press, as well as within the legal profession. This case has many implications for the treatment of people sent on international assignments. For example, the firm involved did not provide enough lead time for the assignee to take care of critical concerns (such as the necessary vaccinations), she was not provided with adequate preparation and advice, she was not provided with adequate support when she arrived, and there was too little concern about the implications of the assignment and its consequences for her career.

Many firms find it important to retain one or more of the travelers' assistance programs or insurance programs that can provide help when the firm's overseas travelers or expatriates and their families experience difficulties. IHRM in Action 13.3 provides a glimpse at the types of services that one of these companies (MEDEX Assistance Corporation, which provides for clients prompt access to medical and related services anywhere in the world) can provide when a traveler (or expatriate) faces a medical problem.[19] Such assistance would be of most help to travelers and expatriates when in remote locations and/or third world countries.

### Death while on assignment

Once in a while (thank goodness, it doesn't happen very often), someone dies while on business travel or while on an international posting.[20] IHR must be prepared to cope with such an event – and help the family involved cope as well. Death may

## International emergency medical assistance

On December 22, MEDEX was informed that a man had been hospitalized in a tiny clinic in the small village of Zinder in the Niger Republic in West Africa. The man – a Dr Shaw – had suffered a serious leg injury when the vehicle in which he was riding overturned during a Young Europe for Africa expedition. Because the clinic lacked the necessary facilities and personnel to treat him, MEDEX personnel immediately arranged a light aircraft to transport him to Niamey, some 1,000 km away.

After assessing Dr Shaw's injuries – torn leg tendons and a fractured left radius – the treating physician in Niamey stated that he could not perform the operation. He added, however, that if an operation was not performed within a very few days, the tendons and nerves might retract to the point that a successful operation could not be performed.

When it became evident that the first available seat on a scheduled flight would not be available for about five days, MEDEX arranged for Dr Shaw to be flown – in the early hours of Christmas morning – to University College Hospital in London. The following day, the broken radius was corrected, the severed tendons were reconnected, and a knee wound was cleaned and closed. Dr Shaw was released from the hospital on January 4.

In a lengthy letter of praise to MEDEX Dr Shaw wrote, "I owe a huge debt of gratitude to your organization. I could have been trapped in Zinder for days, with septic arthritis and in danger of losing my leg. It was a situation where each delay made the risks greater. Your ability to get me out within four days of the accident was remarkable. The French doctors and diplomats were very impressed. I am very thankful.

On a more personal level, I and my family were touched by the care you took to keep us informed of developments. . . . My parents were delighted to be told in separate phone calls that the plane had left, that it was ahead of schedule, and that it had arrived safely."

occur from natural causes or from some other event, such as an auto accident, a terrorist act, or a natural disaster. Whatever the cause, it usually catches everyone by surprise. Thus having thought about the possibility before it happens can make timely and adequate response much more likely. For example, IHR needs to be aware that typical emergency medical insurance and programs do not take care of people after death.[21] The contracts end if death occurs. And treatment of deceased people varies from country to country, so IHR needs to get involved quickly to make sure that the wishes and traditions of the family are pursued.

# Solutions to health and safety challenges for travelers and international assignees

## *Assess the risk*

The first thing IHR professionals need to do is assess the risks. When experts are asked what to tell employees going on international assignments, they often reply, "Drive very carefully on the way to the airport." The point is that there is likely to be greater risk involved in that drive to the airport than in anything else the traveler will experience (with the possible exception of traffic accidents overseas)! When business travelers and IAs and their families leave home and their comfortable, familiar surroundings, their major fears are often of unpredictable and uncontrollable events like acts of terrorism or becoming a hostage or being kidnapped. These are the events that people are most familiar with since they are the ones that make the headlines in the media. But, in reality, there is greater risk from being in an automobile accident driving across town than from serious problems associated with travel or living abroad, even in the post-September 11 world. Consider the:

- *Size of the risk.* Using US statistics, the chances are greater of dying from a dog bite (twenty per year), from being hit by lightning (100), or from drowning in a bathtub (150) than from any act of terrorism (less than twenty in a typical year). Other common risks include being electrocuted in one's own home (900 per year), choking on food (3,000), and dying in auto accidents (about 50,000 per year). Indeed, these types of problems are much more common than unexpected acts of violence of all kinds. Ten thousand Americans even die overseas every year from natural causes like heart attacks and old age. Helping IAs and business travelers to understand the nature of the risks is a first step in planning ways to prepare for the risks that do exist.
- *Types of potential problems for each locale.* This is a short list of possible risks that can exist in any foreign locale. IHR needs to assess (or get assistance from consultants that provide this information) the specific risks that do in fact exist in a particular location. Not every overseas location poses the same level or type of risk.
  - Local concerns, such as crime, health care, food and water, transportation.
  - Potential natural disasters, such as monsoons, volcanoes, and earthquakes.
  - Political situations, such as *coups d'état*, assassinations, and riots.
  - Economic problems, such as potential nationalizations, changes in tariffs, shortages of resources, bad infrastructure.
  - Business environment, such as labor unrest, management problems.
  - Corruption and bribery.
  - Quality and integrity of local contacts.
  - Security of facilities and employees.
  - Emergency medical capabilities; likelihood of accidents.
  - Product theft or tampering/sabotage.
  - Potential for environmental/safety/health disasters.

- *Relative risk for each situation.* IHR also needs to assess the particular individuals being sent abroad as well as the particular destination for varying levels of risk.
  - *The individual.* Not all travelers and IAs face the same risk. Well known and/or prominent and well-to-do business representatives that work in a high-profile job or industry in highly public environments face the greatest levels of risk and require the highest level of protection and attention.
  - *The destination.* In the same way, not all foreign locations present the same levels of risk. Certain destinations often pose many common problems, such as crime, terrorism, kidnapping, problematic legal systems, and corruption. They may also pose more medical system and disease concerns, as well. Identification of such locales can enable IHR to focus attention and resources on personnel assigned to them.

    One critical area to assess is the nature of the legal system. Many people on foreign assignment find themselves in legal trouble. This may be for obvious reasons or for reasons not understood. Often people are jailed until the problem is resolved, within a legal system that may be very different from that which the IA is familiar. And the IA does not have the protection of their home-country laws or solicitors in such circumstances.

    A second area for particular assessment must be the medical system in the foreign location. In many parts of the world, medical facilities are primitive, treatment for many illnesses or injuries is unavailable, and pharmaceuticals are not easily obtained. Clean needles, sanitary facilities, and sterile water are often more the exception than the rule. Indeed, the "normal" medical practices may themselves be foreign, for example, relying of folk treatments, herbal medicines, or shamans, or alternative (to Western medical practices) treatments such as acupuncture.

After performing such assessments, then IHR can determine what actions it needs to take in which circumstances in order to best prepare and/or protect its business travelers and employees sent to foreign postings.

## Prepare a crisis management plan

The second thing IHR needs to do to address global health, safety, and security issues is to prepare a plan for dealing with the issues identified.[22] The following is a short summary of many of the components of such a plan and the procedures that would flow from it.

To begin, IHR needs to get management support. Without this, IHR will never get the resources to carry out the plan nor will the problems themselves get enough attention to keep everyone aware of the importance of the issues (of course, until crises occur – but many issues are very individualized, e.g., illness, and most people may never become aware of their occurrence). Getting a plan prepared (quickly) may be more important than thoroughness. Sensitivity (particularly when dealing with family members and with media) is more important than almost anything. And attrition is an issue when a crisis is handled poorly.

An IA crisis management plan should be regularly tested, under as wide a variety of scenarios as possible, such as civil unrest, extortion or kidnapping, or natural disaster. This is to ensure that the plan is robust enough to deal with all eventualities and to ensure that responsible corporate managers are trained in their necessary reactions. The procedures outlined in the plan should be made known to all parties involved and mock-ups held on a fairly regular basis.

One of the greatest difficulties for many MNEs is to know exactly who they have in any particular location, so that when a crisis arises they know who is at risk. Because of this, one of the first actions of any crisis plan is to track exactly who is traveling in and who is assigned to the area and where is their exact location at that time. (Are they traveling? Are they on holiday? etc.) In addition to tracking their whereabouts, IHR needs to track the status of official documents, such as exit permits, etc.

## Prepare travelers and international assignees

The third component of any plan to deal with global health, safety, and security issues is to develop a program to prepare all business travelers and international assignees and their families. Here are some possible actions:

- *Plan, insure, train, get involved.* IHR needs to develop its own plans for what advice to provide and when. It needs to acquire the necessary insurance to deal with potential problems, from emergency medical evacuation to ransom insurance. It needs to train IHR staff and it needs to develop plans for training travelers and IAs. And, mostly, IHR needs to get involved, up front. If IHR doesn't put attention on these issues (and get top management's attention and support, as well), it is likely no one else will.
- *Focus on high-profile travelers, and IAs.* The highest risk is associated with high-profile travelers and IAs. So IHR needs to place most attention and resources on them.

## Prepare IA homes and subsidiary facilities

A necessary, and sometimes critical, component of any plan will involve providing protection and security for IA homes and foreign facilities in locations of high risk.

## Dealing with civil emergencies/crises

Providing a plan for dealing with potential civil disturbances (in countries of high risk) should also be a major component of any crisis management plan. Such events can creep up on you; while at other times they burst unexpectedly on you. In the former situation, you may have time to develop a response. But in the latter situation, which is often more common, prior preparation is more than important.

IHR (and top management) needs to always keep in focus that the situation is serious: it isn't just someone's paycheck that is at risk (that can be taken care of later), this may be their life.

## Dealing with crises back home

Sometimes the crisis that arises is "back home." That is, it concerns an IA's family that is still at home. IHR must decide what level of support it will provide, for which types of crises. So questions like these will need to be addressed (and, hopefully, a policy developed ahead of time, so IAs know what support is available): Does the firm provide return air fare or provide the tickets? Does it require use of leave days and does it count travel time? What is the definition of family for purposes of providing this support (that is, how close does the family relationship have to be)? What types of emergency or crisis will warrant company support? What type of supporting documentation will be required?

## Sources of information and assistance

One of the most important forms of assistance an organization can provide its business travelers and IAs and their families is information about where they can get additional information and assistance. This would include embassy contacts, web sites for travel, health, safety, and country information, and home company contacts.

## Typical services

The following is a summary of the types of services a well designed plan would involve:

- *Emergency medical services.* These would involve options, depending on the situation, of self-evacuation; medically assisted civil transport; medical evacuation; twenty-four-hour contact information; medical monitoring.
- Financial/legal/travel services.
- Site medical survey, to identify approved clinics and hospitals and medical personnel who speak the IA's language and conduct familiar medicine.
- Pre-departure packages, including country-specific information, vaccinations, insurance, training about any issues specific to the destination locale.

## Crisis management in the MNE

It has been suggested that the following are the stages of crisis management that MNEs typically go through when a crisis actually occurs.[23]

- Recognize/admit that there is a crisis.
- Contain the crisis: stop the hemorrhaging with quick and decisive action, tell the media all you know, decide what is the right thing to do and do it, appoint a single spokesperson for the media, and communicate freely and often with all the necessary stakeholders.
- Resolve the crisis as quickly as possible, at least as far as the firm and its people are involved. Demonstrating a commitment to safety and security, and a dedication to the enterprise's ethical standards for treatment of employees during crises, will ensure that the MNE is regarded even more highly after the crisis than it was before.

## Emergency planning

The following lists the "exemplary practice" steps that an MNE and IHR should go through to effectively plan for and react to emergencies that occur:

- *Basic preparedness.* Do all the things described above, from risk assessment to plan development, with specific attention to country and locale differences; develop a separate plan for each location; determine who is responsible for responding to various types of problems to the media, families, local employees, sources of emergency help, and to activate contingency plans.
- Monitor and anticipate possible problems.
- Stage simulations of alerts and reactions.
- Determine evacuation routes for major crises.
- Belong to an outside service for security, professionals who can be relied on in an emergency.
- Network with the local international business community. Mutual assistance has often proven essential in emergency situations.
- Tap into the embassies. They often can and do provide the necessary information and assistance for people "on the ground."
- Learn to read the "signs." Do not get caught by surprise any more than is absolutely necessary.

## Employee reactions

IHR must be prepared for surprises. Stress in emergency situations and crises causes some people to do the unexpected. So IHR must have contingency plans and back-up personnel identified to deal with such situations. IHR must communicate, communicate, and communicate, so that everyone knows what to do. And IHR, itself, must stay calm (providing a necessary example for everyone else) and, thus, ensure all necessary support is provided.

## *Preparation for evacuation*

In crises that require evacuation, it is suggested that IHR conceive of evacuations in three stages: (1) The first stage is one of ensuring that whatever supplies are needed and necessary transportation options are arranged; that visas and passports are ready; that plans for communication with employees and embassies are ready; that security is alerted; and that general watchfulness is maintained; (2) the second stage involves evacuation of nonessential people, closing down of noncrucial operations, movements of international assignees and families are restricted, and steps are taken to turn local operations over to local management; and (3) the last stage includes closing down operations, handing local operations and facilities over to local management, and insuring that all IA personnel are evacuated.

## Summary of crisis management planning and crisis management

- Planning can lessen the risks and the fears. Plan design is important. Plan execution is key.
- Human resources must take a leading role. If they don't, it is unlikely that anyone else will – and it is HR that deals most directly with travel and relocation/living issues for IAs.
- Don't underestimate or ignore possible threats.
- Don't underestimate how important these issues are to travelers/IAs and families.
- Communication with employees is key.

International assignments are very expensive and very important to global enterprises. Ensuring the health, safety, and security of this small but significant group of employees is essential. The three simple steps of obtaining the relevant information, using that information to create awareness, and being prepared to cope with an IA-related crisis, will go a long way to minimize the risks and maximize the security of international assignees, and by extension, the international business, itself.

## Conclusion

This chapter has discussed three topics of importance to the IHR manager: employee health and safety in the context of the foreign subsidiary and joint venture, health, safety, and security for global business travelers and employees on international assignments and their families and crisis-management planning for MNEs. Often, because health and safety practices differ so much from country to country, responsibility for them is left in the hands of subsidiary (local) HR managers. Nevertheless, MNEs must understand and cope with local and international health and safety regulations, the widely variable practices faced in different countries, and strategic business decisions that may influence workforces and employee relations in multiple locations.

## Points for further discussion

1 What health, safety, and crisis management issues and concerns has Lincoln Electric in China confronted?
2 What steps should Lincoln Electric take to ensure it has a good crisis management plan in the case of an emergency?
3 Who should be involved at Lincoln Electric in establishing a crisis management plan? Should this be a corporate or a country-level action?

# Part III

# The Profession and the department of International Human Resource Management

# 14 The IHR department and the role and future of IHRM

## Learning objectives

After considering this chapter, the reader will be able to describe:

■ The ways the IHR department can obtain more involvement in the MNE
■ Some indicators for an IHR department to show it is world class
■ The complexities and challenges in IHR information systems
■ Services for international relocation and orientation
■ The future of the IHR department and the IHRM profession

## Key terms

■ World-class indicators
■ IHR information systems
■ Professionalizing of IHRM; certification

In the first edition of this book, this chapter began with "In many ways, the future of IHRM is now." Well . . . this is still pretty true. As was said then, and is still true, this is a new field. It is still in its developmental stages, even though some aspects of it have been around for some 100 years, or as long as there have been modern businesses operating in the global arena. The second edition has been written to update the first and to add new material and experience that has developed since the first edition. Most of what has gone before (as reported in the first edition) has not been replaced. Rather, as this edition describes, IHR practices are evolving alongside with new ideas and approaches. Thus, this edition includes new chapters on global culture; global organizational design; cross-border acquisitions, joint ventures, and partnerships; global employment law; global ethics, codes of conduct, and labor standards; an introduction to an expanded concept of global staffing, including global workforce planning; and global performance management. As a consequence, this is a larger book. But the field is still in its infancy with many challenges still in front of it.

As stated in the first edition, there are some aspects of IHRM that have achieved a lot of attention, particularly international assignee management – IA selection, preparation, compensation, and repatriation, and, to a lesser extent, their performance management and health and safety (even though many firms don't yet use what is known about how to improve the probability of success in IA assignments). Yet many other aspects of IHRM have not received the same level of attention. This chapter, then, provides both a view of the profession and its practice as of today and a speculation about what the issues are that are likely to confront IHR managers in the future, as this discipline further develops in its role of becoming a major participant in the strategic management of at least the human resource aspects of the ever-increasing activity of international commerce.

For purposes of description, this chapter is divided into three major sections: (1) the role and nature of the IHR department; (2) the role and nature of IHRM as a profession; and (3) the future of IHRM. As will be seen, there are linkages among these topics, and all are connected by the increasing competency and professionalization of IHRM.

# The IHR department

The first section of this chapter describes the role of the IHR department itself. The rest of this book has primarily concerned itself with what IHR managers do. This section discusses the department within which these activities take place and the role that is evolving for that department. It also discusses some of the support activities that IHR departments are generally called on to provide.

# Organizational advancement of IHRM

Achieving desirable results from ever more complex global business activities requires MNEs to pay increasing attention to more than the development of international operations, research and development, sales forces, and accounting systems. Increasingly, top-level attention must also be paid to the human aspects of cross-border business, to the merger of global workforces and cultures in acquisitions, joint ventures, and alliances, and to the development of the individual employees who represent multiple corporate and national cultures, speak multiple languages, and have widely varying perspectives on customer, product, and business issues. It is IHR which is expected to provide these capabilities and advise the rest of the enterprise on how to ensure performance in this cross-border complexity. MNEs must focus on the difficulties encountered in the development of IHRM systems that deal with global human resource problems, such as global pension and health care systems, management development throughout the global enterprise, global employee and management recruiting, global compensation systems, etc.

In the end, the global and cultural aspects of international business boil down to finding ways for individuals with varying backgrounds and perspectives to work together; that is, finding ways to develop a corporate "glue" that will hold the organization effectively together.[1] One great example of the development and use of such a corporate glue is provided by ABB's 1990 acquisition of Combustion Engineering (CE).[2] The Swedish-Swiss power and transportation conglomerate wasn't sure how to digest its acquisition of the Stamford, Connecticut (US)-based firm. Initially, ABB benefited from a couple of transatlantic personnel moves. It hired an American, General Electric veteran Craig S. Tedmon, Jr, to head the firm's Zurich-based worldwide combustion R&D efforts. And it installed an Austrian who holds an American Ph.D., Gernot H. Gessinger, to run CE's Windsor (Connecticut) combustion lab.

People who transfer from research labs in one country to those in another often experience considerable culture shock. Gessinger found the Connecticut lab dirty, stuffed with unneeded equipment, and unfocused. He ordered a cleanup and canceled dangling projects. And he uncovered considerable distrust of the new European owners. The pragmatic engineers in the US feared intrusions by ABB's combustion theoreticians in Baden, Switzerland. For their part, the Swiss doubted the Americans' credentials. Gessinger built trust by having Windsor help perfect a gas-fired boiler that Baden had developed. Other forms of task-force interaction, as well, led to the hoped-for interaction that encouraged a synergistic sharing of ideas and innovations. It was the management of cross-border and cross-cultural people issues that ultimately led to the integration of European and American labs and operations.

This type of organizational glue – effective cross-national task forces and work teams – will need to be increasingly used to pull together employees from disparate country and corporate cultures. And it will be IHR that will be looked to to provide the global enterprise with the expertise to help design and implement such strategies.

## Involvement of the IHR department

Given the many human resource problems that MNEs encounter in conducting business on a global scale, in the future they will need to encourage the following agenda for their IHR departments.[3] Most of these have been discussed in one or more places earlier in this text. So this provides a way to pull them together and to focus them on the role of the IHR department:

- Ensure IHR contribution as an integral partner in formulating the global strategy for the firm.
- Develop the necessary competence among the senior IHR staff so that they can contribute as partners in the strategic management of the global firm.

- Take the lead in developing processes and concepts for top management as they develop the global strategy. (Indeed, we would suggest they should be part of the top management team developing such strategy, not merely providing input!) These contributions might include developing capacities for information scanning about HR issues throughout the world (particularly for the countries of existing or contemplated operations),[4] for decision making (particularly related to global HR concerns), and for the learning processes that the firm needs to adapt to new global requirements.
- Develop a framework to help top management fully understand the (increasingly complex) organizational structure and people implications of globalization. That is, help top management, individually and as a team, develop the required global mind-set to conduct successful global business.
- Facilitate the implementation of the global strategy by identifying the key skills that will be required by management and employees, assessing current global competencies in IHRM and in the rest of the management team, and developing strategies for locating outside talent that may be required (through consulting, outsourcing, or hiring).
- Distribute and share the responsibilities for IHR. Increasingly, IHR will become a shared responsibility. Line management, IHR managers, and work teams all will share in the objective of ensuring the effective hiring, development, and deployment of the global firm's human resources.[5] This will inevitably lead to the decentralization of IHR decision and policy making, at least in many areas (alongside the pressure for consistent and cost-effective IHR practice). There will be less use of headquarters IHR departments, with IHR responsibilities delegated out to the business units of the firm, or, at least shared and developed with them. Many of the basic administrative activities (particularly for IA program administration, including relocation, cultural and language training, health and safety orientation and management, and benefits administration) will be outsourced to venders with special expertise in these particular areas of IHRM.

## Operation of the department

A world-class IHR department will be operated under these particular guidelines:

- IHRM will be linked with the management of the business at strategic, as well as at operational levels.
- IHRM will shift from being primarily an operational activity (managing issues such as IA staffing, training, and compensation) to more of a strategic role in the management of the global firm; IHRM will shift from being primarily responsive to decisions made by top management to being proactive in the design and application of IHR programs and in the strategic management of the firm – this means they will seek out line managers to get to know their business needs and will try to help solve them; IHRM will shift from doing IHR for line executives to assisting and counseling them on IHR matters; IHRM will shift from operating primarily with a focus on individual employees to a focus on work teams; and

IHRM will shift from focusing primarily on internal problems to focusing on issues external to the firm, even to a societal focus. This will be where senior IHR executives will make their most important contribution to the strategic management of the global enterprise.

## Staffing the department

The IHR department, itself, in order to pursue this new role, will find it has a need for fewer specialists and more generalists; that it will need to be even more business-focused (this means IHR managers will need more line experience – particularly of a global nature – and training, and more line managers will need experience in IHR); that individual IHR managers will need to have more experience working in global teams themselves and more training in how to make teams work effectively together across borders; and that IHR managers will need to develop internal counseling and coaching skills (with line managers, helping them to solve their people problems) and become information specialists (creating, maintaining, and using/interpreting IHR data for the rest of the firm).[6]

## Linking the department with the business and its strategy

In the global firms of the future, IHR departments will need to be more closely linked into the actual management of the business, through development of IHR philosophies (values, culture, vision), policies (guidelines for action), and programs, practices, and processes (involving line managers at every step) that fit the vision and strategy of the firm.

## Demonstrating the contributions of the IHR department

The IHR department of the future will need to learn how to demonstrate that the right things (needed by the organization to be successful) are being done right (as efficiently and effectively as possible, with a positive effect on the corporate bottom line).[7] One aspect of this will be research to determine what the best IHR practices are around the world and to use them both to judge the quality of a firm's IHR activities as well as to develop better IHR practices.

## Indicators of being world class

The following provides a short list of possible criteria and metrics (for use in a "balanced" scorecard)[8] to use to determine whether the IHRM practices in any particular firm are indeed among the best in the world. Some of these are, in fact, being measured by the Saratoga Institute and the Society for Human Resource Management so that they can provide quality benchmarks for IHR departments.[9]

- Inclusion of IHRM in key business issues – including both their formulation and their implementation.
- IHR and organization issues being seen as critical in strategy implementation.
- Ability of IHRM to deal with events proactively.
- Alignment of IHRM policies, procedures, and practices in all businesses, including a clear and shared statement of IHR vision and responsibilities.
- The number of individuals wanting to receive an IHR assignment.
- IHRM meeting its plans and objectives.
- IHRM having a structure, organization, and operation that services the strategic needs and interests of the business.
- IHRM having satisfied customers within the organization.
- IHRM activities being shared and understood by all employees.
- IHRM being flexible and adaptable to new conditions.
- IHRM measuring the effectiveness of its activities.
- IHRM measuring the efficiency of its activities.
- IHRM facilitating, or being capable of facilitating, major organizational change.
- IHRM having competent, adaptive, and flexible staff.

## Support services

In the typical domestic HR department in a large firm, a number of activities are performed that generally support the core HR responsibilities. These include the HR information system (including maintaining records on employees and providing HR reports), human resource planning (including employee forecasts, career plans for managers, and succession planning for executives), job analysis and the writing of job descriptions (for recruiting and training purposes and the setting of performance expectations), job evaluations and wage surveys and the development of job classifications and wage rates, labor market analyses to determine the availability and abilities of potential employees, the development of performance appraisal systems, domestic relocation services, and personnel/HR research.

Today, there is relatively little research on these topics in an international context. Some of them, however, are dealt with in this text, including global workforce planning, cultural issues in IHR research, global performance management, and global management development. Within the purely domestic context, these topics receive a lot of attention, as a glance at any text on Human Resource Management will demonstrate. Indeed, they probably receive a lot of attention in the home (parent) country operations of a large MNE. But little seems to be done with them in extension to the typical MNE's foreign operations, except possibly where the subsidiaries have become major "local" firms in their own right; for example, Ford, IBM, and GM (Opel) in Europe, Unilever in the US (Lever Bros), Siemens or IKEA in the US, or Sony in Mexico. But in these situations, the foreign operations of these firms are for all practical purposes domestic firms in the countries where they have major manufacturing, sales, and R&D activities. And most domestic firms of any size in these countries will have well developed HR support services.

The following discusses four of these support services that play a particularly important role in IHRM: IHR research, IHR information systems, international relocation and orientation, and global administrative services.

## IHR research

A major support activity in many large firms is HR research, an activity staffed, usually, by Ph.Ds in industrial psychology with the mission to study and verify the importance and contribution of HR programs and systems. However, there appear to be few resources in any large firms devoted to research on IHRM programs. Thus, many of the questions raised in this text – for example, determining which hiring practice, job classification system, or compensation system works best in which national context for which type of international employee, or even which type of IA to use when – have not been researched.

Such research still needs to be done. Because of the lack of such research (and possibly because of the relative newness of global business to many firms), MNEs often extend domestic policies to the international level that have been established by experience or by research in the domestic parent (and, thus, also, established within the culture of the parent country and firm). As an interesting example of one such extension of domestic policy, IBM has established a policy to not use graphology (the use of handwriting analysis to help in job candidate screening) anywhere in the world, based on evidence (and attitudes) developed in the US pertaining to its limited usefulness. This prohibition applies even to France, where it is a commonly used technique. Research in multiple countries might verify whether this is a practice that has acceptance and/or usefulness in some countries. Obviously, IHR research could be fruitfully applied to most areas of IHRM responsibility. And as IHR is increasingly expected to provide measures of the effectiveness and contribution of its programs and proposals, developing expertise in IHR research would appear to be highly recommended.

## IHR information systems

As firms internationalize their business operations they eventually reach the point where they also want to internationalize their information systems. This will include the human resource information system (HRIS). But, because the formats and purposes of the HRIS were established to service only HR in the domestic operations (and, if the firm is large enough and has been overseas long enough, or has acquired or merged with existing foreign operations, it probably also has at least some HR information systems established in its subsidiaries to service those operations), internationalizing the HRIS is a very complex and challenging activity.[10] This is described in detail under the following six headings:

*Special problems*   International HR information systems (IHRIS) create special problems for HR. IHRIS systems need to cope with all (and more) of the following special issues (not encountered in a domestic HRIS), all of which can be difficult to deal with:

- Keeping track of international assignees (all different types), including both home-country contact information as well as foreign addresses, etc.
- Keeping track of foreign workforces (a particularly difficult problem for firms like FedEx that operate in about 200 countries).
- Employee ID numbers around the globe (and the way to standardize these, since many countries have their own identification numbers).
- Foreign currency conversions for payroll.
- Standard formatting for compensation and benefit variations from country to country.
- Tracking payroll given various currencies and currency fluctuations.
- Government versus private health and pension benefits in various countries.
- Major variances in paid time off from country to country (even standard definition of what constitutes time off and when someone is included in the active head count).
- Termination liabilities.
- Tracking visas (different types that IAs and families have, schedules for renewal, etc.).
- Tracking family information for IAs, including educational support.
- International job postings.
- Terms and conditions of employment variances from country to country.
- Employment contracts and their differences; etc.

*Management considerations*   There are a number of policy decisions that IHR management must take to develop an IHRIS. It is beyond the scope of this book and this chapter to provide any detail on these issues. So this is only a short list of such policy concerns. They include the following:

- *Separate or connected IHR information systems*. In all of the following areas, does the firm want a centralized IHRIS system? Or is it willing to support separate systems at the local level. Are wholly-owned subsidiaries to be treated differently than joint ventures and partnerships? How are joint ventures and partnerships to be handled?
  - ○ Hardware.
  - ○ Software.
  - ○ Data – what will be maintained and in what form and where.
  - ○ IHR reports.
  - ○ Languages.
  - ○ Networked between countries and between countries and headquarters?
- *Organizational structure*. Will the IHRIS mimic the business's global organizational structure? That is, will the system be centralized, regionalized, or localized? And where will the IHRIS be physically located? With IHR? With the management information system?
- *Control of data flow between locations*. Who will determine who has access to the IHRIS and its information? And under what circumstances and for what purposes will these people be able to gain access to the IHRIS?

- *Privacy protection issues*. How will the firm guarantee protection of employee privacy related to their employment information in the IHRIS? And how will the firm guarantee worldwide that only the necessary information is maintained in the IHRIS?
- *Basic standards*. Who will develop and ensure basic data standards for the IHRIS, such as compatibility across countries, accessibility, and timely data creation, updating, and flow?
- *Policy choices*. Some of the possible policy choices for development of an IHRIS could include the following:
  - Having a central "data depot" for basic information, such as headcount, salary ranges, recruiting information.
  - Localizing the basic data – allowing the thousands of elements that exist around the world, but having only 120 key items available in a central location and available throughout the world.
  - The basic 120 elements must be on all systems (no matter what software used) but must allow entry and access to the system by the central IHRIS.
  - System is handled and maintained by outside vendors, but local HR must keep updated.

*Development and design considerations*
- Legal issues, for example, privacy protection.
- Type of data to be included (who needs what).
- Language of the data.
- Cultural values related to the capture and use of the data.
- Documentation procedures.
- Training in the use and maintenance of the system.
- Access to the data.
- Protection of the data.
- Choice of vendors and technology (hardware and software); who chooses.
- Conversion from existing system(s) to new, international one.
- Integration of new and old systems, both hardware and software.
- Method for handling international assignee compensation data (foreign service premiums, language training expenses, education allowances for dependents, storage of household goods, currency conversions, bonus savings accounts, sale of house, country variances in tax and benefit programs, etc.).

*IHRIS data problems*   All of these (and more) create special problems in the design of a computer database for an IHRIS:

- The way to state the legal nature of a subsidiary or joint venture: for example, XYZ Inc., XYZ PLC, XYZ Gmbh, XYZ FrOres, XYZ SLA, etc.
- Lack of compatibility issues in design of the database (for example):
  - Field lengths and order for postal codes (employee addresses)
  - Formats for stating dates (e.g., of hire, birth dates, etc.): dd-mm-yy versus mm-dd-yy; possibly even other calendars.

     ○  Name fields for varying lengths of names, hyphenated names, two middle initials, etc.; order for surname versus given name; multiple surnames (mother and father's, e.g.).

     ○  Non-English names, words.

     ○  Different educational systems, degrees, value of degrees, certification traditions and standards.

● Context: an IHRIS is developed within a context of varying approaches and traditions and cultural values in terms of what to keep track of on employees (for example, differing traditions in performance evaluations), how to keep track of employee information (e.g., formally versus informally), and who has access to employee data. This makes the creation and maintenance of such data a significant problem. In addition to this, many countries regulate the creation and use of employee information and the transfer of such information, particularly out of country. This makes getting cooperation from foreign operations and managers often quite problematic.

*Special capabilities: IHR websites*[11]   IHR web sites can be designed in many ways and can incorporate various forms of information. They promote the sharing of ideas and resources across borders, allowing firms to benefit from pooled IHR experience and expertise, relying less on outside consultants for routine information. They encourage the exchange of "best practice" and ensure increased effectiveness and efficiencies, as well as increased global awareness. They can include some or all of the following:

● International human resource employee and departmental directories.

● International knowledge and expertise directories or Yellow Pages.

● Country-related HR information (compensation, benefits, labor relations, terms and conditions of employment, legal, payroll and taxation issues, holidays, employment law, and so forth).

● International job postings.

● Listing of worldwide business units, addresses, key personnel, contact information.

● Listing of international HR service providers (IA administrative services, benefits administrators, relocation vendors, employee assistance programs, emergency medical providers, security vendors, tax consultants, etc.).

● International assignment policies and procedures.

● Country-specific culture and local adaptation information.

In addition, the IHR website should offer IHR professionals around the world the ability to interact with each other through the website.

*Special capabilities: automated translation (breaking the language barrier)*[12]   Issues related to language have been presented in a number of places in this text. Even though many people suggest the technology is not yet perfected, this is one additional area where computer technology is already providing some significant service and where the promise of future developments is tremendously appealing. A few years ago, when Federal Express wanted to implement an employee opinion survey throughout its global operations, its Canadian office proposed the use of translation software to help in collecting the survey responses, but also in feeding back to managers and employees the opinions expressed.[13]

The team that was formed to examine the possibilities and how to proceed was cross-functional, international and – because the Canadian operations had both French-speaking and English-speaking employees – bilingual. The team included system analysts, members of the Canadian and corporate employee relations departments, a Canadian operations manager, a Canadian training specialist, and members of the corporate HR team, including an HR analyst, who specialized in research on employee surveys.

The result was a ground-breaking approach to the use of technology in a new way for HR. The software that was used provided an on-line language choice for responding to the survey, which at the time was a first for FedEx, where there were no bilingual systems in operation. The enhanced anonymity, confidentiality, and user-friendliness enabled FedEx HR to implement a more effective and trusted employee feedback system. And it showed that HR can lead the way in the use of technology.

IHRM in Action 14.1 describes what Oracle, a software company that provides some of these services to other companies, did for its own operations in Europe, the Middle East, and Africa.[14] Oracle provides a good example of what is possible in the development of a global IHRIS.

## Relocation and orientation

This area of service can consume much time from IHR managers. To ensure that employees being assigned to foreign posts receive the best possible attention to the very personal concerns of relocation to another country, most of these services are usually sourced from firms that specialize in the delivery of these services directly to IAs and their families.[15] Alternatively, some large MNEs are starting to combine their domestic and international relocation responsibilities. The relocation function evolved out of firms' needs beginning in the 1950s and 1960s, when they began to relocate a much larger number of employees for business and career purposes, to help their relocating employees with problems such as the selling of houses, the shipment of household goods, the location of temporary living quarters in their new location, the purchase of a new house, the control of family in-transit time, and the control of overall relocations costs.[16] These essential relocation activities turn out to be essentially the same for domestic as for international relocations (although the international transfer tends to be much more intense, particularly for spouses and families).

The following six areas provide an introduction to a number of key aspects of the services related to an international relocation.

*Tax and financial advice*   This is one of the first services provided by the IHR department to employees going overseas. Personal income tax preparation becomes quite complicated. And the overall handling of finances, in circumstances in which

# IHR applies Oracle's technology to itself

Oracle has 14,000 employees in thirty-two countries throughout its operations in Europe, the Middle East, and Africa, whose HR needs are met by a staff of 140 people. Oracle began to send certain HR functions to its line managers, using its own Oracle HR system.

"We started with pay slips on the web, instead of having hard-copy pay slips," says Vance Kearney, European HR director. "Then we enabled employees to access and update their own data, and since then we have introduced more and more internet-based processes." The full range of HR activities now available on the internet includes:

- Employee data.
- Pay slips.
- Salary reviews.
- Flexible benefits.
- Management of purchasing products and services bought from internal departments of the company.

This roll-out of computerized and internet-based HR programs has given Oracle's HR department much greater flexibility and enabled it to add service without adding more HR staff. Kearney estimates they could add 50 percent more employees without adding more HR staff. However, Kearney cautions that IHR needs to work out carefully what needs to be different from country to country and what can be similar. He says it doesn't make sense to have thirty-two different systems to do one thing. Yet there will be slight differences in the way things get done in each country. For example, when they started, they had thirty-two different telephone systems. Now they have one global system.

Other systems, like updating employee records, also need to be carefully centralized. Maintaining employee records was a pretty simple process in the UK, but in Switzerland, where taxes vary by the canton in which an employee lives, the firm must track employee residence very carefully and inform tax authorities if an employee moves from one canton to another.

As far as HR is concerned, Kearney says everyone has benefited. "Before this system was set up, we couldn't answer a simple question like 'What is the staff turnover across the company?' because each country had a different way of deciding what this meant. It only took one computer to blow up in Kazakhstan for the whole thing to be out. Now we have one system which works across the world."

income is likely to increase dramatically as well as to involve multiple currencies, new banking systems, varying exchange rates, and so on, is likely to require assistance for the new IA and his or her family. This is generally coordinated by the IHR department.

*Visas and work permits*    It usually falls on the IHR department to obtain the necessary visas for the expatriate (and his or her family) as well as to arrange for whatever work permits are required. Normally, this involves maintaining the personal relations with foreign government officials that are necessary to get these documents in a timely manner, since individual IAs often have limited time to make such preparations after the firm makes the decision to send them abroad (or IHR must maintain relations with consultants or vendors who provide this service, such as local law firms that specialize in visas and work permits). This can be quite complex if the firm tries to also find employment for the trailing spouse or other family members.

*International moving*    There are many complexities in arranging and managing successful international moves for IAs and their families. Needless to say, this is also typically one of the most stressful aspects of moving abroad for most employees and their families. Again, the IHR department usually has responsibility to assure that the employee's move takes place in a smooth, problem-free way.

After a myriad of relocation considerations, the actual physical move overseas of IA, family, and household is often the last item to get "handled."[17] Nevertheless, it is one of the more important considerations in guaranteeing a successful IA experience. At a minimum, managing the overseas move involves the following:

- Making all necessary travel arrangements, including arranging accommodations for when the family initially arrives as well as their permanent housing in the new location.
- Retaining the services of the best possible mover.
- Developing overseas moving policy. Ideally, an MNE sending employees overseas has developed a policy to deal with the major issues confronted in such moves. Overseas movers look for some basic elements in the overseas moving policy. First is the use of an authorization letter, confirming to both the mover and the employee the basic details of the move. Both the mover and the employee need to know what quantity of goods can be shipped (both outgoing and returning, since most IAs acquire additional goods while overseas). In addition, the policy should address restrictions on such items as second pickups or deliveries of household goods, use of local/national carriers, and what items are defined as household goods. Such policies help movers and employees (and their families) avoid problems and make the move go smoothly.
- Determining the proper timing of the move (from the points of view of both the firm and the family).
- Arranging for local housing; either prior to arrival of the IA or after his or her arrival and with his or her involvement.
- Arranging for and ensuring the smooth shipment (and/or storage) of household goods. Given the importance of personal effects on the emotional well-being of an

IA and his or her family, the selection of a mover is critical. The mover must be willing to commit the necessary personnel and resources to ensure that the move is made with the least possible difficulty and disruption and the best possible end results. For the most part, the type and quantity of goods moved is determined by destination.

Weather, local infrastructure, accommodations, customs regulations, and transportation resources all influence how, how much, and what types of goods should be shipped.

*Medical exams for particular foreign locations*   Where medical services may not be up to the parent-country standards, the firm will want to ensure that it isn't going to face any unnecessary health complications.

*Training and orientation*   (About the country, culture, and language of the country of the new assignment for the IA and family). This is discussed in Chapter 10.

*Education and schooling for the IA and family while in the foreign assignment* Sometimes adequate schools for the IA and/or his or her family are not available locally, and the firm must pay for the children to be schooled elsewhere (e.g., in boarding schools), which will also entail extra expense for children to return home periodically or for parents to visit them. The IHR department will be expected to assist the IA family to locate acceptable schooling.

## Administrative services

Most of these services could potentially be provided elsewhere in the firm, but they generally are delegated to the IHR department. All of them are, at least initially, established to ease the process of transferring employees from one country to another. Then because the IHR department has found ways to resolve the availability of these services, they are often extended to other needs of the firm and stay within the responsibilities of the IHR department.

- Travel arrangements (as discussed above – and for everyone in the firm that travels internationally). This can involve acquiring necessary visas, making all necessary travel arrangements (airplane reservations, etc.), and buying travel insurance.
- Housing in the foreign locale (for all international travelers for the firm). This can involve negotiating contracts, signing rental agreements, finding hotel rooms, apartments, and so forth.
- Determining the availability and operation of local transportation in the foreign locale, including rental cars, chauffeurs, Metro maps, bus schedules, and rail systems.
- Office services, such as translation and translators, for business contracts, housing and rental agreements, business letters, and business negotiations.
- Currency conversion. New IAs (and international business travelers) may not have experience with or an understanding of living in another country and having to deal with conversion of their home-country currency into that of the host country.

The IHR department is often tasked with ensuring that the IA understands whatever complications might arise as pay arrangements are worked out to accommodate varying exchange rates and varying local-currency inflation rates.

- Local bank accounts. Since banking systems vary dramatically from country to country, the IA often needs assistance in establishing a local bank account (if indeed that is possible) as well as in understanding how the banking system operates in his or her new country of residence. In many developing countries the banking system is quite underdeveloped (particularly in relation to what the IA may be used to) such that there may not be an established checking system for paying bills or ready access to reliable ATM machines for acquiring cash. The IA will need to be oriented to these realities.
- Government relations. This will initially include familiarity with the proper offices to get visas and work permits but may eventually extend also to local government offices for business services such as telephones and business licenses. The IHR department may find these many services cumbersome and complex, but the successful MNE must have access to them. It makes sense that they be provided by the IHR staff. And they do serve to keep the IHR department closely involved with the firm's international activity.

## Outsourcing

An increasing number of IHR departments are relying on outsourcing as an efficient (read: cost-effective) way of providing certain services for their employees. Typically, the first (and remaining the most common) responsibilities to be outsourced are what are referred to as transactions and administrative processes. Some of these include: visa and immigration processing, language and cultural training, tax compliance and preparation, and, more recently, technology support of IA services. Box 14.1 lists some of the many types of services provided by IHR vendors. And now, some firms are looking at the possibility of outsourcing all IHR activity, with exception of some very high-level strategic involvement by a few highly experienced and senior IHR executives. But, no matter the level of outsourcing used, as Alan Moidel, senior manager of International Assignment Services at Deloitte & Touche LLP, one of the major IHR service vendors, cautions, "While this is proving to be a successful strategy for global workforce management, managers who choose to outsource can't afford to lose control. You need to carefully manage the vendors because, ultimately, you are still responsible for company policy and company employees. And employees want a link back to the company [not just to the vendor]; they don't want to feel isolated."[18]

## Role of IHRM

This next to last section of this last chapter deals with one of the most important topics: the role of the IHR manager, him or herself. This section examines the ongoing professionalization of IHR, the competencies of IHR managers, and the global leadership that can and should be provided by today's IHR manager.

## Box 14.1 Examples of IHR support services provided by external vendors

- *Chase Manhattan Bank.* International employee banking: payroll solutions and banking services, guaranteed foreign exchange rate, delivery of international payroll, single/centralized account worldwide for firm
- *Alliance for Global Mobility* (actual name of the group – but it really is a classic example of an alliance):
  - *Berlitz.* Language and cross-cultural training, global training and development for groups and individuals and families (thirty-five countries)
  - *Ernst & Young.* IA services (global tax compliance, global compensation, global IHR consulting services) (125 countries)
  - *PHH Relocation.* Settling-in assistance, home finding, household goods shipment, property management and resale services (160 countries)
  - *Selection Research International.* Valid and reliable IA assessment and evaluation, selection and development of employees/spouses/families for international assignments
- *William M. Mercer.* Global data base system. Primarily benefits focused, but claims total HR programs. Information on benefits regulations and practice in more than sixty countries
- *FIS Foundation for International Services.* Foreign credential evaluation services: evaluates diplomas and certificates and determines the equivalent degree in parent country
- *Aetna.* Portable benefits and insurance coverage for international employees (medical, life, dental, AD&D), e.g., for highly mobile employees with frequent or unpredictable short-term foreign assignments, international NGO assignees
- *AIG International Services.* Twenty-four-hour worldwide IA support. Single-source solution for IAs, employees with high-frequency travel, training IAs or people on loan from or to foreign affiliates, multilingual assistance, pre-departure assistance, medical assistance/emergency evacuation, legal assistance, travel assistance, global security and protection (all insurances), family adjustment services (e.g., travel, medical and legal referrals, language lessons, cultural training), auto services, destination services, personal security services, lifestyle services (e.g., restaurant discounts, entertainment discounts, etc.)
- *Medpass.* Global emergency medical services, maintain medical records, network of thousands of qualified health-care professionals in more than 180 countries in 1,800 cities, physicians who speak English – the majority of whom are Western board certified
- *Chemical Bank International Employee Banking.* Corporate account manager, discounted (competitive) exchange rates, guaranteed exchange rates,

twenty-four-hour access everywhere, auto-fund transfers and bill payments, repatriation bonus loans, introduction to host-country banks, administration of overseas payrolls, disbursement to foreign accounts, automatic conversion reports, inpatriate services
- *AIU American International Underwriters.* Personal world risk assessment, international security, foreign personal property and liability insurance (including kidnap and ransom, casualty, accident, sabotage, terrorism)
- *Business Health Services.* Employee assistance programs (EAPs) for IAs and families
- *Citibank personal banking for overseas employees*
- *Search Net.* Help for finding and recruiting top people all over the world in virtually all disciplines (i.e., international head hunters)
- *Cendant, and Weichert Relocation.* These two companies assist MNEs in the relocation of international assignees and their families

## Professionalization of IHRM

In order to achieve the above agenda and responsibilities, IHR as a management function will need to continue professionalizing. Organizations that operate in the highly competitive global economy of the future, will need and expect their IHR managers to develop the professional competencies needed to help them successfully steer their organizations through the chaos of global competition.

### Importance of the function

IHRM will need to be recognized by top executives, strategic planners, and line managers in general, as critical to the success of the global enterprise. Research supports that a focus on progressive IHR programs is related to gaining global competitive advantage.[19] Thus IHRM programs and departments must receive high-priority attention and resources. It will be critical for global managers to have experience in the IHR department, and it will be just as important for IHR managers to have experience in line management, and in global assignments, as well.[20]

### Development of IHR managers

Since the IHR function has evolved primarily from the management of expatriates, and is now developing into many other areas of responsibility, a major issue for IHR in the future will be the need to develop a broader perspective on and experience with the global enterprise. MNEs will need IHR executives who can do more than handle the selection, training, relocation, and compensation of expatriates. MNEs will need and expect their IHR executives to assist in the strategic management of their global businesses, to develop IHR policies for operations located around the globe, and hire and develop highly productive workforces in multiple countries. The development of this type of strategic IHR manager is becoming a central focus of the IHR profession.

The typical firm's management and executive development programs are designed and managed by HR, so it should make sense that HR would focus some of that attention on its own development, even though this is often not done. Indeed, if such a focus were aimed at IHR itself, the strengthening of IHR departments and development of more competency in IHR could be accomplished in a number of ways:[21]

- By assigning upwardly mobile domestic HR generalists to overseas regional staffs for two- to three-year periods. For example, Pepsi-Cola has done this successfully, assigning US HR managers to its regional offices in Europe, Asia, and Latin America. However, this is not yet a widespread practice. Note that, at this time, over 90 percent of IHR managers in overseas regions for American MNEs are not Americans.
- By considering assignments of one or more repatriated IAs from any function to IHR in either an operating division or the headquarters staff. Their overseas experiences will add credibility to the IHR function as well as a critical international perspective. In addition, experience in HR should be beneficial to their careers. (Assignment of non-performers, i.e., individuals who had difficulty in their international assignments, should be avoided. Such a move would weaken the IHR function.)
- By assigning several entry-level university graduates with degrees in human resources to overseas subsidiaries and regional positions. Instead of giving them typical expatriate compensation packages, pay them as locals. Indeed, these individuals might even be from the country of assignment, having attended university in the country of the parent firm.

## Education

There are still only limited opportunities to gain an education in IHR, yet this is something that anyone interested in the discipline needs to pursue and is a major component of the professionalization of IHR. There are only a handful of master's degree programs in IHR. However, many universities now offer at least a survey course in IHR, often as part of a master's degree program in HR or as an elective course within a program in international business. But this should only be the beginning of gaining an education in IHR.

Many IHR consulting firms and providers of IHR services offer short seminars and a few host annual conferences on IHR, with topics on various aspects of IHR typically presented by practitioners and consultants. Attendance at these seminars and conferences is one of the available ways to stay current on issues being addressed by

MNEs and on MNE best practices in IHR. The American Society for Human Resource Management has begun (2004) offering a training program for preparation to take the Certificate in Global HR, described in the next section. In addition, there are a number of both university-level curricula and practitioner seminars on cross-cultural management, an area in which IHR practitioners need extensive training. Of course, one of the most important areas for learning for IHR managers should be the experience of living and working (hopefully, practicing HR) in another country and culture (or more than one other country and culture). And self-education must also become (and remain) a cornerstone of any effort to gain knowledge about IHR. This would involve reading the growing number of books and magazines on the subject of IHR as well as networking with other practitioners, including joining one of the growing number of local IHR discussion groups that are being created in many population centers.

The web site that accompanies this book contains many of the references that are mentioned in this section and can be used to locate opportunities for further education in IHRM.

## Certification: testing and the body of knowledge

The Society for Human Resource Management (the US's largest professional society for HR professionals) has commissioned the Human Resource Certification Institute to identify and codify the "body of knowledge" in IHR and to design a testing procedure for certifying professional skill and knowledge in IHR.[22] (For discussion of the certification process in England and elsewhere see the book in this series by Sparrow *et al.*, *Globalizing Human Resource Management*.) The work on identifying the IHR body of knowledge was completed in 2003 and the first certification test was offered in March 2004. Possessing this certificate in IHR (GPHR credential) will signal to employers that the holder has demonstrated a high level of competency in this relatively new discipline.

The IHR professional study identified the following six domains of knowledge in IHR and the certification examination contains sections on each:

- *Strategic international HR management.* The development of HR strategies and programs that can help organizations to meet their short- and long-term business goals.
- *Organizational effectiveness and employee development.* The establishment of organizational structures, programs, and processes that enable corporations to deploy and utilize employees to achieve current and future worldwide business objectives.
- *Global staffing.* The process of planning, developing, implementing, and evaluating staffing initiatives on a worldwide basis to ensure that the organization's staffing goals and objectives are met.
- *International assignment management.* The establishment of international assignment strategy and policies.

- *Global compensation and benefits*. The establishment of global compensation and benefits philosophy and strategy.
- *International employee relations and regulations*. Processes and practices that help to create favorable employment conditions that balance employer needs with employee rights and needs.

This is one additional step in the continuing process of professionalization of the IHR practitioner.

# Competencies (general)[23]

The success of IHR in the future will depend on the ability of companies to develop IHR executives with broad global perspectives (a global mind-set, as discussed in Chapter 10), international experience, and strong technical and strategic business skills. This will include developing the following general competencies for IHR professionals:

- Cross-cultural interpersonal skills.
- Ability to learn about multiple cultures.
- Local responsiveness (develop and maintain relationships with local colleagues and officials, know and understand local markets, regulations, and current affairs).
- Cross-national adaptation.
- Change and diversity management and international team skills.
- Coaching and development of global literacy (in themselves and others).

# Competencies (specific)[24]

In addition, the competent IHR manager of the future will demonstrate a number of skills more specifically related to IHR. He or she will be able to:

- Implement effective recruiting and staffing to attract and retain the best talent for a global workforce.
- Implement formal systems to improve worldwide communications.
- Implement an International Human Resource Information System (IHRIS).
- Foster a global mind-set in all employees through training and development.
- Develop global leadership through design of a program of developmental cross-cultural assignments.
- Position the HR function as a strategic business partner in the organization's global business. (Once considered a bonus for HR managers, business literacy – on a global scale – is now a prerequisite.)
- Demonstrate the worth of IHR programs in terms of their global bottom-line contributions and their being a major source of worldwide strategic advantage.
- Design and implement global HR systems, such as training, compensation, performance management, employee relations, and health and safety.

As described above, development of these competencies within IHR can be partially achieved by including one or more overseas assignments in the career paths of highly skilled HR managers, introducing some of the best foreign-affiliate HR talent into parent-company regional offices and headquarters, assigning repatriating parent-company managers from non-HR functions to IHR, and providing high-potential HR practitioners with international assignments early in their careers. Such experience is certainly just as important for HR as it is for managers in other functions. And yet MNEs rarely give such international development of HR managers any attention, at all.

An IHRM function strengthened by a combination of these approaches would have the capability to develop entirely new IHR technologies to ensure the success of globalization. Some firms, such as Exxon, Unilever, and Chase Manhattan Bank have instituted one of more of these approaches to development of IHR and have made major strides toward increasing the effectiveness of their IHR functions. But many other firms still have a long way to go.

## Future of IHRM[25]

The following is a summary of current trends and challenges in global HR that point to the competencies that IHR managers of the future will need to have. Because these are new, they all will require the development of new skills by IHR managers, and, thus, it is hard to point to specific training or developmental experiences that IHR will need to develop the necessary competencies. Nevertheless, the following challenges do suggest areas for attention.

## Trends in IHR[26]

The following is a list of the trends and challenges now being described by IHR practitioners and consultants:

- Development of global unions and global bargaining.
- The changing role of the subsidiary general manager/managing director/*directeur générale*, with more business decisions, such as parts sourcing being made centrally, and the GM becoming more involved with PR and government relations.
- Global employment litigation (that is, occurring everywhere), over issues such as racial discrimination and sexual harassment.
- Development of global HR programs and departments, rather than decentralized HR programs, with all of their policy exceptions, which are now often the norm in global IHR.[27]
- Global payroll/compensation options, such as global bonus plans and equity incentive plans.
- Global e-HR, HRIS, and HR outsourcing.[28]

- Global employment companies (GECs), with all IAs drawn from this centralized organization.
- Expanded options for international assignments.
- Evolving (and consensus on) international labor standards and ethics.
- Increasing attention to global crisis management due to problems such as terrorism, AIDS, SARS, etc.
- Focus on developing a global learning organization.

## The IHR job of the future

IBM's study of HR practitioners around the globe identified a number of skills which will be increasingly important for IHR in the future. These capabilities were also identified as the ones for which the widest gaps exist between current HR abilities and those which were perceived as needed in world-class organizations of the future. They included:[29]

- The ability to educate and influence line managers on IHR policies, practices, and importance.
- Being computer and technology-literate, so as to be able to create and use global databases for IHR advice and decision making.
- Being able to anticipate internal and external changes, particularly of importance to the availability and qualification of human resources around the world.
- Exhibiting leadership for the IHR function and within the corporation.
- Focusing on the quality of IHR services within the corporation.
- Defining an IHR vision of the future and communicating that to the IHR department and to the firm.
- Developing broad knowledge of many IHR functions.
- Being willing to take appropriate risks in the development and implementation of innovative IHR policies and practices.
- Being able to demonstrate the financial impact of IHR policies and practices.

So, given these trends, what must IHR do? The following seven points summarize many of the suggestions made in this chapter:

- *Hire for international experience*. IHR must convince managers of the MNE of the importance to global competitiveness of having a workforce that knows and understands international business. Thus, the firm needs to appreciate the importance of including international knowledge and experience as criteria in the recruiting and hiring process.
- *Disperse people with international experience throughout the firm* (including HR). One way to improve the firm's overall IB competency is to disperse the people who have the global knowledge and experience throughout the enterprise.
- *Learn how to recruit and assign on a global basis*. IHR must develop the ability to recruit human assets from around the world and to assign such global hires throughout the firm's global operations.

- *Increase the firm's international information diet.* IHR should take a proactive role in providing all locations of the firm with information (e.g., international magazines and newspapers) about not just the firm's global operations, but about global affairs in general, including actions of governments and competitors in countries where the firm operates.
- *Train everyone in cross-cultural communication, etiquette, protocol, negotiation styles, and ethics.* This is one additional, but specific, aspect of providing information to the workforce about global business. These are areas of concern that greatly increase a global firm's competency in the conduct of international business.
- *Ensure international developmental assignments.* IHR must make sure the global enterprise understands and supports the necessary system for ensuring that international assignments are kept as a major component in all executive development programs.
- And, most important, IHR managers need to understand the importance of developing themselves to better carry out their global mandate. This would include developing themselves to be able to better assist their firms in implementing their global value proposition/vision (that is, thoroughly understanding how the enterprise makes money on a global basis and being able to articulate an IHR point of view using the language of business); knowing how to measure global ROI on IHR programs, such as the use of various types of international assignees; developing a global HR balanced scorecard to measure the overall contribution of IHR to the firm's global success; developing relationships throughout the global enterprise; and creating an international HR learning organization, to constantly improve and meet its changing global challenges.

Though the exact nature of the IHR role of the future is still developing, the following roles will likely be among the critical roles being performed by the IHR manager of the future:

- The CFO for global HR, that is, thoroughly knowledgeable about the financial impact of IHR programs.
- The global IHR vendor manager, that is, effectively managing the vendors to which IHR has outsourced its administrative functions.
- The internal consultant to the global business on issues related to the enterprise's human capital and knowledge management.
- The global leader for HR.

And all of this in the context of global culture and business.

Global HR activities – whether they involve planning, designing, structuring, implementing, managing, or developing – are likely to fail unless they are viewed through the filter of the cultures involved. Systems and processes that are spectacularly successful in one culture can fail dismally in another. . . . Not a single aspect of global enterprise is untouched by people – all facets have a human element. . . . The HR function, historically undervalued and underutilized in corporations, has now become a player. In order to step up to the plate, HR professionals must first learn the geography and characteristics of the field.[30]

And once they have done that, IHR can make sure the multinational enterprise does in fact use the filter of culture and the expertise of human resources to achieve its global objectives.

## Conclusion

This chapter has provided a glimpse of the challenges that confront IHRM. These challenges include the organizational advancement and the professionalization of IHRM. International HR managers have to further develop their understanding of their global enterprises and, as a consequence, will become better integrated into the planning and strategic management of those enterprises.

As these challenges are met and IHR managers further develop their global HR competencies, multinational firms will find themselves developing world-class IHR departments with these characteristics:

- Responsive to a highly competitive marketplace and global business structure.
- Closely linked with global business strategic plans.
- Jointly conceived and implemented by line and international HR managers in an equal partnership.
- Focused on global quality, customer service, productivity, employee involvement, teamwork, and workforce flexibility in all the enterprise's operations around the globe.

What this chapter has demonstrated is that only when such an integrated, responsive, and accepted IHRM is developed will IHRM reach its potential and take its rightful place in the management of today's successful global enterprises.

Today there are something more than 220 countries with hundreds of languages and cultures. All of them are market and resource opportunities for global enterprises. In this new world for HR, everything has changed.[31] This book and this chapter have described the role for international human resource management in this new world. New IHR professionals will be business partners and will know the business well enough to align the MNE's human capital with its global business needs, either developing the needed talent or going outside the organization – anywhere in the world – to get it (including IHR skills). IHR will be proactive, that is, it will go looking for global business and HR problems to solve. In this new role, IHR will not just have a seat at the global strategy table, IHR will help set the agenda and set the strategy.

In a profession that is increasingly pressed to align itself with global business goals and to demonstrate the value of every one of its activities with an acceptable business measure of some kind, it is still important for IHR managers to maintain a sense of the importance of the role they play in ensuring the success of their global organizations from the perspective of human resources. In many ways IHR is the multinational enterprise's guardian of worldwide human resource development in the context of a global mind-set and vision. As the MNE demands ever more of its global workforce's energies and talents, IHR must increasingly shoulder the responsibilities for change management and personal and organizational development to meet the constantly changing requirements of this global world of work.[32]

## Points for further discussion

1 Does Lincoln Electric in China reflect a high level of competency in global human resource management?
2 In what ways can Lincoln Electric in China, and in the rest of the world, improve or change its approach to international human resource management?

# Integrative case study
## Lincoln Electric in China
### Ingmar Björkman and Charles Galunic

Jeffrey Kundrach, the general manager of Lincoln Electric (Shanghai) Welding Company, could hardly believe his eyes. One of the small army of professionals dedicated to transplanting Lincoln Electric's operations overseas, Jeffrey was overwhelmed by the growth in the Pudong area of Shanghai, where he helped Lincoln establish its beachhead into China. A forest of buildings now filled the view from his second story office window, where a few years ago there were only marshy fields and dirt roads. All of them had been constructed during the last few years, and most of them hosted foreign companies that took advantage of the Special Economic Zone status available in Pudong. The amazement didn't last long. Kundrach wondered how many of his fellow expatriate managers in China were bothered by the same question: How quickly should a foreign company introduce its management policies into foreign lands, particularly ones so distant from occidental cultures? Should transplantation of foreign practices be avoided altogether, trying to find some made-to-measure path to motivate indigenous employees of multinational firms? For Lincoln Electric, the issue was enormous, having become renowned in the West for a very successful and visible remuneration scheme. At the center of the "Lincoln way" was a piece-rate payment scheme that paid employees only for what they produced, and a bonus system that provided employees with year-end bonuses based on their performance. Many management pundits as well as firm loyalists believed this to be an important factor in Lincoln's longstanding dominant position in its marketplace. But would this work in China?

The Lincoln Electric (Shanghai) Welding Company was Lincoln's first manufacturing investment in China. The plant was opened on May 13, 1998 by Lincoln Electric chairman and CEO, Anthony A. Massaro. The company was established as a wholly-owned subsidiary of a Singapore-based joint venture between Lincoln Electric and its distributor partners. Lincoln Electric was the majority shareholder in the joint venture and solely responsible for the management of the company in Shanghai. After a very successful launch, Kundrach now felt that it was time to review the situation and start focusing more on how to develop the firm's management and labor practices. Furthermore, Michael Gillespie, Lincoln's president and pioneer in Asia, was coming to Shanghai next week and wanted to hear Kundrach's plans for the development of the company.

# The Lincoln Electric tradition

## History and philosophy[1]

John Lincoln established Lincoln Electric Company in 1895. He was joined by his younger brother James in 1907. In these early years the brothers designed and manufactured small electric motors in their Cleveland, Ohio, operation. By 1911 their product line expanded to include battery chargers for electric automobiles and arc welding equipment. The latter soon became the young company's core competency and central revenue generator, with the duo the first to produce a variable, single operator, portable welding machine in the world. In 1998, arc welding and welding products accounted for 94 per cent of the firm's US$1.2 billion in worldwide sales.

In 1914, James Lincoln, the less technically and more managerially minded of the team, took over leadership of the company. His ideas about management and workplace relations strongly shaped the culture of the company. Based on his fervent belief in self-reliance and on the necessity of competition for human progress, he developed an incentive plan that would become the centerpiece of the Lincoln way, based upon a piecework pay system that bucked the wage system pervading many Western corporations.

> Expect that incentive management will cut costs by half or more. Expect that it will make your company dominant in its field. Expect that there will be unlimited progress because of the plan. Expect that your company will write a new chapter in industry.
>
> (James Lincoln)

However, he was also a fervent believer in the equality of management and employees, and also introduced the Employee Advisory Board, a committee focused on major operational issues within the firm which included elected representatives from each department. In 1915, the company gave each employee a paid life insurance policy. The next year, the Lincoln Electric Welding School was established. By 1925 he introduced the first employee stock ownership plan, and one of the first in the United States. In 1929, his Employee Advisory Board introduced an employee suggestion program. During the next three decades the firm developed a job evaluation system to determine base pay rates and instituted a merit rating to determine employee bonuses. Indeed, Lincoln has shared profits with its employees since 1934, based upon James's belief that employees must partake in the direct fruits of the company in order to feel properly motivated to serve the very best interests of the firm.

In 1965, James Lincoln died, some six years after his brother John. William Irrgang became the first non-family member to be appointed president, becoming CEO and chairman in 1972. He was followed by George Willis in 1986 and Donald Hastings in 1992, all having been homegrown and handpicked within the Lincoln organization. Anthony Massaro, who became only the sixth leader in the firm's more than

100 years of operations in 1997, was also the first to be appointed without a long history of Lincoln service.

## The products

At the end of World War II there were more than fifty producers of arc welding equipment in the US. Today, only six major manufacturers remain. Giants such as General Electric and Westinghouse have exited the industry, mainly due to Lincoln's high-quality, competitively priced products. For decades now, Lincoln Electric has been one of the leading producers of arc welding products. In May 1999 Lincoln decided to focus on this business and therefore sold off its electric motors business.

There are three different techniques in the welding industry: manual, semiautomatic, and automatic. The development has been away from the use of manual (stick) welding to semiautomatic and automatic welding. However, stick welding is still widely used in developing countries. Lincoln is a clear leader in the US market for stick electrodes and welding wires, the consumables that constitute the main part of the business. In welding machines, Lincoln competes head-to-head with Miller Electric Manufacturing for the No.1 position.

Customers who buy Lincoln's arc welding equipment are offered a customized cost-reduction program guaranteed to result in a rebate if the company's products and advice fail to help them to save money. It also boasts one of the most comprehensive lines of welding equipment, including stick welders, plasma cutters, engine-driven welders, wire feeder/welders, and robotic/automation systems.

## The incentive management system

In 1951, James F. Lincoln published a book entitled *Incentive Management* in which he outlined his management and labor principles. Incentives at Lincoln have two formal components: (1) wages on a piecework basis, and (2) a year-end bonus.

### *Piecework*

The piecework system was set up in 1914. According to this system, each factory job is rated according to skills, required efforts and responsibilities. A base rate wage comparable to those in similar jobs in the Cleveland area is assigned to the job. The time-study department then sets piece rates so that an average worker can earn the base rate for his or her job. Employees may challenge piecework standards set by the company's time-study department if they think they are unfair. Once they have been determined, the rates are firmly fixed, changing only if there are substantial changes in the production procedures. The firm does not review the base rates periodically to limit earnings. The majority of Lincoln's Cleveland area production workers are on piece rate. The company also employs some production support workers, who are, however, paid on an hourly basis.

The compensation system encourages employees to focus on quantity but also on quality. Workers must rework faulty pieces in their own time, and most products can be traced back to the individuals who produced them. Additionally, quality is one of the ingredients in the merit rating system that determines individuals' annual bonus.

## Year-end bonus

During the Great Depression of the 1930s, when it was impossible for the company to grant pay increases, James Lincoln suggested that they instead share in any increased profits. Hence, since 1934 Lincoln has had a bonus system. A merit rating procedure, done biannually, determines the yearly bonus. Production employees are rated on four criteria:

- *Output*: reviewed by the production department based on the amount of work that the worker produces.
- *Quality*: evaluated by the quality assurance department by tracing who has produced defective product parts.
- *Dependability*: assessed by the department head based on the number of absences, late arrivals, availability for overtime, etc.
- *Ideas and cooperation*: determined by the department head taking account of the individual's participation in the company's suggestion program (approximately fifty suggestions are implemented monthly[2]), how individuals share knowledge with others, cooperating in installing new methods, and the individual's attitude towards superiors, coworkers and the firm.

The firm allocates each department 100 points per employee. If an employee performs at a superior level, he or she can obtain more than twenty-five points for any category, although that means that other employees will receive less than 100 points. Most workers typically get between eighty and 120 points. The actual bonus in dollars depends on the individual's piece-rate earnings.

In years past, the board of directors decided, with management recommendation, the size of the annual overall bonus pool, which depended on such factors as company profits and investment plans. The bonus is now a formula based on and directly tied to the company's profitability. The bonus is paid in December, in time for the Christmas holidays. From the time the bonus system was introduced in 1934 through to 1988, bonuses ranged from 40 per cent to 100 per cent of base pay. In the 1990s, the bonuses were between 53 per cent and 75 per cent. None the less, the workers are still among the highest-paid workers in the US – in 1997, an average piecework employee at Lincoln received approximately US$51,000, while the very top earners received over US$100,000. To many, the incentive structure is one of the most attractive features about Lincoln.

The minute that you walk into Lincoln you sense that there's something different about it – a very high work ethic but with very large bonuses, and that was known for many years. I mean typically people would receive a bonus the size of what they made in an annual salary and that went on for many of the early years. So that was quite an incentive for a lot of people to go to Lincoln.

(Ray Bender, VP Manufacturing, AIA)

## Other features

The company has a stock purchase plan for employees who have been on the job for one year or more. In 1996, more than 60 per cent of the US employees owned shares.[3] Although the Lincoln family and employees still own a large percentage of the Lincoln shares, the first public offering in 1995 pushed outsiders' stake in the company to 40 per cent.[4]

A mainstay of the Lincoln system is their employment guarantee, formally introduced in 1958. Through the company's Guaranteed Employment Policy, at least thirty hours of full-time work is secured for employees with three or more years of tenure (although, in practice, it does not lay off people even with less seniority). In return, employees must be willing to perform any assignment and work overtime when needed. The average work week in Lincoln's US plants is between forty-three and fifty-eight hours, and the company can ask the employees on short notice to work longer hours. In periods of slowdowns, the work is shared so that everybody gets at least thirty hours per week. Sometimes creativity is required. For example, former Chairman Donald Hastings describes how the company responded to a decline in sales during the 1981 to 1983 recession:

The early 1980s were a good example of the lengths our company will go to avoid layoffs. For Lincoln, those years were a time of hardship. Skyrocketing inflation, sharply higher energy costs and a national recession all affected demand for our products. Our sales, which had been strong and steady, dropped 40 per cent during an eighteen-month period. How did we respond? We transferred many of our production people into sales. The very same people who successfully worked to satisfy high levels of demand in earlier years were now working to generate new demand. With their product knowledge, they were good at selling. They brought us new customers, which allowed us to increase production and to weather the recession.[5]

Incompetence, however, can be grounds for dismissal.

The company has fewer supervisors than most organizations per employee (approximately one to 100; in a typical factory in the United States it is one to twenty-five, but it may also be as high as one to ten). There are no reserved parking spaces for any employee and no executive dining room.

An open-door policy is practiced by senior management, who will often know employees by their first names. The Employee Advisory Board meets every two weeks to discuss, though not decide on, issues of concern to the employees. Traditionally the president has run the meetings. The employees in the US plants don't belong to a union and there has never been a strike.

Lincoln has for many decades followed a policy of promoting from within, and all jobs are internally announced. New hires are typically hired to the factory or as a trainee in sales or engineering. Even trainees with college degrees must start by attending welding school for seven weeks, then working on a production line and in several different functional areas. Roughly a quarter of new hires leave during the first three months, although those that remain tend to stay for a long period (turnover rates are 2–4 per cent). A particularly striking feature of the plants in Cleveland is that they have a large number of members of the same family.

Finally, there are no paid holidays or sick days. Employees pay their health care themselves, although the firm does help them with access to collective health insurance plans. It also does not count sick days against workers in their bonus reviews. It also maintains a compassionate stance towards employees in dealing with *ad hoc* situations. For example, several years ago, after formally submitting his resignation (and therefore terminating his insurance privileges), one employee was diagnosed with leukemia. None the less, the company kept his employment contract active during his treatment, thus providing him with access to the group insurance benefits. He was also given back his job at the end of his treatment.

A study carried out by the American Productivity Center in 1985 showed that worker productivity in the US plants was two and a half to three times higher than that in similar manufacturing operations.[6] Today, although the company's direct labor costs are relatively high, its manufacturing operations are still highly competitive because of Lincoln's skilled and productive workforce, process and product innovations, and continued investments in advanced technologies.[7]

## International expansion[8]

By 1986, Lincoln Electric operated five factories in four countries: two in the US, and one in Canada (established in 1925), Australia (1938), and France (1955). The Canadian operation is nearly identical to its Cleveland parent, incorporating the same incentive structures, advisory board, and open-door policy. Holiday pay is, however, required by Canadian law, and health insurance is provided through the provincial government (Ontario). The Australian operation is also similar to Cleveland. The French operation also maintains policies similar to Cleveland, using piecework pay, merit ratings, and the annual bonus scheme (although bonuses tend to be less as a percentage of total compensation). Also, vacation, holiday, and sick pay are in place, following national or industry requirements. On the whole, all operations are competitive in their respective markets and there is a consistent belief that the Lincoln incentive system is an important contributor to their success.

Despite this presence overseas, Lincoln was still primarily an American company, with overseas subsidiaries focusing largely on local markets. Following the appointment of George Willis as chairman in 1986, however, the company embarked on an aggressive expansion campaign, costing approximately US$325 million, mostly directed towards nineteen acquisitions from 1986 to 1991. By 1992, Lincoln Electric maintained manufacturing plants in fifteen nations, including Germany, Ireland, Italy, the Netherlands, Norway, Spain, and the UK in Europe; and Brazil, Mexico, and Venezuela in Latin America. Willis's successor, Donald Hastings, noted that Lincoln was convinced that "because we were so successful in the United States, we could be successful anywhere."[9]

Managing these operations brought unusual and thorny issues. First, because expansion came largely through acquisitions, Lincoln managers faced organizational cultures and practices that were not necessarily amenable to Lincoln's management philosophy and systems. Expatriate managers and mentoring from Cleveland counterparts were put in place to try and overcome these barriers. Second, national and regional differences were also evident and presented obstacles: the presence of very strong unions and the illegality of piecework pay (such as in Germany), supply chain problems (Brazil), regional differences in customers and welding practices along with local managers wishing to remain in firm control of local operations (preventing greater integration of European operations), and a general suspicion of highly incentivized remuneration schemes. Finally, a global recession in the early 1990s left most of these operations starved of the buoyant demand needed to grease the wheels of the Lincoln business model and instill employee trust of the Lincoln way: innovative and extremely dedicated employees are more difficult to generate *de novo* during business slumps, when incentive-based compensation is less likely to reach the customarily mercurial levels Lincoln employees enjoy in the US.

Not surprisingly, even though the parent operation in the US was doing very well, the company lost money for the first time in 1992.[10] The European operations in particular were badly hit, where the recession was compounded with considerable overcapacity in the industry – at one point, the German operation was losing US$1 million every two weeks. The leadership of the company was clearly disturbed by these results and recognized that major steps would need to be taken to stop the hemorrhaging of the firm.

To help manage the situation, two outside executives were hired: Anthony Massaro (a former executive with Westinghouse who had extensive international experience) was appointed Director of International Operations and Jay Elliot (a former international controller for Goodyear Tire & Rubber) was appointed Chief Financial Officer. Following Massaro and Elliott's recommendations, the firm set upon some swift restructuring of the international operations: plants in Brazil, Venezuela, Japan, and Germany were all closed, European operations were restructured with the help of a pan-European general management team plus Cleveland executives, new hires were made in key marketing and sales positions for Europe, local supply chains were improved and local production increased (thus reducing tariff charges), and more products were tailored to European customers.

Massaro also found that Lincoln's naivety regarding the incentive scheme, believing it could be quickly and cleanly implemented in any foreign context, contributed to problems. On this point, outgoing chairman Willis seemingly agreed, estimating that "it's going to take three to four years" to implement the Lincoln system in its international operations.[11] Indeed, by 1994 only plants located in the US, Canada, Mexico, Australia, and France used the piecework and bonus systems.[12] Of these, only the Mexican operation had been added during the rapid internationalization. The plant located in Mexico City was bought in 1990. The unionized plant had roughly 175 workers. Some of the workers and union officials were brought to the US facilities to discuss the incentive system with the US employees, and as an outcome of the trip two of the Mexican workers decided to take a chance on piecework. They also received a minimum income. After they had started to make more money than their fellow workers, others started to ask if they could become part of the system, too. After two years, the entire operation adopted piecework.[13]

Ex-chairman Donald Hastings also agreed with Massaro' s diagnosis, adding:

> The root cause of the crisis was that Lincoln's leaders, including myself, had grown overconfident in the company's abilities and systems . . . We had assumed that the incentive system and culture could be transferred abroad and that the workforce could be quickly replicated.[14]

Lincoln's trouble was not restricted to overseas operations. While Cleveland was performing exceptionally well given the circumstances, lifted by an inspiring local effort to generate sales and boost productivity (e.g., employees gave up a total of 614 weeks of vacation time to meet elevated production and shipping goals), discontent was brewing amongst the ranks. Despite the firm's best efforts to uphold their incentive commitment to these employees (taking short-term loans to pay bonuses in 1992), the company found it difficult to uphold the same level of remuneration that employees were used to, and thus bonuses as a percentage of total compensation dropped to 40–50 per cent. A minority of employees were discontented and there were even murmurs of unionization.[15] However, unionization ideas fizzled out as the firm's fortunes rebounded – in 1997 Lincoln paid out a record US$75 million in bonuses, up from US$65 million in 1996 (in 1996, more than twenty-five workers made over US$100,000[16]). More meetings were also held to try to better understand employee sentiment.

By 1995, international operations started to enjoy growing profitability and competitiveness (but without the full Lincoln incentive system).

After successfully managing the turnaround of the international operations, Anthony Massaro was appointed president and CEO of Lincoln in 1996, and in May of 1997 became chairman of the company. Massaro, better than anyone, understood now the problems Lincoln faced in their internationalization effort. But he also recognized that the future prosperity of the firm relied upon increasing, not decreasing, global presence, and particularly within developing regions, such as Asia, where long-term growth was expected to outpace North America and Europe. To be sure, Lincoln as a whole would have to learn from its recent setbacks. But the lessons were complex – the incentive system was working well in a number of fairly diverse cultural and legal settings, although not in all, and the firm remained committed to this tradition. Could it therefore work in most settings but under more benevolent start-up conditions? Was it mostly an issue of implementation, perhaps requiring the firm to attempt more greenfield start-ups, as opposed to (more culturally challenging) acquisitions? Or would Lincoln have to abandon its incentive system when it came to foreign operations, accepting the norms of each host country when it came to compensating and motivating employees? The next playing field would be in Asia.

## Lincoln Electric in Asia

In the mid-1990s, Lincoln made a new effort at expanding its operations in Asia, following the closure of the Japanese operation. This followed the introduction in 1995 of a new management structure for the corporation consisting of new executive positions (presidents) and accompanying staffs to manage each of five key strategic regions: North America, Europe, Russia–Africa–Middle East, Latin America, and Asia (including Australia). Michael Gillespie was appointed president for the Asian region, of British nationality and having joined Lincoln from ESAB, Lincoln's principal competitor in Asia and in Europe. Asia was now a key target of the firm and Gillespie was called upon by Massaro to provide a fresh and aggressive strategy for the region. Gillespie's plan was to create local (regional) competencies and construct an integrated sales and manufacturing business with Asia.

> The intention was to stop regarding Asia Pacific as a market to which we could export, to which we could sell our surplus production. So what we tried to do was to bring Lincoln to Asia rather than just sending American or Australian products into Asia, and decided that the right thing to do was to produce within the region for the region, products that were appropriate to the region, rather than simply trying to sell products that were right for the US or Europe.
>
> (Michael Gillespie)

A regional office was established in Singapore. The regional organization was to be responsible for strategic planning, technological support to the manufacturing units, and financial control. The regional organization had a high degree of autonomy from headquarters. The principal control consisted of following up that the region achieved its financial objectives. Gillespie was aided by Ray Bender, now the vice-president for manufacturing in the Asia region. Bender was a veteran in the Lincoln organization and had worked for three years on restructuring the company's operations in Europe when, in 1995, he met Gillespie and opted to move to Singapore.

Gillespie and Bender recognized that at least two issues would weigh heavily in their strategy for Asia – welding practices in the region and the management of local employees. With the exception of Japan, manual (stick) welding was still the predominant technique in Asia and the shift to semiautomatic and automatic welding was occurring only slowly and in concentrated areas. While Lincoln was competing, through export channels, in the more automated welding technologies, it was unable to compete in the stick welding market. High tariffs and considerable transportation costs, among other things, made exports of low-end consumables close to impossible. There were also a large number of national and regional competitors who were well established in Asia, although, Lincoln believed, without the dedication to quality and service that Lincoln wanted to bring to the region. While this market on its own did not look attractive, pumping out mainly low-margin products, Gillespie and Bender knew that this was an important vehicle for building brand recognition, boosting the firm's prospects in the automated machinery as new technology was absorbed.

Gillespie and Bender also recognized that motivating and managing employees would be complex. Regional governments could prove to be unstable, legislation regarding the treatment of employees more complex or possibly ambiguous, and local attitudes towards Western firms and practices uncertain – while some might welcome foreign operations, and the technologies and skills they bring with them, others might resent the presence of foreign firms and foreign practices. Moreover, each nation brought with it very specific cultural traits that could inhibit (or, of course, promote) traditional Lincoln management practices.

## A strategy for Asia

Gillespie decided to build operations in three locations: Indonesia, the Philippines, and China. The Indonesian operation was the first to be launched (1996/97), established as a joint venture with Lincoln's local distributor (Lincoln would maintain a 60 per cent stake). The scope of operations, however, would be modest, focusing strictly on stick electrodes. Similarly, the Philippine operation, launched in early 1999, also focused exclusively on stick electrodes. These would be the entry vehicles, along with the Australian operation, for providing the most commonly used products to the region. However, Gillespie recognized that Lincoln would also have to build capacity in the higher-end market, building the groundwork for the region's inevitable technological progress into automated machinery – Lincoln would even contribute to this progress by educating customers on the advantages of the new technology, as Gillespie added:

> Basically the welding industry started with the stick electrode over a hundred years ago. It has moved through the solid wire form of automation to the cored wire. What we have seen in most of Asia is that the majority of the welding has been done with sticks and very little has been done with semiautomatic processes. However, more is being done with automatic and we believe that it will be no different here from anywhere else – first of all, automatic is more productive, secondly it requires somewhat less skill. The downside is the initial investment cost, but this is amply repaid by the productivity once people understand it. We're focusing on it here.

The natural hub for this operation was China. As the general manager, Jeffrey Kundrach, explains:

> A large percentage of the welding you'll see in China is stick electrodes. But there's a move towards the higher technology type of processes, especially, to capitalize on the higher efficiency and productivity of these systems. There is a tremendous number of stick electrode manufacturers and the government is very interested in moving away from that lower end technology into the higher end.

Gillespie added that there are "lots of locally owned stick electrode companies that are fighting each other to death and we saw the opportunity to come in with a good quality [automatic technology], both for the China market and for export."

## Lincoln Electric, Shanghai

### Entering China

Lincoln had established a representative office in Tianjin (northeast China) in the late 1980s, employing mostly local welding engineers who were sent to Cleveland for an eight-month technical training program and returned to China to help push Lincoln products. There were no direct sales efforts, however, as sales were solely through Lincoln's local distributors. Although sales (both stick and automatic technologies) were modest, Lincoln was becoming better known in China and buyers associated Lincoln Electric with good quality. In 1996 a second representative office was added in Shanghai.

Initially, Gillespie believed the best mode of entry for a new operation would be with a local partner, probably a state-owned manufacturing firm. Several meetings took place to discuss a possible joint venture with representatives of the largest Chinese producers of electrodes and welding machines. The belief was that a local company could deliver the important distribution vehicle into the region, where customer contact seemingly required a local touch. In the end, Lincoln decided against a joint venture with a manufacturer, concerned with their outdated manufacturing processes and that Lincoln might not be able to adequately protect its intellectual property. There were also concerns about the Chinese firms' ability to support the company in aggressively selling products in different parts of China. Gillespie and Bender had also done their homework to find that "there were a lot of horror stories of local joint venture partners, so we stepped back and took a breather for a while," as Bender noted.

Instead of a manufacturing partner, Lincoln decided to only seek the collaboration of its distributors. Thus, the investment in the Lincoln Electric (Shanghai) Welding Company was made, with a 68 per cent stake by Lincoln and 8 per cent by each of four of Lincoln's distributors in Asia. Two of the distributors were already active in China and a third soon entered the market. To obtain permission to establish the wholly foreign-owned firm, Lincoln had to agree to a 30 percent export quota.

The decision to build an advanced manufacturing facility in Shanghai had good reasons. For one thing, Shanghai was home to the Pudong New Area, a massive new development area located southeast of the Huangpu river and home to a large number of free trade zones.[17] One of the free trade zones is called the Waigaoqiao Free Trade Zone, lying in the northeast of Pudong. It is adjacent to the mouth of the Yangtze river, 20 km away from the downtown core and 15 km away from the planned Pudong New Airport. It is the first comprehensive and multifunctional free trade zone in China, enjoying easy shipping access and a generous tariff system. For example, supplies could be imported tax free; only if the final products were sold on the Chinese market do customs and VAT have to be paid, and then only on the non-Chinese content. If the products are exported, neither customs nor VAT are paid on the imported supplies. This was a crucial advantage as the plant could be used to serve other Asian markets with advanced consumables products. Lincoln also believed that by locating in Pudong it could avoid possible pressure from local governments wanting to protect their own manufacturing companies. Lincoln decided to lease a building site, providing it with flexibility concerning how to further develop Lincoln's China operations.

## The management team and method

In early 1997, Julius Wu was appointed country manager for China and general manager of the Shanghai operation. Wu was originally from Taiwan and experienced in the electric motor industry in Taiwan and mainland China. Wu was first sent to Cleveland for an eight-week training program, and then returned to Shanghai to start the company's operations out of the representative office in Shanghai.

Shortly after he arrived in Shanghai, Wu met Dr Li Yan. Dr Li was a professor at the Institute of Metal Research at Harbin University and a well known expert in the Chinese welding industry, as one Lincoln manager recounted an encounter with a client representative:

> The young welding engineer at our client's test shop, when he found out who Li was, almost kneeled. Harbin is No.1 for metal research and his qualifications and the way they're written on his business card mean a lot.

Li had also spent three years as a postdoc in the UK, was fluent in English, and a connoisseur of new welding technologies. An advocate for greater cross-cultural understanding, Dr Li was seen as a perfect bridge between Lincoln's foreign technologies and management practices and Chinese business customs and attitudes. Not surprisingly, Wu offered Li the job as plant manager, which Dr Li accepted, having been actively searching for a position with a foreign firm.

In the fall of 1997, Dr Li spent six weeks in Cleveland before starting to work on the start-up of the Shanghai plant. Li decided on all hires for the new company. The first three hires – managers and technicians – were all made through Li's contacts in the welding industry. Because managers and technical people tended to already know the Lincoln brand name they were relatively easy to hire. More difficult would be the skilled operators, who didn't recognize the Lincoln brand name and were relatively scarce. To get skilled people to apply for operator positions Li had to make several visits to people's homes to inform them about the company. Soon, word of mouth helped spread the news of Lincoln's job openings and positions were gradually filled. Virtually all of the employees had worked in the welding industry and would therefore be aware of industry practices in operations and employee management. Finally, most of the employees lived on the other side of the river, in old Shanghai, and were brought to the factory every morning by company bus or van.

All employees had to go through a three-month probation period, some of whom subsequently left the company while others were asked to leave. In several of these cases it appeared the new hires lacked a clear understanding of what Lincoln expected. Dr Li therefore began spending more time assessing and working with candidates.

> I spend one or two days interviewing and working with each of them. I assign some work on the floor to let him have a real feeling for how this operation is functioning. And I try to get a real understanding of how the person is working. I don't want to hire persons and then see them leave.

At this point there was no system of guaranteed employment. Salary levels in the company were on a par with other foreign companies in Pudong, possibly slightly above. All employees, except the managers, were paid normal salaries. Dr Li was the only local person with a bonus clause in his contract.

While Lincoln had transferred its used machinery to the new plant in Indonesia, in China it acquired brand new technology, rolled out simultaneously to both the Cleveland and Shanghai plants – the idea was that each operation's experience could benefit the other.[18] In fact, it turned out that there were fewer problems with the new production lines in China than were experienced in the Cleveland plant, Dr Li having worked extensively with suppliers and operators on the set-up of the machinery. There were also extensive communications between Cleveland and Shanghai. While Julius Wu handled strategic issues, Dr Li was handling most of the technical interactions, spending late evenings communicating with Cleveland (twelve-hour time zone difference). Being responsible for the plant and also being the only technical person fully fluent in English, Li translated all instructions into Chinese. Every operator had a small book with written instructions for their job. Thus, when Anthony Massaro officially opened the plant in May 1998, the operation was on course for a successful beginning.

The final members of the management team were put in place in late 1998. In November 1998, Peter Grant was hired as sales and marketing manager. Grant, an

Australian with a flare for expat life, had four years of experience in China and had worked for one of Lincoln's competitors. All of his sales people were university-qualified welding engineers. The regional finance manager, Jason Foo, initially handled the finance and accounting function from his base in Singapore. In February 1999, Shan Bing, a Chinese accounting expert in his early thirties who had more than five years of experience from foreign investment companies in Shanghai, was hired as finance and control manager.

## Early results and future concerns

By March 1999, Lincoln Electric Shanghai employed forty employees in production, ten engineers and lab technicians, another ten service people, and ten administrative staff. The sales people were affiliated with the representative office in Shanghai and with the other offices in Tianjin, Xian, and Shenyang. By all accounts, the first year of Lincoln Electric Shanghai was a marked success and the company was experiencing "very large growth," despite the slump in other parts of Asia and the downturn in the Asian economy in general. Lincoln executives were already looking into the possibility of expanding their operations into an increasing range of Lincoln products.

Although the future looked bright, many critical issues were looming. First, there were concerns that product quality would be maintained as the operation grew and quality was emphasized as a key advantage of the Lincoln brand. As explained by Ray Bender:

> We took all kinds of steps to hammer in quality, to discuss quality, make sure that what we make is what the market wants . . . We go overboard as far as our quality assurance department is concerned. We invested a lot of money in the [quality assurance] equipment, and we bring auditors in from the United States on a regular basis so that we don't get lulled into thinking that everything is good. So they come in and audit the system.

The company also started to post production outcome and quality data on the board located in the workshop so that all employees could follow how the manufacturing process was running.

Second, Julius Wu fell ill during the fall of 1998 and needed significant time for convalescence. While Jeffrey Kundrach, experienced in several of Lincoln's foreign adventures, would fulfill immediate leadership needs as the general manager, it was uncertain how the leadership would play out in the future.

But perhaps the trickiest issue for the company was if and when to introduce the distinctive Lincoln incentive system. Lincoln devotees remained dedicated to the Lincoln way and believed strongly in the logic of bonuses and piecework. Although Lincoln had not attempted to introduce the incentive system in Shanghai, the issue was being seriously discussed. Regarding bonuses, Bender believed this was an important way of providing both meaningful feedback to employees while also having this feedback linked to something tangible. This was being considered throughout the plant, including the sales force.

Yet bonuses were not considered sufficient motivators by themselves, certainly not as powerful as the piecework logic, as Bender explained:

> There is a definite advantage in sitting down twice a year with all your employees and telling them what their strengths are, where they could do better, what we have to do in order to get our overall goal. If nothing else you need to do that, it's a way of forcing you to sit down and talk to your people to really be frank with them on how they're doing. You can measure piecerate work efficiency so you can discuss their output. A quality system with the number of rejects is also very quantitative so you can sit down and discuss his quality very easily. His attendance can also be discussed.
>
> But I think, if you're looking to get another 20 percent out of your equipment, the best way to do that is on piecework. Piecework is the day-to-day driver. Twice a year there is a sudden realization that the bonus will come up, so maybe there is a lot of activity for two weeks or a month before they are merit rated. But during the other months things are normal. So for me if you're looking at what's going to stimulate a factory it's going to be piecework more than just a bonus system.

The production workers were proving to be an open and amiable group so far. Grant suggested the dividing lines between management and workforce were not necessarily as thick in China as in his native Australia:

> I don't see any of that here, I really don't. It depends on your approach and so on, but you can walk down that line and there's nothing wrong with putting a hand on someone's back and saying, "How are you doing?" or whatever and try and carry on a conversation or even if you can't speak the language, acknowledge them.

Any piecework system would seemingly require such mutual trust.

Nevertheless, there were cultural impediments to consider. For one, the lack of a common language between workers and most managers might hinder effective communication. Also, having the workers bear more of the downside risk for poor company performance might not be acceptable in a country where people were generally not exposed to such remuneration systems. Prolonged depression of people's earnings might even raise accusations of exploitative practices and possibly introduce government intervention. The traditional Lincoln system would also require the ability of the workforce to speak out and make suggestions for improvements in processes, something that would not come easily in the hierarchical Chinese society where superiors were expected to make initiatives and decide on most organizational matters. However, Grant, along with others, was trying to encourage the local employees to become more active:

> I push my people to debate with me, to argue with me at the right time and I welcome them to come in and tell me where they think I am wrong with either a decision or something I've said or what I am planning to do. I push them to do that.

Some, however, did not find the cultural impediments compelling – indeed, they believed many workers would be more than willing to have their pay scheme clear, transparent and rewarding of hard work, the competitiveness involved something Chinese workers were not expected to shy away from. Furthermore, although traditionally there have been very small salary differences in Chinese organizations, a growing number of both foreign and local Chinese companies had recently introduced performance-based compensation systems. Some of the Lincoln managers argued that the main concern was implementation and timing, as Bender noted:

> It's my impression that piecework is a concept that probably could be accepted here, but one of the things that we have to be concerned about is that if it's not done fairly it could end up being a problem. So we have to do a lot of homework to make sure that we're going to keep the person busy in piecework, that the price structure that we set is fair, and that it's going to sustain itself. One of the worst things you could do is set a piecework price and then realize that you made a mistake and then go back and change it. People don't understand why you cut their price when they were making a lot of money.

His views were shared by Kundrach:

> You can't introduce a piece-rate system until you have a steady, stable process. And this is for new equipment. It's new for the corporation, people have to go up a learning curve, and you cannot introduce a piecework system on that learning curve – you would have to adjust the piecework system all the time . . . if you just arbitrarily change the piece rate because somebody is making 20 percent above the basis, then the trust factor is gone.

As Lincoln Electric Shanghai entered its second year it was at least clear that how to sustain growth and boost productivity while maintaining a motivated and committed workforce would have to be closely considered.

## Acknowledgments

Ingmar Björkman is Visiting Professor and Charles Galunic Associate Professor at INSEAD, Fontainebleau, France. This case is intended to be used as a basis for class discussion rather than to illustrate either effective or ineffective handling of an administrative situation. We are grateful for the help and encouragement of Jeffrey Kundrach, Managing Director, Lincoln Electric Shanghai, and Professor John Weeks at INSEAD. Copyright © 1999 INSEAD.

# Notes

## Introduction

1 Discussion of these different terms can be found in many books on international business and international management, such as Bartlett, C.A., and Ghoshal, S. (2002), *Managing Across Borders: The Transnational Solution*, 2nd edn, Boston: Harvard Business School Press, Deresky, H. (2003), *International Management*, 4th edn, Upper Saddle River, NJ: Prentice Hall; Shenkar, O., and Luo, Y. (2004), *International Business*, New York: Wiley; Ohmae, K. (1990), *The Borderless World*, New York: Harper; and articles, including, for example Bartlett, C.A., and Ghoshal, S. (1992), "What is a global manager?" *Harvard Business Review*, September–October, pp. 124–32; Behrman, J.N. (1999), "Why and how managers must develop greater cross-cultural sensitivity," *Global Outlook*, 11 (1): 9–18;

## 1 International business and International Human Resource Management

1 Weidenbaum, M. (1999), "The stake of the average [US] citizen in the world economy," *Global Outlook*, 11 (1): 1–8.
2 Schuler, R. (2003), keynote address to the seventh IHRM conference in Limerick, Ireland, June 4; Bhagwati, J. (2004) *In Defense of Globalization*, Oxford/New York: Oxford University Press; Black, J.S., Morrison, A.J., and Gregersen, H.B. (1999), *Global Explorers: The Next Generation of Leaders*, New York and London: Routledge; Friedman, T.L. (1999), *The Lexus and the Olive Tree: Understanding Globalization*, New York: Farrar Straus & Giroux; Greider, W. (1997), *One World, Ready or Not: The Manic Logic of Global Capitalism*, New York: Simon & Schuster; Micklethwait, J., and Wooldridge A. (2000), *A Future Perfect: The Challenge and Hidden Promise of Globalization*, New York: Crown Business; Rosen, R., with Digh, P., Singer, M., and Phillips, C. (2000), *Global Literacies: Lessons on Business Leadership and National Cultures*, New York: Simon & Schuster.
3 Source: Abrahams, P. (1994), "Getting hooked on fish and chips in Japan," *Financial Times*, May 17, updated in 2003 from web site (www.market-reports.co.uk).
4 Simon, H. (1996), *Hidden Champions: Lessons from 500 of the World's Best Unknown Companies*, Boston, MA: Harvard Business School Press.
5 *Ibid*. Also see Parker, B. (1998), "Charting Unexplored Territory: Leadership Research across Cultures," paper presented at the Western Academy of Management meeting, Istanbul, Turkey.
6 Many authors have presented lists such as this. This particular list is adapted from Ball, D.A., Jr, McCulloch, W.H., Frantz, P.L., Geringer, M., and Minor, M.S. (2001), *International Business*, 8th edn, New York: McGraw-Hill Irwin; Naisbitt, J., and Aburdene, P. (1990), *Megatrends 2000*, New York: Morrow. Also refer to Greider (1997), Naisbitt, J. (1996), *Megatrends Asia*, New York: Simon & Schuster, and references in note 1 in the "Introduction".

7  Schuler (2003); United Nations Conference on Trade and Development (UNCTAD), *World Investment Report 1998*, New York: United Nations (1999).

8  This list is produced every year. The edition reported here is "The *Fortune* Global 500: The world's largest corporations," *Fortune*, July 28, 2003, pp. 97–126.

9  "The *Business Week* Global 1000: The world's most valuable companies," *Business Week*, July 10, 2000, pp. 107–152, and July 9, 2001, pp. 72–90.

10  "Top global companies," *Business Week*, July 14, 2003, pp. 58–62.

11  "The information technology 100," *Business Week*, November 2, 1998, pp. 116–122.

12  "Top global companies."

13  Khermouch, G., with Holmes, S., and Ihlwan, M. (2001), "The best global brands," *Business Week*, August 6, pp. 50–64.

14  "The *Forbes* global 500," *Forbes*, July 21, 2003, pp. 52–56.

15  http//www.forbes.com.

16  See, for example, "Index of foreign billionaires," *Forbes*, July 18, 1994, pp. 152–218; *World Investment Report*, New York: United Nations (1995); "As good times roll: Indonesia's Chinese fear for their future," *Wall Street Journal*, June 5, 1997, p. A18; "Inheriting the bamboo network," *Economist*, December 23, 1995, pp. 79–80; Kao, J. (1993), "The worldwide web of Chinese business," *Harvard Business Review*, March–April, pp. 24–38; Kotkin, J. (1993), *Tribes*, New York: Random House; Seagrave, S. (1995), *Lords of the Rim*, London: Bantam Books; Tanzer, A. (1994), "The bamboo network," *Forbes*, July 18, pp. 138–144; Weidenbaum, M.L. (1996), *The Bamboo Network*, New York: Martin Kessler.

17  See, for example, Mendenhall, M., and Oddou, G. (1995), "White-water rapids of international human resource management" in Mendenhall, M., and Oddou, G. (eds), *Readings and Cases in International Human Resource Management*, 2nd edn, Cincinnati, OH: Southwestern College Publishing.

18  See, for example, Reich, R.B. (1991), *The Work of Nations*, New York: Knopf; Reich, R.B. (1990), "Who is us?" *Harvard Business Review*, January–February, pp. 53–64; Reich, R.B. (1991), "Who is them?" *Harvard Business Review*, March–April, pp. 77–88; Metthee, I. (1994), "Playing a large part," *Seattle Post Intelligencer*, April 4, p. 13; Tranger, C.S. (1989), "Enter the mini-multinational," *Northeast International Business*, March, pp. 13–14.

19  Source: adapted from Schuler, R.S., and Walker, J.W. (1990), "Human resources strategy: Focusing on issues and actions," *Organization Dynamics*, summer, pp. 4–20.

20  Dowling, P.J., Welch, D.E., and Schuler, R.S. (1999), *International Human Resource Management*, 3rd edn, Cincinnati, OH: Southwestern College Publishing.

21  For early writings making this point see Adler, N.J., and Ghadar, F. (1990), "Strategic human resource management: A global perspective" in R. Pieper (ed.), *Human Resource Management: An International Comparison*, Berlin: de Gruyter; Briscoe, D.R. (1989), "International Human Resource Management: What Does it Look Like?" paper presented to the annual conference of the Association of Human Resource Management and Organizational Behavior, Boston, MA, November 1–4; Dulfer, E. (1990), "Human resource management in multinational and internationally operating companies" in R. Pieper (ed.), *Human Resource Management: An International Comparison*, Berlin: de Gruyter; Morgan, P.V. (1986), "International HRM: Fact or fiction?" *Personnel Administrator*, 31 (9): 43–47.

22  Claus, L. (1998), "The role of international human resource management in leading a company from a domestic to a global corporate culture," *Human Resource Development International*, 1 (3): 309–326; Claus, L. (1999), "People Management and Globalization," presentation to the fifty-first annual conference and exposition of the Society of Human Resource Management, Atlanta, GA, June.

23  Claus (1998, 1999).

24  For an article about sources for articles on topics related to IHR see Caliguiri, P.M. (1999), "The ranking of scholarly journals in the field of international human resource management," *International Journal of Human Resource Management*, 10 (3): 515–518.

25 Dowling *et al.* (1999).
26 See, for example, Dowling, P.J. (1988), "International and domestic personnel/human resource management: Similarities and differences," in R.S. Schuler, S.A. Youngblood, and V.L. Huber (eds), *Readings in Personnel and Human Resource Management*, 3rd edn, St Paul, MN: West Publishing. Also discussed in Dowling *et al.* (1999).
27 The first part of this discussion was originally stated by Dowling (1988).
28 Claus (1998); Hendry, C. (1994), *Human Resource Strategies for International Growth*, London: Routledge, particularly chapter 1.
29 See, for example, Doz, Y., and Prahalad, C.K. (1986), "Controlled variety: A challenge for human resource management in the MNC," *Human Resource Management*, 25 (1): 55–71; Evans, P.A.L. (1992), "Human Resource Management and Globalization," keynote presentation at the third biannual conference on International Personnel and Human Resource Management, Ashridge Management College, Berkhamsted, Hertfordshire, England, July 2–4; Evans, P.A.L., Lank, E., and Farquhar, A. (1989), "Managing human resources in the international firm: Lessons from practice" in Evans, P.A.L., Doz, Y., and Laurent, A. (eds), *Human Resource Management in International Firms*, London: Macmillan; Evans, P.A.L., and Doz, Y. (1989), "The two logics behind human resource management," in Evans *et al.* (eds), *Human Resource Management in International Firms*, London: Macmillan; Evans, P.A.L., and Doz, Y. (1989), "The dualistic organization" in Evans *et al.* (eds), *Human Resource Management in International Firms*, London: Macmillan; Halley, J. (1999), "Localization as an ethical response to internationalization" in Brewster, C., and Harris, H. (eds), *International HRM*, London: Routledge; Hendry (1994).
30 Laurent, A. (1986), "The cross-cultural puzzle of international human resource management," *Human Resource Management*, 25 (1): 97.
31 Adapted from Laurent (1986).
32 *Ibid.*
33 Trompenaars, F. (1993–1994), *Riding the Waves of Culture: Understanding Diversity in Global Business*, New York: Irwin, p. 185.
34 Gupta, A., and Govindarajan, V. (2001), "Converting global presence into global competitive advantage," *Academy of Management Executive*, 15 (2): 45–58; Pucik, V. (1992), "Globalization and human resource management" in Pucik, V., Tichy, N.M., and Barnett, C.K. (eds), *Globalizing Management: Creating and Leading the Competitive Organization*, New York: Wiley.
35 Pucik (1992).

## 2 Strategic International Human Resource Management

1 Mendenhall, M.E., Black, J.S., Jensen, R.J., and Gregersen, H.B. (2003), "Human resource challenges in the age of globalization," *Organizational Dynamics*, 32 (3): Z61–74; Schuler, R.S., Jackson, S.E., and Tarique, I. (2003), "Forces in global HRM," virtual document at www.ghrm.rutgers.edu; Oliver, R.W. (1999), *The Shape of Things to Come*, New York: McGraw-Hill.
2 Evans, P., Pucik, V., and Barsoux, J.-L. (2002),*The Global Challenge: Frameworks for International Human Resource Management*, New York: McGraw-Hill Irwin; Marquardt, M.J. (1999), *The Global Advantage: How World-class Organizations Improve Performance through Globalization*, Houston, TX: Gulf Publishing; Brockbank, W. (1997), "HR's future on the way to a presence," *Human Resource Management*, 36 (1): 65–69. Also refer to note 6 for references to the impact of globalization.
3 Evans *et al.* (2003) (2002); Albrecht, M.H. (ed.) (2001), *International HRM: Managing Diversity in the Workplace*, Oxford: Blackwell; Marquardt (1999).
4 Thompson, A.A., Jr, and Strickland, A.J., III (1998), *Strategic Management: Concepts and Cases*, 10th edn, New York: McGraw-Hill: 2.

5  *Ibid.*, pp. 2–3.
6  Pucik, V., and Evans, P. (2004), *People Strategies for MNEs*, London: Routledge. Walker, J.W. (2001), "Are we global yet?" in M.H. Albrecht (ed.), *International HRM*, Oxford: Blackwell; Bartlett, C. (1983), "How multinational organizations evolve," *Journal of Business Strategy,* summer, pp. 10–32; Dowling, P.J., Welch, D.E., and Schuler, R.S. (1999), *International Human Resource Management*, 3rd edn, Cincinnati, OH: Southwestern College Publishing; Fadel, J.J., and Petti, M. (2001), "International HR policy basics" in Albrecht, M.H. (ed.), *International HRM*, Oxford: Blackwell; Harzing, A.-H. (1995), "Strategic planning in multinational corporations" in Harzing, A.-H., and Ruysseveldt, J.V. (eds), *International Human Resource Management*, London: Sage; Lorange, P., and Vancil, R. (1977), *Strategic Planning Systems*, Englewood Cliffs, NJ: Prentice Hall; Miller, E.L., Beechler, S., Bhatt, B., and Nath, R. (1986), "The relationship between the global strategic planning process and the human resource management function," *Human Resource Planning*, 9 (1): 9–23; Tung, R.L. (1984), "Strategic management of human resources in multinational enterprises," *Human Resource Management*, 23: 129–143.
7  Miller *et al.* (1986).
8  Bartlett, C., and Ghoshal, S. (1989), *Managing across Borders: The Transnational Solution*, Boston, MA: Harvard Business School Press; Harzing, A.-W. (2000), "An empirical analysis and extension of the Bartlett and Ghoshal typology of multinational companies," *Journal of International Business Studies*, 31 (1): 101–120.
9  See, for example, Evans *et al.* (2002); Galbraith, J.R. (2000), *Designing the Global Corporation*, San Francisco: Jossey Bass; Heenan, D.A., and Perlmutter, H.V. (1979), *Multinational Organization Development: A Social Architectural Perspective*, Reading, MA: Addison Wesley.
10  Galbraith (2000).
11  There is a good summary of these issues in Segal-Horn, S., and Faulkner, D. (1999), *The Dynamics of International Strategy*, London: International Thomson, and in Galbraith (2000).
12  Adapted from Wetlaufer, S. (1999), "Driving change: An interview with Ford Motor Company's Jacques Nasser," *Harvard Business Review*, March–April, pp. 77–80.
13  Pucik and Evans (2004); Evans *et al.* (2002); Bartlett and Ghoshal (1989); Calori, R., Atamer, T., Nunes, P., *et al.* (2000), *The Dynamics of International Competition*, London and New York: Sage; Friedman, T.L. (1999), *The Lexus and the Olive Tree: Understanding Globalization*, New York: Farrar Straus & Giroux; Galbraith (2000); Greider, W. (1997), *One World, Ready or Not: The Manic Logic of Global Capitalism*, New York: Simon & Schuster; Micklethwait, J., and Wooldridge, A. (2000), *A Future Perfect: The Challenge and Hidden Promise of Globalization*, New York: Crown Business; O'Hara-Devereaux, M., and Johansen, R. (1994), *Global Work: Bridging Distance, Culture and Time*, San Francisco: Jossey Bass; Ohmae, K. (1990), *The Borderless World*, New York: Harper; Reich, R. (1991), *The Work of Nations: Preparing Ourselves for Twenty-first-century Capitalism*, New York: Knopf; Rosen, R., Digh, P., Singer M., and Phillips, C. (2000), *Global Literacies: Lessons on Business Leadership and National Cultures*, New York: Simon & Schuster; Scherer, C.W. (2000), *The Internationalists: Business Strategies for Globalization*, Wilsonville, OR: Book Partners; Segal-Horn and Faulkner (1999). See also Rugman, A.M. (2000), *The End of Globalization*, London: Random House.
14  Adapted from Brandt, E. (1991), "Global HR," *Personnel Journal*, March. Also see Bartlett and Ghoshal (1989); Segal-Horn and Faulkner (1999).
15  Main, J. (1989), "How to go global – and why," *Fortune*, August 28, p. 70.
16  Solomon, C.M. (1993), "Transplanting corporate cultures globally," *Personnel Journal*, October, pp. 78–88.
17  *Ibid.*, p. 78.
18  Pucik and Evans (2004); Bartlett and Ghoshal (1989).
19  Segal-Horn and Faulkner (1999).

20  Adapted from *ibid.*, pp. 172–174.
21  See, for example, the references in note 6 and Kanter, R.M. (1989), *When Giants Learn to Dance: Mastering the Challenges of Strategy, Management, and Careers in the 1990s*, New York: Simon & Schuster; Porter, M.E. (1990), *The Competitive Advantage of Nations*, New York: Free Press.
22  "Thriving on Chaos" seminar (course notebook), Career Track Seminars, presented in San Diego, CA (1990), p. 21.
23  Schuler, R.S., Jackson, S.E., and Luo, Y. (2004), *Human Resource Issues in Cross-border Alliances*, London: Routledge; Chakravarthy, B., and Perlmutter, H.V. (1985), "Strategic planning for a global economy," *Columbia Journal of World Business*, summer, pp. 3–10.
24  Kobrin, S.J. (1994), "Is there a relationship between a geocentric mind set and multinational strategy?" *Journal of International Business Studies*, 25 (3): 493–511; Perlmutter, H.V. (1969), "The tortuous evolution of the multinational corporation," *Columbia Journal of World Business*, January–February, pp. 9–18.
25  Gupta, A.K., and Govindarajan, V. (2002), "Cultivating a global mind set," *Academy of Management Executive*, 16 (1): 116–126; Kedia, B.L., and Mukherji, A. (1999), "Global managers: Developing a mind-set for global competitiveness," *Journal of World Business*, 34 (3): 230–251.
26  Stroh L.K., and Caligiuri, P.M. (1998), "Strategic human resources: A new source for competitive advantage in the global arena," *International Journal of Human Resource Management*, 9 (1): 1–17.
27  Les Real, Corporate Director of International HR, Federal Express, presentation at the faculty development program in International HR, University of Colorado, Denver, CO, June, 2000.
28  Lorange and Vancil (1977).
29  "The Globalization of Human Resources: A Benchmarking Study," Human Capital Consulting Practice, Arthur Andersen (2000).
30  Taylor, W. (1991), "The logic of global business: An interview with ABB's Percy Barnevik," *Harvard Business Review*, March–April, p. 92.
31  The language here is borrowed from the "call for papers" from N. Noorderhaven for the *Management International Review* special issue on the theme of "Can multinationals bridge the gap between global and local?" E-mail message, August 17, 2001, from Academy of International Business.
32  Taylor, S., Beechler, S., and Napier, N. (1993), "Toward an Integrated Theory of International Human Resource Management," paper presented at the National Academy of International Business, Hawaii.
33  Schuler, R.S., Budhwar, P.S., and Florkowski, G.W. (2002), "International human resource management: Review and critique," *International School of Management Review*, 4 (1): 41–70; Schuler, R.S., Dowling, P.J., and De Cieri, H. (1993), "An integrative framework of strategic international human resource management," *Journal of Management*, 19 (2): 419–459; Gupta, A.K., and Govindarajan, V. (2001), "Converting global presence into global competitive advantage," *Academy of Management Executive*, 15 (2): 45–58. See, for example, Milliman, J., Von Glinow, M.A., and Nathan, M. (1991), "Organizational life cycles and strategic international human resource management in multinational companies: Implications for congruence theory," *Academy of Management Review*, 16 (2): 318–339; Ondrack, D. (1985), "International transfers of managers in North American and European MNCs," *Journal of International Business Studies*, 16 (3), pp. 1–19.
34  Beechler, S., Bird, A., and Raghuram S. (1993), "Linking business strategy and human resource management practices in multinational corporations: A theoretical framework," *Advances in International Comparative Management*, 8: 199–215; Engle, A., and Stedham, Y. (1999), "Multinational and Transnational Strategies: Implications for Human Resource Planning," draft sent to author for informal review; Hannon, J.M., Huang, I.-C., and Jaw, B.-S. (1995), "International human resource strategy and its determinants: The case of

subsidiaries in Taiwan," *Journal of International Business Studies*, third quarter, pp. 531–554; Rosenzweig, P.M., and Nohria, N. (1994), "Influences on human resource management practices in multinational corporations," *Journal of International Business Studies*, second quarter, pp. 229–251; Taylor, S., Beechler, S., Najjar, M., and Ghosh, B.C. (1998), "A partial test of a model of strategic international human resource management," *Advances in International Comparative Management*, 12: 207–236.

35  Lei, D., Slocum, J.W., Jr, and Slater, R.W. (1990), "Global strategy and reward systems: The key roles of management development and corporate culture," *Organizational Dynamics*, 18: 63–77; Sheridan, W.R., and Hansen, P.T. (1996), "Linking international business and expatriate compensation strategies," *ACA Journal*, 5 (2): 66–79.

36  Dowling *et al.* (1999); Schuler *et al.* (1993).

37  Kobrin (1994).

38  Luthans, F., Marsnik, P.A., and Luthans, K.W. (1997), "A contingency matrix approach to IHRM," *Human Resource Management*, 36 (2): 183–199; Taylor, S., and Beechler, S. (1993), "Human resource management system integration and adaptation in multinational firms," *Advances in International Comparative Management*, 8: 155–174.

39  Milliman *et al.* (1991).

40  Pucik and Evans (2004); Hamm, S. (2003), "Borders are so twentieth-century," *Business Week*, September 22, pp. 68–73; Caligiuri, P.M., and Stroh, L.K. (1995), "Multinational corporation management strategies and international human resource practices: Bringing international HR to the bottom line," *International Journal of Human Resource Management*, 6 (3): 494–507; Stroh and Caligiuri (1998).

41  Yip, G.S., Johansson J.K., and Roos, J. (1997), "Effects of nationality on global strategy," *Management International Review*, 37 (4): 365–385.

## 3 Organizational structure and design of the multinational enterprise

1  Evans, P., Pucik, V., and Barsoux, J.-L. (2002), *The Global Challenge: Frameworks for International Human Resource Management*, New York: McGraw-Hill; Bartlett, C.A., and Ghoshal, S. (1989), *Managing across Borders: The Transnational Solution*, Boston, MA: Harvard Business School Press; Galbraith, J.R. (1998), "Structuring global organizations," in Mohaman, S.A., Galbraith, J.A., and Lawler, E.E. III (eds), *Tomorrow's Organization: Crafting Winning Capabilities in a Dynamic World*, San Francisco: Jossey Bass; Galbraith, J.A. (2000), *Designing the Global Corporation*, San Francisco: Jossey Bass.

2  Moore, K. (2003), "Great global managers," *Across the Board*, May–June, pp. 40–44; Gupta, A.K., and Govindarajan, V. (2002), "Cultivating a global mind set," *Academy of Management Executive*, 16 (1): 116–126.

3  Galbraith (1998).

4  Based on *ibid*.

5  Adapted from Evans, P.A.L. (1992), "Human Resource Management and Globalization," keynote address presented to the second international conference of the Western Academy of Management, Leuven, Belgium, June 24.

6  Evans *et al.* (2002); Galbraith (2000); Keys, J.B., and Fulmer, R.M. (eds) (1998), *Executive Development and Organizational Learning for Global Business*, New York: International Business Press; McCall, M.W., Jr, and Hollenbeck, G.P. (2002), *Developing Global Executives: The Lessons of International Experience*, Boston, MA: Harvard Business School Press.

7  Gupta, A.K., and Govindarajan, V. (2001), "Converting global presence into global competitive advantage," *Academy of Management Executive*, 15 (2): 45–58.

8  Evans (1992); Evans *et al.* (2002); Galbraith (2000).

9  Evans (1992).

10 Galbraith (2000), p. 1.
11 Trompenaars, F., and Hampden-Turner, C. (2001), "Cultural answers to global dilemmas," *Financial Times*, January 15, pp. 14–15.
12 *Ibid.*, p. 14.
13 *Ibid.*, p. 15.
14 Galbraith (1998), p. 129.
15 Based on Galbraith (2000).
16 This section draws heavily on three sources: Evans *et al.* (2002) and Galbraith (1998, 2000).
17 Most of these organization charts have been adapted from Galbraith (2000). For more on Black & Decker see Mendenhall, M., Black, J.S., Jensen, R.J., and Gregersen, H.B. (2003), "Human resource management challenges in the Age of Globalization," *Organizational Dynamics*, 32 (3): 261–274; also see Rugman, A.M., and Verbeke, A. (2004), "Regional and global strategies of multinational enterprise," *Journal of International Business*, March; and Rugman, A.M. (2003), "Regional strategy and the demise of globalization," *Journal of International Management*, 9: 409–417.
18 Anfuso, D. (1995), "Colgate's global HR unites under one strategy," *Personnel Journal*, October, pp. 44–54.
19 Hall, V. (2001), "International matrix management," *Worldlink*, 11 (1): 2–3.
20 See, for example, *ibid.*
21 Evans (1992); Evans *et al.* (2002); Galbraith (1998, 2000).
22 Evans (1992).
23 *Ibid.*, p. 4.
24 Armstrong D.J., and Cole, P. (1995), "Managing distances and differences in geographically distributed work groups" in Jackson, S.E., and Ruderman, M.N. (eds), *Diversity in Work Teams*, Washington, DC: American Psychological Association; Cascio, W.F. (2000), "Managing a virtual workplace," *Academy of Management Executive*, 14 (3): 81–90; Cramton, C.D. (2002), "Finding common ground in dispersed collaboration," *Organizational Dynamics*, 30 (4): 356–367; Distefano, J.J., and Maznevski, M.L. (2000), "Creating value with diverse teams in global management," *Organizational Dynamics*, 29 (1): 45–63; Duarte, D., and Snyder, N.T. (1999), *Mastering Virtual Teams*, San Francisco: Jossey Bass; Early, P.C., and Gibson, C.B. (2002), *Multinational Work Teams*, Mahwah, NJ: Laurence Erlbaum; Johnson, C. (2002), "Managing virtual teams," *HR Magazine*, June, pp. 69–73; Marquardt, M.J., and Horvath, L. (2001), *Global Teams: How Top Multinationals Span Boundaries and Cultures with High-speed Teams*, Palo Alto, CA: Davies Black; Maruca, R.F. (1998), "How do you manage an off-site team?" *Harvard Business Review*, July–August, pp. 22–35; Montoya-Weiss, M.M., Massey, A.P., and Song, M. (2001), "Getting it together: Temporal coordination and conflict management in global virtual teams," *Academy of Management Journal*, 44 (6): 1251–1262; Moran, R.T., Harris, P.R., and Stripp, W.G. (1993), *Developing the Global Organization*, Houston, TX: Gulf Publishing; Oldenwald, S.B. (1996), *Global Solutions for Teams: Moving from Collision to Collaboration*, Chicago: Irwin; Solomon, C.M. (1995), "Global teams: The ultimate collaboration," *Personnel Journal*, September, pp. 49–58; Solomon, C.M. (1998), "Building teams across borders," *Global Workforce*, November, pp. 12–17; Solomon, C.M. (2001), "Managing virtual teams," *Workforce*, June, pp. 60–65; Townsend, A.M., DeMarie, S.M., and Hendrickson, A.R. (1998), "Virtual teams: Technology and the workplace of the future," *Academy of Management Executive*, 12 (3): 17–29.
25 This section borrows heavily from Cascio (2000).
26 Marquardt and Horvath (2001); Moran *et al.* (1993); Odenwald (1996); O'Hara-Devereaux, M., and Johansen, R. (1994), *Globalwork: Bridging Distance, Culture, and Time*, San Francisco: Jossey Bass.
27 Duarte and Snyder (1999); O'Hara-Devereaux and Johansen (1994).

28  Schuler, R.S., Jackson, S.E., and Luo, Y. (2004), *Managing Human Resources in Cross-border Alliances*, London: Routledge.

29  Trapp, R. (1998), "Glaxo Wellcome's prescription for excellence," *HR World*, November–December, pp. 8–12.

30  Duarte and Snyder (1999).

31  Evans *et al.* (2002).

32  *Ibid.*, pp. 314–315.

33  Armstrong and Cole (1995); Cramton (2002); De Meyer, A. (1991), "Tech talk: How managers are stimulating global R&D communication," *Sloan Management Review*, 32 (3): 49–66.

34  This list is adapted from Solomon (1998, 2001) and Johnson (2002).

35  See, for example, Ahmed, P.K., Kok, L.K., and Loh, A.Y. (2002), *Learning through Knowledge Management*, Oxford: Butterworth Heinemann; Burgoyne, J., Pedler, M., and Boydell, T. (1994), *Towards the Learning Company*, London: McGraw-Hill; Cerny, K. (1996), "Making local knowledge global," *Harvard Business Review*, May–June, pp. 22–38; Choo, C.W. (1998), *The Knowing Organization*, Oxford: Oxford University Press; Davenport, T.H., and Prusak, L. (1998), *Working Knowledge: How Organizations Manage What they Know*, Boston, MA: Harvard Business School Press; Evans *et al.* (2002); Fuller, S. (2002), *Knowledge Management Foundations*, Boston, MA: Butterworth Heinemann; Leonard, D. (1998), *Wellsprings of Knowledge*, Boston, MA: Harvard Business School Press; Marquardt, M.J. (2002), *Building the Learning Organization*, 2nd edn, Palo Alto, CA: Davies Black; Marquardt, M., and Reynolds, A. (1994), *The Global Learning Organization*, Burr Ridge, IL: Irwin; Schwandt, D.R., and Marquardt, M.J. (2000), *Organizational Learning: From World-class Theories to Global Best Practices*, Boca Raton, FL: St Lucie Press; Sparrow, J. (1998), *Knowledge in Organizations*, London: Sage; Stewart, T.A. (1997), *Intellectual Capital: The New Wealth of Organizations*, New York: Doubleday Currency; Watkins, K.E., and Marsick, V.J. (1993), *Sculpting the Learning Organization*, San Francisco: Jossey Bass.

36  Daft, R. (2002), *The Leadership Experience*, 2nd edn, Orlando, FL: Harcourt, p. 582.

37  Prokesch, S.E. (1997), "Unleashing the power of learning: An interview with British Petroleum's John Browne," *Harvard Business Review*, September–October, p. 148.

38  Senge, P. (1990), *The Fifth Discipline*, New York: Doubleday Currency, p. 69.

39  Jackson, S.E., and Schuler, R.S. (2001), "Turning knowledge to business advantage," *Financial Times*, January 15, Special Section, Part Fourteen.

## 4 Cross-border mergers and acquisitions, international joint ventures and alliances

1  See, for example, Schuler, R.S., Jackson, S.E., and Luo, Y. (2004), *Managing Human Resources in Cross-border Alliances*, London: Routledge; KPMG International, *Dealwatch* (1997), Amsterdam, reported in Cartwright, S., "International M&As: The issues and challenges" in Gertsen, M.C., Siderberg, A.-M., and Torp, J.E. (eds) (1998), *Cultural Dimensions of International M&As*, Berlin: de Gruyter; United Nations (2000), *World Investment Report 2000: Cross-border Mergers and Acquisitions and Development*, New York and Geneva: United Nations Conference on Trade and Development.

2  United Nations (2000), p. 152, based on *Financial Times*, July 5, 2000, p. 15.

3  Reported in "*Fortune* 2001 Global 500: The world's largest corporations," *Fortune*, July 23, 2001, p. 144; "The great mergers wave breaks" (2001), *Economist*, January 27, pp. 59–60.

4  See, for example, Lester, T. (2001), "Merger most torrid," *Global HR*, June, pp. 10–12, 15–16.

5  Based on an interview with Heinrich von Pierer, CEO of Siemens, by Javidan, M. (2002), reported in "Siemens CEO Heinrich von Pierer on cross-border acquisitions," *Academy of*

*Management Executive*, 126 (1): 13–15; Karnitschnig, M. (2003), "For Siemens, move into US causes waves back home," *Wall Street Journal*, September 8, pp. A1, A8.

6  Kanter, R.M. (1989), "Becoming PALs: Pooling, allying, and linking across companies," *Academy of Management Executive*, 3 (3): 183–193; Kanter, R.M. (1994), "Collaborative advantage: The art of alliances," *Harvard Business Review*, July–August, pp. 96–108; Kanter, R.M. (1995), *World Class: Thriving Locally in the Global Economy*, New York: Simon & Schuster; and Marks, M.L. (1997), "Let's make a deal," *HR Magazine*, April, pp. 125–131.

7  McKinsey & Co., Coopers & Lybrand, and American Management Association, reported in Marks, M.L. (1997), *From Turmoil to Triumph: New Life after Mergers, Acquisitions, and Alliances*, New York: Lexington Books.

8  Reported in Bates, S. (2002), "Few business alliances succeed, report reveals," in Executive Briefing, *HR Magazine*, May, p. 12.

9  *Ibid.*

10  Bower, J.L. (2001), "Not all M&As are alike – and that matters," *Harvard Business Review*, March, pp. 93–101.

11  Beard, M., quoted in Bourne, S.R., "Merger misery," *Colorado Business*, October, 1996, p. 82.

12  Ohmae, K. (1989), "The global logic of strategic alliances," *Harvard Business Review*, March–April, p. 143.

13  A number of references have been published dealing with the management of mergers and acquisitions. These include: American Compensation Association (1998), *Out of the Vortex: Finding Order in Merger and Acquisition Chaos: A Guide for Compensation and Benefits Professionals*, Scottsdale, AZ: ACA; Ashkenas, R.N., DeMonaco, L.J., and Francis, S.C. (1998), "Making the deal real: How GE Capital integrates acquisitions," *Harvard Business Review*, January–February, pp. 165–178; Charman, A. (1999), *Global Mergers and Acquisitions: The Human Resource Challenge*, Alexandria, VA: Society for Human Resource Management Institute for International Human Resources International Focus; Clemente, M.N., and Greenspan, D.S. (1998), *Winning at Mergers and Acquisitions: The Guide to Market-focused Planning and Integration*, New York: Wiley; Clemente, M.N., and Greenspan, D.S. (1999), *Empowering Human Resources in the Merger and Acquisition Process: Guide for HR Professionals in the Key Areas of M&A Planning and Integration*, Glen Rock, NJ: Clemente Greenspan; Coffey, J., Garrow, V., and Holbeche, L. (2002), *Reaping the Benefits of Mergers and Acquisitions: In Search of the Golden Fleece*, Oxford: Butterworth Heinemann; Galpin, T.J., and Herndon, M. (2000), *The Complete Guide to Mergers and Acquisitions: Process Tools to Support M&A Integration at Every Level*, San Francisco: Jossey Bass; Gertsen, M.C., Siderberg, A.-M., and Torp, J.E. (eds) (1998), *Cultural Dimensions of International Mergers and Acquisitions*, Berlin: de Gruyter; Marks, M.L., and Mirvis, P.H. (2000), "Managing mergers, acquisitions, and alliances: Creating an effective transition structure," *Organizational Dynamics*, winter, pp. 35–47; Mirvis, P.H., and Marks, M.L. (1992), *Managing the Merger: Making it Work*, Englewood Cliffs, NJ: Prentice Hall; Morosim, P. (1998), *Cultural Differences: Effective Strategy and Execution across Cultures in Global Corporate Alliances*, Oxford: Pergamon Press; Rails, J.G., Jr, and Webb, K.A. (1999), *Mastering the Chaos of Mergers and Acquisitions: How to Plan, Negotiate, and Implement Alliances and Partnerships in a Complex World*, Houston, TX: Cashman Dudley; Schmidt, J.A. (ed.) (2002), *Making Mergers Work: The Strategic Importance of People*, Alexandria, VA: Towers Perrin and Society for Human Resource Management Foundation; Schuler, R.S., and Jackson, S.E. (2001), "HR issues and activities in mergers and acquisitions," *European Management Journal*, 19 (3): 239–253.

14  "Border crossings: Three CEOs talk about the dos and don'ts of international alliances," *Across the Board*, November–December, 1994, pp. 41–46; Champy, J. (1997), "Cultural clashes often underlie the urge to merge," *San Diego Business Journal*, July 21, p. 15; Davidson, M. (1996), "The siren call of mergers and acquisitions," *Across the Board*,

October, pp. 37–40; Frank, R., and Burton, T.M. (1997), "Cross-border merger results in headaches for a drug company," *Wall Street Journal*, February 4, pp. A1, A12; Marks (1997); Sunoo, B.P. (1995), "Wedding HR to strategic alliances," *Personnel Journal*, May, pp. 28–30, 32–34. In addition, look at the references in note 13.

15  Coffey *et al.* (2002), p. 9.

16  All of the major references in this chapter that involve mergers and acquisitions, joint ventures, and alliances expand on this point. In addition, some of this section is adapted from McClintock, F.W. (1996), "Due diligence and global expansion," *World Trade Center San Diego Newsletter*, p. 6; and Greengard, S. (1999), "Due diligence: The devil in the details," *Workforce*, October, pp. 68–72.

17  Adapted from Richard, L.J. (2001), "Joining forces," *Global HR*, June, p. 20.

18  Reported in Hopkins, M. (2002), "HR going global . . .," *Global HR*, April, pp. 31–33.

19  Bergh, D.D. (2001), "Executive retention and acquisition outcomes: A test of opposing views on the influence of organizational tenure," *Journal of Management*, 27 (5): 603–622.

20  *Ibid.*

21  Adapted from Kleppesti, S. (1998), "A quest for social identity: The pragmatics of communication in mergers and acquisitions," in Gertsen *et al.*, pp. 147–166.

22  Berry, J.W. (1980), "Acculturation as varieties of adaptation" in Padilla, A.M. (ed.), *Acculturation Theory, Models and Some New Findings*, Boulder, CO: Westview Press; Gertsen, M.C., Siderberg, A.-M, and Torp, J.E. (1998), "Different approaches to the understanding of culture in mergers and acquisitions," in Gertsen *et al.* (1998), pp. 17–38.

23  Gertsen, Siderberg, and Torp (1998).

24  Adapted from Ashkenas *et al.* (1998).

25  See, for example, Owen, G., and Harrison, T. (1995), "Why ICI chose to demerge," *Harvard Business Review*, March–April, pp. 133–142.

26  "M&A cultural considerations," reported in *International Mobility Management Newsletter*, second quarter, 2001, p. 7.

27  Schuler *et al.* (2004); Schuler, R., Tarique, I., and Jackson, S. (2004), "Managing human resources in cross-border alliances" in Cooper, C., and Finkelstein, S. (eds), *Advances in Mergers and Acquisitions*, IV, New York: JAI Press.

28  Schenkar, O., and Zeira, Y. (1987), "Human resources management in international joint ventures: Directions for research," *Academy of Management Review*, 12 (3): 547.

29  Schuler *et al.* (2004); Cyr, D.J. (1995), *The Human Resource Challenge of International Joint Ventures*, Westport, CT: Quorum Books.

30  See, for example, Cyr (1995); Frayne, C.A. and Geringer, J.M. (2000), "Challenges facing general managers of international joint ventures" in Mendenhall, M., and Oddou, G. (eds), *Readings and Cases in International Human Resource Management*, 3rd edn, Cincinnati, OH: Southwestern College Publishing; Geringer, J.M. (1988a), *Joint Venture Partner Selection: Strategies for Developed Countries*, Westport, CT: Quorum Books; Lu, P.X. (2002), "The joint venture organization: The Chinese model" in Jackson, T. (ed.), *International HRM: A Cross-cultural Approach*, London: Sage; Schuler, R.S. (2001), "Human resource issues and activities in international joint ventures," *International Journal of Human Resource Management*, 12 (1): 1–52; Schuler, R., Dowling, P., and De Cieri, H. (1992), "The formation of an international joint venture: Marley Automotive Components," *European Management Journal*, 10 (3): 304–309; Schuler, R.S., Jackson, S.E., Dowling, P.J., and Welch, D.E. (1991), "The formation of an international joint venture: Davidson Instrument Panel" in Mendenhall, M., and Oddou, G. (eds), *Readings and Cases in International Human Resource Management*, Boston, MA: PWS-Kent; Schuler *et al.* (2004); Shenkar, O., and Zeira, Y. (1987), "Human resource management in international joint ventures: Directions for research," *Academy of Management Review*, 12 (3): 546–557.

31  Hladik, K.J. (1985), *International Joint Ventures: An Economic Analysis of US Foreign Business Partnerships*, Lexington, MA: Heath; Liebman, H.M. (1975), *US and Foreign*

*Taxation of Joint Ventures*, Washington, DC: Office of Tax Analysis, US Treasury Department.

32  Barkema, H.G., Shenkar, O., Vermeulen, F., and Bell, J.H.J. (1997), "Working abroad, working with others: How firms learn to operate international joint ventures," *Academy of Management Journal*, 40 (2): 426–442.

33  This list draws heavily on Schuler (2001). See also: Child, J., and Faulkner, D. (1998), *Strategies of Cooperation*, Oxford: Oxford University Press; Culpan, R. (2002), *Global Business Alliances*, Westport, CT: Quorum Books; Cyr (1995); Gomes-Casseres, B. (1989), "Joint ventures in the face of global competition," *Sloan Management Review*, 30 (1): 17–26; Gomes-Casseres, B. (1996), *The Alliance Revolution: The New Shape of Business*, Cambridge, MA: Harvard University Press; Hamel, G., Doz, Y., and Prahalad, C.K. (1989), "Collaborate with your competitors and win," *Harvard Business Review*, January–February, pp. 133–139; Harbison (1996) *Strategic Alliances: Gaining a Competitive Advantage*, New York: Conference Board, Inkpen, A.C. and Dinur, A. (1998), "Knowledge management process and international joint ventures," *Organization Studies*, 9: 454–468. Newburry, W., and Zeira, Y. (1997), "Implications for parent companies," *Journal of World Business*, 32 (2): 87–102; Porter, M.E. (1990), *Competitive Advantage of Nations*, New York: Free Press; Pucik, V. (1988), "Strategic alliances, organizational learning and competitive advantage: The HRM agenda," *Human Resource Management*, 27 (1): 77–93; Shenkar and Zeira (1987); Lei, D., Slocum, J.W., Jr, *et al.* (1997), "Building competitive advantage: Managing strategic alliances to promote organizational learning," *Journal of World Business*, 32 (3): 203–223; Sparks, D. (1999), "Partners," *Business Week*, October 5, p. 106.

34  Cyr (1995), p. 116.

35  Petrovic, J., and Kakabadse, N.K. (2003), "Strategic staffing of international joint ventures (IJVS): An integrative perspective for future research," *Management Decision*, 41 (4): 394–407; Cyr (1995); Geringer, J.M. (1988b), "Partner selection criteria for developed country joint ventures," *Business Quarterly*, 53 (1): 79–90; Schuler *et al.* (2004).

36  Beamish, P.W. (1985), "The characteristics of joint ventures in developed and developing countries," *Columbia Journal of World Business*, 20 (3): 13–19; Harbison, J.R. (1996); Harrigan, K.R. (1986), *Managing for Joint Venture Success*, Boston, MA: Lexington Books; Shenkar and Zeira (1987); Sparks (1999).

37  Shenkar and Zeira (1987), p. 546.

38  Adapted from Barkema, H., and Vermeulan, F. (1997), "What differences in the cultural backgrounds of partners are detrimental for international joint ventures?" *Journal of International Business Studies*, 28 (4): 845–864; Harrigan, K.R. (1988), "Strategic alliances and partner asymmetries" in Contractor, F., and Lorange, P. (eds), *Cooperative Strategies in International Business*, Lexington, MA: Lexington Books; Park, S.H., and Russo, M.V. (1996), "When competition eclipses cooperation: An event history analysis of joint venture failure," *Management Science*, 42 (6): 875–890; Schuler (2001); Goodman, N.R. (2001), "International Joint Ventures and Overseas Subsidiaries," presented at the Society for Human Resource Management Global Forum Audio Conference, December; Cyr (1995); Yan, A., and Zeng, M. (1999), "International joint venture instability: A critique of previous research, a reconceptualization, and directions for future research," *Journal of International Business Studies*, 30 (2): 397–414.

39  Harrigan (1986).

40  Cyr (1995); Geringer (1988), *Joint Venture Partner Selection*; Schuler *et al.* (2004).

41  Cascio, W.F., and Serapio, M.G. (1991), "Human resource systems in an international alliance: The undoing of a done deal?" *Organizational Dynamics*, winter, pp. 63–74; Cyr (1995); Schuler *et al.* (2004).

42  Bruton, G.D., and Samiee, S. (1998), "Anatomy of a failed high technology strategic alliance," *Organizational Dynamics*, summer, pp. 51–63; Cascio and Serapio (1991); Culpan, R. (2002), *Global Business Alliances: Theory and Practice*, Westport, CT:

Quorum Books; Evans, P., Pucik, V., and Barsoux, J.-L. (2002), *The Global Challenge: Frameworks for International Human Resource Management*, New York: McGraw-Hill; Fedor, K.J., and Werther, W.B., Jr (1996), "The fourth dimension: Creating culturally responsive international alliances," *Organizational Dynamics*, autumn, pp. 39–53; Inkpen, A.C. (1998), "Learning and knowledge acquisition through international strategic alliances," *Academy of Management Executive*, 12 (4): 69–80; Isabella, L.A. (2002), "Managing an alliance is nothing like business as usual," *Organizational Dynamics*, 31 (1): 47–59; Kanter (1989, 1994); Ohmae, K. (1989), "The global logic of strategic alliances," *Harvard Business Review*, March–April, pp. 143–154; Parkhe, A. (1998), "Understanding trust in international alliances," *Journal of World Business*, 33 (3): 219–240; Parkhe, A. (1998), "Building trust in international alliances," *Journal of World Business*, 33 (4): 417–437; Sunoo (1995), p. 36.

43  Schifrin, M. (2001), "Best of the web: Partner or perish," *Forbes*, May 21, pp. 26–28.

44  *Ibid*.

45  *Ibid*.

46  Reported in "You are not alone," *Fortune*, special advertising section, May, 2001, pp. S2–S3.

47  Harbison, J., and Pekar, P. (1998), *Smart Alliances*, New York: Jossey Bass.

48  See, for example, Burt, D.N., and Doyle, M.F. (1993), *The American Keiretsu: A Strategic Weapon for Global Competitiveness*, Homewood, IL: Business One Irwin; Ungson, G.R., Steers, R.M., and Park, S.-H. (1997), *Korean Enterprise: The Quest for Globalization*, Boston, MA: Harvard Business School Press.

49  Michaels, J.W. (2001), "Best of the web: Don't buy, bond instead," *Forbes*, May 21, p. 20.

50  Adapted from Applegate, J. (1996), "Alliances quick way to grow: Links to Bombay firm open doors for architect," *Denver Business Journal*, October 4–10, p. 3B.

51  Galbraith, J.R., (2000), *Designing the Global Corporation*, San Francisco: Jossey Bass.

52  See, for example, Cascio and Serapio (1991); Fedor and Werther (1996); Isabella (2002); Schuler *et al.* (2004); Sunoo (1995).

53  Demby, E.R. (2002), "Keeping partnerships on course," *HR Magazine*, December, pp. 49–53.

54  Isabella (2002).

55  Quoted in Demby (2002), p. 50.

# 5 Country culture and MNE culture

1  Source: *The World Competitiveness Report 1995*, by the World Economic Forum and the International Institute for Management Development, reported in *World Business*, January–February, 1996, p. 15. See updates on the *World Competitiveness Yearbook* at www.imd.ch/wcy/ and www.weforum.org.

2  Schell, M.S., and Solomon, C.M. (1997), *Capitalizing on the Global Workforce*, Chicago: Irwin, p. 9. Also see Schneider, S.C., and Barsoux, J.L. (1997), *Managing across Cultures*, New York: Prentice Hall; Earley, P.C., and Erez, M. (eds) (1997), *New Perspectives in International Industrial/Organizational Psychology*, San Francisco: New Lexington Press.

3  Schell and Solomon (1997), p. 8.

4  See, for example, Moore, K. (2003), "Great global managers," *Across the Board*, May–June, pp. 40–44; Black, J.S., Gregersen, H.B., and Mendenhall, M.E. (1992), *Global Assignments: Successfully Expatriating and Repatriating International Managers*, San Francisco: Jossey Bass, chapter 2; Hofstede, G. (1991), *Cultures and Organizations: Software of the Mind*, Maidenhead: McGraw-Hill, chapter 1; Trompenaars, F. (1992/1993), *Riding the Waves of Culture: Understanding Diversity in Global Business*, Burr Ridge, IL: Irwin, chapter 1.

5 Adapted from Black *et al.* (1992) and Hodge, S. (2000), *Global Smarts: The Art of Communicating and Deal-making Anywhere in the World*, New York: Wiley, chapter 3.

6 See, for example, Schell and Solomon (1997); Hofstede (1991); Trompenaars (1992/1993).

7 McCall, M.W., Jr, and Hollenbeck, G.P. (2002), *Developing Global Executives: The Lessons of International Experience*, Boston, MA: Harvard Business School Press.

8 Hofstede, G. (1980), *Culture's Consequences: International Differences in Work-related Values*, Beverly Hills, CA, and London: Sage; Hofstede (1991); Hofstede, G. (2001), *Culture and Organizations: Comparing Values, Behaviors, Institutions and Organizations across Nations*, 2nd edn, Thousand Oaks, CA: Sage; Hofstede, G. (2002), "Cultural constraints in management theories," *CRN News*, 7 (4): 1–3, 12–13, 16, 19, 22–23.

9 See, for example, Hofstede, G. (1984), "Clustering countries on attitudinal dimensions: A review and synthesis," *Academy of Management Review*, 9 (3): 389–398; Hofstede, G. (1983), "The cultural relativity of organizational theories," *Journal of International Business Studies*, 14 (2): 75–90.

10 Saari, L. and Schneider, B. (2001), "Global employee surveys: Practical considerations and insights," paper presented at Going Global: Surveys and Beyond, Workshop at the Annual Conference, Society of Industrial/Organizational Psychology, San Diego, April.

11 Trompenaars, F. (1992/1993); Hampden-Turner, C., and Trompenaars, A. (1993), *The Seven Cultures of Capitalism*, New York: Currency Doubleday.

12 Trompenaars (1992/1993), pp. 31–32.

13 To learn more about GLOBE see Javidan, M., and House, R.J. (2000), "Cultural acumen for the global manager," *Organizational Dynamics* 29 (4): 289–305; GLOBE Research Team (2002), *Culture, Leadership, and Organizational Practices: The GLOBE Findings*, Thousand Oaks, CA: Sage. Also see Earley, P.C., and Erez, M. (1997), *The Transplanted Executive*, New York: Oxford University Press; Schell and Solomon (1997); Triandis, H.C. (1998), "Vertical and horizontal individualism and collectivism: Theory and research implications for international comparative management," *Advances in International Comparative Management*, XII, Greenwich, CT: JAI Press, 7–35.

14 Saari, L., and Schneider, B. (2001).

15 *Ibid.*

16 Ronen, S., and Shenkar, O. (1985), "Clustering countries on attitudinal dimensions: A review and synthesis," *Academy of Management Review*, 10 (3): 435–454; Ronen, S., and Shenkar, O. (1988), "Using employee attitudes to establish MNC regional divisions," *Personnel*, August, pp. 32–39.

17 See, for example, Earley and Erez (1997); Gesteland, R.R. (1999), *Cross-cultural Business Behavior: Marketing, Negotiating and Managing across Cultures*, Copenhagen, Denmark: Copenhagen Business School Press; Hodge (2000); Scherer, C.W. (2000), *The Internationalists*, Wilsonville, OR: Book Partners.

18 Hofstede; Trompenaars (2001); Trompenaars (1992/1993); Triandis (1998); Schell and Solomon (1997).

19 See, for example, Morrison, T., Conaway, W.A., and Borden, G.A. (1994), *Kiss, Bow, or Shake Hands*, Holbrook, MA: Bob Adams.

20 *Ibid.*

21 Gesteland (1999).

22 Brannen, M.Y. (1999), "The many faces of cultural data," *AIB Newsletter*, first quarter, pp. 6–7.

23 *Ibid.*

24 See, for example, all the works by Tom Peters, such as Peters, T., and Waterman, B. (1982), *In Search of Excellence*, New York: Harper & Row; Peters, T. (1992), *Liberation Management*, New York: Knopf; Peters, T. (1997), *The Circle of Innovation*, New York: Knopf; and Collins, J., and Porras, J. (1996), *Built to Last*, New York: Harper.

25 Lubatkin, M.H., Ndiaye, M., and Vengroff, R. (1997), "The nature of managerial work in developing countries: A limited test of the universalist hypothesis," *Journal of International Business Studies*, fourth quarter, pp. 711–733.

26 *International Herald Tribune*, December 1, 1989: 7.

27 *Ibid*.

28 Trompenaars, F., and Hampden-Turner, C. (2001), "Cultural answers to global dilemmas," *Financial Times*, January 15, p. 14.

29 Schuler, R.S., Jackson, S.E., and Luo, Y. (2004), *Managing Human Resources in Cross-border Alliances*, London and New York: Routledge.

30 Pierce, B., and Garvin, G. (1995), "Publishing international business research: A survey of leading journals," *Journal of International Business Studies*, 26 (1): 69–89.

31 Adler, N.J. (1983), "Cross-cultural management research: The ostrich and the trend," *Academy of Management Review*, 8 (2): 226–232; Pierce and Garvin (1995).

32 Boyacigiller, N., and Adler, N.J. (1991), "The parochial dinosaur: Organizational science in a global context," *Academy of Management Review*, 16 (2): 262–290.

33 Thomas, A.S., Shenkar, O., and Clarke, L. (1994), "The globalization of our mental maps: Evaluating the geographic scope of JIBS coverage," *Journal of International Business Studies*, 25 (4): 675–686.

34 *Ibid*.; Hickson, D.J. (1996), "The ASQ years then and now through the eyes of a Euro-Brit," *Administrative Science Quarterly*, 41 (2): 217–228.

35 Inkpen, A., and Beamish, P. (1994), "An analysis of twenty-five years of research in the *Journal of International Business Studies*," *Journal of International Business Studies*, 25 (4): 703–713; Melin, L. (1992), "Internationalization as a strategy process," *Strategic Management Journal*, 13: 99–118; Parker, B. (1998), *Globalization and Business Practice: Managing across Borders*, Thousand Oaks, CA: Sage; Thomas *et al.* (1994).

36 Dowling, P.J. (1988), "International HRM" in L. Dyer (ed.), *Human Resource Management: Evolving Roles and Responsibilities*, Washington, DC: Bureau of National Affairs; Earley, P.C., and Singh, S.H. (2000), "Introduction: New approaches to international and cross-cultural management research" in Earley, P.C., and Singh, S.H. (eds), *Innovations in International Cross-cultural Management*, Thousand Oaks, CA: Sage; McEvoy, G.M., and Buller, P.F. (1993), "New Directions in International Human Resource Management Research," paper presented at the Academy of International Business annual meeting, Maui, HI, October 21–24; Tayeb, M. (2001), "Conducting research across cultures: Overcoming drawbacks and obstacles," *International Journal of Cross-cultural Management*, 1 (1): 91–108; Triandis (1998).

37 See, for example, Dowling, P.J., Welch, D.E., and Schuler, R.S. (1999), *International Human Resource Management*, 3rd edn, Cincinnati, OH: Southwestern College Publishing, appendix A; Graen, G.B., Hui, C., Wakabayashi, M., and Z.-M. Wang (1997), "Cross-cultural research alliances in organizational research" in Earley, P.C., and Erez, M. (eds), *New Perspectives on International Industrial/Organizational Psychology*, San Francisco: New Lexington Press; Mattl, C. (1999), "Qualitative research strategies in international HRM," in Brewster, C., and Harris, H. (eds), *International HRM: Contemporary Issues in Europe*, London: Routledge; Schuler, R.S., and Florkowski, G.W. (1998), "International human resource management" in Shenkar, O., and Punnett, B.J. (eds), *Handbook of International Management Research*, London: Blackwell; Teagarden, M.B., Von Glinow, M.A., Bowen, D.E., Frayne, C.A. *et al.* (1995), "Toward a theory of comparative management research: An idiographic case study of the best international human resources management project," *Academy of Management Journal*, 38 (5): 1261–1287; Von Glinow, M.A., and Chung, B.J. (1989), "Comparative human resource practices in the United States, Japan, Korea, and the People's Republic of China," in *Research in Personnel and Human Resources Management*, Supplement 1, Greenwich, CT: JAI Press.

38 See, for example, Aycan, Z., Kanungo, R.N., Mendonca, M., Yu, K., Deller, J., Stahl, G., and Kurshid, A. (2000), "Impact of culture on human resource management practices: A ten-country comparison," *Applied Psychology: An International Review*, 49, pp. 192–221.

39 Caligiuri, P.M. (1999), "The ranking of scholarly journals in the field of international human resource management," *International Journal of Human Resource Management*, 10 (3): 515–518; House, R.H., Hanges, P.J., Antonio Ruiz-Quintanilla, S., Dorfman, P.W., Javidan, M., Dickson, M., Gupta, V., and GLOBE Country Co-investigators (1999), "Cultural influences on leadership and organizations: Project GLOBE," in Mobley, W.H., Gessner, M.J., and Arnold, V. (eds), *Advances in Global Leadership*, I, Stamford, CT: JAI Press; House, R.J., Wright, N.S., and Aditya, R.N. (1997), "Cross-cultural research on organizational leadership: A critical analysis and a proposed theory," in Earley, P.C., and Erez, M. (eds), *New Perspectives on International Industrial/Organizational Psychology*, San Francisco: New Lexington Press.

40 Saari, L., and Schneider, B. (2001), "Global Employee Surveys: Practical Considerations and Insights," paper presented at "Going Global: Surveys and Beyond," workshop at the annual conference of the Society for Industrial/Organizational Psychology, San Diego, CA, April.

41 *Ibid.*

42 Lubatkin *et al.* (1997) tests these three hypotheses. Also see Sparrow, P., Brewster, C., and Harris, H. (2004), *Globalizing Human Resource Management*, London: Routledge.

43 Punnett, B.J., and Shenkar, O., (eds) (1996), *Handbook for International Management Research*, Cambridge, MA: Blackwell.

44 Dowling *et al.* (1999); Berry, J.W. (1980), "Introduction to methodology" in Triandis, H.C., and Berry, J.W. (eds), *Handbook of Cross-cultural Psychology*, II, Methodology, Boston, MA: Allyn & Bacon; De Cieri, H., and Dowling, P.J. (1995), "Cross-cultural issues in organizational behavior" in Cooper, C.L., and D.M. Rousseau (eds), *Trends in Organizational Behavior* II, Chichester: Wiley; Graen *et al.* (1997); Teagarden, M.B., and Von Glinow, M.A. (1997), "Human resource management in cross-cultural contexts: Emic practices versus etic philosophies," *Management International Review*, special issue, 37 (1): 7–20.

45 Harbison, F. (1959), "Management in Japan" in Harbison, F., and Myers, C.A. (eds), *Management in the Industrial World: An International Analysis*, New York: McGraw-Hill.

46 Mullen, M.R. (1995), "Diagnosing measurement equivalence in cross-national research," *Journal of International Business Studies*, 15 (3): 573–596.

47 Cavusgil, S.T., and Das, A. (1997), "Methodological issues in empirical cross-cultural research: A survey of the management literature and a framework," *Management International Review*, 37 (1): 81.

48 *Ibid.*; Douglas, S.P., and Craig, S. (1983), *International Marketing Research*, Englewood Cliffs, NJ: Prentice Hall; Samiee, S., and Jeong, I. (1994), "Cross-cultural research in advertising: An assessment of methodologies," *Journal of the Academy of Marketing Science*, 22 (3): 205–217.

49 See, for example, Mullen (1995).

50 Yu, J.H., Keown, C.F., and Jacobs, L.W. (1993), "Attitude scale methodology: Cross-cultural implications," *Journal of International Consumer Marketing*, 6 (2): 45–64.

51 Atiyyah, H.S. (1992), "Research Note: Research in Arab countries, published in Arabic," *Organization Studies*, 13 (1): 105–110.

52 See, for example, Mattl (1999).

## 6 Global employment law, and labor relations

1 There are only limited reference works available for information about employment laws on a global basis. Other than individual articles in mostly the practitioner and consultant press, these general references include the following: Bamber, J., Lansbury, D., and

Wailes, N. (2003), *International and Comparative Employment Relations: Globalisation and the Developed Market Economies*, Sydney: Allen & Unwin; Keller, W.L., (ed.) (1997, with extensive annual updates), *International Labor and Employment Laws*, Washington, DC: Bureau of National Affairs, for the International Labor Law Committee of the Section on Labor and Employment Law of the American Bar Association; Maatman, G.L., Jr (ed.) (2000), *Worldwide Guide to Termination, Employment Discrimination, and Workplace Harassment Laws*, Chicago, IL: Baker & McKenzie; Feu, V.D., Edmunds, V., Gillow, E., and Hopkins, M., (eds) (2000, plus annual updates), *EU and International Employment Law*, Bristol: Jordan's, for Evershed's. Watch for G. Florkowski (forthcoming), *Managing Global Legal Systems*, London: Routledge.

2 Much of the information in this section comes from documents of the International Labour Organization, Geneva, Switzerland, such as the report on International Organizations by the Working Party on the Social Dimensions of the Liberalization of International Trade.

3 Berkowitz, P.M. (2003), "Avoidance of Risks and Liabilities through effective Corporate Compliance," paper presented at the fourth Annual Program on International Labor and Employment Law, Center for American and International Law, Dallas, TX, September 10.

4 See, for example, the *World Investment Report* (most recent edition 2004), published by UNCTAD. Refer to the UNCTAD web site at littp://www.unctad.org for information on UNCTAD's work and for access to extensive data about various countries and transnational corporations.

5 Berkowitz (2003).

6 *Ibid.*; Keller (1997, with annual updates).

7 Murphy, E.E., Jr (2001), "The World Trade Organization," in Keller, W.L. (ed.), *International Labor and Employment Laws*, 2001 cumulative supplement to Vol. I, Washington, DC: Bureau of National Affairs and International Labor Law Committee Section of Labor and Employment Law of the American Bar Association, pp. 44–113.

8 See, for example, Nielsen, R., and Szyszczak, E. (1997), *The Social Dimension of the European Union*, 3rd edn, Copenhagen: Handelshøjskolens Forlag/Copenhagen Business School Press.

9 Manley, T., and Lauredo, L. (2003), "International Labor Standards in Free-trade Agreements of the Americas," paper delivered at the fourth Annual Program on International Labor and Employment Law, Center for American and International Law, Dallas, TX, September 30–October 1.

10 See, for example, Baker and McKenzie (2001), *Worldwide Guide to Trade Unions and Works Councils*, Chicago, IL: Commerce Clearing House.

11 Fox, A. (2003), "To consult and inform," *HR Magazine*, October, pp. 87–92.

12 *Ibid.*

13 Adapted from International Labour Organization (2000), *Termination of Employment Digest: A Legislative Review*, Geneva: author; Shillingford, J. (1999), "Goodbye, adios, sayonara," *HR World*, July–August, pp. 27–31 (data on separation practices from Drake Beam Morin).

14 "Employee dismissals can prove costly for companies in Europe," *HR Focus*, August 18, 1992.

15 Hall, L. (2001a), "Protecting your vital assets," *Global HR*, July–August, pp. 46–52.

16 Quoted in Hall (2001a), pp. 46–47.

17 Adapted from *ibid.*

18 *Ibid.*, p. 52.

19 See, for example, Baker and McKenzie (2000), *Worldwide Guide to Termination, Employment Discrimination, and Workplace Harassment Laws*, Chicago, IL: Commerce Clearing House; Conway, M.E. (1998), "Sexual harassment abroad," *Global Workforce*, September, pp. 8–9; Javaid, M. (2002), "Race for knowledge," *Global HR*, November, pp. 59–60; Keller (1997, and annual updates); Mackay, R., and Cormican, D. (2002), "The trouble with religion," *Global HR*, December–January, pp. 26–30.

20  Adapted from a table prepared by Paskoff, S.M. (2003), "Comparison of international employment laws," appendix to his paper "Around the World without the Daze: Communicating International Codes of Conduct," presented at the fourth Annual Program on International Labor and Employment Law, Center for American and International Law, Dallas, TX, September 30–October 1.

21  Hall, L. (2001b), "Data dangers," *Global HR*, October, pp. 24–28; Kremer-Jones, B. (2002), "Think before you send," *Global HR*, July–August, pp. 52–59; "Protecting the privacy of employees based in Europe," *SHRM Global Perspectives*, 1, 1 (2000): 1, 6–7 (originally published in *HR Wire*, by the West Group).

22  "Are you EU privacy-compliant?" (2000) *International Update* (newsletter of the SHRM Institute for International HRM, now the SHRM Global Forum), 3: 10; Martinez, M.N. (1999) "European law aims to protect employee data," *International Update* (newsletter of the SHRM Institute for International HRM, now the SHRM Global Forum), 1: 1, 3; Minehan, M. (2001), "Complying with the European Privacy Data Directive," *SHRM Global Perspective*, 5: 1, 6–8; Minehan, M., and Overman, S. (2000), "Companies to begin EU safe harbor registration," *HR News*, 19 (12): 1–2; Wellbery, B.S., and Warrington, J.P. (2001), *EU Data Protection Requirements and Employee Data,* International Focus White Paper of the SHRM Global Forum, Alexandria, VA: Society for Human Resource Management; Wellbery, B.S., Warrington, J.P., and Howell, R. (2002), "EU data protection requirements: An overview for employers," *Employment Law*, 14 (1): 1–12.

23  Darby, T.J. (2001), "Extraterritorial application of US laws" in Keller, W.L. (ed.), *International Labor and Employment Laws*, 2001 cumulative supplement to Vol. I, Washington, DC: Bureau of National Affairs and the International Labor Law Committee Section of Labor and Employment Law of the American Bar Association, pp. 50–74.

24  Bamber, G.J., and Lansbury, R.D. (eds) (1998), *International and Comparative Employment Relations*, 3rd edn, London: Sage; Rothman, M., Briscoe, D.R., and Nacamulli, R.C.D. (eds) (1992), *Industrial Relations around the World: Labor Relations for Multinational Companies*, Berlin: de Gruyter.

25  Excerpted from a presentation by David Killinger, Director, International Labor Affairs, on Ford Motor Company's global labor relations, delivered at the Faculty Development Seminar on International HRM at the University of Colorado, Denver, June 8, 2000.

26  Newman, B. (1983), "Border dispute: Single-country unions of Europe try to cope with multinationals," *Wall Street Journal*, November 30, pp. 1, 22.

27  Blanpain, R. (1977), *The Badger Case and the OECD Guidelines for Multinational Enterprises*, Deventer, Netherlands: Kluwer; Blanpain, R. (1979), *The OECD Guidelines for Multinational Enterprises and Labour Relations, 1976–1979: Experience and Review*, Deventer, Netherlands: Kluwer; Campbell, D.C., and Rowan, R.L. (1983), *Multinational Enterprises and the OECD Industrial Relations Guideline*, Philadelphia: Industrial Relations Research Unit of the Wharton School, University of Pennsylvania; Jain, H.C. (1980), "Disinvestment and the multinational employer: A case history from Belgium," *Personnel Journal*, 59 (3): 201–205.

28  Rothman *et al.* (1992); Levinson, D.L., Jr, and Maddox, R.C. (1982), "Multinational corporations and labor relations: Changes in the wind?" *Personnel*, May–June, pp. 70–77.

29  Upham, M. (1999), *Trade Unions and Employers' Organizations of the World*, Harlow: Longman.

30  McCullough, G.B. (1977), "Comment," in Banks, R.F., and Stieber, J. (eds), *Multinationals, Unions, and Labor Relations in Industrialized Countries*, Ithaca, NY: New York State School of Industrial and Labor Relations, Cornell University, p. 150, quoted in Grosse, R., and Kujawa, D. (1995), *International Business*, 3rd edn, Chicago: Irwin, p. 436.

31  Bamber and Lansbury (1998); Rothman *et al.* (1992).

32  Paskoff (2003).

## 7 Global ethics and labor standards

1 Digh, P. (1997), "Shades of gray in the global marketplace," *HR Magazine*, April, pp. 91–98; Kumar, B.N., and Steinmann, H. (eds) (1998), *Ethics in International Management*, Berlin: de Gruyter; Gesteland, R.R. (1999), *Cross-cultural Business Behavior*, Copenhagen, Denmark: Copenhagen Business School Press; Morgan, E. (1998), *Navigating Cross-cultural Ethics: What Global Managers Do Right to Keep from Going Wrong*, Oxford: Butterworth Heinemann; Sweeney, J.J. (1998), "Making the Global Economy work for America," presentation by the president of the AFL-CIO to the Economic Strategy Institute Conference, May 5, http://www.aflclo.org/publ/speech98/spO5O5.htm.

2 Donaldson, T. (1996), "Values in tension: Ethics away from home," *Harvard Business Review*, September–October, pp. 48–62; Singer, A.W. (1991), "Ethics: Are standards lower overseas?" *Across the Board*, September, pp. 31–34.

3 Schlegelmilch, B.B., and Robertson, D.C. (1995), "The influence of country and industry on ethical perceptions of senior executives in the US and Europe," *Journal of International Business Studies*, fourth quarter, pp. 859–881.

4 Buller, P.F., and McEvoy, G.M. (1999), "Creating and sustaining ethical capability in the multinational corporation," *Journal of World Business*, 34 (4): 326–343.

5 Fleming, J.E. (1997), "Problems in teaching international ethics," *Academy of Management News*, March, p. 17; Armstrong, R.W. (1996), "The relationship between culture and perception of ethical problems in international marketing," *Journal of Business Ethics*, 15 (11): 1199–1208.

6 The story was related in Digh (1997).

7 This section is adapted from Fisher, C.D., Shoenfeldt, L.F., and Shaw, J.B. (1993), *Human Resource Management*, 2nd edn, Boston, MA: Houghton Mifflin. Original sources: Stace, W.T. (1988), "Ethical relativity and ethical absolutism" in Donaldson, T., and Werhane, P.H. (eds), *Ethical Issues in Business*, Englewood Cliffs, NJ: Prentice Hall; Shaw, W., and Barry, V. (1989), *Moral Issues in Business*, Belmont, CA: Wadsworth; Donaldson, T. (1989), *The Ethics of International Business*, New York: Oxford University Press.

8 Buller and McEvoy (1999).

9 See, for example, Donaldson (1996).

10 Donaldson (1989), p. 103.

11 *Ibid.*, p. 104.

12 This is adapted from a presentation at the annual conference of the Institute for International Human Resource Management by G. Wederspahn (1998), "International Business Ethics," Dallas, TX, April 8.

13 This section is adapted from *International Labor Standards: A Strategic Issues Brief* (1996), Alexandria, VA: Society for Human Resource Management.

14 Reported in "News in Brief. Rights at work: ILO to monitor compliance," *Worldlink*, summer, 2000, p. 3.

15 De George, R.T. (1993), *Competing with Integrity in International Business*, New York: Oxford University Press; Hausman, C. (1996), "Ethics issues circle the globe," *Insights on Global Ethics*, 6 (3): 1, 5.

16 "Bribes can cost the US an edge," *Business Week*, April 15, 1996, p. 30; "Foreign practices: Bribery and pressure tactics are costing American business overseas," *Across the Board*, October, 1996, pp. 11–12; Kaltenheuser, S. (1998), "Schmiergeld," *Across the Board*, November–December, pp. 36–42.

17 Kidder, R.M. (1995), "Measures of corruption," *Insights on Global Ethics*, 5 (8): 2; also related in Jebb, F. (1998), "Moral mazes," *HR World*, November–December, pp. 27–29.

18 Wiehen, M.H. (1998), "Corruption in international business relations: Problems and solutions" in Kumar, B.N., and Steinmann, H. (eds), *Ethics in International Management*, Berlin: de Gruyter.

19 A good overview of this subject can be found in *ibid*. Other references include: "Bribes can cost the US an edge," *Business Week*, April 15, 1996, p. 30; "Foreign practices: Bribery and pressure tactics are costing American business overseas," *Across the Board*, October, 1996, pp. 11–12; "International attention turns to corruption," *Workplace Visions* (Society for Human Resource Management), July–August, 1998, pp. 4–5; James, B. (1997), "OECD takes a first step in the battle over bribery," *International Herald Tribune*, May 29, p. 11; Kaltenheuser (1998); Minehan, M. (1998), "International attention turns to corruption," *HR Magazine*, March, p. 152; Patel, T. (1996), "US seeks to end greasing of palms," *Journal of Commerce*, May 3, pp. 1A, 3A; Webley, S. (1998), "The Interfaith Declaration: Context, issues and problems of application of a code of ethics for international business among those of three major religions" in Kumar, B.N., and Steinmann, H. (eds), *Ethics in International Management*, Berlin: de Gruyter.

20 James (1997); Patel (1996); "International attention turns to corruption," *Workplace Visions*, July–August, 1998, pp. 4–5; Minehan (1998); Kaltenheuser (1998).

21 A good discussion of this issue can be found in Gesteland (1999) and in Wiehen (1998).

22 See, e.g., Dale, R. (1998), "From America, fresh cries of 'Unfair'," *International Herald Tribune*, July 3, p. 13; Collins, S. (1998), *Imports, Exports, and the American Worker*, Washington, DC: Brookings Institution.

23 Reported in *Argus*, March, 1997: original information from "ILO reports even higher child labor figures," Switzerland: Associated Press; Turner, C. (1996), "Child labor widespread, United Nations reports," *Boulder Daily Camera*, December 12, p. 7A.

24 Solomon, C.M. (1996), "Put your ethics to a global test," *Personnel Journal*, January, pp. 236–240.

25 Adapted from *ibid*., p. 239.

26 Jebb (1998).

27 Laabs, J. (1998), "Nike gives Indonesian workers a raise," *Workforce Magazine*, December, pp. 15–16.

28 "Nike raises pay as Indonesia readies wage hike," *San Diego Union Tribune* (Reuter's story), March 24, 1999, p. C3.

29 See Sweeney (1998).

30 From *International Labor Standards: A Strategic Issues Brief*, Alexandria, VA: Society for Human Resource Management, April, 1996, p. A-5.

31 J. Maxwell, of the Global Remuneration Organization, as quoted in Laabs (1998), pp. 15–16.

32 See, for example, the March 7, 1996, issue of *Far Eastern Economic Review:* "Asia's Children: Why so Many Must Work." The issue contains the following articles: Fairclough, G., "Child labour: It isn't black and white," pp. 54–56; Fairclough, G., "Darkness at noon," pp. 56–57; Karp, J., "Caste-iron servitude," pp. 57–58; Gilley, B., "Following the money," p. 58.

33 See, for example, Click, J. (1996), "New business standards focus on human rights," *HR Magazine*, June, pp. 65–72; Gesteland (1999), particularly chapter 9, "Culture, corruption, and bribery"; Kumar and Steinmann (1998).

34 Bernstein, A. (1999), "Sweatshop reform: How to solve the standoff," *Business Week*, May 3, pp. 186, 188, 190.

35 For example, Oakley, J.G. (1999), "Child labor, sweatshops, and the corporate social responsibility of MNCs," *Global Outlook*, 11 (1): 19–32.

36 Nissenbaum, D. (2001), "Ben of Ben & Jerry's plans anti-sweatshop crusade," *Daily Camera*, August 19, p. 7B.

37 Described in Solomon (1996).

38 For more information or a complete copy of the Caux Round Table Principles for Business contact the Caux Round Table Secretariat, 1156 Fifteenth Street NW, Suite 910, Washington, DC 20005–1704 (202–872–9077, www.cauxroundtable.org).

39 Webley (1998); Webley, S. (1996), "An Interfaith Declaration: A code of ethics on international business for Christians, Muslims, and Jews," reproduced in *Business Ethics: A European Review*, 1996, 5 (1): 52–57.

40 "Ethical guidelines for multinationals take the forefront," *World Link*, September–October, 1995, pp. 1, 4.

41 This section is based on Thaler-Carter, R.E. (1999), "Social accountability 8000," *HR Magazine*, June, pp. 106–112; Bernstein, A. (1997), "Sweatshop police," *Business Week*, October 20, p. 39.

42 See, for example, Lee, L., and Bernstein, A. (2000), "Who says student protests don't matter?" *Business Week*, June 12, pp. 94, 96; Van Der Werf, M. (2000), "The Worker Rights Consortium makes strides toward legitimacy," *Chronicle of Higher Education*, April 12, p. A41.

43 Peck, J.K. (1999), "Students rally to eliminate sweatshops," *Colorado Daily*, July 13–15, pp. 1–2.

44 Lee and Bernstein (2000).

45 Digh (1997).

46 Adapted from Tansey, L.A. (1996), "Taking ethics abroad" in *Across the Board*, June, pp. 56, 58; Donaldson (1996).

47 Sweeney (1998).

48 Donaldson (1996).

49 In Digh (1997), p. 92.

50 Donaldson (1996).

51 *Ibid*.

52 Reported in Digh (1997).

## 8 Global workforce planning, forecasting, and staffing the multinational enterprise

1 Wiechman, D., *et al.* (2003), "Designing and implementing global staffing systems" II, "Best practices," *Human Resource Management*, 24 (1): 85–94; Duane, M.J. (2001), *Policies and Practices in Global Human Resource Systems*, Westport, CT: Quorum Books.

2 See, for example, *The International Reference Report: Annual Report of Global Costs, Wages, Salaries, and Human Resource Statistics*, worldwide edition, Redmond, WA: Economic Research Institute; data developed by chambers of commerce, private surveys, and other IHR consultancies.

3 There are many references on this subject. Here are only a few. Boardman, M. (1999), "Worker 'dearth' in the twenty-first century," *HR Magazine*, June, p. 304; Golzen, G. (1998), "Skill shortages around the globe," *HR World*, November–December, pp. 41–53; Herman, R., Olivo, T., and Gioia, J. (2003), *Impending Crisis: Too Many Jobs, Too Few People*, Winchester, VA: Oakhill Press; Johnston, W.B. (1991), "Global work force 2000: The new world labor market," *Harvard Business Review*, March–April, pp. 115–127; Leonard, S. (2000), "The labor shortage," *Workplace Visions*, 4: 1–7; Patel, D. (2001), "HR trends and analysis: the effect of changing demographics and globalization on HR," *Global HR*, July–August, pp. 9–10; Richman, L.S. (1992), "The coming world labor shortage," *Fortune*, April 6, pp. 70–75; Sappal, P. (2000), "Just can't get the staff" (includes articles on skill shortages in various regions of the world), *HR World*, July–August, pp. 53–62.

4 Adapted from "Springs cos. use foreign workers" (2000), *Daily Camera* (Boulder, CO), September 6, p. 3B. For more on the use of offshoring jobs see Greene, J., Carey, J., Arndt, M., and Port, O. (2003), "Reinventing corporate R&D," *Business Week*, September 22, pp. 74–76.

5 Adapted from "Amid shortage of workers, Dutch find reward in hiring the retired," *San Diego Union – Tribune*, April 23, 2000, p. A-29.

6 Adapted from Norris, C.D. (2000), "Already starting: a world marketplace for jobs," *International Herald Tribune*, August 8, p. 6.

7 Golzen, G. (2001), "Winning away from home," *Global HR*, April, pp. 17–20; Hall, L. (2001), "Talent mapped out," *Global HR*, April, pp. 28–34.

8  Hall (2001), p. 30, quoting Alan Tsang, Managing Director for Asia of the search and selection firm Norman Broadbent.

9  See, for example, "European Commission tackles labor mobility" (2002), *BNA Human Resources International Report*, March 11, pp. 1–3.

10  Adapted from Kremer-Jones, B. (2002), "Location, location, location," *Global HR*, July–August, pp. 43–45.

11  Sullivan, J. (2002), "Plan of action," *Global HR*, October, pp. 22–25.

12  See, for example, Black, J.S., Gregersen, H.B., and Mendenhall, M.E. (1992), *Global Assignments*, San Francisco: Jossey Bass; Black, J.S., Gregersen, H.B., Mendenhall, M.E., and Stroh, L.K. (1999), *Globalizing People through International Assignments*, Reading, MA: Addison Wesley; Borg, M., and Harzing, A-W. (1995), "Composing an international staff," in Harzing, A-W., and Van Ruysseveldt, J. (eds), *International Human Resource Management*, London: Sage; Dowling, P., Welch, D.E., and Schuler, R.S. (1999), *International Human Resource Management*, 3rd edn, Cincinnati, OH: Southwestern/ITP Press; Evans, P., Pucik, V., and Barsoux, J.-L. (2002), *The Global Challenge: Frameworks for International Human Resource Management*, Boston, MA: McGraw-Hill Irwin; Gross, A., and McDonald, R. (1998a), "Staffing your Asian operation with Asian returnees: The pros and cons," *International HR Journal*, spring, pp. 3–8; Gross, A., and McDonald, R. (1998b), "Vast shortages in talent keep employers searching," *International HR Update*, July, p. 6; Morgan, P. (1986), "International human resource management: fact or fiction?" *Personnel Administrator*, 31 (9): 43–47; Schell, M.S., and Solomon, C.M. (1997), *Capitalizing on the Global Workforce*, Chicago: Irwin.

13  Morgan (1986).

14  Carpenter, M.A., Sanders, W.G., and Gregersen, H.B. (2001), "Bundling human capital with organizational context: The impact of international assignment experience on multinational firm performance and CEO pay," *Academy of Management Journal*, 44 (3): 493–511.

15  Harzing, A.-W. (2001a), "Of bears, bumble-bees, and spiders: The role of expatriates in controlling foreign subsidiaries," *Journal of World Business*, 36 (4): 366–379; Harzing, A.-W. (2001b), "Who's in charge? An empirical study of executive staffing practices in foreign subsidiaries," *Human Resource Management*, 40 (2): 139–158.

16  Tung, R.L. (1998) "American expatriates abroad: From neophytes to cosmopolitans," *Journal of World Business*, 33 (2): 125–144.

17  Stahl, G.T., Miller, E.L., and Tung, R.L. (2002), "Toward the boundaryless career: A closer look at the expatriate career concept and the perceived implications of an international assignment," *Journal of World Business*, 37 (3): 216–227.

18  For example, Tung, R. (1988), *The New Expatriates: Managing Human Resources Abroad*, New York: Ballinger; Black *et al.* (1992); Evans *et al.* (2002); Borg and Harzing (1995).

19  For example, Barshes, W. (Wm Wrigley Jr Co.) (1997), "Utilization of local Nationals in managing International Operations," presentation at annual International Assignee Forum, KPMG, Chicago; Boyle, T. (Raytheon Systems Co.) (1998), "Local Nationals: Management from afar," presentation at the annual International Assignment Services Conference, Deloitte & Touche, Naples, FL; Greene, G. (Sunglass Hut International) (1998), "Local National Employment Issues," presentation at the annual conference of the Society for Human Resource Management, Institute for International HRM, Miami Beach, FL; Van Ackeren, C. (US West International) (1997), "Enhancing Local Talent within Global Joint Venture Environments," presentation at the annual International Assignee Forum, KPMG, Chicago.

20  Rai, S. (2003), "As it tries to cut costs, Wall Street looks to India," *New York Times*, October 8, pp. W1, 7; Pristin, T. (2003), "One victim when jobs go overseas: US office space," *New York Times*, October 8, p. C7; Fox, J. (2003), "Where your job is going,"

*Fortune*, November 24, pp. 84–94; Schwartz, N. (2003), "Will 'Made in USA' fade away"? *Fortune*, November 24, pp. 98–108.

21  Hays, R. (1974), "Expatriate selection: Insuring success and avoiding failure," *Journal of International Business Studies*, 5 (1): 25–37.

22  For example, Tung, R.L. (1991), "Selection and training of personnel for overseas assignments," *Columbia Journal of World Business*, 16 (1): 68–78; Tahvanainen, M. (1998), *Expatriate Performance Management*, Helsinki: Helsinki School of Economics Press.

23  Edström, A., and Galbraith, J.R. (1977), "Transfer of managers as a coordination and control strategy in multinational organizations," *Administrative Science Quarterly*, 22 (June): 248–263.

24  Harzing (2001a).

25  *Ibid.*

26  Roberts, K., Kossek, E.E., and Ozeki, C. (1998), "Managing the global work force: Challenges and strategies," *Academy of Management Executive*, 12 (4): 6–16.

27  Tung, R.L. (1993), "Managing cross-national and intra-national diversity," *Human Resource Management*, 32 (4): 461–477.

28  Roberts, *et al.* (1998).

29  Adler, N.J. (2002), *International Dimensions of Organizational Behavior*, 4th edn, Cincinnati, OH: Southwestern College Publishing; Bartlett, C.A., and Ghoshal, S. (1989), *Managing across Borders*, Boston, MA: Harvard Business School Press; Black, J.S., Mendenhall, M.E., and Oddou, G. (1991), "Toward a comprehensive model of international adjustment: An integration of multiple theoretical perspectives," *Academy of Management Review*, 16 (2): 291–317; Boyacigiller, N. (1990), "The role of expatriates in the management of interdependence, complexity, and risk in multinational corporations," *Journal of International Business Studies*, 21 (2): 357–381; Boyacigiller, N. (2000), "The international assignment reconsidered," in Mendenhall, M., and Oddou, G. (eds), *Readings and Cases in International Human Resource Management*, 3rd edn, Cincinnati, OH: Southwestern College Publishing; Edström and Galbraith (1977); Hedlund, G. (1986), "The hypermodern MNC: a heterarchy?" *Human Resource Management*, 25 (1): 9–35; Kobrin, S. (1988), "Expatriate reduction and strategic control in American multinational corporations," *Human Resource Management*, 27 (1): 63–75.

30  Bachler, C. (1996), "Global inpats: Don't let them surprise you," *Personnel Journal*, June, pp. 54–56; Forster, N. (2000), "The myth of the international manager," *International Journal of Human Resource Management*, 11: 126; Groh, K., and Allen, M. (1998), "Global staffing: Are expatriates the only answer?" (special report on expatriate management) *HR Focus*, March, p. 75–78; Minehan, M. (1996), "Skills shortage in Asia," *HR Magazine*, 41: 152; Tung, R. (1987), "Expatriate assignments: Enhancing success and minimizing failure," *Academy of Management Executive*, 1 (2): 117–126.

31  Duane (2001).

32  Roberts, *et al.* (1998), p. 96.

33  Black, J.S., Morrison, A.J., and Gregersen, H.B. (1999), *Global Explorers: The Next Generation of Leaders*, New York and London: Routledge; Ferraro, G. (2002), *Global Brains: Knowledge and Competencies for the Twenty-first Century*, Charlotte, NC: Intercultural Associates; Hodge, S. (2000), *Global Smarts: The Art of Communicating and Deal-making Anywhere in the World*, New York: Wiley; Keys, J.B., and Fulmer, R.M., (eds) (1998), *Executive Development and Organizational Learning for Global Business*, New York and London: International Business Press; McCall, M.W., Jr, and Hollenbeck, G.P. (2002), *Developing Global Executives: The Lessons of International Experience*, Boston, MA: Harvard Business School Press; Rosen, R., Digh, P., Singer, M., and Phillips, C. (2000), *Global Literacies: Lessons on Business Leadership and National Cultures*, New York: Simon & Schuster; Scherer, C.W. (2000), *The Internationalists: Business Strategies for Globalization*, Wilsonville, OR: Book Partners.

34 Matherly, C., and Robinson, D. (1999), "Ready for the global workplace?" Special edition of *National Business Employment Weekly*, a publication of the *Wall Street Journal*, 8: 12–13.

35 Cummins, S.E. (1999), "Taking short-term assignments a step further," *International Update*, a publication of the Institute for International Human Resource Management, a division of the Society for Human Resource Management, June, pp. 8–9.

36 Cummins (1999); Morris, D., and Gilbertsen, R. (1998), "Alternatives for structuring international assignments," *International Insight*, summer, pp. 1–5.

37 Fanning, S. (2002), "Short-term assignments: Essential employment issues," *Expatriate Advisor*, winter, pp. 4–5; Hennessey, L. (2002), "Short-term assignments," *Expatriate Advisor*, winter, pp. 2–3; Hunter, J.L. (1998), "Short-term international assignments," *International Insight*, summer, pp. 7–8; Joinson, C. (2000), "Cutting down the days," *HR Magazine*, April, pp. 92–97; Melone, F. (2001), "Changing with the times: Creative alternatives to long-term international assignments," reprinted on-line from National Relocation and Real Estate (November) by Windham International: www.windhamint.com/NewsEvents.asp?ArticleID=51; Ray, M.D. (2001), "Financial factors will determine international assignment length," reprinted on-line from Employee Relocation Council Mobility (November) by Windham International: www.windhamint.com.NewsEvents.asp?ArticleID=16; Sappal, P. (1999), "Spoilt for choice," *HR World*, May–June, pp. 31–34; "Short-term assignments" (2001), *ORC–West News*, February, pp. 1–2, reporting on data from ORC 2000 Global Survey of Short-term International Assignment Policies; Solomon, C.M. (1998), "Today's global mobility: Short-term assignments and other solutions," *Global Workforce*, 3 (4): 12–17; Voigt, K. (2001), "Timing the time abroad: Overseas work assignments are getting shorter," reprinted on-line from the *Asian Wall Street Journal* by Windham International: www.windhamint.com/NewsEvents.asp?ArticleID=36.

38 Hopper, D. (2000), "International assignment management: Facing the challenges of global leadership," *Expatriate Administrator* (KPMG newsletter), summer (http://www.us.kpmg.com/services/tax/ies/tea/summer2000/stories/hopper.html); Melone (2001); Organization Resources Counselors (2000), *2000 Worldwide Survey of International Assignment Practices and Policies*, New York: ORC; Ray (2001); Solomon (1998); Voigt (2001).

39 Evans, *et al.* (2002); Oddou, G., Mendenhall, M.E., and Ritchie, J.B. (2000), "Leveraging travel as a tool for global leadership development," *Human Resource Management*, 39 (2–3): 159–172.

40 "Secrets of success", *SHRM Global Perspectives*, 1, 1 (2001), pp. 6–8 (article on results of 2000 Global Relocation Trends Survey by GMAC Global Relocation Services/Windham International, the National Foreign Trade Council, and the SHRM Global Forum).

41 Yeargan, A. (2000), "International Extended Business Travelers: A Viable Alternative to Long-term Assignments?" *CBI Employee Relocation Report*, May, pp. 25–26.

42 Burchenal, S. (2000), "International Assignment Types," presentation to the Faculty Development Seminar on IHRM, University of Colorado, Denver, June. (Shan described Pepsi-Cola International's split of the traditional expatriate assignment into intermediate and long-term.)

43 "Secrets of success" (2001).

44 *Ibid.*

45 See, for example, Borg and Harzing (1995); Evans *et al.* (2002); Inkson, K., Arthur, M.B., Pringle, J., and Barry, S. (1997), "Expatriate assignment versus overseas experience: Contrasting models of international human resource development," *Journal of World Business*, 32 (4): 351–368; and Pucik, V. and Saba, T. (1999), "Selecting and developing the global versus the expatriate manager: A review of the state of the art," *Human Resource Planning*, 21 (4): 40–54.

46 Burchenal (2000).

47 Andre, R. (2000), "High Technology, Incorporated: The international benefits problem," reprinted in Mendenhall, M., and Oddou, G. (eds), *Readings and Cases in International Human Resource Management*, 3rd edn, Cincinnati, OH: Southwestern College Publishing; "Localization: Moving away from the 'indefinite expatriate'" (1999), *International Mobility Management* (publication of Arthur Andersen), third quarter, pp. 2–3.

48 Hodge (2000); McCall, M.W., Jr, and Hollenbeck, G.P. (2002), *Developing Global Executives: The Lessons of International Experience*, Boston, MA: Harvard Business School Press; Scherer (2000).

49 Frazee, V. (1998), "How to hire locally," *Global Workforce*, 3 (4): 19, 22–23; Morgan (1986).

50 See, for example, Borg and Harzing (1995); Hailey, J. (1999), "Localization as an ethical response to internationalism," in Brewster, C., and Harris, H. (eds), *International HRM: Contemporary Issues in Europe*, London: Routledge.

51 Evans *et al.* (2002).

52 Challenger, J.A. (1999), "Companies initiate foreign policy to fill jobs," *CRN News*, August, p. 16.

53 For example, Gross and McDonald (1998a, b).

54 "Japanese boomerangs" (2003), *Pacific Bridge International Asian HR e-Newsletter*, 2 (12): 2.

55 Grove, B. (2000), Associate Director, San Diego Employers' Association, personal conversation, San Diego, CA.

56 Clague, L. (1999), "GTE: the global just-in-time employee," *CRN News*, August, p. 17; Richards, L. (1999), "The Global Just-in-time Employee," presentation to the annual conference of the Institute for International Human Resource Management, Orlando, FL, April 12.

57 See "Going global with GEC," *International Mobility Management* (an Arthur Andersen publication), second quarter, 2000, p. 7; Pittman, P.W. (2000), "Overseas payroll company: Weapon in the war for talent," *Expatriate Management Update*, February, pp. 1, 7; Greene *et al.* (2003); Hamm, S. (2003), "Borders are so twentieth-century," *Business Week,* September 22, pp. 68–70.

58 Cascio, W. (2000), "Managing a virtual workplace," *Academy of Management Executive*, 14 (3): 81–90; Cummins (1999); Distefano, J.J., and Maznevski, M.L. (2000), "Creating value with diverse teams in global management," *Organizational Dynamics*, 29 (1): 45–63; Evans *et al.* (2002); Germer, E. (2000), "Cross-border commute," *Fast Company*, September, p. 74; "The growing ranks of 'virtual' expatriates," *Wall Street Journal Europe* (France), reported in *Manpower Argus*, October, 2000, p. 10; O'Hara-Devereaux, M., and Johansen, R. (1994), *Global Work: Bridging Distance, Culture and Time*, San Francisco: Jossey Bass; Speier, C., Harvey, M.G., and Palmer, J. (1998), "Virtual management of global marketing relationships," *Journal of World Business*, 33 (3): 263–276; "'Virtual' expatriate assignments expand in the United States," *Les Echos* (France), reported in *Manpower Argus*, October, 1998, p. 2.

59 Inkson *et al.* (1997); Suutari, V., and Brewster, C. (2000), "Making their own way: International experience through self-initiated foreign assignments," *Journal of World Business*, 35 (4): 417–436.

60 Suutari and Brewster (2000).

61 Thaler-Carter, R. (1998), "Using retirees for short-term assignments," *International Update*, a publication of the Institute for International Human Resource Management, a division of the Society for Human Resource Management, September, pp. 3, 11.

62 See, for example, Adler, N., and Ghadar, F. (1990), "Strategic human resource management: A global perspective," in Pieper, R. (ed.), *Human Resource Management: An International Comparison*, Berlin: de Gruyter; Black *et al.* (1992); Black *et al.* (1999); Boyacigiller (2000); Evans *et al.* (2002); Luthans, F., Marsnik, P.A., and Luthans, K.W. (1997), "A contingency matrix approach to IHRM," *Human Resource Management*, 36 (2):

83–199; Shenkar, O. (1995), "Contingency factors in HRM in foreign affiliates," in Shenkar, O. (ed.), *Global Perspectives on Human Resource Management*, Englewood Cliffs, NJ: Prentice Hall.

63 Borkowski, S.C. (1999), "International managerial performance evaluation: A five-country comparison," *Journal of International Business Studies*, 30 (3): 533–555; Briscoe, D.R. (1997), "Assessment centers: Cross-cultural and cross-national issues," in Riggio, R.E., and Mayes, B.T. (eds), *Assessment Centers: Research and Applications*, special issue of the *Journal of Social Behavior and Personality*, 12 (5): 261–270; Caligiuri, P.M. (1997), "Assessing expatriate success: Beyond just 'being there'," *New Approaches to Employee Management*, 4: 117–140; Gregersen, H.B., Hite, J.M., and Black, J.S. (1996), "Expatriate performance appraisal in US multinational firms," *Journal of International Business Studies*, 27 (4): 711–738; Milliman, J., Nason, S., Gallagher, E., Huo, P., Von Glinow, M.A., and Lowe, K.B. (1998), "The impact of national culture on human resource management practices: The case of performance appraisal," *Advances in International Comparative Management*, 12: 157–183; Oddou, G., and Mendenhall, M. (2000), "Expatriate performance appraisal: Problems and solutions," in Mendenhall, M., and Oddou, G. (eds), *Readings and Cases in International Human Resource Management*, 3rd edn, Cincinnati, OH: Southwestern College Publishing.

64 Black, J.S. and Gregersen, H.B. (1999), "The right way to manage expats," *Harvard Business Review*, March–April, pp. 52–63.

65 Edström and Galbraith (1977); Harzing (2001a, b).

66 See, for example, DeFrank, R.S., Konopaske, R., and Ivancevich, J.M. (2000), "Executive travel stress: Perils of the road warrior," *Academy of Management Executive*, 14 (2): 58–71; Harris, H. (2000), "Alternative forms of international working," *Worldlink*, 10 (4): 2–3.

67 Harris (2000).

## 9 Staffing the global enterprise: selection of international assignees

1 For more complete discussion of the management of expatriates refer to Black, J.S., Gregersen, H.B., Mendenhall, M.E., and Stroh, L.K. (1999), *Globalizing People through International Assignments*, Reading, MA: Addison Wesley; Brewster, C. (1991), *The Management of Expatriates*, London: Kogan Page; Carey, P.M. (1998), "Coming home," *CFO*, June, pp. 77–80; Frazee, V. (1997), "Welcome your repatriates home," *Global Workforce*, April, pp. 24–28; Lomax, S. (2001), *Best Practices for Managers and Expatriates*, New York: Wiley; Schell, M., and Solomon, C. (1997), *Capitalizing on the Global Workforce: A Strategic Guide to Expatriate Management*, Chicago: Irwin; Shilling, M. (1993), "How to win at repatriation," *Personnel Journal*, September, pp. 15–19; Shumsky, N.J. (1999), "Repatriation can be the most difficult part of a global assignment," *CRN News*, May, p. 21; Solomon, C.M. (1995), "Repatriation: up, down or out?" *Personnel Journal*, January, pp. 23–29; Stroh, L.K., Gregersen, H.B., and Black, J.S. (1998), "Closing the gap: Expectations versus reality among repatriates," *Journal of World Business*, 33 (2): 111–124; Thomas, D.C. (1998), "The expatriate experience: A critical review and synthesis," *Advances in International Comparative Management*, 12: 237–273; Tung, R.L. (1988), *The New Expatriates: Managing Human Resources Abroad*, Cambridge, MA: Ballinger.

2 Deutsh, C.H. (1988), "Losing innocence, abroad," *New York Times: Business*, July 10, section 3, pp. 1, 26.; Barham, K., and Rassam, C. (1989), *Shaping the Corporate Future*, Ashridge: Ashridge Research Management Group; Shahzad, N. (1984), "The American expatriate manager," *Personnel Administrator*, July, pp. 23–30.

3 For a good overview of the research into the reasons for using expatriates versus local nationals refer to Thomas (1998).

4  GMAC Global Relocation Services/Windham International, National Foreign Trade Council, and SHRM Global Forum (2002 and previous years), *Global Relocation Trends Annual Survey Report*, New York: GMAC GRS/Windham International.

5  Kiechell, M., III (1983), "Our person in Pomparippu: The successful expatriate executive learns to cool heels, live with servants – and come home again," *Fortune*, October 17, p. 213.

6  Brandt, E. (1991), "Global HR," *Personnel Journal*, March, p. 38–44.

7  Davies, J. (1996), "Getting what you pay for," *International Business*, March, pp. 20–23; Halley, J. (1999), "Localization as an ethical response to internationalization," in Brewster, C., and Harris, H. (eds), *International Human Resource Management*, London: Routledge; Kent, S. (1999), "Cultivating home-grown talent," *HR World*, November–December, pp. 24–28; Solomon, C.M. (1995), "Learning to manage host-country nationals," *Personnel Journal*, March, pp. 21–26.

8  Robock, S.H., and Simmonds, K. (1983), *International Business and Multinational Enterprises*, 3rd edn, Homewood, IL: Irwin, p. 559.

9  Quoted from Daniels, J.D., Ogram, E.W., Jr, and Radebaugh, L.H. (1982), *International Business: Environments and Operations*, Reading, MA: Addison Wesley; the original data are from Reynolds, C., "Expatriates in a Changing World Economy," paper presented to the Academy of International Business, November 15, 1978.

10 Howard, C.G. (1992), "Profile of the twenty-first-century expatriate manager," *HR Magazine*, June, pp. 93–100; Laabs, J.J. (1991), "The global talent search," *Personnel Journal*, August, pp. 38–43; Marsick, V.J., and Cederholm, L. (1988), "Developing leadership in international managers: an urgent challenge!" *Columbia Journal of World Business*, winter, pp. 3–11.

11 Adapted from Barnum, C.F. (1992), "John Deere's competitive advantage," *HR Magazine*, February, pp. 74–76, 107.

12 Bartlett, C.A., and Ghoshal, S. (1989), *Managing across Borders*, Boston. MA: Harvard Business School Press; Evans, P., Pucik, V., and Barsoux, J.-L. (2002), *The Global Challenge: Frameworks for International Human Resource Management*, New York: McGraw-Hill; Maljers, F.A. (1992), "Inside Unilever: The evolving transnational company," *Harvard Business Review*, September–October, pp. 46–52; Townley, P. (1990), "Globesmanship" (interview with Paul Oreffice, chairman of the board of Dow Chemical, Michael Angus, chairman of Unilever, and John Young, CEO and president of Hewlett-Packard), *Across the Board*, February, pp. 24–34.

13 Refer particularly to the references in note 1.

14 Rehak, J. (1991), "IRS takes close look at US expatriates," *International Herald Tribune*, August 24 25, p. 15.

15 Brewster (1991); yearly survey reports from consulting firms like GMAC Global Relocation Services/Windham International (2002), and Organization Resources Counselors, for example as reported in Reynolds, C. (1991), "HR must influence global staff strategy," *HR News: International HR*, March, section C, pp. 1–2.

16 See, for example, Franko, L.G. (1973), "Who manages the multinational enterprise?" *Columbia Journal of World Business*, summer, pp. 30–37.

17 Briscoe, D.R., and Gazda, G.M. (1989), "The successful expatriate," *Proceedings*, "Managing in a Global Economy," third biannual international conference, Eastern Academy of Management, Hong Kong, November.

18 See, for example, Black, J.S., and Mendenhall, M. (1990), "Cross-cultural effectiveness: A review and a theoretical framework for future research," *Academy of Management Review*, 15: 113–136; Brocklyn, P. (1989), "Developing the international executive," *Personnel*, March, pp. 44–48; Callahan, M. (1989), "Preparing the new global manager," *Training and Development Journal*, March, pp. 29–31; Hixon, A.L. (1986), "Why corporations make haphazard overseas staffing decisions," *Personnel Administrator*, March, pp. 91–94; Hogan, G.W., and Goodson, J.R. (1979), "The key to expatriate

success," *Training and Development Journal*, January, pp. 50–52; Lanier, A.R. (1979), "Selecting and preparing personnel for overseas transfers," *Personnel Journal*, March, pp. 160–163; Stuart, K.D. (1992), "Teens play a role in moves overseas," *Personnel Journal*, March, pp. 71–78; Tung (1987) "Expatriate assignments: Enhancing success and minimizing failure," *Academy of Management Executive*, 1 (2): 117–126.

19 Miller, E.L., and Cheng, J. (1978), "A closer look at the decision to accept an overseas position," *Management International Review*, 18: 25–33.

20 Adapted from Howard, C.G. (1992), "Profile of the twenty-first-century expatriate manager," *HR Magazine*, June, p. 96.

21 Quoted in Howard (1992), pp. 93–100.

22 See, for example, Donegan, J. (2002), "Effective expatriate selection: The first step in avoiding assignment failure," *Expatriate Advisor*, spring, pp. 14–16; Ondrack, D. (1996), "Key managers 'make or break' a new international operation," *International HR Update*, November, pp. 1, 4; Solomon, C.M. (1994), "Staff selection impacts global success," *Personnel Journal*, January, pp. 12–19.

23 Hawley-Wildmoser, L. (1997), "Selecting the right employee for assignments abroad," *Cultural Diversity at Work*, 9 (3): 1, 12–13.

24 See, for example, the discussion of this point in Black *et al.* (1999).

25 Briscoe, D.R. (1997), "Assessment centers: Cross-cultural and cross-national issues" in Riggio, R.E., and Mayes, B.T. (eds), *Assessment Centers: Research and Application*, special issue of the *Journal of Social Behavior and Personality*, 12 (5): 261–270.

26 See, for example, Baker, J.C., and Ivancevich, J.M. (1971), "The assignment of American executives abroad: systematic, haphazard, or chaotic?" *California Management Review*, 13 (3): 39–41; Hixon (1986); Mendenhall, M., Dunbar, E., and Oddou, G.R. (1987), "Expatriate selection, training, and career-pathing: A review and critique," *Human Resource Management*, 26 (3): 331–345; Mendenhall, M., and Oddou, G. (1985), "The dimensions of expatriate acculturation: A review," *Academy of Management Review*, 10 (1): 39–47; Miller, E.L. (1972), "The overseas assignment: How managers determine who is to be selected," *Michigan Business Review*, 24 (3): 12–19; Miller, E.L. (1973), "The international selection decision: A study of some dimensions of managerial behavior in the selection decision process," *Academy of Management Journal*, 16: 239–252; Tung, R.L. (1981), "Selection and training of personnel for overseas assignments," *Columbia Journal of World Business*, 16 (1): 68–78; Tung (1988); Zeira, Y. (1975), "Overlooked personnel problems of multinational corporations," *Columbia Journal of World Business*, 10 (2): 96–103.

27 Birdseye, M.G., and Hill, J.S. (1995), "Individual, organizational/work and environmental influences on expatriate turnover tendencies: An empirical study," *Journal of International Business Studies*, fourth quarter, pp. 787–813.

28 Nasif, E.G., Thibodeaux, M.S., and Ebrahimi, B. (1987), "Variables associated with success as an expatriate manager," *Proceedings*, Academy of International Business, Southeast Region, annual meeting, New Orleans, November 4–7, pp. 169–179.

29 Refer to sources in previous notes plus Black, J.S., and Gregersen, H.B. (1991), "The other half of the picture: Antecedents of spouse cross-cultural adjustment," *Journal of International Business Studies*, third quarter, pp. 461–477; Black, J.S., and Mendenhall, M. (1991), "The U-curve adjustment hypothesis revisited: A review and theoretical framework," *Journal of International Business Studies*, second quarter, pp. 225–247; Conway (1984); De Cieri, H., Dowling, P.J., and Taylor, K.F. (1989), "The Psychological Impact of Expatriate Relocation on Spouses," paper presented to the annual meeting of the Academy of International Business, Singapore, November 19–22; Foxman, L.D., and Polsky, W.L. (1991), "HR approaches for the Age of Globalization," *Personnel Journal*, April, pp. 38–41; Fuchsberg, G. (1990), "As costs of overseas assignments climb, firms select expatriates more carefully," *Wall Street Journal*, April 5, pp. B-1, B-5; "Gauging a family's suitability for a stint overseas," *Business Week*, April 16, 1979, pp. 127, 130;

Gomez–Mejia, L., and Balkin, D.B. (1987), "The determinants of managerial satisfaction with the expatriation and repatriation process," *Journal of Management Development*, 6 (1): 7–18; Greene, W.E., and Walls, G.D. (1984), "Human resources: Hiring internationally," *Personnel Administrator*, July, pp. 61–66; Harris, J.E. (1989), "Moving managers internationally: The care and feeding of expatriates," *Human Resource Planning*, 12 (1): 49–53; Lanier (1979); Lee, Y., and Larwood, L. (1983), "The socialization of expatriate managers in multinational firms," *Academy of Management Journal*, 26 (4): 657–665; Murray, F.T., and Murray, L.H. (1986), "SMR forum: Global managers for global businesses," *Sloan Management Review*, winter, pp. 75–80; Oddou, G.R., Mendenhall, M.E., and Bedford, P. (1988), "The Role of an International Assignment in an Executive's Career: A Career Stages Perspective," paper presented at the Academy of International Business conference, San Diego, CA, October 20–22; Savich, R.S., and Rodgers, W. (1988), "Assignment overseas: Easing the transition before and after," *Personnel*, August, pp. 44–48; Tung, R.L. (1988), "Career issues in international assignments," *Academy of Management Executive*, 2 (3): 241–244; Tung, R.L. (1987).

30 Conway (1984); Harvey, M.G. (1983), "The multinational corporation's expatriate problem: An application of Murphy's Law," *Business Horizons*, January–February, p. 72; Henry, E.R. (1965), "What business can learn from Peace Corps selection and training," *Personnel*, 42 (4): 17–25; Misa, K.F., and Fabricatore, J.M. (1979), "Return on investment of overseas personnel," *Financial Executive*, 47 (4): 42–46; Murray and Murray (1986); Rahim, A. (1983), "A model for developing key expatriate executives," *Personnel Journal*, April, p. 312; Tung (1981, 1987).

31 Tung, R.L. (1982), "Selection and training procedures of US, European, and Japanese multinationals," *California Management Review*, fall, p. 57–71; Tung, R.L. (1984), *Key to Japan's Economic Strength: Human Power*, Lexington, MA: Heath.

32 Based on Perraud, P., and Davis, A. (1997), "Assignment Success or Failure: It's all in the Family," presentation to the annual conference of the Institute for International Human Resource Management (now the Global Forum, division of the Society for Human Resource Management), Los Angeles, April 15–17.

33 Dolainski, S. (1997), "Are expats getting lost in the translation?" *Workforce*, February, pp. 32–39.

34 Lester, T. (1994), "Pulling down the language barrier," *International Management*, July–August, p. 44.

35 See, for example, "Is there a problem, officer? Second time around expat describes benefits of language skills," *Global Voice*, Berlitz Newsletter of International Communication and Understanding (no date), 6 (1): 1; *Reading across Boundaries*, Newsletter of International Orientation Resources, July, 1994, pp. 1–6.

36 *Reading across Boundaries* (1994), p. 1.

37 *Ibid.*

38 *Ibid.*

39 Solon, L. (2000), "The language of global business," *SHRM Global*, December, pp. 12–14.

40 Naisbitt, J., and Aburdene, P. (1990), *Megatrends 2000*, New York: Morrow.

41 Beeth, G. (1997), "The tale of the cultural translator," *Management Review*, May, p. 10.

42 Refer to surveys by GMAC Global Relocation Services/Windham International, Prudential Relocation, and Cendant International Assignment Services.

43 Adler, N.J. (1984a), "Expecting international success: Female managers overseas," *Columbia Journal of World Business*, 19 (3): 79–85; Adler, N.J. (1987), "Pacific Basin managers: A *gaijin*, not a woman," *Human Resource Management*, 26 (2): 169–191; Adler, N.J. (1984b), "Women do not want international careers – and other myths about international management," *Organizational Dynamics*, 13 (2): 66–79; Adler, N.J. (1984c), "Women in international management: where are they?" *California Management Review*,

26 (4): 78–89; Adler, N., and Izraeli, D. (eds) (1988), *Women in Management Worldwide*, Armonk, NY: Sharpe; Adler, N.J., and Izraeli, D.N., (eds) (1994), *Competitive Frontiers: Women Managers in a Global Economy*, Cambridge, MA and Oxford: Blackwell; "Corporate women: A rush of recruits for overseas duty," *Business Week*, April 20, 1981, p. 120ff. Jelinek, M., and Adler, N.J. (1988), "Women: world-class managers for global competition," *Academy of Management Executive*, 2 (1): 11–19; Kirk, W.Q., and Maddox, R.C. (1988), "International management: the new frontier for women," *Personnel*, March, pp. 46–49.

44 Adler, N.J. (1984d), "Managers perceive greater barriers for women in international versus domestic management," *Columbia Journal of World Business*, 19 (1): 45–53.

45 *Ibid.*

46 See, for example, surveys such as GMAC Global Relocation Services/Windham International annual reports, which consistently show only about 13–15 percent of expatriates to be women.

47 Abraham, Y. (1985), "Personnel policies and practices in Saudi Arabia," *Personnel Administrator*, April, p. 102; Thal, N., and Caleora, P. (1979), "Opportunities for women in international business," *Business Horizons*, December, pp. 21–27.

48 Adler, N.J. (1984b); Golesorkhi, B (1991), "Why not a woman in overseas assignments?" *HR News: International HR*, March, p. C4; Kirk and Maddox (1988).

49 See above, plus Brown, L.K. (1989), *Women in Management Worldwide*, Armonk, NY: Sharpe; Maital, S. (1989), "A long way to the top," *Across the Board*, December, pp. 6–7.

50 Quoted in Grove, C., and Hallowell, W. (1997), "Guidelines for women expatriates," *Solutions*, November, pp. 41–44.

51 *Ibid.*; Sappal, P. (1999), "Sometimes it's hard to be a woman," *HR World*, January–February, pp. 21–24.

52 Caligiuri, P.M., and Cascio, W.F. (1998), "Can we send her there? Maximizing the success of Western women on global assignments," *Journal of World Business*, 33 (4): 394–416; Caligiuri, P.M., and Cascio, W.F. (2000), "Sending women on global assignments," *World at Work Journal*, second quarter, pp. 34–41; Caligiuri, P.M., and Tung, R.L. (1999), "Comparing the success of male and female expatriates from a US-based multinational company," *International Journal of Human Resource Management*, 10: 763–782; Taylor, .S., and Napier, N. (1996), "Working in Japan: Lessons from Western expatriates," *Sloan Management Review*, 37: 76–84.

53 Varma, A., Stroh, L.K., and Schmitt, L.B. (2001), "Women and international assignments: The impact of supervisor–subordinate relationships," *Journal of World Business*, 36 (4): 380–388.

54 Harris, H. (1999), "Women in international management" in Brewster, C., and Harris, H. (eds), *International Human Resource Management*, London: Routledge.

55 See, for example, Ball, L.L. (1991), "Overseas dual-career family an HR challenge," *HR News: International HR*, March, p. C8; Frazee, V. (1998), "Tearing down the roadblocks," *Workforce*, February, pp. 50–54; Harvey, M. (1997), "Dual-career expatriates: expectations, adjustment and satisfaction with international relocation," *Journal of International Business Studies*, third quarter, pp. 627–658; "Problems for dual-career expatriates," *Personnel Journal*, September, 1990, p. 17; Reynolds, C., and Bennett, R. (1991), "The career couple challenge," *Personnel Journal*, March, 1990, pp. 46–49.

56 See the last chapter and Joinson, C. (2002), "No returns: 'Localizing' expats saves companies big money and can be a smooth transition with a little due diligence by HR," *HR Magazine*, November, pp. 70–77.

57 See, for example, Hauser, J. (1997), "Leading practices in international assignment programs," *International HR Journal*, summer, pp. 34–37; Stahl, G.K., Miller, E.L., and Tung, R.T. (2002), "Toward the boundaryless career: A closer look at the expatriate career concept and the perceived implications of an international assignment," *Journal of World Business*, 37: 216–227.

58  Gregson, K. (1997), "Outsourcing international assignments," *International HR Journal*, fall, pp. 38–40; Wadsworth, A. (2003), "Controlling costs through outsourced international assignment administration," *Expatriate Advisor*, summer, p. 12.

59  Joinson, C. (2002), "Save thousands per expatriate," *HR Magazine*, July, pp. 73–77.

60  Harvey, M.G., Novicevic, M.M., and Speier, C. (2000), "An innovative global management staffing system: A competency-based perspective," *Human Resource Management*, 39 (4): 381–394; Hauser, J.A. (2000), "Filling the candidate pool," *World at Work Journal*, second quarter, pp. 26–33.

61  Black, J.S. (2000), "Coming home," *HR World*, January–February, pp. 30–32; Carey, P.M. (1998), "Coming home: Employers are scrambling to combat the loss of returning expatriates," *CFO*, June, pp. 77–80; Feldman, D.C., and Tompson, H.B. (1993), "Expatriation, repatriation, and domestic geographical relocation: An empirical investigation of adjustment to new job assignments," *Journal of International Business Studies*, third quarter, pp. 507–529; Frazee (1997); Lazarova, M., and Caligiuri, P. (2001), "Retaining repatriates: The role of organizational support practices," *Journal of World Business*, 36 (4): 389–401; O'Grady, L. (2001), "Repatriation: the truth about coming home," *CRN News*, October, pp. 10, 15; Poe, A.C. (2000), "Focus on international HR: Welcome back," *HR Magazine*, March, pp. 94–105; RHR International (1993), "Repatriation: The challenge of coming home," *For CEOs Only*, 10 (1): 1–2; Shilling, M. (1993), "How to win at repatriation," *Personnel Journal*, September, pp. 15–18; Solomon, C.M. (1995), "Repatriation: up, down or out?" *Personnel Journal*, January, pp. 21–26; Stroh, L.K., Gregersen, H.B. and Black, J.S. (1998), "Closing the gap: Expectations versus reality among repatriates," *Journal of World Business*, 33 (2): 111–124; "Weigh the risks first on that job abroad," *US News and World Report*, December 2, 1985, p. 82.

62  Black, J.S. (1991), "Returning expatriates feel foreign in their native land," *HR Focus*, August, p. 17; Brewster (1991); Dowling, P.J., Welch, D.E., and Schuler, R.S. (1999), *International Human Resource Management: Managing People in a Multinational Context*, 3rd edn, Cincinnati, OH: Southwestern College Publishing; Harvey, M.G. (1989), "Repatriation of corporate executives: An empirical study," *Journal of International Business Studies*, spring, pp. 131–144; Howard, C.G. (1987), "Out of sight—not out of mind," *Personnel Administrator*, June, pp. 82–90; Welds, K. (1991), "The return trip," *HR Magazine*, June, pp. 113–114.

63  Shumsky, N.J. (1999), "Repatriation can be the most difficult part of a global assignment," *CRN News*, May, p. 21.

64  Martinez, M.N. (1998), "Motorola's sponsorship program helps expats avoid losing their connections," *International HR Update*, July, p. 10.

65  Munkel, N., and Nghiem, L. (1999), "Do multinationals face up to the challenges of repatriation?" *KPMG Expatriate Administrator*, 4: 6–8.

66  Brewster (1991).

67  Adapted from Ettorre, B. (1993), "A brave new world: Managing international careers," *Management Review*, April, p. 15.

68  The term "inpatriates" is less than ten years old. Consequently almost all of the literature about this concept is from practitioner journals and magazines. For example, refer to Bachler, C.J. (1996), "Global inpats: Don't let them surprise you," *Personnel Journal*, June, pp. 54–64; Cook, J. (1998), "A whole new world," *Human Resource Executive*, March 19, pp. 1–2; Copeland, A.P. (1995), "Helping foreign nationals adapt to the US," *Personnel Journal*, February, pp. 83–87; Finney, M. (2000), "Culture shock in America? For foreign expatriates, absolutely," *Across the Board*, May, pp. 28–33; Harvey, M.G., and Buckley, M.R. (1997), "Managing inpatriates: Building a global core competency," *Journal of World Business*, 32 (1): 35–52; Harvey *et al.* (2000); Joinson, C. (1999), "The impact of 'inpats'," *HR Magazine Focus*, April, pp. 5–10; Kent, S. (2001), "Welcome to our world," *Global HR*, February–March, pp. 32–36; Lachnit, C. (2001), "Low-cost tips for successful inpatriation," *Workforce*, August, pp. 42–47; Solomon, C.M. (1995), "HR's helping hand

pulls global inpatriates on board," *Personnel Journal*, November, pp. 40–49; Solomon, C.M. (2000), "Foreign relations," *Workforce*, November, pp. 50–56.

69 Davies, J. (1997), "Getting what you pay for," *International Business*, March, pp. 20–23; Halley, J. (1999), "Localization as an ethical response to internationalization" in Brewster, C., and Harris, H. (eds), *International Human Resource Management*, London: Routledge; Solomon, C.M. (1995), "Learning to manage host-country nationals," *Personnel Journal*, March, pp. 15–21.

70 Kent, S. (1999), "Cultivating home-grown talent," *HR World*, November–December, pp. 24–28.

71 Johnston, W.B. (1991), "Global Work Force 2000: The new world labor market," *Harvard Business Review*, March–April, pp. 115–127.

72 For example, refer to Johnston (1991); Richman, L.S. (1990), "The coming world labor shortage," *Fortune*, April 9, pp. 70–77; Templeman, J., Wise, D.C., Lask, E., and Evans, R. (1989), "Grappling with the graying of Europe," *Business Week*, March 13, pp. 54–56.

73 Lublin, J.S. (1991), "Firms woo executives from 'third countries'," *Wall Street Journal*, September 16, p. B1.

74 Caligiuri, P.M. (1997), "Assessing expatriate success: Beyond just 'being there'," *New Approaches to Employee Management*, 4 (1): 17–140.

75 *Ibid*.

76 Reported in Bennett, R. (1993), "Solving the dual international career dilemma," *HR News*, January, p. C5.

77 *Ibid*.; see also Fitzgerald-Turner, B. (1997), "Myths of expatriate life," *HR Magazine*, June, pp. 65–74; Punnett, B.J. (1997), "Towards effective management of expatriate spouses," *Journal of World Business*, 32 (3): 243–257; Thaler-Carter, R.E. (1999), "Vowing to go abroad," *HR Magazine*, November, pp. 90–96.

78 *Ibid*.

79 Many of the references in this chapter deal with varying aspects of Best Practice in selection of IAs. In addition, refer to Lomax (2001); Berlitz International, PHH Relocation and SHRM Institute for International HRM (1996–1997), executive summary, *International Assignee Research Project*, Berlitz, PHH Relocation, and SHRM Institute for IHRM; Black, J.S., and Gregersen, H.B. (1999), "The right way to manage expats," *Harvard Business Review*, March–April, pp. 52–63; Dolins, I. (2002), "Ready, steady, go," *Global HR*, June, pp. 16–19; Foster, R.D. (1997), "Strategic solutions for effective international assignment," *International HR Journal*, summer, pp. 38–40; Hauser (1997); Herring, L., and Greenwood, P. (2000), "'Best practices' leverage international assignment success in the United States," *International HR Journal*, spring, pp. 21–28; Institute of Personnel and Development (1999), *The IPD Guide on International Recruitment, Selection and Assessment*, London: Institute of Personnel and Development; Martinez, M.N. (1996), "Study targets expatriates' extensive assistance needs," *HR News*, February, pp. B4–B5; Poe, A.C. (2002), "Selection savvy," *HR Magazine*, April, pp. 77–83; Prudential Relocation Global Services (no date), *Leading Practices in International Assignment Programs*, Valhalla, NY: Prudential Relocation; Solomon, C.M. (1995), "Navigating your search for global talent," *Personnel Journal*, pp. 29–32; Usner, J.W. (1996), "A primer on programs and policies for successful foreign assignments," *International HR Journal*, winter, pp. 45–48.

## 10 Training and management development in the global enterprise

1 "GE culture turns sour at French unit" (1990) *Wall Street Journal*, July 31, 1990, p. A11.

2 Keys, J.B., and Fulmer, R.M. (1998), "Introduction: Seven imperatives for executive education and organizational learning in the global world," in Keys, J.B., and Fulmer, R.M.

(eds), *Executive Development and Organizational Learning for Global Business*, New York: International Business Press. Also see the entire special issue of *Human Resource Management*, 39 (2–3), 2000; Sparrow, P., Brewster, C., and Harris, H. (2004), *Globalizing Human Resource Management*, London: Routledge. Also see the entire issue of *Organizational Dynamics*, 33 (1), 2004.

3 Slocum, J., Jr, McGill, M., and Lei, D.T. (1994), "The new learning strategy: Anytime, anything, anywhere," *Organizational Dynamics*, 23 (2): 33–47.

4 Ohmae, K. (1990), *The Borderless World*, New York: HarperCollins, p. 18.

5 See, for example, Ahmed, P.K., Kok, L.K., and Loh, A.Y.E. (2002), *Learning through Knowledge Management*, Oxford and Woburn, MA: Butterworth Heinemann; Argyris, C. (1999), *On Organizational Learning*, 2nd edn, Oxford and Malden, MA: Blackwell; Chawla, S., and Renesch, J., (eds) (1995), *Learning Organizations: Developing Cultures for Tomorrow's Workplace*, Portland, OR: Productivity Press; Davenport, T.O. (1999), *Human Capital: What it is and Why People invest it*, San Francisco: Jossey Bass; DiBella, A.J., and Nevis, E.C. (1998), *How Organizations Learn*, San Francisco: Jossey Bass; Dotlich, D.L., and Noel, J.L. (1998), *Action Learning: How the World's Top Companies are Recreating their Leaders and Themselves*, San Francisco: Jossey Bass; Leonard, D. (1995), *Wellsprings of Knowledge: Building and Sustaining the Sources of Innovation*, Boston, MA: Harvard Business School Press; Liebowitz, J., and Beckman, T. (1998), *Knowledge Organizations: What every Manager should Know*, Boca Raton, FL: St Lucie Press; Marquardt, M.J. (2002), *Building the Learning Organization*, 2nd edn, Palo Alto, CA: Davies Black; Marquardt, M., and Reynolds, A. (1994), *The Learning Organization: Gaining Competitive Advantage through Continuous Learning*, Burr Ridge, IL: Irwin; Sparrow, J. (1998), *Knowledge in Organizations: Access to Thinking at Work*, London: Sage; Stewart, T.A. (1997), *Intellectual Capital: The New Wealth of Organizations*, New York: Doubleday Currency; Vaill, P.B. (1996), *Learning as a Way of Being: Strategies for Survival in a World of Permanent White Water*, San Francisco: Jossey Bass; Watkins, K.E., and Marsick, V.J. (1993), *Sculpting the Learning Organization*, San Francisco: Jossey Bass.

6 De Geus, A. (1980), "Planning is learning," *Harvard Business Review*, March–April, p. 71; also de Geus, A. (1997), *The Living Company*, Boston, MA: Harvard Business School Press; Sparrow *et al.* (2004).

7 Adapted from Geber, B. (1989), "A global approach to training," *Training*, September, pp. 42–47. See also Schuler, R.S., Tarique, I., and Jackson, S.E. (2004), "Managing Human Resources in Cross-border Alliances," in Cooper, C., and Finkelsteins (eds), *Advances in Mergers and Acquisitions*, New York: JAI Press; Odenwald, S.B. (1993), *Global Training: How to Design a Program for the Multinational Corporation*, Homewood, IL: Business One Irwin and Alexandria, VA: American Society for Training and Development; Reynolds, A., and Nadler, L. (1993), *Globalization: The International HRD Consultant and Practitioner*, Amherst, MA: Human Resource Development Press; Miller, V.A. (1994), *Guidebook for Global Trainers*, Amherst, MA: Human Resource Development Press.

8 Adapted from Geber (1989).

9 Described in Kleiman, L.S. (2004), *Human Resource Management*, 3rd edn, Cincinnati, OH: Atomic Dog, p. 450.

10 Sappal, P. (2000), "¿Entiendes? Capiche? Comprenez-vous?" *HR World*, September–October, pp. 28–32.

11 *Ibid.*

12 Quoted in Laabs, J.J. (1991), "The global talent search," *Personnel Journal*, August, p. 13.

13 Gourlay, G. (1989), "Of Coke and cargo cults," *Across the Board*, November, pp. 59–60.

14 Tichy, N., and Charan, R. (1990), "Citicorp faces the world: An interview with John Reed," *Harvard Business Review*, November–December, p. 137.

15 Tyler, K. (1999), "Offering English lessons at work," *HR Magazine*, December, pp. 112–120.

16 Francis, J.L. (1995), "Training across cultures," *Human Resource Development Quarterly*, 6 (1), spring, reprinted in Albrecht, M.H. (ed.), *International HRM*, Oxford and Malden, MA: Blackwell (2001), adapted from Hofstede, G. (1991), *Cultures and Organizations: Software of the Mind*, New York: McGraw-Hill; Pfeiffer, J.W., and Jones, J.E. (1983), *Reference Guide to Handbooks and Annuals*, San Diego, CA: University Associates. Similar efforts are reported in Keys, J.B., and Bleicken, L.M. (1998), "Selecting training methodology for international managers," in Keys, J.B., and Fulmer, R.M. (eds), *Executive Development and Organizational Learning for Global Business*, New York: International Business Press. Also see Earley, P.C., and Peterson, R.S. (2004), "The elusive Cultural Chameleon: Cultural intelligence as a new approach to inter cultural training for the gobal manager," *Academy of Management Learning and Education*, 31 (1): 100–115.

17 Adapted from Jones, M.L. (1989), "Management development: An African focus," *International Studies of Management and Organization*, 19 (1): 74–90.

18 Baker, J.C., and Ivancevich, J.M. (1971), "The assignment of American executives abroad: Systematic, haphazard, or chaotic?" *California Management Review*, 13 (3): 39–41; Black, J.S. (1988), "Work role transitions: A study of expatriate managers in Japan," *Journal of International Business Studies*, 19: 277–294; Oddou, G., and Mendenhall, M. (1991), "Succession planning for the twenty-first century: How well are we grooming our future business leaders?" *Business Horizons*, 34 (1): 26–34; Tung, R.L. (1981), "Selecting and training of personnel for overseas assignments," *Columbia Journal of World Business*, 16 (1): 68–78.

19 See, for example, Black, J.S., Gregersen, H.B., Mendenhall, M.E., and Stroh, L.K. (1999), *Globalizing People through International Assignments*, Reading, MA: Addison Wesley; Brewster, C. (1991), *The Management of Expatriates*, London: Kogan Page; Schell, M., and Solomon, C. (1997), *Capitalizing on the Global Workforce: A Strategic Guide to Expatriate Management*, Chicago: Irwin.

20 Quoted in Blocklyn, P.L. (1989), "Developing the international executive," *Personnel*, March, pp. 44–45.

21 Black *et al.* (1999); Sparrow *et al.* (2004).

22 Black *et al.* (1999); Ward, C., and Kennedy, A. (1993), "Where's the 'culture' in cross-cultural transition?" *Journal of Cross-cultural Psychology*, 24: 221–249.

23 Refer to the references in note 19 as well as Bennett, R., Aston, A., and Colquhoun, (2000), "Cross-cultural training: A critical step in ensuring the success of international assignments," *Human Resource Management*, 39 (2–3): 239–250.

24 Based on Rahim, A. (1983), "A model for developing key expatriate executives," *Personnel Journal*, April, pp. 23–28.

25 Adapted from Black *et al.* (1999), and Ronen, S. (1989), "Training the international assignee," in Goldstein, I.L. and Associates (eds), *Training and Development in Organizations*, San Francisco; Jossey-Bass.

26 Black *et al.* (1999); Francis (1995); Keys and Bleicken (1998); Ronen, S. (1989), "Training the international assignee" in I.L. Goldstein *et al.* (eds), *Training and Development in Organizations*, San Francisco: Jossey Bass.

27 A good summary of this research and application to training programs for IAs is to be found in Keys and Bleicken (1998); also see Black *et al.* (1999); Mendenhall, M.E., and Stahl, G.K. (2000), "Expatriate training and development: Where do we go from here?" *Human Resource Management*, 39 (2–3), pp. 251–265.

28 *Ibid.*

29 See Blocklyn (1989); Black *et al.* (1999); Harris, P. R, and Moran, R.T. (1999), *Managing Cultural Differences: Leadership Strategies for a New World of Business*, 5th edn, Woburn, MA: Butterworth Heinemann.

30 Described in Blocklyn (1989).

31 Lanier, A.R. (1979), "Selecting and preparing personnel for overseas transfers," *Personnel Journal*, March, pp. 160–163.

32 Black, J.S., Gregersen, H.B., and Mendenhall, M.E. (1992), *Global Assignments*, San Francisco: Jossey Bass; Black *et al.* (1999); Black, J.S., and Mendenhall, M.E. (1989), "Selecting cross-cultural training methods: A practical yet theory-based approach," *Human Resource Management*, 28 (4): 511–540; Black, J.S., and Mendenhall, M.E. (1990), "Cross-cultural training effectiveness: A review and a theoretical framework for future research," *Academy of Management Review*, 15 (1): 113–136; Caudron, S. (1991), "Training ensures success overseas," *Personnel Journal*, December, pp. 27–30; Earley, P.C. (1987), "Intercultural training for managers: A comparison of documentary and interpersonal methods," *Academy of Management Journal*, 30 (4): 685–698.

33 Kohls, L.R. (1993), "Preparing yourself for work overseas" in Reynolds, A., and Nadler, L. (eds), *Globalization: The International HRD Consultant and Practitioner*, Amherst, MA: Human Resource Development Press; Budhwar, P.S., and Baruch, Y. (2003), "Career management practices in India: An empirical study," *International Journal of Manpower*, 24 (6): 69–719.

34 *Ibid.*

35 Black *et al.* (1999); Mendenhall and Stahl (2000).

36 Black *et al.* (1999); Mendenhall and Stahl (2000); Black and Mendenhall (1990); Keys and Bleicken (1998).

37 Black, J.S., Morrison, A.J., and Gregersen, H.B. (1999), *Global Explorers: The Next Generation of Leaders*, New York and London: Routledge; McCall, M.W., Jr, and Hollenbeck, G.P. (2002), *Developing Global Executives: The Lessons of International Experience*, Boston, MA: Harvard Business School Press; Pucik, V. (1992), "Globalization and human resource management" in Puik, V., Tichy, N.M., and Barnett, C.K. (eds), *Globalizing Management: Creating and Leading the Competitive Organization*, New York: Wiley; Scherer, C.W. (2000), *The Internationalists: Business Strategies for Globalization*, Wilsonville, OR: Book Partners.

38 See, for example, *Competing in a Global Economy* (1998), executive summary of the Watson Wyatt study *Senior Executives across the Globe*, Bethesda, MD, and Reigate: Watson Wyatt.

39 These paragraphs draw heavily on Evans, P.A.L. (1992), "Human Resource Management and Globalization," keynote address to the third biannual Conference on International Personnel and Human Resource Management, Ashridge Management College, Berkhamsted, England, July 2–4; Evans, P., Lank, E., and Farquhar, A. (1989), "Managing human resources in the international firm: Lessons from practice," in Evans, P., Doz, Y., and Laurent, A. (eds), *Human Resource Management in International Firms*, London: Macmillan; Evans, P., Pucik, V., and Barsoux, J.-L. (2002), *The Global Challenge: Frameworks for International Human Resource Management*, New York: McGraw-Hill Irwin; McCall and Hollenbeck (2002). For a broader look at executive development programs, particularly looking at executive training programs, refer to Keys and Fulmer (1998).

40 Quoted in Evans *et al.* (1989).

41 In addition to the other major references on global management development, most of which make reference to the importance of early identification of candidates for global development, see Spreitzer, G.M., McCall, M.W., Jr, and Mahoney, J.D. (1997), "Early identification of international executive potential," *Journal of Applied Psychology*, 82 (1): 6–29.

42 Bartlett, C.A., and Ghoshal, S. (1989), *Managing across Borders: The Transnational Solution*, Boston, MA: Harvard Business School Press; Bartlett, C.A., and Ghoshal, S. (1990), "Matrix management: Not a structure, a frame of mind," *Harvard Business Review*, July–August, pp. 138–145; Maljers, F.A. (1992), "Inside Unilever: The evolving transnational company," *Harvard Business Review*, September–October, pp. 46–52.

43 Quoted in Bartlett and Ghoshal (1990), p. 143.

44 See, for example, Adler, N.J., and Bartholomew, S. (1992), "Managing globally competent people," *Academy of Management Executive*, 6 (2): 52–65; Black, Morrison *et al.* (1999); Cascio, W., and Bailey, E. (1995), "International human resource management," in Shenkar, O. (ed.), *Global Perspectives of Human Resource Management*, Englewood Cliffs, NJ: Prentice Hall; McCall and Hollenbeck (2002); Minehan, M.E. (1996), "The shortage of global managers" (reports on two major studies, one from thirty countries and one from Europe), *Issues in HR* (Alexandria, VA: Society for Human Resource Management), March–April, pp. 2–3; Rosen, R., with Digh, P., Singer, M., and Phillips, C. (2000), *Global Literacies: Lessons on Business Leadership and National Cultures*, New York: Simon & Schuster; Thaler-Carter, R.E. (2000), "Whither global leaders?" *HR Magazine*, May, pp. 82–88.

45 Reynolds, C. (1991), "HR must influence global staff strategy," *HR News: International HR*, March, p. C2.

46 For the best description of these programs refer to Keys and Fulmer (1998).

47 See, for example, Gupta, A.K., and Govindarajan, V. (2002), "Cultivating a global mind set," *Academy of Management Executive*, 16 (1): 116–126; Morrison, A.J. (2000), "Developing a global leadership model," *Human Resource Management*, 39 (2–3): 117–131.

48 Evans *et al.* (2002); Mendenhall and Stahl (2000).

49 Laabs, J.J. (1991), "Whirlpool managers become global architects," *Personnel Journal*, December, pp. 39–45.

50 *Ibid.*

51 Quoted in *Ibid.*

52 Described in Marquardt, M.J. (1999), *The Global Advantage: How World-class Organizations improve Performance through Globalization*, Houston, TX: Gulf Publishing; Maruca, R.F. (1994), "The right way to go global: An interview with Whirlpool CEO David Whitwam," *Harvard Business Review*, 72 (2): 135–145.

53 "The global CEO," *INC Magazine*, December, 1993, pp. 8–10.

54 See, for example, Bartlett and Ghoshal (1989); Dalton, M., Ernst, C., Deal, J., and Leslie, J. (2002), *Success for the New Global Manager: How to Work across Distances, Countries, and Cultures*, San Francisco: Jossey Bass; Evans *et al.* (2002); Ferraro, G. (2002), *Global Brains: Knowledge and Competencies for the Twenty-first Century*, Charlotte, NC: Intercultural Associates; Hodge, S. (2000), *Global Smarts*, New York: Wiley; McCall and Hollenbeck (2002).

55 Kedia, B.L., and Mukherji, A. (1999), "Global managers: Developing a mind set for global competitiveness," *Journal of World Business*, 34 (3): 230–251.

56 Scherer (2000).

57 Quoted in Talbott, S.P. (1996), "Building a global work force starts with recruitment," *Recruitment Staffing Sourcebook*, supplement to *Personnel Journal*, March, reprinted in Albrecht, M.H. (ed.), *International HRM: Managing Diversity in the Workplace*, Oxford and Malden, MA: Blackwell (2001).

58 McCall and Hollenbeck (2002).

59 Rhinesmith, S.H. (1993), *A Manager's Guide to Globalization: Six Keys to Success in a Changing World*, Homewood, IL: Business One Irwin, and Alexandria, VA: American Society for Training and Development, p. 24.

60 Evans *et al.* (2002), pp. 385–387.

61 Rhinesmith, S.H. (1992), "Global mind sets for global managers," *Training and Development Journal*, 46 (10): 63–68; Rhinesmith (1993).

62 Evans *et al.* (2002), pp. 396–397.

63 See, for example, Black *et al.* (1999); Black, Morrison *et al.* (1999); Claus, L. (1999), "Globalization and HR Professional Competencies," paper presented at the twenty-second annual forum of the Institute for International Human Resources (now called the Global

Forum), Society for Human Resource Management, Orlando, FL, April 13; Dalton *et al.* (2002); Evans *et al.* (2002); Ferraro (2002); Harris, P.R., and Moran, R.T. (1996), "European leadership in globalization," *European Business Review*, 96 (2), reprinted in Albrecht, M.H. (ed.), *International HRM: Managing Diversity in the Workplace*, Oxford and Malden, MA: Blackwell (2001); Harris, P.R., and Moran, R.T. (1999), *Managing Cultural Differences: Leadership Strategies for a New World of Business*, 5th edn, Woburn, MA: Butterworth Heinemann, pp. 41–54; Hodge (2000); McCall and Hollenbeck (2002); Rosen (2000); Scherer (2000).

64  Adler and Bartholomew, (1992); Evans *et al.* (2002).

65  Kets de Vries, M.F.R., and Mead, C. (1992), "The development of the global leader within the multinational corporation" in Pucik, V., Tichy, N.M., and Bartlett, C.K. (eds), *Globalizing Management: Creating and Leading the Competitive Organization*, New York: Wiley.

66  Lancaster, H. (1998), "Managing your career," *Wall Street Journal*, June 2, p. C1.

67  Lobel, S.A. (1990), "Global leadership competencies," *Human Resource Management*, 29 (1): 39–47.

68  Barham, K., and Wills, S. (1992), *Management across Frontiers*, Ashridge: Ashridge Management Research Group.

69  Lancaster (1998).

70  Talbott (1996).

71  *Ibid.*

72  McCall and Hollenbeck (2002).

73  Hall, D.T., Zhu, G., and Yan, A. (2001), "Developing global leaders: To hold on to them, let them go!" in Mobley, W., and McCall, M.W., Jr (eds), *Advances in Global Leadership* II, Stamford, CT: JAI Press.

74  McCall and Hollenbeck (2002).

75  Quoted in Bingham, C.B., Felin, T., and Black, J.S. (2000), "An interview with John Pepper: What it takes to be a global leader," *Human Resource Management*, 39 (2–3): 287–292.

76  Bennett, J.M., and Bennett, M.J. (2003), "Developing intercultural sensitivity: An integrative: approach to global and domestic diversity" in Landis, D., Bennett, J.M., and Bennett, M.J. (eds) *The Handbook of Intercultural Training*, Thousand Oaks, CA: Sage; Hodge (2000).

77  See, for example, Seibert, K.W., Hall, D.T., and Kram, K.E. (1995), "Strengthening the weak link in strategic executive development: Integrating individual development and global business strategy," *Human Resource Management*, 34: 549–567; Yan, A., Zhu, G., and Hall, D.T. (2002), "International assignments for career building: A model of agency relationships and psychological contracts," *Academy of Management Review*, 27 (3): 373–391.

78  Yan *et al.* (2002).

79  Adler and Bartholomew (1992).

80  Black, Morrison *et al.* (1999).

81  Dalton *et al.* (2002).

82  McCall and Hollenbeck (2002).

83  Rosen (2000).

84  *Ibid*, p. 29.

85  Marquardt has published extensively on the subject of organizational learning and the learning organization, including in the global context. This particular information is adapted from Marquardt (1999).

86  Alldredge, M.E., and Nilan, K.J. (2000), "3M's leadership competency model: An internally developed solution," *Human Resource Management*, 39 (2–3): 133–145.

87  Claus, L. (2002), "Cross-cultural savvy and how to acquire it," *Global HR*, June, p. 54.

88  In addition to the many references already provided see Black, S., and Gregersen, H.B. (2000), "High-impact training: Forging leaders for the global frontier," *Human Resource Management*, 39 (2–3): 173–184; Conner, J. (2000), "Developing the global leaders of tomorrow," *Human Resource Management*, 39 (2–3): 147–157; Maznevski, M.L., and DiStefano, J.J. (2000), "Global leaders are team players: Developing global leaders through membership on global teams," *Human Resource Management*, 39 (2–3): 195–208; Nearly, D.B., and O'Grady, D.A. (2000), "The role of training in developing global leaders: A case study at TRW Inc.," *Human Resource Management*, 39 (2–3): 185–193; Roberts, K., Kossek, E.E., and Ozeki, C. (1998), "Managing the global work force: Challenges and strategies," *Academy of Management Executive*, 12 (4): 93–106.

89  Adler, N.J., Brody, L.W., and Osland, J.S. (2000), "The Women's Global Leadership Forum: Enhancing one company's global leadership capability," *Human Resource Management*, 39 (2–3): 209–225.

90  *Ibid.*; Adler, N.J. (1999), "Global entrepreneurs: Women, myths, and history," *Global Focus*, 11 (4): 125–134; Adler, N.J., and Izraeli, D.N. (eds) (1994), *Competitive Frontiers: Women Managers in a Global Economy*, Oxford and Cambridge, MA: Blackwell.

91  Solomon, C.M. (1994), "Staff selection impacts global success," *Personnel Journal*, January, pp. 89–95.

92  See, for example, Brandies, D. (1997), "Developing Global Managers at Rhône-Poulenc Rorer," presentation at the twentieth annual conference of the Institute for International Human Resource Management (now the Global Forum of the Society for Human Resource Management), April 7; Carpenter, M.A., Sanders, W.G., and Gregersen, H.B. (2000), "International experience at the top makes a bottom-line difference," *Human Resource Management*, 39 (2–3): 277–285; Laabs, J.L. (1993), "Building a global management team" (at Gillette), *Personnel Journal*, August, p. 75; Laabs, J.L. (1993), "How Gillette grooms global talent," *Personnel Journal*, August, pp. 65–68, 71, 73, 76; Laabs, J.L. (1995), "International training" (description of Gillette's global management development program), *Global Opportunity*, 40–46; Hodgetts, R.G. and Luthans, F. (2000), "Gillette's prescription for international business success: In-house training and expat experience" (case written specifically for the book), *International Management*, New York: McGraw Hill; Pittman, P., and Gilbert, S. (2000), "Benefits Beyond the Dollar: Articulating the Value of Assignments to Assignee Candidates" (description of JTI's global management development program), presentation at the annual International Assignee Conference of Deloitte & Touche Tomatsu, Scottsdale, AZ, October.

93  Maruyama, M. (1990), "Organizational structure, training and selection of outer space crew members," *Technological Forecasting and Social Change*, 37: 203–212.

94  Mentioned in Maruyama, M. (1994), "Successive modifications of study guidelines for student projects with business firms," *Cybernetica*, 37 (1): 59–72; Maruyama, M. (1992), "Changing dimensions in international business," *Academy of Management Executive*, 6 (3): 88–96.

95  Waugh, D.A. (2000), "Global trends in training and development," *IFTDO* (International Federation of Training and Development Organizations) *News*, 3: 3.

## 11 Global compensation, benefits, and taxes

1  Reynolds, C. (2000a), *2000 Guide to Global Compensation Benefits*, San Diego, CA: Harcourt; Reynolds, C. (1992), "Are you ready to make IHR a global function?" *HR News: International HR*, February, pp. Cl–C3; Reynolds, C. (1997), "Expatriate compensation in historical perspective," *Journal of World Business*, 32 (2): 118–132.

2  See, for example, Crandall, L.P., and Phelps, M.I. (1991), "Pay for a global work force," *Personnel Journal*, February, pp. 28–33; Czinkota, R.M., Rivoli, P., and Ronkainen, I.A. (1989), "International human resource management" in *International Business*, Chicago:

Dryden Press; Green, W.E., and Walls, G.D. (1984), "Human resources: Hiring internationally," *Personnel Administrator*, July, pp. 61–64, 66; Gross, R.E., and Kujawa, D. (1995), "Personnel management" in *International Business: Theory and Managerial Applications*, 3rd edn, Homewood, IL: Irwin; Mesdag, L.M. (1984), "Are you underpaid?" *Fortune*, March 19, pp. 20–25; Stuart, P. (1991), "Global payroll: a taxing problem," *Personnel Journal*, October, pp. 80–90.

3 See, for example, Overman, S. (1992), "The right package," *HR Magazine*, July, pp. 71–74; Senko, J.P. (1991), "Controlling expatriate execs' costs," *Management Review*, March, pp. 38–39.

4 Black, J.S. (1991), "Returning expatriates feel foreign in their native land," *Personnel*, August, p. 17.

5 Clague, L. (1999), "Expatriate compensation: Whence we came, where we are, whither we go," *Corporate Relocation News*, April, pp. 24, 25, 31; Reynolds, C. (1994), *Compensation Basics for North American Expatriates*, Scottsdale, AZ: American Compensation Association; Reynolds, C. (1997), "Expatriate compensation in historical perspective," *Journal of World Business*, 32 (2): 118–132; Reynolds, C. (2000b), "Global compensation and benefits in transition," *Compensation and Benefits Review*, January–February, pp. 28–38; Reynolds, C. (1996), "What goes around comes around," *International HR* (Organization Resources Counselors), Spring, pp. 1–10; Ritchie, A.J., and Seltz, S.P. (2000), "Globalization of the compensation and benefits function," in Reynolds, C. (ed.), *2000 Guide to Global Compensation and Benefits*, San Diego, CA: Harcourt.

6 Adapted and updated from Crandall and Phelps (1991), pp. 28, 30.

7 For good discussions of these issues refer to Dessler, G. (2003), "Managing global human resources" in *Human Resource Management*, 9th edn, Upper Saddle River, NJ: Prentice Hall; Infante, V.D. (2001), "Three ways to design international pay: headquarters, home country, host country," *Workforce*, January, pp. 22–24; Joinson, C. (1999), "Companies tailor benefits, compensation for overseas workers," *HR News*, April, pp. 1, 20; Kearley, T. (1996), "An effective blueprint for international compensation," *Benefits and Compensation Solutions*, November, reprint; Overman, S. (2000), "In $¥N€," *HR Magazine*, March, pp. 86–92; Solomon, C.M. (1995), "Global compensation: Learn the ABCs," *Personnel Journal*, July, pp. 15–19.

8 Stone, R.J. (1986), "Compensation: Pay and perks for overseas executives," *Personnel Journal*, January, pp. 64–69.

9 Czinkota *et al.* (1989), p. 580; Stone (1986).

10 Black, J.S., Gregersen, H.B., Mendenhall, M.E., and Stroh, L.K. (1999), *Globalizing People through International Assignments*, Reading, MA: Addison Wesley; Chesters, A. (1995), "The balance sheet approach: problem or solution?" *International HR Journal*, fall, pp. 9–15; Frazee, V. (1998), "Is the balance sheet right for your expats?" *Global Workforce*, September, pp. 19–26; Infante (2001); Organization Resources Counselors (1998), *Understanding the Balance Sheet Approach to Expatriate Compensation* (pamphlet), New York: ORC; Reynolds, C. (2000), "Expatriate compensation: The basics" and "Expatriate compensation strategies" in Reynolds, C. (ed.), *2000 Guide to Global Compensation and Benefits*, San Diego, CA: Harcourt; Pollard, J. (2000), "Expatriate practices" in Reynolds, C. (ed.), *2000 Guide to Global Compensation and Benefits*, San Diego, CA: Harcourt.

11 O'Reilly, M. (1995), "Reinventing the expatriate package," *International HR Journal*, fall, pp. 58–59; Reynolds (2000b); Sheridan, W.R., and Hansen, P.T. (1996), "Linking international business and expatriate compensation strategies," ACA *Journal*, spring, pp. 66–79.

12 Crandall and Phelps (1991).

13 For discussions of these issues see Gould, C. (1995), "Expatriate compensation," *International Insight*, winter, pp. 6–10; Gould, C. (1998), "Expatriate policy development" in Gould, C. and Schmidt-Kemp, B. (eds), *International Human Resources Guide*, Boston,

MA: Warren Gorham & Lamont; Infante (2001); Kearley (1996); Overman (1992); Pollard (2000); Reynolds (1996, 2000a: chapter 5); Solomon (1995).

14 *Global Relocation Trends Annual Survey Report*, New York: GMAC Global Relocation Services/Windham International, and National Foreign Trade Council, and Alexandria, VA: Society for Human Resource Management (SHRM) Global Forum; Society for Human Resource Management/Commerce Clearing House (1992), *SHRMICCH Survey on International HR Practices*, Chicago: Commerce Clearing House.

15 Overman (1992).

16 Based on 2002 survey by Mercer Human Resource Consulting, reported in *CRN News Update*, 8 July; US Department of State cost of living data (refer to Table 11.1).

17 See, for example, "International cost-of-living variations narrow," *HR Magazine*, September, 2001, p. 29, reporting on surveys by William M. Mercer. Similar surveys by Runtzheimer, AirInc, Windham, Organization Resources Counselors, National Foreign Trade Council, the *Economist*, etc., have found similar results.

18 Senko, J.P. (1990), "The foreign service premium and hardship differential," *Mobility*, May, pp. 10–12.

19 *Ibid.*; *Global Relocation Trends Annual Survey Report*, New York: GMAC Global Relocation Services/Windham International and National Foreign Trade Council, and Alexandria, VA: Society for Human Resource Management (SHRM) Global Forum.

20 Senko (1990).

21 Runzheimer International (consulting firm headquartered in Rochester, WI) (1991), reproduced in *HR Focus*, September, p. 8.

22 Pollard (2000).

23 Senko (1991).

24 Adapted from Russo, S.M., and Orchant, D. (2000), "Expatriate taxation," in Reynolds, C. (ed.), *2000 Guide to Global Compensation and Benefits*, San Diego, CA: Harcourt, p. 165.

25 See, for example, Bishko, M.J. (1990), "Compensating your overseas executives," I "Strategies for the 1990s," *Compensation and Benefits Review*, May–June, pp. 33–43; Brooks, B.J. (1988), "Long-term incentives: International executives," *Personnel*, August, pp. 40–42; Brooks, B.J. (1987), "Trends in international executive compensation," *Personnel*, May, pp. 67–70.

26 Gould, C. (1998: chapter 7); Littlewood, M. (1995), "Total compensation: A new way of doing things," *International HR Journal*, fall, pp. 17–21; Reynolds (2000a: chapter 5); Runzheimer International (2000), *Lump-sum Allowances: The Efficient Approach to Handling Relocation Expenses* (pamphlet), Rochester, WI: Runzheimer International.

27 Gregsen, K.J. (1996), "Flexpatriate remuneration: An alternative method for compensating foreign assignees," *International HR Journal*, winter, pp. 24–28; Reynolds (2000a: chapter 5).

28 Milkman, J., Nason, S., Von Glinow, M.A., Huo, P., Lowe, K., and Kim, N. (1995), "In search of 'best' strategic pay practices: An exploratory study of Japan, Korea, Taiwan, and the United States," *Advances in International Comparative Management*, 5 (10): 227–252; Schuler, R.S. (1998), "Understanding compensation practice variations across firms: The impact of national culture," *Journal of International Business Studies*, 29 (1): 159–177; Toh, S.M., and Denisi, A.S. (2003), "Host-country national reactions to expatriate pay policies: A model and implications," *Academy of Management Review*, 28 (4): 606–621.

29 Based on a table in Russo and Orchant (2000), p. 158.

30 See, for example, Russo and Orchant (2000); Stuart (1991).

31 Presented in Stuart (1991), p. 81. See also surveys such as the *Global Relocation Trends Annual Survey Report* from GMAC Global Relocation Services/Windham International, National Foreign Trade Council, and SHRM Global Forum.

32 Bernstein, Z.S., and Kaplan, C.Y. (2000), "Benefits: Introduction and retirement programs," in Reynolds, C. (ed.), *2000 Guide to Global Compensation and Benefits*, San Diego, CA: Harcourt; Gould (1998); Holleman, W.J. (1991), "Taxation of expatriate

executives," *International Executive*, May–June, pp. 30–33; Russo and Orchant (2000); Stuart (1991).

33  Holleman (1991).

34  Russo and Orchant (2000).

35  Adapted from Stuart (1991), p. 84.

36  Adapted from Outram, R. (2001), "The tax man cometh," *Global HR*, February–March, pp. 22–25.

37  Adapted from Fraser, J.A. (1992), "How to manage international taxes," *INC*, April, p. 129.

38  Crandall, L.P. (1992), "Getting through the global payroll maze," *Personnel Journal*, August, pp. 76–77; Dowling, P.J. (1989), "Hot issues overseas," *Personnel Administrator*, January, pp. 66–72.

39  Crandall (1992).

40  Overman (1992); Andre, R. (2000 and earlier editions), "High Technology, Incorporated: The international benefits problem," in Mendenhall, M., and Oddou, G. (eds), *Readings and Cases in International Human Resource Management*, 3rd edn, Cincinnati, OH: Southwestern College Publishing.

41  See, for example, Gibbons, D. (2002), "Employee benefits for expatriates," *Expatriate Advisor*, spring, pp. 40–41; Joinson (1999); Milkovich, G.T., and Bloom, M. (2000), "Rethinking international compensation," in Mendenhall, M., and Oddou, G. (eds), *Readings and Cases in International Human Resource Management*, Cincinnati, OH: Southwestern College Publishing; Pollard (2000: chapter 7); Reynolds (2000b, 2000a: chapters 4 and 5); Ritchie, A.J., and Seltz, S.P. (2000), "Globalization of the compensation and benefits function" in Reynolds, C. (2000a), *2000 Guide to Global Compensation Benefits*, New York: Harcourt; Russo and Orchant (2000); Sheridan and Hansen (1996).

42  Thanks to Cal Reynolds of ORC, New York, for this phrase.

43  Nemerov, D.S. (1994), "How foreign-owned companies pay their US executives," *Journal of International Compensation and Benefits*, January–February, pp. 9–14.

44  See, for instance, the *Annual CEO Scorecard: International Comparison* from Towers Perrin.

45  *Ibid*.

46  Sparrow, P.R. (1998), "International rewards systems: To converge or not to converge?" in Brewster, C., and Harris, H. (eds), *International HRM: Contemporary Issues in Europe*, London: Routledge; Sparrow, P.R. (1999), "International reward management" in White, G., and Drucker, J. (eds), *Reward Management: A Critical Text*, London: Pitman.

47  Carey, B.P. (1993), "Why inpatriates need special remuneration packages," *Journal of European Business*, May–June, pp. 46–49; De Leon, J. (2000), "International assignments to US headquarters" in Reynolds, C. (2000), *2000 Guide to Global Compensation Benefits*, San Diego, CA: Harcourt.

48  Adapted from Halt, A.G. (1992), "Employee benefits in the global economy," *Benefits Quarterly*, fourth quarter, reprint (no pages).

49  "Towards a global compensation model: Two key concepts," *International Mobility Management Newsletter* (Arthur Andersen), second quarter, 2001, pp. 2–3.

50  Murphy (1998), "Payday around the world," *IBIS Review*, July, pp. 17–20.

51  Latta, G.W. (1995), "Innovative ideas in international compensation," *Benefits and Compensation International*, July–August, pp. 3–7; Luebbers, L.A. (1999), "Laying the foundation for global compensation," *Workforce Supplement*, September, pp. 1–4; Minehan, M. (2000), "The new face of global compensation," *SHRM Global*, December, pp. 4–7; Murphy, E. (1998); Ritchie and Seltz (2000); Sutro, P.J. (1999), "Thinking about a global share plan? Think smart," *Compensation and Benefits Review*, reprint (no pages); "Towards a global compensation model: Two key concepts" (2001); Townley, G. (1999), "Leveling the global paying field," *HR World*, March–April, pp. 75–80.

52 "The cost of doing business," reporting on data from ECA Windham, *Personnel Journal*, 1996, p. 27.

53 "Labor costs in Western Germany are highest in Europe," reported in *Argus* (original data from *Handelsblatt*, Germany), January, 2001, p. 5.

54 "Chief executive pay in twelve countries," reported in *Argus* (original data from *NRC Handelsblad*, Netherlands), February, 1997, p. 4.

55 "2000 Worldwide Remuneration," *CEO Scorecard 2001: International Comparison*, New York: Towers Perrin.

56 See the references in notes 46 and 51 as well as Hempel, P.S. (1998), "Designing multi-national benefits programs: The role of national culture," *Journal of World Business*, 33 (3): 277–294; Outram, R. (2000), "Cherry pickings," *HR World*, March–April, pp. 30–34.

57 Adapted from Kaplan, C.Y., and Bernstein, Z.S. (2000), "Other benefits," in Reynolds, C. (ed.), *2000 Guide to Global Compensation Benefits*, San Diego, CA: Harcourt; "Working practices around the world," *HR World*, November–December, 2000, pp. 18–19.

58 Krupp, N.B. (1986), "Managing benefits in multinational organizations," *Personnel*, September, pp. 76–78; Murdock, B.A., and Ramamurthy, B. (1986), "Containing benefits costs for multinational corporations," *Personnel Journal*, May, pp. 80–85.

59 Bernstein and Kaplan (2000); Spencer, B.F. (1998), "Governments continue to hinder development of centralized approach to funding pensions," *IBIS Review*, July, pp. 10–12; Townley, G. (1999), "In the twilight zone," *HR World*, January–February, pp. 76–79.

60 Di Leopardi, F.A. (1991), "Money makes the world go round", interview with Eugene Barron, assistant treasurer of Johnson & Johnson, *Wyatt Communicator*, spring, pp. 15–19.

61 Freedman, R. (1997), "Incentive programs go global," *Worldwide Pay and Benefits Headlines* (Towers Perrin newsletter), February, p. 1; Gross, A., and Lepage, S. (2001), "Stock options in Asia," *SHRM Global Perspective*, 3 (1): 8–9; "New global share plan survey data released," *International Mobility Management Newsletter* (Arthur Andersen), fourth quarter, 2001, p. 7; Pacific Bridge (2001), "Stock options in Asia: Legal and regulatory roadblocks," *Asian HR e-Newsletter*, May 10, pp. 1–2 ; Perkins, S.J. (1998), "The search for global incentives," *HR World*, November–December, pp. 62–65; William M. Mercer International and Arthur Andersen (1990), *Globalizing Compensation: Extending Stock Option and Equity Participation Plans Abroad*, New York: authors; Solomon, C.M. (1999), "Incentives that go the distance," *HR World*, May–June, pp. 40–44; Thompson, R.W. (1999), "US subsidiaries of foreign parents favor pay incentives," *HR Magazine*, April, p. 10; "US-based long-term incentive plans go global," *International Update* (reporting on a Towers Perrin report, *The Globalization of Long-term Incentive Plans by US-based Companies*), 3 (2000), p. 8; "US version stock plans filter into Europe," *International Update*, February, 1999, p. 9; Veloitis, S. (2000), "Offshore equity compensation plans: Focus of audit activity in many countries," *KPMG e-Newsletter*, *The Expatriate Administrator*, August 28, pp. 1–4.

62 Hewitt Associates (1993), *Granting Stock Options and Restricted Stock to Overseas Employees*, New York: Hewitt Associates.

63 *Ibid.*, p. 1.

64 Adapted from "Canon loves to compete," *Fortune*, July 22, 2002, p. S5.

65 Adapted from Lublin, J.S. (1991), "Employee stock plans run into foreign snags," *Wall Street Journal*, September 16, p. B1.

66 William M. Mercer Fraser (London) (1990), "Options in a shrinking world," *Mercer Fraser Quarterly Review*, 89 (autumn), p. 3.

67 Rodrick, S.S. (ed.) (1999), *Equity-based Compensation for Multinational Corporations*, 2nd edn, Oakland, CA: National Center for Employee Ownership.

68 This section is based on Briscoe, D.R. (1991), "Employee Share Ownership Plans: An International Comparison with Application to Newly Industrializing Economies," presented to the 1991 national conference of the Association for Global Business, Atlanta, GA, November 6–9.

69 For a complete overview of the global situation related to stock ownership and the use of stock options around the world refer to the publication referenced in note 67 above from the National Center for Employee Ownership, edited by S.S. Rodrick.

70 Reported in Kaplan and Bernstein (2000); "Most nations require employers to provide maternity leave, meeting told," *BNAs Employee Relations Weekly*, April 2, 1990, p. 433. For current information on maternity and related leaves refer to Keller, W.L. (ed.), *International Labor and Employment Laws* I (1997), II (2001), and annual updates, Washington, DC: International Labor Law Committee Section of Labor and Employment Law, American Bar Association, Bureau of National Affairs.

71 Adapted from Kaplan and Bernstein (2000) and Keller, *International Labor and Employment Laws*.

72 Johnson, R.E. (1991), "Flexible benefit programs, international style," *Employee Benefits Journal*, 16 (3): 22–25.

73 "Top ten global compensation issues," *Update* (newsletter of the Institute for International Human Resource Management, now the Global Forum, a division of the Society for Human Resource Management), January–February, 1993, p. 1.

## 12 International performance management for international assignees and foreign managers

1 Jackson, S.E., and Schuler, R.S. (2003), *Managing Human Resources through Strategic Partnerships*, 8th edn, Cincinnati, OH: Southwestern College Publishing, chapter 11.

2 Figures from a recent survey by the former Arthur Andersen's Human Capital Services Practice, reported in Juday, H. (1999), "Employee development during international assignments," *Corporate Relocation News*, August, pp. 18, 35.

3 See, for example, Black, J.S., Gregersen, H.B., Mendenhall, M.E., and Stroh, L.K. (1999), "Appraising: Determining if people are doing the right things" in *Globalizing People through International Assignments*, Reading, MA: Addison Wesley; Brewster, C. (1991), "Monitoring performance – and coming home" in *The Management of Expatriates*, London: Kogan Page; Caligiuri, P.M. (1997), "Assessing expatriate success: Beyond just 'being there'," in Aycan, Z. (ed.), *New Approaches to Employee Management*, IV, New York: JAI Press; Davis, D.D. (1998), "International performance measurement and management," in Smither, J. (ed.), *Performance Appraisal*, San Francisco: Jossey Bass; Dowling, P.J., Welch, D.E., and Schuler, R.S. (1999), "Performance management," *International Human Resource Management*, 3rd edn, Cincinnati, OH: Southwestern College Publishing; Gregersen, H.B., Black, J.S., and Hite, J.M. (1995), "Expatriate performance appraisal: Principles, practice, and challenges" in Selmer, J. (ed.), *Expatriate Management: New Ideas for International Business*, Westport, CT: Quorum; Gregersen, H.B., Hite, J.M., and Black, J.S. (1996), "Expatriate performance appraisal in US multinational firms," *Journal of International Business Studies*, fourth quarter, pp. 711–738; Harvey, M. (1997), "Focusing on the international personnel performance appraisal process," *Human Resource Development Journal*, 8 (1): 41–62; Janssens, M. (1994), "Evaluating international managers' performance: Parent company standards as control mechanisms," *International Journal of Human Resource Management*, 5 (4): 853–873; Kleiman, L.S. (2004), *Human Resource Management*, 3rd edn, Cincinnati, OH: Atomic Dog; Milliman, J., Nason, S., Gallagher, E., Huo, P., Von Glinow, M.A., and Lowe, K.B. (1998), "The impact of national culture on human resource management practices: The case of performance appraisal," *Advances in International Comparative Management*, 12: 157–183; Oddou, G., and Mendenhall, M. (2000), "Expatriate performance appraisal: Problems and solutions" in Mendenhall, M., and Oddou, G. (eds), *Readings and Cases in International Human Resource Management*, Cincinnati, OH: Southwestern College Publishing; Schuler, R.S., Fulkerson, J.R., and Dowling, P.J. (1991),

"Strategic performance measurement and management in multinational corporations," *Human Resource Management*, 30 (3): 365–392; Vance, C.M., McClaine, S.R., Boje, D.M., and Stage, H.D. (1992), "An examination of the transferability of traditional performance appraisal principles across cultural boundaries," *Management International Review*, 32 (4): 313–326.

4 See, for example, Oddou and Mendenhall (2000).

5 See, for example, Trompenaars, F. (1994), *Riding the Waves of Culture: Understanding Diversity in Global Business*, New York: Irwin. Dr Trompenaars found that managers from various countries ranked qualities for evaluation in significantly different orders.

6 Beer, M. (1981), "Performance appraisal: Dilemmas and possibilities," *Organizational Dynamics*, 10: 24–36; Cascio, W.F. (2002), *Managing Human Resources: Productivity, Quality of Work Life, Profits*, 6th edn, New York: McGraw-Hill Irwin.

7 Dowling *et al.* (1999).

8 Described in Oddou and Mendenhall (2000).

9 Black *et al.* (1999); Robinson, R.D. (1983), *Internationalization of Business: An Introduction*, New York: Dryden Press.

10 Gregersen *et al.* (1995); Gregersen *et al.* (1996).

11 Oddou, G., and Mendenhall, M. (1991), "Succession planning for the twenty-first century: How well are we grooming our future business leaders?" *Business Horizons*, 34 (1): 26–34.

12 Butler, C., and de Bettignies, H.-C. (2001), "Case: The evaluation," in Albrecht, M.H. (ed.), *International HRM: Managing Diversity in the Workplace*, Oxford and Malden, MA: Blackwell.

13 Gregersen *et al.* (1995); Korn-Ferry International (1981), *A Study of the Repatriation of the American International Executive*, New York: Korn-Ferry International.

14 Mendenhall, M., and Oddou, G. (1985), "The dimensions of expatriate acculturation: A review," *Academy of Management Review*, 10 (1): 39–47.

15 Mendenhall and Oddou (1985).

16 Gregersen *et al.* (1996).

17 Dowling *et al.* (1999); Janssens (1994).

18 Birdseye, M.G., and Hill, J.S. (1995), "Individual, organization/work and environmental influences on expatriate turnover tendencies: An empirical study," *Journal of International Business Studies*, 26 (4): 795–809; Feldman, D.C., and Thompson, H.B. (1993), "Expatriation, repatriation, and domestic geographical relocation: An empirical investigation of adjustment to new job assignments," *Journal of International Business Studies*, 24 (3): 507–529.

19 Torbiörn, I. (1985), "The structure of managerial roles in cross-cultural settings," *International Studies of Management and Organization*, 15 (1): 52–74.

20 Adapted from Logger, E., and Vinke, R. (1995), "Compensation and appraisal of international staff" in Harzing, A.-W., and Van Ruysseveldt, J. (eds), *International Human Resource Management*, London: Sage in association with the Open University of the Netherlands.

21 Borkowski, S.C. (1999), "International managerial performance evaluation: A five-country comparison," *Journal of International Business Studies*, 30 (3): 533–555.

22 Black *et al.* (1999), p. 166.

23 Most of the references in note 3 make this point. In addition, refer to Lomax, S. (2001), *Best Practices for Managers and Expatriates: A Guide on Selection, Hiring, and Compensation*, New York: Wiley.

24 Based on Black *et al.* (1999).

25 *Global Relocation Trends, 1998 and 1998 Survey Reports*, New York: Windham International and National Foreign Trade Council, and Alexandria, VA: Institute for International Human Resource Management (now the Global Forum), a division of the Society for Human Resource Management.

26 Black *et al.* (1999).

27  Logger and Vinke (1995).
28  Gregersen *et al.* (1996).
29  *Ibid.*
30  Cascio, W.F. (2002), *Managing Human Resources: Productivity, Quality of Work Life, Profits*, 6th edn, New York: McGraw-Hill Irwin, pp. 302–303.
31  Black *et al.* (1999).
32  Gardenswartz, L., and Rowe, A. (2001), "Cross-cultural awareness," *HR Magazine*, March, pp. 139–142.
33  Oddou and Mendenhall (2000), pp. 218–219.
34  Brewster (1991).
35  Oddov and Mendehall (2000), p. 274.
36  Tahvanainen, M. (2000), "Expatriate performance management: The case of Nokia Telecommunications," *Human Resource Management*, summer–fall, 39 (2–3): 267–275.
37  Cascio (2002), p. 300.
38  Oddou and Mendenhall (2000).

# 13 Health, safety, and crisis management in the global enterprise

1  The most important reference on country health and safety practices is the *Encyclopaedia of Occupational Health and Safety*, Geneva, Switzerland: International Labour Organization, 1998.
2  Much of this section is based on a discussion in Fisher, C.D., Schoenfeldt, L.F., and Shaw, J.B. (2003), *Human Resource Management*, 5th edn, Boston, MA: Houghton Mifflin. Their discussion is based on these references: Takala, J. (1999), *Introductory Report of the International Labor Office, Occupational Safety and Health Branch*, May; the forty-ninth issue of the *Yearbook of Labor Statistics* (1989–1990), Geneva: International Labour Organization, pp. 982–995; Elling, R.H. (1986), *The Struggle for Workers' Health: A Study of Six Industrialized Countries*, Farmingdale, NY: Baywood, pp. 427–450; Grevers, J.K.M. (1983), "Worker participation in health and safety in the EEC: The role of representative institutions," *International Labor Review*, July–August, pp. 411–428; Chew, D.C.E. (1988), "Effective occupational safety activities: Findings in three Asian developing countries," *International Labor Review*, 127 (1): 111–124; Bixby, M.B. (1992), "Emerging occupational safety issues in the United States, Europe, and Japan," *Proceedings of the Third Conference on International Personnel and Human Resource Management* I, Berkhamsted, July. Also refer to Wokutch, R.E., and McLaughlin, J.S. (1992), "The US and Japanese work injury and illness experience," *Monthly Labor Review*, April, pp. 2–11.
3  Takala (1999).
4  Reported in "Half of the world's workers employed in risky jobs," *Manpower Argus*, February, 1996, p. 5.
5  Breuer, N. (2000), "AIDS threatens global business," *Workforce*, February, pp. 52–55; Itano, N. (2002), "Prevention without cure: HIV/AIDS in the workplace," *Global HR*, March, pp. 17–23.
6  Breuer (2000), p. 52.
7  *Ibid.*, p. 52.
8  Quoted in *ibid.*, p. 53.
9  For a discussion of this case see Hatlevig, T. (1995), "Gray matters: HIV raises global issues," *Personnel Journal*, August, pp. 101–102.
10  See, for example, Copeland, L. (1987), "Traveling abroad safely: some tips to give employees," *Personnel*, February, pp. 18–24; Graebel, B. (2002), "Effects of terrorism on international relocation," *CRN News*, March, pp. 1, 16, 20, 24; Harvey, M.G. (1993),

"A survey of corporate programs for managing terrorist threats," *Journal of International Business Studies*, third quarter, pp. 465–478; Jossi, F. (2001), "Buying protection from terrorism," *HR Magazine*, June, pp. 155–160; Ronkainen, S.A. (1989), "International human resource management" in Czintoka, M.R., Rivoli, P., and Ronkainen, I.A., *International Business*, New York: Dryden Press; Solomon, C.M. (1997), "Global business under siege," *Global Workforce*, January, pp. 18–23.

11 Copeland, L., and Griggs, L. (1985), *Going International*, New York: Random House.

12 Copeland (1987); Gerbman, R.V. (1999), "HR takes on international crime," *HR Magazine*, June, pp. 46–52; Sappal, P. (1998), "Expatriate crimes and misdemeanours," *HR World*, November–December, pp. 32–34.

13 Copeland (1987).

14 Allen, M. (1996), "Maquila execs tighten personal security," *San Diego Business Journal*, August 26, pp. 1, 6; Auerbach, A.H. (1998), *Ransom: The Untold Story of International Kidnapping*, New York: Holt; Bamrud, J. (1996), "Kidnapping, Inc.," *US–Latin Trade*, February, pp. 32–36; Greengard, S. (1997), "Mission possible: Protecting employees abroad," *Workforce*, August, pp. 30–36; Harbrecht, D. (1996), "Dodging danger while doing business abroad," *Business Week*, May 27, p. 151; Harman, L. (1996), "Kidnap sparks interest in ransom policies," *San Diego Business Journal*, August 26, pp. 1, 22; Hanson, M.J. (1999), "One bloody night," *Across the Board*, October, pp. 39–42; Morphy, E. (1996), "The business of kidnapping," *Export Today*, October, pp. 18–22; "Quickie kidnappings grow common in Rio for unwary wealthy," *San Diego Union-Tribune*, November 10, 1995, p. A-24; Taylor, S. (1999), "When workers travel abroad, caution is advisable," *SHRM HR-News*, April, pp. 13, 15.

15 See above, plus Lee, E.L., II (2001), "Keeping expatriates safe abroad: A systematic approach," *CRN News*, July, pp. 1, 18; Robinson, K.-S. (2001), "Violence abroad prompts review of insurance needs," *SHRM HR-News*, April, pp. 5, 16.

16 Dawood, R. (1998), "Bills of health," *HR World*, winter, pp. 57–62.

17 *Ibid.*, p. 61.

18 Adapted from *ibid.*, p. 57.

19 Adapted from "MEDEX Assistance case history," contained in *MEDEX Assistance Corporation* brochure, Baltimore, MD (1992).

20 "American is killed in Mexico City cab holdup," *San Diego Union-Tribune*, September 17, 1997, p. A-21; Evans, G. (2001), "Last rites," *Global HR*, June, pp. 36–40; Evans, G. (1999), "Victim support," *HR World*, May–June, pp. 46–52; Preston, A. (2002), "The international assignment taboo: Expatriate death," *KPMG Expatriate Administrator*, summer, pp. 1–3; "Tragedy on a Turkish roadway," *USAA Magazine*, March–April, 1998, pp. 20–22; York, G. (1996), "American's murder sows fear: Moscow a sinister business partner," *Rocky Mountain News*, November 14, pp. 2A, 58A.

21 Evans (2001).

22 See, for example, Davidson, C., and Busch, E. (1996), "How to cope with international emergency situations," *KPMG The Expatriate Administrator*, April, pp. 6–10; Kroll Associates (2000), *Secure Travel Guide* and *Guide to Personal Security*, New York: Kroll Associates.

23 Sappal, P. (1999), "Global safety net," *HR World*, July–August, pp. 47–64.

## 14 The IHR department and the role and future of IHRM

1 Sparrow, P.S., Brewster, C., and Harris, H. (2004), *Globalizing Human Resource Management*, London: Routledge; Evans, P., Pucik, V. and Barsoux, J-L. (2002), *The Global Challenge: Frameworks for International Human Resource Management*, New York: McGraw-Hill Irwin.

2 Coy, P., with Levine, J.B., Weber, J., Brandt, R., and Gross, N. (1993), "In the labs, the fight to spend less, get more," *Business Week*, June 28, pp. 102–104.

3 Adapted from Reynolds, C. (2000), "The future of global compensation and benefits" in Reynolds, C. (ed.), *2000 Guide to Global Compensation and Benefits*, San Diego, CA: Harcourt; Tichy, N.M. (1988), "Setting the global human resource management agenda for the 1990s," *Human Resource Management*, 27: 1–18.

4 Claus, L. (2000), "Conducting an International HR Environmental Scan: A Strategic Tool of Globalization," paper presented at the twenty-third annual conference and exposition of the Institute for International Human Resources (now the Global Forum), a division of the Society for Human Resource Management, San Diego, CA, April 2–5.

5 Jackson, S.E., and Schuler, R.S. (2003), *Managing Human Resources through Strategic Partnerships*, Cincinnati, OH: Southwestern College Publishing; Caudron, S. (1999), "HR vs. managers," *Workforce*, August, pp. 33–38.

6 Frase-Blunt, M. (2003), "Raising the bar," *HR Magazine*, March, pp. 74–78; Grossman, R.J. (2003), "Putting HR in rotation," *HR Magazine*, March, pp. 50–57.

7 Becker, B.E., Huselid, M.A., and Ulrich, D. (2001), *The HR Scorecard: Linking People, Strategy, and Performance,* Boston, MA: Harvard Business School Press; Fitz-enz, J. (2000), *The ROI of Human Capital: Measuring the Economic Value of Employee Performance*, New York: American Management Association; Philips, J.J., Stone, R.D., and Phillips, P.P. (2001), *The Human Resources Scorecard: Measuring the Return on Investment*, Boston, MA: Butterworth Heinemann; *Transforming the IHR Function for Global Business Success*, New York: Conference Board (1998).

8 Schuler, R. (1991), *The HR Function in Effective Firms in Highly Competitive Environments in the Twenty-first Century*, special report for the IBM Corporation that served as the basis for the global HR survey entitled *A Twenty-first Century Vision: A Worldwide Human Resource Study*, conducted by TPF&C; Schuler, R. (1994) "World-class HR departments: six critical issues," *Singapore Accounting and Business Review*, January, pp. 43–72. Refer to references in note 7.

9 Fitz-enz, J. (1990), *Human Value Management*, San Francisco: Jossey Bass; Fitz-enz (2000); annual reports of the Society for Human Resource Management, Alexandria, VA, and the Saratoga Institute, *Human Resource Effectiveness Report* and *Human Resource Benchmarking*, Saratoga, CA: Saratoga Institute.

10 Briscoe, A.F., Silverman, F., and Noyes, T. (1993), "Internationalizing your HRIS," *HRSP Review*, October–November, pp. 10–14; Greengard, S. (1995), "When HRMS goes global: Managing the data highway," *Personnel Journal*, June, pp. 90–106; Harrington, A. (1998), "Smart thinking about globalization," *HR World*, November–December, pp. 66–70; Harrington, A. (1999), "Well connected systems," *HR World*, pp. 67–74; Meade, J. (1998), "International intranets," *HR Magazine Focus*, May, pp. 10–14; Moidel, A. (1995), "Key factors in choosing technology for your international human resources department," *International Assignment News* (Deloitte Touche Tohmatsu international newsletter), summer, pp. 4–5; O'Connell, S.E. (1997), "Systems issues for international business," *HR Magazine*, March, pp. 36–41; O'Reilly, S. (2001), "Hand it all over," *Global HR*, June, pp. 30–34; Parker, G.L. (2000), "Global human resources information technology" in Reynolds, C. (ed.), *2000 Guide to Global Compensation and Benefits*, San Diego, CA: Harcourt; Rutlen, C. (2001), "Technology tools for international assignments," *CRN News*, July, p. 19; Stambaugh, R. (1993), "Bridging the gap: Global systems and multi-domestic corporations," *HRSP Review*, October–November, pp. 16–21; Wheatley, M. (2001), "Specific solutions," *Global HR*, May, pp. 54–58.

11 Presininzi, P. (1997), "International human resources websites: Another door to global communication," *International HR Journal*, summer, pp. 25–27.

12 Lindahl, R.V. (1996), "Automation breaks the language barrier," *HR Magazine*, March, pp. 79–83.

13 *Ibid*.

14  Adapted from O'Reilly (2001).

15  This subject is a frequent topic for presentations at industry and IHR practitioner conferences demonstrating its importance to IHR professionals. Here is a sample of some of the articles that have appeared in various sources over the last few years: *Global Relocation Trends* (2000), GMAC/GRS/Windham International; Conlan, D.A. (1996), "Outfront in international relocation," *National Relocation and Real Estate*, 12 (6): 42–44; Loewe, G.M. (1994), "Evolution of the relocation function," *Journal of International Compensation and Benefits*, January–February, pp. 43–46; Major, J. (1999), "Relocation as an industry must change," *CRN News*, May, pp. 1, 4, 19–21, 30–31, 35; Mitchell, H.R. (1998), "A moving issue: to outsource or not to outsource," *HR Magazine*, May, pp. 59–68; Morphy, E. (1997), "Expatriate gains," *Export Today*, March, pp. 38–41.

16  Loewe (1994).

17  Siemens, B. (1992), "International moving: Beyond the twilight zone," *HR News: International HR*, February, p. C8.

18  Quoted in "Outsourcing international? Don't lose control," *CRN News* (online public relations services), June 28, 2000.

19  Buyens, D., and de Vos, A. (1999), "The added value of the HR department" in Brewster, C., and Harris, H. (eds), *International Human Resource Management*, London: Routledge; Lawler, E.E., III (1992), *The Ultimate Advantage: Creating the High-involvement Organization*, San Francisco: Jossey Bass; Pfeffer, J. (1994), *Competitive Advantage through People*, Boston, MA: Harvard Business School Press; Pfeffer, J. (1998), *The Human Equation: Building Profits by Putting People First*, Boston, MA: Harvard Business School Press; Stroh, L.K., and Caligiuri, P.M. (1998a), "Increasing global competitiveness through effective people management," *Journal of World Business*, 33 (1): 1–16; Stroh, L.K., and Caligiuri, P.M. (1998b), "Strategic human resources: A new source for competitive advantage in the global arena," *International Journal of Human Resource Management*, 9 (1): 1–17.

20  Grossman, R.J. (2003), "Putting HR in rotation," *HR Magazine*, March, pp. 50–57; Poe, A.C. (2000), "Destination everywhere," *HR Magazine*, October, pp. 67–75.

21  Frase-Blunt (2003); Grossman (2003); Reynolds, C. (1992), "Are you ready to make IHR a global function?" *HR News: International HR*, February, pp. 1–3.

22  McConnell, B. (2003), "HRCI to offer global HR certification in 2004," *HR Magazine*, March, pp. 115, 117; also refer to the HRCI website, www.hrci.org/about/intl.html.

23  Buyens, D., and de Vos, A. (1999), "The added value of the HR department" in Brewster, C., and Harris, H. (eds), *International Human Resource Management*, London: Routledge; Claus, L. (1998), "The role of International Human Resource in leading a company from a domestic to a global corporate culture," *Human Resource Development International*, 1 (3): 309–326; Claus, L. (1999), "Globalization and HR Professional Competencies," paper presented at the twenty-second annual Global HR Forum (Institute for International HR, now the Global Forum, a division of the Society for Human Resource Management), Orlando, FL, April 13; Cuthill, S. (2000), "Globalizing HR: Structure, Strategy, Services," presented at the twenty-third annual Global HR Forum (Institute for International HR, now the Global Forum, a division of the Society for Human Resource Management), San Diego, CA, April 4; Cuthill, S., and Bentzon, K.C. (1998–1999), "Developing the global human resources manager: Meeting the challenges of the next millennium," *HR Director: The Arthur Andersen Guide to Human Capital*, New York: Arthur Andersen; Schell, M.S., and Solomon, C.M. (1997), *Capitalizing on the Global Workforce: A Strategic Guide for Expatriate Management*, New York: McGraw-Hill; Solomon, C.M. (2000), "The world stops shrinking," *Workforce*, January, pp. 48–51; Sullivan, J. (2000), "Ten tenets of twenty-first-century HR," *Workforce*, January, p. 54; Ulrich, D. (1997), "HR of the future," *HR Alliances* (Linkage newsletter), 1 (1): 1, 3; Ulrich, D. (1997), "Judge me more by my future than by my past," *Human Resource Management*, 36 (1): 5–8.

24  Based partially on Stroh and Caligiuri (1998b).

25  Brockbank, W. (1997), "HR's future on the way to a presence," *Human Resource Management*, 36 (1): 65–69; Burke, W.W. (1997), "What human resource practitioners need to know for the twenty-first century," *Human Resource Management*, 36 (1): 71–79; Caudron, S. (1999), "HR vs. managers," *Workforce*, August, pp. 33–38; Gates, S.R. (1996), "Building a global human resources network," *International HR Journal*, winter, pp. 15–23; Kemske, F. (1998), "HR 2008: HR's role will change. The question is *how*," *Workforce*, January, pp. 46–60; Laabs, J. (2000), "Strategic HR won't come easily," *Workforce*, January, pp. 52–56; Pennington, L.P., and Engel, D.W. (1999–2000), "How HR drives successful globalization," *HR Director: The Arthur Andersen Guide to Human Capital*, New York: Arthur Andersen; Poe (2000); Pucik, V. (1997), "Human resources in the future: An obstacle or a champion of globalization?" *Human Resource Management*, 36 (1): 163–167; Schell and Solomon (1997); Solomon (2000).

26  These trends and challenges have been developed over the last few years from attendance at many seminars and presentations by IHR practitioners and consultants in which they have described the challenges they are either now confronting or see developing in the near future.

27  "Policy exceptions now the norm in global IHR," *CRN News*, July, 2001, pp. 1, 10, 14.

28  Lester, T. (1999), "Spare me the detail," *HR World*, July–August, pp. 33–36.

29  Schuler, R.S. (1993), "World-class HR departments: Six critical issues," *Singapore Accounting and Business Review*, 1 (1): 43–72; Towers Perrin (studies conducted for IBM), *A Twenty-first Century Vision: A Worldwide Human Resource Study* (1990) and *Priorities for Competitive Advantage* (1992), New York: authors.

30  Pennington and Engel (1999–2000), pp. 226, 232.

31  Adapted from Bates, S. (2002), "Facing the future," *HR Magazine*, July, pp. 26–32.

32  Partially adapted from Gundling, E. (2000), *International Focus: The Future of Global Management*, in-depth article published by the Society for Human Resource Management Institute for International Human Resources (now the Global Forum), Alexandria, VA.

## Integrative case study: Lincoln Electric in China

1  Professor Norman Berg's account of the Lincoln Electric Company (HBS 376-028) provides a useful account of the firm's longstanding traditions and management philosophy.

2  Wiley, Carolyn (1993) "Incentive plan pushes production," *Personnel Journal*, August, pp. 86–93.

3  *Barrons*, "Highly motivated," November 25, 1996, p. 24.

4  *Business Week* (US edition), "A model incentive plan gets caught in a vise," January 22, 1996, pp. 91–92.

5  Hastings, Donald F. (1996), "Guaranteed employment: A practical solution for today's corporations," *Vital Speeches of the Day*, September 1.

6  Chilton, Kenneth (1993), "Lincoln Electric's incentive system: Can it be transferred overseas?" *Compensation and Benefits Review*, November–December, pp. 24–30.

7  *The Plain Dealer* (Cleveland), "Facing changing times even as it is growing in Asia, Lincoln Electric finds challenges from unions at home," November 26, 1997.

8  This section draws on Professor Christopher Bartlett's *Lincoln Electric: Venturing Abroad* (HBS No. 9-398-095).

9  Hastings, Donald F. (1999), "Lincoln Electric's harsh lessons from international expansion," *Harvard Business Review*, May–June, pp. 163–178.

10  At the end of 1992, the board of directors decided to borrow money to pay bonuses to the employees in Cleveland. In spite of a consolidated loss of US$45.8 million in 1992, Lincoln paid its US employees a US$44 million bonus.

11  Chilton (1993).

12  Lienert, Anita (1995), "A dinosaur of a different color," *Management Review*, February, pp. 24–25.

13  Hodgetts, Richard M. (1999), "A conversation with Donald F. Hastings of the Lincoln Electric Company," *Organizational Dynamics*, winter, pp. 60–66; Hastings (1999).

14  Hastings (1999).

15  *The Plain Dealer* (Cleveland), "Lincoln Electric responds to union drive," October 18, 1997.

16  Hodgetts (1997).

17  For more information on Shanghai and development areas see www.sh.com.

18  An earlier experience in Venezuela necessitated dual entry of new technology, as Kundrach explained. "When we put equipment in Venezuela we couldn't really support it because it was different and we didn't have the knowledge base. We insisted that whatever we put in China, we're going to have it duplicated in Cleveland to be able to support it."

# Author index

# Subject index